T0134760

Lecture Notes in Computer Science 12183

More information about this series at http://www.springer.com/series/7409

Masaaki Kurosu (Ed.)

Human-Computer Interaction

Human Values and Quality of Life

Thematic Area, HCI 2020
Held as Part of the 22nd International Conference, HCII 2020
Copenhagen, Denmark, July 19–24, 2020
Proceedings, Part III

 Springer

Editor
Masaaki Kurosu
The Open University of Japan
Chiba, Japan

ISSN 0302-9743   ISSN 1611-3349 (electronic)
Lecture Notes in Computer Science
ISBN 978-3-030-49064-5   ISBN 978-3-030-49065-2 (eBook)
https://doi.org/10.1007/978-3-030-49065-2

LNCS Sublibrary: SL3 – Information Systems and Applications, incl. Internet/Web, and HCI

This Springer imprint is published by the registered company Springer Nature Switzerland AG
The registered company address is: Gewerbestrasse 11, 6330 Cham, Switzerland

Foreword

The 22nd International Conference on Human-Computer Interaction, HCI International 2020 (HCII 2020), was planned to be held at the AC Bella Sky Hotel and Bella Center, Copenhagen, Denmark, during July 19–24, 2020. Due to the COVID-19 coronavirus pandemic and the resolution of the Danish government not to allow events larger than 500 people to be hosted until September 1, 2020, HCII 2020 had to be held virtually. It incorporated the 21 thematic areas and affiliated conferences listed on the following page.

A total of 6,326 individuals from academia, research institutes, industry, and governmental agencies from 97 countries submitted contributions, and 1,439 papers and 238 posters were included in the conference proceedings. These contributions address the latest research and development efforts and highlight the human aspects of design and use of computing systems. The contributions thoroughly cover the entire field of human-computer interaction, addressing major advances in knowledge and effective use of computers in a variety of application areas. The volumes constituting the full set of the conference proceedings are listed in the following pages.

The HCI International (HCII) conference also offers the option of "late-breaking work" which applies both for papers and posters and the corresponding volume(s) of the proceedings will be published just after the conference. Full papers will be included in the "HCII 2020 - Late Breaking Papers" volume of the proceedings to be published in the Springer LNCS series, while poster extended abstracts will be included as short papers in the "HCII 2020 - Late Breaking Posters" volume to be published in the Springer CCIS series.

I would like to thank the program board chairs and the members of the program boards of all thematic areas and affiliated conferences for their contribution to the highest scientific quality and the overall success of the HCI International 2020 conference.

This conference would not have been possible without the continuous and unwavering support and advice of the founder, Conference General Chair Emeritus and Conference Scientific Advisor Prof. Gavriel Salvendy. For his outstanding efforts, I would like to express my appreciation to the communications chair and editor of HCI International News, Dr. Abbas Moallem.

July 2020   Constantine Stephanidis

HCI International 2020 Thematic Areas and Affiliated Conferences

Thematic areas:

- HCI 2020: Human-Computer Interaction
- HIMI 2020: Human Interface and the Management of Information

Affiliated conferences:

- EPCE: 17th International Conference on Engineering Psychology and Cognitive Ergonomics
- UAHCI: 14th International Conference on Universal Access in Human-Computer Interaction
- VAMR: 12th International Conference on Virtual, Augmented and Mixed Reality
- CCD: 12th International Conference on Cross-Cultural Design
- SCSM: 12th International Conference on Social Computing and Social Media
- AC: 14th International Conference on Augmented Cognition
- DHM: 11th International Conference on Digital Human Modeling and Applications in Health, Safety, Ergonomics and Risk Management
- DUXU: 9th International Conference on Design, User Experience and Usability
- DAPI: 8th International Conference on Distributed, Ambient and Pervasive Interactions
- HCIBGO: 7th International Conference on HCI in Business, Government and Organizations
- LCT: 7th International Conference on Learning and Collaboration Technologies
- ITAP: 6th International Conference on Human Aspects of IT for the Aged Population
- HCI-CPT: Second International Conference on HCI for Cybersecurity, Privacy and Trust
- HCI-Games: Second International Conference on HCI in Games
- MobiTAS: Second International Conference on HCI in Mobility, Transport and Automotive Systems
- AIS: Second International Conference on Adaptive Instructional Systems
- C&C: 8th International Conference on Culture and Computing
- MOBILE: First International Conference on Design, Operation and Evaluation of Mobile Communications
- AI-HCI: First International Conference on Artificial Intelligence in HCI

Conference Proceedings Volumes Full List

38. CCIS 1224, HCI International 2020 Posters - Part I, edited by Constantine Stephanidis and Margherita Antona
39. CCIS 1225, HCI International 2020 Posters - Part II, edited by Constantine Stephanidis and Margherita Antona
40. CCIS 1226, HCI International 2020 Posters - Part III, edited by Constantine Stephanidis and Margherita Antona

http://2020.hci.international/proceedings

Human-Computer Interaction Thematic Area (HCI 2020)

Program Board Chair: Masaaki Kurosu, The Open University of Japan, Japan

- Salah Uddin Ahmed, Norway
- Zohreh Baniasadi, Luxembourg
- Valdecir Becker, Brazil
- Nimish Biloria, Australia
- Scott Cadzow, UK
- Maurizio Caon, Switzerland
- Zhigang Chen, P.R. China
- Ulla Geisel, Germany
- Tor-Morten Groenli, Norway
- Jonathan Gurary, USA
- Kristy Hamilton, USA
- Yu-Hsiu Hung, Taiwan

- Yi Ji, P.R. China
- Lawrence Lam, USA
- Alexandros Liapis, Greece
- Bingjie Liu, USA
- Hiroshi Noborio, Japan
- Denise Pilar, Brazil
- Farzana Rahman, USA
- Manuel Rudolph, Germany
- Emmanuelle Savarit, UK
- Damian Schofield, USA
- Vinícius Segura, Brazil
- Charlotte Wiberg, Sweden

The full list with the Program Board Chairs and the members of the Program Boards of all thematic areas and affiliated conferences is available online at:

http://www.hci.international/board-members-2020.php

HCI International 2021

The 23rd International Conference on Human-Computer Interaction, HCI International 2021 (HCII 2021), will be held jointly with the affiliated conferences in Washington DC, USA, at the Washington Hilton Hotel, July 24–29, 2021. It will cover a broad spectrum of themes related to Human-Computer Interaction (HCI), including theoretical issues, methods, tools, processes, and case studies in HCI design, as well as novel interaction techniques, interfaces, and applications. The proceedings will be published by Springer. More information will be available on the conference website: http://2021.hci.international/.

General Chair
Prof. Constantine Stephanidis
University of Crete and ICS-FORTH
Heraklion, Crete, Greece
Email: general_chair@hcii2021.org

http://2021.hci.international/

Contents – Part III

Learning, Culture and Creativity

Human Values, Ethics, Transparency and Trust

HCI in Complex Environments

HCI for Well-Being and Eudaimonia

Deception of the "Elephant in the Room": Invisible Auditing Multi-party Conversations to Support Caregivers in Cognitive Behavioral Group Therapies

Eleonora Beccaluva[1], Antonio Chiappetta[1], Julian Cuellar Mangut[1], Luca Molteni[1], Marco Mores[2(✉)], Daniele Occhiuto[1], and Franca Garzotto[1]

[1] Department of Electronics, Information and Bioengineering, Politecnico di Milano, Milan, MI, Italy
{eleonora.beccaluva, daniele.occhiuto, franca.garzotto}@polimi.it, {antonio.chiappetta, julian.cuellar, luca7.molteni}@mail.polimi.it

[2] Fraternità e Amicizia Società Cooperativa Sociale Onlus, Milan, MI, Italy
marco.mores@fraternitaeamicizia.it

Abstract. One of the biggest challenges in Group Therapy is to track each patient's experience and feeling without him/her noticing. Altering the familiarity of the mutual support group routine may weaken the therapeutic efficacy of the intervention. It must be avoided the *"Elephant in the room's* Effect": everyone knows is being observed and acts consequently. Therapists struggle and spend years of training on developing the skills they need to "silently" monitor all patients at the same time. From our perspective, we wonder whether and how technology can be a support for therapists in such a challenging task. More precisely, how to provide them with a non-invasive support tool that is invisible to the end-users, but at the same time ever-present for the caregivers. Basically, we asked ourselves: Can we deceive "the *Elephant in the room*"? Therapists may benefit from automatic measures indicating how the participants perceive the session and gathering the participants' feedback is one path to develop valuable mutual support interventions. Our work describes the design, development and assessment of a non-invasive tool to monitor a Group Session.

Keywords: Psychology and cognition: psychological application for user interface · Technology: tools for HCI · UX and usability: evaluation/comparison of usability and UX methods · UX and usability: user experience

1 Introduction

Aural interfaces are gaining a considerable momentum both in research fields and commercial applications. The advances in natural language processing - NLP - and in speech recognition contributed to an ever-growing number of adopters for voice enabled technologies. We take advantage of the thriving aural landscape by integrating commercially available services in our experimental setting. The conversation is at the

© Springer Nature Switzerland AG 2020
M. Kurosu (Ed.): HCII 2020, LNCS 12183, pp. 3–22, 2020.
https://doi.org/10.1007/978-3-030-49065-2_1

center of group interventions. Social or mutual support groups are a common practice in diverse domains: group therapies can mitigate depression [1], promote smoking cessation [2] and encourage women diagnosed with breast cancer [3]. In some cases, group interventions improve the psychological well-being of patients with cancer [4]. Well-being is quite hard to measure, but it is an indicator on the efficacy of the group interventions [5]. As such, it has been investigated in school settings [6] and has recently been examined for older adults as well [6]. The research challenge in our domain dwells in facing the heterogeneity of group interventions when applied to an as much heterogenous user basin. In our study, we evaluate to which extent an external support tool affects how the participants perceive the group therapy. We are interested in evaluating to which extent our support tool influences the intervention. We encompass the different mutual support groups approaches under the umbrella term cognitive behavioral therapy - CBT. CBT is an ensemble of practices for psychological treatment that involve talking therapies to affect the patients' behavior [7]. CBT readiness has been investigated thoroughly in [8], other studies demonstrated which CBT methods are most suited for adults with ASD [9]. Since our participants are young adults with mixed disabilities (mild to severe), we were particularly attentive in avoiding disrupting the group therapy. Interventions for users with disability are brittle and subject to change based on the user cognitive and emotional status during the session [10]. Our participants' conditions include intellectual disability, ASD, epilepsy and bipolar affective syndrome. Our users are very sensitive to small changes in the therapeutic setting. Altering the familiarity of the mutual support group routine may weaken the therapeutic efficacy of the intervention.

Nonetheless, therapists may benefit from automatic measures indicating how the participants perceive the session by means of: (i) the perceived improvements in well-being and (ii) the perceived progresses in self-efficacy. In fact, gathering the participants feedback is one path to develop valuable mutual support interventions. Therefore, the support tool necessary to measure well-being must be non-invasive for participants and informative for therapists. Our ambition is to build a support tool which is invisible to the end users, but at the same time ever-present for the caregivers. We bring into play aural "eavesdroppers" that extract the most relevant topics of the multi-party conversation. First, participants rate the importance of each topic and appraise the enjoyment of the session. Then, therapists consult the feedback and can ameliorate future interventions. In the next section, we present a review on available conversational technologies and how they are applied in multi-party discussions. We revise topic extraction applications in therapeutic settings. Then we explain the design rationale of our system and its implementation. Finally, we report and discuss the results of our study.

2 Background

Named entity recognition - NER - has been widely applied to extract known artifacts in a text. The artifact can be a famous personality, an established company, a popular place. NER takes care to classify a given entity according to its nature and its relationships with peer entities of the domain: e.g., if it belongs to sports, entertainment, food, and the like. Aside from NER, common tasks of natural language processing are tokenization [11], lemmatization [12] and part of speech tagging or simply POS tagging [13]. Tokenization splits a sentence into the words that compose it. Each word is a term of a sample sentence. There is a subtle distinction between term and token: terms consider repetitions, tokens are a collection of different terms.

There are no repeated words in tokenization. Lemmatization is a refinement of stemming; by the stem, we mean the root of a word, and the semantics of the word can change based on the stem affix. For example, the stem for "researching" and "researcher" is in both cases "research" but till the two words do not express the same entity. Finally, POS tagging elicits the syntactic role of each word in the sentence, for example, if it is the noun, the verb or the adjective. Describing a complete NLP toolkit goes beyond the goals of this paper but keeping in mind the fundamental abstractions used in the processing of language will facilitate our understanding of topic extraction. While open source NLP tools exist, the most popular being the Stanford CoreNLP and the NLTK [14, 15], we opted for commercial systems because they may outperform free tools when it comes to named entity recognition alone. Pinto et al. [16] provided a benchmark of the various performances for NLP toolkits in social media texts. We could not find an extensive comparison with the industrial counterpart. Nonetheless, we integrated an external commercial solution due to its high availability, to its robustness and to its support beyond English language. Most of the free alternatives consider only English and we needed the Italian language. Tech companies provide one-click integration for named entity recognition services. Most of the time the services are used to gain insights from customer feedback. The most popular services include but are not limited to: Apple Natural Language Module which supports tokenization, lemmatization and POS tagging, but limits NER to proper names, locations, and organizations [17]; IBM Watson Natural Language Understanding that integrates entity recognition, sentiment analysis, and allows to customize domains [18]; Amazon Comprehend including NER, sentiment analysis, and keywords extraction from the input [19]; Google Cloud Natural Language API which provides NER, sentiment analysis and relationship graphs among the main features [20]. Named Entity Recognition highlights entities, however, we still need to link the extracted entities to topics. Not every entity belongs to a topic: recognized entities may fail in defining a particular topic. For example, the recognized entity "Google" suggests that we are talking about something related to the tech company but fails to capture if we were talking about results of Google search. Keywords are a starting point, and they have been widely used to provide transcripts of meetings [21]. Another approach considers the reactions to an utterance to determine whether to include it or not in the summary [22]. Both previous studies emphasize the fragmentation of transcripts due to the informality of multi-party conversations. The fragmentation leads to a lack in underlining the topics of interest: we do not have the relationships between entities that can improve the topics identification. For this reason, some studies explore how the entities relate to each other. In SemanticTalk, the authors create a network of topics in real-time for supporting face-to-face meetings [23]. In SemanticTalk, each user has its own microphone for recording, which may be invasive for participants. Later, another study insisted on the importance of the relationships among entities in multi-party conversations [24]. Both reports argue that the relationships among entities reduce the fragmentation of the transcript. Using commercial systems, the network of relationships is included in a pre-trained model for the entity extraction. Therefore, we expect the entities to be finer grained than a statistical analysis. However, we still endeavor to identify the actual topics of the conversation starting from the recognized entities. In [25], authors apply the topic extraction to blog posts. They differentiate between leader messages which initiate the topic from follower messages, which do not add information to topics of the conversation. Their approach enhances NER to focus on topics rather than just focus on entities. In our case we do not dispose of blog post: all the conversation is available as a single transcript. We need further clarification to decide which entities belong to the relevant topics of the discussion. We could use statistical approaches to refine the topics, still, we need to keep in mind that the extracted topics come from the mutual support group transcript. It is quite hard to identify the relevant recognized entities without holding a user-model of the participants. Some investigations explored the mechanisms of multi-party conversations in order to guarantee coherence in utterances generated automatically [26]. Other authors went beyond the definition of rules and probed the integration of robots in group conversations [27]. Both studies' results are promising but they cannot be applied in CBT contexts yet. Therefore, we provide the caregivers with an interface where they can select the relevant topics from a list of recognized entities. Moreover, in this way, therapists can add custom topics if needed.

3 Rationale

Together with caregivers, we identified the primary pain points of mutual support group interventions at Fraternità e Amicizia (from now on, F&A), a non-profit organization based in Milan – Italy - which operates in the field of psychosocial disability and offers different services based on the needs of people with disability. Among the services some are psychological-group-support therapies. In this kind of service, people with various disabilities attend group sessions with their peers and a professional therapist to talk about their feelings and to share their problems. One key characteristic is that participants may lose awareness of the discussed topics. In group therapy, there may be topics that are of interest only for a small subset of the participants. Some studies investigated the effects of the participants' roles and the topic changes in professional meetings [28]. To our knowledge, no research tackled the argument for group therapy. Cognitive Behavioral Therapy at F&A focuses on promoting the participants' awareness about themselves and their peers. For this reason, we agreed with therapists to introduce a system that could raise individual awareness about the topics of mutual conversation. In more general terms, we are interested in assessing the user's enjoyment of the therapeutic session. We provide to the subjects the possibility to classify the relevant topics of the discussion and to evaluate how much they liked the session. Behind the scenes, the users rating are used to inform therapists on the condition of the subjects. We solve in this way another pain point of the group therapy: usually, caregivers have no feedback from the participants about the session. With our system, caregivers receive actionable data on the mutual support group. We apply NLP technology in therapeutic intervention; as such, there are several considerations to keep in mind. First, end users may not understand why we register the intervention and what could be the implication of their recordings. To mitigate privacy issues, we never record the participants' voice: all the contributions are mixed in a shared transcript only in textual form (through speech-to-text - STT). If no explicit reference is provided, it is hard to identify a specific participant in the shared transcript. The transcript is deleted periodically as soon as the principal topics are recognized. In the second place, NLP can provide too much information and may fail to include a topic mentioned a few times that still holds great importance for the therapy. Therefore, we enable therapists to "pilot" the topic extraction. They can add custom topics on which they would like to work in each session. Finally, the talking therapy must not be interrupted or altered by the system: in our case, we do not want a bot to be a participant in the mutual discussion. Briefly must remain silent. In this way, we are providing a non-invasive support tool that does not alter the group therapy yet adds value for both participants and caregivers.

3.1 Ethical Issues

Every participant was informed about Briefly before the study. We collected all informed consents from participants and if needed their legal tutor. The informed consents included information about the study itself, procedures, goals, data treatment and withdraws in case of the subjects, at any point of the study, express the willingness not to participate any longer. All informed consents are stored in a safe cabinet. Researchers have no access to sensitive data about the participants. All sensitive information is archived protected by cryptography. Furthermore, both I3Lab and F&A signed a formal agreement for Scientific collaboration and co-titularity of data. The study protocol was submitted to the parties' Legal Department for counseling and approval. The issue of confidentiality and right of the study was solved following all guidelines provided by the Polytechnic of Milan Data Protection Supervisor, including authorization to proceed.

4 Implementation

4.1 Technology

To start, we convert the recording into text, a common task known under the name of speech-to-text - STT. We need a transcript to perform the initial text processing, e.g., to split the dialogue into several tokens in order to improve the accuracy of topic extraction. We employed Apple's Speech framework, available on iOS, to perform STT.

We considered different services to implement the topic extraction: Apple Natural Language Module, DialogFlow, Rakenltk, IBM Watson natural language understanding, Google Cloud Natural Language API, Amazon Comprehend and Aylien. Several factors influenced the selection criterion such as supporting Italian language, online or offline processing, pricing, and functionalities. We needed Italian language support since participants spoke only that language. Online and offline processing influenced the data treatment needed to guarantee the privacy of the users where the recorded dialogues may contain sensitive information. After an extensive evaluation, we opted for Google Cloud Natural Language API. It supports topic extraction with a list of many different categories, and it recognizes keywords with a reasonable degree of accuracy, leaving out stop words and conjunctions. This service supports the Italian language, but Google Translate API has been used to perform translations to English and back to Italian, in order to exploit some additional features only available for the English language. We performed several tests to make sure that the translations did not change the quality of the topics' recommendation. We verified that the extracted topics were the same or synonyms in both languages.

4.2 Architecture

Our system features different modules structured in order to perform at first topic extraction and then topic evaluation. These components are: a mobile application, implemented in iOS, which uses an Apple device to manage the creation of a therapeutic session with the selected participants, performs the recording of the conversation and extracts the principal topics and keywords; a web application which is the interface used by the patients to perform the evaluation and by the therapist to visualize statistics about the sessions; a non-relational, document-based database used to store the content of all sessions; a back-end system which exposes all the APIs needed by the two front-end systems to retrieve or store data, interacting with the non-relational database.

4.3 Mobile Application

The therapist uses the iOS app during the mutual support group sessions. Using a mobile application, we take advantage of developing an accessible UI for the therapist. We simplify the therapeutic session creation; it is enough to insert the participants' codes and select the topics they must rate. Given the delicate context of our research, we highlight how the use of a smartphone does not represent a novelty element for atypical users. As agreed with the caregivers, the presence of a mobile phone during the group therapy session does not represent an element of distraction or emotional distress as the participants regularly use mobile devices in everyday life.

The iOS app presents the following features: manage the creation of a new session by choosing the participants from a list of previously inserted anonymized codes; add a new participant's code to the list; record the conversation among peers; reform the transcription of the conversation; extract topics and keywords from the transcript through Google Cloud NLP API; manage the selection and filtering of topics, ordered by their frequency of appearance in the conversation; save a session document, sending to the back-end the list of participants, the list of selected topics and the date of the session; save the transcript of a session on the device, in order to perform topic extraction later on if there is no connectivity.

4.4   Web Application

We created a web application that serves as an interface for participants to evaluate the session and for therapists to gather feedback. We chose to implement the evaluation and feedback as a web application for its portability across devices. In this way, more participants could fill the evaluation in parallel, and the therapist could consult the results from any device with an internet connection. To present target users with a consistent and responsive interface, we evaluated several front-end frameworks from which we selected Vue.js for its fast learning pace and its broad community support. We integrated external libraries as well to generate the charts displaying the sessions' results. On the one hand, the web application allows the participant to: evaluate the different topics selected by the therapist following three levels of importance in an easy way. We defined the following three levels: "Important", "Neutral" or "Unimportant"; evaluate the session on a Likert scale from 1 star to 7. On the other hand, the web application allows the therapist to: select which session she/he wants to review; select the participants that have to perform the session's evaluation; check out the charts of the results and the general evaluation of a previous session or a specific patient.

5   Method

5.1   Goals and Research Questions

Briefly is, to our knowledge, a unique tool to record a therapy session and extract the main topics from it in real-time. For the study purposes, it was imperative to estimate whether Briefly was perceived as invasive or not from atypical subjects, in a Cognitive Behavioral Group Therapy context. Thus, the goals of this experimental study were to evaluate if Briefly influences the psychotherapeutic setting. Furthermore, therapists' point of view is crucial to understand better if and what type of impact it might have. For this reason, we also evaluated Briefly usability among therapists. A two-condition controlled trial was designed to expose our system's effects on the intervention: the experimental condition incorporates the application in Group Therapy, while the controlled condition does not. We focused our study on four main research questions, considering the novelty of the technological solution, the experimental setting, and the target population.

1. Is Briefly able to influence the subjects' therapeutic experience?
2. Do subjects appreciate the experience with Briefly?
3. Can Briefly be easily used and comprehended by therapists?
4. Are therapists willing to adopt this kind of technology in everyday practice?

5.2   Research Variables

Subjects. In order to investigate Briefly influence on the participants we selected for the study, we considered three variables: well-being, self-efficacy and likability (Table 1).

Table 1. Participants' research variables, measuring tools and methods

Variable	Tool	Method
Well-being	CORE-OM	Pre-post assessment
Self-efficacy	SAT-P	Pre-post assessment
Satisfaction	Likert	Pre-post assessment

Well-being and Self-efficacy. The aim of Cognitive Behavioral Group Therapy at F&A is to help people with disability to be more aware of themselves, of the world around them and to improve their relationships with their peers. Literature in Psychology [29] highlighted that the aspects that influence the most such a perception are those related to: how the subject feels about her/himself (well-being); how and how much she/he feels to be an active agent in her/his life (self-efficacy).

We employ CORE-OM and SAT-P at F&A to measure both well-being and self-efficacy due to the constrains such as validated test, type of subjects, Italian language, and type of setting. CORE-OM is an acronym that stands for Clinical Outcomes in Routine Evaluation-Outcome Measure. It was designed in 1998 by a group of researchers and clinicians, on the wave of the new paradigm of evidence, established on the practice, to evaluate, in an objective way, psychotherapies, with the possibility of comparisons between different psychology and consulting services [30]. According to the authors, this instrument should measure "[...] the core problem domains (Evans, 2002), the heart of the patient's problems, the goal of psychotherapeutic treatment". The CORE-OM is a 34 items questionnaire in which every item can be associated with one possible answer among five options, from "not at all" to "most of the time". The questionnaire investigates 4 domains: well-being (4 items), social functioning (12 items), problems/symptoms (12 items), risk either to self or to others (6 items) [31].

To complete the questionnaire, every participant is asked to fill in a self-report evaluation. The Satisfaction Profile (SAT-P), on the other hand, is a 32 items-test that measures different domains: sleep, eating, physical activity, sexual life, emotional status, self-efficacy, cognitive functioning, work, leisure, social and family relationships, and financial situation. Subjects were asked to evaluate their satisfaction in the above-mentioned domains in the last month on a 10 cm line that goes from "extremely dissatisfied" to "extremely satisfied" [32]. For this study, after the therapists' advice, we agreed not to evaluate the financial situation and sex habits domains, since participants do not have a full understanding of these two notions, and they could be extremely sensitive to both.

Likability. At the end of all sessions, each participant was asked to evaluate the most relevant topics extracted by Briefly and validated by the therapist. Participants had to grade them as "important", "not important" and "neutral". Furthermore, they were asked to evaluate, from 1 to 7, the level of satisfaction for the just-concluded session.

Therapists. For therapists, we considered two variables (Table 2): (i) usability of the application and (ii) its adoption in every-day practice. To investigate usability among therapists we selected the Questionnaire for User Interaction Satisfaction - QUIS [33]. The questionnaire assesses the users' satisfaction analyzing nine different dimensions:

screen factors, terminology and system feedback, learning factors, system capabilities, technical manuals, on-line tutorials, multimedia, teleconferencing, and software installation, if present. To assess the adoption of our system, we administered a questionnaire to the therapists we selected for our study and to a group of psychotherapy students as well. The latter filled the QUIS after showing them a brief presentation and a practical demonstration.

Table 2. Therapists' research variables, measuring tools and methods

Variable	Tool	Method
Usability	QUIS	Post study assessment
Adoptability	Survey	Post study assessment

5.3 Participants

We selected fifteen participants (10 males, 5 females; mean age 26, SD 4.07) for the study. Inclusion criteria were regular attendance of the therapeutic sessions before the beginning of the trial and comparable cognitive levels. Table 3 reports the participants profile identified through anonymized alphanumeric codes. Participants were divided into two groups to ensure a homogeneous sample for the study conditions: experimental vs. control. Subjects were randomly assigned to one of the two conditions according to gender, disability level, and age. The experimental group included 8 people (6 males, 2 females; mean age: 27.25, SD 3.85) whereas the control group was composed of 7 participants (4 males, 3 females; mean age: 24.57, SD 4.12).

Table 3. Participants' profiles

Sub	Age	Sex	Diagnosis
Experimental group			
1	25	M	Genetic syndrome
2	24	M	Severe intellectual disability
3	32	M	Severe intellectual disability with alternating phases of disorientation in space and time
4	29	M	Intellectual disability, facial dysmorphisms
5	24	M	Intellectual disability, mild autism spectrum disorder, chromosome deficiency
6	28	F	Mild intellectual disability, learning disability
7	33	F	Intellectual disability
8	23	M	Intellectual disability, mild bipolar affective syndrome

(continued)

Table 3. (*continued*)

Sub	Age	Sex	Diagnosis
Control group			
9	25	F	Kabuki syndrome with visual deficit (right eye) and moderate auditory deficit
10	32	M	Hydrocephalus, intellectual disability
11	22	F	Periventricular leukomalacia
12	23	F	Sturge-Weber syndrome, right hemiplegia
13	24	M	Kabuki syndrome
14	27	M	Atypical autistic disorder
15	19	M	Intellectual disability, drug-resistant epilepsy, congenital encephalopathy

5.4   Procedure

Number and Duration of Sessions. The study lasted eight weeks, from the 8th of May to the 28th of June 2019. We established one session every seven days, for a total of 8 sessions. Each session lasted 90 min.

Setting. The therapy sessions are organized weekly and carried forward for the entire educational year (September-June). This study was held in the regular therapeutic room, familiar to the subjects, equipped with a round table, some soft lights, and chairs.

Both experimental and control sessions were conducted as the regular weekly therapeutic group sessions, following the standard method: the group accesses the room and takes a sit around the table. The therapist sits with the group in-between participants and, after verifying who is present, starts the session. All participants undergo the CORE-OM and SAT-P questionnaires twice: as a baseline at beginning of the study (before May 8th) and as control at the end of it (after June 28th). The time elapsed between baseline and control allowed us to focus on the application's effects over two months. Paper-based Questionnaires were administered by researchers to all participants in individual sessions to ensure their privacy.

Experimental and Control Group Sessions. All sessions follow a standard and predefined procedure. Before each session, the therapist places the recording device (a smartphone) in the middle of the table and turns on the app. The therapist conducts the intervention as if the device is not there.

After 75 min, the therapist concludes the session. For those in the experimental group the last fifteen minutes are used to assess participants' satisfaction and likability and rate the topics and the session. The therapist selects the most relevant topics on the smartphone. After that, she/he opens Briefly web page on a separated tablet and hands it over to the participants. After all the participants have carried out their evaluations, the session terminates. Throughout the trial, anonymity was ensured by associating to each participant an alpha-numerical code known only by therapists and not by engineers who processed the data and the topics extracted by the system.

As for the experimental group, sessions follow a standardized procedure for the control group as well. The procedure faithfully respects the regular group therapy. Without the tool, the last 15 min are used for free debriefing and to prepare the participants to leave the daycare center.

5.5   Data Gathering

Subjects. To evaluate Briefly impact on participants, we gathered data from 60 questionnaires; 30 CORE-OM (baseline and control) and 30 SAT-P (baseline and control) tests; 16 from the experimental group and 14 from the control group. After collecting paper materials from subjects, we corrected, weighted, and scored the questionnaires according to the standardized charts. CORE-OM results report one score for each domain. Lower scores are associated with better outcomes. Moreover, SAT-P final score is the sum, in centimeters, of all the answers given by participants: the higher the score, the better are participants self-perception and efficacy. Concerning likability, we gathered the data automatically from the in-app evaluation.

Therapists. To evaluate the app impact on therapists, we gathered data from 22 QUIS questionnaires. Therapists scored each item from 0–9 according to their opinion: once again, a high score indicates better usability.

6   Discussion

6.1   Results on Subjects

Well-being. CORE-OM average score is obtained by summing the scores of the individual items divided for the number of answers. Example: Total score 58, divided by 34 items = 1.7, corresponding to the level of psychological distress at the time of measurement. Higher scores correspond to more severe problems.

The differences in pre- and post-assessments after the intervention tells the therapists if the participant's level of discomfort decreased and to what extent. To establish the clinically significant threshold scores, we used Jacobson and Truax's model of reliably change and Clinical significance [34]. The total threshold scores for the clinical populations were 1.19 for males and 1.29 for females. A second threshold of 2.50, for both men and women, demarcates the target population affected by medium-mild disorders, from the population suffering from severe disorders.

Group Analysis. Results over all participants reported in Fig. 1, indicate that both groups, control and experimental, have average scores below the critical threshold of 2.5 (which indicates the presence of medium-severe psychological distress). The average score suggests that all the participants selected for the study have a medium-mild level of psychological distress for B = well-being, P = problems/symptoms, and F = social functioning. None of the participants scored higher than the upper bound set to 2.5. The score also indicates that both groups were homogeneous: no substantial differences emerge between one group and the other.

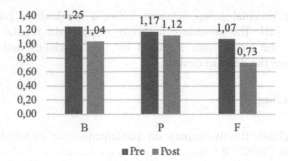

Fig. 1. CORE-OM Mean Scores for all subject in pre- and post-conditions for B = well-being, P = problems/symptoms and F = social functioning

We consider a Δ value for each subject, conveying the score difference between pre- and post-assessment (the baseline score at the beginning and control score at the end of the study), as shown in Eq. (1):

$$\Delta = \text{Control score} - \text{Baseline score} \tag{1}$$

A positive Δ means that the score obtained in the post-assessment is higher than the one obtained for the baseline, underling an improvement. On the contrary, if Δ is negative, the score obtained in the baseline condition is higher than after the intervention, pinpointing a worsening.

As visible in Fig. 2, results are very heterogeneous and differ from individual to individual. Δ mean scores of all subjects were: 0.32 for B = well-being, −0.33 for P = problems/symptoms and 0.03 for F = functioning. So, the difference between the pre and post conditions are to be considered not significant. Results do not differ much if we analyze them separately for the experimental group and the control group as reported in what follows.

Fea74	▼ -0,75	▼ -0,50	▼ -0,17	Fea37	▼ -0,25	▼ -0,83	▲ 0,42
Fea75	▼ -0,50	▼ -0,25	▲ 1,08	Fea57	▼ -0,50	▼ -0,50	▲ 0,25
Fea6	▼ -0,50	▼ -0,33	▼ -0,50	Fea78	▬ 0,00	▼ -0,25	▼ -0,08
Fea77	▬ 0,00	▲ 0,08	▲ 0,50	Fea53	▲ 0,25	▼ -1,50	▼ -0,42
Fea66	▲ 0,25	▲ 0,75	▲ 0,08	Fea30	▲ 0,75	▼ -0,58	▲ 0,67

Fea71	▬ 0,00	▼ -0,08	▼ -0,75
Fea70	▼ -1,50	▼ -0,42	▼ -1,17
Fea17	▲ 1,00	▲ 1,92	▼ -0,17
Fea79	▼ -2,50	▼ -2,09	▲ 0,17
Fea43	▼ -0,50	▼ -0,33	▼ -0,33

Fig. 2. CORE-OM Δ scores for all subjects for well-being, problems/symptoms sand social functioning.

Experimental Group Analysis. Participants in the experimental group obtained lower scores in the post-assessment compared to the pre-assessment. Figure 3 elucidates the mean scores in the pre and post-assessments. Only for social functioning it was possible to observe some improvements. On the other hand, Δ scores, illustrate in Fig. 4, confirm that the subjects remained at a low level of psychological distress.

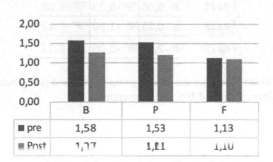

	B	P	F
■ pre	1,58	1,53	1,13
■ Post	1,77	1,51	1,10

Fig. 3. CORE-OM Mean Scores for the experimental group in pre and post-conditions for B = well-being, P = problems/symptoms and F = social functioning.

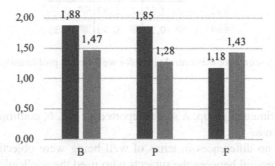

Fig. 4. CORE-OM Δ scores for the experimental group for well-being, problems/symptoms and social functioning

Control Group Analysis. The results of the control group are coherent with those of the experimental group and do not indicate an improvement. Figure 5 illustrates the average score in pre-and post-assessments.

Fea75	▼ -0,50	▼ -0,25	▲ 1,08
Fea77	▬ 0,00	▲ 0,08	▲ 0,50
Fea66	▲ 0,25	▲ 0,75	▲ 0,08
Fea37	▼ -0,25	▼ -0,83	▲ 0,42
Fea57	▼ -0,50	▼ -0,50	▲ 0,25
Fea78	▬ 0,00	▼ -0,25	▼ -0,08
Fea53	▲ 0,25	▼ -1,50	▼ -0,42
Fea79	▼ -2,50	▼ -2,09	▲ 0,17

Fig. 5. CORE-OM Mean Scores for the control group in pre- and post-conditions for B = well-being, P = problems/symptoms and F = social functioning.

Fea74	▼ -0,75	▼ -0,50	▼ -0,17
Fea6	▼ -0,50	▼ -0,33	▼ -0,50
Fea30	▲ 0,75	▼ -0,58	▲ 0,67
Fea71	▬ 0,00	▼ -0,08	▼ -0,75
Fea70	▼ -1,50	▼ -0,42	▼ -1,17
Fea17	▲ 1,00	▲ 1,92	▼ -0,17
Fea43	▼ -0,50	▼ -0,33	▼ -0,33

Fig. 6. CORE-OM Δ scores for the control group for well-being, problems/symptoms and social functioning

As for the experimental group, Δ scores reported in Fig. 6, confirm the low level of psychological distress.

To summarize, no differences in terms of well-being were objectively measurable and statically meaningful between the subjects who used the application and those who regularly underwent the mutual support intervention. Well-being is a broad dimension and an extremely sensitive variable to be measured. It can be influenced by multiple factors such as physiological, motivational, behavioral, and cognitive components and vary on several dimensions such as intensity, duration, and similar [35]. Family, personal interests, social condition, cognitive strategies, time, and age are some of the variables that might affect perceived well-being [36]. Therefore, our results can depend on other aspects not related to the study nor to the presence/absence of the application.

Self-efficacy. SAT-P final score is the sum, in centimeters, of all the answers given by participants. As for CORE-OM and to compare pre and post-assessments, we considered the Δ value for the scores. Once again, a positive Δ emphasizes an improvement. The mean scores for the control group were more promising than those of the experimental one. Table 4 highlights the mean Δ score for every aspect of self-efficacy measured by the test.

Table 4. SAT-P Mean Δ Scores of participants in experimental and control groups. Ps = Psychological, Ph = Physical, Wo = Work, Sa = Satisfaction, So = Social

Ps	Ph	Wo	Sa	So
Experimental group				
83.1	27.2	−13.1	−16.3	64
Control group				
232.4	66.8	9.7	52.4	16.7

In the scores associated with the aspects related to work and satisfactions, participants in the experimental conditions seem to have experienced a worsening in the level of personal satisfaction. However, participants of the control group reported positive Δ in all the aspects measured by the test and therefore possible measurable improvement between the pre- and the post-assessment. Nevertheless, we cannot say that the results are statistically significant.

Likability. Data collected from the 1–7 Likert scale administered to participants at the end of every sessions confirm that most of the participants enjoyed interacting with the application, as illustrated in Fig. 7. From the data collected on subjects, we address the first two research questions:

1. *Is Briefly able to influence the subjects' therapeutic experience?* No data emerging from our study suggest that Briefly influences a subject's therapeutic experience. Outcomes from both CORE-OM and SAT-P showed no difference between subjects that undergo regular therapy and those who experience Briefly during sessions. The results may seem negative for the purposes of our study, but, on the contrary, they are encouraging when we consider the non-invasiveness goal of our system. The primary purpose for which we designed Briefly was for it to be a support tool for patients and therapists, with a specific focus to be non-intrusive. In CBT it is essential to minimize the influence of external factors in the therapy contexts. Results on Briefly led us to consider that, even in the experimental condition, the app had no impact on how the participants perceived the intervention.
2. *Do subjects appreciate the experience with Briefly?* Yes. Likability scores were quite high for all subjects, and they are not bothered by the application running during the session. Participants seem to appreciate the possibility to classify the extracted topics and to rank the overall experience.

Our results confirm that Briefly is an "invisible" non-invasive appreciated support tool during group therapy for people with disability.

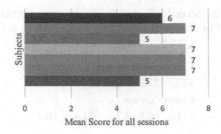

Fig. 7. Subjects' mean likability for all sessions

6.2 Results on Caregivers

Twenty-two caregivers (7 males, 15 females; mean age 39 y/o, S.D. 8.9) were selected for this study. Inclusion criteria were a psychological background and a previous experience in Group Therapy sessions. Caregivers were also assessed for self-perceived level of expertise on technology on a scale from 1 to 7. Most of the participants (15) indicated an expertise level between 3 and 5 and only 3 self-rated themselves between 6 and 7. The low technological expertise of caregivers stresses the need to create an easy system. QUIS use a 10-point scale to rate 21 items related to the system's usability. QUIS results indicate the user's satisfaction about the system's interface [37].

As showed in Table 5, most of the scores were from 7 to 9. QUIS score confirms that Briefly is well designed to support caregivers in the daily interventions. The above considerations allow us to answer our third research question

3. *Can Briefly be easily used and comprehended by therapists?* Mostly yes. Negative mean scores for items 1, 22 and 30 suggest that further improvements need to be done, in order to make Briefly easier to use, even for caregivers who don't have technological background.

To answer our last research question:

4. *Are therapists willing to adopt this kind of technology in everyday practice?* We conducted a workshop with the twenty-two therapist, and we added one specific question to the QUIS: *"Would you recommend Briefly to a colleague?"* The average response score (0–9) was 7. So, most of all therapist included in the workshop would recommend the application to a colleague and use Briefly in their everyday practice.

The fact that Briefly was not perceived by the mutual support group members confirms the non-intrusiveness of our application, repeatedly mentioned in the meeting by many therapists.

Table 5. QUIS results – median over the 22 caregiver questionnaires

QUIS	Score
Overall reaction to the software: 7	
1. Terrible/wonderful	4
2. Difficult/easy	7
3. Frustrating/satisfying	7
QUIS	Score
4. Inadequate power/adequate power	7
5. Dull/stimulating	6
6. Rigid/flexible	7
Screen: 9	
7. Characters on the computer screen	9
8. Highlighting on the screen simplifies task	9
9. Organization of information on screen	9
10. Sequence of screens	9
Terminology and system information: 8.5	
11. Use of terms throughout system	6
12. Computer terminology is related to the task you are doing	9
13. Position of messages on screen	9
14. Messages on screen which prompt user for input	8
15. Computer keeps you informed about what it is doing	8
16. Error messages	9
Learning: 7	
17. Learning to operate the system	7
18. Exploring new features by trial and error	7
19. Remembering names and use of commands	8
20. Tasks can be performed in a straight-forward manner	7
21. Help messages on the screen	9
22. Supplemental reference materials	5
System capabilities: 8.5	
23. System speed	9
24. System reliability	7
25. System tends to be noisy/quiet	9
26. Correcting your mistakes	8
Usability and user interface: 7	
27. Use of colors and sounds	9
28. System feedback	7
29. System response to errors	7
30. System messages and reports	4
31. System clutter	7
32. Interface and UI noise	9

7 Conclusion

Our application reached its goal: to be invisible to the eyes of the patients during the therapeutic session but still appreciated as a tool for topics classification. Furthermore, Briefly does not affect the subject's therapeutic experience and therefore, does not interfere with the intervention. The mutual support group can be carried out using a classic approach, but, at the same time, can provide reliable support for therapists and a valuable source of information on the state of well-being of each individual. From the therapist perspective, being able to monitor each subject in a group context effectively is a concrete need aimed at improving her/his clinical intervention. The potential of Briefly also happens to be more than a tool between patient and therapist. The professionals involved in the study have repeatedly suggested that, given the characteristics listed above, the application would be a valuable tool for the therapists themselves, in the meeting or supervision moments that are an integral part of their profession.

8 Limitations

The first limitation of our study concerns the gathered data: we could not eliminate the missing values depending on the participants' absences. We assume that such values are missing completely at random (MCAR) and decided not to include them in our calculations. We could employ better strategies, e.g., use imputation methods to fill the missing values, but we did not have enough data to obtain accurate results.

We focused mainly on the participants' well-being and self-efficacy. We used standardized questionnaires for both measures, but we could integrate the paper-based methods with automated ones. For example, we could gather data in real-time during the session through video recordings. We will incorporate other measures in the future. Moreover, we paid little attention to the rating the participants gave to each extracted topic. We will investigate further if the topics' rating can suggest a gain in awareness for subjects.

In the end, we can extend the period of the study. We are aware that our work is preliminary, in the sense that we focused mainly on the therapists' perspective. Nonetheless, the usability of Briefly may pave the ground for its adoption in therapeutic practices. Despite the encouraging results of our contribution, we have still to comprehensively address the impact of NLP technologies in mutual support group interventions.

Acknowledgements. This research was supported by *"Psychotherapy School AREA G"* and *"Fraternità e Amicizia No-profit"*. We thank our consultant, Mrs. Barbara Moro from *AREA G.* who provided insight and expertise that greatly assisted the research. We would also like to show our gratitude to Miss Fiorella Gillino, Mr Antonio Montinaro, Miss Federica Corbella and Miss Emily Luciani and all *AREA G.* therapists and students for sharing their pearls of wisdom with us during the course of this research.

References

1. Pfeiffer, P.N., Heisler, M., Piette, J.D., Rogers, M.A.M., Valenstein, M.: Efficacy of peer support interventions for depression: a meta-analysis. Gen. Hosp. Psychiatry **33**(1), 29–36 (2011)
2. Stead, L.F., Carroll, A.J., Lancaster, T.: Group behaviour therapy programmes for smoking cessation. Cochrane Database Syst. Rev. (3) (2017). Article no. CD001007. https://doi.org/10.1002/14651858.CD001007.pub3
3. Cameron, L.D., Booth, R.J., Schlatter, M., Ziginskas, D., Harman, J.E.: Changes in emotion regulation and psychological adjustment following use of a group psychosocial support program for women recently diagnosed with breast cancer. Psycho-Oncol.: J. Psychol. Soc. Behav. Dimensions Cancer **16**(3), 171–180 (2007)
4. Breitbart, W., Rosenfeld, B., Pessin, H., Applebaum, A., Kulikowski, J., Lichtenthal, W.G.: Meaning-centered group psychotherapy: an effective intervention for improving psychological well-being in patients with advanced cancer. J. Clin. Oncol. **33**(7), 749 (2015)
5. Seebohm, P., Chaudhary, S., Boyce, M., Elkan, R., Avis, M., Munn-Giddings, C.: The contribution of self-help/mutual aid groups to mental well-being. Health Soc. Care Community **21**(4), 391–401 (2013)
6. Ruini, C., Belaise, C., Brombin, C., Caffo, E., Fava, G.A.: Well-being therapy in school settings: a pilot study. Psychother. Psychosom. **75**(6), 331–336 (2006)
7. Friedman, E.M., Ruini, C., Foy, R., Jaros, L., Sampson, H., Ryff, C.D.: Lighten UP! A community-based group intervention to promote psychological well-being in older adults. Aging Ment. Health **21**(2), 199–205 (2017)
8. Hawton, K.E., Salkovskis, P.M., Kirk, J.E., Clark, D.M.: Cognitive Behaviour Therapy for Psychiatric Problems: A Practical Guide. Oxford University Press, Oxford (1989)
9. Stott, J., Charlesworth, G., Scior, K.: Measures of readiness for cognitive behavioural therapy in people with intellectual disability: a systematic review. Res. Dev. Disabil. **60** (2017), 37–51 (2017)
10. McConachie, H., et al.: Group therapy for anxiety in children with autism spectrum disorder. Autism **18**(6), 723–732 (2014)
11. Willets, L., Mooney, P., Blagden, N.: Social climate in learning disability services. J. Intellect. Disabil. Offending Behav. **5**(1), 24–37 (2014)
12. Webster, J.J., Kit, C.: Tokenization as the initial phase in NLP. In: COLING 1992: The 15th International Conference on Computational Linguistics, vol. 4 (1992)
13. Plisson, J., Lavrac, N., Mladenic, D., et al.: A rule based approach to word lemmatization. In: Proceedings of IS-2004, pp. 83–86 (2004)
14. Màrquez, L., Rodríguez, H.: Part-of-speech tagging using decision trees. In: Nédellec, C., Rouveirol, C. (eds.) ECML 1998. LNCS, vol. 1398, pp. 25–36. Springer, Heidelberg (1998). https://doi.org/10.1007/BFb0026668
15. Straková, J., Straka, M., Hajič, J.: Open-source tools for morphology, lemmatization, POS tagging and named entity recognition. In: Proceedings of 52nd Annual Meeting of the Association for Computational Linguistics: System Demonstrations, pp. 13–18 (2014)
16. Loper, E., Bird, S.: NLTK: the natural language toolkit. arXiv preprint arXiv:cs/0205028 (2002)
17. Pinto, A., Gonçalo Oliveira, H., Oliveira Alves, A.: Comparing the performance of different NLP toolkits in formal and social media text. In: 5th Symposium on Languages, Applications and Technologies (SLATE 2016). Schloss Dagstuhl-Leibniz-Zentrum fuer Informatik (2016)

18. Apple: Apple Natural Language (2019). https://developer.apple.com/documentation/naturallanguage. Accessed Sept 2019
19. IBM 2019: IBM Natural Language Understanding (2019). https://www.ibm.com/watson/services/natural-language-understanding/. Accessed Sept 2019
20. Amazon: Amazon Comprehend (2019). https://aws.amazon.com/comprehend/. Accessed Sept 2019
21. Google: Google Natural Language (2019). https://cloud.google.com/natural-language/?hl=en. Accessed Sept 2019
22. Liu, F., Liu, F., Liu, Y.: A supervised framework for keyword extraction from meeting transcripts. IEEE Trans. Audio Speech Lang. Process. **19**(3), 538–548 (2010)
23. Galley, M.: Automatic summarization of conversational multi-party speech (2006)
24. Ziegler, J., Jerroudi, Z.E., Böhm, K.: Generating semantic contexts from spoken conversation in meetings. In: Proceedings of the 10th International Conference on Intelligent User Interfaces, pp. 290–292. ACM (2005)
25. El-Assady, M., Sevastjanova, R., Gipp, B., Keim, D., Collins, C.: NEREx: named-entity relationship exploration in multi-party conversations. In: Computer Graphics Forum, vol. 36, pp. 213–225. Wiley Online Library (2017)
26. Li, J., Liao, M., Gao, W., He, Y., Wong, K.-F.: Topic extraction from microblog posts using conversation structures. In: ACL (1). World Scientific (2016)
27. de Bayser, M.G., Guerra, M.A., Cavalin, P.R., Pinhanez, C.S.: Specifying and implementing multi-party conversation rules with finite-state-automata. In: AAAI Workshops (2018)
28. Vázquez, M., Carter, E.J., McDorman, B., Forlizzi, J., Steinfeld, A., Hudson, S.E.: Towards robot autonomy in group conversations: understanding the effects of body orientation and gaze. In: 2017 12th ACM/IEEE International Conference on Human-Robot Interaction (HRI), pp. 42–52 (2017)
29. Sapru, A., Bourlard, H.: Detecting speaker roles and topic changes in multiparty conversations using latent topic models. In: Fifteenth Annual Conference of the International Speech Communication Association (2014)
30. Lucas-Carrasco, R., Salvador-Carulla, L.: Life satisfaction in persons with intellectual disabilities. Res. Dev. Disabil. **33**(4), 1103–1109 (2012)
31. Evans, C., et al.: Towards a standardised brief outcome measure: psychometric properties and utility of the CORE-OM. Br. J. Psychiatry **180**(1), 51–60 (2002)
32. Margison, F., et al.: CORE: clinical outcomes in routine evaluation. J. Ment. Health **9**(3), 247–255 (2000)
33. Majani, G., et al.: A new instrument in quality-of-life assessment: the satisfaction profile (SAT-P). Int. J. Ment. Health **28**(3), 77–82 (1999)
34. Chin, J.P., Diehl, V.A., Norman, K.L.: Development of an instrument measuring user satisfaction of the human-computer interface. In: Proceedings of the SIGCHI Conference on Human Factors in Computing Systems, pp. 213–218. ACM (1988)
35. Diener, E.: Assessing subjective well-being: progress and opportunities. Soc. Indic. Res. **31**(2), 103–157 (1994)
36. Tobia, V., Greco, A., Steca, P., Marzocchi, G.M.: Children's wellbeing at school: a multi-dimensional and multi-informant approach. J. Happiness Stud. **20**(3), 841–861 (2019)
37. Shneiderman, B., Norman, K.: Questionnaire for User Interface Satisfaction (QUIS), Designing the User Interface: Strategies for Effective Human-Computer Interaction. Addison-Wesley Publ. Co., Reading (1992)

An Embodied and Ubiquitous E-coach for Accompanying Older Adults Towards a Better Lifestyle

Mira El Kamali[1(✉)], Leonardo Angelini[1], Maurizio Caon[1],
Denis Lalanne[2], Omar Abou Khaled[1], and Elena Mugellini[1]

[1] University of Applied Sciences and Arts Western Switzerland (HES-SO),
Fribourg, Switzerland
mira.elkamali@hes-so.ch
[2] University of Fribourg, Fribourg, Switzerland

Abstract. The population of people age 65 or over is increasing especially in Europe [3]. Granting to this target population a longer and healthier life is paramount for the European Community. In the context of the H2020 EU funded project "NESTORE" [11], an embodied and ubiquitous e-coach is being developed seeking to change the lifestyle of seniors in different domains of wellbeing. NESTORE e-coach is known as a personalized embodied and ubiquitous e-coach that plays three essential roles in elderly's wellbeing: a coach, a friend and a companion. As a coach, NESTORE will give trainings and advice following a wellbeing path that is proposed by experts in wellbeing. As a friend, this e-coach knows and understands the user. As a companion, this e-coach has the ability to detect the user's emotion and aims at building empathy with the user based by providing support throughout their daily training. The NESTORE e-coach is based on three different intervention medium: a mobile application, a chatbot and an embodied vocal assistant. These interfaces have different forms, different capabilities and different visions. Users can communicate with the NESTORE e-coach through different interfaces exclusively, sequentially, concurrently and synergistically. The interaction can be initiated from the user side to different interfaces and/or from the e-coach side. In this paper, we present the NESTORE's full vision for building the three essential roles of this e-coach which are: a coach, a companion and a friend for seniors. Furthermore, we explain the NESTORE system design, architecture, capabilities and how the different interfaces of this E-coach contribute to make a multi-modal system. Finally, we conclude our work with the state of this H2020 project.

Keywords: Virtual coach · Elderly people · Wellbeing · Human computer interaction

M. Kurosu (Ed.): HCII 2020, LNCS 12183, pp. 23–35, 2020.
https://doi.org/10.1007/978-3-030-49065-2_2

1 Introduction

In most developed countries, especially in Europe, the population of the age group over 65 years is increasing [3]. As getting older, most people will need to stay living a healthy life and to maintain mental and physical autonomy. Thus, a coaching approach can be a solution for retaining their wellbeing. The speedy development of the ICT technology can play a key role in supports of the requirements of the ageing population. Indeed, technology can maximize the successfulness of coaching older individuals at larger scale reducing the economic burden of well-being intervention and at longer term, of their care, However, technology stays advanced for many older adults.

The project NESTORE works to beat the restrictions of current solutions. In fact, most healthcare technological systems tackle two or less wellbeing domains [7]. NESTORE is a virtual coach that addresses healthy older individuals and cover five key dimensions of wellbeing: physical, nutritional, cognitive, social and emotional. Its vision is based on pathways proposed by experts and the experience is personalized on user preferences and needs. SOC and HAPA models [9] known as Behavioral theories are embedded in the coaching algorithms. Data is collected through environmental sensors, wearable devices, beacons, games, sleep monitoring, smart scales and the virtual coach itself, through natural conversation. The whole system is personalized by an intelligent and innovative Decision Support System (DSS) [2] that works on short-term and long-term analysis through analyzing static and dynamic profile. As for the intervention, the virtual coach itself is the only way to deliver data of the whole NESTORE intelligence cloud and devices to the user.

NESTORE e-coach plays three essential roles: a coach, a friend, a companion. We designed NESTORE as a coach that provides coaching activities and plans in each domain of wellbeing in order to give personalized intervention techniques such as short- and long-term goals, feedbacks based on user's score. We designed NESTORE e-coach as a friend giving it the ability of listening to the user upon his or her request and of understanding the user natural language and the powerful intelligence of the system that is able to learn and adapt to users' specific behaviors and context. We also design this e-coach as a companion by being omnipresent via its tangibility or its online availability. Most importantly, we define this sense of companionship by having an empathic relationship with the user using emotions detection algorithm [12]. As a result, our e-coach's final goal is to transform elderly to co-producers of their own health life.

The e-coach is composed of three different interfaces where each interface plays the three roles mentioned before. The three interfaces come in different forms and capabilities: a mobile application, a chatbot integrated in the mobile application, which is a text based conversational agent and a tangible coach, which is an embodied conversational agent that acts as a vocal assistant. These three interfaces can interact with user exclusively, sequentially, concurrently and synergistically. The e-coach interfaces work as a team to act and give the user the sense of coaching, friendship and companionship visioning a long-term human-computer interaction with seniors. In this article, we introduce the NESTORE system with a scenario of an elderly using the e-coach and the role played by the different interfaces. Next, we present the three essential roles of our e-coach by being a friend, coach and companion and how our e-coaches and its three interfaces acts to achieve these roles. Then, we present each interface of the e-coach and the multimodality aspect toward the elderly concluding the article by the status of the project and some future work.

2   Previous Work

We conducted a systematic review to study the previous work for a virtual coach for elderly's wellbeing [7]. We explored the different definitions of the previous e-coaches especially their role as a friend or companion. Most of the papers found mention the importance for e-coaches to be warm, cuddly and useful. However, there were no studies that explore how each role can affect the design of this virtual coach [7]. We also explored the different embodiments and intervention delivery modalities of the virtual coach: a study [13] has built a system that schedules some physical activities for the user: it is a digital human-like coach in computer program. The embodiment here is an animated virtual coach that also spoke up the scheduled messages that appear on the screen for the user using text-to-speech converter. The coach is almost always visually present on the screen for the user. Another study [8] explains a virtual coach called Bandit in a robotic form that mimics human physical activities in order to help elderly to do certain activities. The robot's lip movements are synchronized with the robot's speech so that the lips open at the start until the end of a spoken utterance. Results showed that most elderly were very motivated for such a virtual coach because it is enjoyable, useful and helpful. However, no studies were found that show the multi-modality aspect that we are going to explore in Sect. 6. In fact, most studies explore one type of interface such as [4] and [5]. Finally, most studies were tackling only one domain, which emphasizes the need to explore a multi-domain intervention with multi-modal interaction.

3   E-coach Accompanying Older Adults for a Better Lifestyle: A Scenario

Laura is 65 and has recently retired. She is Italian and lives currently in Milano. She loves cooking and dancing and now that she is free, she would like to spend more time exploring new recipes and re-living her youth dancing in front of the mirror. Sandro, her husband, is also retired and lives with her at home with their dog. Sandro and Laura love gardening together and this is what is helping them to stay fit. To get a healthier lifestyle, Laura got NESTORE e-coach. This virtual coach comes in different forms of interfaces such as a mobile application, a chatbot integrated inside the mobile app and a tangible coach with vocal and tangible interaction capabilities. The chatbot on-boards Laura, introduces her to the system and starts to get to know more about her habits and preferences. Thus, her e-coach chooses "cooking", "dancing" and "gardening" as the main three focuses. The e-coach starts setting quantitative goals for Laura and with time while observing Laura's progress with the e-coach proposed tasks, the e-coach starts sending other goals that optimize Laura's health. Such propositions and recommendations are sent by the chatbot, the mobile application or the tangible coach, according to the user availability or preferences. If the user is not at home, then the e-coach understands her unavailability of having a vocal interaction with the tangible coach and will send its messages to the mobile chatbot instead. Moreover, depending on what the user chooses or uses more often among chatbot or tangible or mobile application, the e-coach will start sending these recommendations to the most used interface over time. In the beginning, Laura is put to a two- week monitoring (motivational) phase to assess her wellbeing path and then she is shifted to the intervention (volitional) phase where Laura conducts a behavioral change and becomes a co-producer on her own health. This behavioral change model called HAPA is proposed by our experts [9]. Daily and weekly progress and proposition of activities are given by the mobile application. The DSS [2] will select coaching plans based on personalized indications, advices on healthy lifestyle and elderly decline prevention. Hence, the e-coach starts monitoring and tracking the progress of Laura, outlines her behavior changes and manages her loss of motivation using different type of intervention techniques such as feedback, recommendations, praise etc. Since all services in the system are proposed by experts in each domain of wellbeing then "dancing" is treated under the umbrella of the physical domain sub-pathways service which is "aerobic fitness" [6]. The e-coach proposes to Laura to "walk her dog" or "gardening" with her husband under the umbrella of combining two domains: the physical and social domain. The chatbot, as its job in the nutritional domain, asks Laura to send a photo of the current meal to analyze her calories and nutrients [14]. On the other hand, the chatbot sends Laura different recipes based on her heathy eating progress and food preferences. In addition, the e-coach, through the mobile application, suggests taking dancing lessons or joining dancing groups nearby Milano. The e-coach, knowing that she and her husband are both fans of gardening, will suggest for them to go to an exhibition on "Italian gardens" via the mobile application interface. Laura can also connect with her friends or family on the platform in order to join them in some activities with them. Not only can the e-coach connect to Laura, but the latter can also ask questions and get an overview of her performance at the end of each day via the tangible coach. These different modalities are activated independently according to the CASE model [10]. The e-coach is also capable of delivering the intervention by combining the multiple interfaces in a synergistic manner [10]. For instance, the tangible coach explains vocally the recipe of a specific food, accompanying Laura step by step during her performance. The tangible coach also sends the full description of the recipe via the chatbot for a visual interaction. Figure 1 shows the user journey through the NESTORE e-coach.

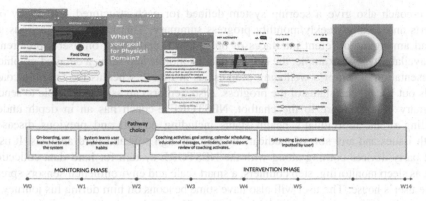

Fig. 1. User journey using NESTORE e-coach

4 Older Adults E-coach Vision and Principles

NESTORE e-coach is based on co-design principles held in 4 different countries: Italy, England, Netherlands and Spain. NESTORE methodology is called after the Greek Nestor, known for his great wisdom, the advisor of Troy. This e-coach guides people to better lives. It plays three essential roles with elderly:

(1) a coach: based on experts in each field of wellbeing to help the user achieve his goals by giving coaching tips, tracking and monitoring the user.
(2) a companion: based on being omnipresent and empathic with the user. It gives the older adults a sense of companionship so that they will not feel alone.
(3) a friend: based on being loyal to the user. It gives also many advices to build a certain trust between the e-coach and the senior.

These three roles allows the e-coach to mediate into the senior's life and recommend the user to change one or more behavior at once.

4.1 NESTORE as a Coach

NESTORE e-coach mentors the senior in five domains: physical, nutritional, cognitive, social and emotional. Domain experts provided specific recommendations that are orchestrated by the coach following a behavioral changing model called HAPA. The e-coach refers to a coaching timeline that is composed of a three-layer system of pathways, coaching activity plans and coaching events. As a coach, the latter helps the user to choose his or her general pathway. In fact, after the 2 weeks motivational phase, the e-coach analyses the user's behaviors and recommend him or her the wellbeing pathway to follow. Next, the e-coach helps the user to select his or her favorite coaching plan activity. The e-coach then helps the user to schedule the proposed coaching activities into his or her calendar matching the user's time availability. Finally, the e-coach guides the users towards their objective by using different intervention techniques such as praise messages, reminders, setting short term to eventually reach long term goals, personalized recommendations, and constructive feedback [7].

The e-coach also give a scoring system defined for each structured activity by our experts and a daily/weekly/monthly progress summary. This kind of interactions are spread among the different interfaces of this e-coach depending on user's preference and availability. For example, the chatbot and the mobile app show a detailed graphical representation of senior's wellbeing progress as in Fig. 2, whereas the tangible coach spells out vocally the status of the progress. Also, seniors can ask the tangible to send a summary of their score to the chatbot. NESTORE e-coach has an in depth understanding of the individual's health status including current and previous diseases, health issues and any sort of medication taken through soft and hard analysis. It uses third party devices coming along with the NESTORE system for hard data collection such as sleep monitoring, step counters, a smart scale and environmental sensors spread in the user's house. The user will also have some beacons on him during his journey in order to detect the amount of social interaction. The chatbot send some questionnaires provided by experts in the cognitive and social domains for soft data collection. The mobile application suggests some cognitive games such as "numerical updating tasks", "digit span backward" and Math problem-solving exercise in order to monitor how well the senior is doing toward his or her wellbeing [6].

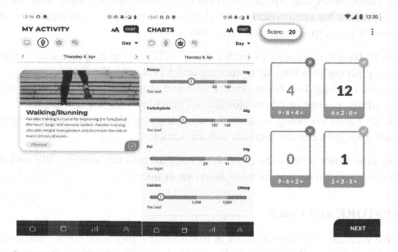

Fig. 2. Mobile application for showing data, scheduling activities and playing games

The chatbot also have food recognition capabilities: it asks the user to send a photo of the current meal he or she is eating. Using machine learning algorithms, the e-coach detects the food in the photo, calculates the calories and the nutrients provided by the meal [14]. To sum up, NESTORE as a coach pushes the individual to convert a habit or follow a healthier routine via a well-studied psychological intervention.

4.2 NESTORE as a Friend

NESTORE e-coach "knows" and "understands" the user which are the two criteria that makes our e-coach a friend. It collects and gathers user's personal data such as the user's health issues, preferences, lifestyle, past experiences, and so many other aspects. Data are collected in two forms: static and dynamic. Static data are basically the user's general information such as users' demographic and environmental characteristics, preferences and baseline data. Whereas, dynamic data are collected via sensors, applications, and contextual APIs. By collecting all these data, the NESTORE e-coach gets to know really well the senior user. On the user side, once the mobile application is downloaded and the tangible coach is installed, the chatbot starts introducing the whole system and switch from formality to informality after a while as a friendship sign. The e-coach will also be able to execute specific tasks for the senior such as weather cast, news updates, general informing and healthy coaching personalized updates that will help seniors to form eventually a sort of a friendship and a bond to the coach. The amount of the use of the e-coach and the type of questions asked by the user will give the e-coach the possibility to become more open to informality. In particular, NES-TORE e-coach implements novel algorithms for detecting and monitoring of important indicators related to user status and behavior. The personalization of the system plays a big role in building a friendship between the e-coach and the senior. The e-coach gives personalized feedback and advice. This latter makes the user feel eventually appreciated, loved and known as a close friend. According to [16], casual friendships are very helpful in relieving stress and depression, but having a close friend takes it to a whole new level of levering. This is what makes e-coach very important in ones' life. This e-coach is the literal definition of "I'm always here for you"; whenever the user calls out for it; it directly replies, which makes it really functional under all circumstances.

In addition to giving advice; e-coach is also a secret keeper. Confidentiality is a one of e-coach's core essence, which strengthen the relationship between the user and e-coach. GDPR is taken into consideration [15] since data collection is consensual and will never be leaked. At longer term, the e-coach will be the best projection of a person you've known your whole life.

4.3 NESTORE as a Companion

Adults encounter all sort of companionship throughout their daily basic day at work, streets, friends and even family. Paper [18] shows that the following does not apply to elderly. The author elaborated that seniors, once retired from jobs and with their children moving away or their friends and/or spouses passing away, do not have always opportunities for social engagement. This might lead to seniors becoming housebound, especially if they lose the ability to drive or become ill. Companionship is a main part of "senior care" and not solely via assistance in daily duties but also via a beneficial conversational interaction. Whenever human companionship is not available for the senior, the e-coach might, at least partially, compensate this lack. In fact, NESTORE e-coach builds an empathic relationship with the user by (1) being omnipresent with the user at any time, (2) understanding the user sentiments and acting upon it and (3) interacting with the user through tangible and vocal interaction. To begin with, the e-coach is always available for the user. Seniors can always have access by opening their mobile application and start chatting with the e-coach. The physical device part of the coach also plays a role of being an omnipresent and a portable battery power e-coach as shown in Fig. 3. Second, the chatbot and the tangible coach can detect the user's feelings based on senior's text input or the senior's voice and tonality. In fact, particular sentences spelled or written by the user are sent to the Emotion Well-Being Engine that analyzes semantically the emotional valence of the phrase. The emotional wellbeing Engine is based on sematic reference model [12] which make understands the user's current affect state. Once the chatbot or the tangible coach detects the user's emotion, they let the user know that they understand his or her feelings and start acting upon it by motivating and supporting the user. The tangible coach, in particular, has a lightning system as shown in Fig. 3 in order to interact with the user. The tangible coach integrates for each emotion lights patterns with different colors for each emotion detected such as "happiness", "sadness", "surprised", "disgust", "anger" and "fear" [12]. These lights follow the Plutchick's diagram colors of feelings [17]. To sum it up, the tangible coach plays a huge role in keeping company by the ability of letting the user to "touch" the coach and "speak" using vocal voice. The user has the opportunity to have a physical device in his or her house, always present and ready to start a conversation with the user.

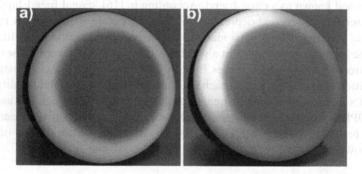

Fig. 3. Tangible coach and the lightning system, listening (a), thinking (b)

5   E-coach Architecture and Interfaces for Multi-modality

The use of digital devices to support elderly's wellbeing has been an open field [7]. Most elderly people, nowadays, own at least one electronic device such as smartphone, smart wearable, tablet, PC or laptop computers and even vocal assistants. In particular, conversational agents have become the center of research and industrial use. According to chatbots.org [19], a conversational agent is a software program which understand and respond the user based on statements sent in ordinary natural language. A conversational agent can be a text-based messaging application such as woebot [20] or a vocal conversational agent such as ALEXA, GOOGLE HOME. They can be used for different purposes such as customer service or information acquisition which make them more useful and popular. Conversational agents can also be used in healthcare.

One of the main goals of the NESTORE virtual coach is to build a ubiquitous interaction with the conversational agents. Commands change with activities across the daily routine and takes place in different time and location. A conversational agent embedded in a mobile application is very useful because it can travel with the user but having a chatbot based conversational agent might decrease the user experience due to its limited modality capability. In fact, a conversational agent which is able to communicate via multiple kind of interfaces preserving the awareness of the user's preferences and context, can enhance the final user experience and provide a more effective interaction [21]. However, the transition from one device to the other should be seamless and opportune to the particular activity performed at that very moment. In order to do that, one should know exactly the capability of each interface. For instance, two of the main advantages of the speech based conversational agent are optimizing time and enabling multi-tasking. Such interface can be used for particularly daily tasks and should be integrated in daily activities that involves having both hands occupied, for example, while cooking. Text-based Chatbots have other principles of interaction. A text-based chatbot is able to perform the demanded tasks effectively and precisely using buttons on user's interface and more importantly visually.

In order to give the best user experience, NESTORE e-coach is constituted of two different types of conversational agents: a vocal tangible coach, a text-based chatbot and the mobile application.

The mobile application is an android app. It contains the senior profile. The latter can also change his or her personal data. The senior can find in the mobile app personalized activities proposed and recommended by the system and can also check his or her progress in each domain of wellbeing. Finally, the user can schedule his or her next activities using the calendar in the mobile app. Such interface shows also feedback on different wellbeing charts.

The chatbot, in NESTORE case, is an intelligent conversational software agent activated by natural language text input. This chatbot provides written and generated conversational output in response using intelligent algorithms and a database. The chatbot, like the mobile application, can also schedule activities for the user, knowing the user's available time, and can propose for the user also activities depending on his health progress through a written scenario of conversations between the chatbot and the user. Users can also chat with the chatbot about their day and their feelings. The chatbot sends also personalized recommendations, feedback, praise messages and notifications on a daily, weekly and monthly analysis. The chatbot can give an overview of the score upon user's request.

The tangible coach is based on vocal and tangible interaction. In the vocal interaction, the tangible coach will listen to the senior and then generate a response to the user depending on his or her question. Through the lighting system of the tangible coach, the senior will know when the tangible is listening, thinking or speaking. The senior can ask any general questions about the system, the weather, global news, general cultural information and the tangible device is always ready to answer. Like the mobile application and the chatbot, the senior can also ask about his or her scheduled and proposed activities and his or her weekly and monthly scores. The answers are all given vocally in the chosen language. Furthermore, the tangible notifies the user every night asking about their sentiments throughout their day to monitor their emotional wellbeing. Finally, like the chatbot, the senior can have a one to one conversation with the tangible coach. The tangible interaction gives the ability to the user to physically control the data collection process. In fact, the tangible coach has two main states, which are the sleep state and the wake state. The user needs to put the tangible coach in the wake state in order to speak with. The two states are differentiated based on the position of the tangible coach. Figure 4 shows the two different states of the tangible coach. As a result, the tangibility and the possibility to caress and to feel this tangible coach can create eventually an emotional bonding with the user.

Fig. 4. Tangible coach in sleep state (a) and wake state (b)

Conversational agents of the e-coach (chatbot and tangible coach) are based on conversations and scenarios managed by the Conversational Coach Engine, which is developed in Node.js. In particular, user's free-text inputs are treated by 4 instances of the RASA Core/NLU Server, each trained in the different languages supported by the chatbot (English, Spanish, Italian and Dutch).

It is easier usually to use just one type of interface and device to get a task done, however this means that the user must actively engage in the task in order to get the job done. For example, if the user focuses only on the tangible interaction, this may lead to the loss of having a visual understanding of the information received.

A multi-modal multi-interface capability is proposed. Interfaces are used sequentially (that is, device A then device B) and are chosen based on their suitability and availability. Different interfaces are used as well simultaneously for task completion (that is, A and B). For instance, since the tangible coach lacks a screen, combining it with the chatbot can expand the tangible coach's capability, by sending links, images or videos.

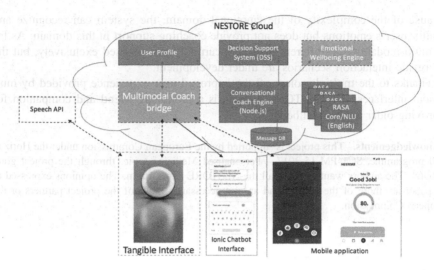

Fig. 5. NESTORE e-coach architecture and the different interfaces of the e-coach (Tangible interface, chatbot, mobile application, serious game, social platform)

The multimodal multi-interface interaction is based on a multimodal bridge shown in the Fig. 5. The Multimodal Coach Bridge decides when each interface interacts with the user, when to trigger recommendations about invoking multiple interfaces, and whether one or more than one interface should interact independently, sequentially or simultaneously.

6 Conclusion

NESTORE project is funded by the European union under the H2020 program and is intended to be finished by year 2021. The NESTORE project is based on a virtual coach that helps the user to maintain and improve his or her wellbeing. This is achieved by designing a multi-modal interaction and giving the e-coach different roles for interacting with the elderly. We presented a user journey with the NESTORE e-coach. We also explained the three roles of the NESTORE e-coach in improving and maintaining senior's wellbeing. NESTORE e-coach is actually a coach, a friend and a companion to older adults. It helps the user to train in different domains in wellbeing by a set of intervention defined by our experts. It also understands the user and act as support system for the user throughout his journey for maintaining or improving the wellbeing. It finally builds an empathic relationship through natural conversation. We also presented the interfaces of this virtual coach and mentioned each roles and capability towards user's wellbeing. Finally, we showed the architecture of our system and multimodal coach bridge for dispatching data for the different interfaces. The current version of the system is currently being tested with 60 users in 3 sites across Europe: Italy, Spain and the Netherlands. At the current stage of the project, NESTORE provides coaching in four domains (physical, nutritional, social and cognitive).

Because of the complexity of the emotional domain, the system can recognize and monitor user's emotions but does not provide coaching support in this domain. As for the multi-modality, the different interfaces currently can be used exclusively, but the synergistic interaction scenarios are under development.

Thanks to the multiple roles and the improved user experience provided by multimodal interfaces, the NESTORE e-coach is a promising friend and companion for improving older adults' wellbeing.

Acknowledgements. This project is supported by the European Commission under the Horizon 2020 programme, SC1-PM-15-2017 – Personalised Medicine topic, through the project grant N.76964. The authors want to thank all the NESTORE Consortium. The opinions expressed in this paper are those of the authors and are not necessarily those of the project partners or the European Commission.

References

1. El Kamali, M., Angelini, L., Caon, M., Andreoni, G., Khaled, O.A., Mugellini, E.: Towards the NESTORE e-Coach: a tangible and embodied conversational agent for older adults. In: Proceedings of the 2018 ACM International Joint Conference and 2018 International Symposium on Pervasive and Ubiquitous Computing and Wearable Computers, pp. 1656–1663. ACM (2018)
2. Orte, S., et al.: Dynamic decision support system for personalised coaching to support active ageing. In: AI* AAL@AI* IA, pp. 16–36 (2018)
3. Chłoń-Domińczak, A., Kotowska, I.E., Kurkiewicz, J., Abramowska-Kmon, A., Stonawski, M.: Population Ageing in Europe: Facts, Implications and Policies. European Commission, Brussel (2014)
4. Miskelly, F.G.: Assistive technology in elderly care. Age Ageing **30**(6), 455–458 (2001)
5. Albaina, I.M., Visser, T., Van Der Mast, C.A., Vastenburg, M.H.: Flowie: a persuasive virtual coach to motivate elderly individuals to walk. In: 2009 3rd International Conference on Pervasive Computing Technologies for Healthcare, pp. 1–7. IEEE, April 2009
6. Angelini, L., et al.: The NESTORE e-coach: accompanying older adults through a personalized pathway to wellbeing. In: Proceedings of the 12th ACM International Conference on Pervasive Technologies Related to Assistive Environments, pp. 620–628. ACM, June 2019
7. Rocke, C., et al.: D5.1 Definition of intervention techniques. https://nestore-coach.eu/deliverables
8. Fasola, J., Matarić, M.J.: A socially assistive robot exercise coach for the elderly. J. Hum.-Robot Interact. **2**(2), 3–32 (2013)
9. Schwarzer, R., Luszczynska, A.: How to overcome health-compromising behaviors: the health action process approach. Eur. Psychol. **13**(2), 141–151 (2008)
10. Dumas, B., Lalanne, D., Oviatt, S.: Multimodal interfaces: a survey of principles, models and frameworks. In: Lalanne, D., Kohlas, J. (eds.) Human Machine Interaction. LNCS, vol. 5440, pp. 3–26. Springer, Heidelberg (2009). https://doi.org/10.1007/978-3-642-00437-7_1
11. Nestore: a companion for better and healthier ageing. European Comission. https://ec.europa.eu/digital-single-market/en/news/nestore-companion-better-and-healthier-ageing

12. Sykora, M.D., Jackson, T., O'Brien, A., Elayan, S.: Emotive ontology: extracting fine-grained emotions from terse, informal messages. In: Proceedings of the IADIS International Conference Intelligent Systems and Agents 2013, ISA 2013, Proceedings of the IADIS European Conference on Data Mining 2013, ECDM 2013, pp. 19–26 (2013)
13. Similä, H., Merilahti, J., Ylikauppila, M., Muuraiskangas, S., Perälä, J., Kivikunnas, S.: Comparing two coaching systems for improving physical activity of older adults. In: Roa Romero, L. (ed.) XIII Mediterranean Conference on Medical and Biological Engineering and Computing 2013. IFMBE, vol. 41, pp. 1197–1200. Springer, Cham (2014). https://doi.org/10.1007/978-3-319-00846-2_296
14. Aguilar, E., Bolaños, M., Radeva, P.: Food recognition using fusion of classifiers based on CNNs. In: Battiato, S., Gallo, G., Schettini, R., Stanco, F. (eds.) ICIAP 2017. LNCS, vol. 10485, pp. 213–224. Springer, Cham (2017). https://doi.org/10.1007/978-3-319-68548-9_20
15. Goddard, M.: The EU general data protection regulation (GDPR): European regulation that has a global impact. Int. J. Market Res. **59**(6), 703–705 (2017)
16. Potts, M.K.: Social support and depression among older adults living alone: the importance of friends within and outside of a retirement community. Soc. Work **42**(4), 348–362 (1997)
17. Chafale, D., Pimpalkar, A.: Review on developing corpora for sentiment analysis using Plutchik's wheel of emotions with fuzzy logic. Int. J. Comput. Sci. Eng. (IJCSE) **2**(10), 14–18 (2014)
18. Tse, T., Linsey, H.: Adult day groups: addressing older people's needs for activity and companionship. Australas. J. Ageing **24**(3), 134–140 (2005)
19. Chatbots.org. Conversational agent. https://www.chatbots.org/conversational_agent
20. Fitzpatrick, K.K., Darcy, A., Vierhile, M.: Delivering cognitive behavior therapy to young adults with symptoms of depression and anxiety using a fully automated conversational agent (Woebot): a randomized controlled trial. JMIR Ment. Health **4**(2), e19 (2017)
21. Sciuto, A., Saini, A., Forlizzi, J., Hong, J.I.: "Hey Alexa, what's up?" A mixed-methods studies of in-home conversational agent usage. In: Proceedings of the 2018 Designing Interactive Systems Conference, pp. 857–868, June 2018

Designing and Testing HomeCare4All:
A eHealth Mobile App for Elderly

Roberta Grimaldi[1], Eliseo Sciarretta[1], Giovanni Andrea Parente[1,2(✉)],
and Carlo Maria Medaglia[1]

[1] Link Campus University, via del Casale di San Pio V 44, 00165 Rome, Italy
robertagrim@gmail.com,
{e.sciarretta,g.parente,c.medaglia}@unilink.it
[2] CoRiS (Dipartimento di Comunicazione e Ricerca Sociale),
Sapienza University of Rome, via Salaria 113, 00198 Rome, Italy

Abstract. Aging population implies an increase in demand for health care
services. This hopefully could be solved by e-health, even if some issues arise
about technology acceptance and adoption among the elderly. In this article, the
authors illustrate HomeCare4All project as a case study to apply Human Centered Design (HCD) process in the field of digital health services, aiming at
design trustworthy mobile applications for elderly people to book healthcare
services at home. Starting from the results achieved from the early step of
design, this paper describes the following steps of the creation of a design
solution by identifying use cases, defining information architecture and prototyping an app mockup. The prototypes are then evaluated through a double
usability test sessions with users, implementing an iterative design process. In
conclusion authors advance suggestions for designing trustworthy mobile
interactions for elderly people or people unaccustomed to technology, showing
the importance of involving end users in the various stages of the design
process.

Keywords: Elderly · Human Centered Design · Iterative design process ·
Digital health services · E-health · Usability test · Mobile app

1 Introduction

"HomeCare4All", from now also HC4A, was a project supported by the POR 2007–
2013 (Regional Operative Programme) co-founded by the FESR (European funds for
the regional districts) and the Italian region of Lazio, Action: VAL (Added Value
Lazio) for the companies assembles for Research, Development and Innovation.

HC4A aimed to develop a brokerage platform for health and social care services at
home. The primary target of the project were the elderly, upon which was focused the
entire design phase, through a Human Centered Design approach.

During the early design phases, not covered in this contribution, the authors have
conducted a survey regarding the needs and habits of the target users of the project
about digital e-health services. Due to survey's results, the authors were able to identify

the smartphone as the most suitable device for the HC4A project, because it allows a direct and intuitive interaction and it's widespread among the project target.

This paper originates from these results and covers the following steps of design, from the creation of use cases to the evaluation of the prototypes, as explained in the following paragraph.

2 Methodology

The Human Centered Design (HCD) is both a design philosophy and a process in which needs, wants, and limitations of the end-users of a system are given extensive attention at each stage of the design process.

Human Centered Design can be expressed by many methodologies, but all of them share a common feature: they're all based upon an international standard, ISO 13407:1999 [1], revised by ISO 9241-210:2010 [2]. This standard defines a general process for including human-centered activities throughout a development life-cycle, still without specifying exact methods. HCD is defined as "an approach to interactive systems development that aims to make systems usable and useful by focusing on the users, their needs and requirements, and by applying human factors/ergonomics, and usability knowledge and techniques. This approach enhances effectiveness and efficiency, improves human well-being, user satisfaction, accessibility and sustainability; and counteracts possible adverse effects of use on human health, safety and performance" [2]. So, a well-designed system is comprehensible and controllable, enables users to complete their task successfully and efficiently, and makes them feel competent and satisfied.

The focus on the HCD is about revolutionizing the data collection phase in order to understand the requirements, obtaining them through research and statistics tools.

In HCD process, four activities form the main cycle of work:

(1) *Specify the context of use*
    This activity allows identifying the people who will use the product, what they will use it for, and under what conditions they will use it.
(2) *Specify requirements*
    The second phase in the system design concern the users' characteristics identification. This activity makes possible to identify any requirements or user goals that must be met.
(3) *Create design solution*
    This part of the process may be done in stages, building from a rough concept to a complete design. The prototype, a representation of all or part of an interactive system, is the core of this phase and it is useful to validate the design choices before proceeding to the graphic and technological development.
(4) *Evaluate design*
    The HCD methodology involves different evaluation test stages, both during and after the design. The best evaluation methods involve the users, in order to know the responsiveness of the product to user needs and requirements.

In the following paragraphs, the authors will deal with the application of phases 3 and 4 to the HC4A case study.

3 The HC4A App

Nowadays the market of health brokerage platforms is dynamic and rich in incentives. In the next few years a consolidation of some features in the intermediation is expected, traditional booking services will become more customizable due to the health specialist filter, the geo-localization feature, the rankings and the evaluation will be always available through the app.

The HC4A platform seems to be suited to its audience's needs. Indeed, the health aspect and the home character of these services are interesting advantages since the former is an essential part of the elderly life and the latter responds to one of the most widespread needs of this specific target. HomeCare4All project takes care of the health of its users and it helps them to remain self-sufficient [3]. Indeed, through the platform, they can manage on their own the access and the booking of the health and social care services.

The implementation of the HC4A platform for mobile devices (smartphones) is an optimal solution for people with mobility limitations, one of the most common problems among elderly. Furthermore, as the authors learned by the results of the questionnaires administered in the early design phases, these devices are quite widespread among the target, ensuring a critical mass of users. The elderly also seem to be able to manage a series of basic functionalities such as registration, login, and search queries.

The HC4A app integrates a voice feature, enabling the data input through natural language, in order to simplify the usability of the system, avoiding problems related to the deterioration of physical and mental capacity and the lack of computer skills.

Based on the studies carried out and the above considerations, the authors had been able to define how to implement the project HomeCare4All.

The mobile application HC4A is a virtual marketplace that offers three main features related to house health and social care services: search, booking and evaluation.

As for the search, the user can benefit from a set of sub-functions: search by service or service provider name; search by voice input; order of the search results based on proximity, cost, date and ranking. The choice of these orders was done taking into account actual market trends.

As for the reservation, the user can also: change date and time of reservations; access and view their history of active reservations and archives of past reservations.

The assessment of the services is carried out by star rating and through comments. Comments may be related to the service in general or to some features in detail (e.g. tidiness, politeness of the staff). The system then assigns an average rating to the service providers, based on the evaluations of their services.

4 Create Design Solution

After the definition of the HC4A app and its features, the authors proceeded through the phase of the Human Centered Design, creating a design solution. So the authors identified the use cases, defined the information architecture, and designed the wireframes of the mobile app.

4.1 Use Cases

The use cases aims to specify the various tasks the user has to perform through the system. 13 use cases have been identified for the HC4A app:

1. User registration on the app
2. Login
3. Research a service
4. Booking a service
5. Send a feedback and comments about a used service
6. Call off the booking of a service
7. Access to the settings of the app
8. Modification of a booking
9. Visualization of a booking
10. Visualization of the service provider details
11. Viewing of the service details
12. Modification of the user profile
13. Research of a services provider

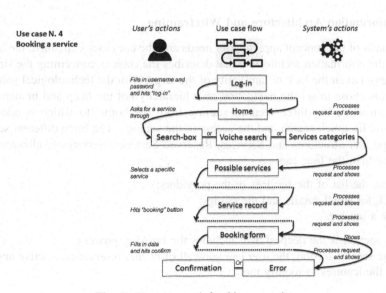

Fig. 1. Use case n. 4: booking a service

Two specific use cases are illustrated in this paper, the most significant ones as they concern the most salient operations the user must carry out in the app. Furthermore, it is in these interactions that the most interesting observations were found (see paragraph "User test and Redesign").

The selected use cases regard the target user and were illustrated below with a description of the interaction and its specific steps: *Use case n. 4: Booking a service* (Fig. 1); *Use Case n. 5: Send a feedback and comments about a used service* (Fig. 2).

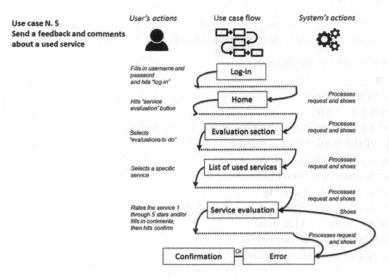

Fig. 2. Use case n. 5: send a feedback and comments about a used service

4.2   Information Architecture and Wireframing

On the basis of the concept app, the user needs and the use cases explained, the authors defined the information architecture that describes the choices concerning the structure of this app. Given the lack of familiarity of the target with the technological solutions, the authors chose to set the navigation on a hierarchy not too deep and branched [4].

The structure has three sections starting from the home, to which is added the search box for quick search and the access to the settings. The three different sections of the app are: Structures and Services, Reserved Services, Services Evaluation.

In the first, the user can:

- Access the list of the services or the providers;
- Check for small details and the ratings;
- Book a service.

This section is the deepest as it includes the booking process.

In the second section, the user can view all of his/her reservations, active and past, and has the features to modify them.

In the third section, the user can evaluate the services they experienced and visualize the past evaluations.

In fact, these three sections contain all the functionalities of the app: to search a service or a structure, to book a service and to evaluate it. The basic idea is to make the functionalities the user may access in each section quite evident.

After the structure of the information, the authors went on prototyping the mobile app interfaces. First, the authors planned the low fidelity wireframes, to define the general frame of each screen with the functions and how to provide them through the elements of the GUI, to test the navigation pattern, to specify how to display the information and their different priorities. This design was based on the use cases and the information architecture previously developed. After these first rough sketches, the wireframes were designed in high fidelity, in order to prototype an interactive demo for the test with the end users.

Stated the general aim of the app, the authors designed the interfaces of the booking service process (Use Case n.4) through one low-fidelity wireframe, and then through the high-fidelity mockups. The first screen the user will see by opening the app is the Home (Fig. 3).

Fig. 3. HC4A app homepage (high-fidelity mockup)

Fig. 4. HC4A app – booking process part 1 (high-fidelity mockup)

This screen is one of the low fidelity wireframes, made by Pencil, an open-source GUI prototyping tool. The layout of this screen is composed by two parts: the first is the top of the screen that remain fixed throughout the navigation; the second is the central part of the screen that changes on the base of the section navigated and the functionalities the user enter. The fixed part is composed by a series of explicit elements to support the orientation: the logo on the left, the buttons to access the user accounts and, on the right, the settings and the header bar indicating the section in which the user are located. Through these fixed elements the users can know at all times important information in the use of an app, as which section they are in and the name of the app too. The authors want to give to the elderly users a certainty that allow them to acquire a sort of self-confidence in the navigation of the app. If this choice of interface design could appear as redundant for a "normal" user, it is necessary for the target of the HC4A app, the elderly, not used to the mobile app.

In the central part of the layout of the Home there are a search box and below three rectangle buttons with a clear label referred to the section. Through the search box users can access one of the distinctive features of the app: the search by voice. Just tapping the microphone icon the user can search a structure or service by saying its name. Then the system asks the user to confirm the term pronounced, through an

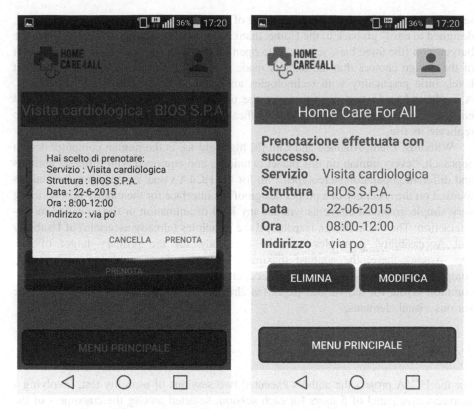

Fig. 5. HC4A app – booking process part 2 (high-fidelity mockup)

overlay confirmation message, and after that it performs the search. At this point the user can choose the order search results are displayed. The authors had assumed that both these interfaces (could have been useful to avoid misunderstanding and mistakes due to the inexperience and the above-written deficit health, as memory or attention deficit, of the target.

The booking feature is designed to be easier to use. Indeed, the procedure consists in a series of steps that, fragmenting the process, require the users to focus on one thing at a time (visit date, time schedule and user address), not overloading their mental workload [5].

Furthermore, during the entire process the system asks the user several confirmations with the booking information in order to, on one hand, avoid accidental touches or mistyping, and on the other hand, clear the user up which step of the process is (Figs. 4 and 5).

As the high fidelity screens show, the button for the settings (at top right) is no longer present. During the high fidelity design, the authors noticed that two buttons were too many for the space available and could cause confusion. So they chose to merge the settings and profile in one button with the profile icon, this way users can easily understand that through this button they can access to all of their data and settings. Moreover, another fixed element of the screens is the button in the bottom, designed to easily go back to the Home, thanks to the explicit label, and preferred to the burger icon (the three bars' icon used to open the side menu). Also this element is part of the design choices that the authors made in view of a target with memory deficit level, little practicality with technologies and little inclination to learn new things. A facilitated navigation aims to make the user experience of this app positive and enjoyable, enhancing the feeling of self-efficacy of the users [3], so as to push them to replicate its use.

Williams, Ulam, Ahamed and Chu [6] highlight as, in the human computer design approach, "every human on this planet is unique, and equipped with different abilities and different population stereotypes". So for the HC4A visual components the authors focused on the necessity of a proper design of the interface for the elderly people, using very simple graphical elements without any kind of animation or the so-called micro-interaction. The visual design respects all the principles (already ascertain) of Usability and Accessibility, principles essential especially for the primary target of this app. Among these: the contrast maximized between foreground and background, complementary colors, only one font face, an adequate space between lines of text, a common layout for the various pages (as already explained), colors consistent in the various visual elements.

5   User Test and Redesign

For the HC4A project the authors executed two sessions of usability test, involving a representative panel of 5 users for each session, selected among the customers of the two health and social care service providers, partners of the project. According to Nielsen and Landauer [7], in fact, 5 is a sufficient number of users to involve to intercept the 80% of the critical issues of an interface. The usability tests can be performed at any stage of the product design and development, both on already existing products and on (interactive or not) prototypes. For this project, the authors opted to carry out the usability test during the final phase of the process design, with a demo of the app, so they could identify the critical issues before the final release.

The protocol of the test consisted in: a brief explanation of the project and the app, a short entry questionnaire, the usability test (composed by a series of tasks) and a final short interview. During the entire test, the user was supported by one of the authors to facilitate the test performance and assisted by the other authors as observers.

The tasks were identified in accordance with certain important factors:

• Criticality, concerns the tasks that could generate more errors in their execution;
• Frequency, concerns all the tasks that are performed more regularly;
• Representativeness, about the tasks that characterize the service.

At the beginning of the test, the users anonymously filled in a short entry questionnaire with some personal information (e.g. age, educational qualification), the technologies and the health and social care services used and the potential interest in the app. Then the user was informed that the session would be video-recorded for analysis needs and he/she was invited to sign the agreement. After that, the users received the list of the requested tasks and he/she began the test. The tasks were 4 and they regarded the use of the main services of the app: registration process, booking of a service, evaluation of an enjoyed service and the voice search.

Following the "Think-aloud" protocol, the users were asked to explain aloud what they were doing and what were their impressions, expectation and considerations about the app experience, while performing the tasks.

At the end of test, the evaluation team conducted a short interview to the users. The questions of the interview were a rework of the multidimensional questionnaire Us.E 2.0 [8] to examine satisfaction, ease of use and pleasantness of the app and to understand the users impressions.

At the end of each session of test, the evaluation team drawn up a report. Thanks to the entry questionnaire, the authors could outline briefly each tester in order to understand the type of users and to analyze adequately the results of the pertinent test. Furthermore, for each task the expected procedure was identified and used as judgment parameter of users' performance. Based on the captured video and the replies of the entry and exit questionnaires, the team noticed a number of critical issues. Rather than on quantitative measurements compared to different performances, the authors focused on qualitative evidence: what is that users have made more effort to understand and use? And why?

Based on the critical issues the authors finally processed a list of recommendations with the improvements to be made. This list was accompanied by an order of priority, to have also a scale of severity of problems emerged. Based on this list, some changes on the app were made for the second session of the usability test. In the end, after the second session of test, the authors identified the outstanding critical issues and defined general recommendations.

6 Discussion and Conclusion

In this article, using the HomeCare4All project as a case study, the authors aimed to explore the most suitable interaction modes and design approach to ease the use of mobile apps by elderly people.

Adopting the Human Centered Design Methodology, the authors were able to define some general suggestions, learning from the experience of the HomeCare4All project, that are more widely applicable to the mobile apps world. The most relevant findings of this study are summed up below.

Labels are easier to understand than icons. An obvious icon for a normal user, as the profile icon, could not be as clear for people with a low practicality of the mobile devices. Although many authors suggest choosing icons on the basis of the background of the specific target, their interpretation is likely to be misleading to these unaccustomed users. Indeed, during the test, the user attention was drawn to what was easy to interpret. In the case of the search task, for instance, the users preferred to use the button with a clear label "Structures and services", than the search box in the home (marked only with a search icon), even if the first option required more steps. On the other side, it is necessary to pay attention to the labeling: each label must be clear and redundant, avoiding to use jargon or more technical terms.

Designing an app for this type of target it is essential to provide support, accompany and lead the users through each process. Often the elderly prove to be anxious and hasty in the use of new technologies, because they do not feel able to use them. This attitude can lead the subject to totally reject these new devices. Offering the right kind of support, increases their confidence and it lowers the chance of rejection. So, the app walkthroughs, the feedback system and the aids provided are fundamental. According with the results of the usability tests, a long process (i.e. the booking in the HC4A app) well structured in various steps, and with different confirmation messages, can give to the users the feeling of being in control of what they are doing in the app. This led all the users to complete the task.

As result of the previous consideration, it is preferable to carefully evaluate if offering more options to the users. In this sense, the tests have confirmed the risk of overstimulation, when the users in the task of the search had reacted negatively to the option of sorting the results. While the authors intended this option as an improvement of the readability of the result list, the users wanted only to get to the results. Arrived at that screen, the majority of the users had a negative reaction to this "yet another request" of attention, which demands another decision. For some types of target, not only the elderly, less freedom means less worries. This suggestion is more efficient for the smartphone device, since space available is less and there is always a risk to have an overcrowded interface (offering more option), which would only cause confusion for the users.

The features and the processes must be designed to be easily understood and simple to carry out, although they must not be necessarily fast to carry out. In spite of the mobile context, that usually implies the need of fast processes, with this specific target the velocity is not a primary goal. Indeed the elderly, even when they are regular users of the web, have different navigation patterns in the web browsing, and they need more time to explore the page. They stare to each section of the page and read most of the text in the page [9].

An interesting result concerns the opposing reaction towards the voice search. This functionality is evaluated useful by the users, although they required support to use it. Probably they intend them closer to their (our) natural mode of interaction: the voice. Once they understood how it works, the users paradoxically exaggerated in the opposite direction, considering the device as a peer, and speaking to it through the natural language (which is not supported in this app). So the users oscillate between two opposite in the use of this hybrid interaction mode: either they were unsure or they overestimated the feature potentials. Probably the hybrid nature of this feature in the HC4A app, which accepts voice input, more natural, but that responds to the specific rules of technology, had brought users to some confusion. However such an attitude is a positive perspective for those future mobile solutions in which the voice will be the primary mode of interaction.

Old users cannot have a full understanding of the process they are performing, both for their little familiarity and for memory and concentration problems due to their age. These limits, in case of unexpected events (as errors, or missing or unexpected feedback), bring the user to the situation of disorientation about the task he/she is performing. These situations in turn make the anxiety and uneasiness take over to the patience and reasoning. During the test, often the authors had noticed the users did not have a clear idea about what they were doing or about what they can expect from the app. In addition to the age health deficit, probably this type of target, unaccustomed to the technology, faces another problem: they have a different type of mental model. It is a mental model, structural and functional, with different references, different logics, different dynamics, not hierarchical but linear [4]. Probably this is caused by the fact that it was formed when the technology did not influence so much the everyday life (and the people). So the users, due to their different mental model, miss the knowledge about how a certain device or system work and how to use it. They cannot predict the effect of any possible sequence of actions. This explains the disorientation of the users during the tests. It is therefore essential not to underestimate the consequences of a mental model not accustomed to the technology, and especially to the mobile device, that is a new entry in the elderly world.

Each of the previous considerations fundamentally contains this basic idea: the designers have to design the mobile app interaction for a target that does not master the technologies. It may seem a basic goal but it is a difficult challenge for the designers, since they (we) are totally encircled by the technology and they (we) no longer remember their (our) life without it. So in the design of mobile apps for the elderly is fundamental, as shown by the case study of HC4A, to engage the end users in several steps of the process design: from the user needs analysis to the validation of the prototype. This represents the key factor of the design process, and allow the designers to get as close as possible to the mental model of this target in order to identify the most suitable modes of interaction to achieve the result of a mobile app really designed for the elderly.

References

1. ISO 13407:1999: Human-centered design process. https://www.iso.org/obp/ui/#iso:std:iso:13407:ed-1:v1:en. Accessed 08 Jan 2020
2. ISO 9241-210:2010: Ergonomics of human system interaction-Part 210: Human-centred design for interactive systems. http://www.iso.org/iso/home/store/catalogue_ics/catalogue_detail_ics.htm?csnumber=52075. Accessed 08 Jan 2020
3. Hernández-Encuentra, E., Pousada, M., Gómez-Zúñiga, B.: ICT and older people: beyond usability. Educ. Gerontol. 35(3), 226–245 (2009)
4. Ziefle, M., Bay, S.: Mental models of a cellular phone menu. comparing older and younger novice users. In: Brewster, S., Dunlop, M. (eds.) Mobile HCI 2004. LNCS, vol. 3160, pp. 25–37. Springer, Heidelberg (2004). https://doi.org/10.1007/978-3-540-28637-0_3
5. Arab, F., Pigot, H., Rabardel, P., Folcher, V., Monnet, A.S.R., Mokhtari, M.: Age, memory and time: practices and support. J. Assoc. Adv. Model. Simul. Techn. Enterp. (AMSE) 71(3), 136–149 (2011)
6. Williams, D., Alam, M.A.U., Ahamed, S.I., Chu, W.: Considerations in designing human-computer interfaces for elderly people. In: 13th International Conference on Quality Software, pp. 372–377. IEEE (2013)

7. Nielsen, J., Landauer, T.K.: A mathematical model of the finding of usability problems. In: Arnold, B., Van der Veer, G. (eds.) Proceedings of the INTERACT 1993 and CHI 1993 Conference on Human Factors in Computing Systems, pp. 206–213. ACM (1993)
8. Di Nocera, F.: Usability Evaluation 2.0: Una descrizione (s)oggettiva dell'usabilità. Ergoproject, Rome (2013)
9. Hanson, V.L.: Influencing technology adoption by older adults. Interact. Comput. 22(6), 502–509 (2010)

Exploring User Expectations of Brain-Training and Coaching Technologies for Cognitive Health

Kyle Harrington[1,2] , Michael P. Craven[1,3(✉)] , Max L. Wilson[4] ,
and Aleksandra Landowska[4]

[1] NIHR MindTech MedTech Co-operative, The Institute of Mental Health,
University of Nottingham Innovation Park, Nottingham, UK
{Kyle.Harrington,Michael.Craven}@nottingham.ac.uk
[2] Division of Psychiatry and Applied Psychology, University of Nottingham,
Nottingham, UK
[3] Bioengineering Research Group, Faculty of Engineering,
University of Nottingham, Nottingham, UK
[4] Mixed Reality Lab, School of Computer Science, University of Nottingham,
Nottingham, UK
{Max.Wilson,Aleksandra.Landowska}@nottingham.ac.uk

Abstract. User-centred evaluation of brain-training and coaching applications is discussed, with a focus on dementia. A brief outline of outcomes measures used for cognitive training is presented. The design of a set of four patient and public involvement workshops is described which are intended to examine user aspects of relevance to brain-training, including motivation, attitudes to learning, trust in technology and cultural relationships to the playing of games and their content. The groups involved researchers, facilitators, three people living with dementia and three care-givers, two of these being dyads. Data was audio recorded and field notes were taken. Initial results are given from the ongoing qualitative study.

Keywords: User-centred design · Evaluation · Pervasive healthcare

1 Introduction

Brain-training commonly refers to digital games or computers or mobile devices which are specifically designed to train a variety of cognitive skills including memory, focus, processing speed and perception. A major criticism of the creators of brain-training apps is that they over claim the strength of evidence and the extent to which they lead to generalisable cognitive benefits that may help with activities of daily living [1]. On the other hand there is evidence that these apps may help older people improve cognitive skill and slow down cognitive decline due to ageing [2].

Dementia is a syndrome that results from changes in brain pathology where an individual's engagement with mentally stimulating activities as well as social engagement and a healthy lifestyle, could influence its onset or progression [3]. Whilst there are difficulties in showing the benefits of specific cognitive training or

© Springer Nature Switzerland AG 2020
M. Kurosu (Ed.): HCII 2020, LNCS 12183, pp. 49–60, 2020.
https://doi.org/10.1007/978-3-030-49065-2_4

interventions, there is growing interest in and consensus about which psychosocial factors contribute to cognitive reserve, defined as the capacity of the brain to compensate for brain pathology [4]. The potential to intervene with a mixture of cognitive training exercises and lifestyle coaching begs the question of how best to support people with digital technologies. For those who are encouraged to improve cognitive health, and in particular persons living with dementia for which medical treatment is currently very limited, in considering technological solutions it is important to understand user expectations, both positive and negative. Expectations are influenced by a number of internal and external factors which need to be understood in more detail.

The work described in this paper is part of a larger project which is seeking to develop and evaluate cognitive training programmes supported by digital technology that are aimed at promoting good cognitive health and encouraging behaviours that promise to reduce the risk of dementia [5]. In addition it aims to provide a cognitive measurement and monitoring function to assist in the detection of cognitive impairment, with a potential to screen for or diagnose dementia at a pre-symptomatic stage [6]. The goal of better understanding expectations is to guide the choice of a viable set of evaluation measures for such technologies.

It is known that persons with lived experience of dementia wish to be included in the development of assistive technologies [7]. As part of the evaluation of new healthcare technologies, Patient and Public Involvement (PPI) can be employed effectively to inform the design and conduct of clinical trials [8] and it increases the quality of health and social care research in general [9]. PPI ensures a focus on the topics which concern health service users the most; Brett et al. showed that the involvement of users at an early stage in research can help to prioritise research questions, assist in the development of experimental protocols including patient reported outcome measures, and inform the analysis and dissemination of results [10]. It thus ensures that research is grounded in the lived experience of affected groups, increasing its relevance and helping to enable the long-term sustainability of research. PPI will be used most immediately in our current research to inform the design of an upcoming longitudinal brain imaging study, which will investigate the potential for brain-training programs to reduce the mental workload required to undertake specific cognitive activities [11]. It will also influence the design of the brain-training and coaching app being designed in the wider Horizon 2020 research programme and inform its future evaluation.

2 Background

The scientific literature is replete with examples of observed benefits of cognitive training. Numerous studies have investigated the effects of cognitive training on a variety of outcomes within diverse populations, with many studies showing moderate benefits within areas such as verbal memory, nonverbal learning, attention, verbal cognition, psycho-social functioning and general cognition and large gains in working memory [12]. Meta-analysis has demonstrated that computer-based cognitive interventions can have moderately beneficial effects in cognition, anxiety and depression in persons living with dementia [13]. However, due to differences in how individual studies measure occupational and educational attainment, differences in populations being measured and differences between the types of cognitive training provided, definitive and comprehensive models of the efficacy of these interventions remain elusive [14, 15].

2.1 Outcome Measures

Amongst the important outcome measures for assessing cognitive training with people who have cognitive impairment are those that aim to reveal subjective and objective change in the performing of activities of everyday life. Whilst there are a variety of methods to assess people's capabilities to perform everyday tasks [16–18], activities of daily living (ADL) are generally taken to mean people's regular self-care activities and extent these can be done independently. ADL provides a measurement functional status, particularly in regard to older people, people who have suffered an injury, or people living with dementia. An individual's ability to perform ADL is sometimes assessed by self-reported questionnaire [16, 19, 20] but can also be assessed using task-based assessments such as the Timed Instrumental Activities of Daily Living (TIADL) [21, 22]. Here, instrumental activities include tasks such as food preparation, driving, medication use and financial management.

In a notable previous study of a cognitive intervention; the Advanced *Cognitive Training* for Independent and Vital Elderly (ACTIVE) trial [23], measures of cognitively demanding real-world activities were largely assessed using self-reports, including the 'minimum dataset', but task-based assessments were also used, including processing speed using complex tasks, a road-sign test and the above TIADL test. Other studies have linked cognitive remediation and cognitive training to improvements in the activities of daily living. Carter, Oliveira, Duponte and Lynch [24] highlight two studies in which cognitive skills training helped to support people perform the activities of daily living. In the first study, they performed a post-hoc analysis of ADL improvement scores collected on acute stroke patients who were either assigned to a cognitive skills remediation programme or given an alternative course of treatment. It was discovered that those with higher scores showed significantly better personal hygiene, bathing and toilet activity improvements. Using a separate dataset the authors also showed significant correlations between cognitive skills and ADL.

Self-reported questionnaires are a less objective measure of cognitive improvement than observation. However, self-reported measures of ADL do tend to correlate highly with important real world outcomes, including the likelihood of institutionalisation [25]. Whilst there are a wide variety of outcome measures which are typically reported in cognitive training studies, many of these focus specifically on clinical or cognitive outcomes and there is a great deal of heterogeneity of selected outcome measures between studies [26].

By adopting a user-centred approach via PPI, we aim to explore whether and how people living with dementia and their carers conceptualise cognitive changes through a medical lens or otherwise. In order to improve the face validity on future research and to investigate which possible benefits of cognitive training would be meaningful and important to people living with dementia and their caregivers the topic of 'What counts as meaningful improvement?' was chosen for our first focus group in consultation with stakeholder groups (see later). It is intended that these insights will enable us to better understand the key areas of concern in the lived experience of people affected by dementia and so to ensure that any training or rehabilitation regime is able to focus upon relevant and meaningful improvement metrics.

2.2   Motivation & Learning, Trust and Barriers to Inclusion

As for any healthcare or assistive technology, potential for non-use or abandonment [27] is an issue for individuals living with dementia and their carers. Motivation and engagement are key factors likely to impact upon the success of cognitive training regimes [28] and it is suggested that gamified aspects offer the promise of personalised strategies to improve engagement [29]. To investigate factors which influence motivation and engagement, the paradigm of Dweck's Mindset [30] is useful as a theoretical framework. Dweck suggests that those who believe that their intelligence is fixed are likely to see any difficulties as failures whilst those who believe their intelligence is malleable will view difficulties as a challenge and an opportunity for growth. For this reason, exploring factors associated with motivation and life-long learning is another important topic of discussion with potential users of technologies designed for improving cognitive health. Given that game mechanics can influence engagement and adhesion [31] and subsequently, motivation and commitment to 'serious gaming' regimes [28, 29], we specifically wanted to explore whether the literature reflected the understandings of our participants.

Digital brain-training and cognitive rehabilitation programs also offer the opportunity for monitoring cognition, wellbeing and overall health. Developing digital methods for monitoring healthcare needs, may help to facilitate more timely intervention and optimize the allocation of health and community care resources [32]. However, patient views around cognitive screening tools are complex and multifaceted and it is unclear which specific factors promote or reduce the acceptance of screening tools [33].

In addition to factors surrounding trust and motivation, we also wanted to explore barriers to digital inclusion which may leave some of the most marginalised in society without access to promising new developments in health technologies [34]. Whilst exclusion is decreasing over time, it is suggested that numerous barriers still remain and these may be a particular issue for at-risk groups [35].

3   Method

3.1   Focus Groups

In order to investigate attitudes and perceptions of cognitive training and screening technologies, we conducted a series of focus group meetings with people with dementia and caregivers. After reviewing the literature and in conjunction with our consortium partners, the following topics were chosen, as introduced in the last section:

1. What counts as meaningful improvement?
2. Motivation and learning
3. Trust in digital diagnosis
4. Barriers to digital inclusion

Prior to commencement, we also discussed the acceptability and relevance of these discussion topics with members of our organisation's standing PPI groups which have expertise in mental health and dementia respectively. Focus group sessions were designed to be three and a half hours in total and involved lunch and regular breaks. Each was split into two sessions; one before and one after lunch to cover a sub-topic within each main topic. Data collection was conducted through audio recordings and handwritten field notes by the researchers present.

3.2 Participants

Participants for the focus group were recruited via Join Dementia Research (www.joindementiaresearch.nihr.ac.uk/); an online platform which supports research involving participants affected by dementia. Our focus groups (those conducted to date) comprised of the same six participants, three living with dementia and three carers of people with a diagnosis of dementia. PPI members are experts-by-experience, due to their firsthand knowledge of dementia diagnoses and cognitive difficulties as well as their own perceptions of technology designed with dementia in mind.

There was an equal gender split and the group included two dyads of spouses where in one dyad the participant with dementia was male and in the other was female. The group was also ethnically diverse, and represented a variety of different backgrounds and experiences. Up to three members of our institute's standing PPI groups were also present in each workshop to assist with facilitation, who also contributed their lived experience of memory or mental health problems, their relationships to technology and opinions about these.

3.3 Ethics

Whilst PPI activities do not always require ethical approval [36], in order to maximise data yield we wished to record each of our sessions with a voice recorder to provide additional data for subsequent review and analysis. Prior to seeking ethical approval, one of our standing PPI team members reviewed the ethics application and supporting documents (participant information sheet, consent form, protocol documents) and checked the documents for readability and acceptability. Ethical approval was granted by the Faculty of Medicine and Health Sciences Research Ethics Committee (Approval number: 333-1906). Participants were fully informed as to the purpose and methods of the study and given an opportunity to ask questions. We understood consent according to the legal definition of the Mental Capacity Act Code of Practice (Mental Capacity Act 2005) and adhered with best-practice guidance for assessing capacity provided by the British Medical Association. Under the Mental Capacity Act 2005, capacity relates to the ability to make and understand the consequences of specific decisions. We would not make any legal judgments which related to diagnosis, power of attorney or capacity in general. All participants were provided with an information sheet prior to their involvement and asked to sign a consent form confirming they understood the purposes and method of the study. Transportation was provided for participants and they were each paid an involvement fee in line with INVOLVE guidelines [36].

3.4   Materials

All participants, including workshop facilitators were provided with name badges in order to facilitate an informal, first name basis tone to the discussions. During our first session, we used short power-point presentations to introduce concepts related to cognition, and clinical trial design which served as the basis of our discussion. In the second session participants were asked to bring in some personal items to guide the discussion and on opposite walls of the room were pinned up sheets of paper containing dichotomous statements about motivation. In the third session a set of ideation cards from the UnBias project [37] were used in order to facilitate discussions around fairness and algorithmic bias. In the fourth and final workshop a flip-chart was used to record part of the group discussion.

4   Results

The four workshops were conducted between October 2019 and January 2020. To date, an initial analysis has been conducted of the first two of them from field notes and a first pass of listening to the audio recordings. As the project is work-in-progress, full thematic analysis will be completed once all of the audio recordings have been transcribed using a professional transcription service.

4.1   Meaningful Improvement

In the first workshop, participants began by exploring the concept of cognition, and how technology might be used to help mitigate its decline. At first participants appeared skeptical about the use of technology in general, and in particular, how games might be used to improve cognition. Many participants considered themselves to have low technological literacy, yet towards the end of the session it transpired that many of the participants were familiar with and regular played a host of phone and tablet-based word-based and numerical puzzle games, such as Scrabble and Sudoku. Participants were enthusiastic about these types of applications, although conceptualised them as puzzles rather than computer games. Those who discussed playing puzzle games were also enthusiastic about competitive and social gaming and the dyads mentioned playing the same games or playing with others online. Other participants mentioned using a Kindle or an iPad to build their own up their own confidence in technology. Participants discussed concepts relating to cognitive offloading, such as calendar, navigation and scheduling applications. One participant added mentioned that he felt technology helped him to stay organised:

"My brain is better now with computers".

These examples from the group discussion demonstrate a potential disconnect between people's own familiarity and use of technology with that of their self-perception.

The main topic for the day, meaningful improvement, was discussed at length, with participants drawing upon examples in their own lives. However, a consensus formed that improvement was hard to quantify, may fluctuate over time, and may be subjective and difficult to define. Participants with dementia also stated that often, it was their partners who noticed changes before they did themselves, meaning that assessing one's own cognition may be difficult. Despite this, participants also mentioned the importance of functional measures of well-being, such as the activities of daily living, physical health and self-care. Participants discussed that although they were aware that dementia was a progressive neurodegenerative disease, they held a firm belief that staying active and keeping the brain active was a central feature in slowing or mitigating their cognitive decline and maintaining independence. The link between mood, cognition and self-care was discussed at length, with many participants saying that they often felt unable to think properly or to focus when they had low mood.

Attendees of the focus group also mentioned a variety of hobbies and group activities such as 'Singing for the Brain' and 'Forget Me Notts', the latter referring to a local Nottinghamshire-based community group. However, one participant mentioned that many of the activities in these groups were Euro-centric or were particular to the local area and thus were difficult to relate to and could be exclusionary.

4.2   Motivation and Learning

In the second session, participants explored motivation and learning. They were asked to bring into the session a specific item or story which represented something which had motivated them or something which they had accomplished. One participant brought a hand-drawn picture they were proud of. Another mentioned the pleasure of working on an allotment, another the achievement of cooking from memory and one participant mentioned that they had taken up tennis in later life. We used these examples as an ice-breaker to explore motivating factors which may be harnessed in cognitive training and coaching applications. Participants mentioned that involvement in their hobbies allowed them to challenge the myths about what older people were capable of. This included personal perceptions of their limitations. Hobbies and social activities were seen as a way to mitigate the decline of cognition, and some participants mentioned they had seen others who were less active, deteriorate very quickly. Participants also discussed the social nature of some of their hobbies which helped them to stay motivated over a longer period of time. One participant mentioned both the importance of saying active in retirement, in addition to how his own hobby enabled him to become part of a community:

"I took up gardening again when I retired ... fill the time in, because I'd seen too many people, before I retired, who'd packed up work, and they'd just go downhill ... they'd got nothing to do, and anytime I ran into 'em [they said], 'Oh don't retire, there's nothing to do, all you do is watch the telly'. Well, we watch the telly in the evening, but I can always find plenty to do since

I've retired, with the garden, and I took up bowling, bowls...You've got to give yourself an interest. Gardening, I've found is ideal, if you've got an allotment, you've got a community".

In the second part, participants explored their attitudes to learning and motivation by means of dichotomous statements which were broadly related to Dweck's concepts of fixed and growth mindsets, as introduced earlier. The statements were placed on opposite walls and participants were asked where on the continuum they stood between diametrically opposed positions such as 'I am naturally good at things' versus 'I am good at things because I have practiced them.'

There was a wide range of differing views on people's own conceptions of the malleability of their cognitive skills, thus suggesting that a single approach to framing the benefits of cognitive training would be insufficient.

5   Discussion

Participants who attended the focus group may not necessarily have been aware of the concept of cognitive reserve or the research which lay behind it, nevertheless, participants had a good intuitive understanding of the concept, which they were able to discuss at length. Perhaps somewhat surprising in our discussion groups were participant attitudes towards acquiring new skills later on in life. One participant claimed he had "never really been a reader", yet had become an avid reader after retirement, suggesting that people are often very eager to pick up new skills later on in life. Our discussions suggest that there are many factors which motivate people to stay cognitively, physically and socially active later in life, and that maintaining good cognitive health is an important priority for people living with dementia and their carers.

5.1   Limitations

Participants were invited to join the focus group using the research recruitment tool, Join Dementia Research. We specifically invited only participants who had stated that the severity of their dementia was mild to moderate. This of course excludes people living with dementia whose symptoms are more severe, and therefore the findings from this focus group are most likely not representative of people living with dementia at a later stage. However, we were fortunate to be joined by a participant who had experience in caring for his wife in the later stages of dementia, which allowed for a broader discussion. There is often a tension between carers' wishes to ensure that their care recipients are safe and well, and the desire to respect individual autonomy [38]. The relative importance afforded to each of these considerations may change as the symptoms of dementia progress and a person's capacity to understand the consequences of their decisions deteriorates.

Participants who chose to list themselves on Join Dementia Research, are also much more likely to be actively involved in other dementia research (as some of our participants were), and therefore their experiences and expectations of research may be different from the general population. Nevertheless, for our purposes of helping to guide future clinical research, participants were able to bring their own experiences of how trials work in practice to the specific research questions, particularly around the discussion about meaningful improvement. Some participants in the group also had firsthand experience of other dementia research programs, which they were able to draw on for the purposes of discussion.

5.2 Further Work

We are continuing to analyse the data generated from our workshops, and intend to use Thematic Analysis [39] to systematically identify salient and important issues which arose during discussions. PPI volunteers involved in the workshops will also be invited to help during the analysis phase of our research. Involving those with lived experience in the data analysis can help to create meaning from the data and provide valuable perspectives in interpreting findings [40].

Using insights gained from the PPI workshops, we will be conducting iterative longitudinal trials on the effectiveness of the Brain+ Recover app on various cognitive abilities. In particular, we will investigate whether the brain-training app reduces the mental workload places on participants for similar tasks following a training regime. It has been shown that functional Near Infra-Red Spectroscopy (fNIRS) can be used to estimate mental workload, and therefore enables an objective, continuous and detailed insight into mental effort on cognitively demanding tasks [11, 41]. We also intend to use the insights garnered from PPI to provide guidance on future clinical validation as well as further development of the commercial Brain+ software.

6 Conclusions

Patient and public involvement in digital health research is essential in enabling high quality understanding of areas of importance which are guided by the lived experiences of the target user-group. As experts-by-experience, people living with dementia and carers are willing and able to offer detailed opinions, which are relevant to the development and evaluation of technologies for cognitive health. By taking into account their expectations and life experiences and from understanding potential barriers, research goals can be orientated towards people's actual needs, rather than the perceived needs of technology developers alone. Furthermore, methodological issues which relate to adherence of study protocols, and general willingness to participate in research, can be explored in full with the hope of increasing the quality of future work.

Acknowledgements. Funding was provided by the European Commission Horizon 2020 EIC-FTI-2018-2020 grant no. 820636, coordinated by Brain+ ApS (Denmark). The research reported in this paper was also supported by the NIHR MindTech MedTech Co-operative and the NIHR Nottingham Biomedical Research Centre. The views represented are the views of the authors alone and do not necessarily represent the views of the Department of Health and Social Care in England, the NHS, or the NIHR. The authors wish to thank the PPI volunteers who attended the workshops for their enthusiastic and insightful contributions. We were very pleased to work with such a diverse, pro-active and knowledgeable group of people. We also thank group facilitators Njoki and Izzy who provided support and advice throughout the project, including documentation review, and Dr. Julie Gosling who contributed to the planned activities in the later three sessions.

References

1. Simons, D.J., et al.: Do "brain-training" programs work? Psychol. Sci. Public Interest **17**, 103–186 (2016)
2. Nouchi, R., et al.: Brain training game improves executive functions and processing speed in the elderly: a randomized controlled trial. PLoS ONE **7**, e29676 (2012)
3. Stern, Y.: What is cognitive reserve? Theory and research application of the reserve concept. J. Int. Neuropsychol. Soc. **8**, 448–460 (2002)
4. Vernooij-Dassen, M., et al.: Bridging the divide between biomedical and psychosocial approaches in dementia research: the 2019 INTERDEM manifesto. Aging Ment. Health, 1–7 (2019)
5. Harrington, K., Craven, M.P., Wilson, M.L.: AD prevent-detect: evaluation of cognitive screening and cognitive training for people at risk of dementia (2019). http://motrin.media. mit.edu/mentalhealth/wp-content/uploads/sites/15/2019/04/CMH2019_paper_25.pdf
6. Dong, M., et al.: Alzheimer's disease (AD) detect & prevent-presymptomatic AD detection and prevention. In: International MinD Conference 2019 - Designing with and for People with Dementia: Well-being, Empowerment and Happiness, pp. 151–154. TUD Press, Dresden (2019)
7. Meiland, F., et al.: Technologies to support community-dwelling persons with dementia: a position paper on issues regarding development, usability, effectiveness and cost-effectiveness, deployment, and ethics. JMIR Rehabil. Assist. Technol. **4**, e1 (2017)
8. Bagley, H.J., et al.: A patient and public involvement (PPI) toolkit for meaningful and flexible involvement in clinical trials–a work in progress. Res. Involv. Engagem. **2**, 15 (2016)
9. Tomlinson, J., Medlinskiene, K., Cheong, V.L., Khan, S., Fylan, B.: Patient and public involvement in designing and conducting doctoral research: the whys and the hows. Res. Involv. Engagem. **5**, 23 (2019)
10. Brett, J., et al.: Mapping the impact of patient and public involvement on health and social care research: a systematic review. Health Expect. **17**, 637–650 (2014)
11. Wilson, M.L., Sharon, N., Maior, H.A., Midha, S., Craven, M.P., Sharples, S.: Mental workload as personal data: designing a cognitive activity tracker. In: 3rd Symposium on Computing and Mental Health (2018). http://eprints.nottingham.ac.uk/50630/
12. Hill, N.T.M., Mowszowski, L., Naismith, S.L., Chadwick, V.L., Valenzuela, M., Lampit, A.: Computerized cognitive training in older adults with mild cognitive impairment or dementia: a systematic review and meta-analysis. Am. J. Psychiatry **174**, 329–340 (2016)
13. García-Casal, J.A., Loizeau, A., Csipke, E., Franco-Martín, M., Perea-Bartolomé, M.V., Orrell, M.: Computer-based cognitive interventions for people living with dementia: a systematic literature review and meta-analysis. Aging Ment. Health **21**, 454–467 (2017)
14. Sajjad, A., Bramer, W.M., Ikram, M.A., Tiemeier, H., Stephan, B.C.M.: Exploring strategies to operationalize cognitive reserve: a systematic review of reviews AU - Harrison, Stephanie L. J. Clin. Exp. Neuropsychol. **37**, 253–264 (2015)
15. Martin, M., Clare, L., Am, A., Mh, C., Zehnder, F.: Cognition-based interventions for healthy older people and people with mild cognitive impairment (review). Cochrane Database Syst. Rev. **1**, CD006220 (2011)
16. Galasko, D., et al.: An inventory to assess activities of daily living for clinical trials in Alzheimer's disease. Alzheimer Dis. Assoc. Disord. **11**, S33–S39 (1997)
17. Spector, W.D., Katz, S., Murphy, J.B., Fulton, J.P.: The hierarchical relationship between activities of daily living and instrumental activities of daily living. J. Chronic Dis. **40**, 481–489 (1987)

18. Lawton, M.P., Brody, E.M.: Assessment of older people: self-maintaining and instrumental activities of daily living. Gerontologist **9**, 179–186 (1969)
19. Bucks, R.S., Ashworth, D., Wilcock, G., Siegfried, K.: Assessment of activities of daily living in dementia: development of the bristol activities of daily living scale. Age Ageing **25**, 113–120 (1996)
20. Pincus, T., Swearingen, C., Wolfe, F.: Toward a multidimensional health assessment questionnaire (MDHAQ): assessment of advanced activities of daily living and psychological status in the patient-friendly health assessment questionnaire format. Arthritis Rheum.: Off. J. Am. Coll. Rheumatol. **42**, 2220–2230 (1999)
21. Owsley, C., Sloane, M., McGwin Jr., G., Ball, K.: Timed instrumental activities of daily living tasks: relationship to cognitive function and everyday performance assessments in older adults. Gerontology **48**, 254–265 (2002)
22. Wadley, V.G., Okonkwo, O., Crowe, M., Ross-Meadows, L.A.: Mild cognitive impairment and everyday function: evidence of reduced speed in performing instrumental activities of daily living. Am. J. Geriatr. Psychiatry **16**, 416–424 (2008)
23. Jobe, J.B., et al.: ACTIVE: a cognitive intervention trial to promote independence in older adults. Control. Clin. Trials **22**, 453–479 (2001)
24. Carter, L.T., Oliveira, D.O., Duponte, J., Lynch, S.V.: The relationship of cognitive skills performance to activities of daily living in stroke patients. Am. J. Occup. Ther. **42**, 449–455 (1988)
25. Luppa, M., Luck, T., Weyerer, S., König, H.-H., Brähler, E., Riedel-Heller, S.G.: Prediction of institutionalization in the elderly. A systematic review. Age Ageing **39**, 31–38 (2009)
26. Harrison, J.K., Noel-Storr, A.H., Demeyere, N., Reynish, E.L., Quinn, T.J.: Outcomes measures in a decade of dementia and mild cognitive impairment trials. Alzheimers Res. Ther. **8**, 48 (2016)
27. Phillips, B., Zhao, H.: Predictors of assistive technology abandonment. Assist. Technol. **5**, 36–45 (1993)
28. Garris, R., Ahlers, R., Driskell, J.E.: Games, motivation, and learning: a research and practice model. Simul. Gaming **33**, 441–467 (2002)
29. Orji, R., Vassileva, J., Mandryk, R.L.: Modeling the efficacy of persuasive strategies for different gamer types in serious games for health. User Model. User-Adap. Inter. **24**, 453–498 (2014)
30. Dweck, C.: Carol Dweck revisits the growth mindset. Educ. Week **35**, 20–24 (2015)
31. Craven, M.P., Fabricatore, C.: Game features of cognitive training. In: 2016 International Conference on Interactive Technologies and Games (ITAG), pp. 42–49. IEEE (2016)
32. Harrington, K., Fulton, P., Brown, M., Pinchin, J., Sharples, S.: Digital wellbeing assessments for people affected by dementia. In: Kurosu, M. (ed.) HCI 2015. LNCS, vol. 9171, pp. 409–418. Springer, Cham (2015). https://doi.org/10.1007/978-3-319-21006-3_39
33. Martin, S., et al.: Attitudes and preferences towards screening for dementia: a systematic review of the literature. BMC Geriatr. **15**, 66 (2015)
34. Robotham, D., Satkunanathan, S., Doughty, L., Wykes, T.: Do we still have a digital divide in mental health? A five-year survey follow-up. J. Med. Internet Res. **18**, e309 (2016)
35. Greer, B., Robotham, D., Simblett, S., Curtis, H., Griffiths, H., Wykes, T.: Digital exclusion among mental health service users: qualitative investigation. J. Med. Internet Res. **21**, e11696 (2019)
36. Vale, C.: Public involvement in clinical trials. NIHR Involve (2012). http://www.invo.org.uk/posttypepublication/public-involvement-in-clinical-trials/
37. Horizon UnBias Toolkit. https://unbias.wp.horizon.ac.uk/2018/09/06/unbias-fairness-toolkit/
38. Harrington, K.: Decision making within missing person incidents. Ph.D. thesis. University of Nottingham, Faculty of Engineering (2019). http://eprints.nottingham.ac.uk/56597/

39. Braun, V., Clarke, V.: Using thematic analysis in psychology. Qual. Res. Psychol. **3**, 77–101 (2006)
40. Jennings, H., Slade, M., Bates, P., Munday, E., Toney, R.: Best practice framework for patient and public involvement (PPI) in collaborative data analysis of qualitative mental health research: methodology development and refinement. BMC Psychiatry **18**, 213 (2018)
41. Maior, H.A., Pike, M., Wilson, M.L., Sharples, S.: Continuous detection of workload overload: an FNIRS approach. In: Contemporary Ergonomics and Human Factors 2014: Proceedings of the International Conference on Ergonomics & Human Factors 2014, Southampton, UK, 7–10 April 2014, p. 450. CRC Press (2014)

Emotional Responses to Health Data Visualization

Chloé Lourdais[1]($\boxtimes$), Emilie Poirson[1], and Liang Ma[2]

[1] Laboratory of Digital Sciences of Nantes (LS2N),
Ecole Centrale de Nantes, Nantes, France
{chloe.lourdais,emilie.poirson}@ls2n.fr
[2] Department of Industrial Engineering, Tsinghua University, Beijing,
People's Republic of China
liangma@tsinghua.edu.cn

Abstract. The current development of telemedicine and m-health services has changed the way in which individuals monitor their health information. These services offer the possibility to receive and consult health data through computers or mobile devices at home, without medical support at any time. Could this new way of approaching our health data have an impact on our psychophysiological state? This study investigated with an experiment individual reactions to health data visualization on an interface. These reactions were investigated in terms of perceived emotion and stress, behavior and physiological changes (cardiac and electrodermal activities). This study compared individual responses to the visualization of different types of data: health data of the user, health data of another person and weather data. The statistical analysis was performed, based on ultra-short-term features for the physiological responses. The results confirmed that the visualization of personal health data entails the most important responses in terms of perceived stress, duration of data visualization and heart rate variability. Therefore, this study suggests that the conception of health interfaces would require particular attention concerning their content, their design, and their accessibility, in order to limit stress elicited by remote health data consultation.

Keywords: Remote health monitoring · Health interface · Data visualization · Physiological responses · Emotional user experience

1 Problem Statement

1.1 The Development of E-health Usage and the Quantified-Self Movement

The usage of remote health services, under the field of connected health (e-health), is currently undergoing important worldwide growth, mainly explained by the rapid advancement in information and communication technologies in the health domain [1, 2]. Firstly, through telemedicine, patients can receive remote healthcare services from health professionals. Telemedicine includes video consultation with specialists, medical result transmission, e-prescribing system, teleassistance, etc. Then, mobile-health

M. Kurosu (Ed.): HCII 2020, LNCS 12183, pp. 61–74, 2020.
https://doi.org/10.1007/978-3-030-49065-2_5

(m-health) refers to the use of wireless mobile devices in a medical setting, such as smartphones or tablets. M-health allows doctors and patients to continually monitor patients' health. It includes medical records, health guidance, medication or health information reminders, as well as a variety of applications on wellness, sport, nutrition or sleep [3]. This service could be based on the usage of health connected devices, such as connected electrocardiogram, pulse oximeter, glucometer, thermometer, pill reminder or system detecting falls. To go further, outside a medical setting, the new phenomenon, quantified self, refers to the usage of wearable technologies for self-monitoring personal data in a pleasant, wellness or sportive usage, with the objective to continually improve health. User physiology, activities and environment are evaluated with quantified parameters [4]. A wide range of connected devices supports this practice. The most common is the connected watch, allowing users to monitor and share cardiac and activity parameters. Other connected devices can be quoted: balance, pedometer, sleep analyzer, fertility tracker, toothbrush, smart clothing, etc.

The current development of these practices gives rise to new issues. Among the field of human factors, some barriers to the integration of the technologies into the daily life of patients have been identified. They mainly concern the usability, the safety and the flexibility of the technologies [1, 5]. However, other aspects can be considered. Indeed, individuals have direct access to personal health information, at home, without medical support and at any time. They can also receive health alerts at any time. With this study, we intended to find out if the remote self-monitoring of health information can impact users' psychophysiological states, especially in terms of emotional load and stress.

1.2 Emotional Responses to Computer-Related Activities

In remote health usage, communication between patients, hospitals, health professionals or connected devices is performed through an interface. From the patient perspective, the interface represents the primary access to her or his health information. It can be an application or a website, used through a computer or a mobile device. However, computer interaction can play an important role in users' emotional states [6, 7]. Several studies showed that computer-related activities can elicit emotions, stress, behavioral changes, and physiological changes, either in the case of an interaction with a robot [8], with virtual agents [9], with computer games [10] or with interfaces [11, 12]. In particular, in the case of an interface, Lockner et al. [12] presented the different interface components eliciting emotion: (1) the content, referring to the information displayed on the interface, (2) the design, referring to the way to transmit and present the information, and (3) the task, referring to the activity requested by the interface. For instance, concerning the design component, Fang et al. [13], showed that the way to display health data can elicit different emotional loads on the elderly. However, our study focused on the content component and intended to examine emotion elicited by health content on an interface.

Firstly, it is important to define emotion. Emotion can be interpreted as a reaction to a stimulus after a cognitive process based on an appraisal [14]. Individuals constantly evaluate their environment with their own concerns. Stimulus, such as an object, a situation, a person or a thought, can immediately entail short emotional reactions.

Emotions are specific to individuals [7]. The circumplex model of affect established by Russell [15] defines emotion by the two dimensions of valence and arousal. Valence refers to the evaluation of pleasantness and arousal refers to the intensity level of the activation. Contrary to emotion, the mood is an affective experience that lasts over hours, with a low-intensity level and for which the cause is difficult to identify. The mood can affect emotion, that is why it is important to consider the influence of mood on emotion [6, 7]. Then, stress is not considered as an emotion, but stress is linked with emotion and vice versa. Stress refers to a state that occurs when individuals deal with something that they would like to change [16]. In our study, we intended to focus on emotion and stress as a response to a specific stimulus related to health content display on an interface.

Emotion and stress are important in the daily life of individuals. Emotion can affect individual attention, memory, decision-making and judgment [6, 7]. In the case of health interface usage, emotion and stress may cause wrong data interpretation and disturb users' life. Moreover, in the longer term, they may have an impact on the mental and physical health of the users.

Different methods for assessing emotion have been developed. Firstly, emotion is an affective experience that can be subjectively evaluated. Self-reports allow individuals to evaluate their experienced emotional state [7]. In this study, perceived emotional valence and arousal were evaluated with the Self-Assessment Manikin (SAM) [17]. Furthermore, changes in individual behavior and physiological state could be interpreted as emotional or stress reactions. They represent objective measures. Some studies reviewed the physiological methods that can be used in human-computer interaction research [7, 18, 19], such as electrodermal activity, cardiac activity, eye tracking, blood pressure, electromyogram, and respiration. In this study, we focused on the measures of cardiac and electrodermal activities. Firstly, the cardiac activity can be analyzed by a lot of parameters on Heart Rate (HR) and Heart Rate Variability (HRV) [20]. These parameters are based on the time intervals between successive heartbeats. In this study, we focused on ultra-short measurement windows (less than 5 min) for assessing acute physiological changes related to the stimulus. Ultra-short windows can be useful for measuring acute emotion and stress during interface interaction [21, 22]. On the other hand, the electrodermal activity, more precisely, the skin conductance can be divided into two signals: the phasic and the tonic signals. Whereas the tonic signal is considered as a general level of activation, the phasic signal is more appropriate to reflect specific stimulus responses. The phasic signal is composed of discrete peaks, called SCRs (Skin Conductance Responses), which can be interpreted as stimulus reactions.

1.3 Research Objective

The objective of this study was to analyze the emotional load and stress elicited by the usage of remote health services from the patient perspective. In particular, the study focused on the usage of patient health interface at home. First, we proposed and conducted an experimental protocol that intended to evaluate emotion and stress elicited by health data visualization. Secondly, the data collected were analyzed. Finally, we concluded the study and discussed the limitations and future work.

2   Experiment

2.1   Experiment Description

An experiment was conducted to determine if the visualization of health content on an interface without medical support could entail an important emotional load on individuals. In order to evaluate the importance of emotional responses, reactions to the visualization of three types of data were compared: physiological data of the subject, physiological data of another person and weather data (Fig. 1). Weather data were used as the comparison condition.

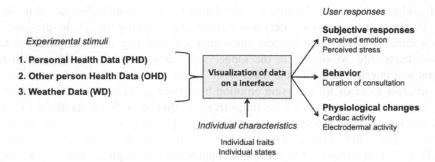

Fig. 1. Experiment objectives

Reactions to data visualization were considered in terms of subjective emotion and stress, behavior and physiological changes. Perceived emotion and stress were assessed with questionnaires, physiological changes were based on cardiac and electro-dermal activities and finally, the duration of data consultation was used as an indicator of behavior. Individuals may have different approaches to how they consult data and then have different reactions. The influence of the user profile was analyzed in terms of individual traits and individual states. Individual traits refer to permanent characteristics that stay stable during a long period, such as personality or character. Individual states refer to a state of mind, feelings or thoughts, at the precise moment of the experiment.

2.2   The Main Sequence

The main part of the experiment was a test lasting 30 min during which participants visualized the three types of data one by one. While participants watched a movie on an interface, some notifications were triggered, followed by a display of data. After visualizing data, participants could click a button to return to watch the movie. Data consultation durations and physiological activities were recorded.

Visualized Items. Each type of data included four items (Fig. 2). The items are data usually consulted at home in the e-health or weather areas. The physiological data included cardiac frequency (bpm), respiratory frequency (bpm), body temperature (°C) and skin conductance (µS). The weather data included outside temperature (°C), probability of precipitation (%), relative humidity (%) and wind speed (km/h). All the information was the instantaneous item values at the moment of the data page display. To the right of the current data, the variations of the data compared to the last data consultation were displayed. This information helped the users to monitor the data during the experiment. The data were represented with the same design features in order to minimize the impact of confounding variables on responses. The background colors were chosen white and light blue, considered as neutral colors for physiological and weather domains. To ensure that participants understood the meaning of the data, an explanation of the items was provided at the beginning of the experiment. Also, icons helped users to easily recognize the sense of the data.

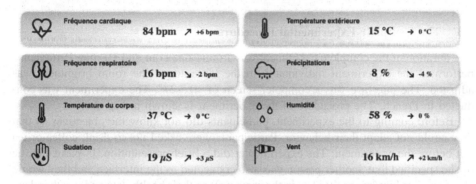

Fig. 2. Visualized data: physiological items and weather items

The Notifications. The notification system was identical for all the participants. Notification messages appeared on the upper right corner of the interface, asking participants to monitor the data. A short audible alarm accompanied the notifications to inform users. Data displayed 10 s after the triggering of the notification and the movie automatically stopped. To avoid the surprise effect of the page change, a 5-s countdown was programmed.

Nine notifications were programmed per participant: three notifications of each type of data (Fig. 3). The time interval between each notification was irregular. However, a minimum of two minutes between two consecutive notifications was set, so that users could return to their rest state. Each consecutive group of three notifications contained the three types of data but in different orders. In this way, participants could not predict the next notification and the three types of data were visualized at similar times.

The Movie. The movie was the same for all the participants. It was relaxing and calm, with a low and constant level of emotional arousal. The objective was to occupy participants with a familiar activity while reducing emotional state and then detect emotional responses to the data visualization. We have chosen an extract of the documentary film Home (2009, Yann Arthus-Bertrand).

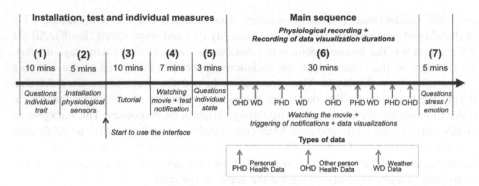

Fig. 3. Experimental procedure

2.3 The Complete Experimental Procedure

The duration of the complete experiment was around one hour and 10 min. Participants performed the experiment individually in the laboratory. The room brightness was adjusted. The interface was a computer screen of size 27″. The experiment was conducted in French. The procedure of the experiment is shown in Fig. 3.

Before coming to the experiment, participants did not know the objectives so that they could not adapt their behavior. Participants were asked not to drink coffee or tea 2 h before the experiment. The experimenter did a brief presentation. In particular, he or she specified that another person was also connected to the interface and they would also visualize him/her health data in the same way as their health data and weather data. Participants also signed an informed consent to participate.

In the first step, (1) participants answered the questionnaires on individual traits in a paper-pencil format. Then, (2) helped by the experimenter, participants were equipped with the physiological sensors. The physiological measurements were used to show participants their health data on the interface, and also to analyze physiological responses to data visualization during the statistical analysis.

All the next steps were performed on the interface, which was programmed for the experiment. Participants just needed to follow the instructions. All the participants had the same experimental procedure. In (3), the interface operation, the notification system, and the visualized items were explained with a tutorial. Then, (4) a test similar to the main sequence was performed: participants began to watch the movie and a notification test was triggered. Participants could become familiar with the interface, the notification system, and the data meanings. These steps were used to minimize the impact of the interface discovery and data misunderstanding on emotional responses. Next, (5) participants were asked to answer the questions about their individual states. Participants could answer these questions in the same context as the main sequence. We considered that individual states were identical throughout the main sequence.

After that, (6) the main sequence automatically began, as well as the recordings of physiological activities and data visualization durations. At the end of the experiment, (7) participants were automatically asked to answer the questions about experienced emotion and stress when they visualized the three types of data.

2.4 Questionnaires

Individual Traits and States. Questionnaires were used to assess some individual aspects that can change the way in which individuals react to the data visualizations. The following questionnaires were used:

- Demographic characteristics: age, gender and nationality.
- Health Anxiety: Individual tendency to worry about health was assessed with the short version of the Health Anxiety Inventory [23]. It is composed of 14 questions presented in a multiple-choice format.
- Habits of using mobile devices: We elaborated a questionnaire of 7 items for which individuals rated each item on a 5-point agreement scale. For instance "I spend a lot of time on my smartphone compared to other people".
- Habits of using e-health applications: We elaborated a questionnaire of 7 items for which individuals rated each item on a 5-point agreement scale. For instance "It is essential for me to regularly check my health data on my applications".
- Mood: The mood was assessed by using the bi-dimensional approach of the Russell's Circumplex Model [15]. The questionnaire included two 10-point scales. The first scale concerned the valence dimension, from negative to positive, and the second scale concerned the arousal dimension, from calm to active. The subjects rated these scales on how their mood was during the last hours.
- Anxiety state: The short and state version of the State-Trait Anxiety Inventory was used [24]. It includes 6 items where subjects rated each item on 4-point intensity scales.

Perceived Emotion and Stress. The questionnaires were asked for each type of data.

- Subjective emotion: The Self-Manikin Assessment (SAM) [17] was used. We used the two scales of valence and arousal dimensions. The scales are based on graphic characters to describe the 9-point scales. For the valence dimension, the graphic character range from happy to sad. For the arousal dimension, the graphic characters range from calm to active.
- Subjective stress: We elaborated a questionnaire of 4 questions. For instance, "Does this situation make me feel tense?". Each item was rated on a 5-point scale. The score was obtained by summing the scale values across the 4 items.

2.5 Physiological Measurement

The physiological measurement was performed with the BioNomadix Wireless Wearable Physiology device; from BIOPAC Systems Inc. Cardiac (ECG), respiratory (RSP) and electrodermal (EDA) activities were measured. The ECG sensors were composed of three electrodes that must be placed on the subject's chest, the RSP sensor was a belt that must be placed around the chest and the EDA sensors were two electrodes placed on fingers.

Firstly physiological data were transferred in real-time to the interface when participants visualized their current health data. Then physiological recordings were saved to study physiological responses to data visualization during the statistical analysis. Before that, ECG and EDA signals were prepared on the AcqKnowledge software.

ECG and EDA signals were filtered to reduce noise. Artifacts were identified and eliminated. Heartbeat times of the ECG signal were extracted: RR intervals (interbeat time intervals) and NN intervals (interbeat time intervals without artifact). Next, the phasic signal and the SCRs (Skin Conductance Responses) of the EDA activity were extracted for the analysis.

2.6   Participants

24 subjects took part in the experiment: 11 females and 13 males, from 23 to 85 years old (Mean = 43.71, Median = 39, SD = 19.71), with three different nationalities: French, Indian and Portuguese. All subjects could understand French. The subjects did not have any particular pathology. Each participant performed the complete experiment in the same conditions.

3   Result

3.1   Method of Statistical Analysis

With the objective and perceptive data collected, we firstly checked the absence of outliers, with the outlier boxplot method. Atypical values but correct were kept. Errors (from measurement or data collecting) were corrected.

Then we conducted a statistical hypothesis test: (H_0) Individual responses are the same for all three types of data visualized; (H_a) Individual responses are not the same for all three types of data visualized. A paired-sample analysis was performed to take into account the within-subject aspect: a repeated measures ANOVA was used. Because of the relatively small number of participants, it was important to check the assumptions for applying the repeated measures ANOVA. Firstly, the normality was checked with the Shapiro-Wilk test ($\alpha = 0.05$): responses must be approximately normally distributed for each experimental condition. Then the sphericity was checked with the Mauchly's test ($\alpha = 0.05$): the variance of the response differences between conditions must be equal. If the condition of sphericity was violated, the Greenhouse-Geisser correction could be applied. In the case of not normally distributed data, the non-parametric Friedman test for paired-sample measures was used. Then, post-hoc tests were performed to identify differences between stimuli. In the case of a repeated measures ANOVA, we used multiple paired t-tests between conditions. The Bonferroni correction method was applied for adjusting the p-values. In the case of the Friedman test, we used the Nemenyi post-hoc test. The effect size was also analyzed. In the case of a repeated measures ANOVA, the generalized eta-squared (n_G^2) was used and in the case of the Friedman test, the Kendall's coefficient of concordance (W_K) was used.

3.2   Analysis of Perceived Emotion and Stress

Emotion. Emotional valence was rated from 1 (very pleasant) to 9 (very unpleasant). The emotional valence scores were not normally distributed at each condition, as assessed by Shapiro-Wilk test ($p < 0.05$). The Friedman test was used and did not show significant differences between stimuli ($X^2 = 4.59$, df = 2, p = 0.10, $W_K = 0.76$). Next, emotional arousal was rated from 1 (very calm) to 9 (very active). The Friedman test was used (Shapiro-Wilk test, p < 0.05) and showed significant differences ($X^2 = 8.71$, df = 2, p = 0.013, $W_K = 0.66$). However, the Nemenyi post-hoc test did not report any differences for multiple comparisons (p > 0.05). Therefore, the global subjective emotional state did not differ between the three types of data visualizations.

Stress. Stress was rated from 4 (no stress) to 16 (high stress). The stress scores were not normally distributed at each condition (Shapiro-Wilk test, p < 0.05). The Friedman test was significant ($X^2 = 10.61$, df = 2, p = 0.0050, $W_K = 0.59$). According to the Nemenyi post-hoc test, personal health data visualization (M = 6.29, SD = 2.64) was more stressful than weather data visualization (M = 4.96, SD = 2.48) (p = 0.031) (Fig. 4).

3.3   Analysis of Duration of Data Consultation

Responses were collected for 19 subjects. According to the Shapiro-Wilk test, the duration (in seconds) of data consultations were not normally distributed at each condition (p < 0.05). The Friedman test was used and reported highly significant results ($X^2 = 13.95$, df = 2, p = $9.37.10^{-4}$, $W_K = 0.84$). According to the Nemenyi post-hoc test, durations of personal health data visualization (M = 10.6, SD = 3.09) was highly longer than durations of weather data visualization (M = 8.79, SD = 3.47) (p = 0.0019) and also highly longer than durations of visualization of another person health data (M = 9.68, SD = 3.49) (p = 0.0098) (Fig. 4).

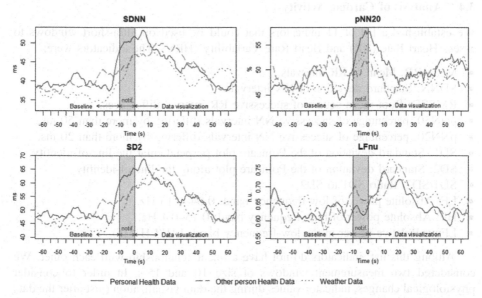

Fig. 4. Indicator variations during notifications (Indicator values on sliding windows of size 15 s – Mean for the notifications of the same type of data – Mean for all the participants).

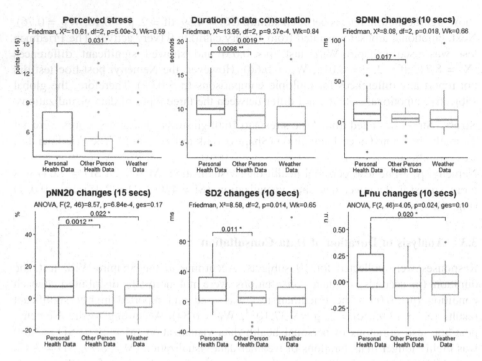

Fig. 5. Statistical results of the subjective, behavioral and physiological indicators showing significant differences between the three types of data visualizations. *p < 0.05, **p < 0.01.

3.4 Analysis of Cardiac Activity

We established a list of 11 indicators that could be used on ultra-short windows to assess Heart Rate (HR) and Heart Rate Variability (HRV). The indicators were:

- Mean RR: Mean of RR intervals,
- SDNN: Standard deviation of NN intervals,
- RMSSD: Root mean square of successive RR interval differences,
- pNN50: percentage of successive NN intervals differing by more than 50 ms,
- pNN20: percentage of successive NN intervals differing by more than 20 ms,
- SD1: Standard deviation of the Poincaré plot perpendicular the line-of-identity,
- SD2: Standard deviation of the Poincaré plot along the line-of-identity,
- SD1/SD2: Ratio SD1 to SD2,
- LF: Absolute power of low-frequency band: 0.04–0.15 Hz,
- HF: Absolute power of high-frequency band: 0.15–0.4 Hz,
- LFnu: Relative power in the low-frequency band: LH/(LH+HF).

Among this list, indicators do not have a linear relationship with each other. We considered two measurement windows of size 10 and 15 s. In order to consider physiological changes, indicator values during the data visualization (just after the data page change), were compared by a subtraction, with indicator values during the baseline stage (just before the notification triggering of the same notification) (Fig. 4).

The statistical analysis was performed with the same procedure, for all the indicators and for the two measurement windows. Among this list, 4 indicators reported significant differences between stimuli: SDNN, SD2 and LFnu, within the measurement window of 10 s, and pNN20, within the measurement windows of 10 and 15 s. The Fig. 4 shows indicator variations during the notifications for the three types of data and the Fig. 5 reported the statistical results for these indicators.

Changes in SDNN (ms) were more important for the visualization of personal health data (M = 12.5, SD = 29.1) than for health data of another person (M = 3.36, SD = 22.7). Likewise, changes in SD2 (ms) were also more important for the visualization of personal health data (M = 18.4, SD = 38.2) than for health data of another person (M = 3.58, SD = 29.7). Then, changes in LF (n.u.) were more important for the visualization of personal health data (M = 0.108, SD = 0.317) than weather data (M = −0.030, SD = 0.301). And finally, changes in pNN20 were more important for the measurement windows of 15 s. Changes in pNN20 (%) were more important for the visualizations of personal health data (M = 9.86, SD = 19.7) than health data of another person (M = −2.14, SD = 20.9), as well as weather data (M = 0.833, SD = 19.3).

Therefore, the type of data visualized on the interface had an impact on certain aspect of heart rate variability, especially on the indicators SDNN, SD2, pNN20, and LFnu. The changes in the indicators between the data visualization and the baseline windows were always more important for personal health data visualization.

3.5   Analysis of Electrodermal Activity

Among the 24 participants, electrodermal measures could be analyzed for only 15 participants because of too much noise in some recordings. Four indicators of phasic activity were studied: the mean and maximum amplitude of the phasic activity, the sum of the SCR amplitudes and the ISCR (Integrated Skin Conductance Responses). We used a common measurement window that starts 1 s after the stimulus beginning and ends 6 s after the stimulus beginning. For each notification, indicator values in this window were compared, by a subtraction, with indicator values in the baseline window of the same size. The statistical analysis was performed for these indicators. However, no significant results were found. We supposed that the small number of subjects with valid recordings could explain the lack of results.

3.6   Analysis of Individual Characteristics

Among parameters showing significant differences between experimental stimuli, impacts of individual traits and states were analyzed. We conducted a Principal Component Analysis to detect interactions of individual characteristics on the responses to the three types of data. No significant result was found. This result needs to be confirmed with a wider participant panel.

4 Conclusion and Discussion

Some responses analyzed in this study showed significant differences between visualizations of personal health data and weather data (perceived stress, duration of data consultation, LFnu and pNN20). Other responses showed significant differences between visualizations of health data of the user and heath data of another person (duration of data consultation, SDNN, SD2, and pNN20). For all these features, responses to personal health data visualization were always more important than responses to the other types of data. These results confirmed that the visualization of personal health data without medical support could elicit important emotional load, compared with other types of data, and especially concerning the perceived stress, the duration of the data consultations and the heart rate variability changes.

Moreover, we did not find any differences in the reactions between visualizations of health data of another person and weather data. The visualization of health data of another person seemed not to have a strong impact on the user's emotional state. It is important to restate that the other person was unknown to the user. Moreover, this result also confirmed the experimental protocol, especially, the minimization of confounding variable effects on responses, such as the effect of the design features and the data understanding.

The study of physiological activities reported that HRV important changes associated with the data visualization happened during the first 10 s. However, the indicator pNN20 showed stronger differences during the measurement window of 15 s than 10 s. Further work would be to study the durations of differences between conditions. Indeed, the longer the duration of physiological change is, the stronger the impact may be.

Moreover, the experiment showed significant results on participants without particular pathology. We can suggest that emotional load, especially physiological changes, would be more important for subjects with a particular disease, such as a chronic disease. It would be interesting to study this phenomenon in future work.

To conclude, daily health data visualization could entail important acute stress and emotion, reflected by stress, behavioral and cardiac changes. In the short and long term, this phenomenon could impact user's daily life, mental and physical health.

With the current development of e-health usage and the quantified-self phenomenon, the results pave the way to other considerations to analyze. The usage and the conception of health interfaces would require specific attention to reduce emotional load elicited on users. The design of health interfaces can be though to reduce emotional responses. The design can refer to colors and illustrations, the way to display the data, the way to explain data meanings, the way to transmit alerts to the user, etc. Also, the health content could be studied: what health data can individual access? For instance, health data comparisons with norms, the evolution of data over time, specific data related to a disease, etc. Finally, another aspect to consider would be the interface accessibility: who can access the data, when can the user consult the data, when are the data updates?

References

1. Tuckson, R.V., Edmunds, M., Hodgkins, M.L.: Telehealth. N. Engl. J. Med. **377**, 1585–1592 (2017)
2. Grigsby, J., Rigby, M., Hiemstra, A., House, M., Olsson, S., Whitten, P.: Chapter 7: The diffusion of telemedicine. Telemed. J. E Health **8**, 79–94 (2002)
3. World Health Organization: mHealth: New Horizons for Health Through Mobile Technologies. World Health Organization, Geneva (2011)
4. Lupton, D.: Self-tracking, health and medicine. Health Sociol. Rev. **26**, 1–5 (2017)
5. Genaro Motti, V., Caine, K.: An overview of wearable applications for healthcare: requirements and challenges. In: Adjunct Proceedings of the 2015 ACM International Joint Conference on Pervasive and Ubiquitous Computing and Proceedings of the 2015 ACM International Symposium on Wearable Computers, pp. 635–641. Association for Computing Machinery, Osaka (2015)
6. Brave, S., Nass, C.: Emotion in human-computer interaction. In: Sears, A., Jacko, J.A. (eds.) The Human-Computer Interaction Handbook: Fundamentals, Evolving Technologies and Emerging Applications, pp. 103–118. CRC Press, Boca Raton (2007)
7. Lottridge, D., Chignell, M., Jovicic, A.: Affective interaction: understanding, evaluating, and designing for human emotion. Rev. Hum. Factors Ergon. **7**, 197–217 (2011)
8. Tiberio, L., Cesta, A., Olivetti Belardinelli, M.: Psychophysiological methods to evaluate user's response in human robot interaction: a review and feasibility study. Robotics **2**, 92–121 (2013)
9. Prendinger, H., Becker, C., Ishizuka, M.: A study in user's physio logical response to an empathic interface agent. Int. J. Humanoid Robot. **3**, 371–391 (2006)
10. Van Reekum, C., Johnstone, T., Banse, R., Etter, A., Wehrle, T., Scherer, K.: Psychophysiological responses to appraisal dimensions in a computer game. Cogn. Emot. **18**, 663–668 (2004)
11. Ward, R.D., Marsden, P.H., Cahill, B., Johnson, C.: Physiological responses to well-designed and poorly designed interfaces. In: Proceedings of CHI 2002 Workshop on Physiological Computing (2002)
12. Lockner, D., Bonnardel, N., Bouchard, C., Rieuf, V.: Emotion and interface design. In: Proceedings of the 2014 Ergonomie et Informatique Avancée Conference-Design, Ergonomie et IHM: quelle articulation pour la co-conception de l'interaction, pp. 33–40 (2014)
13. Fang, Y.-M., Chou, Y.-P., Chu, B.-C.: Health information display for elderly people: interface attributes, usability, and emotional reaction. In: 2016 International Conference on Applied System Innovation (ICASI), pp. 1–4 (2016)
14. Ellsworth, P.C., Scherer, K.R.: Appraisal processes in emotion. In: Handbook of Affective Sciences, pp. 572–595. Oxford University Press, New York (2003)
15. Russell, J.A.: A circumplex model of affect. J. Pers. Soc. Psychol. **39**, 1161–1178 (1980)
16. Lazarus, R.S.: Stress and Emotion: A New Synthesis. Springer, New York (2006)
17. Bradley, M.M., Lang, P.J.: Measuring emotion: the self-assessment manikin and the semantic differential. J. Behav. Ther. Exp. Psychiatry **25**, 49–59 (1994)
18. Park, B.: Psychophysiology as a tool for HCI research: promises and pitfalls. In: Jacko, J.A. (ed.) HCI 2009. LNCS, vol. 5610, pp. 141–148. Springer, Heidelberg (2009). https://doi.org/10.1007/978-3-642-02574-7_16
19. Dirican, A.C., Göktürk, M.: Psychophysiological measures of human cognitive states applied in human computer interaction. Procedia Comput. Sci. **3**, 1361–1367 (2011)

20. Shaffer, F., Ginsberg, J.P.: An overview of heart rate variability metrics and norms. Front. Public Health **5**, 258 (2017)

21. Schaaff, K., Adam, M.T.P.: Measuring emotional arousal for online applications: evaluation of ultra-short term heart rate variability measures. In: 2013 Humaine Association Conference on Affective Computing and Intelligent Interaction, pp. 362–368 (2013)

22. Salahuddin, L., Cho, J., Jeong, M.G., Kim, D.: Ultra short term analysis of heart rate variability for monitoring mental stress in mobile settings. In: 2007 29th Annual International Conference of the IEEE Engineering in Medicine and Biology Society, pp. 4656–4659. IEEE (2007)

23. Salkovskis, P.M., Rimes, K.A., Warwick, H.M.C., Clark, D.M.: The health anxiety inventory: development and validation of scales for the measurement of health anxiety and hypochondriasis. Psychol. Med. **32**, 843–853 (2002)

24. Marteau, T.M., Bekker, H.: The development of a six-item short-form of the state scale of the Spielberger State-Trait Anxiety Inventory (STAI). Br. J. Clin. Psychol. **31**, 301–306 (1992)

Improving Dialogue Design and Control for Smartwatches by Reinforcement Learning Based Behavioral Acceptance Patterns

Rainer Lutze[1]([✉]) and Klemens Waldhör[2]

[1] Dr.-Ing. Rainer Lutze Consulting, Wachtlerhof, Langenzenn, Germany
rainerlutze@lustcon.eu
[2] FOM University of Applied Sciences, Nuremberg, Germany
klemens.waldhoer@fom.de

Abstract. Dialogue control for health-oriented smartwatch apps is a multi-dimensional task. In our application scenario, the intended purpose of the smartwatch app is the prevention and detection of health hazards jeopardizing the smartwatch wearer (e.g. exsiccosis because of insufficient drinking); the designated target group of the app are elderly people. The dimension of a potential simultaneity of health hazards and ethical considerations how to position the wearer always in control of the app have been presented before. In this paper we focus on the third dimension of the mandatory acceptance conditions of the app. The intended assistance functionality of the app can be only realized, if the interventions of the app occur only in daily life situations, when the wearer will accept such interventions. We present a machine learning approach, by which the app will learn from the wearer over time, when such interventions are appropriate and accepted - and when the app will be expected to remain silent. Of course, this decision has to take into account also the urgency of the intervention with respect to the severity of the threating health hazard.

Keywords: Acceptance patterns for smartwatches · Machine learning · Assistance for the elderly · Health hazard handling · Ambient assisted living

1 Introduction

For supporting a *safe*, *healthy* and *self-determined life* of elderly people *in their familiar home* setting, the use of assisting *non-stigmatizing information technology* is widely accepted. Smartwatches are suitable devices, because (i) they will be typically worn from dawn to dusk, inside the home and on the road, (ii) upfront models (e.g. Apple Watch™ 3 and later, Samsung Galaxy Watch Active2™) include LTE communication modules for autonomous alerting, and (iii) they can be programmed via apps.

Our smartwatch assistance app [1–3] monitors about a dozen health hazards simultaneously typically in the background, whenever the smartwatch is worn. The monitoring is based on the activity patterns of the smartwatch wearer, observed vital parameters (pulse) and the location of the smartwatch wearer. Whenever the

© Springer Nature Switzerland AG 2020
M. Kurosu (Ed.): HCII 2020, LNCS 12183, pp. 75–85, 2020.
https://doi.org/10.1007/978-3-030-49065-2_6

smartwatch app concludes about a threatening present health hazard, it initiates a dialogue with the user in order to prevent an emergency service while no factual health hazard occurred (false alert), or, to motivate the wearer to start short-time counter measures (in the described examples: to drink something), or, to include external human help by placing a phone call via the integrated mobile radio within the smartwatch (e.g. call to a home emergency call center, if no liquids are reachable for the user). We denote this dialogue as *health hazard handling dialogue* as constituent of a more comprehensive health hazard handling process [1]. For implementing a structured, complete and standardized execution of such health hazard handling dialogues, the concept of a *critical dialogue section*, CDS, has been proposed in [4].

The first problem dimension needed to be handled by the dialogue control is the potential simultaneity of health hazards. Typically, only one health hazard can be handled by an user dialogue at a time. This challenge will be solved first via a prioritization of health hazards, in that simultaneous health hazards will be discussed with the user following decreased severity. Second, via the concept CDS an ongoing, model-based dialogue for health hazard handling will never be disrupted by another handling dialogue for a higher prioritized hazard detected in the meantime [4]. This stringent approach is feasible because an individual handling dialogue takes only a very few minutes.

The second problem dimension of dialogue control is governed by ethical considerations. The smartwatch wearer shall be always left in control, whether he wants entering a dialogue with the smartwatch app and which of his or her person-related information, especially vital data and/or movement profiles, will be disclosed to third parties. Whenever the smartwatch assistance app – within the course of a health hazard handling dialogue - calls in for external human help, such help will be only effective if the actual person related information from the smartwatch user will be made available to an external human specialist. It will therefore be transferred automatically by the app just before the external call will be established. This means, that within the course of the user dialogue, an explicit consent from the user will be mandatory for disclosing such person-related information and calling-in external human help [5]. The user consent is collected by executing a prealert on the smartwatch. The process flow for doing so has been modelled by declarative description of the complete health hazard handling process via UML state machines [1, 2, 4]. The only exception to such an indispensable user permit is a situation, in which the smartwatch app assumes a potentially life-threatening health hazard as well as an unconscious user.

The third problem dimension of dialog control is determined by the acceptance conditions of corresponding apps by the users. Our experiences from the implementation of smartwatch assistance apps based on the principles described above have shown that dialogue offers from the app will be accepted by the smartwatch wearer in some situations but will be regularly rejected in others. These aspects must be considered by a careful, user centered design. Otherwise the app will lose acceptance and will not be used due to perceived "false alerts". We propose to solve this challenge by including a new machine learning component, which will observe and learn the situational parameters, in which proactive dialogues from the smartwatch will be accepted by its wearers.

2 Requirements Specification

A key problem is how the system can learn when an app-initiated health hazard handling dialogue will not be situationally appropriate from an user's perspective (e.g. when driving a car at high speed or while talking to other persons). Especially in the scope of a situation, when the smartwatch wearer basically has no interest to disclose his or her specific reasons to the app. For acquiring this information, we have decided to use machine learning, specifically *reinforcement learning*. This learning will result in an *individual adaption* of the app behavior when to proactively entering dialogues with the smartwatch wearer.

In implementing this new approach, first of all a new unobtrusive *("shut up")* gesture had to be added to the smartwatch repertoire of recognized gestures[1]: *slapping the opposite hand on the wrist where the smartwatch is worn in order to stop a situationally unwanted app initiated dialogue.* Alternatively, a spoken command could be implemented *("not now")*. Clearly, the execution of this *shut up* gesture resp. command indicates a negative reward to the learning algorithm. The immediate interrupt of an initiated CDS[2] is the maximum *negative reward*, the complete execution of such a section (and cooperative participation of the smartwatch wearer) is the maximum *positive reward* to the algorithm.

Based on this dialogue evaluation, the proposed learning algorithm initially has to learn *from examples,* when a health hazard handling dialogue has been allowed by the wearer in the past, and when not. To do so, potential situational parameters within the smartwatch's sensorial horizon must be collected, which were present at the moment of allowance, interruption or denial of the dialogue. These situational parameters include the current geographic location of the smartwatch wearer, his/her movement speed, the time and day of the week, ..., see Sect. 3 below for the details. The sum of these parameter values, the *situational setting,* is supposed to determine the acceptance of the dialogue in a specific situation.

Although, the event of allowing, interrupting or denying a health hazard handling dialogue will typically occur *only infrequently* in everyday life of the smartwatch user. A second essential requirement for the learning algorithm therefore is to *generalize* the experienced event and to transfer and apply it to *comparable situations,* when the same behavior of the algorithm will be probably expected from the user's point of view. This generalization will be achieved by mapping the n parameter values of a situational setting into a data point within a n-dimensional data space, »hypercube« (Fig. 1). This hypercube will be populated not only with data points for each experienced health

---

[1] These gestures include: *drinking, eating, hand washing, run_away, sleeping/snoozing, steering (a vehicle/bicycle), teeth brushing, tumbling,* and, of course, the *»unclassified«* gesture [2].

[2] It should be noted that the *critical dialogue section* concept proposed in [4] is asymmetric in its nature: by definition, a *critical dialogue section* will be always executed completely by the smartwatch app, as soon as it has started. But, the smartwatch wearer, user, is free to interrupt the execution of the section by application of the "shut up" gesture or command at any time.

hazard dialog event. Additionally, whenever an EDL/ADL has been recognized by the assistance app, the situational setting of the EDL/ADL will be written as a data point to the hypercube. Based on experiences from our field test with the smartwatch app, in this way the hypercube will be populated with a about a new dozen data points for ADLs recognized per day and smartwatch wearer. Now, when a data point for an experienced health hazard dialog event will be added to the hypercube, we consider the uniform distribution of data points within the hypercube. If the data point for the experienced event is contained within a *cluster* in this hypercube based on the relative proximity of data points within the hypercube, the experienced behavior (decline or acceptance of the dialogue) will be extended to *all elements within this cluster,* if - and only if - this can be done in a non-contradictory way. The last restriction is of relevance, because the success of the learning process cannot be assured by technical means.

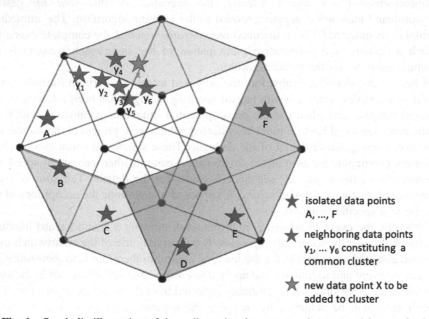

Fig. 1. Symbolic illustration of the n-dimensional parameter data space (»hypercube«)

The constructed, more and more populated hypercube constitutes a very personal profile of *what* the wearer is typically doing *when* and *where*. This is *extremely sensitive personal information,* and will be deliberately stored exclusively in the smartwatch assistance app. The profile must not be calculated outside the smartwatch app and cannot be exported and/or transferred to other devices, in order to prevent any potential misuse (»*privacy by design«,* [6], Principle 3: *"Privacy **Embedded** into Design").* This is a very basic requirement and boundary condition to the solution described below.

3 System Design

3.1 Suitability and Scope of Machine Learning

Machine learning (ML) is the most successful AI approach currently used. Machine vision is one example where convolutional neuronal network (CNNs) and deep learning [7] as an example of ML are extremely successful. Three types of ML approaches are used nowadays: *supervised learning* (SL) where the data set is trained against labels, *unsupervised learning* (UL) which identifies patterns in the data set without using labels and reinforcement learning (RL) where the learning algorithm receives feedback on its actions and learns from that feedback. A major condition of those approaches is that they depend on relatively big training data sets in order to provide correct results. RL may be to some extent different as the reinforcement can be done by algorithms (e.g. using game rules, [8]). Nevertheless, for our application domain health hazards handling dialogues – the examples to learn from - occur relatively rare.

Therefore, our approach is based on *learning by examples* ([9], chapter 18) and *a maximal utilization* of those examples *for similar situational settings.*

In order to determine the potential scope of machine learning, we have to consider the relation between the factual presence of a health hazard in reality and the identification resp. classification of the same situation as hazardous to the user's health by the assistance app. The four possible combinations of values and *standardized denominations* for such binary value combinations are depicted in Table 1.

Table 1. Classification matrix for health hazards.

Reality vs. App Classification	health hazard **factually present**	health hazard factually **not present**
assistance app **identifies** health hazard	**True Positives (TP)** **Appropriate action** proposed by app	**False Positives (FP)** **User harassed** by superfluous action proposal
assistance app **does not identify** health hazard	**False Negatives (FN)** Action required by app, but **no proposal to user**	**True Negatives (TN)** **No action** proposed by app, nothing necessary

In principal, for TPs and FNs, the app behavior is ok, nothing needs to be improved. This statement is valid, as long as the user will always allow TP health hazard handling dialogues. But what, if the user also trains the app to keep silent in TP situations, because he wants to keep his peace of mind, ignoring the threatening or already manifested health hazard? Following the second problem dimension described above, the postulated dominance of control principle for the user would result in a reticence of the assistance app against better knowledge. This may be questionable with respect to health implications but is mandatory from ethical principles favoring the *primacy of self-determination of the user*.

FPs are covered by the proposed learning algorithms targeting to learn a user accepted communication behavior. For a rational user, which would always correctly decline FP health hazard handling dialogues, the learning algorithm would result in a flawless assistance app communication behavior.

For FN, the situation is complicated for two reasons. First of all, the proposed simple learning algorithm is incapable to learn or improve the necessary healthcare knowledge even for *already known* resp. hazards already managed by the assistance app. For improving this implemented behavior of the assistance app, either new SL training samples would be required to improve the artificial neuronal network executing the EDL/ADL recognition process within the app [2, 3]. Or, the declarative knowledge representation embodying the healthcare handling process itself[3] based on such recognized EDLs, ADLs would have to be improved [1, 4]. Especially a full automatization of the structural knowledge acquisition for the latter case is currently out of scope [10, 11]. Furthermore, the assistance app is trained to conclude a fixed number of health hazards based on sensorial values, EDLs/ADLs recognized from them and their sequencing and combination in time. Thus, the app will not detect health hazards beyond the sensorial horizon of the sensors and/or conclusion principles applicable. But, these hazards would be also subsumed as FN. As an example, the app is not trained for detecting injuries form car accidents which obviously is a very relevant category of health hazards.

3.2 Modelling Situational Settings

The following parameters for characterizing a situational setting of (i) a recognized EDL/ADL, or (ii) the execution of a health hazard handling dialogue - via execution of the corresponding CDS - will be considered by the smartwatch assistance app:

- The *geographic location* of the smartwatch wearer: (lat, long) acquired from the GPS sensor of the wearer outdoor. When being at home, a room based indoor localization can be achieved by utilizing the Wi-Fi signature of the specific room.
- The specific *time of the day* (digitized in a 15 min grid).
- The *specific day of the week*. The day of the week is additionally categorized either as (1) a regular workday (Monday to Friday), (2) a Saturday or private holiday, or (3) a Sunday or public holiday.
- The *speed* by which the wearer is moving, digitized into four discrete speed intervals, like: *steady, walking, running, driving*.

The corresponding parameters values will be aggregated into a 4-dimensional data point. If this data point does not already exist in the hypercube, it will be added, when (i) a EADL/ADL has been recognized or (ii) a CDS has been executed. Let x denote this considered data point. Data point x will be associated with a set of values, denoted $vals_x$. Initially, these values $v \in vals_x$ describe the events which caused the creation of

---

[3] Currently described via an extended notion of UML finite state machines.

the data point x. Later on, the values will be amended by the experiences learned for the situational setting data represented by x. The potential elements v in the value set $vals_x$ of data point x set can be:

1. an atomic denominator **ea** for an recognized ADL/EDL.
2. a triple **(c, r, ea)** describing the category **c** of a CDS executed (Table 2), the execution result **r** (Table 3) and eventually the perceived occasion of the CDS execution, given by the recognition of an EDL/ADL with denominator **ea** in close temporal proximity to the CDS execution. ea may be empty, special denominator *nil,* if no such EDL/ADL has been recognized in close temporal proximity to the execution of a CDS.

Table 2. Categories of CDS indicating the severity with respect to the involved health hazards

Category of a CDS	Threat progress	Examples
High	Immediate	Injuries as a consequence of a fall, cardiovascular problems due to inappropriate pulse rate with respect to physical activity
Medium	Foreseeable	Exsiccosis to due insufficient drinking
Low	Precautions	Returning home as a prevention against getting lost

Table 3. Possible result values for a CDS execution

CDS execution result	Meaning
r_1	CDS allowed by user and completely executed
r_2	CDS execution interrupted by user, incomplete
r_3	CDS execution immediately stopped by user

For example, a recognized EDL »tumble« typically causes immediately the execution of a CDS, so it is useful to associate the CDS execution directly with the occasion of this recognized EDL. A similar close temporal proximity is typically between the ADL »runaway« and the CDS execution for handling the foreseeable health hazard resulting from the runaway situation. On the other site, an *"insufficient drinking"* health hazard handling dialogue takes place significantly later than the last recognized »drinking« ADL and independently from other EDL/ADLs. Therefore, it does not make sense to associate the data point for corresponding CDS execution with any EDL/ADL. Only, if an EDL/ADL incidentally would be recognized in close temporal proximity to the *"insufficient drinking"* dialogue execution, it would be added as the incidental occasion of the CDS execution. In the latter case, this really makes sense, because the corresponding EDL/ADL could have in fact influenced the specific user reaction to the *"insufficient drinking"* dialogue execution.

The designated purpose of the association of values with data points within the hypercube is to derive a recommendation for (dialogue) action behavior of the assistance app. It is therefore essential to construct *unambiguous* recommended actions. Therefore, if the value set $vals_x$ of data point x already contains a value $v_o = (c, r, ea)$ and a new value $v_n = (c, s, ea)$ shall be added to the value set with $r = r_1 \wedge s = r_3$ or vice versa, i.e. a contradictory recommendation for action, the new value v_n will replace the existing value v_o in the value set $vals_x$. New experience replaces old experience. By incorporating EDLs/ADLs in the value tripel, whenever possible, we also reduce the reach of contradictory recommendations for (dialogue) action for the future app behavior.

The inclusion of only the category of a CDS executed instead of the specific health hazard handled by this CDS into a value element of a data point x will help to extend the validity of the specific example represented by this data point x. The learned example will be assumed to be applicable for all other data points y in the same cluster than x, executing a health hazard dialogue of the same category and on the occasion of the same EDL/ADL than for the example. If a CDS handles more than one health hazard at a time, the most severe health hazard category with respect to the Table 2 determines the categorization of the CDS.

3.3 Extending the Reach of Learned Examples

Shortly after a new data point x resulting from a CDS execution and with a specific value $v = (c_v, r_v, ea_v) \in vals_x$ due to the execution of this CDS has been added to the hypercube, the assignment of x to the already computed *clusters* of other data points will be done. The agglomerative clustering of data points within the hypercube (cf. [11], chapter 6.8) favorably will be done at night, when the smartwatch is typically not worn and recharged.

We use an easy computable *manhattan metric* [12] for data points defining the distance two data points as the sum of the absolute differences of the data points within each dimension of the parameter space: for the location we use a logarithmic *euclidean distance,* the *time difference* between the (relative) times of the day, the *difference of suitable ordinal numbers* for the day of week, and also for the speed intervals by which the smartwatch wearer is moving.

As soon as data point x has been assigned to a cluster, the learned dialogue behavior for the situational setting represented by x and encoded in the value v of x can be transferred and extended to all elements of the cluster. We thereby assume that the dialogue behavior of x will be also appropriate for "similar" situational settings. Such similar situational setting will be given by all elements belonging to the same cluster than x. Let y denote such a data point within the same cluster than x and let $w = (c_w, r_w, ea_w)$ denote an arbitrary tripled value element within the value set $vals_y$ of y.

Then the value transfer and extension process from x to y is specified by the following rules:

- If $vals_y$ does not contain value elements in the form of triples, value v of x is added to $vals_y$. [Data point y did not contain any dialogue control behavior, which will be added hereby.]
- If, for all values $w \in vals_y$, category c_v is different from category c_w, or, categories c_v and c_w are the same and ea_v and ea_w are different, again value v can be added to

vals$_y$. [In this case, the dialogue control behavior of v will be amended by the dialog control behavior of v.]

- If, for a value w $\in$ vals$_y$, c$_v$ = c$_w$ and ea$_v$ = ea$_w$, but r$_v$ $\neq$ r$_w$, we have contradictory execution results for the same category of CDS and executed on the same occasion. We need a *graceful*, non-contradictory local *adaption* of x to its neighborhood in the cluster. Therefore, let y now denote such a cluster element in defined maximal proximity to x with respect to the 4-dimensional parameter space and a value w as specified above.

  - If r$_w$ = r$_2$, then r$_w$:= r$_v$. In this way, the stratified execution result r$_v$ = r$_1$ r$_3$ will replace the - so far - *ambiguous* execution result r$_2$ in the neighborhood of the data point x, because the value combinations r$_1$, r$_2$ and r$_2$, r$_3$ are estimated as *non-contradictory*.

  - If r$_v$ = r$_1$ and r$_w$ = r$_3$, or vice versa, *contradictory* execution results, then r$_w$:= r$_2$. Thus, we *lessen* the contradiction in the neighborhood of the new data point x.

If the new data point x cannot be added to a cluster, x remains an *isolated, non-clustered* data point in the hypercube, and due to its isolation an extension of the reach of the learned example seems inappropriate.

3.4 Applying Learned Experience to New Health Hazard Handling Dialogues

Whenever a new health hazard handling dialogue shall be started and a corresponding CDS has been selected for execution, the acquired values of data points within the hypercube will be used as a recommendation for action. First of all, the situational setting of the CDS to be executed will be determined as a data point x in the hypercube. If x does not contain any triple value in its value set vals$_x$, there is no learned experience for controlling the execution of the CDS, the execution of the CDS can start.

Otherwise, we have to check within the value set vals$_x$ of x whether there is applicable learned experience for the execution of the CDS. First of all, we need to determine the category of the CDS with respect to Table 2, let c denote this category. Then, if the value set of x does contain a value triple v = (c, r, ea$_v$), and the CDS would be executed on the occasion of an EDL/ADL ea which has been recognized in closed temporal proximity to the scheduled CDS execution, and ea = ea$_v$, this triple v contains the learned experience for the execution of the CDS.

Now c and r will be used for a lookup in Table 4 on how to proceed with the execution of the CDS. A "retry execution" command means that for the selected CDS the same procedure as described above in this Sect. 3.4 will be repeated at the designated point of time in the future. Although, there is no guarantee that the selected CDS will be executed at that point of time in the future. The CDS might compete at that time with other concluded health hazards, which will have a higher priority on the blackboard described in [4]. In such a case one of those higher prioritized CDS will be selected for execution by the blackboard scheduler algorithm described in [4].

Table 4. Application of acquired experience for dialogue control within the assistance app

c = ↓	r = →		
	r₁ [successful]	r₂ [interrupted]	r₃ [prohibited]
High	Execute CDS immediately	Execute CDS immediately	Retry execution after short time (e.g. 5 min)
Medium	Execute CDS immediately	Retry execution after short time (e.g. 5 min)	Retry execution after longer time (e.g. 30 min)
Low	Execute CDS immediately	Retry execution after longer time (e.g. 30 min)	Cancel execution

4 Discussion

Up to now, it is an open question what is the actual decisive factor for the successful and complete interaction flow for a health hazard handling dialogue via CDS execution? Our hypothesis, implemented in the presented approach, is that this factor is *the occasion* on which the CDS is executed. Alternatively, the decisive factor might be also the *real cause of the health hazard* handled by the dialogue. These alternatives need to be further explored and verified for optimizing the future app behavior.

The effectiveness of the proposed learning algorithm presupposes a "rational" smartwatch wearer, who deliberately and *consistently* accepts and rejects health hazard handling dialogues for TP and/or FP situations. If this consistency will be not the case - or the sensorial horizon of the smartwatch would be incomplete with respect to the actual acceptance pattern of the smartwatch app wearer -, this would result in even the same or nearby data points in the parameter hypercube with contradictory values. No extension of the reach of learned experience to *similar situational settings* within a cluster will take place. As a consequence, the algorithm will never improve its conversational behavior and acceptance from the smartwatch wearer's perspective. For example, if the acceptance of health hazard handling dialogues would be dependent of the presence of the smartwatch wearer's companion, because the smartwatch wearer wants not to be disclosed as being dependent on technical aids in the presence of other persons, the learning would not work at all. The smartwatch app would never be capable to detect the presence of other persons by its current sensors, and thus would not be possible to include this decisive parameter in its situational settings.

Unfortunately, an automatic improvement of the app's behavior for FN situations seems not realistic for the foreseeable future without significant scientific breakthroughs.

Another point which needs to be handled by future work is if the user wants to reactivate suppressed alerts. The current descriptions, esp. for low risks, would result once an alert is suppressed it will be suppressed forever and therefore no deviant behavior could be ever learned in the future. A relaxation approach, by which the learned experience (suppression) will be "forgotten" in the course of time, or a specific maintenance tool for the hypercube, could be effective remedies.

5 Conclusions

As a result, our experiment demonstrates that the acceptance of health-based smartwatch apps can be discernibly improved for the anticipated target group of elderly persons, if the app's behavior respects the favored individual usage patterns. Such behavioral patterns can be automatically acquired by reinforcement machine learning during the (initial) usage of the app with economic effort and in presence of a rational, consistently acting user.

References

1. Lutze, R., Waldhör, K.: A smartwatch software architecture for health hazard handling for elderly people. In: 3rd IEEE International Conference on HealthCare Informatics (ICHI), Dallas, USA, 21–23 October, pp. 356–361 (2015)
2. Lutze, R., Waldhör, K.: Personal health assistance for elderly people via smartwatch based motion analysis. In: IEEE International Conference on Healthcare Informatics (ICHI), Park City, UT, USA, 23–26 August, pp. 124–133 (2017)
3. Lutze, R., Waldhör, K.: Utilizing Smartwatches for Supporting the Wellbeing of Elderly People. 2nd International Conference on Informatics and Assistive Technologies for Health-Care, Medical Support and Wellbeing (HealthInfo), Athens, Greece, 10–12 October, pp. 1–9 (2017)
4. Lutze, R., Waldhör, K.: Model based dialogue control for smartwatches. In: Kurosu, M. (ed.) HCI 2017. LNCS, vol. 10272, pp. 225–239. Springer, Cham (2017). https://doi.org/10.1007/978-3-319-58077-7_18
5. Lutze, R.: Practicality of smartwatch apps for supporting elderly people – a comprehensive survey. In: 24th ICE/IEEE International Technology Management Conference (ITMC), Stuttgart, Germany, 17–20 June, pp. 427–433 (2018)
6. Cavoukian, A.: Privacy by design - the 7 foundational principles – implementation and mapping of fair information practices. http://dataprotection.industries/wp-content/uploads/2017/10/privacy-by-design.pdf. Accessed 28 Jan 2020
7. Goodfellow, I., Bengio, Y., Courville, A.: Deep Learning. The MIT Press, Cambridge (2017)
8. Sutton, R.S., Barto, A.: Reinforcement Learning: An Introduction. Adaptive Computation and Machine Learning. The MIT Press, Cambridge (2018)
9. Russel, S., Norvig, P.: Artificial Intelligence – A Modern Approach, 3rd edn. Pearson Education Limited, Harlow, Essex (2016)
10. Bishop, C.M.: Pattern Recognition and Machine Learning. Springer, New York (2006)
11. Witten, I.H., Frank, E., Hall, M.A.: Data Mining – Practical Machine Learning Tools and Techniques, 3rd edn. Morgan Kaufmann Publishers/Elsevier, Burlington (2011)
12. https://en.wikipedia.org/wiki/Taxicab_geometry. Redirected from "manhattan metric". Accessed 28 Jan 2020

FaceForward – An AI-Based Interactive System for Exploring the Personal Potential

Elisabeth Veronica Mess$^{(\boxtimes)}$, Dennis Rockstein, and Christian Märtin

Augsburg University of Applied Sciences, An der Hochschule 1,
86161 Augsburg, Germany
{elisabethveronica.mess,dennis.rocksteinl,
christian.maertin}@hs-augsburg.de

Abstract. This paper explores the idea of the human body as an interface between self- and outside perception as well as verbal and nonverbal communication. Based on this perspective, the visual appearance can be viewed as a display of personality which indicates certain traits or even hidden potentials to a significant point. It allows the individual as well as other individuals to develop a deeper understanding, acceptance, and even tolerance for each other, if those individual traits and potentials are recognized. The concept behind this is an integrated approach, *FaceForward*, which is based on an analog face reading system. It is combined with as well as supported by the possibilities of AI within an interactive prototype. It intertwines the historical, but still applied integrated knowledge of human nature by face/body reading with a combination of algorithms and AI-based learning. The main goal is to analyze face and body based on their expression, structures, and, most of all, geometric shapes. Portraits of individuals are selected and pass through two different pipelines. One operates as a pre-processing module. The other for training the AI based on the principles of the face reading system. In the end, the results achieved with the AI approach shall be compared to a survey outcome of self- and outside perception based on psychologic concepts.

Keywords: Human perception · Authentic personality · Body language · Personality psychology · Face reading · Face detection · Artificial intelligence · Neural networks · Deep learning

1 Initial Situation

Everyone has the potential to grow into the best version of oneself and share this version with fellow human beings. This version describes a personality consisting of an even balance of temper and character, which leads to an authentic individual (Fig. 1) as well as communication within the self and external perception [1]. Unfortunately, this growth distorts easily due to social standards as upbringing, education, general surroundings, relationships, or mental as well as physical health problems [2]. This can lead to the situation that the individual is partly or not at all being perceived as authentic, what again could lead to a distorted verbal and nonverbal communication [3].

© Springer Nature Switzerland AG 2020
M. Kurosu (Ed.): HCII 2020, LNCS 12183, pp. 86–102, 2020.
https://doi.org/10.1007/978-3-030-49065-2_7

Fig. 1. How do we perceive and communicate authentic personality? [16]

This fundamental problem of human growth and communication increases due to superficial tools or methods used for self-portrayal or staging as well as the pervasive digitalization of our community. As a result of this focus, the desired integrated combination of self and outside perception shifts to a mere focus of outside perception. The 'true authentic self' degenerates, and the true potentials of an individual are often neither detected nor exploited. This can lead to further disturbed personality development or growth. Thus, people who are highly influenced by outside perceptions or are highly aware of the opinions of others around them are more likely to lose themselves. A possible consequence of this 'personality error' can be a distinct feeling of futility of one's existence or, as an extreme result, depersonalization.

1.1 FaceForward – Origins and Concept

FaceForward is a research project that proposes a possible way for finding a solution for this severe problem. The idea explores the perspective of the human body as a key to explore one's personality and potentials. Simplified, the visual appearance of an individual could be viewed as an interface between self- and outside perception, verbal and nonverbal communication.

Therefore, the concept behind FaceForward focuses on the methods of a scientifically controversial and ethically biased analog face reading system, aka *psychophysiognomics* (in the following named as *PPI*). Within this project and also in future explorations this system is examined critically as well as applied experimentally. In doing so three main steps for researching and testing PPI within the prototype FaceForward will be followed:

1. research of a possible connection between personality and an outer appearance by comparing internal and external perception (following psychology standards, e.g., Big Five Model, The Color Code)
2. developing an analysis process (following the main rules of PPI), and,
3. implementing it within an interactive environment as visible, tangible, and thereby understandable as possible.

To achieve that, an interdisciplinary approach is pursued, which applies deep-learning algorithms to the toolset of PPI, especially, because they are similar to the human learning process. This combination is used for generating a comprehensive database for analysis and comparison. Secondly, for developing and analysis process as simple and transparent as possible. And finally, for exploring actual individual or economic benefits as well as disadvantages of learning/using the feature protocol of PPI (see Sect. 1.2).

To wrap this in a proper visual style FaceForward has to be accompanied, as other innovative private services and technologies which are used for individualization of viable designs, by appropriate design methods for detecting unwanted ethical conflicts and for respecting moral and human values [14, 15]. Especially, if the integration of a controversial method is a topic.

Precisely for this reason the first interface design sketch has focused on a playful and almost childish exploration of the own personality within a jungle expedition as a game *FaceForward – Explore yourself and be part of a marvelous adventure* (Fig. 2).

Fig. 2. The index screen of the planned online application FaceForward

Two personas help the user to navigate through the different steps and make the process transparent and understandable. It is also possible to stop the journey at every point to give users as much control about their analysis as they need (Fig. 3).

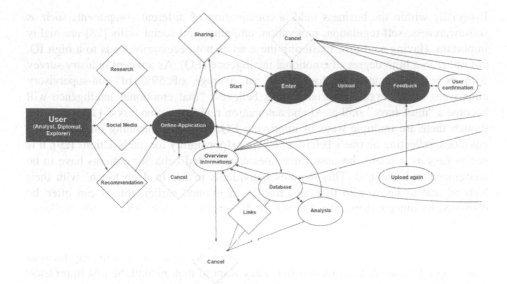

Fig. 3. Extract of the planned agile and incremental user flow of the FaceForward prototype guiding the user through the analysis with several milestones.

If the user gives her consent, the collected data during the user journey are used for expanding the database.

1.2 Relevance

FaceForward combines two highly controversial areas: psycho-physiognomics and artificial intelligence. Even though PPI is still in practical usage, no scientific research concerning the potentials and risks of this pseudo-science is available. Neither has it been researched with respect to ethnic, ethical, and moral matters, especially in connection with technologies such as face or emotion reading, face tracking and face perception.

The latter could be a problem due to similar prejudices toward PPI and some AI approaches, such as racial segregation, discrimination, unethically, or unlawful usage [20, 32, 33]. But, on the other hand, it could also possess an exceptional and significant relevance to our society. And that is because within those emerging technologies such as face recognition, face- and emotion tracking, expression reading, or facial integration into humanoid robots, visual appearance, and the personality of humans gain more significance and power. But there is even more to it than that.

Firstly, as PPI's main philosophy is about helping people to understand themselves and the people around them better, as experts of the field claim, its relevance rises higher primarily due to the growing interest of people for personality, identity, and individual growth in the areas of self-development, self-growth, self-optimization, and self-marketing. These areas are important when it comes to growing into the 'best' version of oneself or assessing the personality/potentials of others [8, 21–24].

Especially within the business field, a combination of different components such as self-awareness, self-regulation, motivation, empathy, and social skills [28] are highly important. Having said this, mastering these areas not necessarily leads to a high IQ, but rather to a high degree of emotional intelligence (EQ). As a recent industry-survey with N = 1,500 employees found out, an average of 59% of non-supervisory employees in 11 large industrial nations believes, "that emotional intelligence will become a "must-have" skill as AI and automation replace routine tasks" [12, 13]. Even though there are multiple ways of improving EQ, such as controlling one's negative emotions, reflecting on one's behavior, taking responsibility for one's actions [29], it is not as easy as it seems, because sometimes deep-rooted behavior patterns have to be recognized and changed. This requires individuals to be 'in deep touch' with their 'selves' and to know who they are. But, as mentioned earlier, this is can often be disrupted by other factors. The difficulty and sometimes complexity of this challenge could be one of the reasons why PPI creates a great fascination in our society which has experts from different fields e.g. coaching, profiling, human resource management or consulting [7, 34, 35] educating themselves in PPI. They believe it will help them to understand themselves and others better. They want to look behind the first impression of the visual appearance and develop their EQ even further.

Secondly, recent studies in the context of cognitive and social psychology [30, 31] roll up PPI again as it has a certain impact on these fields. For instance, a Yale University study has researched the influence of face structures in terms of human perception. The results point out a very interesting perspective. Facial features of strangers have an even more substantial impact on how personality is perceived, and this perception influences the way we interact with others far more than we thought until now. And this doesn't necessarily focus on the attractiveness of a person. They also point out that the problem behind this perception most of the time is unconscious. Thus, we are not aware of the 'pull' people have on us [25], and in some situations, this can lead to wrong prejudices.

Thirdly, within the field of computer science, the visual appearance of the human body, especially the face, holds a magical attraction. The motives behind this exploration may vary between an entertaining (e.g. Facebook Face Recognition, Instagram Face Filters etc.), economic (e.g. marketing, IT security, etc.), or even a political perspective. The problem behind this is, if the usage exceeds the entertainment field, any individual can be affected in either a positive or negative way. A recent and significant example of this is the data leak of Facebook. Millions of users' privacy [was] misused as a company used the harvested data without consent for political advertising purposes [27]. The difficulty about this is not the technology itself, but how and with what intention it was or is used. Thus, in terms of combining computer science, or more specifically, AI and PPI, the ethical principles and long-term effects of, e.g., face or emotion reading data, have to be researched thoroughly in the future as well as the commercial exploitation of such data.

And finally, the wish to manipulate one's staging and performing is another considerable factor, which gets more attention every day, especially in the U.S. due to diverse platforms in the internet [9]. In the long term this can lead to a disrupted, even superficial way of viewing one's own personality. That is a severe problem in terms of the three-perspective self[1] where the outside perception, in this case, is more important than the self-perception [26]. Due to this, the individual is mainly reduced to her or his visual appearance, and this can lead to diverse prejudices.

Due to these evolving trends and developments PPI especially in combination with AI could have an even greater impact on self-optimization and personal growth. But it could also create disadvantages or even risks if it is misused. Due to this vague outcome PPI needs to be explored in a scientific manner in the context of HCI, computer science, psychology, sociology and design.

2 Related Work

The field of artificial intelligence that assigns character traits to facial structures, as applied in PPI, is scientifically unchaited territory, as this topic is a new field of AI research. In this paper facial structure recognition is used as a foundation stone. The procedure for the facial structure recognition is relatively similar to the recognition of emotions.

Random multimodel deep learning for classification (RMDL) deals with the topic of classification in the field of deep learning. RDML is able to guarantee to find the best possible structure or architecture by means of parallel optimizations, in fact, robustness and accuracy depending on the deep learning architecture. RDML offers a wide range of input, including texts, videos, pictures, and symbols. Furthermore, the algorithm consists of three different deep learning architectures, a deep neural network (DNN), a convolutional neural network (CNN), and a recurrent neural network (RNN). A DNN is based on a simple multi-layer perceptron architecture consisting of several hidden layers. Such architectures are mostly used for classification. Besides, the algorithm uses a CNN that operates with a feed-forward mechanism. In the last step, an RNN is used, which reuses the output of the neurons as input for the next iteration step. This architecture is used for the RMDL algorithm in order to have it carry out classification.

Face recognition is also based on images, whereby parallels can be found [10]. Besides the general optimizations in the field of face recognition and image classification, some works are researching primary problems related to the recognition of faces per se. Challenges, such as different poses of a face, blur, and blurriness, or different positions of a face in an image, including image depth, are still problems that cannot be solved completely so far [11]. The main problem here is that most detectors have only been trimmed for frontal facial poses and therefore have high error rates with pictures with different poses. The difficulty is the matching of position marks of the faces, which are anchored in the classifier Haarcascade [18], for example. These position markers, also called *landmarks*, compare significant features in the face to make features easier to discover, which in turn may or may not detect a face. These features include eyes, nose, mouth and ears, each of which is defined by an area to support the robustness of

---

[1] The neuroscientist, medical specialist and psychotherapist Joachim Bauer explains in his book "Wie wir werden, wer wir sind" (2019) the three-perspective self as three perceptions; you, me and us, which correlate a field of verbal and nonverbal resonance which is needed to develop personality.

the classifier. The algorithm *Retina Face* focuses on the efficient localization of faces in images. The image should be iterated pixel by pixel to create different scales of a possible face. On a single instance, a detector is receiving these scaled images afterwards in order to locate a face with the help of its own, and an additional parallel supervised learning algorithm. In addition, both learning methods work together to create a robust detector. For the training five landmarks for face recognition in the data set *WIDER Face* are annotated to show significant improvements afterwards [19].

The AI part of this paper was inspired by these publications, especially parts of the classification.

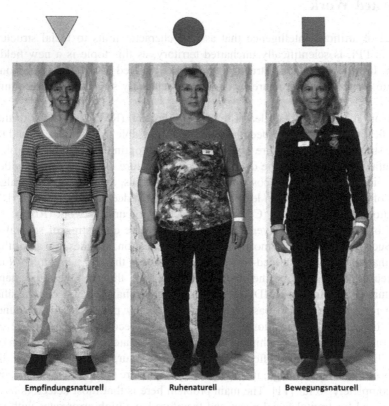

Empfindungsnaturell   Ruhenaturell   Bewegungsnaturell

Fig. 4. Extract of the feature protocol of psycho-physiognomics. The three archetypes visualized [17]

3   Fundamentals of the Analog Face Reading

The history of PPI goes way back to ancient times when people already felt the urge to connect the personality of a human with the outer body [4, 5]. It is an old toolset that over-crosses multiple disciplines such as biology, psychology, medicine, and art, and even though it was misused countless times in history (discrimination, segregation), it is still in use today.

PPI exploits a comprehensive feature protocol (up to 300 properties) by which the face and the body are analyzed based on composition and structure. In further detail, it can be divided in macro- and micro-analysis, which classify the face into its geometrical shapes. Those can be either rectangle, circle, or triangle, as well as any mixture of these three forms (Fig. 4).

In subsequent steps, spaces between the forehead, nose, and chin are analyzed as well. The micro-analysis examines, how these different forms and spaces influence each other by exemplarily measuring, how thin or thick lips are, what shape the eyes have, or how fleshy the earlobes are just to name some examples. For instance, a firm and forward pushing chin could stand for a dominant personality with a focus on practical matters.

But attention, compared to a triangle face shape, this feature can be interpreted very differently as the triangle shape stands for an individual with a focus on numbers, data, and facts combined with an overall diplomatic nature [6]. If looking at all features within an integrated approach, in accordance with the rule set of PPI, it is not possible to exclude any characteristics as they correlate with each other.

4 Method

4.1 Conceptual Approach

The concept for the implementation consists of an artificial intelligence approach that should be able to map the structure of a face to a physiognomic class. The implemented prototype was divided into two pipelines, where both parts flow into each other. The first part of the pipeline (pipeline A) is responsible for the automated normalization of the images, the acquisition of the facial structure and the support of pipeline B. The second part is responsible for learning and testing a trained model and contains the entire structure for classification using artificial intelligence.

In the beginning, the prototype consisted of only one part, the AI, but this had to be extended as the data acquisition turned out to be more complex than was supposed at the beginning of the research. Especially the lack of data sources of appropriate facial images and physiognomic characteristics caused great problems for the training of the AI. In order to meet these challenges, Pipeline A is used, which makes it possible to extract images from all available sources and prepare them for research. For this purpose, some tools from image preprocessing are used, which normalize the images with the faces to a defined shape. In addition to the tools derived from the Python library *OpenCV,* the algorithm *Haarcascade* by Viola and Jones, and the segmentation function *Active Countour* are used. *Haarcascade* is responsible for recognizing the faces in the respective image and using their positions and the previously mentioned tools to normalize the image individually and dynamically. What exactly the standardization of methods and algorithms involves is explained in detail in the next section, Implementation. *Active Contour* is capable of interpreting the contour for each recognized face and marking it by means of coloring.

Pipeline B, which includes the entire structure of a Convolutional Neural Network (CNN), under the training and validation of the model and subsequent testing, was designed using the artificial intelligence of *FaceNet* [36]. A part of the structure of *FaceNet* was taken over and rebuilt for the purpose of this topic. The goal of *FaceNet's* algorithm is different; it specializes on the recognition of faces in images with a very small amount of training data. Especially because of this characteristic, this architecture offers a decisive advantage over others for this prototype. Due to the non-existent data collection and the independent preparation of standardized image data, only a small data set could be made available for training. With the support of *FaceNet*, the training of a model can be realized in spite of the small amount of data, whereas conventional architectures usually require a large data set. The structure consists of a feed-forward CNN supported by a composite of two architectures, *Inception* and *ResNet*. The specific advantage of this combination is the following: *ResNet* has a special feature, i.e. it is working with *identity shortcut connections*. This allows it to jump over certain layers in order to skip unnecessary calculations. If the result of a layer does not affect the next weight, then it can be discarded, which can otherwise affect the performance of the entire architecture. This kind of calculations can be achieved mainly by the architecture of *Inception* since it is working with several blocks in parallel. A block consists of several layers that previously use and calculate the input parameters from the blocks. If one of these parallelized, nested blocks is faster, and the weights of the other blocks have no effect in the results, they can be skipped.

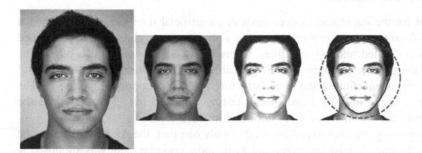

Fig. 5. Simplified structural plan for the conceptual approach

These blocks are called residual blocks. In addition, due to the architecture of *Inception*, several features can be matched more frequently via template matching. The two pipelines are not only used to normalize raw image data to a fixed dimension but are also used directly afterwards for the training of the model by a CNN that is responsible for assigning the correct classes with a classification task at the end. These classes are still prototypically rough structures of physiognomies. The diagram in Fig. 5 provides an overview of the two conceptualized pipelines. The next chapter describes the individual steps shown in the figure in detail. It also refers to the algorithms and functions used in the two pipelines.

4.2   Implementation

The prototype consists of two parts, whereby the first pipeline (image pre-processing) is not only crucial for normalizing image data per se, but also for testing the model in pipeline B. To understand the process of image data better, pipeline A here is explained in detail. The starting position of pipeline A is as follows: Images with faces, whereby only one face may be shown per image. Furthermore, the direction of the face should always be the same, in this case, straight ahead. The goal of this pipeline is to extract the contour of a facial structure from a normalized facial image in order to feed the artificial intelligence. For this purpose, each image is treated individually in order to be able to capture a broad spectrum of different images. After downloading the images, the location of the face in the image is determined first. This information is used to crop the image to a fixed format of 400 pixels for both width and height without losing important image information.

The face is also centered in the image so that the subsequent *Active Contour* algorithm can initially recognize the contour of the face. To prevent errors, the algorithm has been extended by an additional iteration. If a face is not recognized, the initial radius is moved and adjusted using the positioning of *Haarcascade*. In addition, the initial radius, which is a kind of ellipse, can be adapted more finely to the face structures. After the image has been normalized, the contour of the face can theoretically be scanned and saved separately. During our research it was noticed that the *Active Contour* algorithm could not recognize every facial structure. After analyzing this problem, it was found out that by calculating the contour through the pixels using a threshold, a calculation is made. If the contrast between the face and the background is very high, the contour can be correctly recognized; otherwise, it causes distortions.

To prevent this problem, the entire image is contrast-optimized, meaning the contrast is increased by a certain factor. This optimization produces larger differences in contrast, which is good for the *Active Contour* algorithm. The last part of Pipeline A consists of extracting the facial structure using the above-mentioned algorithm, which creates a separated image and places it in a hierarchy with the class name. With this intermediate step, Pipeline B can easily and directly take over the image data and prepare them for training.

In order to obtain an overview of the entire steps of the first pipeline, each sub-step was stored separately as an image and summarized in a diagram (Fig. 6). The figure consists of five small pictures, which are to illustrate a sequence.

The first image is an original image (raw), which was downloaded from the Internet, for example. The second image contains the scaling with the individual tools of image preprocessing. The third image shows the contrast optimization. The fourth image shows the initial radius (red, dashed line) and the recognized face structure (blue, solid line). The last image shows only the contour of the detected face structure, which is saved separately in the correct folder as a new image.

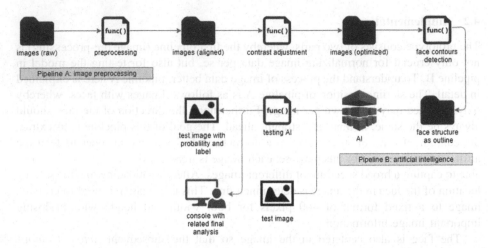

Fig. 6. Overview of the entire steps of the first pipeline (Pipeline A) (Color figure online)

The second pipeline takes over seamlessly and acts semi-automatically. Due to the structure of *FaceNet*, the hierarchy could easily be set up, but almost the entire implementation had to be replaced. Many customizations and additions were enhanced with custom functions, such as the normalization of raw images. Also, the function for testing the classification was rebuilt; only the architecture *Inception-ResNet* could be taken over almost completely. For creating, loading and saving of models *TensorFlow* supports the procedure, more precisely the API *Keras* does. Both in combination offer the necessary functions to set up a feed-forward CNN. In addition, *TensorFlow slim* offers for the best-known architectures the schemes with which it is possible to train the model according to a certain pattern. The settings and hyperparameters for the CNN were taken from an already existing research work. This research work dealt with a comparison of architectures *(AlexNet, Inception-ResNet,* and *VGGNet16)*, which achieved the highest accuracy for a classification with a small data set. The classification included the recognition of persons, whereby different challenges, such as noise in the image, different poses of the faces, or blurring in a benchmark, were set. The result showed that *Inception-ResNet* achieved the highest accuracy with the settings used for the research. The training data set with about 50 images per class (3 classes) is relatively small for this prototype, but it is especially difficult to get labeled and normalized image data. In addition, not all images are suitable for classification or training, as certain facial structures must be taken into account. After the training has been completed, the learned model is evaluated with a test script. Two results are generated, one of which is written to the test image with the class that is to be tested. The other result is directly dependent on the physiognomy so that the text and the corresponding properties for the respective class are displayed on the console. It should be noted that the research involves a prototypical application, which needs to be explored in more detail, before valid statements can be made.

To better understand the second pipeline, a simple example is used to show what pipeline B does with the test pattern in the individual steps (Fig. 7).

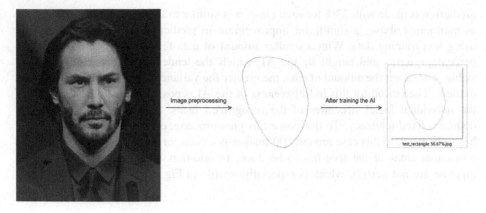

Fig. 7. Showcase of pipeline B using a simple example (Image Source: [37])

It can be seen that in the second pipeline, the algorithms of the first pipeline are also used to get the image into the right shape and to extract the contour based on the face. Since the AI has only worked with this type of image data during training, these data must not differ in the test scenario. With the support of Pipeline A, data consistency is maintained. Finally, the result and the associated probability is written into the name of the image, as mentioned above, and stored separately in order not to distort the original test image.

5 Results

In this section the research results in the fields of computer science and PPI are discussed. Before describing the perspectives from both different areas, the quantitative as well as the qualitative results are presented. With a training data set of about 50 images per class, 5% of which were used for validation, an accuracy of almost 60% was achieved. Since the research is still at the beginning of the study and a data source had to be created, a value of 60% is a good starting point. However, during testing, the trained model still showed its weaknesses, so the data set and the hyperparameters of the CNN were adjusted. With a smaller data set of about 15 images per class, the same accuracy for training and validation could be achieved, and the results of testing were much better. This phenomenon is explained in the following from the perspective of computer science and PPI. Since this research is the result of a cooperation among two different disciplines and both views on the results are completely different, they are now considered separately.

5.1 Results in Terms of AI

From the point of view of computer science, more precisely of AI, a bad result is usually determined by an ambiguous prediction of a class. If, e.g., a class is predicted with 90% or higher, the AI is very sure about the assignment of the test pattern. If a prediction is made with 33% for each class, it is similar to throwing a dice. In addition, as mentioned above, a significant improvement in predictions could be achieved by using less training data. With a smaller amount of data fewer outliers are detected in percentage terms and taught by the AI, which the tendency in forecasting remains stable. The larger the amount of data, the greater the variance of the special features and outliers. The reason for this indecisiveness of the AI is possibly due to the variation of the individual facial structures of the recognized faces, from which the AI cannot deduce a fixed tendency. To overcome this phenomenon, either a much larger data set has to be used, in this case around 500 images per class, or an analysis focusing on the prominent areas of the face has to be done. In addition, also the results of the first pipeline are not perfect, which is especially visible in Fig. 8.

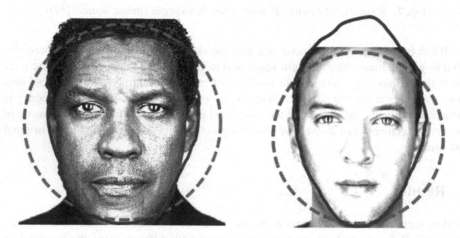

Fig. 8. Results of pipeline A using examples

It is too obvious that the facial structure of the left image could be seen in great detail, whereas the right image was slightly distorted by cropping the image. Such outliers can also influence the learning of the AI.

5.2   Results in Terms of PPI

Normally, AI focuses on only one result (highest/lowest), whereas PPI needs all three values to interpret the result correctly, as there are different variations between the shapes (mix-types). Also, all features correlate with each other. That is why it is not possible to exclude a value. The current dataset is divided into three categories, so the AI had to be adjusted with respect to the resulting output. Now the prototype provides the user with three different results, i.e. three different percentages of the three categories. Connected to these results, the content output (written analysis) will differ according to the results.

Even though the analysis could be already accurate, if one result were, e.g., 77%, the percentages for the other classes are still needed for future microanalysis. As mentioned in the beginning, the feature protocol consists of up to 300 features, and even if one feature would mean something, another could direct the analysis into a different direction. For example: Let us assume an output of 77% for triangle, 13% for circle, and 10% for rectangle. That indicates that the test subject has an almost clear archetypal face with one solid basic facial form. In this case, it is the triangle. Circle and rectangle are distinct, very low, and in terms of AI, this would be a good result as only one result is very high. Even though the current prototype is not capable of analyzing more than this basic shape, it is planned for future versions, to go deeper into the feature protocol.

Even if the values for circle and rectangle are pretty low, we still have to look at the other features to find out, whether they support this result or contradict it. One possible next step in the PPI reading of a human expert could be to look at the height or length of the forehead, nose part, and chin. Each of them is connected to one of the basic shapes with their features, but varies a bit. If we go further with the example, the next analysis output could be a hierarchy of (1) chin, (2) nose and (3) forehead. In the beginning, the analysis of the subject could have been interpreted as someone with a very visionary, thinking, creative, but also diplomatic nature. Usually not so involved in realization but more in the planning and organizing. According to the second result, the subject could now be interpreted as someone, who is a visionary thinking person, but tends to be more active or even possesses a hands-on-mentality, unlike a usual thinker would do. That is just a little example of how things might develop during the analysis process.

Another example could be that we initially had a result of 33% for each basic shape, which would indicate a mixed type. The second round could then find an equal hierarchy of forehead, nose, and chin, which would support the first result. In terms of PPI analysis, this could indicate a very balanced person who easily connects with others on different levels as they have characteristics of each type.

The analysis process would continue until most of the characteristics are analyzed and interpreted in relation to each other. Only then it might be possible to state an almost accurate result according to the feature protocol analysis of PPI.

6 Conclusion and Future Work

There are several aspects that will determine the future of this project.

First: Even though the current prototype includes the feature protocol of PPI, our main goal has changed to creating a unique face reading system without it. Our future face reading system will be based on self-, outer-, and visual perception, only. These are going to be analyzed by several empiric studies, surveys, etc.

Second: The AI prototypes database will be based on the feature protocol of PPI, until significant results of the empiric studies are available. This is acceptable, because the developed AI for this prototype focuses more on the analysis of face structures, landmarks, etc., rather than on determining personality.

Fig. 9. A possible scenario of the implemented prototype FaceForward and its users. The UI shall be easy to use as well as a fun experience to learn easily more about one's personality especially the (hidden) Potentials [16].

Although our research project is still in its early stage, we are expecting deep insights. If our future research will discover essential relationships between self-, outside- and visual perception, the prototype shall be changed to the key elements of these relationships and be tested first in a laboratory study using educational test scenarios.

Later studies can be conducted in educational environments, like schools or universities (Fig. 9). The educational field seems to provide a relatively safe environment to learn more about both disciplines, their potentials, and how they could change our overall communication and learning behavior.

As a matter of fact, this research focuses a lot on subjective perception and multiple factors that have to be taken into account. To research and certify or even refute any future face/body reading system an even greater quantity of pictures of different individuals is needed in order to arrive at valid results. Obviously, those pictures need to be classified and labeled accordingly.

Only then it might be possible to receive an overall result of the perception as well the condition of the personality of the individual. And only then it is possible to state, if the visual appearance could be a key to one's personality and potentials from a scientific perspective.

References

1. Saucier, G., Srivastava, S.: Personality dimensions. What makes a good structural model of personality? Evaluating the big five and alternatives. University of Oregon, p. 3 (2012). https://pdfs.semanticscholar.org/d13d/3f7a620b884e3c5660e63bb4d029de96089d.pdf. Accessed 29 Oct 2019
2. Eisenberg, N., Duckworth, A.L., Spinrad, T.L., Valiente, C.: Conscientiousness: origins in childhood? Developmental psychology. US National Library of Medicine, National Institutes of Health (2017). https://www.ncbi.nlm.nih.gov/pmc/articles/PMC3610789/. Accessed 29 Oct 2019
3. Popescu, M.: Psychology of communication – between myth and reality. Int. J. Acad. Res. Acc. Finance Manag. Sci., 321–325 (2012). http://hrmars.com/admin/pics/1045.pdf. Accessed 29 Oct 2019
4. Law, B.C.: Designation of Human Types (Puggala Pannati). English translation. Pali Text Society, p. 29 (2006)
5. Aristoteles: Physiognomonica. Translated and commented by Vogt, S., Volume 18: Opuscula, Part VI, p. 196f. Akademie-Verlag, Berlin (1999)
6. Horn-Lingk, A.: Einstieg in die Psycho-Physiognomik. Lehrbuch der ganzheitlichen Menschenkenntnis. Vertraudich Verlag (2017)
7. Mess, E.: Physiognomik. Potenziale & Gefahren. Interviews mit Experten der Physiognomik & Designern im Bereich der Interaktiven Medien (2018). https://www.emconcep-tual.de/physiognomy-ii
8. Renata, C.: The Actor's Guide to Self-Marketing: How to Brand and Promote Your Unique Image. Skyehorse Publishing, New York (2019)
9. LaRosa, J.: The $10 Billion Self-Improvement Market Adjust to a New Generation (2018). https://blog.marketresearch.com/the-10-billion-self-improvement-market-adjusts-to-new-generation. Accessed 07 Nov 2019
10. Kowsari, K., Heidarysafa, M., Brown, D.E., Meimandi, K.J., Barnes, L.E.: RMDL: random multimodel deep learning for classification. In: ICISDM 2018: 2018 2nd International Conference on Information System and Data Mining ICISDM 2018, Lakeland, FL, USA, 9–11 April, 10 p. ACM, New York (2018). https://doi.org/10.1145/3206098.3206111
11. Li, Z., Tang, X., Han, J., Liu, J., He, R.: PyramidBox++: high performance detector for finding tiny face. Computer Vision and Pattern Recognition. Journal DBLP:journals/corr/abs-1904-00386 (2019)
12. Sonka, M., Hlavac, V., Boyle, R.: Image Processing, Analysis and Machine Vision. Springer, Boston (1993). https://doi.org/10.1007/978-1-4899-3216-7
13. Capgemini Research Institute: Emotional intelligence – the essential skillset for the age of AI, p. 7. Capgemini (2019)
14. Friedmann, B., Hendry, D.G.: Value Sensitive Design: Shaping Technology with Moral Imagination. MIT Press, Cambridge (2018)
15. Thew, S., Sutcliffe, A.: Value-based requirements engineering method and experience. Requirements Eng. 23, 443 (2018). https://doi.org/10.1007/s00766-017-0273-y
16. Unsplash.com. https://www.unsplash.com. Accessed 15 Nov 2019
17. Horn-Lingk, A.: Einstieg in die Psycho-Physiognomik, p. 25. Vertraudich Verlag, Munich (2017)
18. Viola, P., Jones, M.J.: Rapid object detection using a boosted cascade of simple features. In: Proceedings of the 2001 IEEE Computer Society Conference on CVPR 2001, vol. 1, p. I.511. IEEE(2001)

19. Deng, J., Guo, J., et al.: RetinaFace: single-stage dense face localisation in the wild. Computer Vision and Pattern Recognition, Journal DBLP:journals/corr/abs-1905-00641 (2019)
20. Devlin, H.: AI programs exhibit racial and gender biases, research reveals (2017). https://www.theguardian.com/technology/2017/apr/13/ai-programs-exhibit-racist-and-sexist-biases-research-reveals. Accessed 02 Jan 2020
21. Beals, J.: Self Marketing Power: Branding Yourself as a Business of One. Keynote Publishing, Montclair (2008)
22. Focus Money: Selbstmarketing – Mit Xing und Twitter Karriere machen. 10 Goldene Regeln für die Selbstvermarktung. N.k., p. 5. https://www.focus.de/finanzen/karriere/berufsle-ben/tid-15059/selbstmarketing-zehn-goldene-regeln-fuer-die-selbstvermark-tung_aid_422310.html. Accessed 07 Nov 2019
23. Careerplus: Die Kunst der Selbstvermarktung. N.k. (2017) https://www.career-plus.ch/blog/kunst-der-selbstvermarktung. Accessed 07 Nov 2019
24. Serafinelli, E.: Identity: a visual presentation. In: Digital Life on Instagram: New Social Communication of Photography, p. 157. Emerald Publishing (2018)
25. Veronon, R.J.W., Sutherland, C.A.M., Young, A.W., Hartley, T.: Modelling first impressions from highly variable facial images. PNAS (2014). https://doi.org/10.1073/pnas.1409860111. Accessed 29 Jan 2020
26. Bauer, J.: Wie wir werden, wer wir sind. Die Entstehung des menschlichen Selbst durch Resonanz. Karl Blessing Verlag, München (2019)
27. Cadwalladr, C., Graham-Harrison, E.: Revealed: 50 million Facebook profiles harvested for Cambridge Analytica in major data breach (2018). https://www.theguardian.com/news/2018/mar/17/cambridge-analytica-facebook-influence-us-election
28. Asiegbu, J.E.: The analysis of the components of emotional intelligence at workplace: the case of the nigerian telecommunication inudstry. Eastern Mediterranean University, p. 6 (2016). https://pdfs.semanticscholar.org/6690/f8259b81353fa28a3f0b25d985e9a3b8ace2.pdf
29. Reddington, S.: How to Improve Emotional Intelligence. JNR Publishing Group (2017). https://books.google.de/booksid=xlmZDwAAQBAJ&pg=PT37&dq=is+it+easy+to+develop+a+high+EQ&hl=en&sa=X&ved=0ahUKEwiJoOCr5f7mAhXNCuwKHYJGAGkQ6AEISTAE#v=onepage&q=high%20EQ&f=false. Accessed 01 Jan 2020
30. Hassin, R., Trope, Y.: Facing faces: studies on the cognitive aspects of physiognomy. J. Pers. Soc. Psychol. **78**, 837–852 (2000). https://doi.org/10.1037/0022-3514.78.5.837
31. Mohammed, A., Pathath, A., Al-Kuwaity, K., Ibrahim Ali, S.: Rhino physiognomy: a myth or science? J. Craniofac. Surg. **29**(1) (2017). https://doi.org/10.1097/scs.0000000000004082
32. Robitzski, D.: Left unchecked, artificial intelligence can become prejudiced all on its own (2018). https://futurism.com/artificial-intelligence-prejudiced. Accessed 01 Jan 2020
33. Smith, R.E.: Rage Inside the Machine: The Prejudice of Algorithms, and How to Stop the Internet making Bigots of Us All. Bloomsbury Publishing Plc, London (2019)
34. Grieger-Langer, S.: Profiling. https://profilersuzanne.com/profiling/. Accessed 14 Jan 2020
35. Orth, M.: Menschen[er]kenntnis. https://menschenerkenntnis.com. Accessed 14 Jan 2020
36. Schroff, F., Kalenichenko, D., Philbin, J.: FaceNet: a unified embedding for face recognition and clustering. arXiv:1503.03832v3 [cs.CV] (2015)
37. Men's Hairstyles X. 20 Keanu Reeves Hairstyles. https://www.menshairstylesx.com/celebrity-hairstyles-for-men/keanu-reeves-hairstyles/. Accessed 20 Nov 2019

Designing an Assisted Self-help Mobile App to Cope with Panic Disorder: Preliminary Results and Open Issues

Maria Teresa Paratore[✉]

Istituto di Informatica e Telematica – CNR, Via Moruzzi 1, 56100 Pisa, Italy
`maria.paratore@iit.cnr.it`

Abstract. During the latest years, mental health disturbances related to anxiety have become more and more widespread. Among them, panic disorder is fairly common and affects a significant percentage of people in the U.S. and in Europe, regardless of their instruction level, social state and culture, with obvious consequences to the health and social care systems. Many approaches exist to the treatment of panic disorder, and all of them share the requirement of making the patient feel actively involved as the main responsible of the success or failure of the therapy. This has led to increasing interest among specialists in developing strategies based on pure or assisted self-help. Mindfulness-based psychotherapy, which has been proved to be particularly effective with anxiety disorders, is often delivered in self-help formats. Many mobile applications exist which guide users through step-by-step training programmes and provide general information about this kind of practice, but the supervision of a psychotherapist, although advisable, is seldom provided. In this paper, we introduce the prototype of a mobile application based on the key concept of self-efficacy, whose goal is to help users prevent and cope with panic and anxiety disturbs under the guidance of mental health professionals. We will describe the theoretical background we relied upon and the different phases involved in the design of the application. Preliminary results, future work, and open issues will also be discussed.

Keywords: mHealth · Panic disorder · Mindfulness · Self-help · Self-management collaborative design · Persuasive design

1 Introduction

The aim of our work is to explore the potentialities offered and the challenges posed by mobile technologies applied to an existing traditional psychoeducational programme. We will describe the process of design and development which led to the first prototype of *Calma*, a self-management mobile app tailored on the needs of users affected by PD and designed in co-operation with a group of patients and clinicians.

1.1 Mental Disorders and Mobile Health

Anxiety disorders are a heterogeneous group of pathologies which affect the normal behaviour of patients and undermine their quality of life. A thorough and quite recent

© Springer Nature Switzerland AG 2020
M. Kurosu (Ed.): HCII 2020, LNCS 12183, pp. 103–116, 2020.
https://doi.org/10.1007/978-3-030-49065-2_8

review of the existing epidemiologic literature [1] shows a worldwide percentage of anxiety disorders of 7.3%, with a greater relevance among western developed countries (7.0%–15.5%). Other studies [2, 3] show different percentages and data analysis, but all of them highlight the heavy burden represented worldwide by these diseases, which are identified as chronic conditions.

The World Health Organization (WHO) in their Mental Health Action Plan 2013–2020 [6] warn about "the need for a comprehensive, coordinated response from health and social sectors at the country level" and encourage mobile health (mHealth) applications as a means of promoting self-care to cope with the global burden of mental disorders. mHealth can be used by governments to spread knowledge, help prevention and reduce the stigma associated to mental illness. Mobile applications can help overcome geographical and economic barriers and deliver treatment to patients who otherwise would not undergo any form of therapy, at the same time reducing costs. If properly delivered, psychological care via mobile technology presents many positive aspects both for patients and for mental health providers [7, 8]: patient-therapist communication can be extended beyond face-to-face sessions via instant messaging; symptoms can be tracked and reported on a daily basis; training sessions and coping strategies can be delivered on the patient's device in multimedia formats; real-time aid (such as relaxation quick tips) can be automatically triggered whenever anomalous physiological conditions are met. Research2Guidance, in their 2017 mHealth economics report [9], show that mHealth applications are gaining larger shares of the market every year, with a supply growing in perspective faster than the demand. In such a scenario, the amount of apps for psychological well-being, and in particular for anxiety disorders, is growing at a fast rate [15, 16].

1.2 Panic Disorder: Symptoms and Therapeutic Approaches

Panic disorder (PD) is a common anxiety disorder, diagnosed when recurring panic attacks occur. A panic attack is described by a series of very strong sensations and physical symptoms, such as dizziness, excessive sweating, shaking, hyperventilation, chest pains; in a typical panic attack physical symptoms happen suddenly, rapidly rise, reach their peak and disappear within 10 to 20 min and are associated with disturbing thoughts and feelings. These episodes, despite their relative shortness, very often end with conditioning the social lives of who experiences them; subjects who have suffered from a panic attack tend in fact to live in constant fear on having another one [28] and this vicious cycle undermines their social and family relationships as well as productivity on the working place. Other disturbances such as Generalised Anxiety Disorder (GAD) and mood disorder may be present in co-morbidity, making the quality of life even poorer [4]. Most of the patients affected by PD seek for a pharmacological or psychotherapeutic aid according with their economic means. Either combined treatment or psychotherapy alone—rather than medication alone—should be the first options offered to patients [9]. The therapy, be it pharmacological or psychotherapeutic or a combination of both, must anyway be focused on making patients feel active part of a changing process that will lead them to achieve good and stable results.

Cognitive Behavioural Therapy (CBT), which takes into account how thoughts affect emotions and behaviour, has been proved to be effective for anxiety disorders, especially when combined with psychopharmacology. Recently, mindfulness and Acceptance and Commitment Therapy (ACT) have also emerged as effective approaches to contrast anxiety disorders [11, 12]. Mindfulness involves techniques such as meditation and awareness of our own body sensations, that help in the process of staying focused and connected to the present moment, while the main goal of ACT is to make patients be aware of their sensations and feelings in a non-judging way. A peculiar aspect of CBT, ACT and mindfulness is that they provide techniques which patients can learn autonomously and practice in short sessions during their everyday life. Many resources such as books, web sites and multimedia exist that aim at teaching and practising such techniques, which has led to an increasing interest among specialists in adopting them in the context of self-management programmes. The outcomes of such self-aid strategies, even when delivered through mobile apps, seem generally promising [10, 13], albeit some studies [14] suggest that clinical guidance should always be provided to achieve good results.

2 Designing the App

2.1 Key Features for Effective Self-help Mobile Applications

As pointed out by Luxton, Bush et al. [7] a mobile application can be successfully adopted in order to improve the effectiveness of a psychoterapeutic programme throughout the phases of data gathering, self-report, self-assessment and two-way communication between patients and psychoterapists; moreover, features such as geolocation and integration with wearable sensors can be exploited to allow a continuous monitoring of the patient that otherwise would be difficult if not impossible to achieve. The use of mHealth for mental healthcare is actually being encouraged by governments in many countries, including Europe [24], anyway, a huge amount of applications for psychological self-help is currently available on the market, making it is difficult for both patients and therapists to choose a reliable software. Despite the proved effectiveness of applications for mental health based on the mentioned therapeutic approaches [10], thorough investigations show that the software available on the market don't always meet basic quality requirements such as a solid therapeutic background, proved quality contents or good usability [17]; moreover, accurate testing is seldom provided [15].

When designing a software application devoted to mental healthcare, it is essential to keep in mind the needs of its target users [19] as well as the therapeutic background it relies upon. Users' engagement issues such as poor adherence (when the app is not able to capture the users' interest for a proper amount of time and hence fails in delivering its contents) and dropout (when users do not complete required actions, such as compiling questionnaires) must also be addressed. A successful app should be designed in such a way that users feel motivated to use it on a regular basis and actively involved in a process of improvement of their condition, which is also the key to success of any psychotherapy. In this perspective, it is advisable to adopt a participatory design strategy which involves both patients and healthcare providers [20].

2.2 Therapeutic Background

Our goal was to build a patient-centred mobile application based on a psychoeducational programme [22] that was conducted by a team of psychosomatic experts (psychiatrists and psychologists) in the context of a research on self-management of chronic conditions [23]. The programme adopted self-efficacy [25], ACT and mindfulness as means of achieving self-management skills.

During the programme, patients were given some basic notions of mindfulness and ACT. Many learning multimedia resources were provided in digital format in order to encourage home practising (audio and pdf files describing guided meditation sessions and stretching exercises), moreover, patients were asked to keep a journal on a daily basis and were interviewed by telephone once a week. Questionnaires were also administered by e-mail (as pdf attachments to be filled in and sent back) in order to provide data about general conditions of the patients and their perceived level of self-confidence. Group sessions were held periodically, during which the psychotherapists asked the patients to share their experiences, enhancements and failures; the evolution of disturbs for each patient was shown during this sessions thanks to charts obtained on the basis of data collected through interviews and questionnaires.

2.3 Defining the Functionalities in a Collaborative Way

For our study, we recruited 12 patients diagnosed with PD who were undergoing the programme. Patients (11 women and one man) were aged in a range from 40 to 70 and shared good knowledge of mobile technologies. A participatory design strategy [20] ensured us to build ad hoc functionalities as well as tailored solutions that could encourage the use of the application. Co-design sessions were held on a regular basis and involved all of the 12 patients, 2 psychotherapists and an ICT engineer.

Beginning from the first session, use-cases were prepared and discussed. We started our design process by proposing a first set of core features related to the phases of data gathering and information exchange between therapists and patients. It was agreed that questionnaires should have been proposed periodically by the app via forms to be compiled and submitted. Similarly, it was required a digitized form of diary. From the therapists' point of view, these functionalities simplified the process of data gathering (also reducing the amount of time needed to transcribe data and manually analyse them), while patients appreciated the possibility to provide their data conveniently without the need of pencil and paper (saving paper was also perceived positively). During the following co-design sessions new functionalities were added upon request of one or the other stakeholder; among these, the tracking of emotions and feelings was a major requirement. Enabling users to check the evolution of their disturbs constitutes in fact a good form of engagement [15]; it has a positive outcome on the willingness to proceed on the therapeutic itinerary, possibly modifying some strategies of coping or asking for help. As a further means of self-monitoring, a mood-tracker was requested in order to compare mood levels with the other data gathered by the app. This was deemed particularly useful by therapists, given the proved co-morbidity of PD with mood disorders, while patients were eager to have a means of linking their specific mood to other events registered in the diary. Patients required to keep track of the places where situations of distress may occur, since panic attacks are often associated to specific places or situations. A further functionality strongly requested by patients was that the app should provide first aid assistance whenever they felt a panic attack approaching.

A final agreement on the main features provided by the app is shown in Fig. 1, where three functional areal are identified:

- *Practice*: functionalities to access multimedia resources such as audio files or external links related to ACT and mindfulness. Resources such as coping strategies for stress and anxiety and first-aid tips to contrast panic are provided.
- *Diary*: a set of forms and widgets to help users provide information about their psychological situation in a convenient and intuitive way. Data are gathered by the app and sent to specialists in a format that will be easy for them to analyse.
- *Report*: diagrams that show the evolution over time of a patient's situation based on data gathered through diary entries and questionnaires.

2.4 Designing for Persuasiveness

Shaping or changing attitudes and/or behaviours is a typical requirement for any mHealth intervention. Behaviour change interventions in eHealth are referred to as "persuasive technologies" and imply a whole range of design criteria, many of which strictly related to cooperative design. In our case, using *Calma* on a regular basis should train patients to correct the way they perceive disturbing real life situations.

Oinas-Kukkonen and Harjumaa in [30] define a theoretical framework to assess and design persuasive digital systems. Based on the previous work by Fogg [31], they suggest four persuasive software features: Primary Task Support, Credibility Support, Dialogue Support and Social Support; it is worth to note that these features reflect those empirically identified by Luxton et al., in their analysis of the capabilities required to identify effective mHealth interventions for mental health [7]. Thanks to our co-design approach, primary task support (i.e. the features supporting and optimizing the carrying out of the application's requirements from the users' perspective) was basically ensured by construction. In a similar way, to ensure the pleasantness of the app, GUIs' mock-ups were submitted, discussed and re-submitted to users until a final agreement was found. Credibility support was at first not deemed useful by some of our users, since they claimed they already knew and trusted the source of information delivered by the application, but they were convinced when it we highlighted the importance of providing the app with proper references about authors and contents in the perspective of its usage among a wider audience of patients. Forms of social support were not appreciated by users, nor were they deemed useful by therapists, who pointed out that symptoms, situations and coping strategies involved in PD are extremely subjective; as a consequence social sharing of individual problems and experiences would have been of little use in this specific case. Features related to dialogue support such as praises, notifications and reminders were accepted, but with some limitations. Notifications play an important role in mHealth, anyway developers must consider carefully how to integrate them into their applications [27]. Forms of automatic communication should be issued in a proper amount and with a proper timing, moreover, when a notification is issued it should be ensured that its content is relevant for the user in that precise moment, otherwise engagement would be negatively affected. Many of our users were particularly concerned about unobtrusiveness, and they did not show much enthusiasm for dialogue support. Reminders for practising, compiling the diary and the questionnaires were appreciated and considered very useful, provided that their timings could be customised via the app itself; praises were accepted as an incentive to practice, while other gaming strategies were considered too demanding and of little use. The final agreement achieved for dialogue support is shown in Fig. 1.

Fig. 1. The core functionalities of *Calma* as they were defined at the end the co-design process.

3 Developing the Prototype

Once that the functional requirements were defined, a first prototype of *Calma* was developed. As the development of the application was carried out, users were asked to test it, especially from the usability and attractiveness points of view so that, after some cycles of testing, a final version of the Android prototype was validated and approved. Users agreed that the requirements emerged during the co-design sessions had been met and that the software was an effective means to make it easier and more engaging to follow the self-management programme. The following sections describe the key features of this version of the application.

3.1 The Mood Tracker

The mood-tracker was conceived in order to let users collect data about their mood in a simple way and whenever they wanted. The UI is based on the so-called Circumplex Model of Affect [32]. According to this model, emotions can be visually organised on four quadrants in a two-dimensional space depending on their pleasantness (x-axis) and the arousal level they are associated to (y-axis). Figure 2 shows a representation of the Circumplex model and the UI of our mood-tracker, that is a coloured wheel where the current mood can be selected by scrolling with one finger. Each mood entry is stored in the local database, making it possible to show the evolution of a user's mood over time by means of a linear chart.

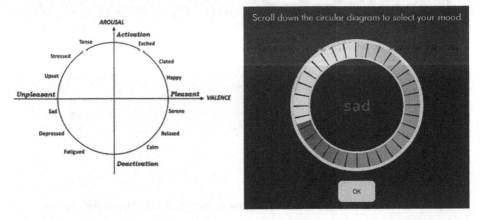

Fig. 2. The Circumplex model of emotions and the mood-picker wheel used in the app.

3.2 The Practice Section

"Here and now" are the keywords related to mindfulness and seem to be the ideal premises for the section of our app devoted to practising. This section is organised in four contexts (home, open air, travel, office) where a panic attack may occur and users may want or need to practice. Patients suffering from panic disorder are very likely to develop avoidance behaviours, as they tend to fear places or situations where a previous attack took place. It is hence important to associate a stressful event with the place where it occurred. Four large clickable areas with coloured figures make it very simple to get the exercises and start to practice. Each context is related to a certain number of exercises/strategies to help the user concentrate on the present moment and stay connected to the surrounding environment in a mindful way. The user is invited to read the text and then start to practice by pressing the upper "play" button. The duration of the practice is customizable. Exercises can be browsed through by swiping left or right.

Some of the proposed exercises are more likely than others to be practised in short sessions as quick strategies to cope with panic symptoms. Since the access to first-aid capabilities needs to be straightforward, such tips are proposed by default and a switch button can be used in order to commute on more complex exercises (see Fig. 3); on the contrary, more articulated mindfulness sessions are presented by default when a practising reminder is issued.

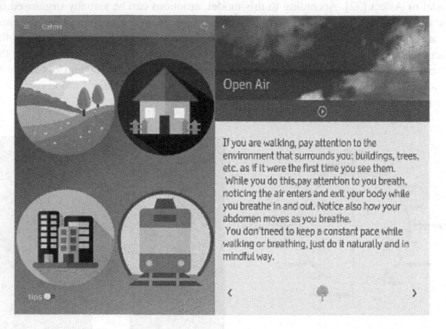

Fig. 3. The Practice main page and a suggested strategy for the "Open Air" context.

3.3   The Diary Section

This is the section where users can describe their experiences in a guided way through a wizard and fill in questionnaires. A summary of all the records inserted is available. The insertion date and a symbol next to each entry reminds when and where the corresponding event took place (see Fig. 4). Entries are stored in a local database and users can review, edit and delete them in any moment. Information about where a stressful episode took place must be provided, as well as the amount of stress and the quality and intensity of the emotions, the feelings and the thoughts experienced. According to ACT principles, users are asked to assess the stress level on a scale from 0 to 10. Then a description of quality and strength of the experienced emotions must be given through a guided mechanism of multiple choices. This kind of verbal self-assessment makes it possible to describe the dominance dimension of emotions (i.e. their controlling and dominant nature), which is not possible when using only pictorial methods [33]. Six basic emotions are provided (anger, fear, sadness, shame, confusion, happiness) and three levels of intensity (light, moderate, strong) for each of them. In a similar way, users are asked how much control they have over the emotions and to describe their rational and irrational thoughts by choosing among pre-defined descriptions. Finally, users are asked to auto-assess their motivation degree (i.e. their willingness to change) by means of a ruler ranging from 0 to 10 (Fig. 5).

Fig. 4. Summary of the diary entries.

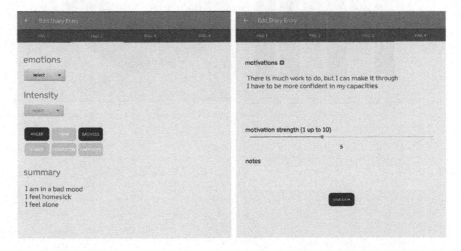

Fig. 5. The "emotions" and "motivations" sections of the diary wizard.

3.4   The Report Section

All of the collected data are periodically sent to the therapists by the app, anyway in the Report section users can find different graphical representations of their disturbs over time, according to data collected up to the present moment (up to 60 sequential diary entries can be considered). The following reports are available:

- *Basic Emotions.* A stacked candle chart that shows for each diary entry the associated emotions and their strength.
- *Stressful Contexts.* A doughnut chart that represents the distribution of the diary events registered with a stress level equal or higher than 5 (on a scale from 0 to 10).
- *Stress and Motivation Levels.* Two linear charts that compare stress and motivation levels reported at each diary entry.
- *Mood Levels.* A linear chart represents the evolution of mood over time using data entered by means of the mood-picker.

Samples of the mentioned charts are shown, clockwise, in Fig. 6.

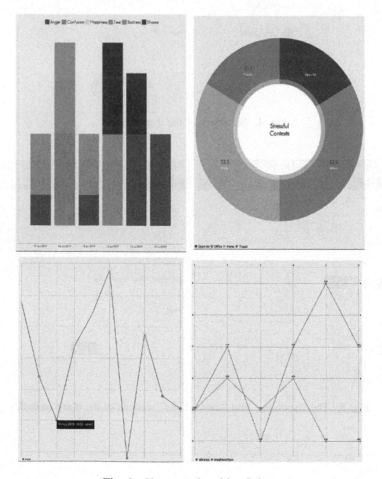

Fig. 6. Charts produced by *Calma.*

4 Open Issues and Future Work

This prototype met the requirements of a limited set of patients who were undergoing the same self-efficacy programme. In order to better assess the efficacy of our application, a wider number of patients should be involved and a compared study between the outcomes of a traditional pencil-and-paper self-efficacy programme and the same programme delivered through *Calma* should be performed.

We are planning to make the prototype available for evaluation to a larger set of users interested in an assisted psychoeducational programme. At the same time we are motivated to add new features in order to make the app more effective as a first-aid tool as well as a healthcare instrument in support of less experienced users.

4.1 Integration with Wearable Technologies

Hyperventilation, tachycardia and high blood pressure are often associated with stressful conditions and are very common when a panic or anxiety attack is approaching. These symptoms are related to the rising of anxiety that usually precedes a panic attack and can be effectively used by the app to "autonomously" detect a possible need of help by the user. Wearable devices can provide constant monitoring of a users' physical condition, which is a desirable feature for many mHealth applications [15]. Given the extreme popularity of devices such as smart bracelets, we are planning to develop real-time notifications for a next prototype of our app, to be issued whenever a suspiciously high arousal level is reported.

According to Fogg's Behaviour Model for persuasiveness [26], a target behaviour can be successfully induced by an application when a good compromise is reached between ease of use and user's motivation (the so-called Activation Threshold). A trigger is more likely to induce a certain behaviour to the user if it is issued when two conditions are met: the user is strongly motivated towards a goal (e.g. lower their heart rate) and the action required to achieve that goal is simple. In our case, the app would intercept an abnormal physiological condition via the wearable device's API and then it would issue a push notification to the user. The user would access to a first-aid hint by simply responding to the notification (Fig. 7).

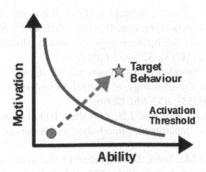

Fig. 7. How to trigger a target behaviour according to the Fogg model.

This functionality, based on objective parameters, could flank the available on-demand help feature, which on the contrary is based on the patient's subjective perceptions.

4.2 Reaching a Broader Audience

Recently, popularity of mindfulness has grown and reached also people not in need of psychiatric or psychological help, but just interested in improve their quality of life by reducing stress or anxiety. This made us think about a new version of *Calma* meant for "less experienced" users, who have never sought psychological support before.

The broader catchment area of such an application poses new design issues with respect to the current prototype, mainly related to user engagement, credibility and social support. New mechanisms of interaction with therapists such as video conference and instant messaging should also be investigated.

5 Conclusions

We have presented the first prototype of Calma, an assisted self-help application for the management of panic and anxiety disturbs designed in co-operation with mental health experts and patients. We have discussed the co-design process and described the guidelines and best practices adopted. We have highlighted how persuasiveness design was influenced by users during the co-design phase. A further evolution of the app towards a broader audience has been prospected as a future work, as well as a possible integration with wearable technologies. The need of more extensive user tests has nonetheless been pointed out.

Acknowledgments. We wish to thank Dr. Antonella Ciaramella and the Alypsia non-profit organisation (http://www.istitutogift.it/aplysia-onlus/) for their hints and the precious contribute throughout the co-design process.

References

1. Baxter, A.J., Scott, K.M., Vos, T., Whiteford, H.A.: Global prevalence of anxiety disorders: a systematic review and meta-regression. Psychol. Med. **43**(5), 897–910 (2013)
2. Bandelow, B., Michaelis, S.: Epidemiology of anxiety disorders in the 21st century. Dialogues Clin. Neurosci. **17**(3), 327–335 (2015)
3. Girolamo, G.D., et al.: Prevalence of common mental disorders in Italy: results from the European Study of the Epidemiology of Mental Disorders (ESEMeD). Soc. Psychiatry Psychiatr. Epidemiol. **41**(11), 853–861 (2006)
4. Kroenke, K., Spitzer, R.L., Williams, J.B., Monahan, P.O., Loewe, B.: Anxiety disorders in primary care: prevalence, impairment, comorbidity, and detection. Ann. Intern. Med. **146**(5), 317–325 (2007)
5. Olatunji, B.O., Cisler, J.M., Tolin, D.F.: Quality of life in the anxiety disorders: a meta-analytic review. Clin. Psychol. Rev. **27**(5), 572–581 (2007)

6. World Health Organization: Mental health action plan 2013–2020, Geneva, 02 May 2013/21 February 2015. http://apps.who.int/iris/bitstream/10665/89966/1/9789241506021_eng.pdf? ua=1

7. Luxton, D.D., McCann, R.A., Bush, N.E., Mishkind, M.C., Reger, G.: mHealth for mental health: Integrating smartphone technology in behavioral healthcare. Prof. Psychol.: Res. Pract. Public Domain 42(6), 505–512 (2011)

8. East, M.L., Havard, B.C.: Mental Health Mobile Apps: From Infusion to Diffusion in the Mental Health Social System. MIR Ment. Health 2(1), e10 (2015)

9. Combination therapy for panic disorder. Harvard Mental Health Letter, June 2008. https:// www.health.harvard.edu/newsletter_article/Combination_therapy_for_panic_disorder

10. Mak, W.W.S., et al.: Efficacy and moderation of mobile app–based programs for mindfulness-based training, self-compassion training, and cognitive behavioral psychoeducation on mental health: randomized controlled noninferiority trial. JMIR Ment. Health 5 (4), e60 (2018)

11. Hayes, S.C., Luoma, J.B., Bond, F.W., Masuda, A., Lillis, J.: Acceptance and commitment therapy: model, processes and outcomes. Behav. Res. Ther. 44(1), 1–25 (2006)

12. Hofmann, S.G., Sawyer, A.T., Witt, A.A., Oh, D.: The effect of mindfulness-based therapy on anxiety and depression: a meta-analytic review. J. Consult. Clin. Psychol. 78(2), 169–183 (2010)

13. Cavanagh, K., Strauss, C., Forder, L., Jones, F.: Can mindfulness and acceptance be learnt by self-help?: a systematic review and meta-analysis of mindfulness and acceptance-based self-help interventions. Clin. Psychol. Rev. 34(2), 118–129 (2014)

14. French, K., Golijani-Moghaddam, N., Schröder, T.: What is the evidence for the efficacy of self-help acceptance and commitment therapy? A systematic review and meta-analysis. J. Context. Behav. Sci. 6, 360–374 (2017)

15. Bush, N.E., Armstrong, C.M., Hoyt, T.V.: Smartphone apps for psychological health: a brief state of the science review. Psychol. Serv. 16(2), 188–195 (2019)

16. Van Ameringen, M., Turna, J., Khalesi, Z., Pullia, K.: There is an app for that! The current state of mobile applications (apps) for DSM-5 obsessive-compulsive disorder, posttraumatic stress disorder, anxiety and mood disorders. Depress. Anxiety 34(6), 526–539 (2017)

17. Coulon, S.M., Monroe, C.M., West, D.S.: A systematic, multi-domain review of mobile smartphone apps for evidence-based stress management. Am. J. Prev. Med. 51(1), 95–105 (2016)

18. https://research2guidance.com/the-mhealth-app-market-reaches-31-billion-by-2020/

19. Chiauzzi, E., Newell, A.: Mental health apps in psychiatric treatment: a patient perspective on real world technology usage. JMIR Ment. Health 6(4), e12292 (2019)

20. Clemensen, J., Larsen, S.B., Kyng, M., Kirkevold, M.: Participatory design in health sciences: using cooperative experimental methods in developing health services and computer technology. Qual. Health Res. 17(1), 122–130 (2007)

21. Oinas-Kukkonen, H.: A foundation for the study of behaviour change support systems. Pers. Ubiquit. Comput. 17(6), 1223–1235 (2013)

22. Lorig, K., Holman, H.R.: Self-management education: history, definition, outcomes, and mechanisms. Ann. Behav. Med.: Publ. Soc. Behav. Med. 26(1), 1–7 (2003)

23. Chiusalupi, M., et al.: The role of anxiety on the outcome of a self-management program for subjects with chronic pain. In: Poster n. 283, Annual Conference of the European Association of Psychosomatic Medicine, EAPM 2017, Barcelona, Spain, 28 June–01 July 2017 (2017)

24. https://ec.europa.eu/digital-single-market/en/news/green-paper-mobile-health-mhealth

25. Bandura, A.: Self-efficacy: toward a unifying theory of behavioral change. Psychol. Rev. 84 (2), 191–215 (1977)

26. Fogg, B.J.: A behavior model for persuasive design. In: Persuasive 2009 Proceedings of the 4th International Conference on Persuasive Technology, Article no. 40. ACM, New York (2009)

27. Bidargaddi, N., Pituch, T., Maaieh, H., Short, C.E., Strecher, V.J.: Predicting which type of push notification content motivates users to engage in a self-monitoring app. Prev. Med. Rep. 11, 267–273 (2018)

28. Clark, D.M.: A cognitive approach to panic. Behav. Res. Ther. 24(4), 461–470 (1986)

29. Wildeboer, G., Kelders, S.M., van Gemert-Pijnen, J.E.W.C.: The relationship between persuasive technology principles, adherence and effect of web-based interventions for mental health: a meta-analysis. Int. J. Med. Inform. 96, 71–85 (2016)

30. Oinas-Kukkonen, H., Harjumaa, M.: Persuasive systems design: key issues, process model, and system features. CAIS 24, 28 (2009)

31. Fogg, B.J.: Persuasive Technology: Using Computers to Change What We Think and Do. Morgan Kaufmann Publishers, San Francisco (2003)

32. Posner, J.E., Russell, J.W., Peterson, B.S.: The circumplex model of affect: an integrative approach to affective neuroscience, cognitive development, and psychopathology. Dev. Psychopathol. 17(3), 715–734 (2005)

33. Desmet, P.M.A., Vastenburg, M.H., Romero, N.: Mood measurement with Pick-A-Mood: review of current methods and design of a pictorial self-report scale. J. Des. Res. 14(3), 241–279 (2016)

Digital Overload Warnings - "The Right Amount of Shame"?

Aarathi Prasad[✉] and Asia Quinones

Skidmore College, Saratoga Springs, NY, USA
aprasad@skidmore.edu

Abstract. Media is rife with articles regarding smartphone addiction and how digital overload may be harming the mental well-being of children and young adults. As a response to the negative backlash about digital overload, Apple and Google released ScreenTime and Digital Well-being on iOS and Android devices to help users make informed decisions about their smartphone app usage. However, we expect that reminding users about their digital overload may have a negative effect, especially in undergraduate students, who are avid users of smartphones, and maybe also struggling with mental health issues. We conducted a survey among 230 undergraduate students to understand whether they use the Screen-Time feature on their iOS devices to manage app usage and if so, how the tool affected their emotions. We discovered that ScreenTime was effective in changing smartphone usage behavior, but also triggered negative emotions in undergraduate students who are avid smartphone users and also struggle with mental health issues. We expect the tools can be improved by changing the way users are warned about increased phone usage, by incorporating positive mindfulness techniques. We also emphasize the need to have more studies, like ours, to understand the effectiveness of digital overload reminder tools.

Keywords: Smart home · Smartphones · Tablets · Children · Privacy · Trust · Security · Safety · Family

1 Introduction

Smartphones have increasingly become an integral part in people's daily lives, allowing them to manage activities [46], keep track of health and wellness [15] and also stay connected with family and friends [16]. However, the media is rife with articles regarding smartphone addiction and how *digital overload* may be harming users, especially young adults [43,44]. In this paper, we use the term digital overload to indicate the phenomenon where people are constantly using their smartphones, computers and tablets to obtain immediate access to messages from their loved ones, news updates and information from hundreds of networked apps. Researchers have shown that digital overload can lead to stress, anxiety, depression and lack of sleep, especially in undergraduate students [6,10].

© Springer Nature Switzerland AG 2020
M. Kurosu (Ed.): HCII 2020, LNCS 12183, pp. 117–134, 2020.
https://doi.org/10.1007/978-3-030-49065-2_9

As a response to the negative backlash about digital overload, Apple and Google released ScreenTime and Digital Wellbeing on iOS and Android devices to help users make informed decisions about their smartphone app usage [29]. For example, the ScreenTime app feature allows iOS users to set a specific allotted time of usage per app [49]. When the timer is up, iOS shows a warning and temporarily blocks the user from returning to the app. ScreenTime also presents weekly reports about the users' overall app usage including apps opened and websites visited while analyzing how they use their device.

Researchers have shown that nudging users about the time they spent on their devices helps them manage their smartphone use [34] so it is possible that ScreenTime may help users reduce their digital overload. However, we expect that reminding users about their digital overload may have a negative effect, especially in undergraduate students, who are avid users of smartphones [2] and may also be struggling with mental health issues such as anxiety and depression [1]. We wanted to understand whether digital overload warnings were effective in helping undergraduate students reduce their screen time, without adding to their mental health burden.

We conducted a survey among undergraduate students to understand whether they use the ScreenTime feature on their iOS devices to manage app usage and if so, how the tool affected their emotions; we chose to focus on iOS users who use ScreenTime to manage their iPhone usage because iPhones were more popular than Android phones on our campus.

In this paper, we provide the following contributions. We present the survey questionnaire and findings from the survey we conducted with 230 undergraduates to understand the effect of digital overload warnings on their smartphone app usage behavior. Our exploratory study revealed that participants mostly experienced negative emotions on receiving a warning they had exceeded the time allotted for an app and despite receiving the warning, most participants went back to the app. However, we also discovered that most participants felt content after viewing the summary of their daily app usage and believed that ScreenTime helped them understand and in some cases, alter their app usage behavior. We also present a discussion on why participants may ignore digital overload warnings, and provide design recommendations for nudging techniques to motivate users to reduce screen time.

2   Background and Related Work

It is important for users to learn to control their smartphone use as smartphone overuse distracts users while at work, in class, or while driving [3,13,28,35]. On the other hand, researchers also discovered that vague examples of problematic smartphone use provided by popular media have influenced people's notions of smartphone overuse, causing them to be overcome by negative emotions such as guilt even when they used their smartphones for a useful task [25].

Emotions have been defined as feelings, expressive behavior or a responsive state [19]. Scherer defined emotions as a sequence of events – feelings that a person experiences, action taken as an immediate reaction to the feeling such as crying, an appraisal to evaluate events that caused the feeling, communicate our feelings through facial expressions such as a smile or a hug when we are happy, and finally, the physical response in our body, such as rush of blood flow when we are angry [41]. Plutchuk identified that every emotion also has an opposite emotion, so he presented eight primary emotions with varying intensity on a wheel with the opposite emotions represented on opposite sides of the wheel [37]. Stressors typically lead to increased negative emotions [11] and negative emotions have been shown to lead to problematic use of smartphones, especially in young adults [4,5]. On the other hand, the Broaden-and-Build theory of positive emotion posits that when people are likely to broaden their thoughts and action and bring about change when they experience positive emotions, even if only for a moment [12]. So in our survey, we wanted to understand both the negative and position emotions participants experienced when attempting to control digital overload.

Researchers identified social media and communication as the most addictive apps for undergraduate students [8]. Lee et al. discovered that college students who spent more time on their phones daily, especially immediately after receiving a push notification, were more likely to be addicted to their smartphones [27]. A survey of 612 participants showed that a lack of self control and low willpower also contributed to digital overload [24]. Prior research showed that college students are drawn to smartphones when they experience stress in their personal and academic lives [23,47] and also when they have low self-esteem and high anxiety levels [21]. Researchers have shown that digital overload also can lead to stress, anxiety, depression and lack of sleep, especially in undergraduate students [6]. Prior research shows that smartphone use increased anxiety, stress, and feelings of impatience in college students, even when their phone was not with them [10]. Additionally, Toma discovered that self-comparison on social media sites such as Facebook led to depression, especially among people with psycho-social problems [45].

Tools that track a user's device usage can be very useful, since it has been shown that users are often unable to quantify the time they spend using apps on devices [26]. A study conducted with an app usage tracking tool called ScreenLife revealed that personal tracking of device use is desirable for increasing productivity, and controlling device use [40]. Prior research also shows that nudging users about the time they spent on their devices helps them control their device use [34]. However, is it enough to just track how long you spend on different applications to understand smartphone usage? Harwood et al. discovered that it was the nature of smartphone use, and not the extent of use, that affected stress and depression [20]. Mehrotra et al. conducted a study to understand the relationship between user's emotional state and their app usage [30]. Our survey is the first that we know of, that studies the effectiveness of digital overload warning tools and specifically, how they affect users' emotions.

3   Research Methods

We conducted a survey of 233 undergraduate students to understand whether they use the ScreenTime feature on their iOS devices to make informed decisions about their app usage and what emotions they experienced when using different aspects of the ScreenTime tool. In our work, we considered emotion as the first event in Scherer's emotion model, i.e., the feeling that a person experiences. We addressed the following research questions:

- How many undergraduate students are aware of and use digital overload tools available on their phones?
- What time limits do they select for daily use of social media, entertainment and games; we have anecdotal evidence that students consider apps in these three categories to be most distracting.
- What emotions do they feel when they use an app for which they set a daily time limit?
- What emotions do they feel when they see the warning that they have exceeded the time set for an app?
- What action do they take as a response to the warning?
- How effective are digital overload warnings in changing users' smartphone usage behavior?

The survey was administered using the Qualtrics software. The study was approved by the college's institutional review board (IRB) and we recruited the participants through an email sent to all undergraduate students at our institution. All participants were incentivized with a $5 Starbucks gift card for completing the survey, irrespective of whether they had used the ScreenTime tool on their phones. We only considered iOS users for the following reasons: iPhones were more popular on our campus than Android, and ScreenTime was available on all iPhones unlike Android's Digital Wellbeing – we excluded the 2 Android users from the 233 participants who responded to the survey. It is unclear whether we excluded users from poor socio-economic background by only considering iOS users; we did not collect demographic information because it was not relevant to our research questions.

The survey included questions about the participants' ScreenTime usage, emotions they felt when using ScreenTime, such as using an app with a time limit, when receiving a warning about exceeding time limit, and when reviewing daily smartphone usage summary, actions they took as a response to the time limit warnings, and any changes in their smartphone usage behavior. The questionnaire is included in the Appendix section at the end of this paper. The list of emotions included in the survey questions was compiled from public American Psychology Association test records and articles in psychology journals about emotions and moods [14,31,42].

4 Findings

We coded and grouped the qualitative data into themes that we present below, as well as analyzed the quantitative data using independent t-tests. We classified emotions as positive and negative using Plutchik's wheel of emotions [37].

Familiarity of ScreenTime. Out of the 228 participants we considered, 206 were familiar with ScreenTime functionality, but only 37 participants used the ScreenTime tool on their iPhones.

Time Limits for Social Media, Entertainment and Games. In the survey, we asked participants to choose the time limits they set for three categories - social media, entertainment and games. Most participants were concerned more about the time they spent on social media than entertainment apps and games. Using independent t-tests, we discovered that participants who had chosen a time limit of less than or equal to 2 h for daily social media app use were more likely to experience negative emotions when they saw a time out warning ($p < 0.05$).

Out of the 37 participants, 34 had set time limits for social media use; the mean time was 4.5 h, median time 2 h, with an interquartile range (IQR) of 5 h. 31 participants set time limits for games; the mean time was 4.13 h, the median time 1.5 h with an IQR of 3 h. 29 participants set time limits for entertainment; the mean time limit was 3.93 h, the median time was 1 h with an IQR of 7 h.

Reasons for Using Social Media, Entertainment and Gaming Apps. The participants used social media, entertainment and gaming apps when they were bored or as a way to relax when they were stressed or having a panic attack. For example, one participant said, "I distract myself from panic with games and humor." while another said, "I use games and social media mainly as a distraction for when I'm bored or am kinda stressed [and] when [I] don't want to do something."

Participants associated negative and positive emotions with smartphone apps. One participant said, "When it comes to playing games I feel relaxed and happy to take my mind off of things but social media apps tend to make me happy but cause me lots of anxiety." Another participant said "sometimes social media can be overwhelming and anxiety inducing." Social media apps also invoked positive emotions, for example one participant found that Instagram, "[provided them] great inspiration for art and cooking and lifestyle habits", while another found comfort in using social media apps.

Participant Emotions When Using Smartphones with ScreenTime Enabled. As shown in Fig. 1a, participants mostly feel positive emotions, though many participants also reported feeling stressed, ashamed, unsatisfied, over-whelmed and anxious when using apps for which they had chosen a daily usage time limit. Participants' emotions were affected by their perception of their smartphone use.

Some participants were not worried about their smartphone use but wanted to track the time they spent using their phones; one participant said, "I set the

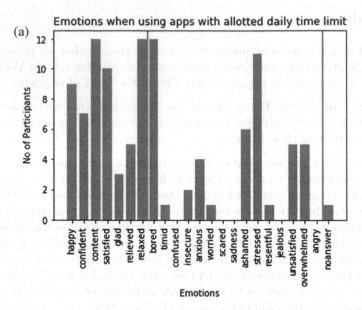

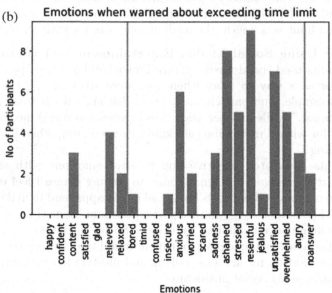

Fig. 1. (a) Emotions when using apps with daily time limits. The first green line separates the emotions into positive and negative; the last bar shows the number of participants who did not answer the question. Participants mostly feel positive emotions, though many participants also report that they were stressed, ashamed, unsatisfied, overwhelmed and anxious. (b) Emotions when receiving warning about exceeding time limit. The first green line separates the emotions into positive and negative; the last bar shows the number of participants who did not answer the question. Participants mostly feel negative emotions when receiving the warning.

limits, but I don't really care if I go over them. [It is] just a way for me to know how long Ive spent on my phone."

Others were relieved after learning, from ScreenTime data, that they used their phone less than they expected; one participant said, "I feel more satisfied because I know that my free time is not wasted by using these apps and it feels relieving when I am spending less time attached to my device."

However, some participants considered their smartphone use as problematic and experienced emotions such as shame and guilt when they were on their phone. One participant said, "I enjoy using the apps I often limit, but I feel guilty about using them, or almost ashamed". Another said, "I know I should be doing better things with my time, but the allure of social media is often difficult to overcome."

Other participants were able to use the apps without experiencing negative emotions, until they exceeded the time limit. One participant said, "I generally like using the app I set a time limit for (Instagram), but I know I spend too much time on it which makes me feel a little ashamed."

Participant Emotions About Exceeding Time Limit Warnings. As shown in Fig. 1b, participants experienced mostly negative emotions when receiving the warning that they have exceeded the time allotted for an app. Participants experienced positive emotions when they had chosen a time limit that they were comfortable with, while other reported feeling resentful, ashamed, unsatisfied, anxious, stressed, overwhelmed, sad, angry and worried when they realized that they had spent a significant time on certain apps that they were trying to reduce use of.

Some participants felt guilty for exceeding the allotted time limit; they associated the warnings with negative traits such as being addicted to their smartphone, lacking self-control, procrastinating and being disconnected from their surroundings.

Some participants felt upset on seeing the warnings because they enjoyed using their smartphones. One participant said, "My phone and apps are a safety blanket and a distraction to what's going on around me and it gets upsetting that I don't have much to hide from." The other participant said, "I love being on my phone so when I get the notification I feel pretty sad."

Some participants experienced negative emotions based on the time of the day when they received the warnings, especially if the warnings appeared earlier in the day. One participant said, "I think I am always a bit surprised at what point in the day the timer alarms. Most days it is close to when I am going to bed, other days it is much earlier in the evening and that is when I feel a bit ashamed about how much I am on my phone." Another said, "I sometimes feel resentful that I have used all my time especially when it's early in the morning."

Some participants experienced positive emotions because they were able to stop using the phone when seeing the warning while others felt negative emotions for wanting to continue using the app despite the warning; one participant was "ashamed that I want to go over the limit". One participant said, "I feel content

124   A. Prasad and A. Quinones

because I know that I won't be using my phone as much as I used to". while the other said, "I feel better knowing I am consciously controlling my screentime."

Some participants felt negative emotions when receiving the time limit warnings but were able to reflect on the positive consequence of reducing smartphone use. One participant said, "I get annoyed sometimes BUT generally it's a good reminder to get the heck back to work" while another participant said, "The time warning makes me feel bad because it makes me aware of how much time I waste on the app. Ultimately I feel relieved though because I know that because of the time limit I am spending less time on the app." A third participant said, "I am sad because it shows that I've spent the day using the apps with all the time available to me, but I am glad that the timer helps me control the amount of time spent on my phone." Another participant was happy they did not have to monitor their own app usage, they said, "I'm vaguely resentful when the app locks because I want to keep using it, but I'm glad that the choice to use it has been (mostly) taken out of my hands, as I don't think my impulse control is very good."

Participants also liked the flexibility that ScreenTime provided, by not restricting their access to apps even after exceeding usage time limit. One participant realized that they could set high time limits to avoid seeing the digital overload warning. This participant said, "I feel positive feelings because the time limits I set are so high that it discourages me from getting anywhere close to that amount of time." Another participant also felt happy that ScreenTime did not lock them out of the app when they exceeded the time limit; this participant said, "I picked 'content' because the setting does not permanently lock me out of the app, so I do not worry when I can extend the time if needed."

Actions Taken by Participants as a Response to the Time Limit Warning. Only 3 participants reported that they rarely went back to the app after seeing the warning. 13 participants said that they sometimes went back, 10 often went back and 4 always went back.

One participant felt better that ScreenTime made them consciously reduce the time spent on smartphone apps, but felt that they were missing out on the benefits provided by the apps, which made them want to use the app; this participant said, "It makes me feel better to know I'm spending less time on my phone, but I am still always wondering if someone has messaged me on one of the blocked apps and sometimes I ignore the time limit".

Some participants were unhappy that they continued using the apps despite getting the warning of exceeding the time limit; one participant said, "I picked "stressed" because I feel like I extend the time too often."

Participant Emotions About Their Smartphone Use, Based on ScreenTime Data. As shown in Fig. 2a, participants experienced a mix of both positive and negative emotions (most participants felt content) when viewing a summary of their daily app usage, while others were unaffected by daily app usage summary; one participant said, "I dont care how long I spent in the apps".

Some participants noticed a decrease in their screen time and believed that the ScreenTime was indeed helping them reduce their smartphone usage. One

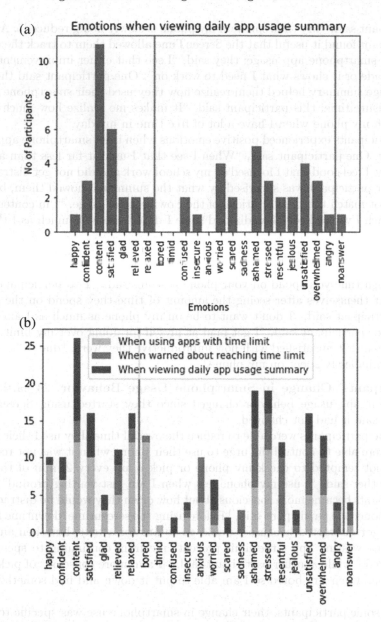

Fig. 2. (a) Emotions when viewing the app usage summary. Participants felt a mix of positive and negative emotions, though most participants felt content when viewing a summary of their daily app usage. (b) Summary of emotions participants experienced in three different situations when using ScreenTime. The first green line separates the emotions into positive and negative; the last bar shows the number of participants who did not answer the question. The figure clearly shows that participants felt strong negative emotions when viewing the warning about exceeding time limit, both positive and negative emotions when using apps with allotted time limits and mostly positive emotions when viewing the daily app usage summary.

participant said, "My time spent on my phone is slowly being reduced". Another participant found it useful that the ScreenTime allowed them to track the change in their smartphone app usage; they said, "I see that either improvements have been made or it shows what I need to work on". One participant said the daily app usage summary helped them realize how they used their smartphone during their leisure time; this participant said, "It makes me realize how much time I spent on my phone when I have a lot of free time in my day."

Participants experienced positive emotions when their smartphone app usage was low. One participant said, "When I see that I used it far less than average that day, I feel good that I focused on my school work and did not get distracted." Another participant was surprised by what the summary showed them, because it did not match their expectations of their own digital usage. "I'm content with how much I've used social media and since I didn't use it as much as I thought I did."

On the other hand, participants experienced negative emotions when they realized their smartphone usage was high. One participant said, "When it shows how much time you spend on your phone it seems sad." Two participants were angry at themselves after seeing the amount of time they spend on the phone; one participant said, "I don't want to be on my phone as much as I am" while the other participant said, "I get mad at myself for going over my limit.". One participant felt unsatisfied with how unproductive they were, "due to how much time I mindlessly spent on my phone."

Participants' Change in Smartphone Usage Behavior. 23 participants said their app usage behavior changed since they started using ScreenTime, while 5 said it had not changed.

Some participants were able to reduce the overall time they used their phone. Some were able to control the urge to use their phone when it was not required, "I am not tempted to check my phone or pick it up every 20 min of the day" and another said, "I use my phone less when I am just waiting around". Some participants became more conscious about how often they would be distracted by their phone; one participant said, "Before using the screentime/downtime feature I often got distracted because I would go to answer a text, but then autopilot to a time wasting app - the limit prevents me from continuing to spend time distracted." while another participant said, "[I am] more conscious of picking up the phone when I'm bored so I am able to put it down and find something else to do."

For some participants, their change in smartphone use was specific to social media apps. For example, one participant said, "I actually stopped being on social media for so many hours and now it has lessened to one or sometimes two." One participant deleted social media apps once they realized they spent a lot of time on them.

However, for most participants, their change in behavior came at the cost of negative emotions. One participant used their phone less on purpose because they were worried about seeing time limit warnings. Another participant experienced negative emotions when they used an app after seeing the warning, they said,

"I still override the lock from time to time, and I don't use my locked apps too much less, I just feel worse when I do use them." Another participant said that ScreenTime made them realize how much time they were "wasting" on using smartphones, when they could "put [that time] to better use".

On the other hand, some participants ended up using their smartphone more than they wanted to because they had not reached the time limit. One participant said, "Sometimes I am happy I didnt use all the screen time but sometimes i want to use more so when i get the notification it stresses me out or makes me annoyed that i used so much."

Overall, participants became aware of their app usage behavior better after using ScreenTime; one participant said, "I have become more conscious of how much mindless scrolling I do on Instagram and opening random things on Snapchat for example (I think most college kids can relate to this)".

Participants Experience Mixed Emotions About the Data Provided by ScreenTime. One participant felt overwhelmed with the data while others found the data helpful in understanding their device usage behavior. One participant said, "I notice that when I'm more stressed, I use it more, and vice versa."

One participant was satisfied with the amount of information provided by ScreenTime; this participant said, "I think more information would just make me feel worse honestly, this is about the right amount of shame."

Some participants wanted more detailed information about their app usage. For example, one participant said, "I wish you could breakdown the usage on specific apps, and how long the individual durations of use are per day.". Other participants wanted "a countdown [timer] and usage per app", "what times of the day I use them" and "what app I click on the most".

Two participants also had suggestions that were not related to time spent on apps; they wanted to know "how many times the phone is picked up" and "how much battery [the phone] uses and what that equates to in energy costs and environmental impacts."

5 Discussion

The goal of the ScreenTime feature was to help people make informed decisions about their digital overload, not to prevent people from going back to apps. But digital overload tools are expected to help people understand their smartphone app usage behavior and learn to reduce their screen time. Our survey revealed that users go back to the app despite getting a warning that they had exceeded the time limit, and that the warnings may make them feel negative emotions such as stress, dissatisfaction, shame and guilt. In this section, we discuss why people go back to apps even though they feel guilty when doing so, and explore design techniques could be used in order to encourage users to reduce their screen time, without inducing negative emotions.

5.1 Reasons for Going Back to Apps

Many users reported feeling "addicted" to their devices causing them to feel insecure, stressed and anxious. This addiction could be the result of an *attachment* created between the individual and their smartphone, given how much users rely on their smartphones now. Kim et al. studied whether avoidant attachment could predict smartphone addiction and concluded that avoidant attachment may lead to low self-esteem and anxiety in college students, which in turn may lead to smartphone addiction [21]. We plan to work with psychologists to explore attachment theory further to understand why users go back to using their smartphones despite feeling negative emotions such as guilt and shame on being warned about digital overuse.

Some participants also mentioned that they used smartphones to escape from the stress in the "real world". This could be the result of social phobia among users. For example, Ding et al. discovered that social and communication apps are considered most addictive among college students [8]. Yen et al. showed that people with social phobia prefer to communicate with others via the Internet than in person [50]. It is important to take into consideration users struggling with social phobia when designing tools for digital overload; for example, users with social phobia will not benefit from tools that force users to interact with each other and not use their phones when in the presence of others, such as Lock n' LoL [22].

Another reason for digital overload could be the phenomenon called Fear of Missing Out (FoMo). Przybylski et al. define FoMo as the constant fear that others might be having rewarding experiences from which one is absent, which makes people stay continually connected with what others are doing [38]. In our study, many participants reportedly went back to their apps even after receiving a warning that they exceeded the time limit allotted for the app, due to the fear of "missing out" on something while not using their phones. Digital overload tools such as ScreenTime are supposed to help reduce users' tendency to overuse apps but our survey revealed that reminders to stop using the app are only causing users to feel left out, making users go right back to the app. Pielot et al. demonstrated that users felt connected with others if they respond quickly to app notifications [36]. Designers might want to use positive reinforcement techniques that help users feel connected with others without being tempted to open an app, in order to help them reduce their screen time.

5.2 Techniques for Behavior Change

Digital overload tools, such as ScreenTime, are designed to help a user make informed decisions about the app usage. ScreenTime allows a user to choose a daily time limit for popular apps, and then warns the user when they exceed the time limit. ScreenTime does not force a user to stop using the app, but merely shows a warning screen, which a user can easily bypass to go back to the app if needed.

Some participants also pointed out how they were unaware of how long they had been using an app during the day; Okeke et al. developed a feedback mechanism that allowed a user to see how long they used the app during the day and how many times they opened the app [34]. This nudging technique also "primes" a user for the warning once they exceed the time limit, and could potentially also reduce the negative emotions a user may experience when suddenly being shown the warning screen [32].

Instead of using a negative reinforcement technique by warning users to stop using apps when they exceed their time limits, digital overload tools could use a positive reinforcement technique such as rewarding a user for not using the app beyond the time limit; one participant said they went back to apps despite warnings because they were not rewarded for quitting the app. Providing users with rewards, such as badges, have been shown to help change their behavior; for example, in mobile health apps, badges encouraged users to adopt a healthy lifestyle [9,39].

Designers can also re frame the warning message to provide a message that encourages the user to stop using the app. For example, the warning message could suggest other activities the user could do, such as take a walk, meditate, or listen to music, instead of going back to the app.

Participants often felt guilty and ashamed for spending a lot of time on popular apps, especially social media, because they believed the time they spent on these apps exceeded social expectations. Digital overload tools can provide actual data on how others use the app; for example, the tools could give feedback based on the average time the users' friends, or people in their town, state or country spent on the app every day. However, as our survey showed, this could make users feel positive or negative depending on whether they spent less or more time on the apps than others.

Participants often enjoyed using their smartphones; in some cases, participants considered smartphones as an escape from their stressful lives. These participants often experienced negative emotions when they saw the digital overload warnings. To prevent users from spiraling into negative emotions, designers can incorporate context-sensing to determine whether a user is already stressed or experiencing some negative emotion and take the outcome of the learning algorithm into account when deciding whether to warn users about digital overload; researchers have used smartphone data such as a user's app usage, call and sms statistics, and location traces to determine a user's mood and mental health state [17,18,30,48].

6   Limitations

We conducted a survey to understand what emotions undergraduate students experience when using digital overload tools. We are aware that survey responses may not reflect the actual emotions participants may feel when using the tool, but given our study was exploratory, our goal was to get a sense of the range of emotions participants may experience when using digital overload tools. In our future studies, we plan to incorporate ecological momentary assessment (EMA) techniques to learn about users' actual emotions when using digital overload tools as well as conduct post-study interviews to better understand the reasons behind the emotions.

In our survey, we did not collect any personal information about the participants such as gender or age because they were not pertinent to our research questions. Other researchers have studied how age and gender affect digital overuse [7,8,33].

Our survey results are specific to the ScreenTime tool. We chose an existing digital overload tool instead of developing a new tool for the study because we did not want the users to experience additional negative emotions due to a steep learning curve.

Finally, it is possible that participants' responses were affected by factors external to the study such as academic or relationship stress.

7 Summary

In this paper, we presented the findings from a survey conducted among undergraduate students to understand the effect of digital overload reminder tools. Our analysis revealed that participants mostly experienced negative emotions such as resentment, shame, and anxiety when the phone warned them that they had exceeded the time allotted for an app and most participants went back to the app despite receiving the warning. However, most participants were happy with their daily app usage and also found that ScreenTime had changed their app usage behavior. We also presented a discussion on why participants may ignore digital overload warnings to continue using apps, and provide design recommendations for nudging techniques to reduce screen time.

Survey Questionnaire

1. Do you use an iPhone every day?
   (a) Yes
   (b) No
2. Are you familiar with the ScreenTime functionality on your phone?
   (a) Yes, I want to continue with the survey.
   (b) No. I wish to quit the survey.
3. Have you set any time limits for apps using ScreenTime?
   (a) Yes
   (b) No
   (c) I do not wish to answer
4. Choose the time limits (in hours) that you set in ScreenTime. Go to Settings−>ScreenTime−>App Limits on your phone to view the time limits you have set.
5. Choose from below, the emotions you feel when you use an app for which you set a time limit

   (a) Happy
   (b) Confident
   (c) Content
   (d) Satisfied
   (e) Glad
   (f) Relieved
   (g) Relaxed
   (h) Bored
   (i) Timid
   (j) Confused
   (k) Insecure
   (l) Anxious
 (m) Worried
   (n) Scared
   (o) Sadness
   (p) Ashamed
   (q) Stressed
   (r) Resentful
   (s) Jealous
   (t) Unsatisfied
   (u) Overwhelmed
   (v) Angry
  (w) I do not wish to answer

6. In one or two sentences, explain why you selected the emotions in the previous question?
7. Choose from below, the emotions you feel when your phone warns you that your time is up? [Same list as 5]
8. In one or two sentences, explain why you selected the emotions in the previous question?
9. Typically, when the time is up, how often do you go back to the app using the snooze option?
   (a) Rarely go back to app
   (b) Sometimes go back to the app
   (c) Often go back to app
   (d) Always go back to app
   (e) I do not wish to answer
10. Choose from below, the emotions you feel when you look at your summary for today [Same list as 5].
11. In one or two sentences, explain why you selected the emotions in the previous question?
12. Have you changed your behavior since you started using ScreenTime?
   (a) Yes
   (b) No
   (c) I do not wish to answer
13. In a few words, explain how your behavior has changed?
14. What additional information do you want about your app usage?

References

1. National College Health Assessment. Technical report, American College Health Association (2017). http://www.acha-ncha.org/docs/NCHA-II_SPRING_2017_REFERENCE_GROUP_EXECUTIVE_SUMMARY.pdf
2. Social Media Use in 2018. Technical report, Pew Research Center (2018)
3. Anshari, M., Almunawar, M.N., Shahrill, M., Wicaksono, D.K., Huda, M.: Smartphones usage in the classrooms: learning aid or interference? Educ. Inf. Technol. **22**, 3063–3079 (2017). https://doi.org/10.1007/s10639-017-9572-7
4. Beaudry, A., Pinsonneault, A.: The other side of acceptance: studying the direct and indirect effects of emotions on information technology use. MIS Q. **34**(4), 689–710 (2010)
5. Chen, L., Yan, Z., Tang, W., Yang, F., Xie, X., He, J.: Mobile phone addiction levels and negative emotions among Chinese young adults: the mediating role of interpersonal problems. Comput. Hum. Behav. **55**, 856–866 (2016)
6. Demirci, K., Akgönül, M., Akpinar, A.: Relationship of smartphone use severity with sleep quality, depression, and anxiety in university students. J. Behav. Addict. **4**, 85–92 (2015)
7. van Deursen, A.J., Bolle, C.L., Hegner, S.M., Kommers, P.A.: Modeling habitual and addictive smartphone behavior: the role of smartphone usage types, emotional intelligence, social stress, self-regulation, age, and gender. Comput. Hum. Behav. **45**, 411–420 (2015)
8. Ding, X., Xu, J., Chen, G., Xu, C.: Beyond smartphone overuse: identifying addictive mobile apps. In: Proceedings of the CHI Conference Extended Abstracts on Human Factors in Computing Systems, pp. 2821–2828. ACM (2016). https://doi.org/10.1145/2851581.2892415
9. Edwards, E.A., et al.: Gamification for health promotion: systematic review of behaviour change techniques in smartphone apps. BMJ Open **6**(10) (2016). https://bmjopen.bmj.com/content/6/10/e012447
10. Faiola, A., Vatani, H., Srinivas, P.: The impact of smartphone use on the psychosocial wellness of college students. In: Alexandrov, D.A., Boukhanovsky, A.V., Chugunov, A.V., Kabanov, Y., Koltsova, O. (eds.) DTGS 2018. CCIS, vol. 859, pp. 264–276. Springer, Cham (2018). https://doi.org/10.1007/978-3-030-02846-6_21
11. Feldman, P.J., Cohen, S., Lepore, S.J., Matthews, K.A., Kamarck, T.W., Marsland, A.L.: Negative emotions and acute physiological responses to stress. Ann. Behav. Med. **21**, 216–222 (1999)
12. Fredrickson, B.L.: Positive emotions broaden and build. In: Advances in Experimental Social Psychology, vol. 47. Academic Press (2013). http://www.sciencedirect.com/science/article/pii/B9780124072367000012
13. Gill, P.S., Kamath, A., Gill, T.S.: Distraction: an assessment of smartphone usage in health care work settings. Risk Manag. Healthc. Policy **5**, 105–114 (2012)
14. Gobl, C., Chasaide, A.N.: The role of voice quality in communicating emotion, mood and attitude. Speech Commun. **40**, 189–212 (2003)
15. Higgins, J.P.: Smartphone applications for patients' health and fitness. Am. J. Med. **129**, 11–19 (2015)
16. Hope, A., Schwaba, T., Piper, A.M.: Understanding digital and material social communications for older adults. In: Proceedings of the SIGCHI Conference on Human Factors in Computing Systems (CHI), pp. 3903–3912. ACM, New York (2014). https://doi.org/10.1145/2556288.2557133

17. Huang, Y., et al.: Assessing social anxiety using GPS trajectories and point-of-interest data. In: International Joint Conference on Pervasive and Ubiquitous Computing (Ubicomp). ACM (2016)
18. Huang, Y., Tang, Y., Wang, Y.: Emotion map: a location-based mobile social system for improving emotion awareness and regulation. In: Conference on Computer Supported Cooperative Work & Social Computing (CSCW). ACM (2015)
19. Izard, C.E.: The many meanings/aspects of emotion: definitions, functions, activation, and regulation. Emot. Rev. **2**, 363–370 (2010)
20. Harwood, J., Dooley, J.J., Scott, A.J., Joiner, R.: Constantly connected-the effects of smart-devices on mental health. Comput. Hum. Behav. **34**, 267–272 (2014)
21. Kim, E., Koh, E.: Avoidant attachment and smartphone addiction in college students: the mediating effects of anxiety and self-esteem. Comput. Hum. Behav. **84**, 264–271 (2018)
22. Ko, M., et al.: Lock n' LoL: mitigating smartphone disturbance in co-located social interactions. In: Proceedings of the 33rd Annual ACM Conference Extended Abstracts on Human Factors in Computing Systems, pp. 1561–1566. ACM (2015). https://doi.org/10.1145/2702613.2732819
23. Kuang-Tsan, C., Fu-Yuan, H.: Study on relationship among university students' life stress, smart mobile phone addiction, and life satisfaction. J. Adult Dev. **24**(2), 109–118 (2017)
24. Lachmann, B., Duke, É., Sariyska, R., Montag, C.: Who's addicted to the smartphone and/or the Internet? Psychol. Pop. Media Cult. **8**, 182–189 (2017)
25. Lanette, S., Chua, P.K., Hayes, G., Mazmanian, M.: How much is "too much"?: the role of a smartphone addiction narrative in individuals' experience of use. In: Human-Computer Interaction, vol. 2 (2018)
26. Lee, H., Ahn, H., Nguyen, T.G., Choi, S.W., Kim, D.J.: Comparing the self-report and measured smartphone usage of college students: a pilot study. Psychiatry Invest. **14**, 198–204 (2017)
27. Lee, U., et al.: Hooked on smartphones: an exploratory study on smartphone overuse among college students. In: Conference on Human Factors in Computing Systems (2014)
28. Leynes, P.A., Flynn, J., Mok, B.A.: Event-related potential measures of smartphone distraction. **21**, 3063–3079 (2018)
29. Macworld: iOS screen time vs. android digital wellbeing: which phone addiction fighter is best for you? (2018). https://www.macworld.com/article/3295880/ios/android-digital-wellbeing-vs-ios-screen-time.html
30. Mehrotra, A., Tsapeli, F., Hendley, R., Musolesi, M.: MyTraces: investigating correlation and causation between users' emotional states and mobile phone interaction. In: Interactive, Mobile, Wearable and Ubiquitous Technologies (2017)
31. Meyers, R.J., Roozen, H.G., Smith, J.E., Evans, B.E.: Feelings about coming for treatment questionnaire. In: PsycTESTS (2014)
32. Mirsch, T., Lehrer, C., Jung, R.: Digital nudging: altering user behavior in digital environments. In: International Conference on Business Informatics (2017)
33. Oberst, U., Wegmann, E., Stodt, B., Brand, M., Chamarro, A.: Negative consequences from heavy social networking in adolescents: the mediating role of fear of missing out. J. Adolesc. **55**, 51–60 (2017)
34. Okeke, F., Sobolev, M., Dell, N., Estrin, D.: Good vibrations: can a digital nudge reduce digital overload? In: International Conference on Human-Computer Interaction with Mobile Devices and Services (MobileHCI) (2018)

35. Ortiz, C., Ortiz-Peregrina, S., Castro, J., Casares-López, M., Salas, C.: Driver distraction by smartphone use (WhatsApp) in different age groups. Accid. Anal. Prev. **117**, 239–249 (2018)
36. Pielot, M., Rello, L.: Productive, anxious, lonely: 24 hours without push notifications. In: MobileHCI (2017)
37. Plutchik, R.: Emotion: A Psychoevolutionary Synthesis. Harper and Row, New York (1980)
38. Przybylski, A.K., Murayama, K., DeHaan, C.R., Gladwell, V.: Motivational, emotional, and behavioral correlates of fear of missing out. Comput. Hum. Behav. **29**, 1841–1848 (2013)
39. Rabbi, M., et al.: Sara: a mobile app to engage users in health data collection. In: Proceedings of the 2017 ACM International Joint Conference on Pervasive and Ubiquitous Computing and Proceedings of the 2017 ACM International Symposium on Wearable Computers (UbiComp), pp. 781–789. ACM (2017). https://doi.org/10.1145/3123024.3125611
40. Rooksby, J., Asadzadeh, P., Rost, M., Morrison, A., Chalmers, M.: Personal tracking of screen time on digital devices. In: Conference on Human Factors in Computing Systems (2016)
41. Scherer, K.R.: What are emotions? And how can they be measured? Soc. Sci. Inf. **44**(4), 693–727 (2005)
42. Siemer, M.: Moods as multiple-object directed and as objectless affective states: an examination of the dispositional theory of moods. Cogn. Emot. **9**, 815–845 (2005)
43. A.H.N.Y. (Times): Is Your Child a Phone 'Addict'? January 2018. https://www.nytimes.com/2018/01/17/well/family/is-your-child-a-phone-addict.html
44. B.C.N.Y. (Times): Is screen time bad for kids' brains? December 2018. https://www.nytimes.com/2018/12/10/health/screen-time-kids-psychology.html
45. Toma, C.L.: Taking the good with the bad: effects of Facebook self-presentation on emotional well-being. In: Handbook of Media Use and Well-Being, pp. 170–182. Taylor & Francis (2014)
46. Wang, D., Xiang, Z., Fesenmaier, D.R.: Smartphone use in everyday life and travel. J. Travel Res. **55**, 52–63 (2014)
47. Wang, J.L., Wang, H.Z., Gaskin, J., Wang, L.H.: The role of stress and motivation in problematic smartphone use among college students. Comput. Hum. Behav. **53**, 181–188 (2015)
48. Wang, R., et al.: StudentLife: assessing mental health, academic performance and behavioral trends of college students using smartphones. In: Conference on Ubiquitous Computing. ACM (2014)
49. Welch, C.: How to use Apple's new screen time and app limits features in iOS 12, September 2018. https://www.theverge.com/2018/9/17/17870126/ios-12-screen-time-app-limits-downtime-features-how-to-use
50. Yen, J.Y., Yen, C.F., Chen, C.S., Wang, P.W., Chang, Y.H., Ko, C.H.: Social anxiety in online and real-life interaction and their associated factors. In: Cyberpsychology, Behavior and Social Networking, vol. 15 (2012)

Design of Digital Coaches for Health and Wellness in the Workplace

Alessandra Rinaldi(✉) and Kiana Kianfar

Innovation in Design and Engineering Lab, Department of Architecture,
University of Florence, Via della Mattonaia 8, 50121 Florence, Italy
{alessandra.rinaldi,kiana.kianfar}@unifi.it

Abstract. Aging of the workforce is a growing problem for many developed and developing countries. In Europe, the current demographic trend is towards an increasingly aged workforce [1]. This happens while, industry appears increasingly dependent on the knowledge of their older workers [2]. For this reason, companies are pushed to explore ways to keep older workers employed for a longer period of time [3].

On the other hand, work is undergoing technological upgrading and innovation driven by digitization, the so called Fourth Industrial Revolution [4]. The technological advancement makes possible to achieve higher levels of work and total factors productivity [5, 6].

In this context, the challenge is how smart technologies, particularly AI innovations and IOT technologies, can meet the needs of a growing number of older adults at workplaces, and how these technologies can be introduced to enable aging-workforce good health, aging labour market participation, and aging-worker security known as active aging in the workplace [7]. (AAiW)

This paper presents the result emerged at IDEE Lab (Innovation in Design & Engineering Lab), of University of Florence, based on the methodological approach of *design sprint* and *design thinking*, through the exploration of the opportunities offered by smart technologies (AI and IoT) for the design of digital coaches and tangible interfaces, aimed at active aging in the workplace, and able to help people stay healthy for longer at work and to promote them smart aging.

Keywords: Workplace 4.0 · Active aging at work · Human-centred design · Artificial intelligence

1 Introduction and Background

Europe is being severely challenged by the ageing of the population. The discussion about the demographic change in Europe's population can be reduced to one simple formula: the number of young people is sharply declining, the number of older people rising. Three basic trends are responsible for this change: i) the continued rise in life expectancy owing to a significant improvement in the health and quality of life of Europeans; ii) the increase in the over 65 age group until 2030 when the children of the "baby boom generation" reach retirement age; iii) a constantly low birth rate owing to numerous factors [8]. The 2002 report from the UN on World Population Ageing 1950-2050 presented an alarming statistic on the aging of the world population, a fact that

© Springer Nature Switzerland AG 2020
M. Kurosu (Ed.): HCII 2020, LNCS 12183, pp. 135–146, 2020.
https://doi.org/10.1007/978-3-030-49065-2_10

would change the cultural, social, political and economic structure of the entire planet, unprecedented in the history of humanity: in 2050, for the first time, the number of elderly people in the world will be greater than the number of young people. In developed countries about 1/5 of the total population was over 60 years old already in 2000 and by 2050 this percentage should become 1/3 [9].

These pronounced demographic changes influence all the social structures and the basic infrastructures of a society. In the last 50 years, many industrialized countries have witnessed a change in the age structure of the population [10]. The International Labour Organization has estimated that by 2025, there will be a 32% increase in the number of people aged over 55 years. In Europe, the current demographic trend is towards an increasingly elderly workforce [1].

1.1 About Ageing at Work

Ageing is a gradual process in which, long-term health problems and chronic diseases increase. Therefore, about 30% of men and women in the age group 50–64 years need urgent adjustments at work due to their health problems to prevent the risks of work disability and early retirement [11]. Musculoskeletal and mental disorders are the major health problems associated with ageing including decline in vision, hearing and psychomotor coordination and are estimated to start as early as the age of 50. Depression is also currently one of the most common reasons for work disability and early retirement. There are wide individual differences in functional capacity and health status at any given age. Although health and physical capacity deteriorate as we get older, we have to mention that several other functions improve with age [11].

Mental growth is the success story of ageing. For example, strategic thinking, considerateness, sharp-wittedness, ability to deliberate, ability to rationalize, wisdom, control of life, language skills and holistic perception improve with age. Older workers are also committed and engaged with their work, loyal towards their employer, and are often responsible for less absenteeism than other age groups. Life management and Work experience improve with age, too. Studies have shown that when measuring the work performance in the workplace, work experience compensates for the decline of some basic cognitive processes such as memory functions and psychomotor skills [11].

Older workers are also an important human resource because with ageing and the increase of work experience, older workers improve their valuable social capital: (i) professional competence, tacit knowledge, cooperation skills grow, (ii) structural awareness about the organization and its functions improve, and (iii) customer contacts and networks expand, and understanding about changes in operational environment improves [11]. Therefore, industry related more and more to the knowledge, skills and experience of older workers [2]. For this reason, many EU governments were led to raise the official retirement age and to restrict the possibilities of early retirement, with the result of a longer working life and greater exposure of workers to hazards and risks [12]. Consequently, companies are exploring ways to keep older workers employed for a longer period of time and to support them in maintaining their work ability and increasing their employability [3].

Old workers are capable of learning new things. Learning is not dependent on age, but the learning process changes with age. Therefore, it is very important that these workers have possibilities to access training and equal opportunities to learn new skills and update their professional skills [11].

All these work world changes require novel solutions so as to help ageing workers maintain workability and productivity, along with a balance between work and personal life, which supports them in finding a good quality of life, active and healthy ageing [3]. In order to mitigate the impact of demographic ageing on society and economy, the concept of active aging has emerged. The WHO (World Health Organization) defines the concept of active aging as "the process of optimizing opportunities for health, participation, and security in order to enhance quality of life as people age. It allows people to realize their potential for physical, social, and mental well-being throughout their life course and to participate in society, while providing them with adequate protection, security and care when they need it" [13]. The concept of active ageing encourages flexible working practices. Workplace ergonomics and job design strongly influence the quality of an employee's work performance. According to Walker (2005) "for those workers that are experiencing physical decline it is possible to modify the workplace in order to assist them to maintain their productivity" [14].

Parallel to these challenges related to the ageing workforce and its effect, work is undergoing technological upgrading and innovation driven by digitization, the so called Fourth Industrial Revolution [4], which has produced an irreversible change in contemporary industrial society. Industry 4.0 technologies have shown considerable potential in augmenting job quality and satisfaction through an improvement in working conditions [15, 16]. The technological advancement makes it possible to achieve a higher quality of work and total factors productivity and to implement the Sustainable Development Goals [5, 6]. Through implementation of occupational safety and health (OSH) practices, companies are capable to meet the challenges posed by an ageing workforce [12]. Progress has been notable: user-centric, responsive, active systems employ state-of-the-art technologies spanning from AI to advanced collaboration tools, visual analytics and big data to make work life easier for workers in the office and factory [3]. These systems, however surprising, are rarely applied in combination [17] and remain remote from OSH and ageing territory [3].

Current research and the applications of smart technologies in the AAiW context, emerging from the scientific literature, are mainly consolidated to identify the measures that enhance the health, participation and security of people in the workplace with the advancement of intelligent technologies [7].

Workability and productivity can be fostered by the enhancement tools and novel services enabled through a series of highly adaptive, personalized ICT technologies with aims for promoting the workers' active and healthy ageing, maintaining their employability and the balance between work and personal life to achieve an overall well-being. AR/VR based context-awareness, AR telepresence and visual analytics are some different domains offered by a wide variety of cutting-edge technologies to support ageing workers in every respect [3]. For example, improving job satisfaction, as far as possible, through reward systems or providing a major collaboration with colleagues, knowledge sharing and optimizing task performance and personal health and lifelong learning through virtual and digital coaching.

In this context, the challenge is discovering how digital and smart technologies, particularly AI innovations, IOT technologies or smart automation, can meet the needs, desires and aspirations of a growing number of older adults at workplaces, how these technologies can be introduced to ensure the ageing-workforce good health, labor market participation, and ageing-worker security known as active ageing in the workplace [7] (AAiW). This research project focused on how design can play a fundamental role in bringing these technologies to a final form that can be felt and perceived by users.

The solutions found are tangible interfaces, which mean user interfaces that allow easy and friendly interaction with digital information through physical products.

2 Methodological Approach

The research is based on the design and innovation methodology of *sprint design* and *design thinking*, for building and testing the prototypes of IDEE Lab (Innovation in Design & Engineering Lab). This methodology has been used to explore the opportunities offered by smart technologies (AI and IoT) for the design of digital coaches and tangible interfaces aimed at active ageing in the workplace, and able to help people stay healthy for longer at work and to promote smart ageing. As already mentioned in the previous part, based on the WHO framework, *active ageing* is built on three pillars: *participation, health, and security* [13]. In this research we focused on health and well-being (physical and mental) at work as an important research area for promoting active ageing in the workplace, enabled by the new generation of ever attentive personalized systems called *virtual coaches* [18] and *tangible interface*. Virtual coaches can be understood as computer systems capable of sensing relevant context, determining user intent and providing useful feedback with the aim of improving certain aspects of the user's life [19].

The project development process according to the *sprint design* approach, entailed a workshop during which different design teams were created, involving about 40 designers (5 teams of 8 people each). The design teams addressed these topics:

1) imagine a tangible interface for a *virtual coach* in a working environment;
2) choose the kind of services that the *virtual coach* provides to users:
   - Supporting employees' healthy lifestyle;
   - Enhancing teamwork and teambuilding;
   - Promoting company culture;
   - Guiding and counseling employees for their careers;
   - Boosting creativity;
   - Supporting sustainable behaviors;
3) imagine the physical embodiment of the *virtual coach* and how users can interact with it.

For the *idea generation phase*, the How Might We (HMW) method were used, that represent an essential design sprint methodology, to capture opportunities during lightning talks and throughout the *understand phase*.

This method allowed the teams to take the ideas, to mark the points that emerged and to positively reformulate them. HMWs in fact created an active framework for resolving the challenges. Then, HMW sharing, affinity diagram, HMW voting tools were used to share all the research questions and to categorize them into themes.

In this way we have had a systematic view of all the ideas, and we could manage to have a better look at the various opportunities and to prioritize identified opportunity areas for our users and focus on the best ideas. After that, by using *crazy 8's*, that is a core *design sprint* method, each team tried to sketch some fast design solutions. The goal was to push beyond the first idea, frequently the least innovative, and to generate a wide variety of solutions to our challenge. The same process of sharing and voting was utilized to identify the best sketch and we expanded it through the *solution sketch* method. In this way each team spent more time articulating one idea they were most interested in. For the development of the specified concept as the final step, *storyboard* and *paper prototype* tools were adopted. The storyboard method brought each design sprint team together on their own prototype concept and helped the team to make critical decisions during the prototyping process (Fig. 1).

Fig. 1. Workshop conducted by IDEE Lab and one of paper prototype developed.

2.1 Concepts and Ideas Developed During the Workshop

During the research process conducted by the IDEE Lab team, with the participation of 40 designers, new ideas were generated. The main ideas can be divided into the following macro-categories:

Macro categories	Micro categories	Description
Virtual Assistant	Smart Wearable Device	Wearable devices have a huge potential to be integrated in the office environments in terms of health and productivity. Such idea consists i.e. in designing earphones equipped with a voice recognition system that can receive and process the information and create a vocal output. This type of device can be developed more by adopting the sensors which can measure the stress and strain caused by heavy work and communicate them to the worker
Virtual Assistant	Smart Portable Device	This idea includes a series of small devices (pocket-size) that aim to improve the user's health and working status, through the involvement of the 5 (mainly tactile and visual) senses, leaving a positive feedback that encourages socialization and collaboration between colleagues in the office environment. Each device is basically connected with an App
Productivity Enhancement Tool	Intelligent Office Worktop Interactive Screen	Office desks seem inseparable furniture from the office environments. Those can be completed with interactive touch screens, and have a variety of functions for the workplace, such as: - Interactive meeting desk for video calls; - Interactive desk for files transfer, highlighting issues, digital notes, wireless charging; - Interactive desk equipped with a weight relief system which can offer a set of services: relieve the weight of the water bottle by reminding you to drink
Personalized System	Personalized Workplace	This concept addresses motivating the office worker during the long hours at work and personalizing the work environment. The idea consists on an App connected to a video projector with which the workplace can be customized by the user, screening the different videos, images and textures
Reward System	Smart office furniture	The objective of this idea is to improve efficiency and employee satisfaction, through the design of a tangible interface. Connecting to the concept of business growth, a tree structure is imagined, located inside the company headquarters, associated with AR. When a corporate goal is achieved by the employees, the leaf relating to this result is fixed on the tree, and can be visualized in AR, to improve visual satisfaction

3   Final Results

The final idea developed by IDEE Lab team consists of the design of a product-service system aimed at increasing social connection and sense of belonging between distant collaborators, and to enhance teamwork and teambuilding. By creating an abstract visualization of colleagues and the ability to communicate visually and verbally with them, as if they were in the same room, a higher level of productivity, creativity and personal motivation of each member can be achieved.

The device includes a physical pocket-size product connected to an APP by adopting IoT and AI technologies.

The project focuses on two main challenges in the office environments: i) how productivity can be increased, ii) how motivation can be maintained.

Productivity is the unit of measurement of efficiency in the work process. Efficiency is understood as a reference to a level of performance that requires the minimum amount of input to generate the greatest amount of output.

Regarding productivity aspects, some important factors to be integrated in the project have been identified, such as improving work processes and working wellbeing.

3.1   Improving Work Processes

Personal and team productivity depends heavily on the organization and planning of tasks. Starting the day or an entire project without a detailed plan and an adequate organization will cause tension, confusion, delays and, almost certainly, failures. Time management must be considered first for organization and planning. There are some instruments that serve to plan the project, to facilitate the decision-making process and to reduce both time and costs necessary to complete a project, such as: the Gantt chart and the Pert diagram. The product-service includes an APP, which allows you to insert the tasks and the time available for each of them, based on the Gantt chart. All the members directly or indirectly involved in the project can have an overview of the scheduled tasks and are informed of their deadline (Fig. 2).

In this way, the task's progress can be visualized in every work phase, and this has the following advantages:

- Clarity: giving a clear overview of different activities and timeline in a one simple panorama.
- Communication: by updating the project progress status, it becomes more intuitive and commutative for the members.
- Motivation: with a clear overview, team members can better understand their overall performance and are able to incorporate their work habits into the project planning. They will have a better awareness of the dependencies between tasks and of the impact of delays on the project. This promotes closer collaboration and encourages better organization of tasks.
- Time management: by setting realistic times, it is easy to understand within which time interval a particular task should be completed. In this way, you can ensure that other projects that consume resources and time are not compromised.

- Flexibility: projects are often subject to change. Having an overview of unexpected changes in activity or timing, activities and resources can be adopted accordingly.

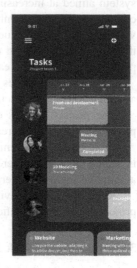

Fig. 2. Mobile application with possibility to insert the tasks and create Gantt chart. Design by Francesco Colucci, IDEE Lab team member.

3.2   Improving Work Wellbeing

As already mentioned before, physical and mental well-being has a crucial effect on the office-worker performance and achievement of personal and business objectives, and also on their health. That's because a right balance between work and personal life is so important. Thanks to the generation of new technologies, different aspects relative to health can be measured and communicated to users. Drinking enough water for correct hydration, and having regular breaks are two main health needs that have been addressed in the project.

Workers who use video terminals and display screen equipment are entitled to a break of 15 min every two hours of continuous work. It is sufficient that the employee stops working in front of a display for that time frame. Waiting for the response from the electronic system is not considered as a break. This APP is able to calculate the time necessary to have a break and to drink water during working hours, reminding the user through notifications (visual and sound feedback) (Fig. 3).

Fig. 3. The notifications keep the user aware of his health state and remind him to take a break and drink water.

3.3   Increasing Motivation

Motivation is a key concept in today work world, characterized essentially by the competitiveness and flexibility of employees and collaborators. Often, determination and motivation make the difference in the success or failure of a project. In addition, to keep the team motivated, special techniques and attention to the following aspects are required:

- Objectives: transfer strategies and translate objectives as general vision and as personal input;
- Personal relationships: connect people, facilitate acquisition and exchange of useful strategies and knowledge, pursuit of a peaceful atmosphere in the team;
- Motivations: work on unintended emotional components to encourage teamwork and virtuous behavior;
- Emotions: keep the emotional level high in the team, especially in times of high pressure, when the achievement of the goals seems really distant; it is necessary to keep the passion high in one's own and in the work of others;
- Awareness: strengthen individual skills and identify strengths and weaknesses to make work more efficient and effective.

In order to keep office workers motivated and to provide them with a sense of belonging, the project also includes a device, as a tangible interface. The product is connected to the mobile application. Each user is assigned a color at the time of registration on the APP and during any conversation by the device everyone is recognized by their color. The user can communicate with the team visually and vocally though the device (Fig. 4).

Fig. 4. The device provides the belonging sense to the work team through a tangible interface which create a colorful avatar for each member of the group and keep them participate during the work hour. Design by Francesco Colucci.

4   Discussion and Conclusions

The adoption of different digital tools and cutting-edge technologies has introduced the new office-work paradigms to ensure satisfactory conditions in work environments, from productivity conditions to a state of physical and mental wellbeing, from personal motivation to sustainable attitudes. All these factors influence healthy and active ageing at work. Supporting the office worker's healthy and friendly ageing in all respects is an added value for the company and society, with consideration of the importance of elderly workers in terms of know-how and experience. Tangible interfaces introduce a new concept in the office, such as educational, social and communicative aspects by involving the human senses rather than just a PC screen or a Smartphone. The social and communicative aspects provide incentives toward high motivation and a sense of belonging for office worker, by keeping them interacting and participating actively with the context and by creating connections with others, with attitudes of collaboration, individual receptivity and shared responsibilities.

References

1. European Commission - Directorate-General for Economic and Financial Affairs: The 2015 Ageing Report. Underlying Assumptions and Projection Methodologies. European Economy 8-2014 (2014). http://ec.europa.eu/economy_finance/publications/european_economy/2014/pdf/ee8_en.pdf. Accessed 10 Feb2020/02/10
2. Schinner, M., Calero Valdez, A., Noll, E., Schaar, A.K., Letmathe, P., Ziefle, M.: 'Industrie 4.0' and an aging workforce – a discussion from a psychological and a managerial perspective. In: Zhou, J., Salvendy, G. (eds.) ITAP 2017. LNCS, vol. 10298, pp. 537–556. Springer, Cham (2017). https://doi.org/10.1007/978-3-319-58536-9_43
3. Giakoumis, D., Votis, K., Altsitsiadis, E., Segkouli, S., Paliokas, I., Tzovaras, D.: Smart, personalized and adaptive ICT solutions for active, healthy and productive ageing with enhanced workability. In: Proceedings of the 12th ACM International Conference on PErvasive Technologies Related to Assistive Environments, pp. 442–447. ACM (2019)
4. Schwab, K.: The fourth industrial revolution. In: World Economic Forum, Geneva, Switzerland (2016)
5. Horne, R., Khatiwada, S., Kuhn, S., Milasi, S.: World employment and social outlook: trends 2016, World employment social outlook, ILO, Geneva (2016). https://www.ilo.org/wcmsp5/groups/public/—dgreports/—dcomm/—publ/documents/publication/wcms_443480.pdf. Accessed 10 Feb 2020
6. Dodds, F., Donoghue, A.D., Roesch, J.L.: Negotiating the Sustainable Development Goals: A Transformational Agenda for An Insecure World, 1st edn. Routledge, Abingdon (2017)
7. Yang, Q., Shen, Z.: Active aging in the workplace and the role of intelligent technologies. In: Proceedings of the 2015 IEEE/WIC/ACM International Conference on Web Intelligence and Intelligent Agent Technology (WI-IAT), vol. 01, pp. 391–394. IEEE Computer Society (2015)
8. Morschhäuser, M., Sochert, R.: Healthy Work in an Ageing Europe. Federal Association of Company Insurance Funds, Essen (2006)
9. United Nations, Dept of Economic and Social Affairs. Population Division. World Population Ageing, pp. 1950–2050, Edizione 207. UN (2002)
10. Granville, G., Evandrou, M.: Older men, work and health. Occup. Med. **60**(3), 178–183 (2010)
11. Ilmarinen, J.: Promoting active ageing in the workplace. Safety and health at work (2012). EU-OSHA. https://osha.europa.eu/en/publications/articles/promoting-active-ageing-in-the-workplace/view. Accessed 10 Feb 2020
12. EU-OSHA: Healthy workplaces for all ages: promoting a sustainable working life (2016). https://osha.europa.eu/en/publications/healthy-workplaces-good-practice-awards-2016-2017-0/view. Accessed 10 Feb 2020
13. World Health Organization: Active ageing: a policy framework (No. WHO/NMH/NPH/02.8). WHO Press, Geneva, Switzerland (2002)
14. Walker, A.: The emergence of age management in Europe. Int. J. Organ. Behav. **10**(1), 685–697 (2005)
15. Lithoxoidou, E.E., et al.: Improvement of the workers' satisfaction and collaborative spirit through gamification. In: Kompatsiaris, I., et al. (eds.) INSCI 2017. LNCS, vol. 10673, pp. 184–191. Springer, Cham (2017). https://doi.org/10.1007/978-3-319-70284-1_15
16. Arena, D., et al.: Towards a semantically-enriched framework for human resource management. In: Lödding, H., Riedel, R., Thoben, K.-D., von Cieminski, G., Kiritsis, D. (eds.) APMS 2017. IAICT, vol. 513, pp. 306–313. Springer, Cham (2017). https://doi.org/10.1007/978-3-319-66923-6_36

17. van den Broek, E.L.: Monitoring technology: The 21st century pursuit of well-being? EU-OSHA, Discussion paper (2017)
18. Siewiorek, D., Smailagic, A., Dey, A.: Architecture and applications of virtual coaches. In: Proceedings of the IEEE, vol. 100, no. 8, pp. 2472–2488. IEEE (2012)
19. French, B., Tyamagundlu, D., Siewiorek, D.P., Smailagic, A., Ding, D.: Towards a virtual coach for manual wheelchair users. In: 2008 12th IEEE International Symposium on Wearable Computers, pp. 77–80. IEEE (2008)

The Influences of Media Naturalness and Mental Model Alignment on Reducing Patient Uncertainty in Virtual Consultation

Yuxi Vania Shi[✉], Sherrie Komiak[✉], and Paul Komiak[✉]

Memorial University of Newfoundland, St. John's, NL, Canada
{ys8378, skomiak, pkomiak}@mun.ca

Abstract. Virtual consultation (VC) can be simply referred to as a telemedicine service that enables patients to access doctors remotely. Many patients still have uncertainties regarding the consultation process and results, which mostly concern communication with doctors. This motivated us to explore the answers to the following question: How do media naturalness and mental model alignment influence patients' uncertainties in virtual consultation and how do these uncertainties affect patient satisfaction towards the consultation?

A two (naturalness: low vs. high) by two (mental model alignment: low vs. high) field experiment was conducted to answer this question. For each group, participants were asked to answer corresponding questions regarding their uncertainties and their satisfaction towards the consultation. 327 valid questionnaire was obtained at the end.

The results show that during patient-doctor communication, more natural the VC system is, the less uncertainties patients will have during their communication with doctors. Meanwhile, higher level of mental model alignment the VC system has, the less uncertainties patients will have during the communication. The results suggest that healthcare providers should select systems which are more natural to patients, and design them to align with patients' mental models of visiting doctors to reduce patients' uncertainties. The results also show that higher level of uncertainty leads to lower level of patient satisfaction towards the consultation.

The findings of this study will redound to the benefit of academic society in virtual consultation considering that naturalness and mental model alignment play important roles in reducing patients' uncertainties during their communication to doctors.

Keywords: Virtual consultation · Uncertainty · Healthcare · Naturalness · Mental model · Patient satisfaction

1 Background

It is widely accepted that virtual consultation (VC) has many benefits in delivering healthcare compared to face-to-face (FTF) doctor's visits. Traditionally, the patient may make a phone call to book an appointment, then the doctor or specialist discusses the patient's medical problem in person and begins the process of a treatment plan. The

© Springer Nature Switzerland AG 2020
M. Kurosu (Ed.): HCII 2020, LNCS 12183, pp. 147–164, 2020.
https://doi.org/10.1007/978-3-030-49065-2_11

entire consultation process is face-to-face communication. This scenario is looking more and more obsolete, making the traditional doctor visit yet another procedure transformed by the age of online healthcare (Rosenzweig and Baum 2013). The rapid proliferation of VCs is challenging the norm, with the benefits of eliminating the need for patients to leave the comfort of their office or home, accessibility of the same quality healthcare services in large cities and rural areas, and reduced charges for both patients and caregivers. Some researchers attested that up to 70% of all patients who seek care do not even need face-to-face interaction (Palen et al. 2012).

VC benefits patients in many formats. One of the best-known and freely available internet video applications to conduct VC is Skype. Previous reviews of the clinical uses of Skype provided evidence to support it clinically (Armfield et al. 2015; Armfield et al. 2012). Armfield et al. (2015) reviewed twenty-seven articles and concluded that Skype was reported to be feasible and beneficial (Armfield et al. 2015), especially in the management of chronic diseases such as cardiovascular diseases and diabetes. Their results showed that Skype allowed excellent communication between individuals and health professionals and was mostly used in developed countries. While not many studies considered the economic effects associated with using Skype and similar free or inexpensive tools to do VC, those that agreed that Skype was more economical than face-to-face appointments with savings from avoided travel and waiting (Armfield et al. 2015; Daniel et al. 2012; Travers and Murphy 2014).

The feasibility of clinical use of these tools, including Skype, telephone, message, and others, motives the development of various VC systems. One popular commercial type is systems that enable patients to select certified doctors from a list of options, regardless of whether they are familiar with the doctors, to do VCs online (Greenhalgh et al. 2016; Tejera Segura and Bustabad 2016; Zilliacus et al. 2010). With these systems, patients can access professional healthcare anytime and anywhere, without the risk of getting infected by other patients in the hospital (Ellenby and Marcin 2015; Greenhalgh et al. 2016; Klaassen et al. 2016).

Besides the benefits of VC for patients, other parties, including physicians, nurses, and healthcare institutes, also receive massive conveniences and benefits. VC improves the efficiency of physicians, and largely reduces the rate of no-show appointments (Hanna et al. 2012). VC can complement nursing in cost-effective ways and increase the intimacy between patients and nurses (Reed 2005; Stern 2017). It can also benefit hospitals and other healthcare providers with more accessible doctor-physicians-specialists-hospitals connections. For example, Patterson and Wootton (2013) carried out a questionnaire survey of referrers and specialists over a six-month period and found that the patient management and diagnosis efficiency improved due to the use of telemedicine technology (Patterson and Wootton 2013).

Despite its undeniable potential, fears have been expressed about VC that it may be clinically risky and less acceptable to patients or staff, and it brings significant technical, logistical, and regulatory challenges (Greenhalgh et al. 2016). Also, the influence of VC varies greatly depending on where and how the technology is applied (Porter and Lee 2015). Thus, there are many challenges to the adoption of VC and make full use of VC.

There is currently little theoretical guidance to address the emerging challenges of VC. Although how to boost patients' attitudes has been studied extensively in VC area, traditional approaches to studying VC solely focused on outcomes and were from a positive perspective (Alrubaiee and Alkaa'ida 2011; Lazar et al. 2013; Meesala et al. 2017). In these traditional healthcare research, it is considered important to connect patient satisfaction with VC benefits and advantages. This becomes problematic as the patients' negative feelings play a comparably important role to form their perceptions on the consultation experience, despite all the benefits of VC. In virtual consultation, patients communicate with doctors through VC systems which has different level of naturalness according to media natural theory (Kock 2009, 2010). These systems were designed to align differently to patients' mental models of visiting doctors according to mental model theory (Payne 2003; Scott 2018; Van Der Henst 2000). While VC systems with different levels of naturalness and mental model alignment were found to influence patients' uncertainties (Stefan Timmermans et al. 2018), few literature studied how. This paper fills above gaps by answering the following research question: How do media naturalness and mental model alignment influence patients' uncertainties in virtual consultation and how do these uncertainties affect patient satisfaction towards the consultation?

2 Literature Review

2.1 Media Selection and Content in Patient-Doctor Communication in Virtual Consultation

Numerous studies have explored the complex effects and contradictory roles of the Web in altering healthcare delivery and the physician-patient relationship (Wald et al. 2007). Instead of direct communication between patients and doctors in a traditional face-to-face consultation, VC involves media during patient-doctor computer mediated communication (CMC). Trevino et al. (1987) proposed that various media differ in their ability to accurately convey information cues (Trevino et al. 1987) and to provide communication functions (Huang et al. 2016). Daft et al. (1987) suggested that correct media selection is expected to be related to communication effectiveness, and hence to communicators' performances (Daft et al. 1987). Also, mass communication theorists have included orientation to the environment or uncertainty reduction as an important function played by the media (Berger 1986; Katz et al. 1974).

Media selection has long been studied in different areas for different purposes. For example, Kuang et al. (2017) conducted an experiment to study strategies to select social media for more effective promotion (Kuang et al. 2017). Lapointe (2018) studied the impact of media selection for better design of ballasted flocculation processes (a technology consisting of injecting ballast medium to increase floc specific gravity and size in the water industry) (Lapointe and Barbeau 2018). Liu and Chang (2016) examined the role of media involvement in game addiction (Liu and Chang 2016). Some research focused on the factors that influence people's media selection instead of the opposite. For example, Ambrose et al. (2008) explored factors on the choice of communication media and concluded that media selection is affected by the communication needs of the participants, the stage of relationship development, and the purchasing context (Ambrose et al. 2008). Though media selection is not new in the information system area, little research on media selection has been done on patient-doctor communication (Mao 2015).

2.2 Uncertainty

Unlike other negative aspects in VC, uncertainty is an critical factor that can affect communication results (Antheunis et al. 2012; Duronto et al. 2005). Since the scope of this paper is restrained to patient-doctor communication, it is naturally to focus on patient uncertainty instead of other similar concepts to investigate how to improve patient-doctor communication results. Uncertainty refers to "an interactant's subjective sense of the number of alternative predictions available when thinking about a partner's future Behaviour, or the number of alternative explanations available when thinking about a partner's past Behaviour" (Bradac 2001). There are two types of uncertainty, including cognitive uncertainty and Behavioural uncertainty (Berger and Bradac 1982). Cognitive uncertainty refers to the level of uncertainty associated with the beliefs and attitudes of each other in the communication, while Behavioural uncertainty refers to the extent to which Behaviour is predictable in a given situation (Berger 1986; Berger and Bradac 1982). Research has shown that managing uncertainty is a central process that affects our communication with people, especially strangers (Duronto et al. 2005).

In healthcare, uncertainty is everywhere in clinical practice (Danczak and Lea 2017). Diagnosis, referral, arranging treatment and teamwork difficulties may all give rise to troubling uncertainties for doctors (Danczak and Lea, 2017). Clinical uncertainty can give patients stress, and mis- or over-use of medicines (Srivastava 2011). Many studies have been done to reduce doctors' uncertainty during diagnosis. For example, Andre et al. (2016) interviewed 25 general practitioners to describe strategies of coping with uncertainty in patients (Andre et al. 2016). Their results showed that the use of guidelines as well as the use of more patient-centered tests associate to reduce uncertainty. Patient-centered care is the newest trend in medicine (Srivastava 2011). It is suggested that adhering to patients can reduce either diagnosis uncertainty for doctors or patients' stress and prognosis uncertainty (Schapira 2014; Stieglitz and Dang-Xuan 2013).

In the traditional face-to-face consultation, patients have feelings of uncertainty, anxiety, depression, and other psychological difficulties because of patients' limited understanding of medical problems and treatment (Ong et al. 1995). In the context of VC, patients can be uncertain about many things both on doctors and systems (Panlaqui et al. 2017). These uncertainties could stem from feelings of lacking information as traditional consultation, or from the selected communication media (Timmermans et al. 2018). These uncertainties can affect their cognitions, feelings, as well as decision makings (Schapira 2014). Communicating uncertainty is the first and critical step in helping patients to manage uncertainty about the consultation quality in order to make a good quality decision (Politi and Street 2011). Good patient-doctor CMC should give patients confidence that their doctor is an advocate who will not abandon them in order to reduce their uncertainty (Srivastava 2011). In the face of uncertainties, healthcare organizations must be reprogrammed and renewed, repositioning themselves for the future (Cheng Lim and Tang 2000). Therefore, understanding patients' uncertainties during communication with doctors would allow healthcare organizations to receive guidance to improve system design.

2.3 Patient Satisfaction

According to O'Connor et al., "It's the patient's perspective that increasingly is being viewed as a meaningful indicator of health services quality and may, in fact, represent the most important perspective" (Andaleeb 2001). Patient satisfaction is considered as one of the most important quality dimensions and key success indicators in healthcare (Pakdil and Harwood 2005). Oliver (2014) defined satisfaction as "the consumer's fulfillment response", a post-consumption judgment by the consumer that a service provides a pleasing level of consumption-related fulfillment, including under- or over-fulfillment (Alrubaiee and Alkaa'ida 2011; Oliver 2014). Zineldin (2006) defined satisfaction as an emotional response (Alrubaiee and Alkaa'ida 2011; Zineldin 2006).

A comprehensive and critical review of the patient satisfaction literature was first done by Ware et al. (1978). The conclusion revealed empirical studies of patient satisfaction dealt with many items which could be grouped into constructs which were implicitly intended to measure (Ware 1978; Ware et al. 2017). Linder-Pelz (1982) argued that while the result was informing us of the multidimensionality of the phenomenon, it still did not tell what is the nature of the phenomenon to begin with (Linder-Pelz 1982), and this issue had never been confronted concerning patient satisfaction (Linder-Pelz 1982). Patients make judgments about the care they received from healthcare providers. Their judgments are based largely on their perceptions of how care is administered (Pakdil and Harwood 2005). That is, patient satisfaction is created through a combination of responsiveness to the patient's views and needs, and continuous improvement of the healthcare services, as well as continuous improvement of the overall doctor-patient relationship (Zineldin 2006).

Determining the factors associated with patient satisfaction is an important topic for people to understand what is valued by patients, how the quality of care is perceived by patients, and to know where, when and how service change and improvement can be made (Mair and Whitten 2000; Williams et al. 1998; Zineldin 2006). Much research has been done on the impact of characteristics of doctors and systems on patient satisfaction in the healthcare area. Studies have investigated how far the doctor's level of information provision, information seeking, and communication skills during consultations are related to patient satisfaction (Agha et al. 2009). This paper suggested an impact of patient-centered uncertainty on patient satisfaction in the context of VC.

3   Theoretical Foundation

3.1   Media Naturalness Theory

Media naturalness is an important concept to explain the differences between computer-mediated and face-to-face communication (Blau and Caspi 2010). The degree of naturalness of a medium can be assessed based on the degree to which it incorporates five key elements of face-to-face communication: a) collocation, which would allow individuals engaged in a communication interaction to share the same context, as well as see and hear each other; b) synchronicity, which would allow the individuals to quickly exchange communicative stimuli; c) the ability to convey and observe facial expressions; d) the ability to convey and observe body language; and e) the ability to convey and listen to speech (Kock 2005). According to Kock (2002, 2005), the naturalness of the communication medium created by an e-communication technology can be defined as the degree to which the technology selectively incorporates (or suppresses) those five elements. That is, other things being equal, the degree of incorporation of one of the media naturalness elements correlates with the degree of naturalness of an e-communication medium (Kock 2002).

Ned Kock (2002) developed the media naturalness hypothesis to answer the question: What happens when we selectively suppress face-to-face communication elements (e.g., colocation,) through e-communication technologies? The hypothesis argued that, other things being equal, a decrease in the degree of naturalness of a communication medium (or its degree of similarity to the face-to-face medium) leads to the following effects in connection with a communication interaction: (1) increased cognitive effort, (2) increased communication ambiguity, and (3) decreased physiological arousal.

3.2   Mental Model Theory

Humans are able to reason by manipulating symbolic representations and translating them back into actions or nothing correspondence between the external events and their internal representations (Staggers and Norcio 1993). That is, the image of the world around us, which we carry in our head, is just a model. Nobody in his/her head images all the world, government or country. Humans have only selected concepts, and relationships between them, and use those to represent the real system (Forrester 1971). In short, a mental model is an explanation of someone's thought process about how something works in the real world. Craik defined the term model as: "any physical or chemical system which has a similar relation-structure to that of the process it imitates" (Craik 1967). The notion of mental model has been used to study humans' reasoning and learning process (Chiou and Anderson 2010; Johnson-Laird 1989; Payne 2003; Van Der Henst 2000; Yang et al. 2016)

Numerous studies have shown that deep comprehension of discourse involves the construction and manipulation of mental representations that reproduce the state of affairs described (Cutica and Bucciarelli 2011; Zwaan et al. 1995). The listener builds such representations based on the semantic and pragmatic information contained in the text, together with his or her prior knowledge and any inferences that are drawn. Depending on the different theoretical frameworks within which this phenomenon has been studied, these mental representations are called mental models (Johnson-Laird 2006; Johnson-Laird 1989). A mental model is a mental representation that analogically reproduces a perceived or described state of affairs; it consists of elements, which stand for the perceived or described entities, and relationships between such elements, which stand for relationships between the entities (Cutica and Bucciarelli 2011). Several authors have demonstrated that the more a listener is able to make links and place the information that is received within an integrated network, the higher his/her level of comprehension (Cutica and Bucciarelli 2011).

Mental models are small-scale models that the individual believes is analogous to how the world works (Craik 1967). Beyond this general definition, more detailed theory on mental models varies between authors (Jones et al. 2011; Scott 2018). Also, mental models are periodically used to describe the entire range of mental representations and cognitive processes (Scott 2018), or a smaller subset of these processes (Doyle and Ford 1998). They are considered by some authors to be temporary structures that reside in the working-memory (Johnson-Laird 1989; Wilson and Rutherford 1989).

There is no way to study mental models directly (Gentner and Stevens 1983). Mental models cannot be elicited without distortion (Doyle et al. 2008; Gentner and Stevens 1983). Scott (2018) conducted a study to investigate the measurement of a mental model. The study relied on an inference that enduring changes in decision preferences are indicative of changes to deeper and more stable cognitive structures, such as mental models (Kuhneman and Tversky 1984). Scott (2018) concluded that there were two significant considerations to the study: separating measurement of mental models from the measurement of their change, and measuring change rather than perceived change (Scott 2018).

Therefore, this study does not attempt to elicit mental models, but rather to investigate their alignment with the existing models in patients' minds. Research has shown that both mental model alignment and transfer influence a range of related outcomes, such as immersion (Biocca 2006), flow (Sherry 2004), and learning (Martinez-Garza and Clark 2017) in the context of game playing (McGloin et al. 2018).

4 Research Framework and Hypothesis

4.1 Research Model

The URT theory suggests three strategies (passive, active and interactive) to reduce uncertainty during the three phases (entry, personal and exit) (Berger and Calabrese 1975). Focusing on patient-doctor communication process which mostly belongs to the personal phase, this paper aims to investigate interactive factors that can reduce patients' uncertainties about VC. The interactive strategy requires the VC system to provide a friendly and natural environment for patients to communicate with doctors. Therefore, it is important to select appropriate communication media and media design. Media selection and content play important roles in patient-doctor communication (George et al. 2013). Different media have different level of naturalness which affects communication efficiency and effectiveness (Kock 2010). Different design of media has different level of mental model alignment which affects patients' attitudes and concerns (Yang et al. 2016). In this study, we use media naturalness and mental model alignment as our independent variables, which influence patient satisfaction through uncertainty in the context of virtual consultation.

Naturalness is one of the independent variables. Patients can select different types of media to communicate remotely with doctors, including telephone, email, text, video and other platforms. According to media naturalness theory, these different forms of media have different levels of naturalness compared to face-to-face encounters, which enable people to use the media to deliver assorted quantities and different types of information to the receiving party. Humans evolved to be more comfortable communicating in a natural way (Kock 2004). It is reasonable to propose that patients have more confidence during communication through mediums which provide them with a more natural way to communicate with doctors.

Mental model alignment is another independent variable. Patients rely on the content of media to get information, evaluate situations and form mental models, which makes the media design very important when it comes to reducing patient's uncertainty. According to the mental model theory (Legrenzi et al. 1999; Van Der Henst 2000), people rely on the models in their mind to perform reasoning and decision-making tasks. During the patient-doctor communication process, patients are more likely to believe/decide it is true when the situation matches or aligns with the pre-conceived mental models in their minds. That is, patients will be more confident about the situation, therefore reducing the uncertainty level.

When patients are uncertain about the doctor, they are not able to communicate with confidence and coherence. Patients' level of satisfaction may decrease if they cannot communicate well with their doctors. They will not get the best communication results, which influences patient satisfaction. Therefore, we propose that there is a path from uncertainty to patient satisfaction. The research model is present in Fig. 1, as follows.

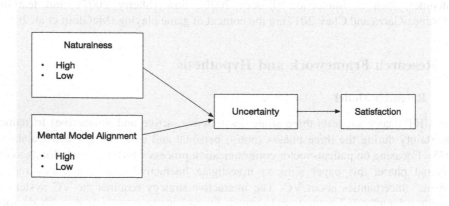

Fig. 1. Research model to reduce uncertainty during patient-doctor communication in VC

4.2 Hypothesis

Selected media enables patients to communicate with doctors in different formats. The more natural the communication is, the more certain patients feel about both doctors and the media/system. That is, different media may have a different impact on uncertainty level during patient-doctor CMC, due to various levels of naturalness. Therefore, it is proposed in this study that media naturalness can influence patients' uncertainty about doctors and systems during patient-doctor CMC. The more natural the system is, the more certain patients feel about doctors and the system, and more positive on the communication results with the doctors. For example, in instant messaging, people communicate without seeing one another. Conversely, video conferencing gives patients opportunities to see the doctor whom they may not be familiar with and sometimes enables doctors to see and hear the symptoms. From a media naturalness point of view, video conferencing offers multiple channels to deliver verbal and non-verbal information, and it is more natural than instant messaging. Patients who consult doctors through video conferencing feel that the interaction is more natural and closer to traditional FTF consultation than instant messaging. Therefore, during patient-doctor CMC, video conferencing is proposed to give patients more certainty and more positive attitudes towards the consultation, while instant messaging fails to be perceived as natural by patients. Therefore, the hypothesis is as follows:

H1: Increased media naturalness will reduce uncertainty during patient-doctor CMC.

One important assumption in this study is that people have certain mental models formed about visiting a doctor in their minds, either based on traditional consultation experiences or their imagination or expectations, before taking part in VC. If system design aligns with the mental model patients already have, they tend to believe that the situations are reliable and represent the real world, according to mental model theory. In this situation, patients are more certain and confident about the communication process and results. Therefore, patients have a lower level of uncertainty, in comparison to the situations when the design does not align with their mental models.

The misalignment between system design and patients' pre-conceived mental model could lead to misunderstanding and confusion during patient-doctor communication, which affects patients' description of symptoms and doctors' diagnosis. Patients are not sure how to deal with this situation as they cannot retrieve relevant information from existing mental models. So, they predict negative results, as people tend to make negative assumptions about situations that are unfamiliar (Scare 1983). Contrarily, they are more confident about familiar situations in which their predictions are accurate, based on their previous experience.

Certain aspects of communication can vary widely among different doctors or patients (Verlinde et al. et al. 2012). There are roughly two different types of VC systems in Canada, regarding the "ownership" of doctors. While many VC systems have certified doctors provided for patients to select (one example is https://www.getmaple.ca/), some systems serve solely as a platform which provides patients remote access to communicate with their family doctors (one example is https://livecare.ca/). For these systems, the VC systems do not "own" or certify many new doctors to be selected by patients. Instead, they require both patients and their family doctors to register on the system, which gives users greater access to one another by all means, including messaging and/or video conferencing. Patients already knew the doctors and likely had FTF consultations with the doctor before. Therefore, when patients remotely visit their doctors through these platforms, they are more certain about the doctor and the entire consultation process based on prior interaction, compared to systems where most doctors are new to patients. The prior interaction with family doctors can be viewed as the process by which patients build mental models of consulting doctors. From the mental model perspective, systems providing accesses to patients' familiar doctors aligns better with patients' mental models of doctor's visits. In this scenario, patients feel more comfortable about the communication and more confident about the consultation diagnosis by doctors whom they are familiar with. Therefore, we have the following hypothesis:

H2: Increased mental model alignment will reduce uncertainty during patient-doctor CMC.

When patients cannot fully understand the situation, they have doubts and hesitations about doctors and the system. It is hard for them to believe they will get an accurate and comprehensive diagnosis under these conditions. They may feel frustrated and be unable to maintain positive attitudes toward the consultation. That is, they may not be satisfied with either the consultation process or results. Therefore, it is proposed in this study that uncertainty levels can influence the level of patient satisfaction. The hypothesis is as follows:

H3: Increased uncertainty will reduce patient satisfaction during patient-doctor CMC.

5 Data Collection

An artefactual field experiment methodology was used to investigate the above hypothesis. An artefactual field experiment is one that employs a nonstandard subject pool, an abstract framing, and an imposed set of rules, according to Harrison and List (2004). It is a suitable methodology, considering the randomness and geographically distributed nature of VC. We selected new and family doctors as the method to represent low and high levels of mental model alignment because doctor selecting is an important difference in VC compared to traditional face-to-face (FTF) doctor's visits, and it's also a crucial factor that can affect patient-doctor communication. We selected instant messaging and video conferencing as representatives of low and high levels of naturalness due to their popularity in VC. Therefore, four groups (family vs. new doctor, video consultation vs. instant messaging) were built for the experiment. We developed the measure items for patient uncertainty and satisfaction based on the work of Shi et al. (Shi et al. 2019) and Ware et al. (Ware et al. 1983).

Given that actual consultation is time-consuming and hard to control in experiment conditions, we chose to simulate the consultation process with scenario descriptions instead of making participants actually consult a doctor. The scenario description includes both text and snapshots for full immersion. Each group is expected to fully understand the condition and consultation process and be able to finish the task of answering related questions after going through the description.

Participants were randomly assigned to one online group with their consent. The scenario description and questionnaire were displayed to each group. After fully understanding the group conditions, participants were required to answer the questionnaire items on conditions, constructs, prior experience with VC, and basic demographic information. We used 7-scale Likert-type questions for the measurement items of the five constructs (values of 1–7 for strongly disagree-strongly agree). Participants finished the experiment by submitting the questionnaire. The whole process was done online. 327 valid questionnaires were collected to conduct data analysis.

6 Data Analysis

PLS-SEM was chosen in this study to analyze data because the research model is formative. The software we used for data analysis was SmartPLS 3.0 because it was considered as one of the superior tool to do PLS-SEM for formative models (Hair et al. 2014; Henseler et al. 2012; Ringle et al. 2014; Ringle et al. 2012). The general results and significance level values are presented in Fig. 2 and Table 1.

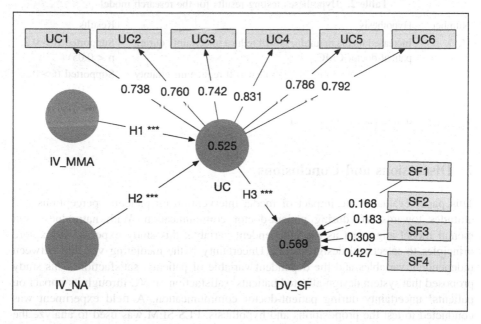

Fig. 2. General data analysis results (NA: Naturalness; MMA: Mental Model Alignment; UC: Uncertainty; SF: Satisfaction)

The R^2 values in Fig. 2 reveal that the research model explains about 53% of the variation in UC and about 57% of the variation in SF. In general, R^2 values of 0.75, 0.50, or 0.25 for the endogenous constructs can be described as respectively substantial, moderate, and weak (Hair et al. 2016). Following this rule, the R^2 values of uncertainty (0.525) and satisfaction (0.569) can be considered moderate.

Looking at the relative importance of the exogenous driver constructs for uncertainty in Table 1, one finds that the construct *Naturalness* and *MMA* are almost equally important with path coefficient value (0.381) for naturalness being slightly higher than it (0.355) for MMA. It is advisable for healthcare providers to focus on both the selection of media and the design of the content to align with patient's mental models. The path coefficient value being 0.685 suggests a strong positive relationship between uncertainty and patient satisfaction. Table 1 also shows that all relationships in the research model are significant. Therefore, it is concluded that the hypothesis proposed in this study were well supported as shown in Table 2.

Table 1. Significance testing results of the path coefficients

	Path coefficients	t Values	Significance levels	p Values
NA-> UC	0.381	6.391	***	.000
MMA-> UC	0.355	6.363	***	.000
UC-> SF	0.685	22.192	***	.000

(Note: $*p < .05$. $**p < .03$. $***p < .01$)

Table 2. Hypotheses testing results for the research model

Number	Hypothesis	Results
H_1	Increased media naturalness will reduce uncertainty during patient-doctor CMC.	Supported (t > 0.2; p < 0.05)
H_2	Increased mental model alignment will reduce uncertainty during patient-doctor CMC.	Supported (t > 0.2; p < 0.05)
H_3	Increased uncertainty will reduce patient satisfaction during patient-doctor CMC.	Supported (t > 0.2; p < 0.05)

7 Discussions and Conclusions

This paper evaluated the impact of media intervention on patients' perceptions and attitudes towards VC during patient-doctor communication. With naturalness and mental model alignment as the independent variable, this study expected to explore principles to select and design media. Uncertainty is the mediating variable between independent variables and the dependent variable of patients' satisfaction. This study proposed that system design affected patients' satisfaction on VC through its impact on patients' uncertainty during patient-doctor communication. A field experiment was conducted to test the propositions and hypothesis. PLS-SEM was used to analyze the obtained data.

The quantitative results showed that there were significant effects of media naturalness and mental model alignment on patients' uncertainty and their satisfaction, during patient-doctor CMC in the VC, thus providing support for hypothesis one, two and three. The results provided evidence for the importance of system selection and content design to reduce patient uncertainty in the context of VC.

The findings of this study will redound to the benefit of academic society in virtual consultation considering that naturalness and mental model alignment play important roles in reducing patients' uncertainties during their communication to doctors. By revealing the influences of naturalness and mental model alignment on reducing uncertainty, researchers can conduct further studies on this basis to investigate specific design features to improve the naturalness and mental model alignment levels of VC systems, and consequently to reduce patients' uncertainties. For healthcare providers, the study can guide them on what should be emphasized in the design of VC systems to reduce patients' uncertainties, and to improve patient satisfaction as a result.

There are several limitations that present opportunities for future research. First, although it provides better manipulation on the experiment with simulation of the consultations by describing the scenario instead of demanding the participants actually to consult a doctor, there is a limitation that patients completed the required tasks based on their personal experience instead of the scenario description, especially for patients who had the VC experience before. Future research could conduct some pilot studies or experiments which allow patients actually consult doctors instead of just snapshots and text description. A second limitation is on the participants of the experiment. The demographic results showed that the majority (83%) of participants were females, which may cause a bias for data analysis. It remains uncertain whether the analysis results would be the same if the demographic structure is different. Future study can test the moderating effects of factors such as gender, age and others.

References

Agha, Z., Schapira, R.M., Laud, P.W., Mcnutt, G., Roter, D.L., San Diego, V.A.: Patient satisfaction with physician-patient communication during telemedicine. Telemed. E-Health 15(9), 830–839 (2009). https://doi.org/10.1089/tmj.2009.0030

Alrubaiee, L., Alkaa'ida, F.: The mediating effect of patient satisfaction in the patients' perceptions of healthcare quality – patient trust relationship. Int. J. Mark. Stud. 3(1), 103 (2011). https://doi.org/10.5539/ijms.v3n1p103

Ambrose, E., Marshall, D., Fynes, B., Lynch, D.: Communication media selection in buyer-supplier relationships. Int. J. Oper. Prod. Manag. 28(4), 360–379 (2008). https://doi.org/10.1108/01443570810861561

Andaleeb, S.S.: Service quality perceptions and patient satisfaction: a study of hospitals in a developing country. Soc. Sci. Med. 52(9), 1359–1370 (2001). https://doi.org/10.1016/S0277-9536(00)00235-5

Andre, M., Gröndal, H., Strandberg, E.-L., Brorsson, A., Hedin, K.: Uncertainty in clinical practice-an interview study with Swedish GPs on patients with sore throat (2016). https://doi.org/10.1186/s12875-016-0452-9

Antheunis, M.L., Schouten, A.P., Valkenburg, P.M., Peter, J.: Interactive uncertainty reduction strategies and verbal affection in computer-mediated communication. Commun. Res. 39(6), 757–780 (2012). https://doi.org/10.1177/0093650211410420

Armfield, N.R., Bradford, M., Bradford, N.K.: The clinical use of Skype—For which patients, with which problems and in which settings? A snapshot review of the literature. Int. J. Med. Inform. 84, 737–742 (2015). https://doi.org/10.1016/j.ijmedinf.2015.06.006

Armfield, N.R., Gray, L.C., Smith, A.C.: Clinical use of Skype: a review of the evidence base. J. Telemed. Telecare 18(3), 125–127 (2012). https://doi.org/10.1258/jtt.2012.SFT101

Berger, C.R.: Uncertain outcome values in predicted relationships uncertainty reduction theory then and now. Hum. Commun. Res. 13(1), 34–38 (1986). https://doi.org/10.1111/j.1468-2958.1986.tb00093.x

Berger, C.R., Bradac, J.J.: Language and social knowledge : uncertainty in interpersonal relations. E. Arnold (1982). http://mun-primo.hosted.exlibrisgroup.com/primo_library/libweb/action/display.do?tabs = detailsTab&ct = display&fn = search&doc = Alma-MUN2131106924000 2511&indx = 1&recIds = Alma-MUN2131106924000 2511&recIdxs = 0&elementId = 0& renderMode = poppedOut&displayMode = full&frbrVer

Berger, C.R., Calabrese, R.J.: Some explorations in initial interaction and beyond: toward a developmental theory of interpersonal communication. Hum. Commun. Res. 1(2), 99–112 (1975). https://doi.org/10.1111/j.1468-2958.1975.tb00258.x

Biocca, F.: The Cyborg's dilemma: progressive embodiment in virtual environments. J. Comput.-Mediat. Commun. **3**(2) (2006). https://doi.org/10.1111/j.1083-6101.1997.tb00070.x

Blau, I., Caspi, A.: Studying invisibly: media naturalness and learning. In: Kock, N. (ed.) Evolutionary Psychology and Information Systems Research, pp. 193–216. Springer, Boston (2010). https://doi.org/10.1007/978-1-4419-6139-6_9

Bradac, J.J.: Theory comparison: uncertainty reduction, problematic integration, uncertainty management, and other curious constructs, pp. 456–476 (2001)

Cheng Lim, P., Tang, N.K.H.: A study of patients' expectations and satisfaction in Singapore hospitals. Int. J. Health Care Qual. Assur. **13**(7), 290–299 (2000). https://doi.org/10.1108/09526860010378735

Chiou, G.L., Anderson, O.R.: A study of undergraduate physics students' understanding of heat conduction based on mental model theory and an ontology-process analysis. Sci. Educ. **94**(5), 825–854 (2010). https://doi.org/10.1002/sce.20385

Craik, K.: The nature of explanation. 1943. Cambridge University, Cambridge (1967)

Cutica, I., Bucciarelli, M.: "'The more you gesture, the less i gesture'": co-speech gestures as a measure of mental model quality. J. Nonverbal Behav. **35**, 173–187 (2011). https://doi.org/10.1007/s10919-011-0112-7

Daft, R.L., Lengel, R.H., Trevino, L.K.: Message equivocality, media selection, and manager performance: implications for information Systems. MIS Q. **11**(3), 355 (1987). https://doi.org/10.2307/248682

Danczak, A., Lea, A.: The psychology of uncertainty in difficult decisions. InnovAiT **10**(8), 466–472 (2017). https://doi.org/10.1177/1755738017709034

Good, D.W., Lui, D.F., Leonard, M., Morris, S., McElwain, J.P.: Skype: a tool for functional assessment in orthopaedic research. J. Telemed. Telecare **18**(2), 94–98 (2012)

Doyle, J.K., Ford, D.N.: Mental models concepts for system dynamics research. Syst. Dyn. Rev. **14**(1), 3–29 (1998). https://doi.org/10.1002/(SICI)1099-1727(199821)14:1%3c3:AID-SDR140%3e3.0.CO;2-K

Doyle, J.K., Radzicki, M.J., Trees, W.S.: Measuring change in mental models of complex dynamic systems. In: Qudrat-Ullah, H., Spector, J., Davidsen, P. (eds.) Complex Decision Making. Understanding Complex Systems, pp. 269–294. Springer, Heidelberg (2008). https://doi.org/10.1007/978-3-540-73665-3_14.   https://link-springer-com.qe2a-proxy.mun.ca/content/pdf/10.1007/978-3-540-73665-3_14.pdf

Duronto, P.M., Nishida, T., Nakayama, S.-I.: Uncertainty, anxiety, and avoidance in communication with strangers. Int. J. Intercult. Relat. **29**, 549–560 (2005). https://doi.org/10.1016/j.ijintrel.2005.08.003

Ellenby, M.S., Marcin, J.P.: The role of telemedicine in pediatric critical care (2005). https://doi.org/10.1016/j.ccc.2014.12.006

Hair Jr, J.F., Sarstedt, M., Hopkins, L., Kuppelwieser, V.G.: Partial least squares structural equation modeling (PLS-SEM). Eur. Bus. Rev (2014). https://doi.org/10.1108/EBR-10-2013-0128

Forrester, J.: World dynamics (1971). http://documents.irevues.inist.fr/handle/2042/29441

Gentner, D., Stevens, A.L.: Mental Models, 1st edn. Erlbaum, New York (1983)

George, J.F., Carlson, J.R., Valacich, J.S.: Media selection as a strategic component of communication. MIS Quart. **37**(4), 1233–1251 (2013)

Greenhalgh, T., et al.: Virtual online consultations: advantages and limitations (VOCAL) study. BMJ Open **6**(1), e009388 (2016). https://doi.org/10.1136/bmjopen-2015-009388

Hair, J.F., Hult, G.M., Ringle, C.M., Sarstedt, M.: A Primer on Partial Least Squares Structural Equation Modeling (PLS-SEM) [1st]. Sage publications (2013)

Hanna, L., May, C., Fairhurst, K.: The place of information and communication technology-mediated consultations in primary care: GPs' perspectives. Fam. Pract. **29**(3), 361–366 (2012). https://doi.org/10.1093/fampra/cmr087

Henseler, J., Ringle, C.M., Sarstedt, M.: Using partial least squares path modeling in advertising research: basic concepts and recent issues. In: Handbook of Research on International Advertising, p. 252 (2012). https://doi.org/10.4337/9781848448582.00023

Huang, Y., Yang, C.G., Baek, H., Lee, S.G.: Revisiting media selection in the digital era: adoption and usage. Serv. Bus. **10**(1), 239–260 (2016). https://doi.org/10.1007/s11628-015-0271-4

Johnson-Laird, P.: How We Reason (2006). https://books.google.ca/books?hl=en&lr=&id=UjYsJN0krNYC&oi=fnd&pg=PR9&dq=Johnson+Laird+2006&ots=JcWhHBd5uP&sig=t4nVa_n0EAS0YSvventnno6VFfg

Jones, N.A., Ross, H., Lynam, T., Perez, P., Leitch, A.: Mental Models: an interdisciplinary synthesis of theory and methods. Ecol. Soc. **16**(1) (2011). https://about.jstor.org/terms

Kahneman, D., Tversky, A.: Choices, values, and frames. Am. Psychol. **39**(4), 341–350 (1984). https://doi.org/10.1037/0003-066X.39.4.341

Katz, E., Blumler, J.G., Gurevitch, M.: The uses of mass communications: current perspectives on gratifications research. Pub. Opin. Q. (1974). https://doi.org/10.1086/268109

Klaassen, B., Van Beijnum, B.J.F., Hermens, H.J.: Usability in telemedicine systems—a literature survey. Int. J. Med. Inform. **93**, 57–69 (2016). https://doi.org/10.1016/j.ijmedinf.2016.06.004

Kock, N.: Evolution and media naturalness: a look at e- communication through a Darwinian theoretical lens. In: International Conference on Information Systems (2002). http://aisel.aisnet.org/icis2002

Kock, N.: The psychobiological model: towards a new theory of computer-mediated communication based on Darwinian evolution. Organ. Sci. **15**(3), 327–348 (2004). https://doi.org/10.1287/orsc.1040.0071

Kock, N.: Media richness or media naturalness? The evolution of our biological communication apparatus and its influence on our behavior toward e-communication tools. IEEE Trans. Prof. Commun. **48**(2), 117–130 (2005). https://doi.org/10.1109/TPC.2005.849649

Kock, N.: Information systems theorizing based on evolutionary psychology: an interdisciplinary review and theory integration framework. MIS Q. **33**(2), 395–418 (2009). http://www.jstor.org/stable/20650297

Kock, N.: Evolutionary psychology and information systems theorizing. In: Kock, N. (ed.) Evolutionary Psychology and Information Systems Research. Integrated Series in Information Systems, vol. 24, pp. 3–37. Springer, Boston (2010). https://doi.org/10.1007/978-1-4419-6139-6_1

Kuang, K., Jiang, M., Cui, P., Sun, J., Yang, S.: Effective promotional strategies selection in social media: a data-driven approach. IEEE Trans. Big Data **4**(4), 1 (2017). https://doi.org/10.1109/TBDATA.2017.2734102

Lapointe, M., Barbeau, B.: Selection of media for the design of ballasted flocculation processes. Water Res. **147**, 25–32 (2018). https://doi.org/10.1016/j.watres.2018.09.041

Lazar, E.J., Fleischut, P., Regan, B.K.: Quality measurement in healthcare (2013). https://doi.org/10.1146/annurev-med-061511-13554

Legrenzi, P., Girotto, V., Legrenzi, M.S.: Naive probability : a mental model theory of extensional reasoning, **106**(1) (1999)

Linder-Pelz, S.: Toward a theory of patient satisfaction. Soc. Sci. Med. **16** (1982). https://ac-els-cdn-com.qe2a-proxy.mun.ca/0277953682903112/1-s2.0-0277953682903112-main.pdf?_tid=d4c078e2-602d-4758-a92a-555f8616dc55&acdnat=1538102201_5453b4e9240c6636fcf6901805db0e13

Liu, C.-C., Chang, I.-C.: Model of online game addiction: the role of computer-mediated communication motives. Telematics Inform. **33**, 904–915 (2016). https://doi.org/10.1016/j.tele.2016.02.002

Livecare - Doctors delivering healthcare through telehealth. (n.d.). https://livecare.ca/. Accessed 27 Jan 2019

Mair, F., Whitten, P.: Systematic review of studies of patient satisfaction with telemedicine. Med. J. **320**(7248), 1517–1520 (2000). https://www-jstor-org.qe2a-proxy.mun.ca/stable/pdf/25224711.pdf?refreqid=excelsior%3Aeee56d7ef6167a3a5efccf3ca2d59fa2

Mao, Y.: Investigating Chinese migrants' information-seeking patterns in Canada: media selection and language preference. Glob. Media J. **8**(2), 113–131 (2015). Canadian Edition

Maple: Online Doctors, Virtual Health & Prescriptions in Canada. (n.d.). https://www.getmaple.ca/. Accessed 27 Jan 2019

Martinez-Garza, Mario M., Clark, Douglas B.: Two systems, two stances: a novel theoretical framework for model-based learning in digital games. In: Wouters, P., van Oostendorp, H. (eds.) Instructional Techniques to Facilitate Learning and Motivation of Serious Games. AGL, pp. 37–58. Springer, Cham (2017). https://doi.org/10.1007/978-3-319-39298-1_3

McGloin, R., Wasserman, J.A., Boyan, A.: Model matching theory: a framework for examining the alignment between game mechanics and mental models. Media Commun. **6**(2), 126 (2018). https://doi.org/10.17645/mac.v6i2.1326

Meesala, A., Paul, J., Ambedkar, B.R.: (2017). Service quality, consumer satisfaction and loyalty in hospitals: thinking for the future. https://doi.org/10.1016/j.jretconser.2016.10.011

Oliver, R.L.: Satisfaction: A Behavioral Perspective on the Consumer. Routledge (2004). https://doi.org/10.4324/9781315700892

Ong, L.M.L., De Haes, J.C.J.M., Hoos, A. M., Lammes, F.B.: Doctor-patient communication: a review of the literature. Soc. Sci. Med. **40**(7), 903–918 (1995). https://pdf.sciencedirectassets.com/271821/1-s2.0-S0277953600X0038X/1-s2.0-027795369400155 M/main.pdf?X-Amz-Security-Token = AgoJb3JpZ2luX2VjEIz%2F%2F%2F%2F%2F%2F%2F%2F%2F%2F%2FwEaCXVzLWVhc3QtMSJHMEUCIA6%2BYKuq8YHdDzkx4xsiN4RKJjfIO02g-T7ruRDlZB2QgAiEAvFqnK%2FtEJ

Johnson-Laird, P.N.: Mental models. In: Posner, M.I. (ed.) Foundations of Cognitive Sciences, pp. 469–499. MIT Press, Cambridge (1989)

Pakdil, F., Harwood, T.N.: Patient satisfaction in a preoperative assessment clinic: an analysis using SERVQUAL dimensions. Total Qual. Manag. Bus. Excell. **16**(1), 15–30 (2005). https://doi.org/10.1080/1478336042000255622

Palen, T.E., Ross, C., Powers, J.D., Xu, S.: Association of online patient access to clinicians and medical records with use of clinical services. JAMA – J. Am. Med. Assoc. **308**(19), 2012–2019 (2012). http://jama.jamanetwork.com/data/Journals/JAMA/25500/joc120103_2012_2019.pdf%5Cnhttp://ovidsp.ovid.com/ovidweb.cgi?T=JS&PAGE=reference&D=emed10&NEWS=N&AN=2012673220

Panlaqui, O.M., Broadfield, E., Champion, R., Edington, J.P., Kennedy, S.: Outcomes of telemedicine intervention in a regional intensive care unit: a before and after study. Anaesth. Intensive Care **45**(5), 605–610 (2017)

Patterson, V., Wootton, R.: A web-based telemedicine system for low-resource settings 13 years on: insights from referrers and specialists. Glob. Health Action, **6**(1) (2013). https://doi.org/10.3402/gha.v6i0.21465

Payne, S.J.: Chapter 6 – Users' mental models: the very ideas. In: HCI Models, Theories, and Frameworks, pp. 135–156 (2003). https://doi.org/10.1016/B978-155860808-5/50006-X

Politi, M.C., Street, R.L.: The importance of communication in collaborative decision making: facilitating shared mind and the management of uncertainty. J. Eval. Clin. Pract. **17**(4), 579–584 (2011). https://doi.org/10.1111/j.1365-2753.2010.01549.x

Porter, M.E., Lee, T.H.: Virtual visits-confronting the challenges of telemedicine. New Engl. J. Med. **372**(18), 1681–1684 (2015). https://doi.org/10.1056/NEJMp1502419

Reed, K.: Telemedicine: benefits to advanced practice nursing and the communities they serve. J. Am. Acad. Nurse Pract. **17**(5), 176–180 (2005). https://doi.org/10.1111/j.1745-7599.2005. 0029.x

Ringle, C.M., Da Silva, D., Bido, D.D.S.: Structural equation modeling with the smartpls. Revista Brasileira de Mark. **13**(02), 56–73 (2014). https://doi.org/10.5585/remark.v13i2.2717

Ringle, C.M., Sarstedt, M., Straub, D.W.: Editor's Comments: a critical look at the use of PLS-SEM in MIS quarterly. MIS Q. **36**(1) (2012). http://ssrn.com/abstract=2176426

Rosenzweig, R., Baum, N.: The virtual doctor visit. J. Med. Pract. Manag. **29**(3), 195–198 (2013). http://www.scopus.com/inward/record.url?cid=2-s2.0-84896459731&partnerID=40& md5=ea2962b69e8a9b553da8948785bc99b3

Williams, S., Weinman, J., Dale, J.: Doctor patient communication and patient satisfaction. Fam. Pract. **15**(5), 480–492 (1998)

Scare, D.O.: The person-positivity bias. J. Pers. Soc. Psychol. **44**(2), 233 (1983). http://citeseerx. ist.psu.edu/viewdoc/download?doi=10.1.1.464.1318&rep=rep1&type=pdf

Schapira, L.: Handling uncertainty. Support. Care Cancer **22**(3), 859–861 (2014). https://doi.org/ 10.1007/s00520-013-2086-y

Scott, R.: Mental model alignment. Group Model Building. SOR, pp. 55–68. Springer, Singapore (2018). https://doi.org/10.1007/978-981-10-8959-6_6

Sherry, J.L.: Flow and media enjoyment. Commun. Theory **14**(4), 328–347 (2004). https://doi. org/10.1111/j.1468-2885.2004.tb00318.x

Shi, Y.V., Komiak, S.Y.X., Komiak, P.: Understanding patient uncertainty during patient-doctor computer- mediated communication in virtual consultation. In: SIG-Health Pre-ICIS Workshop, Munich (2019)

Srivastava, R.: Dealing with uncertainty in a time of plenty. New Engl. J. Med. **365**(24), 2252–2253 (2011). https://doi.org/10.1056/NEJMp1109456

Staggers, N., Norcio, A.F.: Mental models: concepts for human-computer interaction research. Int. J. Man-Mach. Stud. **38**, 587–605 (1993). http://userpages.umbc.edu/~norcio/papers/ 1993/Staggers-MM-IJMMS.pdf

Timmermans, S., et al.: Does patient-centered care change genital surgery decisions? The strategic use of clinical uncertainty in disorders of sex development clinics. J. Health Soc. Behav. **59**(4), 520–535 (2018). https://doi.org/10.1177/0022146518802460

Stern, A.: Exploring the benefits of telehealth. Trustee **70**(10), 4 (2017)

Stieglitz, S., Dang-Xuan, L.: Emotions and information diffusion in social media—sentiment of microblogs and sharing behavior. J. Manag. Inf. Syst. **29**(4), 217–248 (2013). https://doi.org/ 10.2753/MIS0742-1222290408

Tejera Segura, B., Bustabad, S.: A new form of communication between rheumatology and primary care: the virtual consultation. Reumatología Clínica **12**(1), 11–14 (2016). https://doi. org/10.1016/j.reumae.2015.03.001. English Edition

Travers, C.P., Murphy, J.F.: Neonatal telephone consultations in the National Maternity Hospital. Irish Med. J. (2014)

Trevino, L.K., Lengel, R.H., Daft, R.L.: Media symbolism, media richness, and media choice in organizations. Commun. Res. (1987). https://doi.org/10.1016/j.fertnstert.2007.12.031

Van Der Henst, J.-B.: Mental model theory and pragmatics. Behav. Brain Sci. **23**(2), 283–284 (2000). https://doi.org/10.1017/S0140525X00212442

Verlinde, E., et al.: The social gradient in doctor-patient communication. Int. J. Equity Health **11** (1), 12 (2012). https://doi.org/10.1186/1475-9276-11-12

Wald, H.S., Dube, C.E., Anthony, D.C.: Untangling the web—the impact of internet use on health care and the physician–patient relationship. Patient Educ. Couns. **68**, 218–224 (2007). https://doi.org/10.1016/j.pec.2007.05.016

Ware, J.E.: The measurement of patient satisfaction. Health Med. Care Serv. Rev. **1**(1), 5–15 (1978). https://www.popline.org/node/499534

Ware, J.E., Profile, S., Hays, R.D.: Methods for measuring patient satisfaction with specific medical encounters PCAR (NCI) view project estimation of medical care total expenditures view project (2017). https://doi.org/10.1097/00005650-198804000-00008

Ware, J.E., Snyder, M.K., Wright, W.R., Davies, A.R.: Defining and measuring patient satisfaction with medical care. Eval. Prog. Plan. **6**(3–4), 247–263 (1983). https://doi.org/10.1016/0149-7189(83)90005-8

Wilson, J.R., Rutherford, A.: Mental models: theory and application in human factors (1989). http://journals.sagepub.com.qe2a-proxy.mun.ca/doi/pdf/10.1177/001872088903100601

Yang, Y., Narayanan, V.K., Baburaj, Y., Swaminathan, S.: Team mental model characteristics and performance in a simulation experiment. Manag. Res. Rev. **39**(8), 899–924 (2016). https://doi.org/10.1108/MRR-02-2015-0036

Zilliacus, E., Meiser, B., Lobb, E., Dudding, T.E., Barlow-Stewart, K., Tucker, K.: The virtual consultation: practitioners' experiences of genetic counseling by videoconferencing in Australia. Telemed. E-Health **16**(3) (2010). http://online.liebertpub.com/doi/pdf/10.1089/tmj.2009.0108

Zineldin, M.: The quality of health care and patient satisfaction: An exploratory investigation of the 5Qs model at some Egyptian and Jordanian medical clinics. Int. J. Health Care Qual. Assur. **19**(1), 60–92 (2006). https://doi.org/10.1108/09526860610642609

Zwaan, R.A., Magliano, J.P., Graesser, A.C.: Dimensions of situation model construction in narrative comprehension. J. Exp. Psychol. Learn. Mem. Cogn. **21**(2), 386–397 (1995). https://doi.org/10.1037/0278-7393.21.2.386

Design and Research of Intelligent Products for the Management of Chronic Diseases of the Elderly

Xinxin Sun[✉], Zhenzhou Li, and Minlin Yang

School of Design Arts and Media, Nanjing University of Science
and Technology, Xuanwu Area, Nanjing 210094, China
sunxinxinde@126.com, 1720664827@qq.com,
1356554252@qq.com

Abstract. This paper aims to explore the design of intelligent products based on the needs of elderly users. Based on the existing literature results, the possibility of design intervention in the management of chronic diseases of the elderly was proposed, and the general characteristics and behavioral characteristics of the elderly users were studied by questionnaire method, the acceptability and subjective attitude of the elderly in using intelligent products and services were found, and the survey results were analyzed by mathematical statistics. The results showed that older people who considered it necessary to record physical data were higher than those who did not. With the increase of education, the proficiency of using mobile phone also increases; According to the elderly's score of functional needs, the function with the highest score is automatic detection, followed by automatic analysis, remote consultation, diet therapy and community communication. Finally, based on the questionnaire survey results, this paper developed the design practice of intelligent medical products for hypertension, a common chronic disease of the elderly, and proposed the design strategy of intelligent products and services for chronic disease management of the elderly.

Keywords: Chronic disease management · Smart product design · Smart endowment

1 Introduction

As of December 2018, China had 140 million elderly people aged 65 or above, accounting for about 10.5% of the country's total population, according to official data. China has entered a serious aging society. At the same time, researchers from the Chinese center for disease control and prevention published survey data showing that 75.8% of Chinese people aged 60 and over suffer from one or more chronic diseases, and one suffers from multiple chronic diseases. Common chronic diseases mainly include cardiovascular and cerebrovascular diseases, cancer, diabetes, chronic respiratory system and other diseases. Among the Chinese residents aged 60 and above surveyed, 58.3% had hypertension, 19.4% had diabetes and 37.2% had dyslipidemia. To enrich the supply of smart health service products for the elderly, the development

© Springer Nature Switzerland AG 2020
M. Kurosu (Ed.): HCII 2020, LNCS 12183, pp. 165–177, 2020.
https://doi.org/10.1007/978-3-030-49065-2_12

of health management wearable devices, portable health monitoring equipment, chronic disease monitoring equipment, home service robots and other smart home products and services will become a real demand. The reality is that at present, the research on intelligent products for the management of chronic diseases of the elderly in China is still in its infancy, and the existing intelligent products do not fully consider the functional needs, cognitive styles, behavioral patterns and experience needs of the elderly user group. With the aggravation of the aging of Chinese society, it is urgent to carry out the research on intelligent products for the management of chronic diseases of the elderly under the background of smart pension. And the elderly due to the decline of body functions and a reduction in the ability to follow up study, presents the particularity of different from the general population, led to the elderly in the use of smart home products produced in cognition, understanding, decision-making, implementation, feedback in the process of friction, resulting in inaccurate operation, switch function is not smooth, information is not natural, and a series of related to products and services system function, operation, design problem of the experience of the interactions, thus deepening the intelligent products and digital divide between older users.

At present, China is implementing a scientific and technological old-age care plan in line with its national conditions, which requires the use of information technology and the Internet to achieve efficient and high-quality old-age care management, so as to basically form a old-age care industry system covering the whole life cycle by 2020. Hope to introduce the pension services of the Internet, use the Internet for information exchange, information processing, data storage, information maintenance, big advantages of data mining, make the old man in the life care, health management, health care get personalized service, so that it can help pension institutions, community greatly enhance management efficiency, and makes the endowment satisfaction greatly improved. In 2019, the state issued the "healthy China action (2019-2030)", in Chinese action to promote health committee held in Beijing on July 29, 2019: are mentioned in the press conference of elderly health promotion action advocated the elderly themselves well slow disease management, delay condition, reduce the complications, at the same time, encourage and support enterprises by taking advantage of information technology, such as "Internet+" developing wearable healthy elderly support technology and equipment, etc. This greatly supports the development and promotion of new intelligent products.

2 Background

2.1 Chronic Diseases of the Elderly in China

With the development of society, the degree of population aging is getting deeper and deeper, and the elderly group as a special social group is gradually enlarged. With the increasing degree of population aging, the disease burden of the elderly population caused by age-related chronic non-communicable diseases (chronic diseases) will continue to increase [1]. Disability adjusted life year (DALY) is the total number of years of healthy life lost from onset to death, including YLL due to premature death and YLD due to illness. DALY is a comprehensive measure of quantity of life and quality of life in terms of time [2]. DALYs comprehensively analyzed the incidence, disability and death of the disease [3]. In China, the prevalence of chronic diseases in the elderly is as high as 71.8% [4], and 51.3% of DALYs is caused by health problems in the elderly aged $\geq$ 60 years. Chronic diseases cause 178.91 million DALYs in the elderly, accounting for 92.7% of the total disease burden of the elderly [5]. In the elderly group, the common chronic diseases are hypertension, cervical spondylosis, diabetes, arthritis and so on.

2.2   Design the Possibility of Intervening in the Management of Chronic Diseases of the Elderly

With the increasing incidence of chronic diseases, chronic diseases have become one of the major concerns of the medical industry [6]. Traditional medical treatment has been unable to meet the needs of our aging chronic disease treatment and rehabilitation control [7]. The development and popularization of intelligent products bring the dawn to solve these problems. The European Union, the United States, Canada, Japan and other developed countries have implemented the use of pervasive computing (UPC) and background intelligence (AmI) technology to assist the elderly in their daily lives at home since the 1990s. Functions include automatically detecting the elderly's independent completion of daily activities related to housework, and providing prompt or assistance when necessary. Medical care testing and environmental monitoring were conducted for the elderly, and automatic rescue and alarm were conducted in emergency situations (Gustafsson 2010). EMTapia (2004) believes that sensors can be applied everywhere in residential buildings, and simple and tiny sensing facilities can be designed to bring convenience to the life of the elderly. Zouba (2009) proposed that changes in daily activities (ADL) of elderly users should be intelligently monitored and analyzed to detect and treat health problems before they get worse. Wang Lin (2015), a Chinese scholar, conducted an investigation on the current situation of the use of information technology products by the elderly, as well as the functions and design requirements of the products. Xing Zhudi (2015) pointed out that smart home for the elderly needs to pay attention to special needs from health equipment, intelligent voice technology, intelligent detection and other aspects, and fit the functions with the needs. Liu Shulao (2015) the elderly intelligent household property can be divided into interaction and support attribute, interaction properties including operability, visual perceptual, representative, situation, spatial interaction and social interaction six classes, support properties include mathematical degree, barrier-free supportive, safety, convenience, the sensory function of self control and promote. However, current smart products attach great importance to "intelligence" and "high technology", and face more young people, while ignoring the "suitable aging" of smart products and services in specific applications [8].

In addition, China released the "healthy China action (2019-2030)" this year, and mentioned in the press conference of the healthy China action promotion committee held in Beijing on July 29, 2019: the health promotion action for the elderly advocates the elderly to manage chronic diseases, delay the disease and reduce complications, and encourages and supports enterprises to develop wearable health support technologies and devices for the elderly by using "Internet+" and other information technologies. Therefore, the use of intelligent products to intervene in the management of chronic diseases of the elderly has a great possibility. In the whole exploration process, several directions have been gradually formed: social service management, hardware management, software management, software and hardware combination, and network end system management.

2.2.1 Space for Design Intervention in Hardware Management Classes

Medical product hardware is generally used to detect relevant disease data or directly treat patients. Most medical product hardware will have direct contact with human body. Therefore, in the use of the process of contact with the human body to fully consider ergonomics and product usability design. After extensive research on medical products, this paper concludes that the main pain points in the hardware of medical products are: first, with the decline of physical quality and learning ability of the elderly, bulky and complex hardware products are no longer suitable for the elderly group. At present, most medical products on the market are too specialized in appearance and function, which cannot well meet the cognitive and aesthetic needs of the elderly. In addition, the product features complex operation, many buttons, the partition is not scientific and reasonable, bringing some obstacles to the elderly users; Second, due to the large size of some medical products hardware, in the storage process will take up more space, it is not convenient to carry; Third, there are different medical products hardware for the same chronic disease, while there are few products specially designed for the elderly, so there is not enough space to choose.

Therefore, there is still a lot of room for development in medical product hardware design, including product interaction mode, humanized emotional design and other contents. But also products have begun to explore in this field at present. The product form can better reflect the product function. The cuff is used for collecting physiological data and controlling the subject for data processing and transmission. The product can better meet the operation mode and function of the elderly group.

2.2.2 Space for Design Intervention in the Software Management Class

A growing number of mobile applications software products applied to the management of chronic diseases. However, there are still some design breakthroughs at present. First, although the whole medical treatment process system is relatively complete, the tracking of postoperative recovery, especially the tracking of chronic diseases, mainly relies on the traditional follow-up, which still has great deficiencies in software functions, which will be the entry point for future design intervention. Second, the current product interface information structure design is not reasonable, the product usability is insufficient, coupled with the elderly for the intelligent product operation is not skilled lead to the decline in information acceptance, will also become a breakthrough in software design; Three is that of a software product visual design can not fully meet the aesthetic and cognitive of older users, such as font, font size, color and symbol design, the optimization of visual elements to improve the operation of older users experience.

2.2.3 Design Intervention Space in the Combination of Hardware and Software

The combination of hardware and software is a popular way at present, that is, medical products hardware and supporting software complement each other to jointly prevent and manage chronic diseases. In the combination of hardware and software, there are several points worth paying attention to: First, emotional design of medical products for the elderly, the hardware is a cold instrument, how to bring the elderly a warm feeling through the combination of hardware and software. Second, the way hardware and software interact will be a breakthrough in design. That is, what functions are implemented by hardware and what functions are implemented by software, the interaction between the two also needs to be designed. In addition, because the elderly are slow to accept new things, shortening the strangeness between the product and the elderly through design will make the product win in the competition. How to integrate the product into the life of the elderly naturally is also the breakthrough point of design.

3 Methods and Processes

3.1 Questionnaire Design

Based on the preliminary basic research, this paper will carry out the design and research of intelligent products for the management of chronic diseases of the elderly. In order to study the demand degree of chronic diseases management of the elderly, the experience of using intelligent products and the management form of chronic diseases of the elderly, this experiment adopts the questionnaire method to carry out the design and research. In the process of setting up the questionnaire, reference was made to relevant literature on chronic diseases of the elderly. A total of 20 questions were set in the questionnaire, including chronic diseases monitoring of the elderly, attitudes to recorded data, personal daily living habits and other aspects.

3.2 Questionnaire Distribution and Collection

Six major cities in China, including nanjing, Shanghai, Xi'an, Shenzhen, Jinan and Shenyang, were selected according to the comprehensive factors of urban economic development level, geographical location and city type. A total of 105 questionnaires were distributed online, of which 35 were filled by the elderly themselves and 70 were filled by their children according to the actual situation.

19 invalid questionnaires were removed, leaving 86 valid questionnaires, with an effective rate of 81.9%.

The gender ratio and age distribution of users are reasonable, which can provide a reasonable basis for the questionnaire results. After the questionnaire was collected, SPSS software was used for data statistics and analysis.

4 Research Results

4.1 Analysis of the Needs for Chronic Disease Management of the Elderly

According to the analysis of the independent sample T test, as shown in Table 1, there are significant differences in the degree to which the elderly who record data consider it necessary to record data. The significance (double-tail) is 0.001 and 0.000 respectively, both less than 0.05.In daily life, the data records statistics is recognized by the majority elderly and there is indeed a need for data records. However, 64.26% of the elderly only performed data recording due to various reasons, such as inconvenient recording and unknown how to analyze after recording.

Table 1. Independent sample T test for recording data and necessity of recording data

	Levin's variance equality test		Mean equality t test		Mean equality t test				
	F	Significance	t	Degree of freedom	Significance (two-tailed)	Mean difference	Standard error difference	Difference 95% confidence interval lower limit	Difference 95% confidence interval upper limit
Assume that such variance	7.210	.010	3.448	56	.001	.860	.249	.360	1.360
The equal variance is not assumed			8.686	49.000	.000	.860	.099	.661	1.059

As can be seen from the analysis in Table 2, the significance value of the education level of the elderly and the degree of necessity of recording data is 0.723, greater than 0.05, so there is no significant difference. We cannot reject the former hypothesis: the elderly with all education levels feel it necessary to record data. The homogeneity test of variance showed that the significance was 0.102 greater than 0.05, so multiple comparative analysis was unnecessary.

Table 2. ANOVA

	Sum of squares	Degrees of freedom	The mean square	F	Significant
Between groups	.299	2	.150	.326	.723
Within the group	25.218	55	.459		

To test the old design demand in the area of chronic disease in statistical measurement data, necessity will be divided into three levels: almost no need, general and special necessary need, shown in Table 3, Among them, 23.3% think it is almost unnecessary to count chronic diseases, and 50% think it is generally necessary, and 26.7% think it is necessary to special old man. Therefore, it is proved that the elderly pay more attention to the necessity of chronic disease measurement data recording and have design requirements.

Table 3. Statistical necessity scale for the elderly

	Frequency	Percentage	Effective percentage	Cumulative percentage
Hardly necessary	20	23.3%	23.3%	23.3%
Generally necessary	43	50%	50%	73.3%
Especially necessary	23	26.7%	26.7%	100.0
Total	86	100.0%	100.0%	

Through observation and in-depth interviews, the functional requirements for chronic disease management of the elderly are divided into automatic detection, automatic analysis, remote consultation, community communication and diet therapy. Based on the elderly's score of functional requirements, descriptive statistics were made for the score, as shown in Table 4. The highest scoring function is automatic detection (M = 4.56, SD = 0.60), followed by remote consultation (M = 4.31, SD = 0.68), diet therapy (M = 3.93, SD = 0.89), automatic analysis (M = 3.68, SD = 0.91), and community communication (M = 3.56, SD = 0.99).

Table 4. Statistical necessity scale for the elderly

Functional requirements	N	Mean	Standard deviation	Standard error	95% confidence interval of the mean	
					The lower limit	The upper limit
Automatic monitoring	86	4.5625	0.6092	0.1523	4.2272	4.8978
Automatic analysis	86	3.6875	0.9164	0.2291	3.1832	4.1918
Remote inquiry and consultation	86	4.3125	0.6818	0.1704	3.9373	4.6877
Community exchange	86	3.5625	0.9980	0.2495	3.0132	4.1118
Diet diet	86	3.9375	0.8992	0.2248	3.4426	4.4324

4.2   Correlation Between the Use Experience of Smart Products and the Education/Experience of the Elderly

The research group conducted the correlation analysis of education background and experience in using intelligent products, and the correlation analysis of education background and whether medical intelligent products were used.

As can be seen from Table 5, 75.0% of the elderly with a bachelor's degree or above are proficient in using smart products, 51.1% of the elderly with a college degree are proficient in using smart products, and 28.5% of the elderly with a high school education or less are proficient in using smart products.

Table 5. Cross tabulation of education and experience in using smart products

Degree	No use at all	Inproficiency	General skilled	More skilled	Very skilled	Total
High school education or below	28.6%	42.9%	14.3%	14.2%	0%	100.0%
Junior college	10.5%	38.4%	41.1%	10.0%	0%	100.0%
Undergraduate or above	3.1%	21.9%	49.2.0%	25.0%	0.8%	100.0%

This indicates that the degree level is positively correlated with the proficiency of using smart products, and the higher the degree, the higher the proficiency of using smart products.

According to the chi-square test, as shown in Table 6, Pearson chi-square, likelihood ratio and linear correlation between the education background of the respondents and their experience in using intelligent products were 0.003, 0.002 and 0.001, respectively, all of which were less than 0.05.

Table 6. Chi-square test

	Value	Degree of freedom	Asymptotic significance (bilateral)
Pearson chisquare	19.592^a	6	.003
Likelihood ratio (L)	21.478	6	.002
Linear correlation	11.304	1	.001
Number of valid cases	86		

As can be seen from Table 7, the proportion of the elderly with bachelor's degree or above who frequently use medical intelligent products is 14.3%, the proportion of the elderly with college degree who frequently use medical intelligent products is 21.0%, and the proportion of the elderly with high school education or less who frequently use medical intelligent products is 9.4%. The overall performance is that

Table 7. Cross-tabulates the frequency of education and use of smart products of medical type for the elderly

Degree	Never used	Rarely used	Occasionally used	Often used	Frequently used	Total
High school education or below	56.2%	25.0%	9.4%	6.3%	3.1%	100.0%
Junior college	21.1%	31.6%	26.3%	15.8%	5.2%	100.0%
Undergraduate or above	28.6%	28.3%	28.8%	14.3%	0%	100.0%

with the increase of education, the proportion of the elderly using medical intelligent products is increasing. With a high school education or below, the majority of people who seldom use medical smart products are not proficient in using smart products. A considerable proportion of the elderly can operate and use smart products under the guidance of others.

According to the chi-square test, as shown in Table 8, there is a linear correlation between the education background of interviewees and whether they use medical intelligent products, which is 0.02, less than 0.05.

Table 8. Chi-square test

	Value	Degree of freedom	Asymptotic significance (bilateral)
Pearson card square	10.708^a	10	.381
Likelihood ratio (L)	12.637	10	.245
Linear correlation	5.385	1	.020

5 Design Practice

5.1 Design Concept

Based on the previous questionnaire survey results and combined with the cognitive ability and learning ability of the elderly, this paper designed a medical intelligent product for hypertension, a common chronic disease of the elderly, for the elderly over 60 years old who can use smartphones independently.

The product is divided into two parts: hardware and software. The hardware part mainly collects blood pressure data, wears it on the upper arm, and measures blood pressure at any time. The data is uploaded to the mobile phone through bluetooth, enabling the elderly to view timely data and relevant data analysis in the APP. Through the "power switch", "start", "end" simple keys to achieve the measurement of blood pressure, the basic need for assistance, easy to operate.

5.2 Functional Design

The software APP is mainly composed of 4 parts, as shown in Fig. 1. The first part is data statistics and analysis. Most elderly people do not record data due to the tedious recording of data. Second, emergency call for help. Patients can call their children or other guardians with one key after their condition suddenly intensifies and they take medicine to stabilize their condition. The third is the function of doctor's advice, showing the doctor's suggestions for the treatment of patients, etc., which can be checked at any time to prevent forgetting; The fourth is related to hypertension text, video recommended, with voice reading function.

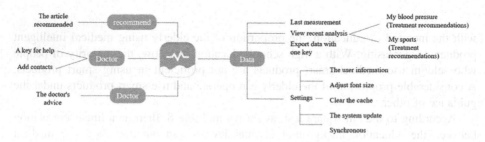

Fig. 1. Software function design

Let the intelligent medical products really integrate into life and play their due roles, instead of being a burden to use.

5.3 Software Interface Design

The overall interface is simple and adopts graphic design to reduce the cognitive burden of information receivers. The interface displays the latest measurement data, and red and blue represent different blood pressure values. When red values appear, abnormal blood pressure is indicated. At the same time, in the interface designed for the elderly, the font size is larger, such as the key call interface design. In addition, the color contrast in the interface is relatively strong, the graphical language is relatively rich, and the use of the product conforms to the operation habits of the elderly (Figs. 2 and 3).

Fig. 2. Software interface design 1

Fig. 3. Software interface design 2

6 Discussion and Conclusion

With the improvement of living standards and the widespread use of electronic technology products, more and more elderly people are learning to use smart products. According to the above data analysis, with the increase in education level of elderly people, their proficiency in using mobile phones is also increasing. However, among the respondents, the vast majority of the elderly have a high school education or lower, and they are more worried that they will not use smart technology products. With the growth of age, the physical function and learning ability of the elderly group decline, and they are unable to skillfully use smart products. Part of the reason is that the products themselves are not designed properly and cannot adapt to the operation habits of the elderly group. Therefore, the operation mode of smart products is more convenient and the interaction mode is more direct. The elderly group can use smart products autonomously with less time.

In terms of product functions, the management of chronic diseases can establish a bottom-up level of "seeing – insight – foresight" intelligent services, including: first, "seeing" the daily posture activities of the elderly and displaying the daily activity information and data of the elderly in a visual form. For example, for old people with heart disease, it can transform the sleeping position, body language such as movement through intelligent mattress monitoring the elderly, forming the number of times the elderly get up at night, body weight, sleep in the body such as heart rate, breathing frequency data, and displayed on the terminal equipment, in the form of visualization for doctors, children in a timely manner to understand the elderly health and sleep patterns, preventing incidents, forming a closed loop of sleep detection - sleep analysis - professional consultation.

Second, "insight" and analysis of the elderly body language data, adaptive response and intelligent processing; For the elderly users with arthritis and hypertension, falling can not only seriously damage the elderly's ability to move, but also cause the elderly to have tension, anxiety, depression, irritability and other psychological disorders. In terms of fall and fall prevention technology, a variety of technical solutions are currently being studied, some of which are to install sensors on the floor, when the old man falls down, the instrument will alarm; There are infrared sensor or camera, according to the attitude of the elderly to determine whether there is a fall. Sensing devices equipped with the elderly will be active alarm, according to the walking posture to determine the state of the fall.

Third, according to the reasonable action effect of the elderly to "foresee" the behavior results, take the initiative to recommend the service information. The smart nursing technology products integrated with medical, psychology, ergonomics and other professional knowledge can not only monitor the physical condition of the elderly for early monitoring and early warning, but also predict the health risks of the elderly through the accumulation of big data, or provide medical reference. Equipped with an electronic blood pressure meter with data transmission function, the blood pressure data of the elderly can be automatically uploaded to the data platform as long as the elderly take blood pressure measurement without any other operation, and the children and caretakers of the elderly can timely check the blood pressure data and various warning information of the elderly. It can monitor its health status in real time by means of wearing and implanting. For example, "wearable ecg monitoring suit" can monitor the elderly's heartbeat frequency and other health information in real time and continuously, and cooperate with the corresponding expert system and service system to achieve effective chronic disease management and risk management.

In terms of product interaction, body language shows a dynamic evolution trend according to age. For example, older people compared to the general user community of body language, facial expressions, head movements and gestures in sports, arm and hand movement, leg and foot movement etc. There is a big difference in these aspects. So the attitude of the behavior type and transformation rules, the relationship between behavior and space will be changed, therefore, intelligent product design for elderly users need to pay attention to: one is that targeted mapping between function and the function of the body of the elderly. Second, is that targeted mapping among the product interaction form, low attention, situational interaction semantics with the elderly cognitive patterns and interactive habits; Third, the product captures, transforms and explicitly expresses the implicit and empirical body language of the elderly, which will more effectively provide a basis and breakthrough point for innovative design. For example, provide certain visual operation clues and effective guidance to help users quickly understand the operation skills; The fourth is to reduce the difficulty of operation and design according to the behavioral ability of the elderly, so that the product brings real convenience to the user group.

Acknowledgements. This research was financially supported by MOE (Ministry of Education in China) Youth Project of Humanities and Social Sciences Fund, 2018: "Design and Research of Intelligent Home Products and Services System Based on the Body Language of the Elderly" (No. 18YJCZH158) and "the Fundamental Research Funds for the Central Universities", No. 330919013233.

References

1. Prince, M.J., et al.: The burden of disease in older people and implications for health policy and practice. Lancet **385**(9967), 549–562 (2015)
2. Li, L. (ed.): Epidemiology, vol. 11, pp. 20–21. People's Medical Publishing House, Beijing (2008)
3. Devleesschauwer, B., Havelaar, A.H., Charline, M.D.N., et al.: Calculating disability-adjusted life years to quantify burden of disease. Int. J. Public Health **59**(3), 565–569 (2014). https://doi.org/10.1007/s00038-014-0552-z
4. Statistical Information Center of the National Health and Family Planning Commission. The Fifth National Health Service Survey and Analysis Report of 2013 (2015)
5. World Health Organization: Global Health Estimates 2016: Disease burden by Cause, Age, Sex, by Country and by Region, 2000-2016, Geneva (2018)
6. Zhang, L., Kong, L.: Prevention of chronic diseases: a critical investment – report of the world health organization. China Chronic Dis. Prev. Control **14**(1), 1–4 (2006)
7. Niu, H., et al.: Intervention of health management model on chronic diseases of the elderly. Value Eng. **37**(19), 236–237 (2008)
8. Chen, G., Chen, X., Hua, S.: Research on "suitable for aging" design of smart home products. Sci. Technol. Innov. Appl. (24), 44–46 (2009)

The Efficacy of Virtual Reality Exposure Therapy for Fear of Falling (FOF) in the Elderly

Morihiro Tsujishita[1][✉], Hiroshi Noborio[1], Yashuhiro Masutani[2], Masanao Koeda[2], and Katsuhiko Onishi[2]

[1] Nara Gakuen University, Nakatomigaoka, Nara 631-8524, Japan
tuzisita@nara-su.ac.jp
[2] Osaka Electro-Communication University, Shijo-Nawate, Osaka 575-0063, Japan

Abstract. Fear of falling down is common among older people because it occurs on average in 50% of those who have fallen in the previous year. Our main aim was to investigate the reduction of FOF in elderly fallers using a virtual reality exposure therapy. To pursue this aim we developed a virtual reality exposure therapy system to clarify the following two experiments, let the subject wear it and watch it, collect various vital data of the subject, and confirm the effectiveness of our VR exposure therapy. In this study, we conducted a preliminary study on two elderly people who had fallen previously effect of reducing fear of falling by VR exposure therapy is confirmed.

Keywords: Fear of falling · Virtual reality exposure therapy · Elderly fallers

1 Introduction

In recent years, there has been increased attention to falling as a public health problem. Fear of falling is known to affect more than half of older people over 60 years of age.

This fear is associated with physical and psychological effects that increase the risk of falling. About 30% of people older than 65 years fall at least once per year. Fear of falling is common in older people, occurring on average in 50% of those who have fallen in the previous year [1].

The consequences of falls often are severe, leading to loss of functional independence, social isolation, disability, and death [2]. Since the identification of the post-fall syndrome and use of the term "ptophobia" (the phobic reaction to standing or walking) in the early 1980s, fear of falling (FOF) has gained recognition as a health problem of older adults [3].

Our main aim was to investigate the reduction of FOF in elderly fallers using virtual reality exposure therapy. To pursue this aim we developed a virtual reality exposure therapy system to clarify the following two experiments, let the subject wear it and watch it, collect various vital data of the subject, and confirm the effectiveness of our VR exposure therapy.

© Springer Nature Switzerland AG 2020
M. Kurosu (Ed.): HCII 2020, LNCS 12183, pp. 178–187, 2020.
https://doi.org/10.1007/978-3-030-49065-2_13

[Experiment 1] An elderly subject who has experienced a fall in a house is asked to view the fall scene by VR technology, and it is confirmed whether or not a fear of falling can be caused.

[Experiment 2] When experiment 1 is confirmed, it is confirmed whether the fear of falling caused by watching a VR scene can be reduced by VR exposure therapy (Fig. 1).

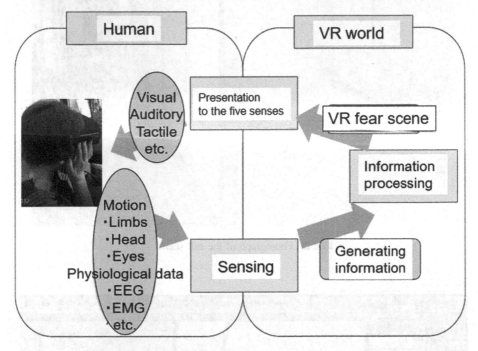

Fig. 1. Schematic diagram of VR exposure therapy system.

In this study, we conducted a preliminary study on one elderly person who had fallen.

Ethical approval for the present study was provided by the Ethics Committee of the Nara Gakuen University (approval number 30-008) and Osaka Electro-Communication University (approval number 19-005). The participant was properly informed about the study and signed written consent forms prior to participation in accordance with the Declaration of Helsinki.

2   Experiment 1

We asked to cooperate with two elderly participants with a cognitive function who had a fall experience in the house within one year and was able to walk independently. We photographed the fall scene with the permission of the elderly participants (Fig. 2). VR scene data on site was created using a VR creation system (VR solution, MEGASOFT Inc, Japan) (Fig. 3). Using this VR data, a room-scale VR is constructed in which the

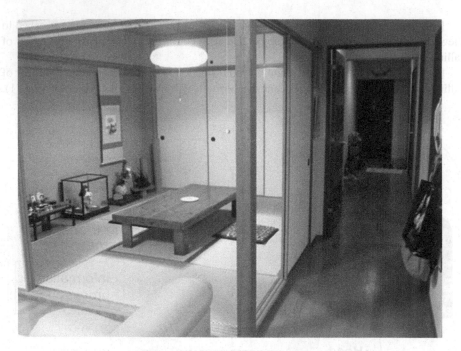

Fig. 2. Photograph of the fall scene.

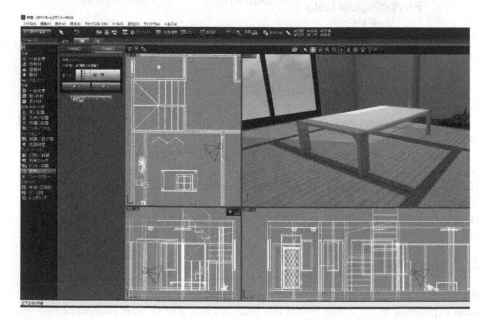

Fig. 3. VR creation system.

VR space moves in conjunction with the elderly participant actually moving in the room. After the fall scene VR was completed at a later date, the elderly participant came to the facility to take part in the research, wearing Oculus goggles (Irvine, CA). The participant experienced psychophysiological fears while watching the fall scene the VR performed (Fig. 4).

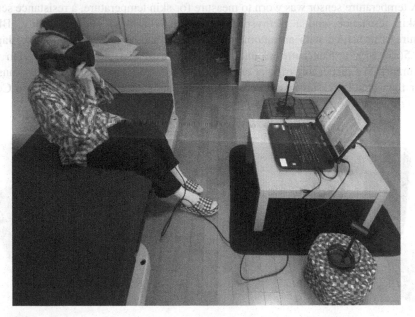

Fig. 4. Elderly participant wearing VR goggles and experiencing VR environment.

2.1 Participant and Methods

The elderly participant was examined for sex, age, height, weight, history of falling, and the Modified Fall Efficacy Scale (MFES) [4] and Physical Self Efficacy Scale (PSES) [5] (Table 1).

Table 1. Baseline characteristics of participants.

Characteristics	Subject
Sex	Female
Age, y	87
Height, cm	148.6
Body weight, kg	52
History of fall	6 months ago
MFES (range 36–140)	108
PSES (range 15–75)	61

Skin temperature, skin resistance, heart rate variability, blood pressure, and electromyogram measurements were used to measure psychophysiological fears. Measurements were performed with Oculus goggles not installed, with eyes open in a resting position (resting condition), VR room viewing in a model room that was not the scene of the fall using Oculus goggles (non-fall VR conditions), and VR scene viewing fall (VR condition). All measurements use non-invasive methods.

A temperature sensor was worn to measure for skin temperature, a resistance sensor for skin resistance, and a plethysmogram sensor for heart rate variability. Blood pressure is measured with an automatic sphygmomanometer (Crosswell Ltd., Japan) (Fig. 5(a)) with a manchette around the upper arm, and an electromyogram was measured with a disposable tripolar electrode on the epidermis of the eyebrows muscle. Other than blood pressure, we recorded four channels simultaneously with ProComp (Thought Technology Ltd., Quebec, Canada) (Fig. 5(b)).

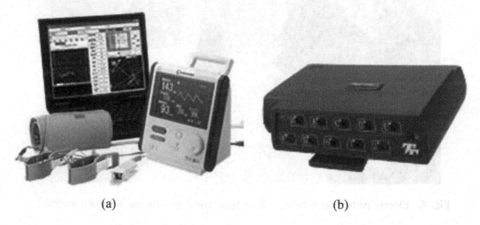

(a)   (b)

Fig. 5. The psychophysiological measurement systems. (a) Blood pressure; (b) ProComp multimodality encoder.

The measurement procedure was as follows. Each measurement sensor installation and equipment adjustment (10 min) → 10 min measurement under resting conditions → 5 min rest after VAS evaluation → Oculus goggles wearing (5 min) → 10 min measurement under non-falling VR conditions → After VAS evaluation 5 min sitting break after removing Oculus goggles → measured for 10 min under falling VR conditions → after VAS evaluation Oculus goggles and each measurement sensor were removed and the experiment was completed (5 min). Based on the data obtained from the above experiments, the extent of the fear of falling by the falling scene VR was confirmed.

2.2   Results

As a result of the measurement, there was a change in a part of the psychophysiological data under the non-fall VR condition. However, a large change in psychophysiological data was observed under the fall VR condition, suggesting that viewing the fall VR could cause fear (Fig. 6, 7 and 8).

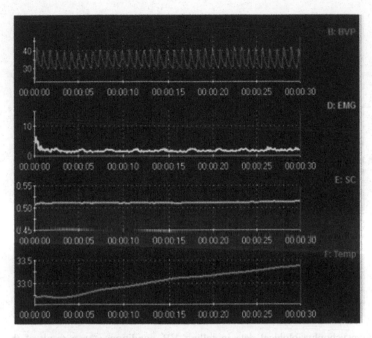

Fig. 6. The psychophysiological data at resting condition. As a result of the resting condition, an increase in body temperature (F:Temp) was observed, but other data were stable.

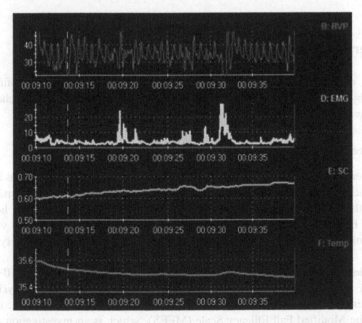

Fig. 7. The psychophysiological data at non-falling VR conditions. As a result of the non-fall VR condition, slight fluctuations in heart rate variability (B:BVP), muscle activity (D:EMG), increased skin conductance (E:SC) and decreased body temperature (F:Temp) were observed.

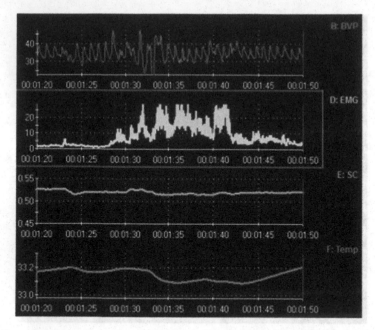

Fig. 8. The psychophysiological data in falling VR conditions. As a result of the fall VR condition, large fluctuations in heart rate variability (B:BVP), large increases in muscle activity (D:EMG), and fluctuations in skin conductance (E:SC) and body temperature (F:Temp) were observed.

3   Experiment 2

The effect of reducing the fear of falls by VR exposure therapy was confirmed for elderly subjects who have confirmed the occurrence of subjective and psychophysiological fear by the fall scene VR in Experiment 1.

3.1   Procedure of VR Exposure Therapy

The fall scene VR is the one from Experiment 1, and the same Oculus goggles are worn and relaxation training by heartbeat fluctuation biofeedback was performed while watching the fall scene VR. Heart rate coherence method was used for heart rate variability biofeedback, and heart rate coherence (the degree of consistent variation) was presented to elderly subjects by auditory feedback through respiratory control (Fig. 9).

For elderly subjects, this training was conducted for 2 min with a set of 10 min and a break for 10 min. During VR exposure therapy, subjective and psychophysiological measurements of fear were conducted in the same way as in Experiment 1, and after two sets, the Modified Fall Efficacy Scale (MFES), which is an investigation scale for fear of falling, and the body Survey of the self-efficacy scale.

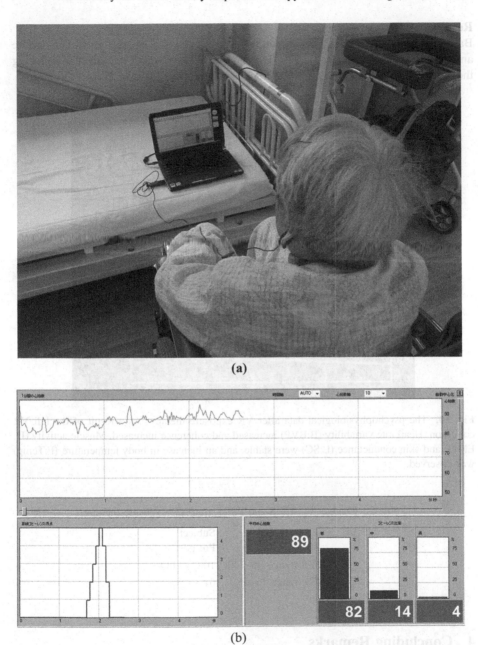

Fig. 9. Heart rate variability biofeedback using emWave Pro (Heartmath LLC, USA). (a) Heart rate coherence is presented to elderly subjects by auditory feedback through respiratory control. (b) emWave Pro collects pulse data and translates coherence information into a user-friendly graphics display.

Results

Based on the changes in subjective and psychophysiological measurement data before and after VR exposure therapy (Fig. 10) and the fall fear scale, the effect of reducing the fear of falling by VR exposure therapy was confirmed (Table 2).

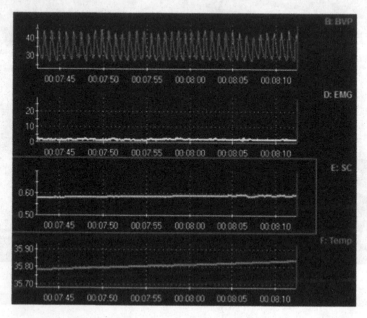

Fig. 10. The psychophysiological data after VR exposure therapy. As a result of the fall VR condition, Heart rate variability (B:BVP) increased and coherence increased. Muscle activity (D: EMG) and skin conductance (E:SC) were stable, and an increase in body temperature (F:Temp) was observed.

Table 2. Changes in MFES and PSES after VR exposure therapy.

	Subject Pre post
MFES (range 36–140)	108 → 114
PSES (range 15–75)	61 → 69

4   Concluding Remarks

In this study, the results of psychophysiological data revealed that elderly people who had previously fallen experienced fear of falling by watching the fall VR. We also found that exposure therapy using fall VR reduces the fear of falling by using HRV biofeedback. However, in this study, since there was only one subject, we would like to increase the number of subjects and conduct verification in the future.

Acknowledgment. This research has been partially supported by the Collaborative Research Fund for Nara Gakuen University.

References

1. Wilson, M.M., Miller, D.K., Andresen, E.M., et al.: Fear of falling and related activity restriction among middle-aged African Americans. J. Gerontol. A Biol. Sci. Med. Sci. **60**, 355–360 (2005)
2. Evitt, C.P., Quigley, P.A.: Fear of falling in older adults: a guide to its prevalence, risk factors, and consequences. Rehabil. Nurs. **29**, 207–210 (2004)
3. Bhala, R.P., O'Donnell, J., Thoppil, E.: Ptophobia: phobic fear of falling and its clinical management. Phys. Ther. **62**, 187–190 (1982)
4. Tinetti, M.E., Mendes de Leon, C.F., Doucette, J.T., Baker, D.I.: Fear of falling and fall-related efficacy in relationship to functioning among community-living elders. J. Gerontol. A Biol. Sci. Med. Sci. **49**, M140–M147 (1994)
5. Davis-Berman, J.: Physical self-efficacy, perceived physical status, and depressive symptomatology in older adults. J. Psychol. **124**, 207–215 (1990)

A New Analysis Method for User Reviews of Mobile Fitness Apps

Peihan Wen and Mo Chen[(✉)]

Chongqing University, Chongqing, People's Republic of China
1048632863@qq.com

Abstract. Keeping fit has always been the focus of public attention, so the emergence of fitness apps has been highly sought after. However, after the outbreak, updates to fitness apps often disappoint their users. Therefore, it is eager for developers to learn about the real requirements and opinions to their apps. To investigate users' requirements, we take data mining on user reviews, and apply sentiment analysis to obtain users' evaluations and suggestions on the attributes and functions of fitness apps. The users of fitness apps have a high follow-up, and usually have been using these apps for a long time, leaning to treat them as daily applications, and can clearly perceive the experience brought by apps during the process. Therefore, users are very serious when evaluating the apps, and the reviews include user requirements, ideas for improvements, positive and negative sentiments about specific features, and descriptions of experiences with these features. Based on the characteristics of the reviews, we use the P-N deep analysis method to perform sentiment analysis on user reviews. For each review, we extract the active and negative evaluations of the corresponding features separately to avoid errors in evaluating features of apps only based on the star rating of the reviews. And when extracting sentiment words in sentiment analysis, verbs are added as features words and adverbs are added as emotion words because users of fitness apps use more adverbs than that of other apps to express their feelings and many nouns can be expressed by verbs in Chinese.

Keywords: Fitness apps · User reviews · P-N deep analysis

1 Introduction

Obesity has been plaguing many people around the world, and health has always been a matter of great concern to everyone. In the past, people often sought professional guidance by going to the gym to exercise for losing weight, bodybuilding, and shaping. And now, through fitness apps everyone can take advantage of fragmented time to receive professional guidance for exercise training anytime, anywhere. In the Chinese market, the fitness industry has entered a blowout period since 2015. More and more fitness apps have appeared on the market, and more and more people are used to using mobile fitness apps to assist in daily fitness exercises. However, in recent years, there have been serious problems with homogeneity of content, biased towards female users, single function and single profit model problems in fitness apps [1]. Developers want to change the status, but the updates of apps usually result in user dissatisfaction and disappointment. Therefore, developers eagerly need to know the real needs and preferences of users. Zhang Xiaoping, Zhao Shurong and Yang Yulong use college students as research objects to explore their experience feedback on some attributes of fitness apps through questionnaire surveys and give improvement opinions based on statistical results [2]. Wang Xuan, Zhou Yaqian and Cao Gang constantly collect feedbacks from trial users in the process of improving and developing a fitness app to understand users' requirements and make targeted improvements to the app [3]. At present, there are few researches on the review analysis of fitness apps in China, but the user reviews of fitness apps contain a lot of information. The users of fitness apps have a high follow-up, and usually have been using these apps for a long time, leaning to treat them as daily applications, and can clearly perceive the experience brought by apps during the process. Therefore, users are very serious when evaluating the apps, and the reviews include user requirements, ideas for improvements, positive and negative sentiments about specific features, and descriptions of experiences with these features. In order to dig deeper into the review information, we will not filter neutral reviews and will use P-N deep analysis method to analyze all user reviews. For each review, we extract all positive and negative emotion words of the respective features separately to avoid mistakes in evaluating app features based on the star rating of the review. And when extracting sentiment words in sentiment analysis, verbs are added as features words and adverbs are added as emotion words because users of fitness apps use more adverbs than that of other apps to express their feelings and many nouns can be expressed by verbs in Chinese. The analysis of user reviews will help developers improve the apps in a more targeted way. By analyzing user reviews and mining users' actual needs, developers can improve applications and expand their competitive advantage.

2 Related Work

In the field of reviews analysis, many scholars have done a lot of research and proposed many methods for many applications and software. Jiang M, Song D, Liao L, et al. proposed a Bayesian model that links a traditional Collaborative Filtering (CF) technique with a topic model seamlessly to analyze the preferences of consumers on e-commerce platforms [4]. Emitza Guzman, Walid Maalej proposed an automated approach that helps developers filter, aggregate, and analyze user reviews of apps in App stores [5]. Li Hanyu, Qian Li and Zhou Pengfei also analyzed the emotional polarity of e-commerce platform commodity reviews [6]. Most articles take electronic platform user reviews and reviews of some movie or book websites as research objects [7, 8], or propose an analysis method for user reviews of all kinds of apps, but there are certain characteristics that are ignored in the application and the results are biased. There are almost no articles on analysis methods that take user reviews of fitness apps as research objects. Therefore, this article proposes a new analysis method for user reviews of fitness apps in the Chinese market.

Sentiment analysis can be divided into three categories: sentiment analysis based on simple statistics analysis, sentiment analysis based on correlation analysis, and sentiment analysis based on machine learning. Tsou et al. comprehensively considered the semantic intensity, polar element distribution and density to make statistics on the semantic tendency of news texts and judge the public's evaluation of celebrities [9]. Taboada puts forward the emotion analysis method based on thesaurus. The main idea of this method is to build a lexicon of emotion words and phrases, which have the tendency and intensity information of emotion. Based on this, they use the intensive method to calculate the emotion score of the text, and finally judge the emotion category of the text according to the score [10]. Wang Xiaoyun et al. quantified the emotional value of commodity reviews through emotional dictionaries, and then constructed a commodity scoring model to make consumers understand commodities more intuitively [11]. The commonly used methods are structural extraction of text syntactic information and semantic role labeling of sentences (SRL) [12]. Turney proposed the semantic analysis idea based on PMI-IR, combined with information retrieval method (IR) and mutual information (PMI) to build a semantic based emotional analysis model. And the method is applied to the review of automobile, movie and other services or commodities, and good results are obtained [13]. Considering the influence of word frequency on feature extraction, Guo Song and others improved the Ig algorithm and improved the accuracy of classification [14]. Meng Jiana et al. solved the problem of poor effect of emotional tendency analysis in different fields by establishing the relationship between words in different fields and transferring domain knowledge [15]. Li Tiancai and others trained word vectors with a large number of Chinese text data through deep learning method, and gained the tendency of micro blog emotion by adding word vectors [16]. There is not much research on sentiment analysis for Chinese short texts, most of which are based on the extraction of sentiment and statistical features of the text. Dongwen Zhang et al. used the word2vec tool to expand the emotion lexicon, and used support vector machines to train text sentiment classification models based on sentiment word features and part-of-speech features [17]. Huang Ren et al. also extended the sentiment lexicon through the word2vec tool, using a statistical model based on sentiment feature words to score users' emotion on text [18].

Each of the three types of sentiment analysis has advantages and disadvantages, and this article will perform a sentiment analysis on user reviews of fitness apps to obtain the user's true views and needs for the features of the app. The correspondence between feature terms and sentiment terms is extremely critical, so we use sentiment analysis based on correlation analysis. Establish feature lexicon and emotion lexicon respectively and form corresponding feature-emotion rule base. The method we propose will perform sentiment analysis on the features (functions, user experience, etc.) of the app, so feature words and sentiment words will be extracted and mapped accordingly, and gain users' positive and negative evaluations of the features of the fitness app and their proportions, so that developers know where to keep and where to improve in the updates of apps.

3 P-N Deep Analysis Method

The main goal of our method is to identify the application functions mentioned in user reviews and the emotions related to these functions, and show the user's positive or negative preference for a certain feature through the proportion of positive and negative emotions. To this end, we use natural language processing and data mining techniques. Figure 1 describes the method. First, we collect users' reviews of the fitness apps from professional platforms. Then, we preprocess the text data to remove noise to get pure text. Then, we apply text mining technology to extract features from the reviews and establish the feature lexicon, extract emotion words from the reviews and form the emotion lexicon, and build a feature-emotion rule base based on the correspondence between features and emotions. Then according to the feature lexicon, dependency syntax analysis, feature-emotion rule base, sentence similarity analysis, we extract feature-emotion word pairs of reviews. Finally, we use KANO model classify users' requirements.

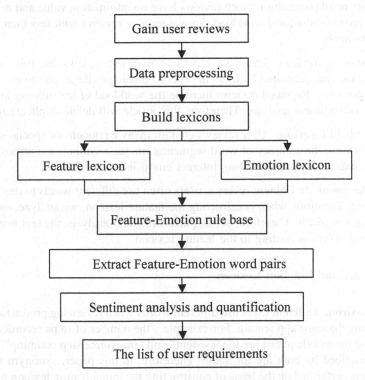

Fig. 1. Overview of the method.

3.1 Review Collection and Preprocessing

Obtaining reviews data and preprocessing the data is the first and crucial step. It lays the foundation for the extraction of feature words and emotion words.

Review Collection. The data source can be achieved by a crawler program, but now there are too many obstacles to crawl some websites or software. It will be more convenient to seek a professional mobile promotion data analysis platform, such as Qimai and Kuchuan. They provide data query for iOS, Android application market, WeChat, etc. Through these platforms, all reviews data (including date, users' name, rating, and evaluation content) of users in a specific market for a specific app can be obtained. The data we will analyze is user reviews of fitness apps in the Chinese Android market. We obtained 14041 user reviews of Huawei Sports Health, a famous fitness app, in China's Android market from professional data platform Qimai.

Data Preprocessing. There is a lot of useless information in reviews, such as spam reviews (reviews made up of symbols, reviews with fewer words), repetitive reviews, etc. In order to ensure that the collected data is valuable for research, we will clean up the useless data from the following aspects to reduce the interference of experimental data with noise data.

Delete Spam Reviews. There are many reviews that contain only a few words, a string of characters or all punctuation. Such reviews have no information value and need to be deleted to reduce subsequent workload. So, we remove reviews with less than 3 words and pure symbols.

Delete Duplicate Reviews. There are repetitive reviews: reviews are full of "brush reviews", which are generated by users in order to obtain privileges etc. to meet one of their own purposes. Repeated reviews increase the workload of text mining and affect the results of sentiment analysis. Therefore, this article will delete duplicate reviews.

Special Symbol Processing. User reviews contain many emoticons or special symbols. In order to ensure the accuracy of word segmentation, such symbols are removed from the review data set by using existing Internet emoji lists.

Word Replacement. In Chinese reviews, users often use different words to describe the same feature. Therefore, when constructing the feature lexicon, we analyze and merge the synonyms of words. Therefore, before performing text analysis, the text needs to be replaced with words according to the feature lexicon.

3.2   Feature and Emotion Lexicon

Feature Lexicon. Different users use different words when reviewing products, even if they evaluate the same app feature. For example, "the number of steps recorded by the bracelet and the mobile phone are inconsistent" and "inaccurate step counting", the app features described by both are the same. Therefore, in this paper, synonym merging processing is performed on the basis of constructing the initial feature lexicon to reduce the dimension of the feature lexicon.

Secondly, the extraction granularity is not fine enough when performing feature extraction. For example, the following reviews "the intensity of the video is very moderate" and "the video is very rich". The former evaluates the strength of the video and the latter is the diversity of the video. However, most of the researches attribute the above reviews to the evaluation of videos when extracting features from user reviews. In feature extraction, we use a "feature-attribute" two-layer structure, such as video-intensity and video-diversity, to obtain user requirements in a finer granularity, and more examples are shown in Table 5.

Therefore, the construction of the feature lexicon in this paper has the following two purposes: to synthesize and replace synonyms based on word similarity analysis, to reduce the app feature dimension of user reviews; and to establish feature-attribute subordinate relationships between features. The specific construction process is as follows, as shown in Fig. 2.

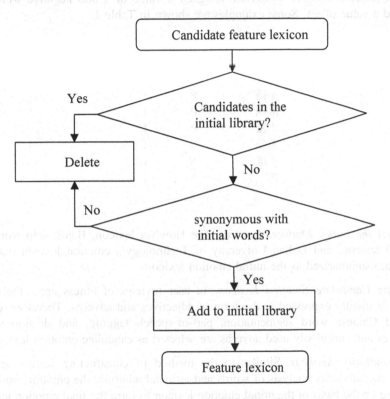

Fig. 2. Construction process of feature lexicon

Construct the Initial Feature Lexicon. We sort out app features according to the details of the fitness app the general situation of the reviews, including the feature-attribute membership relationship as the initial feature lexicon.

Screening Candidate Feature Lexicon. App features usually appear in the form of nouns or noun phrases in user reviews. Sometimes verbs are also a kind of feature expression in Chinese expressions. Therefore, based on Chinese word segmentation and part-of-speech tagging, stop words are removed and nouns, noun phrases and verb nouns are filtered as candidate feature lexicon.

Word Similarity Analysis. According to these papers [17, 18], the Word2vc tool is very effective for expanding feature lexicons and emotion lexicons. Therefore, the Word2vc similarity calculation model was trained based on the corpus to analyze the synonymous relationship. The words with synonymous relationship were merged and replaced with the feature words in the initial feature lexicon.

Emotion Lexicon. The emotion lexicon is very important for text mining sentiment analysis, but the currently published emotion lexicon is updated too slowly, and the development of network languages is extremely fast. Therefore, this article is based on a public emotion lexicon, with the help of word similarity analysis, to expand the emotion lexicon. Positive words are assigned a value of 1 and negative words are assigned a value of −1. Some examples are shown in Table 1.

Table 1. Examples for values of the emotion lexicon

Emotion words	P or N	Values
不错	P	1
准确	P	1
丰富	P	1
卡顿	N	−1
不准	N	−1
差	N	−1

Construct the Initial Emotion Lexicon. The HowNet lexicon, Baidu stop word list, NTUSD lexicon, and Dalian University of Technology's emotion lexicon ontology library are summarized as the initial emotion lexicon.

Screening Candidate Emotion Lexicon. In user reviews of fitness apps, the user's attitude is usually expressed in the form of adjectives and adverbs. Therefore, on the basis of Chinese word segmentation, part-of-speech tagging, and de-stop words, adjectives and commonly used adverbs are selected as candidate emotion lexicon.

Word Similarity Analysis. Similar to the method of constructing feature lexicon, through the similarity analysis of words and artificial addition, the emotion words are expanded on the basis of the initial emotion lexicon to form the final emotion lexicon.

3.3 Feature-Emotion Rule Base

According to the study of Chinese entity relationship [19], the Dependency Parsing (DP) analysis method is very effective for feature-sentiment analysis based on Chinese text. We use this method to analyze the grammatical structure of user reviews and extract grammatical components. Sentence components can be divided into 14 types, such as subject-verb relations (SBV), attribute-headword relations (ATT), and adverb-headword (ADV) relations. The natural language processing tool of Harbin Institute of

Technology, LTP is used to analyze the dependency syntax of text. Some examples of types of are sentence components shown in Table 2.

According to the research on user reviews and common Chinese expression habits, we find that the relationship between emotion words and feature words in the reviews mostly appears as the dependency relationship of SBV, ATT, and ADV. Therefore, on the basis of DP analysis, the word pairs containing both emotion words and feature words, and the dependency relationships are SBV, ATT, and ADV are selected as the candidate word pair set of the emotion-feature rule base. The user will choose to use the same adjective to modify multiple objects when reviewing, such as "the courses of the app is rich" and "the recommended recipes offered by the app is rich", "rich" can both modify the course and recipes, so we divide the emotion-feature rule base into two categories: 1V1 rule base, this kind of emotion words only modify one feature word, which can directly infer the characteristics evaluated by users based on emotion words; 1Vn rule base, one emotion word modifies multiple feature words, which is more common.

In the reviews, select the (feature, emotion) word pairs whose dependencies are ATT, ADV, and SBV and exist in the feature lexicon and emotion lexicon, and count the frequency. Some examples of emotion-feature rule bases are shown in Table 2.

Table 2. Examples of 1V1 and 1Vn feature-emotion rule base

Emotion words	Feature words	1V1 or 1Vn	Relationships	Frequency
卡顿	连接	1V1	SBV	182
贵	价格	1V1	SBV	24
有用	课程	1Vn	ATT	69
有用	指导	1Vn	ATT	13
丰富	课程	1Vn	SBV	99
丰富	食谱	1Vn	SBV	6

3.4   Sentiment Analysis

Initial Score. The initial score of the feature words is based on the assignment of the emotion words in the emotion lexicon, and then a four-dimensional array (feature, attribute, emotion, initial score) is obtained. Considering the influence of the degree adverb, we will weigh the polarity of the emotion words of the degree adverb. The HowNet dictionary divides the degree adverb polarity values (V_{ad}) of different emotional intensity into 4 levels, as shown in Table 3:

Table 3. The degree adverb polarity values (V_{ad})

Degree adverb	V_{ad}
非常, 太, 完全, 无比, 最, 超级	2
比较, 稍微, 略微, 更	1.5
略, 微, 有点, 有些	0.5
Positive words with no modified by degree adverbs	1
Negative words with no modified by degree adverbs	−1

Weighted Score. The initial score is weighted according to the polarity value of degree adverbs. For emotion words modified by degree adverbs, the initial sentiment score is weighted according to the polarity values of degree adverbs:

$$weighted\ score = V_{ad} \times initial\ score \qquad (1)$$

On the contrary, the initial score is maintained.

Final Score. Because some users tend to use encouraging statements, the positive rate of some features is very high. In order to balance the impact of the encouraging reviews on the final score, we calculate the positive and negative sentiment mean of each feature. And the revised sentiment score is calculated as follows:

$$Score = \overline{P} + \overline{N} \qquad (2)$$

Among them, $\overline{P}$ and $\overline{N}$ represent the mean of positive emotions and negative emotions respectively. After the score calculation and the calculation of the positive and negative sentiment ratios, the final sentiment analysis results (features, attributes, frequency, positive ratio, negative ratio, and final score) are obtained. The analysis results are shown in Table 4:

Table 4. The results of sentiment analysis

Features	Attributes	Frequency	Positive ratio	Negative ratio	Final score
课程	多样性	99	83.2%	16.8%	0.77
课程	数量	69	79.7%	20.3%	0.65
设备	连接	201	11.1%	88.9%	−0.21
功能	计步	186	5.6%	94.4%	−0.12
数据	同步率	98	19.2%	90.8%	−0.08
音乐	连接性	87	14.5%	85.5%	−0.14
界面	布局	56	88.7%	11.3%	1.12

3.5 Requirement Analysis

In similar research [20], the KANO model is very effective in determining the weight of features. Based on sentiment analysis, we use KANO model to mine and classify user needs. First, based on the sentiment dictionary analysis, the initial sentiment scores are 1 and -1. According to Sect. 3.4, the extreme value of the degree adverb is 2, so the score interval is $[-2, 2]$.

The types of user requirements included in the KANO model are attractive requirements, performance requirements, basic requirements, non-differentiated requirements, and reverse requirements. Attractive requirements refer to features that exceed user expectations. When the app does not have such features, user satisfaction will not decrease, and when the app has such features, user satisfaction will increase significantly. For performance requirements, user satisfaction is positively related to such features, that is, when the app has such features, user satisfaction increases, and vice versa. Basic requirements refer to the necessary features of the apps. When developers optimize such features, user satisfaction will not increase, but when the app does not have such features, user satisfaction will be greatly reduced. Non-differentiated requirements mean that the user's satisfaction will not change based on the availability of such features. Reverse requirements refer to the features that users don't need. When the app has such features, user satisfaction will decrease.

When the score is bigger than 1, the user's emotional tendency is stronger, the app features exceed the user's expectations, and the user satisfaction is high. Therefore, app features with an emotional value bigger than 1 are attractive requirements; if the score is in the [0, 1] interval, it indicates that the user's satisfaction is not high, the app features have not exceeded user expectations, and users are eager for a better experience. Therefore, the app features with emotional values in the [0,1] range are performance requirements; when the score is less than 0, the user is dissatisfied and the app features do not meet the basic needs of the user and need to be further improved. Based on the requirements classification, we also comprehensively consider the user's attention to the feature-attribute of the apps, the ratio of the number of feature-attribute evaluations to the total number of evaluations, to obtain the final list of user requirements.

The results of the user requirements are shown in Table 5.

Table 5. The results of user requirements analysis

Features	Attributes	Final score	The type of requirement	Frequency
课程	多样性	0.77	Performance	8.2%
课程	数量	0.65	Performance	6.4%
设备	连接	−0.21	Performance	15.9%
功能	计步	−0.12	Basic	14.8%
数据	同步率	−0.08	Basic	7.4%
音乐	连接性	−0.14	Basic	6.3%
界面	布局	1.12	Attractive	4.7%

The requirement list and the type and priority of the requirements indicate that the developer of the app should maintain the layout and style of the app interface, because users have a high degree of attention and satisfaction with the interface. At the same time, it should be noted that the device connection, music playback, data synchronization, and step counting functions are in urgent need of improvement, because users do not get a good experience in these aspects. Finally, the number and diversity of fitness classes should be appropriately improved to meet the needs of more users.

4   Conclusion

We propose a new analysis method (P-N depth analysis method) based on user reviews of fitness app in China market. This method extracts the features and emotion words of each review and word pairs, and assigns sentiment words and degree adverbs to quantify sentiment analysis. Determine and calculate the positive and negative word pair frequencies of the same feature during word pair extraction. Finally, according to the sentiment value and the positive and negative sentiment ratios of the reviews in the sentiment analysis, we understand the user's main requirements and the types of those requirements. The results of the example verification are basically consistent with the results of manual statistical analysis.

Our method maximizes the use of textual data and avoids analysis bias caused by deleting neutral reviews and judging sentiment just based on ratings. The final analysis results can provide developers with suggestions for improving the apps. They can improve the specific feature attributes and profit model, bring users a better user experience, expand the advantages of the industry, and prevent problems such as content homogeneity which cause user churn.

We still have a lot of work to do on the research of user reviews of mobile fitness apps. When extracting features from reviews, we mainly consider explicit features. But users sometimes don't directly describe the feature when they express their opinions, or even don't mention the feature. In the future, we can extract implicit features based on the relationship between semantics and feature words, to get more data of features, and to get more accurate evaluations of features by users.

References

1. Wu, R., Wang, Q.: Research on development status, problems and countermeasures of sports fitness app. J. Shandong Inst. Phys. Educ. **04**, 22–26 (2015)
2. Zhang, X., Zhao, Y., Yang, Y.: Research on the experience of college students using fitness apps under the new media environment. China School Phys. Educ. (High. Educ.) **05**, 7–12 (2017)
3. Wang, X., Zhou, Y., Cao, G.: "Xingxiu"—research on mobile phone APP for college students. Mod. Bus. Ind. **03**, 70–71 (2019)
4. Jiang, M., Song, D., Liao, L., et al.: A Bayesian recommender model for user rating and review profiling. J. Tsinghua Univ. (Engl. Version), **20**, 634–643 (2015)

5. Guzman, E., Maalej, W.: How do users like this feature? A fine-grained sentiment analysis of app reviews. In: 2014 IEEE 22nd International Requirements Engineering Conference, RE 2014 – Proceedings, pp. 153–162 (2014). https://doi.org/10.1109/re.2014.6912257

6. Li, H., Qian, L., Zhou, P.: Sentiment analysis and mining for product review texts. Inf. Sci. **01**, 53–57 (2017)

7. Ma, S., Xu, X.: Research on user online evaluation based on comment sentiment analysis—taking Douban movie as an example. Libr. Inf. Serv. **10**, 95–102 (2016)

8. Li, H., Zhang, H.: A method for sentiment analysis of book reviews based on word vector and CNN. J. Test Measur. Technol. **02**, 165–171 (2019)

9. Tsou, B.K.Y., Yuen, R.W.M., Kwong, O.Y., et al.: Polarity classification of celebrity coverage in the Chinese press, 105–111 (2005)

10. Taboada, M., Brooke, J., Tofiloski, M., et al.: Lexicon-based methods for sentiment analysis. Comput. Linguist. **37**, 267–307 (2011)

11. Wang, X., Shi, L.: Commodity comprehensive scoring model based on emotion quantification of web reviews. J. Hangzhou Dianzi Univ.: Soc. Sci. Ed. **03**, 8–15 (2016)

12. Chen, Y., Huang, Z., Shi, X.: An SNN-based semantic role labeling model with its network parameters optimized using an improved PSO algorithm. Neural Process. Lett. **44**, 245–263 (2016). https://doi.org/10.1007/s11063-015-9449-y

13. Turney, P.D.: Thumbs up or thumbs down?: semantic orientation applied to unsupervised classification of reviews. In: Proceedings of Annual Meeting of the Association for Computational Linguistics, pp. 417–424 (2002)

14. Guo, S.: Improving the algorithm of information gain feature selection in text classification. Comput. Appl. Softw. **30**, 139–142 (2013)

15. Meng, J., Duan, X., Yang, L.: Tendency analysis of cross-domain product reviews based on feature transformation. Comput. Eng. **10**, 167–171 (2013)

16. Li, T., Wang, B., Mao, E., et al.: Analysis of sentiment orientation of Weibo based on Skip-gram model. J. Comput. Appl. Softw. **07**, 114–117 (2016)

17. Zhang, D., Yang, P., Xu, Y.: Research of Chinese comments sentiment classification based on Word2vec and SVMperf. Comput. Sci. **43**, 418–421 (2016)

18. Huang, R., Zhang, W.: Study on sentiment analysis of internet commodities review based on word2vec. Comput. Sci. **43**, 387–389 (2016)

19. Gan, L., Wan, C., Liu, D., et al.: Chinese entity relation extraction based on syntactic and semantic features. J. Comput. Res. Dev. **53**, 284–302 (2016)

20. Tang, Z., Long, Y.: Research on personalized demand acquisition method based on Kano model. Soft Sci. **02**, 131–135 (2012)

How to Present Calorie Information on the Electronic Menu to Help People Order More Healthily

Shiyuan Zhang[✉], Liang Zhou[iD], and Ying Zhao[iD]

School of Public Administration, Sichuan University, Sichuan, China
519704936@qq.com, zhouliang_bnu@163.com,
zhaoying@scu.edu.cn

Abstract. A large study published in THE LANCET in 2014 showed that the number and proportion of obese and overweight people in the world have been increasing in the past 30 years. The problem of high obesity rate has attracted people's attention. At the same time, the frequency of people eating out shows a rapid increase, and eating out often will increase the risk of overweight and obesity. Because of changes in the ordering methods of restaurants, the electronic ordering system affects people's food choices and also has an important impact on obesity. Therefore, how to design an electronic ordering system that can effectively promote consumers' healthy diet is a key issue. In this research, the authors use factorial experiments and laboratory experiments to explore the impact of calorie labels on the electronic menu and the perceptual fluency of calorie labels on users. Studies have found that electronic menus presenting calorie labels would guide people to choose foods with lower calorie values, and calorie labels with low perceptual fluency would better guide people to choose foods with lower calorie values. The results can complement the research in the field of electronic menus and calorie labels, and provide a theoretical basis for the menu design of restaurants using electronic menus. Through this study, more people and restaurants will focus on dietary health issues, thereby effectively reducing the obesity rate in China.

Keywords: Electronic ordering system · Calorie label · Perceptual fluency

1 Introduction

In recent years, eating out has become the norm in people's lives, and the frequency of people eating out has shown a rapid increase. Eating out will increase the consumption of meat, sweets, alcohol, etc., and reduce the intake of vegetables and fruits [1, 2]. Because eating out is related to high-energy, high-density foods, eating out often increases the risk of overweight and obesity [3]. In 2014, THE LANCET published a large-scale study report on the world's obese population. The report shows that the global number and proportion of obese and overweight people have been increasing in the past 30 years, and the peak obesity rate is gradually becoming younger. The number of obese people in China is increasing year by year, and a series of diseases caused by obesity are also endangering people's lives. For adults, being overweight and

M. Kurosu (Ed.): HCII 2020, LNCS 12183, pp. 200–212, 2020.
https://doi.org/10.1007/978-3-030-49065-2_15

obese is a major risk factor for cardiovascular disease, diabetes, musculoskeletal diseases, and some cancers. For children, obesity also causes great health risks, which is not conducive to their growth and development [4–6]. With the popularization of smart electronic products and the development of mobile Internet, more and more restaurants have replaced traditional paper menus with electronic ordering systems. Therefore, how to design an electronic ordering system that can promote consumers' healthy diet is a key issue.

Many restaurants have stated the calories in their menus. In response to this situation, researchers have visited restaurants that indicate the calories of food. Some customers who focus on dietary management say that the menus with calories are very useful for them. Roberto's research [7] shows that presenting calorie labels on menus can affect consumers' choice and intake of food during meals. Participants who use the menus that present calorie labels for ordering chose foods with fewer calories than those who use the menus that do not present calorie labels. Whether or not presenting calorie labels on an electronic menu would have the same effect is a question we want to explore.

At the same time, some studies have suggested that calorie labels do not affect people's choices of food at mealtime. Therefore, we considered a moderator of calorie labels, namely the perceptual fluency of how calorie labels are presented on electronic menus. The effect of calorie labels is affected by whether people are aware of it on the one hand, and on the other hand, it is regulated by people's cognition degree of the label. Perceptual fluency will affect people's subjective experience of information cognition [8]. Previous studies have shown that changing contrast of background and legibility of fonts can effectively change the perceptual fluency of information [9]. Song's research [10] changed the perceptual fluency of information by changing the legibility of the font, and explores the impact of perceptual fluency on people's information processing methods. It was found that under the condition of low perceptual fluency, participants were more inclined to read the material carefully. Therefore, the perceptual fluency of the information in the electronic menu will affect the subjective experience of people when reading, and will also affect the way people process the menu information.

On this basis, this paper studied the impact of calorie label presentation on people's order choices in the electronic ordering system, and designed experiments to explore whether the presence of calorie labels and the perceptual fluency of calorie labels affect people. We believe that a menu that presents calorie labels will lead people to choose foods with low calorie values, and a calorie label with low perceptual fluency will enable people to choose foods with lower calorie values. In the presentation of calorie labels, we have chosen two ways to display the calorie value directly and describe the calorie value, to explore whether different calorie labels have different effects on guiding people's healthy diet. The study adopted the research methods of factorial design and laboratory experiment method. By designing experiments, the participants are tested in groups, and the data are analyzed.

This study aims to design an electronic ordering system that can better guide people to have a healthy diet. Today, consumers pay little attention to dietary health issues during meals, and few restaurants guide consumers' awareness of dietary health during their ordering process. This has led consumers to still ignore whether the dishes have an impact on their health or even cause them to become obese. In the society with high obesity rates, an electronic ordering system that focuses on the healthy diet can not only provide consumers with healthy meals, but also serve as a marketing strategy for restaurants. On the one hand, the conclusion has theoretical contributions. It can supplement and make certain contributions to the research on the theories related to healthy diet and calories, which will be helpful for the future research in this field and have a positive impact on the future effective reduction of obesity rate in China. It can provide theoretical support for other researchers concerned with electronic menus and diet health. Based on this research, researchers can further explore the effect of other calorie label presentation methods such as aging-booth on people's food choices, and complete a more comprehensive study. On the other hand, the conclusion has practical significance. The results can be extended to more restaurants that use electronic menus, provide theoretical basis for their electronic menu design and consideration of users' health, and provide ideas and development direction for the design of electronic ordering system in the future. We hope that through this research, more and more consumers and restaurants will pay attention to dietary health issues, and consumers will consider the impact of calories on their bodies during ordering process, effectively reducing the obesity rate in China.

2 Theoretical Background

2.1 Calorie Label

Calorie label means that the restaurant's menu contains detailed information on the energy content of all dishes. Its goal is to make consumers make healthier eating choices by posting calorie labels in a visible and transparent way for consumers [6].

Regarding the effect of calorie labels on the menu on consumers during meals, some scholars believe that it has the effect of promoting consumers to choose healthier, lower-calorie foods. In 2017, Ontario Province became the first province in Canada to be required to indicate calorie content on the restaurant chain's menu. Samantha [11] and other researchers collected data on the use of nutritional information in restaurants in the province and provinces that do not have a menu calorie labeling policy, as well as dining choices for young people aged 16-30 before and after Ontario implemented the policy. They studied differences in the level of attention to nutritional information across provinces. The results showed that nutritional information in Ontario was significantly more concerned than in other provinces, and nutritional information had a greater impact on dietary choices among respondents in Ontario than in other provinces. Krešić's research shows that by providing energy information, people can choose foods with fewer calories and less fat [12]. Research by Roseman and other researchers confirms that menu calorie labels have a significant positive effect on students' intentions to choose low-calorie foods [13].

Other researchers have found that calorie labels in menus have different effects on different people's diet choices. A study [14] by Larson et al. Found that the calorie information on the menu does not similarly affect everyone's choices. About half of the participants in his study noticed the calorie information while dining in the restaurant, and used this information to do ordering decision. At the same time, the effects of calorie labels may provide guidance for people with eating disorders or other weight problems. Shikdar and Suzuki found that, with the exception of Hispanics, the higher the use of calorie labels, the more willing people are to choose a healthy diet [15]. Because people of different races have different dietary habits and attention to calorie labels, the calorie labels on the menu may exacerbate the difference in obesity between races [16].

However, some researchers believe that calorie labels have no significant effect on people's dietary choices [17, 18]. A study [19] of the effects of calorie labels on fast food diets found that McDonald's calorie labels have nothing to do with calorie changes in foods purchased by adults, teens, and children. Even though people may focus on calorie labels on the menu, their ability to accurately estimate the calorie value of the food they buy has not improved. Because of the results of such studies, Dallas [20] considered that the reason why calorie labels did not affect consumers' diet choices was that they did not consider the order in which people processed information when setting calorie labels, so they studied the presentation of calorie information. It was found that the position of the calorie label has an impact on consumers' diet choices.

In this study, we introduce the concept of calorie labels to explore the impact of calorie labels on consumer dietary choices. We believe that calorie labels have an impact on food choices when dining out, and an electronic menu showing calorie labels will guide people to choose foods with lower calorie values.

2.2 Perceptual Fluency

Perceptual fluency refers to the subjective experience of individuals in processing information at the perceptual level when processing information [8]. Related concepts include conceptual fluency, information retrieval fluency, language fluency, coding fluency, etc. [21] Perceptual fluency can also be divided into object perceptual fluency and temporal perceptual fluency. The degree of perception of the physical properties of the stimulus, and the duration of the stimulus, will have an effect on the perceptual fluency.

Perceptual fluency is related to the difficulty of processing information in the task [22]. Therefore, researchers usually judge the perceptual fluency by inquiring about the difficulty level of the processing information perceived by the participants, and can also judge the perceptual fluency by measuring the response speed of the participants [23].

In order to adjust the perceptual fluency in experiments, researchers in related fields mainly control the experimental materials. In the past, researchers used to control text materials during experiments. By changing the font and gray scale of reading materials, they adjusted the perceptual fluency of text materials to easily and effectively achieve low perceptual fluency. For example, adjusting the grayscale of text materials to 50% grayscale is a simple and effective way to reduce perceptual fluency [24].

In daily life, people tend to choose smooth processes for information processing. The smooth information processing process can increase the processing speed, reduce the processing time and improve the processing efficiency. However, some researchers have found a boost in low-perception fluency [25]. Alter's research shows that low perceptual fluency can promote individuals to process information in more detail and in depth, which is helpful to the development of individual cognition [8]. And related research believes that the effect of learning difficult-to-read materials is better than that of easy-to-read materials, and unsmooth materials help alleviate overconfidence during learning.

As for the relationship between perceptual fluency and learning effects, researchers in related fields have come to different conclusions. Some researchers believe that low perceptual fluency can improve learning effectiveness [26]. The researchers changed the perceptual fluency by changing the font, gray scale, font size, and other factors of the text material. It was found that the participants in the experimental group whose text was not fluent had better learning results [24]. And some researchers believe that low perceptual fluency is not conducive to the improvement of learning effects. Carole's study found that the participants did not produce significantly different learning effects due to the clarity of the experimental materials [27]. Current researches have not yet reached a consistent answer to this question, and there is still much room for research on perceptual fluency.

In this study, we add the concept of perceptual fluency to the electronic ordering system. The level of perceptual fluency of the system interface text will affect consumers' subjective experience and processing difficulty of dish information when ordering. We believe that calorie information with low perceptual fluency can deepen the user's impression of calorie information when ordering, enable users to process calorie-related information in more detail, and enable users to choose foods with lower calorie values.

3 Hypothesis Development

As mentioned earlier, researchers have come to different conclusions about the effect of presenting calorie labels on the menu on consumers' intentions to choose low-calorie foods. Some researchers believe that menus that present calorie labels have a positive effect on consumers 'choice of low-calorie foods, while some researchers believe that calorie labels have no significant effect on consumers' diet choices. And when consumers pay attention to calorie label, the effect of processing information is related to the perceptual fluency of the information, and the research conclusions about perceptual fluency and learning effects are also different.

Calorie labels provide consumers with calorie information in a way that is visible and transparent to consumers. Dining out will increase the consumption of meat, sweets, alcohol, etc., and reduce the intake of vegetables, fruits, etc., and is related to high-fat foods. If there is no calorie label on the menu in the restaurant, consumers cannot effectively estimate the calorie content of the food when ordering, and the accuracy of the calorie estimation is low. When choosing food, by using a calorie label to focus on the health of the food, consumers will respond faster to health attributes and respond less to taste attributes, thereby increasing health choices [28]. Prolonged exposure to menus that present calorie labels may increase consumer awareness of calories and healthy diet [29]. So we propose the first hypothesis as follows:

H1: A menu showing calorie labels will lead people to choose foods with lower calorie values.

Part of the studies on perceptual fluency have shown that low perceptual fluency can promote individuals to process information more meticulously and deeply. If the individual feels that the difficulty of information processing is low, the individual generally activates the first processing system, that is, the fast and intuitive system. At this time, the individual uses heuristic thinking. If the individual feels that the information processing is more difficult, the individual generally activates the second processing system, that is, the slow and intentional system. At this time, the individual will invest more effort and adopt analytical thinking [30]. When choosing food, consumers tend to think more about taste preferences than health [31]. When the perceptual fluency of calorie labels is lower than the perceptual fluency of other information, consumers perform fast and intuitive processing of other information with high perceptual fluency. Calorie labels with low perceptual fluency will trigger consumer calorie label stimuli for systematic and sophisticated processing, making consumers more focused on calorie labels. And calorie labels can make consumers aware of the health aspects of food. As a result, consumers are paying more attention to the health aspects of foods, so they can respond faster to health attributes and less to taste attributes. From this we propose the second hypothesis as follows:

H2: Calorie labels with low perceptual fluency enable people to choose foods with lower calorie values.

Our research on the presentation of calories mainly includes the two presentation methods of displaying calorie values and describing the calories in text. People have different degrees of recognition for data-based labels and text-based nutrition information labels [32]. It can be seen that when the same information is presented in different ways, people's understanding of it will also be different. Therefore, we believe that the two presentation methods, which directly display the calorie value and the text description of calories, have different degrees of understanding of calorie information during the ordering process, and have different effects on people's ordering choices. And further explore the effect of perceptual fluency on the two presentation methods.

H3: In the presentation of calorie labels, the menu that directly presents the calorie value and the menu that describes the calorie value have different effects on people's choice of food.

4 Research Design

4.1 Research Method

The study adopts the research methods of factorial design and laboratory experiment method. The laboratory experiment method strictly controls the experimental conditions and eliminates errors caused by irrelevant factors as much as possible. And the laboratory experimental method is usually used to investigate the cause and effect relationship, which is suitable for the research purpose of this research, so this method is adopted.

80 participants are randomly recruited and randomly divided into four groups for experiments. Each group of participants use different interfaces of the electronic ordering system to order food. We record the dishes selected by each group of participants, calculate the total and average calories of the selected dishes, and the time taken to select the dishes. At the same time, some of the control factors affecting the experiment are statistically processed through questionnaire design. The control factors such as the participants' height, weight, and subjective feelings about the information are designed as questionnaire questions. Participants of each group fill in the questionnaires after ordering food. The purpose of the questionnaire questions is to explain the errors generated in the experiment and to statistically summarize the subjective feelings of the participants in their daily dining choices.

Data analysis is performed using a one-way analysis of variance. One-way analysis of variance refers to an experiment in which only one factor is changed, and by analyzing the experimental data, it is tested whether multiple normal population means with equal variances are equal to determine whether each factor has a significant effect on the experimental index. Because the two groups of experiments for comparative analysis are controlled so that only one factor changes at a time, this analysis method is used. By comparing and analyzing the data obtained from the experiment, we explore whether the dishes selected by the participants when ordering would cause significant differences due to different menu designs, and verified whether the research hypothesis is valid.

4.2 Participants and Experimental Materials

In this experiment, 80 participants are randomly recruited to participate in the experiment in universities, institutions and other places, and all participants participate in the experiment voluntarily. The 80 participants include students, teachers, corporate employees and persons in other fields. Because the participants are recruited and grouped by random recruitment and allocation, the influence of different groups on the dependent variable could be offset each other, so the subjective impact of the crowd is solved by the randomization of the recruitment of subjects.

Because there are four groups in the experiment, four different types of electronic menus need to be designed as one control group and three experimental groups. The electronic menu designed in this experiment is provided to the participants for experimentation in the form of a webpage front-end interface.

The experimental materials mainly include the menu design and interface design of electronic menu. This electronic menu prototype is a fictional restaurant menu. Because it is not a real restaurant, the influence of the restaurant itself on the experimental results can be ruled out. The dishes are vegetarian and balanced, with a total of 26 dishes, which can meet the ordering needs of most participants, and the dishes in the four experimental electronic menus are consistent. The interface design of the four groups of experimental prototypes are all different. The first group is used as the control group. The introduction of the dishes mainly includes the names of the dishes, the pictures of the dishes, and the introduction of the dishes. The second to fourth groups are experimental groups. In addition to the name of the dish and the picture of the dish, the display of the calorie value and the text description of the calorie value are added.

The calorie information in the interface of the experimental group is real data obtained from a special food data website, www.boohee.com. The perceptual fluency of calorie labels in the second to fourth groups is also different. The interface of the second group of experiments uses a high perceptual fluency calorie value and a text description of the calorie value. The perceptual fluency of the caloric value of the interface of third group of experimental is low, and the perceptual fluency of the text description of the calorific value is high. The interface of the fourth group of experimental uses a high perceptual fluency calorie value and a low perceptual fluency calorie text description. At the same time, the factors controlling the other non-independent variables of the second to fourth groups are the same, so as not to affect the experimental data. The text with high perceptual fluency in this experiment uses Microsoft Yahei font, the font color code of the calorie value is # 2894FF, and the font color code of the calorie description is #FFFFFF (the shading is black). The text with low perceptual fluency uses KAIU.TTF font and is in italic. The font color code of the calorie value is # ACD6FF, and the font color code of the calorie description is # 9D9D9D (shading is black). At the same time, in order to highlight the calorie information contained in the experimental group, the calorie-related information of the menu is displayed directly below the name of the dish, and it is displayed in a large font to ensure that it is eye-catching and to avoid participants ignoring this information and affecting the experimental results.

After design, the interfaces design of the four groups of electronic ordering systems are shown in Fig. 1, Fig. 2, Fig. 3, and Fig. 4:

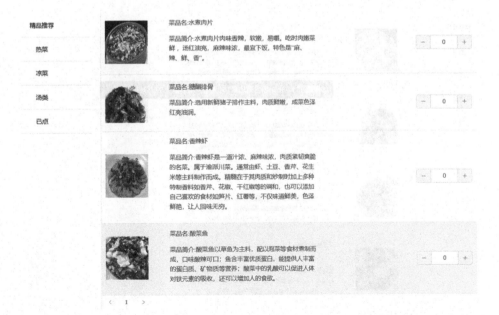

Fig. 1. Interface of the electronic ordering system used in the first group of experiments

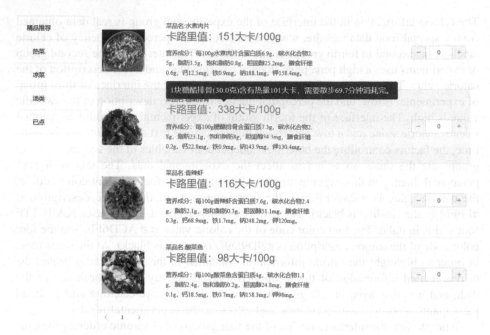

Fig. 2. Interface of the electronic ordering system used in the second group of experiments

Fig. 3. Interface of the electronic ordering system used in the third group of experiments

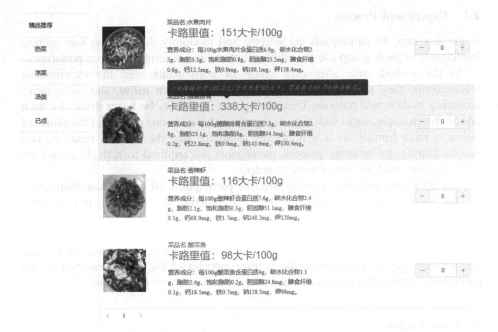

菜品名:水煮肉片
卡路里值: 151大卡/100g
营养成分：每100g水煮肉片含蛋白质6.9g，碳水化合物2.
5g，脂肪3.5g，饱和脂肪0.8g，胆固醇25.2mg，膳食纤维
0.6g，钙12.5mg，铁0.9mg，钠188.1mg，钾158.4mg。

卡路里值: 338大卡/100g
营养成分：每100g糖醋排骨含蛋白质7.3g，碳水化合物2.
8g，脂肪23.1g，饱和脂肪8g，胆固醇34.3mg，膳食纤维
0.2g，钙22.8mg，铁0.9mg，钠143.9mg，钾130.4mg。

菜品名:香辣虾
卡路里值: 116大卡/100g
营养成分：每100g香辣虾含蛋白质7.6g，碳水化合物2.4
g，脂肪2.1g，饱和脂肪0.3g，胆固醇51.1mg，膳食纤维
0.3g，钙68.9mg，铁1.7mg，钠248.2mg，钾120mg。

菜品名:酸菜鱼
卡路里值: 98大卡/100g
营养成分：每100g酸菜鱼含蛋白质4g，碳水化合物1.1
g，脂肪2.4g，饱和脂肪0.2g，胆固醇24.8mg，膳食纤维
0.1g，钙18.5mg，铁0.7mg，钠158.3mg，钾98mg。

Fig. 4. Interface of the electronic ordering system used in the fourth group of experiments

4.3 Measurement of Variables

According to the research purpose, we design a questionnaire to measure other variables. The questionnaire is designed with a total of 11 questions, including the following aspects: 1. Personal information of the subjects, such as gender, age, height, weight and education; 2. The experimental group of the participants; 3. Participants' degree of attention to the effect of calorie information of dishes on their health when dining out; 4. When the participants used the prototype of the experimental menu, the degree of influence of the four factors of the basic information of the dishes, the caloric value, the text description of the caloric value, and the nutritional component information on the choice of the participant when ordering; 5. When the participants read the menu, whether the calorie value and the description of the calorie value make the participants feel comfortable; 6. In the process of using the menu, whether the calorie value and the description of the calorie value will affect or hinder the reading experience of the participants and the choice of ordering; 7. The degree of satisfaction of the participants with the electronic menu used; 8. The data collection of the participants after the ordering step, including uploading screenshots of the selected dishes and the total time to fill in the ordering. Except for the questionnaire's personal information, experimental group and data recovery after the experiment, other questions are designed using Likert 7-level scale. Participants are required to indicate their degree of agreement or disagreement with the attitude-related statements stated in each question.

4.4   Experiment Process

In the first step, 80 participants are selected and randomly divided into four groups. Participants of each group use four different electronic ordering interface prototypes.

In the second step, after each group of participants read the experimental requirements, they start to use the prototype of their own menu, and order meals according to their two portions. Considering that there may be fewer dishes for each person (for example, a girl with a small appetite only needs one dish), and the choice of dishes is more limited, so it is uniformly stipulated that the order is based on two people. During the ordering process, participants are required to actively record the selected dishes and the time it took to order.

The third step, after the ordering step, the participants fill out the questionnaire.

The fourth step is to collect data. After the experiment, the participants are numbered according to the serial number when filling out the questionnaire, and the experimental data is sorted into an Excel file.

The fifth step is to import all experimental data into the SPSS software, perform a one-way analysis of variance on the average calories of the dishes selected by the participants, output the test results, and analyze and interpret the results.

5   Conclusion

Experimental results support research hypotheses. The study mainly drew the following two conclusions. First, calorie labels have an impact on people's food choices when dining out. An electronic menu showing calorie labels will guide people to choose foods with lower calorie values. Second, calorie labels with different perceptual fluency have different degrees of influence on people's food choices. And calorie labels with low perceptual fluency can better guide people to choose foods with lower calorie values. In addition, although both the calorie value and the description of the calorie value will affect people's dining choices, the effect of the calorie value on people's choice of ordering is different from the effect of the description of the calorie value. Therefore, the research results show that the menu interface of an electronic ordering system showing calorie labels with low perceptual fluency can best guide people to choose foods with lower calorie values during the ordering process. The results can complement the research in the field of electronic menus and calorie labels, and provide a theoretical basis for the menu design of restaurants using electronic menus. Through this study, more people and restaurants will focus on dietary health issues, thereby effectively reducing the obesity rate in China.

Acknowledgment. This work is supported by Fundamental Research Funds for the Central Universities, Sichuan University (Grant No. skbsh201808).

References

1. Murakami, K., Sasaki, S., Takahashi, Y., Uenishi, K., the Japan Dietetic Students' Study for Nutrition and Biomarkers Group: Neighborhood restaurant availability and frequency of eating out in relation to dietary intake in young Japanese women. J. Nutr. Sci. Vitaminol. **57**(1), 87–94 (2011)
2. O'Dwyer, N.A., Gibney, M.J., Burke, S.J., Mccarthy, S.N.: The influence of eating location on nutrient intakes in Irish adults: implications for developing food-based dietary guidelines. Public Health Nutr. **8**(3), 258–265 (2005)
3. Bezerra, I.N., Sichieri, R.: Eating out of home and obesity: a Brazilian nationwide survey. Public Health Nutr. **12**(11), 2037 (2009)
4. Ayala, G.X., Rogers, M., Arredondo, E.M., Campbell, N.R., Elder, J.P.: Away-from-home food intake and risk for obesity: examining the influence of context. Obesity **16**(5), 1002–1008 (2008)
5. Wootan, M.G., Osborn, M.: Availability of nutrition information from chain restaurants in the United States. Am. J. Prev. Med. **30**(3), 0–268 (2006)
6. Lando, A.M., Labiner-Wolfe, J.: Helping consumers make more healthful food choices: consumer views on modifying food labels and providing point-of-purchase nutrition information at quick-service restaurants. J. Nutr. Educ. Behav. **39**(3), 157–163 (2007)
7. Roberto, C.A., Larsen, P.D., Agnew, H., Baik, J., Brownell, K.D.: Evaluating the impact of menu labeling on food choices and intake. Am. J. Public Health **100**(2), 312–318 (2010)
8. Alter, A.L., Oppenheimer, D.M.: Uniting the tribes of fluency to form a metacognitive nation. Pers. Soc. Psychol. Rev. **13**(3), 219–235 (2009)
9. Alter, A.L., Oppenheimer, D.M.: Predicting short-term stock fluctuations by using processing fluency. Proc. Nat. Acad. Sci. **103**(24), 9369–9372 (2006)
10. Song, H.: The effects of processing fluency on judgment and processing style: three essays on effort prediction, risk perception, and distortion detection (2009)
11. Goodman, S., Vanderlee, L., White, C.M., Hammond, D.: A quasi-experimental study of a mandatory calorie-labelling policy in restaurants: impact on use of nutrition information among youth and young adults in Canada. Prev. Med. **116**, 166–172 (2018)
12. Krešić, G., Liović, N., Pleadin, J.: Effects of menu labelling on students' food choice: a preliminary study. Br. Food J. **121**(2), 479–491 (2019)
13. Roseman, M.G., Joung, H.W., Choi, E.K.C., Kim, H.S.: The effects of restaurant nutrition menu labelling on college students' healthy eating behaviours. Public Health Nutr. **20**(5), 797–804 (2017)
14. Larson, N., Haynos, A.F., Roberto, C.A., Loth, K.A., Neumark-Sztainer, D.: Calorie labels on the restaurant menu: is the use of weight-control behaviors related to ordering decisions? J. Acad. Nutr. Diet. **118**(3), 399–408 (2018)
15. Shikdar, S., Suzuki, S.: Racial disparities in menu-labeling usage: analysis of the 2012 Behavioral Risk Factor Surveillance System (BRFSS) sugar-sweetened beverage and menu-labeling module. J. Racial Ethn. Health Dispar. **5**(3), 514–521 (2018)
16. Feng, W., Fox, A.: Menu labels, for better, and worse? Exploring socio-economic and race-ethnic differences in menu label use in a national sample. Appetite **128**, 223–232 (2018)
17. McGeown, L.: The calorie counter-intuitive effect of restaurant menu calorie labelling. Can. J. Public Health **110**(6), 1–5 (2019)
18. Cantu-Jungles, T.M., McCormack, L.A., Slaven, J.E., Slebodnik, M., Eicher-Miller, H.A.: A meta-analysis to determine the impact of restaurant menu labeling on calories and nutrients (ordered or consumed) in US adults. Nutrients **9**(10), 1088 (2017)

19. Petimar, J., et al.: Evaluation of the impact of calorie labeling on McDonald's restaurant menus: a natural experiment. Int. J. Behav. Nutr. Phys. Act. **16**(1), 99 (2019)
20. Dallas, S.K., Liu, P.J., Ubel, P.A.: Don't count calorie labeling out: calorie counts on the left side of menu items lead to lower calorie food choices. J. Consum. Psychol. **29**(1), 60–69 (2019)
21. Oppenheimer, D.M.: The secret life of fluency. Trends Cogn. Sci. **12**(6), 237–241 (2008)
22. Rummer, R., Schweppe, J., Schwede, A.: Fortune is fickle: null-effects of disfluency on learning outcomes. Metacogn. Learn. **11**(1), 57–70 (2016)
23. Schooler, L.J., Hertwig, R.: How forgetting aids heuristic inference. Psychol. Rev. **112**(3), 610 (2005)
24. Diemand-Yauman, C., Oppenheimer, D.M., Vaughan, E.B.: Fortune favors the bold (and the italicized): effects of disfluency on educational outcomes. Cognition **118**(1), 111 (2011)
25. Sungkhasettee, V.W., Friedman, M.C., Castel, A.D.: Memory and metamemory for inverted words: illusions of competency and desirable difficulties. Psychon. Bull. Rev. **18**(5), 973 (2011)
26. Hafner, M., Stapel, D.A.: Information to go: fluency enhances the usability of primed information (Retraction of vol 49, pg 73, 2009). J. Exp. Soc. Psychol. **49**(2), 318 (2013)
27. Yue, C.L., Castel, A.D., Bjork, R.A.: When disfluency is—and is not—a desirable difficulty: the influence of typeface clarity on metacognitive judgments and memory. Mem. Cognit. **41**(2), 229–241 (2013)
28. Hare, T.A., Malmaud, J., Rangel, A.: Focusing attention on the health aspects of foods changes value signals in vmPFC and improves dietary choice. J. Neurosci. **31**(30), 11077–11087 (2011)
29. Block, J.P., Roberto, C.A.: Potential benefits of calorie labeling in restaurants. JAMA **312**(9), 887–888 (2014)
30. Alter, A.L., Oppenheimer, D.M., Epley, N., Eyre, R.N.: Overcoming intuition: metacognitive difficulty activates analytic reasoning. J. Exp. Psychol. Gen. **806**(4), 569 (2007)
31. Glanz, K., Basil, M., Maibach, E., Goldberg, J., Snyder, D.A.N.: Why Americans eat what they do: taste, nutrition, cost, convenience, and weight control concerns as influences on food consumption. J. Am. Diet. Assoc. **98**(10), 1118–1126 (1998)
32. Lyu, X., Zhao, J., Luo, L., Wenliu, X.: The application and evaluation of the nutritional information of dishes in ordering of inpatients. J. Hyg. Res. **46**(4), 663–665 (2017)

Learning, Culture and Creativity

Development and Technical Experience of Plastic Injection Machine for STEAM Education

Jui-Hung Cheng[1](✉) and Hsin-Hung Lin[2]

[1] Department of Mold and Die Engineering, National Kaohsiung University
of Science and Technology, No. 415, Jiangong Road, Sanmin District,
Kaohsiung City 80778, Taiwan
rick.cheng@nkust.edu.tw
[2] Department of Creative Product Design, Asia University,
No. 500, Lioufeng Road, Wufeng, Taichung City 41354, Taiwan

Abstract. Traditional technical education exhibitions for high-school or elementary school students used static posters, demo tools or oral presentation ways to introduce different kinds of professional technical education. For Mechanical engineering and product design fields, limits by learning space, budget, safety issues that hadn't similar industrial level machines for them to operate and experience those real-world technologies. Normally those exhibition results did not as their prediction, still had a gap between schools and industries. For solving this issue, we introduced how to implement an industrial level plastic injection machine to be education applications for STEAM (Science, Technology, Engineering, Arts and Mathematics). By a small machine structure and simple UI/UX design of HMI (Human-Machine-Interface) control panel indication, the visitors could operate the table type plastic injection machine and produces toys by themselves via play experience. This innovation STEAM teaching model could enhance learning interesting and motivation for younger students before them entrance the technical colleges or universities, let them understand the latest technology trends and assist them chose appropriate development fields and found career plan directions in the future.

Keywords: STEAM education · Technical & vocational exhibition · HMI · Plastic injection machine · Toy design

1 Introduction

1.1 STEAM and PBL Education

For educators and policymakers around the world, when worry about the country's economy and abilities to work in the future, there is a growing emphasis on the need to expand students' pursuit of STEAM education in science, technology, and engineering. From research surveys, problem-oriented learning (PBL) can address this need, especially PBL teaching for STEAM, effectively enhancing students' interest in pursuing a career, as well as learning science and mathematics motivations and abilities [1]. For

© Springer Nature Switzerland AG 2020
M. Kurosu (Ed.): HCII 2020, LNCS 12183, pp. 215–230, 2020.
https://doi.org/10.1007/978-3-030-49065-2_16

technical vocation education, it is a complex activity for integrated interdisciplinary vocational education, which requires some ongoing decision-making and response in carrying out pre-planned tasks. However, in the field of education, PBL (Problem-Oriented Learning) and STEAM's teaching activities combine science, technology, engineering, art, and mathematics, as well as other interdisciplinary learning, and use well-designed observation and evaluation tools to assess teaching effectiveness [2]. And, this study is particularly meaningful for research teaching practice. The focus remains on how to educate students to identify problems and how to solve real-life problems through interdisciplinary and professional learning [3].

1.2 Technical Experience for Product Design

Whether from academic institutions, businesses or governments, the three-track cooperation provides their resources to improve the country's economic competitiveness and create a win-win situation, and such success stories often occur in practical technical and vocational education and production cooperation. If the Government can actively play a cooperative partner role, strengthen science and technology legislation, and promote the transformation of technical and vocational education and industrial research and development results, and promote and stimulate enterprise development [4–7]. From the perspective of research and development results in talent training, universities can drive regional development through the input and interaction of resources between the industries. As a result, Governments have also developed policies to support them, providing incentives to plan for the implementation of re-engineering pro-grams. This is a fairly specific and feasible approach and a measure of performance [8–10]. In the technical education of mechatronics, product integrated design is defined as products from the beginning of the raw materials, to the finished product process, and even finally to the hands of consumers through so many stages, designers must be able to know each manufacturing process, including the company's production and supply of raw materials process, quality yield, production and delivery days and so on can be quite clear, even more effective, to provide innovative innovation abilities [11–13]. In the overall product design innovation, what is needed is selection, induction and effective integration. With mechatronic of product design, it is a new era of the design concept, more and more attention by academia and the business communities, which is also one of the important models of the innovative design of enterprise project products [14–16].

1.3 HMI Design for Plastic Injection Machine

The global manufacturers faced new challenges, including waste of resources, short delivery times, increased work costs, lack of work capacity, etc. Therefore, the plastics manufacturing industries, into automated production and the intelligent manufacturing stage, increase productivity, prevent human error, and solve a lack of workforces. In particular, through the network knowledge-driven platform manufacturing information system, to the design, tool, molding, and other science and technology, to co-ordinate plastic products to increase the injection molding experience, improve traditional productivity, effective scheduling of production plans, and through IoT (Internet of

Things) technologies for equipment and processing monitoring. More importantly, those manufacturing data can be accumulated, saved, and reused in each session. As these machines and facilities become more and more complex in functioning, it is no longer possible to rely solely on the human experience of masters, but with the assistance of information systems or databases. Allows staff to operate plastic injection machines through a simple and clear human-machine interface (HMI), which is a key component for operators and industrial machines to ensure safety and proper operation. In general, the lifecycle of the HMI software on the industrial machine is often longer than the office computer software. Over time and with new requirements, the maintenance costs of the machines will continue to increase, and the education and training of basic technical skills may become more difficult to adapt to new needs. In particular, the needs of each business or school are different, and to design HMI for a specific application domain, it sometimes needs to be significantly modified or completely rebuilt. If users can learn basic principles and program coding, it is easy to modify HMI content to meet the requirements of the enterprise or teaching [17]. For schools, industrial-grade plastic injection machine operation learning belongs to a specific professional department, like mold and die or mechanical engineering. Based on safety, acquisition costs, and teaching purposes, it is more difficult to promote each student's learning. If there is a small educational plastic injection machine as a teaching tool, it is easier to promote and enhance the learning effect of students. So, the micro-injection molding technology is very important, in the computer, communications, consumer and medical industries, etc., has lots of application value. In general, the micro-injection molding mechanism takes two-stage reciprocating screw and plunger mechanisms. Through the screw and plunger, the plastic plus heating melt into the mold cavities, for the pressure and cooling process. The micro-injection molding module and the human-machine interface can effectively calculate the filling amount accurately [18]. Most of the plastic machine dimension of market existing are designed for adults, if you want to give primary and secondary school students to use the teaching-level machine, it is necessary to carry out ergonomics improvements for the product. New design methods for integrating technology and optimizing human-machine interfaces increase appeal. As well as simulating the main postures of student mannequins, development and comfort people are engineered by ergonomics. It allows users to ensure personal safety and increase comfort when operating machines and helps solve some of the problems with the product [19].

2 Interactive Experience of Vocational Education Exhibition

The traditional static technical education exhibition is less interactive and attractive to the students who visit. However, in the field of entertainment and educational applications, schoolchildren can effectively help children develop abilities such as space, mathematics, creative problem solving, etc. in the process of playing with building blocks and assembling toys [20]. The RTA (Ready-to-Assemble) model of self-assembled products is becoming more common today because it reduces transportation and manufacturing assembly costs. However, even though the user manual is provided to assemble similar simple graphic parts, most users who lack technical assembly experience are prone to errors during the assembly process and tend to be confused and frustrated with the assembly process. In contrast, building blocks toys that are easy to connect to structures do not have this problem. The study points out that this kind of assembled children's toys can be used as a teaching tool to teach schoolchildren to calculate the volume of the body, through simple graphic interlocking joint mechanisms, such as slide-in, straight and tilt-type joints, to assemble the body toys. In particular, the more complex the structure, the more likely it is that the user will find it esoteric and the more likely it is that something will go wrong during assembly. As a result, users can cope with such self-assembled products without difficulty after practice [21]. Also, 3D burr puzzles are often used to attract visitors to museum exhibitions. The reason for this is that a puzzle can be seen as a game that is thought of by reassembling fragments. Simplify the task of creating puzzle-style activities, increase the interaction between visitors and museums, and achieve the effect of education and play games [22, 23].

The traditional introduction of technical education exhibitions are mostly used static booth so that schools put up stalls to introduce departments, but this cannot attract the public visitors like parents, and students, they hard to understand the connotation of technical vocational education and the development of industries. Therefore, to solve the above problems, Taiwan's Ministry of Education for the first time in conjunction with the universities of science and technology and public education institutions set up an exhibition held a "New Paradise of Technology" exhibition, its show concept mainly from the concept of exploring the park, the overall explore camp will be the theme park, and the application of computers, video, object demonstration, scenario simulation, and other exhibition technologies to create entertainment environment, the scenario game of knowledge also can be explored, discover and experience the connotation of technical education in the game of breaking through, and understand the future development of technical and vocational skills. In the past, technical education rarely has to experience the career scenario pattern, so that students can easily discover their interests and potential. About students' potential, sometimes even to themselves or their parents do not know, after the opportunities to contact, will know what interests are, let the students explore their personality learning direction and potential career plan. The technical exhibition that provided the professional experience during visiting, let students understand the learning direction of technical and vocational education and the future industrial environment, as an assessment of the development of promotion and employment suitability. Starting from the understanding of themselves, and then explore the professional development of various groups, through the in-depth experience of the connotation and advantages of technical and vocational education, but also to explore their future possibilities. Let the participants play the role of professional, the experience of six groups (mechanical, electrical and electronics, design, chemical, civil and architectural, and aquatic groups) research and development for the future learning. About students' potential, sometimes even to themselves or their parents do not know, after the opportunities to contact, will know what interests are, let the students explore their personality learning direction and potential career plan. The technical exhibition that provided the professional experience during visiting, let students understand the learning direction of technical and vocational education and the future industrial environment, as an assessment of the development of promotion and employment suitability. Starting from the understanding of themselves, and then explore the professional development of various groups, through the in-depth experience of the connotation and advantages of technical and vocational education, but also to explore their future possibilities. Let the participants play the role of professional, the experience of six groups (mechanical, electrical and electronics, design, chemical, civil and architectural, and aquatic groups) research and development for the future learning.

3 Development of Educational Plastic Injection Machine

3.1 Design Objectives

This study focuses on the interactive exhibition of technical and vocational education in mechanical groups, that designs and develops an educational plastic injection machines so that students can see through their operating plastic injection machine, making their toys of plastic parts during experience activities. At the same time, to promote the technical and vocational education hands-on creative spirit, this study also simplifies complex technologies, and arrange the DIY courses so that visitors can get up close and personal with the machine, feel the new look of various types of science and technology. Mainly for the user groups divided into two categories: in primary and secondary school students, the main learning the basic operation of an injection machine, to understand the process of making toys knowledge. In the training section of college students, it focuses on HMI, UI/UX, IoT, and other principles and practical technology development, for example, the teaching platform can learn stepper motor control, cylinder movement control, etc., these focus on the STE field (Science, Technology, and Engineering) of STEAM education. The knowledge skills such as PLC program cording and UI/UX design of human-machine surface, internet and intranet setup and web monitoring programming that belong to the AM field (Art and Mathematics) of STEAM Education. The design objectives of this machine:

1. Provide an educational plastic injection machine teaching platform that is portable and can demonstrate the actual operation of each control component.
2. Allows users to operate the machine, making their toy plastic parts experience activities.
3. Through the simple modular design, the use of compatibility components, with expandable human-machine interface design, consider ergonomic easy to operate, simulation industries actual control applications.
4. The intelligent monitoring system of the Smart Machine Box (SMB) provides the information data collected by various sensors on the local side mold or the machine and enables remote real-time monitoring of the production data of the mold or machine through the Internet of Things (IoT) uploaded to an external cloud database and dynamically updated.
5. Through those data monitoring and analysis, it can also be further integrated to MRP/ERP system, as the basis for process improvement or manufacturing parameter adjustment, to achieve factory automation and intelligence.

6. For Small and Medium-sized Enterprises (SMEs) or teaching research institutes, basic entry-level training equipment can be obtained at a low cost, reducing access to intelligent manufacturing.

3.2 System Architecture and Development Processes

The development of an educational plastic injection machine, mainly a large quantity production of plastic injection products. Considering the portable mobility use in different teaching environments, it is designed as a fully electric floor-to-ceiling aluminum extruded machine. On the platform, a small horizontal plastic injector is placed, which consists of stepper motor mechanisms, the programmable logic controller (PLC), heating mechanisms, temperature sensors, injection mold (male mold and female mold), and AC/DC power converter and other components. Through the operation process, training students to understand the acting method of the plastic injection machine and the operating process, practical operation to obtain physical experience. And can be used in research and development production test samples, small batch testing needs. External IoT intelligent monitoring module to monitor device movements and machine operation in remote real-time.

The operation of the plastic injection machine and the system production process of toys are shown in Fig. 1, 1) after drying the plastic raw materials, 2) putting the dried plastic materials into the filling bucket, 3) through heating tube melting the solid plastic materials into liquid status, 4) filling the liquid plastic into the injection gate through pressure to the mold cavities, 5) holding the injection mold and then cooling plastic parts for seconds, 6) after the toy is formed and it will be ejected off the mold and dropped into slide portion, 7) the final product of the toy will be assembled and packaging shipment. This educational plastic injection machine can be applied to the

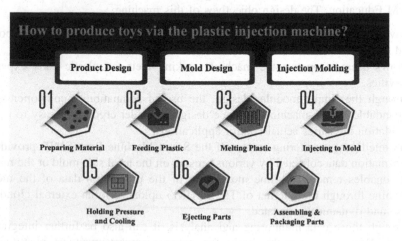

Fig. 1. The injection process for toy producing

research and development phase, for making initial engineering prototyping and test-ing. As well as the demand for small-volume trial production. It can also add an external IoT intelligent manufacturing monitoring module. When visitors scan QR code or barcode and they could through mobile devices, such as smartphones, tablets, lap-tops, etc. And can be in remote real-time monitoring the equipment action and machine operation status. Includes parameters such as time, temperature, pressure, etc.

3.3 Development of Small Plastic Injection Module

The main components of this small plastic injection module are feed mechanism, heating mechanism, moving screw mechanism, transmission mechanism, stepping motor, injection mold, etc. (showed as Fig. 2). In the small plastic injection control module setting aspect, in the HMI panel, users can set up the mechanical action operation and the relevant parameters, to control the feed screw supply plastic material filling amount, confirm whether the plastic materials be put into the filling bucket. When after closing the safety door and letting the sensor sensed, then the injection machine can be operated, we could adjust the male and female mold to reach the joint mold position, and then carry out the plastic injection action procedure, that the plastic material is heated and melted into the mold cavities via the feed tube. After the completion of the plastic injection molding action, open the injection mold to the specified position, so that the injected products can be successfully removed, that is, to complete the entire plastic injection manufacturing process (showed as Fig. 3 and Fig. 4). In terms of control systems, as shown in Fig. 5, there are several major modules, including the power switch, AC/DC converter, motor drivers, PLC controller, SMB, and IoT Module, etc.

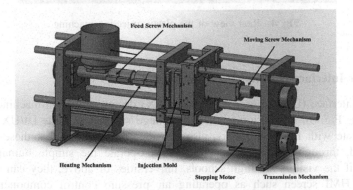

Fig. 2. The small plastic injection modules

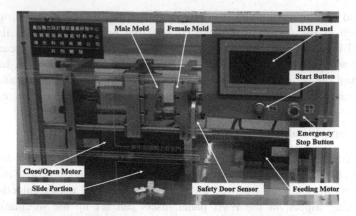

Fig. 3. Front view of the plastic injection machine

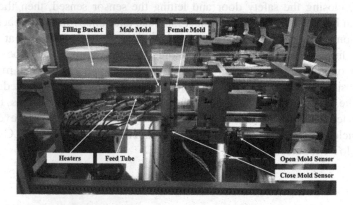

Fig. 4. Rear view of the plastic injection machine

3.4   User Interface (UI) and User Experience (UX) Design

The user interface (UI) and user experience (UX) design of human-machine interface (showed as Fig. 6), in addition to training college students to code UI/UX programs and integrate with PLC controllers, also consider the contents that these users can understand, through the touch panel icons to operate the simple human-machine interface, if the visitors are high schools, universities or above, they can set up the advanced HMI screen such as operating air pressure control components of the cylinders, the stepper motor modules, or practice the movement mechanisms, etc. Users are guided by those interactive icons of the touch panel and can also adjust numerical parameters to change the moving speed and distance of the stepper motors. In the intuitive display screen, users could change the system is automatic, manual, or stop status by LED indicators. It is also possible to work with the Raspberry Pi control board in the SMB (Smart machine box), combined with the wireless AP router communication mechanism, delivery information to the wireless device with IoT intelligent monitoring in remote sites. Users can also use portable devices to monitor the various sensor information on the machine, such as air pressure cylinder, gripper scours open or close, stepper motor current position, moving speed and another system status.

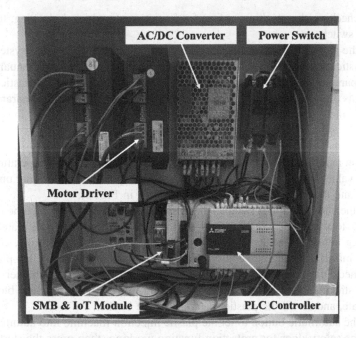

Fig. 5. Control panel of the plastic injection machine

Fig. 6. UI/UX design and PLC logical program integrated by college students

3.5   UI/UX Interface Operating Procedure

The main operating procedures of the machine are several: 1) pour the plastic materials into the filling bucket, 2) adjust the plastic injection machine parameters, 3) inject melted plastic materials into the mold cavities, 4) take off formed plastic parts and then to assemble the burr puzzle toy. The details of the following steps:

1. After checking the machine surface for foreign materials and cleaning, turn on the power switch.
2. Enter the parameter setting interface of the main screen of the HMI system, setting the plastic melting temperature, mold temperature, automatic or manual state and other parameters (showed as in Fig. 7). If there are different plastic injection materials or mold structures, according to the system recommended parameter table to make the set adjustment. If the setting process is completed, press the production quantity zero key to recalculate.
3. Entering the manual operation screen, press the close mold button firstly, let the injection mold in the forming condition to warm, wait until the temperature reaches the set value, wait 30 min for the overall mold temperature to be better uniform and stable, and then the adjustment test (showed as in Fig. 8).
4. When the above action is completed, press the open mold button, let the mold open moving to touch to the open mold sensor position, and then press and hold the injecting button to let the melted plastic liquid continue to shoot out, confirm the plastic material discharge condition and the flow status of the melted plastic. And then check the connection with the injection gate and mold, whether there is a curing sticking block of plastic or overheating, to remove it to avoid blocking the feed gate, and re-fill the plastic materials in the bucket.
5. Press the automatic button to let the plastic injection machine into automatic mode, close the safety door for protection function working, then press the start button to start production (showed as Fig. 9). At the beginning of production, there will be

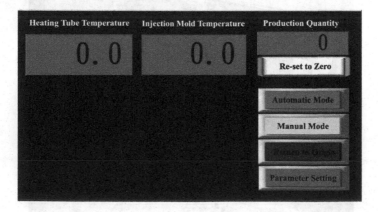

Fig. 7. Main screen of UI/UX design

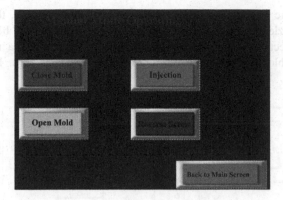

Fig. 8. Manual operation for open or closed mold

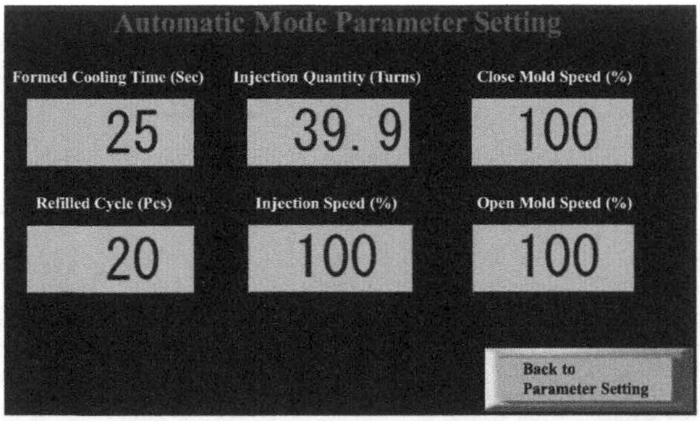

Fig. 9. Automatic setting screen

short-shot that cannot be filled phenomenon, about inject 5–10 pieces and the injection conditions will stabilize, forming a complete finished product and confirming it had dropped, press the start button to continue the next production.

3.6 The Burr Puzzle Toy Design and Plastic Injection Mold Development

The interlock burr puzzles are disassembled and reed from notched sticks. During assembly, all building blocks are etched into each other except the single key building blocks that maintain activity. What's interesting is that it's stable, it can be interlocked with each other, and we don't need glue or screws to fix it. Even the burr puzzles made up of a small number of building blocks can sometimes be difficult to solve the assembly problems without careful logical thinking. Because building blocks are assembled in a certain order, the complexity of the arrangement of different puzzle blocks can become very high. The main technical or logistic challenges of the game is that each piece of part is a single feature that ensures the height interlock of the standing-volume blocks during assembly or removal. Therefore, to attract students to operate the plastic injection machine and self-made toys purposes, the main components of burr puzzle toys, including simple 2 "C" blocks and an "O" block, limited in a small plastic injection mold for educational machine, designing a mold with three cavities to form blocks for the burr puzzle toys (showed as in Figs. 10 and 11).

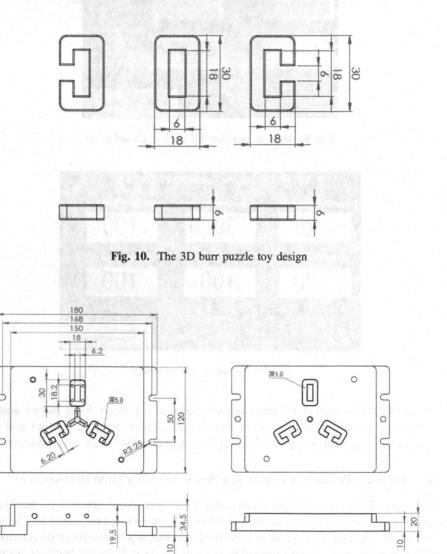

Fig. 10. The 3D burr puzzle toy design

Fig. 11. Injection mold design for burr puzzle toy (left is male mold and right is female mold)

4   Interactive Teaching and Results in an Exhibition

To ensure the safety of operation and simplify the operating procedures for visiting students, firstly by the college students setup the injection parameters, including the plastic filling quantity, cycle time, heating and cooling temperature, injection speed or pressure, etc., the operating of HMI will be kept in a simple start screen, and then invite students to personally operate the plastic injection machine. As shown in Figs. 12 and 13, when the injection start key is pressed, it will be automatically close the injection mold, heat the plastic material to melt into the mold cavities through the injection tube. The injection machine will automatically execute the molding-related procedure according to the set parameters. After the burr puzzle toy is formed and cooled, it will be ejected out of the mold and complete the injection procedure. If the injection machine is set to manual mode, the action stops each time a finished product is formed. If the machine is set to automatic mode, that is, according to the set quantity, repeatedly shot out of production, and then stop the action. As shown in Fig. 14 and Fig. 15, the finished product will be shot out, allowing the students to use the tool themselves, cutting off the required "C" and "O" blocks. Then the visiting students from the game, according to the instructions DIY (do-it-yourself) completes the simple 3pcs blocks of burr puzzle toy assembled. In the further development of game expansion, they can also take different amounts of blocks, change the shape of the burr puzzles, give full play to the creativity and imagination (showed as in Fig. 16, 17 and 18). The assembled blocks can also be brought home as a valuable and meaningful souvenir after visiting the technical and vocational exhibition (showed as in Fig. 19). The study results as well as interactive teaching practice contents, for toy design, molding education and the assembly of burr puzzle toy games, the visiting students can understand the concept of STEAM education and related technical connotations, will be a profound impression on the technical and vocational education exhibition, achieve the advanced industrial-level plastic injection machine to be simplify the entry-level of educational plastic injection machine that visiting students can understand to establish the direction of future technical or professional learning and career planning.

Fig. 12. Toy ejecting from male mold   **Fig. 13.** The plastic injection blocks

Fig. 14. Cutting toy blocks

Fig. 15. The C & O blocks

Fig. 16. Explaining to students how to play

Fig. 17. Assisting students to solve problems

Fig. 18. Students assembled the DIY blocks

Fig. 19. Burr puzzle toy as visiting souvenir

5   Conclusion

This study by the development and technical experience of educational plastic injection machine, so that visiting students can contact and operate the injection machine, experience the injection molding to produce the burr puzzle toys, reverse the traditional industrial-grade equipment are not easy to get close to the stereotype. Whether it is the development of the plastic injection machine needs a variety of science, technology, engineering, and other knowledge, or human-machine interface required aesthetics for UI/UX design and program coding, etc., need STEAM education knowledge of all disciplines fully integrated. The burr puzzle toys to carry out mechanical puzzle game, although this cheap plastic toy is not high-level teaching aids, belonging to simple functional blocks, it very much needs to rely on intellectual and mechanical science principles. And in the process of blocks puzzle-solving and assembly, students' pursuit of three-dimensional shape can also be regarded as an art education, which can bring strong interactive experience, give full play to students' creativity to overcome problems and integrate the interdisciplinary learning disciplines of STEAM education, and effectively enhance the interactive and interesting of technical and vocational education exhibition. This innovative and interactive exhibition concept validates visiting users of different ages and is guided by design and education practices, whether the mechanical design, human-machine interactive design, toy design, and interactive experience exhibition design, providing theoretical and practical reference values.

References

1. LaForce, M., Noble, E., Blackwell, C.: Problem-based learning (PBL) and student interest in STEM careers: the roles of motivation and ability beliefs. Educ. Sci. 7(4), 92 (2017)
2. Stearns, L.M., Morgan, J., Capraro, M.M., Capraro, R.M.: A teacher observation instrument for PBL classroom instruction. J. STEM Educ. Innov. Res. 13(3), 7–16 (2012)
3. Asghar, A., Ellington, R., Rice, E., Johnson, F., Prime, G.M.: Supporting STEM education in secondary science contexts. Interdisc. J. Prob.-Based Learn. 6(2), 4 (2012)
4. Tamaki, K.Y., Park, Y., Goto, S.: A professional training programme design for global manufacturing strategy: investigations and action project group activities through industry-university cooperation. Int. J. Bus. Inf. Syst. 18(4), 451–468 (2015)
5. Szücs, F.: Research subsidies, industry–university cooperation and innovation. Res. Policy 47(7), 1256–1266 (2018)
6. Hong, E.Y., Choi, J.I., Kwon, K.H.: Study on the sustainability of the industry-university cooperation center: focusing on the US Industry-University Cooperative Research Centers (I-UCRCs) and Korea SMEs industry-university cooperation center. Korean Bus. Educ. Rev. 32(1), 79–100 (2017)
7. Nomakuchi, T., Takahashi, M.: A study about project management for industry-university cooperation dilemma. Procedia Comput. Sci. 64, 47–54 (2015)
8. Han, S.S., Yim, D.S.: Path dependence in industry-university cooperation-in terms of industry's voluntary participation. Int. J. Ind. Distrib. Bus. 9(3), 45–56 (2018)
9. Seo, B.D., Park, M.K., Ju, J.Y., Lee, W.H.: Developing a core competence model for LINC (Leaders in Industry-university Cooperation) at K-University: A case study. Int. J. Softw. Eng. Appl. 10(2), 171–180 (2016)
10. Bao, X.Z., Dong, Y.H., Wang, Y.: R&D cost allocation and income sharing for industry-university cooperation in open innovation context. NTUT J. Intellect. Prop. Law Manag. 5(1), 11–32 (2016)
11. Hartmann, J., Germain, R.: Understanding the relationships of integration capabilities, ecological product design, and manufacturing performance. J. Clean. Prod. 92, 196–205 (2015)

12. Hehenberger, P., Vogel-Heuser, B., Bradley, D., Eynard, B., Tomiyama, T., Achiche, S.: Design, modelling, simulation and integration of cyber physical systems: methods and applications. Comput. Ind. **82**, 273–289 (2016)
13. Koller, R.W., Ricardez-Sandoval, L.A.: A dynamic optimization framework for integration of design, control and scheduling of multi-product chemical processes under disturbance and uncertainty. Comput. Chem. Eng. **106**, 147–159 (2017)
14. Liu, J., Cheng, Z., Ma, Y.: Product design-optimization integration via associative optimization feature modeling. Adv. Eng. Inform. **30**(4), 713–727 (2016)
15. Naghizadeh, M., Manteghi, M., Ranga, M., Naghizadeh, R.: Managing integration in complex product systems: the experience of the IR-150 aircraft design program. Technol. Forecast. Soc. Change **122**, 253–261 (2017)
16. Nguyen, V.D., Martin, P.: Product design-process selection-process planning integration based on modeling and simulation. Int. J. Adv. Manuf. Technol. **77**(1–4), 187–201 (2015)
17. Dorninger, B., Beer, W., Moser, M., Zeilinger, R., Kern, A.: Automated reengineering of industrial HMI screens by static analysis. In: Proceedings of the 2014 IEEE Emerging Technology and Factory Automation (ETFA), pp. 1–4 (2014)
18. Yang, C.C., Hwang, S.J., Lee, H.H., Huang, D.Y.: Control of hot runner type micro injection molding module. In: IECON 2007 33rd Annual Conference of the IEEE Industrial Electronics Society, pp. 2928–2933 (2007)
19. Naddeo, A., et al.: Postural analysis in HMI design: an extension of OCRA standard to evaluate discomfort level. J. Achiev. Mater. Manuf. **30**(1), 60–70 (2010)
20. Lin, J., Yang, W., Gao, X., Liao, M.: Learning to assemble building blocks with a leap motion controller. In: Li, Frederick W.B., Klamma, R., Laanpere, M., Zhang, J., Manjón, B. F., Lau, Rynson W.H. (eds.) ICWL 2015. LNCS, vol. 9412, pp. 258–263. Springer, Cham (2015). https://doi.org/10.1007/978-3-319-25515-6_25
21. Jiang, P., Wongwichai, T., Yanpanyanon, S., Tanka, T.: Identifying the impact of shape in assembly of an "easy-to-understand" interlocking joint cube puzzle. J. Sci. Des. **3**(2), 2_21–2_28 (2019)
22. Echavarria, K.R., Samaroudi, M.: Digital workflow for creating 3D puzzles to engage audiences in the interpretation of archaeological artefacts. In: The 16th EUROGRAPHICS Workshop on Graphics and Cultural Heritage (EG GCH) (2018)
23. Xin, S., Lai, C.F., Fu, C.W., Wong, T.T., He, Y., Cohen-Or, D.: Making burr puzzles from 3D models. ACM Trans. Graph. (TOG) **30**(4), 1–8 (2011)

Bringing Digital Transformation into Museums: The Mu.SA MOOC Case Study

Massimiliano Dibitonto[✉], Katarzyna Leszczynska, Elisa Cruciani, and Carlo M. Medaglia

DASIC, Link Campus University, via del Casale di S. Pio V, 44, 00165 Rome, Italy
{M.Dibitonto, K.Leszczynska, E.Cruciani, C.Medaglia}@unilink.it

Abstract. Mu.SA. - Museum Sector Alliance [1], is an EU funded project that aims to fill the gap between formal education and training and the Museums' need of competencies to drive digital transformation in order to be competitive in the digital era. The project will reach its goal building new European profiles of emerging job roles in museums, creating a training program and delivering a pilot, that will be used to test the methodology and the contents developed.

In this paper, we will present the result of the evaluation of MOOC, that represents the first part of the course that has been delivered, trying to understand the strengths and weaknesses in order to improve it.

The results of the evaluation of the MOOC were generally positive indeed and the level of interest shows that this strategy is considered particularly useful at sectoral level and as an opportunity for employment growth. The number of participants involved highlights the ability of the MOOC tool to attract and interest a wide audience of a heterogeneous age group covering several professional fields.

Keywords: Digital transformation · Museum professionals · Digital skills · MOOC · Learning design · Usability

1 Introduction

1.1 Digital Transformation and New Professional Skills in Museums

Museums are currently experimenting a transformation process: they are moving from being quiet, static and predictable institutions to complex cultural organisms rooted in the life of different communities and connected to global platforms.

The new directions that museums are about to take will mostly be determined by external happenings and developments, so the main challenges in the future will have to do with balancing physical and digital reality, measuring the social impact of new cultural trends, closing the gap between museum insiders and outsiders, using means familiar to all of them [2].

One of the biggest challenges of digital transformation is to embrace all these changes and its success depends on how museums integrate into the digital ecosystem

M. Kurosu (Ed.): HCII 2020, LNCS 12183, pp. 231–242, 2020.
https://doi.org/10.1007/978-3-030-49065-2_17

and use emerging technologies, recognizing the power of digital culture to transform the identity and behaviour of a society.

The heritage sector is a developing field, as varied and complex as the emerging professions in the cultural heritage sector. The introduction of information technology, digitization and changes in information have led to new emerging professions in the field of heritage, merging the humanist community with the technological industry.

While Tait [3] addresses the problem of lack of qualifications for practitioners and also denounces a large part of the use of voluntary and not well-trained resources for this purpose, Conway [4] questions whether the professions that traditionally dealt with the care and preservation of physical objects are able to redefine themselves in the digital age.

As the taste and needs of the "new generation" of museums' visitors are changing and the museum offering is evolving at the same time, it has become necessary to recruit and train a new generation of heritage specialists who are ready to face all these new challenges.

Mandarano [5] stresses that in order to initiate the technological and digital transformation of a museum, it is essential that the director understands the needs deriving from this change and introduces actions to support it, such as hiring professionals and experts who do not belong directly to the historical-artistic field. It is also crucial that employees become flexible and ready to update their skills or dialogue with hybrid professional profiles, to achieve a common goal.

The final report produced by J.A. van Lakerveld et al. [6], not only identifies the emerging professions of the near future - e.g. collection managers, conservators, restorers, education, interpretation and outreach staff, researchers, ICT and technology professionals, entertainment, hospitality and visitors services staff, sustainability staff, marketing and fundraising staff - but offers an in-depth overview of how the tasks of these figures are changing in the technological era and consequently, the report highlights the new skills the market requires. One way to promote innovation in this area is through professional development processes, consisting of targeted recruitment of professionals and the provision of continuous training throughout their working life.

From the many examples observed, we believe that innovation is a result of a process that involves human and technological aspects, especially regarding organizational aspects and the development of human resources. In this perspective, the training and professional development of the entire organization are central points of reflection.

That is why we aim to bring Mu.SA project as an example of a training path for museum experts interested in introducing digital innovation and transformation in museums.

2 Mu.SA - Museum Sector Alliance

Mu.SA - Museum Sector Alliance - is a three-year project (funded by the European Erasmus Plus Programme - Sector Skills Alliances) whose main purpose is to address the increasing disconnection between formal education and training and the employment field as a result of the emergence of new job roles due to the quickening pace of the adoption of ICT in the museum sector. Mu.SA addresses directly the shortage of digital and transferable skills identified in the museum sector and supports the continuous professional development of museum professionals [1].

To achieve this goal the first part of the project aimed at the identification of emerging job profiles through the analysis of the needs in the museum sector and the offer of formal education programs. To do this, international qualitative and quantitative researches were carried out in Greece, Italy and Portugal, the three countries of the consortium, from December 2016 to March 2017. A number of 81 museums expert was involved through interviews, focus groups and questionnaires [7]. The study output the following profiles:

- Digital Strategy Manager;
- Digital Collections Curator;
- Digital Interactive Experience Developer;
- Online Community Manager [7].

The research highlighted the common digital and transferable competencies needed by these professional figures, as an upskilling starting point to help them face current and future challenges closely related to the implementation of new technologies within the museum sector.

2.1 The Mu.SA Course

Based on these outcomes, specific VET curricula were designed for each one of the four new job profiles identified. The design of the curricula was based on the e-CF skills (European Framework for e-Competence) [8], DigComp skills (Digital Competence Framework for Citizens) [9] and 21st Century skills [10]. More than 40 digital and transferable competencies were selected. Then a blended course was designed and implemented, providing three main phases:

- A Massive Open Online Course (MOOC) to cover the essential skills common to all the profiles (8 weeks) combining eight e-CF, nine DigComp and five 21st Cent skills divided in 22 modules, divided in turn in Units. The platform tracked the completion of the single units assessed through true/false, fill in the blank or matching questions. The pilot of the MOOC has run from January to March 2019 [11].
- A Specialization Course, divided in 4 curricula, to deepen the topics specific for each profile. A blended course, structured with an online part, and face to face meetings, organized in every country of the partnership. The duration of this phase of the course was 24 weeks (360 h in total), including Face to Face learning (24 h split in 6 days training), online and self-study (288 h) and assessment (48 h). The online modules were assessed with the same strategy used for the MOOC but, in addition to that, the students had also to complete "practical assignments" with an estimated effort of 2 h each and characterized for each profile. The pilot of the Specialization Course started in September 2019 and is expected to end in March 2020 [1].

- A Work-Based Training, to practice in a real context with the support of tutors form the VET provider and Social Partners. It consisted of 200 h of practical learning in a museum or other cultural organization (in Greece, Italy and Portugal) and five hours of assessment. It has started in October 2019 and during this period, the student had to work on activities related to the job profile chosen and develop a project work [1].

The partnership contributed with their experts to create the contents and implement the courses. The materials were mainly videos, presentations and essays together with external OERs. The course was implemented on an instance of the Moodle platform.

A pilot of each phase of the course was accomplished in order to test the effectiveness and the quality of the methodology and tools produced and to upgrade them. In the following chapter, we will present the results of the evaluation of the MOOC training course as the first feedback on the project.

3 MOOC Evaluation

The Mu.SA project provides a series of evaluation activities aimed at assessing the quality of the modular European VET curriculum, the methodology and the tools provided by the project. It involves students, stakeholders, partners and experts, and it is focused on:

- Methodology and tools developed;
- MOOC;
- Specialization Course;
- Work-Based Training.

The evaluation activities will promote communication between the partnership and the stakeholders in order to assess the extent to which the main project outcomes effectively meet the educational needs of their future beneficiaries. Moreover, this part is important as it allows to test the success and the quality of the project pilot and will be the base for future improvements. Indeed, in order to impact on a wider scale, the outcomes of the pilot will be used to upgrade and expand the course, to attract new partners, creating a dynamic upskilling process for museum professionals, supported by communities of practice and empowered by open source tools and digital content. In the following paragraph, we will present the results of the MOOC evaluation.

3.1 Objectives and Strategy

The evaluation of the MOOC reported here aimed to achieve the following evaluation objectives:

- Quality in Use: to assess the functionality, usability and accessibility of the online platform (technical level);
- Learning Design: to assess the learning activities and content delivery (learning level);

- Learning Outcomes: to assess the quality of the contents and subject coverage (learning outcomes level).

During the project an evaluation strategy has been developed, defining the methodologies and the tools to be used. The evaluation methods used are a mix of qualitative and quantitative data collection techniques: a pre-course and a final evaluation survey, quantitative monitoring data extracted from the logs of the MOOC platform, feedback collected by the tutors during the interaction with the students on the platform, interviews.

The data analysis was performed both through statistical and qualitative content analysis of the open answers of the questionnaires and of the text emerging from interviews and focus groups. Moreover, the logs of the MOOC platform were used to analyze the students' activity.

On the overall level, the present evaluation is compliant with the Quality Reference Framework (QRF) for the Quality of Massive Open Online Courses (MOOCs) [12], which indicates the standards of MOOCs evaluation to be met in order to guarantee the pedagogical, strategic and technological relevance of the evaluation.

Table 1. QRF criteria met by Musa evaluation strategy.

	Quality reference framework	Mu.SA evaluation
E-1	QRF standards for evaluation planning	Evaluation strategy
E-2	QRF standards for evaluation realization	Questionnaires, interviews, focus group, log analysis
E-3	QRF standards for evaluation review	Internal review process among project partners
E-4	QRF standards for improvements and optimization	Consultation process among project partners and stakeholders with evaluators

3.2 Participants

The MOOC started in January 2018 and 3803 persons (out of 5291 that expressed their interest) registered to the platform. From the analysis of the platform log, it resulted that 659 (17,3%) were male and 3144 female (82,7%). The overall number of respondents to the pre-course survey among the participants of the MOOC was 1391, indicating a response rate of 36% on a total number of 3803 participants.

The distribution of participants by age shows a homogeneous situation in the two age groups in the middle, namely those related to the 24–34 and 35–44 classes, respectively at 42% and 34% of the total, followed by the <44 class (16%) and the 18–24 class (7,5%).

In addition, the majority of participants have a high level of education: 58% of them have a master's degree, 22% have a bachelor's degree, while 11% have a doctorate. Only the remaining 9% have a lower qualification (professional or high school).

The majority of participants reported being unfamiliar with MOOCs (37%), while the remaining 63% of responses were distributed quite homogeneously.

In most cases (36%) participants indicated to have a medium-high level of knowledge and understanding of the topics covered by the course. Analyzing the values of the answers for each topic, it emerges that, on average, the level of knowledge and understanding is medium-high: 3.67 on a scale from 1 to 5, with a fairly low Standard Deviation (0.26) and a variation of 0.98 points between the maximum scores (netiquette) and minimum scores (forecast development). The situation depicted, not showing any strong variation within the target group, suggests that the course was able to attract a homogenous target group, thus enhancing the probability of teachings to be in line with the level of each participant.

The ex-ante expectations of participants in terms of personal and professional objectives for the Mu.SA MOOC were collected through a set of eight options, presented as multiple choices. As shown below (see Fig. 1), the majority of participants aimed to acquire new skills (17,9%) and knowledge (17,6%) and, to a slightly less measure, to develop new competencies (16,3%). Some objectives, such as collaborating with other people or getting in touch with experts in the field, received less preferences (respectively, 7% and 8,2%), compared with other ones as getting a certification (13,7%), accessing educational resources (13,1%) and gaining a competitive advantage (10,7%).

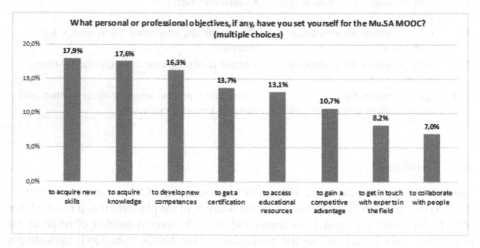

Fig. 1. Pre-course survey: objectives of participants of the MOOC.

Similarly, the opinion of participants in terms of expected personal and professional impacts of the Mu.SA MOOC was collected through a set of eight options, presented as multiple choices. The majority of participants expected to be able to apply the learnings to their job (77%) and to be able to get more job opportunities (72%). Only one example of impact, namely being able to affect regional or national policies on the subject, scored less than 30%, while the others placed in the middle, such as being able to improve the current job, being able to get a better job (both scoring above 40%) and, to a slightly less measure, being able to change "how things work" in their organization (which scored below 40%).

3.3 Quality in Use

The Quality in Use objective is referred to the overall usability and easiness of use of the platform and the contents. The metrics used were: effectiveness (ability to complete tasks on the platform), efficiency (task time), and satisfaction (rating of the experience on the platform). As it was challenging to perform usability tests in the three countries, we referred mainly to the final evaluation questionnaire, interviews, platform logs and feedback from the tutors.

Participants' opinion on the learning environment was generally positive, indicating a strong appreciation on the easiness of the learning platform and a noticeable level of satisfaction with the modalities of interaction with the educational contents provided. Indeed the 62% of the respondents agreed that the online learning platform was easy to use, while the percentage is slightly lower for the interaction with contents (46% fully satisfied, 40% moderately satisfied). However, a slightly less positive appreciation was observed also for the easiness of interaction with other students through the platform (22% fully satisfied, 44% moderately satisfied). The platform, indeed, only offered a forum while it was noticed that students autonomously created a Facebook group for further discussions (without the presence of "staff" members).

Students were asked to provide a more detailed opinion about some usability related attributes of contents and educational resources (that contributes also to the objective "Learning Outcomes").

Table 2. Final evaluation survey: usability of contents and of educational resources.

Question	Very satisfied	Moderately satisfied	Slightly satisfied	Dissatisfied	ND
1. Aesthetic quality of graphics	31%	40%	22%	6%	0%
2. Usability in browsing	39%	39%	17%	4%	0%
3. Organization of the sections and elements	40%	39%	16%	3%	2%
4. Interaction methods through different communication tools (forums, direct messages, emails etc.)	29%	40%	24%	7%	0%
5. Easiness in accessing training materials	51%	38%	9%	2%	0%
6. Availability of training materials	47%	38%	13%	2%	0%

On average the results illustrated in Table 2 show a high level of satisfaction. In particular, the easiness in accessing the training materials and their availability were considered two very satisfactory elements, as well as, to a minor extent, the organization of the sections and elements and the usability in browsing. Slightly less positive was the level of satisfaction expressed towards the aesthetic quality of graphics and towards the interaction methods through different communication tools. The efficiency was related to the ability to complete the weekly activities on time (36% strongly agrees, 38% moderately agrees).

The opinion of the average of the participants was very positive in the case of the level of satisfaction with their performance in the MOOC (51% very satisfied). It is also worth underlining that the 40% of the participants declared to feel very secure, gratified, content, relaxed and complacent about their Mu.SA MOOC learning, while only very few people have reported a very negative judgement on any aspect of the course. Within those people, it should be highlighted that a relatively higher proportion was found in response to the question related to the adequacy of time given for studying and doing the activities: this represented a negative outlier.

In conclusion, the MOOC has allowed participants to complete tasks on the platform in an effective manner and using a reasonable expenditure of time resources, leading to a high level of satisfaction regarding the overall experience of the platform. These elements indicate a high level of quality in the use of it.

3.4 Learning Design

The Learning Design objective was about the ability of the methodology, tools and contents to reach the project goals also in relation to the students' characteristics and needs. The metrics used were: activity level on the platform, drop-out, time-demand (are the students on time with their assignments?), cognitive demand (does the effort required matches the students' level?).

The most relevant data about the activity on the platform is the final drop-out rate. Indeed out of the 3803 people registered, 2607 (49,3%) attended and 1371 (25,9%) succeeded. This ratio could be considered a good result if compared with the rates observed by Onah et al. [13]. We tried to investigate the reason for the drop-out but we only collected a few answers that couldn't be considered representative. However, some students gave up for personal reasons while others (especially workers) did not have enough time to follow the course. On the other hand, the interview with some students has shown that the respondents of the course to the expected outcomes were an important driver for the self-motivation. This is also confirmed by the positive opinion about the respondents to the initial expectation (cfr. learning outcomes and Fig. 2). Regarding the workload (time-demand), the opinion of participants on average was moderately positive. Indeed, from the feedback collected on the forum (qualitative), we can see that many students struggled to be on time with their assignments. The majority of the students responded that the course requires a moderate cognitive effort. An issue that could have affected the cognitive workload should be related to the clarity of the contents (discussed in the next paragraph).

The analysis of the platform logs helped to discover patterns in the activity of the students. Analyzing the number of assessment completed by the ones that have attended at least one Unit of the course, we can see that a significative number of students completed less than eight assessments. Observing also the completion of the assessment per week, we can observe that the drop-out happened after the first 2 weeks (that have 8 assessments each).

The analysis of users' activity on the platform revealed that it was not uniform and some modules required more "views". However, we did not find a clear correspondence with the level of satisfaction expressed with the single methods. Moreover, the views of the assignments were not considered as the system blocks the user after the second attempt.

The analysis of the activity on the Forum allowed to point out the weeks that triggered more interaction. An analysis of the posts helped to better understand this activity. As an example, in the first weeks, many questions were generally related to the MOOC. In the other cases were mainly related to the comprehension of some topics or questions in the assessments.

In conclusion, despite participants' drop-out rate was noticeable (68%), considering other aspects, it seems that the learning design was well constructed. Indeed, as resulted from the questionnaire, the time and cognitive demand of the course resulted to be coherent with the students' level, indicating a high level of the learning design.

3.5 Learning Outcomes

The evaluation of Learning Outcomes aimed at the assessment of contents' quality and subject coverage. Metrics: Quality of contents (usefulness, understandability, presentation, scientific relevance, technical relevance, relevance related to the initial expectations), and subject coverage (do the modules cover the subjects of the course? Do they fit the initial expectations?).

The quality of contents was analyzed in the final questionnaire as mentioned above. Items 1 and 3 of Table 1 are related to the quality of contents and their presentation, indicating a good satisfaction level.

Moreover, regarding the contents and the structure, 38% of the respondents fully agrees and 48% moderately agrees that the strategies/educational activities implemented in the teaching practice have been adequate in comparison with the course's training goals. 43% fully agrees while 44% moderately agrees that the resources have been adequate. 38% were fully satisfied and 44% moderately satisfied with the general structure of the course.

The average of respondents was moderately positive in relation to the elaboration and the clarity of exposition and presentation of the contents. The feedback from the tutors reports some requests, through the forum and with direct messages, for further explanation or additional materials for certain subjects. These comments were evaluated in order to improve the material in the further development of the course.

At the overall level, the satisfaction of participants towards the various training modules was rather high, ranging mostly from moderately satisfactory to very satisfactory. The four most favoured modules were: "creative thinking skills"; "creatively using technologies"; "netiquette" and "team working", scoring respectively 52%, 50% and 49% (both for "team working" and "netiquette") of responses indicating to a high satisfaction level. However, considering the mean value of the ratings given to each module, there is little variance among them: only 0,4 points from the maximum score to the minimum score.

Regarding the correspondence to the initial expectations, 39% of the students think that the course has reached the intended training goals, 49% agree that it was moderately successful and only 1% answered: "not at all".

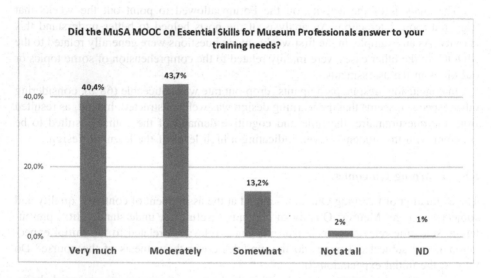

Fig. 2. Final evaluation survey: perceived coherence with learning needs.

Finally, the opinion of participants on the coherence with their learning needs shows a very positive rating, having more than 84% of responses ranging homogeneously from moderately coherent to very coherent. Only 13,2% of participants considered the course as only somewhat coherent with their learning needs, while just 2% of them did not perceive any coherence between the topics and their learning needs.

3.6   Synthesis

The quantitative and qualitative elements collected allow expressing some summary considerations, based on the five evaluation criteria generally adopted at EU level: relevance, efficiency, effectiveness, impact and sustainability.

Relevance and Coherence. The strategy implemented within the project appears to be consistent with the needs of the participants and the potential of the museum sector and is considered particularly useful at sectoral level and as an opportunity for employment growth. The number of participants involved highlights the ability of the MOOC tool to attract and interest a wide audience of a heterogeneous age group covering several professional fields. The level of this criteria is therefore considered satisfactory.

Efficiency. Efficiency levels are adequate and in line with expectations; for many participants, the project represented the first moment of use of the MOOC; despite this, no significant critical issues emerged. MOOC was easy to use and fully usable.

Effectiveness. Both in terms of content and methodologies used, the MOOC has proved to be an effective tool. In general terms, the design logic highlights innovative methodologies and appears able to achieve good results in terms of skills and experience. The structure was judged to be consistent with both requirements and initial expectations.

Impact. To date, an impact assessment would be insignificant since the only element is the number of participants who decided to continue with the path through the candidacy for the Specialization Course. Therefore, the level of these criteria cannot be assessed.

Sustainability. The elements of sustainability are mainly those related to the future usability of MOOC as an element of both in-depth analysis and further dissemination and transferability. The project can be qualified as a pilot experience and could play a significant role also for future training interventions and for strengthening skills in the museum sector. The level of this criteria is therefore considered satisfactory.

4 Conclusions and Future Works

4.1 A Subsection Sample

Market conditions and needs are constantly evolving and the working environment is becoming increasingly demanding in terms of skills, which must be in line with the most innovative trends and technologies. This is also happening in the museum context, where, first of all, it is necessary to spread a digital culture and train all professionals involved. Nowadays, they need multidisciplinary knowledge that includes not only the cultural domain but also competencies in the fields of ICT, communication, business strategy, marketing, etc.

With the intention of addressing this challenge, the Mu.SA vocational training course has been designed to support students and professionals in the acquisition of hybrid and transversal skills. The results achieved in the first phase of the project are encouraging, considering the engagement of the students and the ability of the course to fulfill the initial expectations.

At the present moment, the course is still active and many measurement data are being processed. In this paper, we have presented the first results of MOOC, which represents the first phase of the three-year project. It is our intention to propose in future works the analysis of the data of the Specialization and Work-Based training course, with the aim of understanding the general progress of the project, analyzing its potential and critical issues, and the impact of digital transformation in museums. One thing is certainly positive: the European Commission has proposed the Mu.SA project as a good practice in the field of "Opportunities for Cultural Heritage Professionals".

Acknowledgement. This research was carried out within the Museum Sector Alliance – Mu.SA project (Project Number 575907-EEP-1-2016-1-EL-EPPKA2-SSA) under the Erasmus + programme/Action KA2: Cooperation for innovation and the exchange of good practices – Sector Skills Alliances.

References

1. Mu.SA official website. http://www.project-musa.eu/
2. Giannini, T., Bowen J.: Of museums and digital culture: a landscape view. In Conference: Electronic Visualisation and the Arts (2018)
3. Tait, P.: Skills needs analysis: repair, maintenance and energy efficiency retrofit of traditional (pre-1919) buildings in England and Scotland (2013). https://historicengland.org.uk/content/heritage-counts/pub/2013/skills-needs-analysis-2013-repair-maintenance-energy-efficiency-retrofit/. Accessed 24 Jan 2020
4. Conway, P.: Preservation in the age of google: digitization, digital preservation, and dilemmas. Libr. Q. **80**(1), 61–79 (2010)
5. Mandarano, N.: Musei e media digitali. Carocci Ed, Rome (2019)
6. Van Lakerveld, J.A., Vroonhof, P., Broek, S., Stoutjesdijk, F.D., Van Loo, S.B.: Skills, training and knowledge transfer: traditional and emerging heritage professions (2017). https://www.panteia.com/uploads/2017/07/final-report-on-emerging-heritage-professions-23062017.pdf. Accessed 24 Jan 2020
7. Silvaggi, A., Pesce, F.: Job profiles for museums in the digital era: research conducted in Portugal, Italy and Greece within the Mu. SA project. J. Cult. Manag. Pol. **8**, 56 (2018)
8. European e-competences Framework 3.0 (e-CF). https://www.ecompetences.eu. Accessed 20 Jan 2020
9. Digital Competence Framework for Citizens (DigComp) document. https://publications.jrc.ec.europa.eu/repository/bitstream/JRC106281/web-digcomp2.1pdf_(online).pdf. Accessed 20 Jan 2020
10. 21st Century skills. https://www.aeseducation.com/career-readiness/what-are-21st-century-skills. Accessed 20 Jan 2020
11. Polymeropoulou, P., Pierrakeas, C., Borotis, S., Kameas, A.: Implementing a MOOC course for museum professionals with a worldwide effect. In: 2019 10th International Conference on Information, Intelligence, Systems and Applications, IISA, pp. 1–8. IEEE (2019)
12. Stracke, C.M., et al.: The quality of open online education: towards a reference framework for MOOCs. In: 2017 IEEE Global Engineering Education Conference, EDUCON, pp. 1713–1716. IEEE (2017)
13. Onah, D.F., Sinclair, J., Boyatt, R.: Dropout rates of massive open online courses: behavioural patterns. EDULEARN14 Proc. **1**, 5825–5834 (2014)

Pincello: An Affordable Electronics Kit for Prototyping Interactive Installations

Emanuel Felipe Duarte(✉) ⓘ and M. Cecília C. Baranauskas

Institute of Computing, University of Campinas,
Av. Albert Einstein, Campinas 1251, Brazil
{emanuel.duarte,cecilia}@ic.unicamp.br

Abstract. Interactive artifacts and environments that involve more aspects of life other than work (*e.g.*, social relations, entertainment, art etc.) are gaining more attention within the Human-Computer Interaction (HCI) field. This includes interactive art and installations. Do-It-Yourself (DIY) technologies, such as Arduinos with sensors and actuators, are often used in interactive installations. These technologies, however, are often oriented towards hobbyists and engineers. Moreover, easy-to-use commercial kits have a relatively high cost and a lack of flexibility. In this paper, we present Pincello: an affordable electronics kit for prototyping interactive installations. Pincello is not a commercial product, but rather a recommendation of components accompanied by meaningful hands-on documentation. We present and discuss the main components of the kit, including suggestions on how they can be used to allow different forms of interaction. We also present three case studies in which Pincello was used, involving 105 Human-Computer Interaction (HCI) students. Considering how the kit received positive feedback in the three case studies, and how it was successfully used to create 18 installations of varied themes, Pincello has shown to be a promising tool for the design and construction of interactive installations.

Keywords: Interactive installation · Interactive art · Electronics kit · Do-It-Yourself · Arduino

1 Introduction

The understanding of the interaction between a human and a computer has significantly changed since the beginning of the HCI field. The concept of a computer is constantly changing along technological innovation; besides the pervasiveness of personal computers and smartphones, we now have a wide variety of "things" and even environments embedded with computational technology, effectively rendering the computer "invisible", as foretold by Weiser [19]. Following Wieser's concept of ubiquitous computing, as the computer reaches out of the screen it becomes necessary for HCI researchers and practitioners to be able to design interactive artifacts and environments capable of sensing and actuating in varied ways. Consequently, HCI communities show a growing interest in

© Springer Nature Switzerland AG 2020
M. Kurosu (Ed.): HCII 2020, LNCS 12183, pp. 243–261, 2020.
https://doi.org/10.1007/978-3-030-49065-2_18

pervasive Do-It-Yourself (DIY) technologies, such as Arduinos, Raspberry Pis, and related gadgets.

Coincidentally, this growing interest in pervasive DIY technologies is aligned with how HCI has been expanding its boundaries with new waves of thought and is no longer limited to well-defined and/or workplace problems [2,3,14,17]. In practical terms, HCI is now concerned with more than graphical user interfaces and user tasks, it is considering interactive artifacts and environments that encompass more aspects of life other than work, such as social relations, entertainment, art *etc.* In this paper, we focus on a context of practice that has been gaining attention among HCI researchers [7] and benefits significantly from pervasive DIY technologies, which is the creation of interactive art, and more specifically, interactive installations.

DIY technologies have been used in many creative ways in the creation of interactive installations for quite some time. Currently, perhaps the most popular of these technologies is the Arduino microcontroller. Gibb [13] discusses some of the main qualities that defined Arduino's success, which are: (i) its relatively low cost; (ii) it can be programmed via Universal Serial Bus (USB) through an easy to use Integrated Development Environment (IDE); and (iii) it is supported by an engaged community. According to Gibb [13], as the Arduino is introduced in art museums and galleries, it closely resembles the route taken by photography in the 1800s: at first, it was seen as a new technology that belonged only to science museums rather than art ones but is now easily featured in any art museum or gallery. The Arduino has evolved over the years both in terms of hardware and software, but perhaps the most important change is how the word "arduino" became a synonym to a wider range of devices (from other microcontrollers to single-board computers), platforms and sometimes even an entire technological DIY culture (*e.g.*, "the age of the arduino" [4]).

Although DIY technologies are already being used to create interactive installations, one challenge that hinders a more widespread use is how these resources are often documented with a technical language more suited for engineers and hobbyists, while tutorials often involve solving mundane well-defined problems (*e.g.*, home automation). There are commercial products that address this entry-barrier problem with electronic kits designed to simplify circuit making, however, these proprietary kits are often aimed at children in educational contexts, are relatively expensive (usually costing a few hundred US dollars for more complete versions), and lack the flexibility for being extended, modified, and used in unconventional ways, as is often the case of interactive installations. To address these challenges, in this paper we present Pincello, an affordable electronics kit designed specifically for the prototyping of interactive installations. With Pincello, the entry barrier is reduced through a documentation that is practical, illustrative, and not too technical, and the flexibility is ensured by a selection of universal components that can be installed and used in different ways. Pincello was already used in three case studies, InterArt, InstInt, and InsTime, which, combined, involved a total of 105 Computer Science and Computer Engineering undergraduate and graduate students attending HCI courses. The students succeeded in creating a combined total of 19 interactive artworks and installations with varied themes, aesthetics, and innovative approaches to interaction with computational systems.

This paper is structured as follows: in Sect. 2 we provide, without exhausting the subject, an overview of relevant literature about the use of DIY technology in the creation of interactive installations; in Sect. 3 we present Pincello, detailing what it is, its online documentation, and its components; in Sect. 4 we discuss, as case studies, the three instances in which Pincello was used; lastly, in Sect. 5 we present our conclusions.

2   Literature Review

Both Bannon and Ehn [1], and Kostakos [16] argue that HCI literature often shows a tendency to focus on results, products, and services instead of processes and practices. This is no different in the more specialized topic of interactive art, as Duarte, Gonçalves and Baranauskas [8] argue how the design processes and practices for the creation of interactive installations often lack thorough presentation and discussion in the literature. Although a scarce topic, in this section we will briefly discuss, without exhausting the subject, some academic works, and commercial products in the context of the explicit and at least mildly explained use of pervasive DIY technologies for the creation of interactive installations.

In the context of multi-modal installations, the work of Jaimovich [15] describes the use of an Arduino microcontroller to create an interactive sound installation called *Ground Me!*. The installation uses an electrically grounded floor in conjunction with copper poles hanged from the ceiling and connected to the positive side of low voltage batteries. The role of the microcontroller is to detect and communicate to a computer when a circuit is closed, which happens when a barefoot person standing on the floor (or with any other part of its skin touching the floor) touches a copper pole. The value that is detected by the Arduino microcontroller will vary according to skin conductivity and body impedance, and this value is used by the computer to generate a sound related to electricity, such as shocks and sparks. As no specific sensor was used, the author had to engineer the circuit from scratch with batteries, cables and other conductive materials, resistors, and multiplexers. As another example of a multi-modal installation, Yang *et al.* [20], in turn, describe the use of an Arduino microcontroller in their *Light Up!* interactive installation. The authors make use of a computer connected to the Arduino microcontroller to analyze both the volume and pitch of the music being played in the environment. There are also pressure sensors on the ground to capture the dance movements of the people experiencing the installation. After combining the data from the music and how people are dancing, the installation triggers multiple Light-Emitting Diodes (LEDs) according to this data combination, creating visual feedback about both the music and the dancing taking place.

In the topic of cultural heritage, the work of Feng and Wang [11] describes the use of an Arduino microcontroller for the design of their *Urban Memory Accessor* interactive installation. The microcontroller is used to control the interactive process of creating a resin cube containing debris from demolished old buildings, intended as a form of preservation of urban culture. When someone activates the installation with a smartphone through a QR code, the Arduino microcontroller commands a series of servo motors responsible for inserting raw materials into a cube mold, injecting the resin, turning on a source of ultraviolet light to cure the resin for five minutes, and then releasing the completed cube. The mechanical complexity of this installation required a formal engineering approach to design the moving parts activated by servo motors. Also on the topic of cultural heritage, the work of Dimitropoulos et al. [5] discuss the use of Arduino sensors in the creation of an interactive simplified loom replica connected to an interactive digital application, intended at educating about the millennial weaving process. Although the authors mention design and prototyping, evaluation and testing, and technological tests (regarding microcontrollers, sensors, and connectivity) as steps of their research, they do not provide more detail about how the circuitry was built or which kind of sensor was used in the loom.

On the subject of promoting awareness, the work of Gardeli et al. [12] presents 8 projects in the theme of environmental awareness, of which 6 are interactive installations that make use of the Arduino microcontroller. The authors describe the use of varied components for the creation of the installations besides the Arduino microcontrollers, such as infrared motion sensors, Near-Field Communication (NFC) tags and readers, speakers, and even a valve and a small water pump. Also related to awareness, but in this case, real-time awareness of audience engagement during a talk, the work of Röggla et al. [18] describes the Tangible Air interactive installation. In their experiment, the authors provided the audience with a custom-built wireless Galvanic Skin Response (GSR) sensor, and the presenter wore a sweater with integrated sensors. The data collected from the sensors was shown in real-time to everyone, allowing awareness about the engagement of the audience as a whole, the individual engagement of 10 random people from the audience, and physiological data from the presenter. Besides stating that the wireless GSR sensor was custom-built, the authors do not explain why or how it was engineered.

From our literature review, we can highlight relevant technological challenges that emerge in the design of interactive installations. For instance, there is often a need to create a form of communication between microcontrollers and more powerful computers responsible for more computation-intensive tasks (e.g., from projecting images and playing music to more complex data algorithms). Another aspect to be observed is how often there is a need to engineer electronic circuits and create custom-built components for specific purposes, which can be a complex and demanding task. At a first impression, some commercial products that simplify the use of electronics and the making of things seem to mitigate these challenges. For instance, Bare Conductive's touch board kit with electric paint[1] has many creative uses showcased in the company's website, Furthermore, other commercial options such as Circuit Scribe's circuit drawing kits[2] and LittleBits's

---

[1] https://bareconductive.com/.
[2] https://circuitscribe.com/.

maker kits[3] have a playful approach aimed mostly at children education. However, even though these products are suited for exploring, playing, and learning, products that are designed to be easily assembled and disassembled will often lack the flexibility for being extended, connected in unintended ways, tuned and modified. To illustrate, Bare Conductive's electric paint does not go much beyond touch detection, and both Circuit Scribe's and LittleBits's kits seem more useful to prototype toy gadgets, rather than designing interactive environments in which the technology becomes pervasive.

As our literature review shows, pervasive DIY technologies can be a substantial tool in the creation of interactive installations. However, even with a high number of commercial kits, documentation, and tutorials available online, these tools usually have at least one of two limiting factors: low flexibility, limiting what can be created to mostly reproductions of existing projects; or a documentation that is too technical and oriented towards the solution of well-defined day-to-day problems, such as home automation. These options may work fine for hobbyists and educational contexts, but they fall short for HCI researchers and practitioners interested in designing and prototyping open-ended interactive artifacts and environments, such as interactive art and installations. Therefore, it is our understanding that an electronics kit that is both flexible and well-documented, but also affordable, could be of interest to the HCI community.

3   Pincello

Pincello is an affordable electronics kit to support the design and prototyping of interactive art and installations. It is important to emphasize that Pincello is not a commercial product and is not being sold anywhere. It instead acts as a recommendation of components that can be used together to compose an electronics kit. Anyone interested in creating interactive installations with these technologies can assemble a Pincello kit by individually buying the recommended components. The hardware will have an approximated cost between US$20.00 and US$60.00 depending on country, taxes and local availability of components. Pincello has two equally important parts: the hardware itself, and an accompanying original online documentation with practical tutorials[4].

The hardware is composed by two single-board microcontroller units, 12 different kinds of sensors, and 6 different kinds of actuators (there are also other components in Pincello, such as breadboards, jumper cables, and resistors, but we will not discuss these in detail in this paper as they are not pertinent to our HCI focus). We briefly describe all these components in the following subsections. The online documentation, in turn, has a kickstart tutorial aimed at creating an interactive artifact with physical and digital counterparts that is simple, illustrative, and easily modified and extended. Figure 1 illustrates this interactive artifact, which can be used as a starting point to explore more sensors

---

[3] https://littlebits.com/.
[4] https://efduarte.github.io/pincello.

and actuators and extended into actual interactive installations. The kickstart tutorial is organized into three main steps:

1. The first step is the configuration of an online Message Queuing Telemetry Transport (MQTT) broker to mediate the communication between physical and digital counterparts. The recommended MQTT broker is shiftr.io[5], which is well documented, has a useful graph visualization of the connected clients and exchange of messages and is free to use;
2. The second step is the setup of the programming tools to write, compile and upload code to the microcontrollers. Although the Arduino IDE can be used without major problems, a more professional (yet still straightforward) setup with Sublime Text[6] and PlatformIO[7] is recommended; and
3. The third and final step is the creation of the physical and digital counterparts that will communicate through the Internet and the MQTT Broker. As illustrated in Fig. 1, the physical counterpart is a circuit created with a microcontroller, a sensor, and an actuator, while the digital counterpart is a webpage with information and controls. Each counterpart is well documented to be easily modified and extended, and more physical or digital artifacts can be included in the communication.

Furthermore, after the kickstart tutorial, the online documentation has also more technical, individual tutorials for every sensor and actuator in the kit. Always with a focus on HCI, these individual tutorials go deeper in explaining how the component works, how it can be used in interactive installations, how it should be wired to the microcontroller, as well as provide both minimal and more robust code examples that help explore and use the components.

3.1 Microcontrollers

Microcontrollers usually have a relatively low processing power, which means they are more suited for simple tasks, such as receiving information from sensors and sending information to actuators and other devices. This limitation, however, can be worked around with the use of wireless communication and Internet access. For instance, a microcontroller may not be able to project and play high-definition images and sounds, but it can communicate with a computer that will be able to do these tasks. With an emphasis on versatility and low cost, we chose two different microcontrollers to be included in Pincello, they are:

NodeMCU DEVKIT 1.0. This single-board microcontroller, illustrated in Fig. 2a, has built-in Wi-Fi, allowing wireless communication and Internet access. The NodeMCU DEVKIT 1.0 can be used to create artifacts that not only have sensors and actuators but are also able to wirelessly communicate with other

---

[5] https://shiftr.io/.

[6] https://www.sublimetext.com/.

[7] https://platformio.org/.

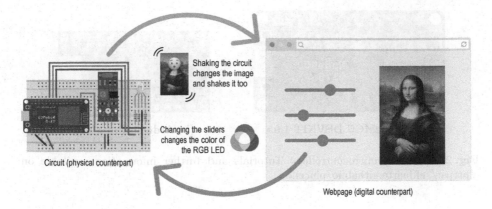

Fig. 1. Illustration of the interactive artifact created with Pincello's tutorial. Full tutorial available on: <https://efduarte.github.io/pincello>.

devices and the world through the Internet. Furthermore, its low size and energy consumption allow the use of mobile power sources (such as a power bank) to create devices that are relatively portable and low-profile. For instance, if an interactive installation needs to be composed by multiple components (*e.g.*, physical objects that can be picked up and played with, projections, social media presence *etc.*), by embedding the NodeMCU DEVKIT 1.0 into physical objects, these components can all be connected through the Internet and communicate with each other. Lastly, while technically not an Arduino, the NodeMCU DEVKIT 1.0 can be programmed with the Arduino IDE and similar tools that use the Arduino language, benefiting on the high availability of documentation, tutorials, and software libraries online.

Arduino Pro Micro. This microcontroller, illustrated in Fig. 2b, complements the NodeMCU DEVKIT 1.0. Both microcontrollers are similar in size, appearance, and compatibility with the Arduino language and its libraries. Regarding differences, while the Arduino Pro Micro lacks built-in Wi-Fi, it can mimic the inputs of a mouse and keyboard when connected to a computer through USB. Considering that data sent through Wi-Fi and the Internet will inevitably have a delay (usually between tens and hundreds of milliseconds) and be subject to bad connections, this mimic is useful when there is a need for an extra-reliable, low-latency communication between the microcontroller and a computer, even though it is only a one-way channel. For instance, if an interactive installation needs to be instantly responsive to small events, even a sensor with dozens of readings per second can still be used with the Arduino Pro Micro to dynamically control the response with virtually no latency.

(a) NodeMCU DEVKIT 1.0.   (b) Arduino Pro Micro.

Fig. 2. Pincello's microcontrollers. Tutorials and further information available on: <https://efduarte.github.io/pincello>.

3.2 Sensors

Considering that Pincello emphasizes wireless communication over the Internet, every sensor from a device that takes part in this communication can be used in interactive installations built with Pincello. For instance, even the webcam of computer communicating with the NodeMCU DEVKIT 1.0 can be considered a sensor, and it can be used to detect objects, faces, emotions *etc.* In this section, however, we focus on the sensors from the electronics kit. With an emphasis on being able to capture a wide variety of human interactions, we selected the following 12 kinds of sensors to be included in Pincello:

Humidity and Temperature (DHT11). This sensor, illustrated in Fig. 3a, uses a hygrometer and a thermistor to measure relative air humidity and temperature. It can be used to monitor the temperature and humidity of an ambient, but it can also detect some forms of human interaction. For instance, by directly blowing on the sensor, or even holding it in your hand, you will likely see an increase in both temperature and humidity. The downside is that the sensor is not very responsive to short interactions, as readings occur only every second.

Capacitive Touch Button (TTP223). This sensor, illustrated in Fig. 3b, can be activated by touch regardless of the applied pressure. Besides its use as a button, this sensor can be used to create touchable surfaces or objects with the use of additional conductive material. For instance, by attaching a copper tape to the plating behind the sensor and then covering a tangible object with this tape, you can detect when someone touches that object.

Accelerometer and Gyro (MPU-6050). This sensor, illustrated in Fig. 3c, contains both an accelerometer and a gyroscope in the same component. It captures in real-time both acceleration and rotation in the x, y and z axes. This sensor can be used in many ways, from simply detecting when a tangible object is picked up or laid down, to more complex tasks, such as detecting at which speed and direction an object (for instance, a crank) is being rotated or even tracking the absolute orientation of a physical object.

Ultrasonic Distance (HC-SR04). This sensor, illustrated in Fig. 3d, uses the speed of sound to calculate distance, like the sonar system of a submarine, or the parking sensor of a car. Differently from the reflexive obstacle sensor presented next, this sensor can be used not only to detect something but also return a numeric distance. For instance, the sensor can be used to detect when someone approaches an interactive installation, but also respond in different ways according to how far (or close) the person is.

Reflexive Obstacle (FC-51). This sensor, illustrated in Fig. 3e, detects anything that reflects light (someone's hand, or any object that is not black) positioned a few centimeters from the sensor. Differently from the ultrasonic distance sensor presented above, this sensor can only be used to return a binary detection and not a numeric distance. For instance, the sensor can be used to detect if an object was placed in a specific position right in front of a sensor, or even if someone waived his/her hand over it.

Digital Luminosity (LDR). This sensor, illustrated in Fig. 3f, detects if the luminosity is above or below a certain threshold, adjusted in the included potentiometer. Differently from the analog Light-Dependent Resistor (LDR) presented next, this sensor returns only a binary value according to the threshold, and not a numeric luminosity value. Besides the luminosity of an ambient, this sensor can be used to detect touch-less interactions. For instance, certain actions from a person (like placing his/her hand in a specific spot) may block light from reaching the sensor, and therefore be detected by it.

Analog Luminosity (LDR). This sensor, illustrated in Fig. 3j, changes its resistance according to the amount of light it is exposed to. Differently from the digital luminosity sensor presented above, this sensor provides a numeric luminosity value that ranges from 0 to 1023 when used with the NodeMCU DEVKIT 1.0. Besides the luminosity of an ambient, this sensor can be used to detect touch-less interactions. For instance, certain actions from a person (like pointing a smartphone flashlight towards an object) may increase the amount of light reaching the sensor and therefore result in increased values.

Hall Effect (A3144). This sensor, illustrated in Fig. 3g, detects the presence of magnetic fields. The output can be both digital or analog, and the precision can be adjusted in the included potentiometer. This sensor can be used to detect if a magnet is close to the sensor (a small magnet will need to be at least a few centimeters away). For instance, by embedding magnets into tangible objects of an interactive installation, these objects can then be used to activate the interactivity by positioning them near the sensors.

Vibration (SW-420). This sensor, illustrated in Fig. 3h, detects vibrations above a certain threshold, adjusted in the included potentiometer. It only detects the presence or absence of vibration, not its intensity. This sensor can be used as a motion detector that is both simpler and easier to use when compared to an accelerometer, with the downside of not detecting any details about the motion. For instance, by embedding this sensor into a tangible object (like a rattle), it becomes possible to detect when this object is picked up and shaken.

Sound (KY-038). This sensor, illustrated in Fig. 3i, uses an electret to detect sound. The output can be both digital or analog, and the precision can be adjusted in the included potentiometer. It does not make distinctions between different kinds of sounds, and it may require fine calibration to avoid background noise, but it may be useful in musical installations. For instance, the sensor can be placed inside a drum to detect when someone is playing that instrument with the precision of detecting every beat.

Tilt (SW-200D). This sensor, illustrated in Fig. 3k, uses gravity to detect if it is turned upwards or downwards. This sensor can be used in interactive installations to detect the change of orientation of tangible objects. For instance, by embedding the sensor into a tangible object over a table it becomes possible to detect when that object is flipped over.

Push Button. Push buttons, illustrated in Fig. 3l, close a circuit when they are physically pressed. Besides their use as traditional buttons, these sensors can be used to create pressable surfaces with a satisfying "click" (tactile and sound) feedback. For instance, by gluing cardboard surfaces with different textures on the top of push buttons, it is possible to create tactile pressable surfaces that look and feel much more interesting than conventional buttons.

3.3 Actuators

In the same way as with sensors, every actuator from a device that communicates with the NodeMCU DEVKIT 1.0 can be considered an actuator to be used in interactive installations build with Pincello. For instance, a computer may display images through a projector, or play high-definition sounds through a set of speakers. In this section, however, we focus on the actuators from the electronics kit. With an emphasis on being able to impact and influence the physical world beyond the use of screens, we chose the following 6 kinds of actuators to be included in Pincello:

LED. This actuator, illustrated in Fig. 4a, is present in the following colors: red, green, blue, yellow, and white. Differently from the Red, Green, and Blue RGB LEDs presented next, a common LED does not change its color, but its brightness can be controlled. LEDs can be used in interactive installations in various ways, such as decoration, indicators of system status, or as feedback for human actions.

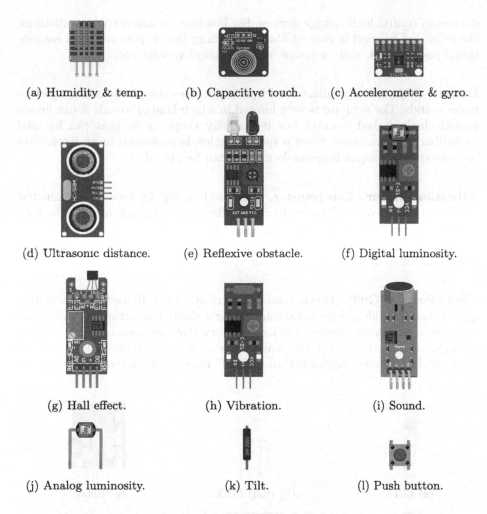

(a) Humidity & temp.   (b) Capacitive touch.   (c) Accelerometer & gyro.

(d) Ultrasonic distance.   (e) Reflexive obstacle.   (f) Digital luminosity.

(g) Hall effect.   (h) Vibration.   (i) Sound.

(j) Analog luminosity.   (k) Tilt.   (l) Push button.

Fig. 3. Pincello's sensors. Tutorials with wiring, coding and further information available on: <https://efduarte.github.io/pincello>.

RGB LED. This actuator, illustrated in Fig. 4b, differently from the common LEDs presented above, can be changed to any color in the RGB spectrum (except for black, as black is the absence of color in light sources). RGB LEDs can be used in interactive installations in various ways, such as decoration, indicators of system status, or as feedback for human actions.

Relay. This actuator, illustrated in Fig. 4c, uses a magnetic switch to turn on or off high voltage devices. While Arduinos and similar electronics usually operate between 3.3 and 5 V, most domestic devices operate between 100 and 250 V, therefore this actuator is intended to bridge the difference by using low voltage devices to control high voltage devices. For instance, in interactive installations, the relay can be used to control almost anything that is powered by a conventional power outlet, such as lamps, motors, sound systems *etc.*

Buzzer. This actuator, illustrated in Fig. 4d, uses the piezoelectric effect to make sounds. The actuator is very limited in which kind of sounds it can create (mostly high-pitched sounds), but it can play simple notes that can be used as feedback. For instance, when a specific action is performed in an interactive installation a corresponding simple melody can be played.

Vibration Motor. This actuator, illustrated in Fig. 4e, uses an asymmetric weight attached to a small motor to create vibrations. This actuator can be used to create haptic feedback in interactive installations. For instance, the vibration motor can be attached to an object that is supposed to be picked up, and it can vibrate in different intensities according to how that object is manipulated.

Micro Servo (SG90). This actuator, illustrated in Fig. 4f, uses a motor with a gear train to provide precise angle control over a shaft. This actuator can be used to create controllable physical motion in interactive installations. For instance, an object can be attached to the shaft of the micro servo to allow this object to be rotated to different angles within the 180° range of the servo.

(a) LED.   (b) RGB LED.   (c) Relay.

(d) Buzzer.   (e) Vibration motor.   (f) Micro servo.

Fig. 4. Pincello's actuators. Tutorials with wiring, coding and further information available on: <https://efduarte.github.io/pincello>.

4 Case Studies

Pincello has already been used in three case studies in the context of undergraduate and graduate HCI courses, and we received positive feedback from the students regarding Pincello in all of them. These three case studies are named:

InterArt [6]; InstInt [8]; and InsTime [10]. In the following subsections, we will present a brief overview of each case study, with emphasis on how Pincello was used and what kind of interactive installation was created with it.

4.1 InterArt

The InterArt case study took place in the first semester of 2017 at the University of Campinas (Unicamp). A total of 55 Computer Science and Computer Engineering undergraduate students attending an HCI undergraduate course, distributed into 9 teams, designed and constructed 9 interactive artworks based on a theme of their choosing [6]. Within a comprehensive design process with many design activities, Pincello was presented to the students along some interactive artifact examples to inspire them by illustrating a kind of interaction design that goes beyond the computer screen. Each of the 9 teams received a Pincello kit to be used throughout the semester. Only one team opted for not using Pincello (its use was not mandatory), and instead focused on the use of a Microsoft Kinect. At the end of the semester, the teams presented their projects, and, as illustrated in Fig. 5, some of these installations (Monolito, Lobo-Guará, and Memoção) were later exhibited at the Exploratory Science Museum of Unicamp [9]. A brief summary of the interactive installations created in the InterArt case study is presented in the following list:

- **500cc**: a sensory dancing platform with a visual drawing of the dancing;
- **Autorretrato**: a dynamic display of famous self-portrait paintings based on physiological measurements of the audience;
- **Loneliness**: a "notgame" exploring the concept of social isolation;
- **MusicBoard**: a musical instrument for people without musical skills;
- **Monolito**: a monolith to interact with the projection of a psychedelic scene from Kubrick's 2001: A Space Odyssey;
- **Lobisomem Atacando o Galinheiro**: a farm mock-up to explore storytelling involving chickens and a werewolf;
- **Lobo-Guará**: an interactive maned wolf designed for museums;
- **Nychos**: an interactive interpretation of famous Nychos' dissections; and
- **Memoção**: a tactile exploration experience based on Internet memes.

Except for the team that used the Microsoft Kinect (500cc), all the installations have wireless communication between the NodeMCU DEVKIT 1.0 microcontroller and a computer responsible for displaying images and playing sounds (during this case study, Pincello did not have yet the alternative Arduino Pro Micro microcontroller, and it was later added due to the need of some of these installations for a more low-latency one-way communication). Regarding sensors, the students used all the sensors available in Pincello at the time of this case study, which were: humidity & temperature, accelerometer & gyro, reflexive obstacle, vibration, sound, analog luminosity and push buttons. With regard to actuators, with the exception of the buzzer which was not used at this time, the students used the other two actuators available in Pincello at the time: LEDs

(a) Memoção.   (b) Lobo-Guará.

Fig. 5. Two examples of interactive installations from the InterArt [6] case study, exhibited at the Exploratory Science Museum of Unicamp.

and RGB LED. The usage of components included creative uses, such as a proximity (reflexive obstacle) sensor on the head of the interactive maned wolf in the Lobo-Guará installation to detect attempts to pet it, or covering push buttons with rectangular surfaces with different textures to create a tactile installation, namely the Memoção installation. The teams also used sensors that were not included in Pincello, such as heart rate and gesture, highlighting how Pincello is flexible and can be customized.

4.2   InstInt

The InstInt case study took place in the second semester of 2017 at Unicamp. A group of 5 Computer Science graduate students with different backgrounds attending an HCI graduate course co-designed and constructed a small-scale interactive installation for public spaces [8]. Within a comprehensive design process with many design activities, as in the InterArt case, Pincello was presented to the students along some interactive artifact examples to inspire them by illustrating a kind of interaction design that goes beyond the computer screen. Each of the 5 students received a Pincello kit to be used throughout the semester in a co-design process [8]. At the end of the semester, the students presented their project, illustrated in Fig. 6. The installation, which has a physical form that resembles something between a large umbrella and a carousel with ribbons attached around it, initially plays an instrumental music at a low volume (played from a computer), blinks some colorful lights (with the use of LEDs) and spins at a low speed (with the use of a micro servo) as it waits for interaction. When a person approaches, this person can touch the ribbons (activated by capacitive touch buttons extended with conductive copper tape). Touching each ribbon controls the volume of a different instrument in the music also changes the blinking of lights, which follows the music.

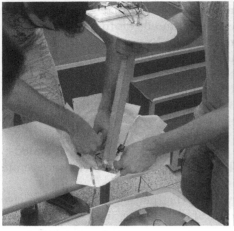 

(a) Prototype being constructed.   (b) Small-scale interactive installation.

Fig. 6. Construction and final physical artifact of the small-scale interactive installation from the InstInt [8] case study.

This interactive installation also required a wireless communication between the NodeMCU DEVKIT 1.0 microcontroller and a computer responsible for playing the music. Regarding sensors and actuators, this interactive installation used only the capacitive touch button as a sensor (the specification for the real-scale installation also specifies the use of the ultrasonic distance, but it was not used in the small-scale prototype), and LEDs and the micro servo as actuators. The use of capacitive touch button sensors extended with conductive copper tape illustrates how Pincello is flexible and can be used in creative, unforeseen ways. Furthermore, one design solution illustrates another important aspect of Pincello that emerged in this case study: the participants first envisioned an installation that continually rotates in the same direction, like a carousel. However, when experimenting with the available micro servo motor that can only rotate 180°, participants ended up implementing it to rotate back and forth in a semicircle, resembling a waltz dance that further corroborated to the captivating experience provided by the small-scale installation. Therefore, Pincello is not only a tool to build predetermined interactive installations, but it is also a tool that is supposed to be part of the design process of interactive installations.

4.3   InsTime

The InsTime case study took place in the first semester of 2018 at Unicamp. A total of 45 Computer Science and Computer Engineering undergraduate students attending an HCI undergraduate course, distributed into 9 teams, designed and constructed 9 interactive installations based on the theme of "deep time" [10]. Within a comprehensive design process with many design activities, Pincello was presented to the students along some interactive artifact examples to inspire them by illustrating a kind of interaction design that goes beyond the computer screen. Each of the 9 teams received a Pincello kit to be used throughout the semester. At the end of the semester, the teams presented their deep time projects. Two examples of the final projects are illustrated in Fig. 6. Similarly to what happened in the InterArt case study, some of these installations (CronoBit and Temporário) were also later exhibited at the Exploratory Science Museum of Unicamp. A brief summary of the interactive installations created in the InsTime case study is presented in the following list:

- **Chronos**: an interactive mock-up of a timeline with five geological periods;
- **CronoBit**: a set of drums to play with how humans can drastically accelerate natural processes that would otherwise take much longer;
- **De Volta Para o Futuro**: a memory game that plays with how we perceive the passage of time when we are concentrated or having fun;
- **General Purpose Timer**: an interactive mock-up to play and learn about the impacts of different methods of garbage disposal;
- **Limbo**: a hand crank to control a visual simulation of earth's history;
- **Looper**: a blowable miniature windmill to play with the age of the universe;
- **Rolex**: a set of light bulbs of different technologies and increasing power efficiency, turned on by ironic applause;
- **Temporário**: an educational video display that is aware about how many people are watching it, and adjusts the playback accordingly; and
- **Time**: a mock-up city about the positive and negative sides of nuclear energy.

Because InsTime was chronologically the third case study in which Pincello was applied, it benefited from lessons learned and improvements to the kit and the online documentation. For instance, this is the first case study in which the Arduino Pro Micro alternative microcontroller was used, and it was fundamental in allowing the CronoBit installation, illustrated in Fig. 7a, to be highly responsive, capable of detecting every beat of the drums regardless of how fast was the drumming. Besides the De Volta Para o Futuro memory game installation that also used the Arduino Pro Micro to have low-latency input, the other seven teams created installations with wireless communication through the NodeMCU DEVKIT 1.0 microcontroller. Regarding sensors, the students used the following components available in Pincello: capacitive touch button, accelerometer & gyro, ultrasonic distance, reflexive obstacle, vibration, sound, and push buttons. With regard to actuators, with the exception of the vibration motor which was not used at this time, the students used the other five actuators available in Pincello at the time: LEDs, RGB LED, relay, buzzer, and micro servo. The usage of components included creative uses. For instance, in the Limbo interactive installation, the accelerometer & gyro was attached to a hand crank (recycled from a bicycle pedal) to calculate angular velocity and acceleration, which controlled a virtual visualization of earth's history.

(a) CronoBit.   (b) General Purpose Timer.

Fig. 7. Two examples of the interactive installations from the InsTime [10] case study, openly addressing the theme of "deep time".

5 Conclusion

Considering how the field of HCI is increasingly interested in interactions that go beyond work-related and well-defined problems, the use of pervasive DIY technology by researchers and practitioners is a substantial step towards the design and construction of more open-ended physical interactive artifacts and environments. In this context, Pincello has achieved its objective of being a relatively easy-to-use and flexible tool for the creation of interactive installations. As has been evidenced in the three case studies, the feedback from the involved students was positive and the resulting interactive installations were varied in theme, aesthetic, and innovative approaches to interaction with computational systems. Finally, Pincello also achieved its objective of being relatively affordable when compared to commercial kits. With these positive results, we see Pincello as a promising tool for the HCI community that is now openly available to be explored, learned, modified and transformed.

Acknowledgments. This study was financially supported by the National Council for Scientific and Technological Development (CNPq) through grant #306272/2017-2 and by the São Paulo Research Foundation through grants #2015/16528-0, #2015/24300-9 and #2017/06762-0. Figures 2, 3 and 4 were generated with the Fritzing open-source software.

References

1. Bannon, L.J., Ehn, P.: Design: design matters in participatory design. In: Simonsen, J., Robertson, T. (eds.) Routledge International Handbook of Participatory Design. Routledge International Handbooks. Routledge, London (2013)
2. Bødker, S.: When second wave HCI meets third wave challenges. In: Proceedings of the 4th Nordic Conference on Human-Computer Interaction: Changing Roles, NordiCHI 2006, pp. 1–8. ACM, New York (2006). https://doi.org/10.1145/1182475.1182476

3. Bødker, S.: Third-wave HCI, 10 years later–participation and sharing. Interactions **22**(5), 24–31 (2015). https://doi.org/10.1145/2804405
4. Cressey, D.: Age of the arduino. Nature **544**(7648), 125–126 (2017)
5. Dimitropoulos, A., et al.: The loom: interactive weaving through a tangible installation with digital feedback. In: Ioannides, M. (ed.) Digital Cultural Heritage. LNCS, vol. 10605, pp. 199–210. Springer, Cham (2018). https://doi.org/10.1007/978-3-319-75826-8_17
6. Duarte, E.F., Baranauskas, M.C.C.: InterArt: learning human-computer interaction through the making of interactive Art. In: Kurosu, M. (ed.) HCI 2018. LNCS, vol. 10901, pp. 35–54. Springer, Cham (2018). https://doi.org/10.1007/978-3-319-91238-7_4
7. Duarte, E.F., Baranauskas, M.C.C.: Revisiting interactive art from an interaction design perspective: opening a research agenda. In: Proceedings of the 17th Brazilian Symposium on Human Factors in Computing Systems, IHC 2018. Association for Computing Machinery, New York (2018). https://doi.org/10.1145/3274192.3274227
8. Duarte, E.F., Gonçalves, F.M., Baranauskas, M.C.C.: Instint: enacting a small-scale interactive installation through co-design. In: Proceedings of the 30th Australian Conference on Computer-Human Interaction, OzCHI 2018, pp. 338–348. ACM, New York (2018). https://doi.org/10.1145/3292147.3292158
9. Duarte, E.F., Maike, V.R.M.L., Mendoza, Y.L.M., de Lima Tenório Brennand, C.V., Baranauskas, M.C.C.: "The magic of science:" beyond action, a case study on learning through socioenaction. In: Anais do XXV Workshop de Informática na Escola (WIE 2019), pp. 501–510. Sociedade Brasileira de Computação (SBC), Porto Alegre, November 2019. https://doi.org/10.5753/cbie.wie.2019.501. https://www.br-ie.org/pub/index.php/wie/article/view/8541
10. Duarte, E.F., Mendoza, Y.L.M., Baranauskas, M.C.C.: Instime: a case study on the co-design of interactive installations on deep time (2020, publication pending)
11. Feng, W., Wang, Y.: Urban memory accessor: mechanical design of interactive installation based on arduino. In: Yuan, P.F., Xie, Y.M.M., Yao, J., Yan, C. (eds.) CDRF 2019, pp. 346–354. Springer, Singapore (2020). https://doi.org/10.1007/978-981-13-8153-9_31
12. Gardeli, A., Vosinakis, S., Englezos, K., Mavroudi, D., Stratis, M., Stavrakis, M.: Design and development of games and interactive installations for environmental awareness. EAI Endorsed Trans. Serious Games, **4**(12) (2017). https://doi.org/10.4108/eai.8-12-2017.153402
13. Gibb, A.M.: New media art, design, and the Arduino microcontroller: a malleable tool. Master's thesis, Pratt Institute, School of Art and Design (2010)
14. Harrison, S.R., Tatar, D.G., Sengers, P.: The three paradigms of HCI. In: Alt. Chi. Session at the SIGCHI Conference on Human Factors in Computing Systems, pp. 1–18. ACM, San Jose (2007)
15. Jaimovich, J.: Ground me! an interactive sound art installation. In: Proceedings of the International Conference on New Interfaces for Musical Expression, Sydney, Australia, pp. 391–394 (2010). http://www.nime.org/proceedings/2010/nime2010_391.pdf
16. Kostakos, V.: The big hole in HCI research. Interactions **22**(2), 48–51 (2015). https://doi.org/10.1145/2729103
17. Rogers, Y.: HCI theory: classical, modern, and contemporary. Synth. Lect. Hum.-Cent. Inform. **5**(2), 1–129 (2012). https://doi.org/10.2200/S00418ED1V01Y201205HCI014

18. Röggla, T., Wang, C., Perez Romero, L., Jansen, J., Cesar, P.: Tangible air: an interactive installation for visualising audience engagement. In: Proceedings of the 2017 ACM SIGCHI Conference on Creativity and Cognition, C&C 2017, pp. 263–265. Association for Computing Machinery, New York (2017). https://doi.org/10.1145/3059454.3078708

19. Weiser, M.: The computer for the 21st century. Sci. Am. **265**(3), 94–104 (1991)

20. Yang, Y., Wang, S., Tseng, Y., Lin, H.K.: Light up! creating an interactive digital artwork based on Arduino and MAX/MSP design. In: 2010 International Computer Symposium (ICS 2010), pp. 258–263, December 2010. https://doi.org/10.1109/COMPSYM.2010.5685506

Research on Design of Intelligent Creeping Blanket for Infants Based on Sustainable Design

Han Gao[(✉)]

Nanjing University of Science and Technology, Xiaolingwei 200, Nanjing, Jiangsu, China
630184112@qq.com

Abstract. With the continuous improvement of parents' educational level in China, parent has been paid more and more attention to the early education of their children. There is only visual and tactile interaction between traditional crawling blankets and infants. The value of early education is small. The application of thinking and intelligent information technology to the design of infant crawling blankets can develop greater potential for early education for infant crawling blankets and solve a certain waste of resources. Therefore, it is very important to fully consider the development characteristics of all aspects of the baby and comprehensively consider the application of sustainable design thinking in the intelligent crawling blanket, so as to design a growth intelligent crawling blanket that enhances the infant's early education experience. This article takes the intelligent crawling blanket of infants 0–3 years old as the research object, and adopts a combination of qualitative research and quantitative research to summarize the design principles and design strategies of infants and young children's intelligent crawling blankets based on the development characteristics of infants and the needs of parents. Intelligent crawling blanket for infants not only meets the development needs of infants but also achieves product sustainability.

Keywords: Sustainable design · Smart crawling blanket · Baby development characteristics

1 Introduction

The market potential of intelligent crawling blankets is huge for infants and toddlers in China. At present, resources are wasted due to unscientific function settings. It can meet the growing market demand of infants and toddlers in the early education industry, improve the early childhood education experience, and reduce the waste of resources on intelligent crawling blankets by applying sustainable design thinking to intelligent crawling blankets for infants. Intelligent crawling blankets for infants and toddlers based on sustainable design can not only meet the development characteristics of infants in various aspects, improve the early education experience of infants, fully explore the external and intrinsic value of the product, but also achieve sustainable product extension Service life, reducing waste of resources. The product's life cycle

M. Kurosu (Ed.): HCII 2020, LNCS 12183, pp. 262–275, 2020.
https://doi.org/10.1007/978-3-030-49065-2_19

can be briefly summarized as the whole process of a product from its production to its disposal. The life cycle of a product specifically includes the four life stages of the product's raw material extraction and processing, manufacturing, circulation, and waste recycling. The design link in the manufacturing stage played a key role in the sustainable development of the entire product. Based on this, this article researches sustainable design thinking, conducts user surveys on infants and parents, makes market research on crawling blankets, and analyzes the sustainability indicators of various links in the life cycle of infant crawling blanket products to provides a real and reliable basis for baby crawling blanket design.

2 Characteristics of Infant Development

2.1 Physiological Development Characteristics of Infants

Infant hood is the fastest period of natural growth. The infants' body and bones grow rapidly, from basic instincts such as swallowing, vomiting, exhaling, and sucking, to "touching and rolling." The coordination of brain tissues and limb movements is an important part in the physiological development of infants and toddlers. With the development of infants and toddlers' brain functions, the development of their limb movements exhibits regularity. The development of random movements is directional and sequential. Babies around 6 months have been able to master head movements freely, and then slowly learn to crawl and turn around, and begin to cooperate with brain and limb movements and stand even walk with the help of external forces, finally achieved complete coordination of brain and limb movements. In the early childhood stage, it promotes the coordinated development of brain and limb movements by playing with various items and appliances. At this stage, it can effectively help infants grow and develop by using hands-on brain toys.

2.2 Characteristics of Infant Psychological Development

The psychological development of infants presents a specific logical sequence in development characteristics according to the increase of age. The psychological development of infants is divided into three stages. The first stage is the development of sensory perception. Infants 3–4 months can sense the surrounding environment through sensory organs such as eyes, ears, nose and nose. The second stage is the stage of psychological activity. Based on the development of sensory perception, infants' thinking, Psychological experiences have developed rapidly such as will and interest. Babies learn to crawl is an important sign of this stage, because crawling is the first completely autonomous movement in the life of infants and young children. Crawling completes a certain goal and indicates the generation of ideas. The process of completion requires thinking and will activity. After the goal is completed, an emotional experience will be produced, and the goal will be continuously completed while promoting the development of the brain. Elementary interpersonal communication activities are the third stage of the psychological development of infants. Infants at this stage gradually have basic language skills and physical movement skills.

During the period of infant psychological development, the development of emotions and emotions is also an important aspect. Emotions are the instincts of infants. They have characteristics such as congenital, situational, and volatility. For example, newborn babies often produce crying emotions because of physical factors such as hunger, sleepiness, and physical discomfort. Emotions are more inclined to the influence of social factors, often manifested in social interaction activities, showing characteristics such as Sociality, durability and stability. About 3 months, the babies' emotions usually express happiness, disgust, and anger by crying and smiling; about 6 months, the babies' emotions gradually become rich, and then start to use body movements to express joy, fear, and sadness, such as nodding, shake your head, kick your legs, wave your hands, etc. At the age of one and a half, young children begin to learn to talk and walk on their legs, slowly integrating into the social activities of life.

2.3   Cognitive Development Characteristics of Infants

The cognitive development of infants is a staged development process, and education is carried out at different levels according to the cognitive characteristics of different stages. The specific cognitive characteristics of infants and young children at different stages are shown in the figure below (Tables 1, 2 and 3).

Table 1. Cognitive development characteristics of infants aged 0–1

	0–6 m	7–9 m	10–12 m
Tactile	Can simply grasp	Throw, tear, grab, pinch, etc.; love to stuff things into mouth	Can graffiti, turn pages
Vision	Gradually follow the object	Have a certain understanding of the outline of the object	Can see the details of the object
Auditory	Can identify sound sources, easy to be attracted by sounds	Can heard imitating sounds, wave limbs with music	Distinguish faster more flexible sound
Attention	Can gradually follow objects, can notice strangers or things	Like to explore the surroundings Environment	Focus on the things of interest
Thinking ability	Observe and identify Small differences in objects	Prolonged concentration of attention	Lack of objective existence concept

Table 2. Cognitive development characteristics of infants aged 1–2

	13–15 m	16–18 m	19–21 m	22–24 m
Tactile	Hands are more coordinated and can hold small objects	Can build blocks and easily hold a spoon	Like graffiti	Can draw simple graphics profile
Vision	Have a certain distinction between colors, like warm tones	Can distinguish simple common objects, enhanced visual matching	Can distinguish the different characteristics of the object	Can recognize color better, express object characteristics through distinguishing graphics simply
Auditory	Active search Source, like familiar sounds	Enhance imitation ability	Can distinguish different people's voices	Smooth hearing and movement coordination
Attention	Staring at an object for a long time	Attention will move with the movement of the object	Can distinguish the main and secondary of things	Staring at an object for a long time
Thinking ability	Preliminary understanding of existence, category concepts	Ability to compare the characteristics of two objects	Preliminary cognition of right and wrong	Preliminary understanding of existence, category concepts

Table 3. Cognitive development characteristics of infants aged 2–3

	0–6 m	7–9 m
Tactile	Enhanced control of both hands	Flexible control of fine movements, such as origami
Vision	Distinguishable graphics and colors	Began to have their own aesthetic consciousness
Auditory	Perfect hearing	Can distinguish between different instruments
Attention	Can observe and identify Small differences in objects	More concentrated, like to repeat
Thinking ability	A certain degree of space, time cognition	Enhance memory and problem solving ability

3   Research on the Status of Smart Crawling Blanket Market

3.1   Smart Crawling Blanket Market Status

According to the "2018 China Children's Family Insight White Paper" released by Tencent Data Labs, the size of China's children's consumer market has exceeded 4.5 trillion yuan, which is a huge cake. It has attracted giants to make frequent attempts in children's education. In this huge number, It has played an important role that the second-child policy has been open since 2016. When the post-80s and 90s were upgraded to the main force of parents, their better economic foundation and the pursuit of consumption upgrades also raised childcare expenditures. Data show that a family's parental expenditure for the whole year accounts for about 22% of the total family income, and this proportion is still increasing. In addition, research released the "Insight Report on Young Parenting Families in China in 2019", through investigating the parenting behaviors and parenting concepts of young parenting families, it was found that the intelligence of early education toys has become a new development trend.

Baby crawling blanket market rugs originated in Japan and South Korea first, and have matured in the Japanese and Korean markets. The awareness of the Chinese market is gradually forming and has great potential for development. The market demand is large, but the current intelligent crawling has the problems of homogenization, the lack of value of early education, and waste of resources in the market.

3.2   Survey of Excellent Competitive Products for Smart Creeping Carpets

CNPP big data platform provides store data support, based on online store product sales, store design image, user evaluation attention and other strength data as a reference, comprehensively organized by maigoo.com The top three on the list are Fisher, Parkeron and Goodbaby. Then using the SWOT to analyzes the three brands of smart crawling blankets, the following design pain points are obtained: (1). The function setting of the smart crawling blanket is single and the intelligence level is not high; (2) The homogeneity of the flat pattern design is seriouson the smart crawling blanket; (3) It does not take into account that the cognitive development of infants is a increasing process, so the sustainability of crawling carpets is poor (Fig. 1).

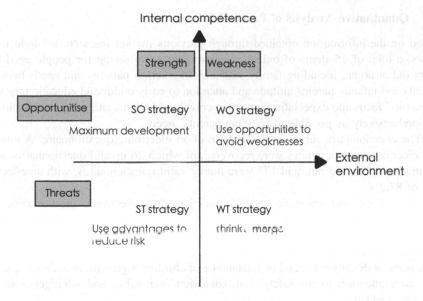

Fig. 1. SWOT matrix chart

4 Research on User Demand Extraction

4.1 Qualitative Analysis of Parental Needs

Analysis of Literature Research. This article mainly uses the co-word analysis method to conduct literature research on intelligent crawling blankets, and uses the keywords "crawling blanket", "smart crawling blanket" and "sustainable" to search and analyze relevant literature in the domestic infant and early childhood education industry for the past five years. Then it imports literature data to citespace analysis literature keyword by using the China Knowledge Network's bibliographic information export function. It can be concluded that the current crawling blanket can play an auxiliary role in the cognitive development of infants, more and more of which are applied to Intelligent technology, and pay great attention to the interaction, safety and humanity between crawling blankets and infants.

Analysis of Interview Content. After formulating the interview outline, face-to-face interviews with two parents from different families were conducted to understand the parent's methods and processes of early childhood education. Observe and record the interaction between parents and infants. Based on the interview records, dig deeper into the parents' smart crawling blanket The needs are summarized as follows: (1) parents' lack of a systematic understanding of the methods and processes of early childhood education; (2) the value of positioning blankets for crawling blankets by parents is much greater than the value of early education; (3) crawling blankets and infants Children's interaction is poor; (4) Parents hope that the intelligent crawling blanket is more intelligent and has a record of monitoring the physical changes of infants and young children.

4.2 Quantitative Analysis of Parental Needs

Based on the information obtained through previous market research and field interviews, a total of 15 items of online questionnaires were set up for people aged 0–3 years old at home, including family structure, interaction patterns and needs between parents and infants, parents attitude and attention to early childhood education, as well as parents' focus and expectations on smart crawling blankets, and grasp information as comprehensively as possible to fully tap parents' needs.

The questionnaire survey is in the form of an electronic questionnaire. A total of 203 electronic questionnaires were recovered, of which 26 invalid questionnaires were automatically filtered out, and 177 were finally valid questionnaires, with an effective rate of 87.2%.

According to the automatic statistical function of the electronic questionnaire, it is found that young parents spend less time with their children, and they need to bear the energy burden of the child. However, parents hope that they can assist the early education of the child and promote the child in the process of companionship and know all aspects of development and understanding of children's growth. In addition, parents pay more attention to the safety, fun, education, versatility and intelligence of the crawling blanket.

5 Sustainable Design Thinking

5.1 Sustainable Design

At present, there is no precise and consistent definition of "sustainable design" in academic circles. It has been developing, being explored and being explored. Among them, Carlo Vezzoli, a well-known scholar at the Politecnico di Milano, put forward: "Sustainable design is a design practice, design education and research to achieve sustainable development." Sustainable design theoretically studies sustainable design and the relationship between people and things, people and nature, through the application of design practices, make the functions, structures, shapes, colors, and surrounding environmental conditions of the product more reasonable to meet people's material and spiritual needs. For product design, it means that its functionality has been extended and the product life cycle has been extended, minimizing the waste of resources and promoting the harmonious development of people and the natural environment (Fig. 2).

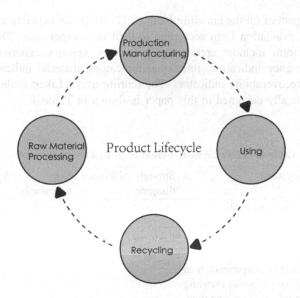

Fig. 2. Product lifecycle

5.2   Analysis of Sustainable Indicators

Research Purposes and Methods. At present, sustainable development is a development model strongly advocated globally. For all designers, it is worthy of careful consideration to think how to apply sustainable design thinking in the design link. The analysis of the product's life cycle and the assessment of sustainable indicators have become important means to effectively solve this problem. In addition, although China's intelligent technology has developed rapidly, it has started late, and intelligent crawling blankets are also in the initial stage of development, and have great potential for development. Therefore, this article evaluates the parents' sustainable indicators in the interaction process with infants using smart crawling blankets, collects data, analyzes and summarizes them. Then it provides data support for the later design of smart crawling blankets based on sustainable design thinking.

Positioning of the Tested Population. The trial conducted an objective screening of the participating population in the early stage: (1) the parents are 22–40 years old and the infants are 0–3 years old; (2) have a certain understanding of smart devices; (3) have children with children independently By the. A total of eight experimenters and their children were selected, four male and four female.

Experimental Process and Data Statistics. The experimental equipment used in this test is the McGrady smart crawling blanket with high sales volume, comprehensive functions and high intelligence. The test's test steps are divided into: (1) first let the testes and their children experience the McGrady smart crawling blanket for half an hour. The operation tasks are set to guide children to pay attention to the flat pattern of the smart crawling blanket, guide infants to crawl and guide infants to trigger the voice attached to the pattern on the crawling blanket; (2) After the experience is over, testes fill in the index evaluation form according to their own experience. The indicators of the evaluation form include: appearance indicators, sensory experience indicators, emotional experience indicators, functional indicators, material indicators, structural indicators, and recoverability indicators. The scoring uses a Likert scale with 16 items. The scale specifically designed in this paper is shown in Table 4:

Table 4. Table captions should be placed above the tables.

Sustainability indicators	Strongly disagree	Disagree	Not necessarily	Agree	Strongly agree
Sustainability in appearance (the appearance of smart crawling blankets can attract infants and toddlers for a long time, suitable for infants)					
Sustainability in sensory experience (can use the voice and light of smart crawling blankets to attract infants for a long time, Sound decibels and light intensity are in line with the characteristics of infants)					
Sustainability in emotional experience (parents can communicate with each other emotionally through intelligent crawling blankets, and the interaction between crawling blankets and infants is naturally smooth)					
Sustainability in function (multifunctional integration, practical and efficient, comfortable and flexible)					
Sustainability in material (safe green material, stable performance, easy to process, wear-resistant and durable)					
Sustainability in structure (structural safety, growth, portability, easy assembly and disassembly, maintenance)					
Sustainability in recoverability (easy to disassemble, simple looking back, green and pollution-free materials, recyclable)					

Each statement has five types of answers: "strongly agree", "agree", "not necessarily", "disagree", and "strongly disagree", which are recorded as 5, 4, 3, 2, 1, respectively indicate how much you agree with the statement. Among them, A–H represents 8 testers, and the specific test results are shown in the table (Tables 5 and 6):

Table 5. Sustainability indicator evaluation form

Sustainability indicators	A	B	C	D	E	F	G	H
Appearance index	2	3	4	3	2	3	3	3
Sensory experience index	2	3	2	3	3	3	2	3
Emotional experience index	3	2	3	4	3	2	3	4
Functional index	3	2	3	3	2	3	4	3
Material index	2	2	3	2	3	2	3	3
Structural index	1	2	2	3	3	3	3	2
Recyclability index	2	1	2	2	3	2	3	2

Table 6. Sustainability indicator evaluation form

Sustainability indicators	Median	Average
Appearance index	3	2.875
Sensory experience index	3	2.625
Emotional experience index	3	3
Functional index	3	2.875
Material index	2	2.5
Structural index	2	2.375
Recyclability index	2	2.125

After 8 people and their children experienced the McGrady smart crawling blanket for half an hour, they evaluated 7 sustainable indicators such as its appearance and form. The evaluation results show that the smart crawling blanket has a better emotional interaction experience for parents and infants., but the average sustainability of the remaining six indicators did not exceed 3, in general, the current smart crawling blanket has not reached the satisfaction of parent users in terms of sustainability. Among them, when observing the testes and their children to perform the designated tasks, it was found that there are also problems, such as some parents guiding their children to trigger the flat pattern on the crawling blanket, and the duration of their children's attention is short. The comprehensive test results show that the current intelligent crawling blanket has a certain auxiliary effect on the physical, psychological and cognitive development of infants and young children, but its sustainability is poor in all aspects.

6 Research on Intelligent Creeping Blanket Design Based on Sustainable Design

6.1 Smart Creeping Blanket Design Principles

According to the results of previous market research, user demand research, and sustainable index evaluation experiments, sustainable design thinking is applied to the design of smart crawling blankets, and it is advocated that product functions and effects are maximized while taking into account resource conservation and environmental friendliness. Follow these principles in product design.

Security principles. Infants' intelligent crawling blankets must first consider safety, infants' immunity is weak, and they do not have the awareness and ability to protect themselves. If parents take care of them improperly, they can easily cause accidents. Therefore, the design of intelligent crawling blankets must ensure the safety of materials, structures, and manufacturing processes for infants.

Personality Principles. The functional design of the intelligent crawling blanket should not only take into account the differences in infants' individual cognitive levels caused by different ages of the infants, but also take into account the differences in infants' interests and hobbies, so as to provide infants more suitable in their individual personalized functions and interaction modes for capacity development. Personalized design not only makes infants more efficient to use, but also allows infants to have an interaction mode more suitable for their own ability development.

Interest Principle. Interest is an indispensable function of intelligent crawling blanket for infants. The interest design of intelligent crawling blanket can attract infants' long-term attention by enriching the appearance pattern, interactive voice, and interactive behavior of crawling blanket.

Interaction Principle. The interactivity of the intelligent crawling blanket is not only the natural interaction between infants and crawling blankets, but also the interaction between infants and parents, which enriches parent-child interaction methods and increases parent-child companionship time.

Intelligent Principle. Intelligence is an important means to support the function of the intelligent crawling blanket. The intelligence of the intelligent crawling blanket is mainly reflected in its personalization and growth. According to the behavior trajectory of infants, active hot zones, pressing pressure, and accuracy of touch, etc. Judging the level of children's physical development and cognitive ability, and even identifying the interests of infants and young children through factors such as the number of touches and dwell time.

Intellectual Principle. The starting point of the intelligent crawling blanket is to coordinate the development of infants' physical limbs and improve the cognitive ability of the infants. In the design, the development characteristics of all aspects of the infants must be taken into consideration, so as to play the real value of smart crawling blanket.

Growth Principle. The growth in the design of the intelligent crawling blanket is specifically reflected in the continuous updating of functions and playing measures, so that infants continue to love the intelligent crawling blanket. The characteristics of infants' physical development and cognitive development are the characteristics of continuous development, which is also an important reason for the growth of intelligent crawling blankets.

6.2   Smart Creeping Blanket Design Strategy

Under the guidance of design principles, this article combines the needs of users, and uses a combination of baby products and parent apps in the design of smart crawling blankets. Next, it proposes the design strategy of smart crawling blanket products for infants and the apps used by parents.

Design Strategies for Infant and Child Smart Creeping Blanket Products

Structural Safety, Environmental Protection of Materials, Soft Colors, Appropriate Voice Decibels. Safety is the primary consideration for infant products. Since smart crawling blankets require various sensors and power supply devices such as pressure sensors and temperature sensors, power supply devices usually use batteries to ensure safety. Some smart crawling blankets use household batteries. However, this type of battery has a short life and will cause environmental pollution, so energy storage batteries should be considered. The materials of infant crawling blankets must meet the relevant standards for hygiene and safety. Although the material of the cloth velvet is soft and feels good, it is easy for infants to grab the fluff and stuff it into their mouths, which endangers the health of infants and young children. The paint uses green environmentally friendly, safe and non-toxic plant inks. The colors of the inks are soft, and the color matching is mostly warm. When the pattern of the crawling blanket is pressed, the light and voice packet are triggered. The color of the light can be customized to adjust the color number and brightness. The sound decibel of the voice packet is based on the research of existing articles. 40–70 dB is the most comfortable hearing valve for infants.,so the speech in this listening interval is most suitable.

Modular Design. The modular design makes infant crawling blankets have their own value whether they are single or combined. Smart crawling blankets are divided into modules with different themes, and the teaching voice package content of each module is also different. For example, there are piano, drums, guitars on the music module. They can be used to make musical instrument sounds or music songs. The animal module can teach infants to know animals, and can also tell fable stories related to them. Parents can choose one or several modules according to their needs, which is more humane.

Simple and Convenient Way of Interaction. Infants trigger the pattern on the smart crawling blanket through physical pressing by single pressing and long pressing. It can trigger the voice. Pressing again after 1 s will not cause repeated playback of the voice even affect the user experience. It provide light and voice feedback through the pressing of the infant and the intelligent crawling blanket between he infant and the intelligent crawling blanket t, which is simple and clear.

Childhood of Patterns. The pattern childish refers to the appearance of the smart crawling blanket. The flat pattern style cartoon is flattened. Adding interesting entertainment elements makes the image information more visual and easier to attract the attention of infants. It not only improves the visual level of infants but also promotes attention Development of thinking skills.

Multi-sensory Multi-level Interaction. The multi-sensory simultaneous participation of infants can promote the coordinated development of infants' abilities. The intelligent crawling blanket integrates vision, hearing, and touch to provide cognitive training for infants at different levels.

Growth Functional Design. The growth function refers to the growth of the function according to the age of the infant. The parents can set the corresponding voice package teaching through the supporting app. As the infant grows, the voice package can also be upgraded and updated in real time.

Parent-Child Interaction and Enhanced Emotional Communication. Parents play an irreplaceable role in the growth of infants. Parents are eager to participate in the early education of infants. Intelligent crawling blankets use artificial intelligence, sensors, Bluetooth and other technologies, which will bring more to children. The entertaining game experience promotes their physical and mental cognitive development, cultivates hobbies, increases the interest of learning, promotes parent-child interaction, and strengthens the emotional communication between parents and children during the playing process.

Parental App Design Strategies

Closely Connected with the Product. The app is closely connected to the product. The parent app is connected to the smart crawling blanket via Wi-Fi or Bluetooth. The teaching content of the crawling blanket is set on the app. Various sensors of the crawling blanket record the baby-related data and transmit it to the parent's app. The hardware and software are closely connected to enhance the interaction between parents and infants.

Scientific and Reasonable, and Have Certain Auxiliary. The matching parent app must first play a certain supporting role. Scientifically guide parents to set the teaching content of the intelligent crawling blanket to avoid that the early educational value of the intelligent crawling blanket is not really exerted due to the unreasonable teaching content.

The Interface Information is Clear and Concise. The core function of the matching parent app is to set the voice pack of the crawling blanket. Parents can also customize the recording of the voice pack. The auxiliary function is to transfer the baby-related data recorded by the sensor to the app, and perform record analysis to generate a weekly report. Parents can directly check the data report on the app to understand the child's body, crawling and other related conditions. In the app interface design, follow the logical order, concise and clear, to avoid tedious operations that cause parents to spend too much attention.

Unified Style and Emotional Design of the Interface. The parent's matching app interface style be unified, and the appearance flat style of the smart crawling blanket also be unified. The entire interface uses soft and warm colors. The theme colors of each module correspond to the modules of the crawling blanket. In addition, considering that it is an app related to infants, but the user is a parent, the interface design of the app should consider the emotional communication between infants and their parents It is the interaction between the app interface and the crawling blanket.

7 Conclusion

For China in the continuous development of intelligent technology, it is of great significance to apply sustainable design thinking to the infant market. In the design stage, it should redefine the intelligent crawling blankets' function through sustainable design thinking, so it can not only meet the needs of infants' development and parents' needs, but also promote the healthy development of all abilities of infants, and to meet the social background of saving resources, environmentally friendly and sustainable, and protect the world we live on better.

In the design of intelligent crawling blankets for infants, it should be considered that the particularities of the infant group and the psychology and needs of parents, and the intelligent crawling blankets should be analyzed and improved from the perspective of sustainable design to extend the life of products and reduce resources waste. In the process of using the smart crawling blanket by parents and their children, the teaching content of the crawling blanket is set according to the age of their children to more scientifically and reasonably meet the cognitive development needs of infants and young children of different ages, so that the smart crawling blanket has a certain growth. In addition, the modular design allows parents to choose modules with different topics according to their needs. Each module has different topics and functions, which is more user-friendly.

In general, this article analyzes the existing problems of smart crawling blankets on the market, and takes the natural development law of children as the premise, extracts the needs of users and buyers, and refines the design principles and strategies of smart crawling blankets. What is more important, it provides an innovative idea and method for the design of intelligent crawling blanket that is scientific and reasonable and consistent with the concept of sustainable development.

References

1. Vezzoli, C.: Design for Environmental Sustainability. Cape Peninsula University of Technology, Cape Town (2009)
2. Bauman, K.: Tinker Bots: Modular Robotic Toys a la Living Lego [EB/OL]. Core 77's TOY, 14 April 2014
3. Chang, T.W.: Interacting play—design as a metaphor for developing interactive games. In: Jacko, J.A. (ed.) HCI 2007. LNCS, vol. 4553, pp. 190–197. Springer, Heidelberg (2007). https://doi.org/10.1007/978-3-540-73111-5_22
4. Anonymous. Toy and Game Companies: Mattel plays responsibly with "Design It, Make It, Live It" sustainability strategy. Comput. Netw. Commun. (2011)

Extraction and Reuse of Pattern Configuration for Personalized Customization of Cantonese Porcelain Based on Artificial Intelligence

Yi Ji, Xiaohong Sun[⊠], Xingyang Dai, Sean Clark, Yutong Liu, and Tieming Fu

School of Design Arts, Guangdong University of Technology, 729, Dongfeng Street, Guangzhou 510000, Guangdong, China
jiyi001@hotmail.com, 1415748506@qq.com

Abstract. To solve the problems of inefficient learning caused by the complexity, fragmentation and lack of personalization of traditional handicraft learning resources. Based on the method of pattern configuration extraction and reuse, this paper takes the innovative design of Canton Porcelain pattern as an example. For the first time, sorting the knowledge of Cantonese Porcelain according to different cultural attributes (labels), to establish the knowledge base and pattern sample base of Canton Porcelain, and build a semantic relationship between the them, recommend Cantonese Porcelain elements that meet users' needs through semantic search. Then, shape context was used to extract patterns of Cantonese Porcelain, and topological methods was combined to establish the configuration rules of patterns. Shape grammar based on character encoding were improved in the process of generation of personalized customization patterns of Cantonese Porcelain, used to describe the transformation of shapes during pattern filling, thereby generation of personalized customization patterns of Cantonese Porcelain based on element extraction will be completed. Develop a personalized customization system for Cantonese Porcelain crafts, and tests the method feasible through an application example.

Keywords: Cantonese Porcelain · Semantic search · Configuration rules · Personalized customization

1 Introduction

At present, in the traditional handicraft personalized customization, the pattern design is still a time-consuming and laborious work, the design of the pattern still needs to be completed by the designer manually. Due to a large number of original pattern cases, how to quickly extract the cases that meet the requirements of the large number of original cases and reuse them is the key to the personalized customization of handicraft patterns. In the existing researches in China, there are few methods aim at design pattern and configuration rapid extraction and reuse, which is difficult to meet users' demand for personalized customization of traditional handicrafts. Facing demand for handicraft customization industry, there is a lack of knowledge connotation mining and the integration and management of the whole knowledge, and there is a shortage in quickly taking cases that meet the needs of users. Drawing on existing research on knowledge management of cultural relics, Through the integration and management of cultural relics knowledge [1, 2], establishing database of cultural relics [3], the cultural heritage ontology model [4, 5], cultural relics resources data model, network cultural heritage resources management system [6] and so on, defines the semantic information of knowledge of cultural relics, is used to express the knowledge in the information retrieval system structure [7], fulfil from cultural relics from knowledge to guide the design of process [8]. The research focuses on the expressive language of cultural relic knowledge, so it is necessary to further explore the excavation and reasoning of cultural relic knowledge in product personalized design. In the study of pattern and configuration extraction, shape grammar is a common method, mainly to express the transformation of the shape, the transformation rules are complicated, low reusability. Existing in the study, by improving the shape grammar, based on the imitation of natural language to improve shape grammar [9], hierarchical shape grammar [10], the shape of the parametric design of grammar [11] and the establishment of ontology model and the relationship between the shape grammar [12], arts and crafts oriented pattern design, shape grammar expression is difficult to meet the design configuration of handicraft in the personalization design configuration extraction and reuse requirements.

This paper starts from the traditional handicraft design and takes Cantonese Porcelain as an example, by using the method of pattern configuration extraction and reuse. First, analyze the application of Cantonese Porcelain knowledge in the personalized customization of crafts, classify and express the knowledge of Cantonese Porcelain, establish the ontology information dictionary based on the knowledge of Cantonese Porcelain, and apply it to the semantic retrieval of the personalized customization system of Cantonese Porcelain; The upper and lower grammars and topological structures of shapes were used to extract patterns and configuration, and the improved grammars based on character coding were used to transform shapes in the process of pattern filling. Finally, a system for customization of Cantonese Porcelain crafts was developed to verify that this method is helpful to improve the efficiency of the customization of Cantonese Porcelain crafts.

2 Knowledge Classification of Cantonese Porcelain

2.1 Knowledge Sources and Classification of Cantonese Porcelain

The knowledge of Cantonese Porcelain for personalized customization comes from many aspects, mainly from Guangzhou Cantonese Porcelain masters, Cantonese Porcelain researchers and other experts to provide knowledge related to Cantonese Porcelain, which provides rich cultural, experience and technical support for the personalized customization of handicrafts. Through the investigation and visit of Guangzhou Cantonese Porcelain workshop, we found that local Cantonese Porcelain masters provided modeling knowledge and technical knowledge, while Cantonese Porcelain researchers provided basic knowledge, cultural knowledge and partial functional knowledge. Through collection and reading of Cantonese Porcelain books, more specific pattern knowledge and functional knowledge were obtained. Based on the demand analysis of Cantonese Porcelain knowledge in the process of handicraft customization, the Cantonese Porcelain knowledge oriented to handicraft customization can be divided into 5 categories, namely basic knowledge, modeling knowledge, pattern knowledge, functional knowledge, technical knowledge and cultural knowledge. The classification framework is shown in Fig. 1.

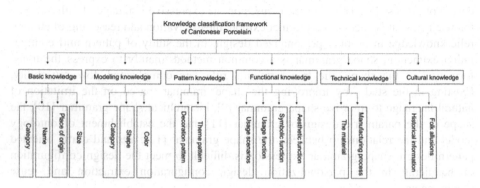

Fig. 1. Classification of knowledge framework for personalizing customization for Cantonese Porcelain

2.2   Acquisition of Knowledge Concepts and Vocabulary of Cantonese Porcelain

In the selection of Cantonese Porcelain cases, according to the existing knowledge of Cantonese Porcelain, Cantonese Porcelain was selected in the following categories: bottles, plates, cups, basins, bowls, pot, tank, paintings, handleless cup and others. Themes include animals, people, flowers and birds, plants, badges, landscapes, ships and more. The begonia window includes Ruyi begonia window, butterfly begonia window, nail begonia window, pillow begonia window and so on. The corner spacing includes dog's teeth, hand drag, pig's nose cloud, wishful banana, fish's eye, top work, double top work, hanging beads, cord edge corner spacing, etc. Brocade pattern (Jindi pattern) mainly includes four-character brocade, scroll brocade, three-line- brocade, herringbone brocade, swastika brocade, shark skin brocade, etc. 317 cases of Cantonese Porcelain were selected from the works collected through field research to construct a case library of Canton glazed porcelain. According to the classification framework of Cantonese Porcelain knowledge oriented to arts and crafts, this paper analyzes the cases of Cantonese Porcelain and constructs the knowledge base of Cantonese Porcelain. According to the attributes and connotations of Cantonese Porcelain, conceptual vocabulary was extracted, and the concept of knowledge of Cantonese Porcelain customized for arts and crafts was shown in Table 1.

Table 1. Knowledge concept for personalized customization for Cantonese Porcelain

Knowledge category		Specific description	Concept subextraction
Basic knowledge	Serial number	The name of Cantonese porcelain, encoding each Cantonese porcelain pattern according to the attributes and types, such as attributes: picture, A01; Project category: glair color, B02: source: physical shooting, C002: classification code: disk, DOI: level 2 Classification code: flower plate, EOI: file number F(9digits): 000000001	A01B02C002D01E01F000000001 A01B02C002D01E01F000000002...
	Collecting place	Cantonese porcelain workshop, such as Cantonese Porcelain Museum of He Lifen from Liwan district, Guangzhou	
	Size	Description the size of Cantonese porcelain, including length, width, height, e.g: length of 30 cm	
Modelling knowledge	*Ware category*	*Vessels of Cantonese porcelain according to existing classification methods, such as bottles and plates*	*Bottle; Plate; Bowl; Pot; Painting*
	Shape	*An illustration of the shape of Cantonese porcelain, such as a circle*	*Circle; Diamond; Rectangle; Gourd shape...*
	Color	*A description of the colors of Cantonese porcelain, such as vermilion and magenta*	*Vermilion; Magenta; Lake blue; White...*
Pattern knowledge	Decoration pattern	Descript the decoration pattern elements of Cantonese porcelain, such as the Begonia Window on the plate	Begonia Window; organization pattern; Brocade pattern; Cord edge corner spacing..
	Theme pattern	A description of the main encounter patterns painted on Cantonese porcelain, such as the theme of character	Character theme; Animal theme; Plant theme..
Functional knowledge	*Use situation*	*The use of Cantonese porcelain, such as a wedding*	*Cooking; Birthday; New Year..*
	Usage function	*The usage form of Cantonese porcelain, such as a decoration*	*Decoration; Hanging ornaments; living utensils...*
	Symbolic function	*The meaning expressed by the cantonese porcelain motif or patterns, such as good luck and happiness*	*Many sons and many blessings, Career success; Business flourished; Family harmony*
	Aesthetic function	*Analysis and interpretation of the overall aesthetics of Cantonese Porcelain, such as the Bat coin character's Cantonese porcelain, auspicious wealth and happiness*	*The composition is symmetrical, full and lively*

(continued)

Table 1. (*continued*)

Knowledge category		Specific description	Concept subextraction
Technical knowledge	The tools of technology	The tool such as a brush, used in making Cantonese porcelain	Color bowl; Ink; Brush; Water cup; Pillow case...
	Technological process	Cantonese porcelain production process, method, such as the hook line	Selection of magnetic blank; Open; Manuscript; Tick; Color
Cultural knowledge	*Historical information*	*The development history of Cantonese porcelain for more than 300 years, such as the formation of Cantonese porcelain in the Qianlong dynasty*	*The formation of Cantonese porcelain; The rise of Cantonese porcelain; The prosperity of Cantonese porcelain*
	Folk allusions	*Historical stories related to Cantonese porcelain, such as "master's birthday of Cantonese porcelain"*	*A Dream in Red Mansions; Story of The Three Kingdoms...*

2.3 Knowledge Organizations and Expression of Cantonese Porcelain

Ontology Modeling of Cantonese Porcelain. Through sorting out and summarizing the knowledge of Cantonese Porcelain and extracting the concept vocabulary, and through grammatical analysis, semantic analysis and pragmatic analysis, the natural language processing of the knowledge of Cantonese Porcelain is carried out to determine the definition of the natural language sequence of each case of Cantonese Porcelain. Language sequence is the feature vector representing the statement set. The statement includes subject-verb-object and various modifiers. The feature vector is obtained through the relationship between these components. Then, the semantic and pragmatic information about Cantonese Porcelain cases is extracted by analyzing the meaning and use of sentence components and their mutual relations. According to the rules, for example: through Cantonese Porcelain case A01B02C002D01E01F0000 00001 ontology information for its grammatical information = {round, scarlet magenta, flower plate mouth, bat}, pragmatic information = {place adorn}, interior decoration, semantic information = {many children f}, and its syntax, semantics and pragmatics information items are stored as a basic attributes to Cantonese Porcelain all information dictionary. By analogy, the ontology model of each Cantonese Porcelain case is established. The basic information items are taken as input, association rules are mined by using FP- growth, and then collated to establish constraint rules. Use the rule representation format in Jena, which consists of the rule name, rule condition, and rule conclusion. For example, there is a rule about grammatical information and semantic information: if the pattern of "bat" is included in a case of Cantonese Porcelain, it means "many children, many blessings", and the representation format is as follows: [rule-name: (X RDF: type qiwu: Cantonese Porcelain) college (X qiwu: design is qiwu: bat) from college to college (X qiwu: pattern is qiwu: "many children fu")].

Building the Database of Cantonese Porcelain. Building the database of Cantonese Porcelain, Combining Cantonese Porcelain Cases with Cantonese Porcelain Knowledge Content, to realize the semantic relation between the knowledge and the instance of Cantonese Porcelain, lay the foundation for semantic retrieval. The case base of Cantonese Porcelain for the Personalized customization of traditional handicrafts includes three databases: original pattern database, pattern database and configuration rule database, laying the foundation for the Personalized customization of traditional handicrafts.

Semantic Retrieval is Based on Cantonese Porcelain Ontology Knowledge. The process of semantic retrieval based on the ontology knowledge of Cantonese Porcelain is as follows: ① Input user requirements, use the ICTCLAS word segmentation system to participle segmentation on user-entered words or sentences, the synonyms are mapped to the words in the perfect information dictionary of Canton Porcelain, form a key character string; ② Semantic analysis of key words will be carried out through the knowledge base of Cantonese Porcelain, Map keywords with the concepts in the knowledge of Cantonese porcelain and examples in Cantonese Porcelain case base. Using semantic similarity, retrieve the conceptual vocabulary sequence with the highest similarity to keywords in Cantonese Porcelain knowledge base. Ultimately translate user needs into vocabulary sequences, recommend a number of cases of Cantonese Porcelain that most meet the needs of users (Fig. 2).

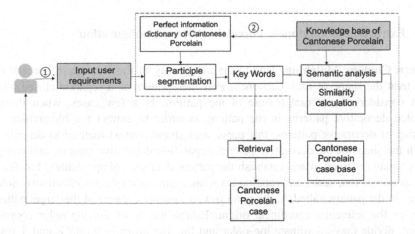

Fig. 2. Semantic retrieval is based on Cantonese Porcelain ontology knowledge

3   Knowledge Classification of Cantonese Porcelain

3.1   Classification of Cantonese Porcelain Decoration Patterns

The pattern of Cantonese porcelain decoration pattern mainly includes the Begonia Window organization pattern Brocade pattern and Cord edge corner spacing. This paper has analyzed the decoration patterns in the database of Cantonese porcelain, as shown in Fig. 3, the decoration pattern ontology model is shown in Fig. 4.

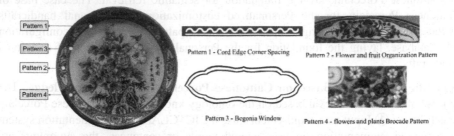

Fig. 3. Decoration patterns of Cantonese Porcelain

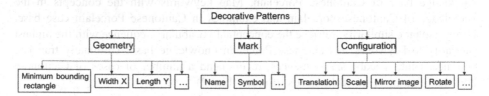

Fig. 4. Pattern ontology model for configuration rules

3.2   Extraction of Cantonese Porcelain Pattern Configuration

Pattern Contour Matching. Due to the irregularity of the Cantonese Porcelain pattern, treat the shape of each Cantonese Porcelain pattern as a separate closed outline, don't consider the internal texture of the pattern. In a few cases, when there are repeated decorative patterns in the pattern, in order to extract the hierarchical relationship of decorative patterns, this paper uses shape context method to describe and match the shape of the decorative pattern, separation decorative pattern, and complete the automatic extraction and establish the pattern database. Shape context has features such as translation, scale, and rotation invariance can match shapes effectively. Select a pattern in the pattern called A, the point $p_i(x_i, y_i)$ on the contour of the target pattern is taken as the reference coordinate origin. Establishment of the log-polar coordinate system, divide they-coordinate log-polar and the x-coordinate θ into Z and T respectively, the whole space is divided into $Z \times T$. Record the number of point distributions at the relative positions of point PI to other points, its statistical distribution histogram $h_i(k)$ is called point PI in the shape context, an algorithm is as follows:

$$h_i(k) = \#\{p \neq p_i : p \in bin(k)\} \tag{1}$$

In this, k = {1, 2, ... , K}, K = Z × T.

Set a point on the contour of pattern B to be matched as q_j, calculate the matching cost C_{ij} between the histograms of points pi and q_j distributions, namely:

$$C_{ij} = C(p, q) = \frac{1}{2} \sum_{k=1}^{k} \frac{\left[h_i(k) - h_j(k)\right]^2}{h_i(k) + h_j(k)} \tag{2}$$

Among them, $h_i(k)$ is the point PI on the contour of the target pattern, $h_j(k)$ is the point q_j on the contour of the pattern to be matched. The smaller C_{ij}, the smaller the cost of matching 2 points, greater similarity. Pattern contour matching is shown in Fig. 5.

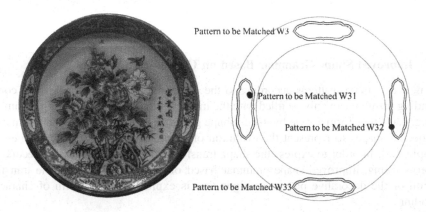

Fig. 5. Decoration pattern contours matching

Configuration Extraction. According to the shape context matching method, extract the decorative patterns that are most similar to the target decorative pattern in the Cantonese Porcelain pattern, extraction of the configuration of the Cantonese Porcelain pattern using the rules of topological structure [13], take the central coordinate of Cantonese porcelain pattern as the origin, determine the center coordinates of each decorative pattern in the pattern. Abstract the central coordinates of each decorative pattern into points, Abstract the path between each point into a line, the topology of these points and lines is called the pattern configuration rule. Extraction rules according to pattern configuration, extracting configuration rules of each pattern in the case base, establish a configuration rule base.

Cantonese Porcelain decorative pattern W = {W1, W2, ⋯ , Wa}, a is the total number of different patterns in a Cantonese Porcelain pattern. A decorative pattern in Cantonese Porcelain pattern Wa = {Wa1, Wa2, ⋯ , Waf}, f is the number of time a decorative pattern appears in a Cantonese Porcelain pattern. According to the above configuration rules, mark the position of the decorative pattern from left to right according to the number of times each decorative pattern appears in the pattern. Figure 6 shows the extraction process of pattern configuration rules.

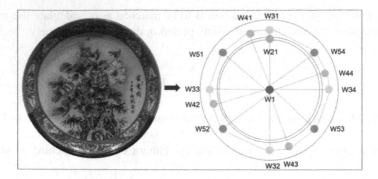

Fig. 6. Pattern configuration rules extraction process

4   Reuse of Configuration Rules

4.1   Improved Shape Grammar Based on Character Encoding

Fill new decorative patterns according to the extracted configuration rules, the corresponding position can only be filled with the initial state of the pattern during automatic filling, can't transform a style by itself. Shape grammar mainly uses the transformation of specific shapes to represent the evolution of graphics, the transformation rules are complicated. In order to express the shape transformation in the process of decorative patterns filling, improved shape grammar based on character encoding, the transformation of the decorative pattern configuration is expressed in the form of character encoding.

The configuration rule coding mainly includes 5 items such as attributes, type, style, status, and others. (1) Attribute, which indicates the keywords and symbols appearing during the encoding process, and its meaning, parameters and interpretation; (2) Type, which indicates the name and center coordinates of the decorative pattern (x, y); (3) Style, indicating the transformation state, transformation parameters and specific process of decorative pattern; (4) The symbols "{" and "}" are used to represent the two states of the beginning and the end of the decorative pattern transformation respectively; (5) Others, indicating the comments and intervals in the process of representing the decorative pattern configuration. The code of configuration rules is shown in Table 2.

Table 2. The code of configuration rules

Attribute	Keywords/Symbols	Meaning	Parameter	Explain
Type	W	Decorative pattern	$v\,x\,y$	Number of patterns and center coordinates (x, y) Refer to the central coordinate of the pattern (0,0)
Style	TRAN	Translation	$d_X d_Y$	X, Y direction translation distance
	ROTA	Rotate	$\theta_\circ$	The Angle and direction of rotation around its center (1 is clockwise and 0 is counterclockwise)
	SCAL	Scaling	$S_X S_Y$	Scaling in the X and Y directions
	MIRR	Mirror image	uc	The axis of symmetry x = u and whether to retain the original graph (1 is retained, 0 is not retained)
	CLAR	Circular array	$v\delta$	Quantity and interval angle, the angle range can be evenly distributed
	LNAR	Linear array	$d_X d_Y\,d_Y d_Y$	X and Y interval and number
	ASPR	Spiral array	$b\zeta s_d$	Radial increment, interval angle, scaling
	...	...	...	...
Status	{	Start	–	No parameters, 1 line
	}	End	–	No parameters, 1 line
Other	//	Annotation	1	Annotation content
	.	Interval	–	No parameters

4.2 Reuse of Configuration Rules

After the decorative pattern is filled in the extracted configuration rules, change the decorative pattern according to the original pattern's configuration rules. Scale the pattern, representing the decorative pattern size with the smallest enclosing rectangle, the width of the smallest enclosing rectangle of the original decorative pattern is T and the length is S, the minimum enclosing rectangle of the fill decorative pattern is H in width and M in length, the scaling formula in X and Y directions is:

$$S = \min\left\{\frac{T, S}{H, M}\right\} \tag{3}$$

The process of filling decorative patterns without eliminating overlap is shown in Fig. 7. Reuse pattern configuration rules are extracted in Section 2.3.2, users can select similar decorative patterns recommended by the system for filling, as is shown in Fig. 8.

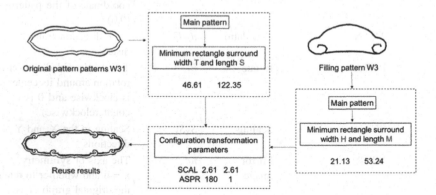

Fig. 7. Filling decorative patterns without eliminating overlap

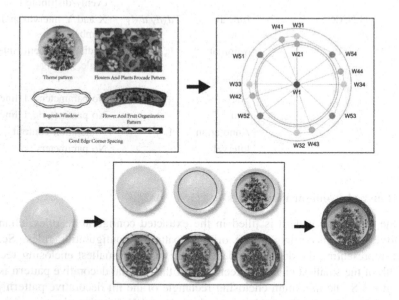

Fig. 8. The decoration pattern filling process

5 Cantonese Porcelain Personalized Customization System

According to the knowledge of Cantonese Porcelain personalized customization for traditional handicrafts, Develop Cantonese Porcelain's personalized customization system to realize effective management and reuse of Cantonese Porcelain knowledge. This system provides knowledge integration services and personalized customization services for Cantonese Porcelain process designers and learning users. The research content of this paper has been partially input into the system website of "Lucky Strike". The system includes Cantonese Porcelain knowledge database, vector image database, information retrieval, user management and Cantonese Porcelain personalized customization. This paper mainly introduces the traditional handicraft personalized customization system based on the knowledge of Cantonese Porcelain.

5.1 Cantonese Porcelain Knowledge Management Platforms

The system administrator logs into the system background to enter the knowledge management interface, as shown in Fig. 10. The left side of the interface is the system function navigation bar, including the work information management diagram and the work information import diagram, etc. The right side is the system operation interface, which realizes the retrieval and viewing of the knowledge of Cantonese Porcelain. The system administrator submits the information of Cantonese Porcelain knowledge such as concepts, attributes, rules and cases to the server, and saves them to the database through computer logic processing. Users can view the knowledge information of Cantonese Porcelain through the browser.

5.2 Cantonese Porcelain Personalized Customization Platforms

Users log in "Lucky Strike" system, the main functions of the system home page including project classification, keyword retrieval, case display, etc. According to the classification of Cantonese Porcelain knowledge, users can select the Cantonese Porcelain cases they need, such as the begonia window of Bogu. According to the previous period association between the words in the perfect information dictionary of Cantonese Porcelain knowledge and the constraint rules established, the user can enter keywords to retrieve related cases of Cantonese Porcelain. The system home page is shown in Fig. 9.

A user uses "characters" and "beautiful" as keywords, from the system to retrieve the conform to the requirements of Cantonese Porcelain case to start the whole process of customization is: the system from the words in the perfect information dictionary to retrieve a number of keywords related Cantonese Porcelain case for the user to choose from. After selecting a Cantonese Porcelain case, the user enters the Cantonese Porcelain personalized customization details interface, as shown in Fig. 10. Cantonese Porcelain personalized customization includes plates, bowls, basins, bottles, pot, cups, paintings and other products. In this paper, the application example selects the plate as

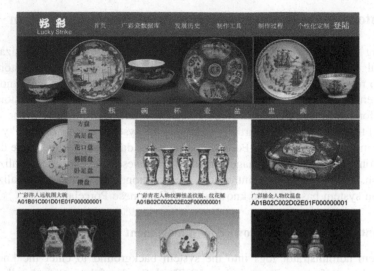

Fig. 9. Home page of "Lucky Strike"

Fig. 10. Cantonese Porcelain personalized customization system page [14]

the custom object, and the personalized customization details interface of the plate includes the basic information, knowledge information, and historical information about the case. After the user selects a case that meets the need, he can start personalized customization.

Enter the personalized customization interface of Cantonese Porcelain. Users in Cantonese Porcelain plate custom interface configuration rules corresponding to the choice of pattern, pattern recommended box will display system recommended by the similar pattern, the user can choose favorite pattern, the system will automatically fill in the pattern configuration rules of corresponding position, generation products, if you are not satisfied, can press the "reset" key to select patterns. Besides, it is a real-time interaction between the user and Cantonese Porcelain in the real environment based on the AR recognition function in the mobile device. Users acquire information through scanning real objects. Additionally, users can also scan images 2D and then the system will automatically convert to 3D. This stage is mainly experiential learning mid-term from reflective observation (watching and thinking) to abstract conceptualization (doing and thinking) (Fig. 11).

Fig. 11. Model from 2D to 3D based on AR [14]

6 Result

Figure 12 shows some Cantonese Porcelain works customized by the user on the "Lucky Strike" system. Users create new works through the innovation and combination of elements. It also makes it easier for users to grasp the constituent elements of Cantonese Porcelain and the intrinsic value of traditional culture.

Fig. 12. Examples of custom work by system users

Secondly, we conducted a questionnaire test for system users. The design of the questionnaire mainly refers to the QUIS scale (questionnaire for user interface satisfaction), It is a tool to measure user satisfaction with human-computer interaction, Many scholars have tested the reliability and validity of the scale, and the results are good [15]. To conduct the evaluation experiment, we created a survey website using the SO JUMP system and invited twenty-five subjects (aged between 18 and 34) to evaluate "Lucky Strike" system for user interface satisfaction. The SO JUMP is a professional platform for the online questionnaire survey, evaluation, voting, focused on providing users with powerful, humanized design online questionnaires, collect data, custom reports, and results of the survey analysis. The subjects are recruited from Guangdong University of Technology student population and Guangzhou citizen in China. Finally, the user interaction satisfaction results obtained from the QUIS scale were analyzed. As the Table 3 shows, user satisfaction with the system is close to 72%, and then we will continue to improve the system according to the problems reported by users.

Table 3. Analysis of questionnaire for user interface satisfaction

Scoring interval	1–40	40–80	80–120	120–160	160–200	200–243
Number	0	2	6	8	6	3
Ratio		A(0%)	B(8%)	C(24%)	D(35%)	E(24%)	F(12%)

7 Conclusion

In view of the demand of personalized customization of Cantonese Porcelain knowledge, this paper proposes a method of extracting and reusing patterns of Cantonese Porcelain patterns personalized customization for traditional handicrafts based on Artificial Intelligence, and develops a personalized customization system of Cantonese Porcelain accordingly. Firstly, a knowledge base of Cantonese Porcelain patterns personalized customization for traditional handicrafts was established to classify the knowledge of Cantonese Porcelain, and an ontology model of Cantonese Porcelain knowledge was established. Through semantic retrieval, cases of Cantonese Porcelain that met users' needs were matched. Then, the shape context method and topological structure are used to obtain the pattern and configuration rules of the pattern to construct the pattern library and the configuration rule library. In the pattern filling process, an improved shape grammar based on character encoding is proposed to describe the pattern configuration transformation. This method improves the reuse rate of Cantonese Porcelain in the field of traditional handicraft personalized customization.

References

1. Luo, S., Dong, J.: Knowledge integration and management of objects for cultural and creative design. Comput. Integr. Manuf. Syst. **24**(4), 964–977 (2018)

2. Luo, S., Dong, J.: Research on the classification of object knowledge for creative design investigate. J. Zhejiang Univ.: Eng. Ed. **51**(1), 113–123 (2017)
3. Zhu, K.: Research and discussion on the construction of basic database of cultural relics. Cultural relic protection. Sci. Conserv. Archaeol. **23**(3), 16–21 (2011)
4. Doerr, M.: The CIDOC conceptual reference module: an ontological approach to semantic interoperability of metadata. Archive **24**(3), 75–92 (2003)
5. Gong, H., Hu, C., Liu, C.: Research on information resource classification and metadata design of digital cultural relic museum. Intell. Mag. **33**(1), 183–189 (2014)
6. Meyer, É., Grussenmeyer, P., Perrin, J., et al.: A web information system for the management and the dissemination of Cultural Heritage data. J. Cult. Herit. **8**(4), 396–411 (2007)
7. Yang, Y., Du, J., Ping, Y.: Intelligent information retrieval system based on ontology. J. Softw. **26**(7), 1675–1687 (2015)
8. Leong, B.D., Clark, H.: Culture-based knowledge towards new design thinking and practice- a dialogue. Des. Issues **19**(3), 48–58 (2003)
9 Zhang, X., Wang, J., Lu, G., et al.: Pattern configuration and reuse based on ontology and shape grammar. J. Zhejiang Univ. Eng. Ed. **52**(3), 461–472 (2018)
10. Cui, J., Tang, M.X.: Integrating shape grammars into a generative system for Zhuang ethnic embroidery design exploration. CAD Comput. Aided Des. **45**(3), 591–604 (2013)
11.   Sayed, Z., Ugail, H., Pakmer, I., et al.: Parameterized shape grammar for n-fold generating islamic geometric motifs. In: 2015 International Conference on Cyberworlds, Chongqing, pp. 79–85. IEEE Press, New York (2015)
12. Grobler, F., Aksamija, A., Kim, H., Krishnamurti, R., Yue, K., Hickerson, C.: Ontologies and shape grammars: communication between knowledge-based and generative systems. In: Gero, J.S., Goel, A.K. (eds.) Design Computing and Cognition 2008, pp. 23–40. Springer, Dordrecht (2008). https://doi.org/10.1007/978-1-4020-8728-8_2
13. Jiang, Y., Jin, Y.: Full information acquisition and utilization based on natural language understanding in knowledge construction. Libr. Inf. Serv. **59**(6), 104–112 (2015)
14. Ji, Y., Tan, P.: Exploring personalized learning pattern for studying Chinese traditional handicraft. In: Proceedings of the Sixth International Symposium of Chinese CHI - Chinese CHI 2018, Montreal, QC, Canada, 21–22 April 2018, pp. 140–143. ACM Press (2018)
15. Chinese magazine editorial board of otolaryngology head and neck surgery, Chinese medical association otolaryngology head and neck surgery branch of nasal science group. Diagnosis and treatment of allergic rhinitis guide. J. Chin. Clin. Doctors (6), 67–68 (2010). https://doi.org/10.3969/j.iSSN.1008-1089.2010.06.028
16. Belongie, S., Malik, J., Puzicha, J.: Shape matching and object recognition using shape contexts. IEEE Trans. Pattern Anal. Mach. Intell. **24**(4), 509–522 (2002)
17. Zhang, L., Lu, D., Zhang, L., Pan, Y., et al.: Composition knowledge generation model based on comprehensive reasoning. J. Comput. Aided Des. Graph. **12**(5), 384–389 (2000)
18. Bibri, S.E., Krogstie, J.: ICT of the new wave of computing for sustainable urban forms: their big data and context-aware augmented typologies and design concepts. Sustain. Cities Soc. **32**, 449–474 (2017)
19. Wei, X., Weng, D., Liu, Y., Wang, Y.: Teaching based on augmented reality for a technical creative design course. Comput. Educ. **81**(C), 221–234 (2015)
20. Russon, J.: Sites of Exposure: Art, Politics, and the Nature of Experience. Indiana University Press, Bloomington (2017)
21. Pine, B.J., Gilmore, J.H.: The Experience Economy. Harvard Business School Press, Boston (1999)

22. Mou, Q.C., et al.: Making children's education products of "TuTuLe" based on AR technology. Comput. Inf. Technol. (2017)
23. Wei, S., Wang, B.: Application of AR technology in intangible cultural heritage and cultural tourism industry. J. Jianghan Univ. 44(4), 364–368 (2016)
24. Ilic, U., Yildirim, O.G.: Augmented reality and its reflections on education in Turkey. In: International Dynamic, Explorative and Active Learning (2015)
25. Hirve, S.A., Kunjir, A., Shaikh, B., Shah, K.: An approach towards data visualization based on AR principles. In: International Conference on Big Data Analytics and Computational Intelligence, pp. 128–133. IEEE (2017)
26. Heun, V., Kasahara, S., Maes, P.: Smarter objects: using AR technology to program physical objects and their interactions. In: Extended Abstracts on Human Factors in Computing Systems CHI 2013, pp. 2817–2818. ACM (2013)
27. Zhang, Y., Zhu, Z.: Interactive spatial AR for classroom teaching. In: De Paolis, L.T., Mongelli, A. (eds.) AVR 2016. LNCS, vol. 9768, pp. 463–470. Springer, Cham (2016). https://doi.org/10.1007/978-3-319-40621-3_34
28. Augmented Reality. In: IEEE International Conference on Trust, Security and Privacy in Computing and Communications, pp. 1666–1675. IEEE, fchencq
29. Puyuelo, M., Higón, J.L., Merino, L., Contero, M.: Experiencing augmented reality as an accessibility resource in the UNESCO heritage site called "la lonja", Valencia. Proc. Comput. Sci. 25, 171–178 (2013)
30. Mendoza, R., Baldiris, S., Fabregat, R.: Framework to heritage education using emerging technologies. Proc. Comput. Sci. 75, 239–249 (2015)
31. Kim, E., Kim, J., Woo, W.: Metadata schema for context-aware augmented reality applications in cultural heritage domain. In: Digital Heritage, vol. 2, pp. 283–290. IEEE (2016)
32. Dieck, M.C.T., Jung, H.: Value of augmented reality at cultural heritage sites: a stakeholder approach. J. Destin. Mark. Manag. 6(2), 110–117 (2017)
33. Anonymous. Related Content Database, Inc.: RCDb Licenses BD-Live Software to Netflix for PS3 Instant Streaming Disc. Information Technology Newsweekly (2009)
34. Big Data for Development: Challenges & Opportunities [DB/OL], 01 May 2012. http://www.unglobalpulse.org/sites/default/files/BigDataforDevelopmentUNGlobalPulseJune2012.pdf
35. [7][12][13][14] Enhancing Teaching and Learning through Educational Data Mining and Learning
36. Analytics [DB/OL], 12 October 2012. http://www.ed.gov/edblogs/technology/files/2012/03/edm-la-brief.pdf
37. Jara, C.A., Candelas, F.A., Puente, S.T., Torres, F.: Hands-on experiences of undergraduate students in automatics and robotics using a virtual and remote laboratory. Comput. Educ. 57(4), 2451–2461 (2011)
38. Bacca, J., Baldiris, S., Fabregat, R., Graf, S., Kinshuk: Augmented reality trends in education: a systematic review of research and applications. J. Educ. Technol. Soc. 17(4), 133–149 (2014)
39. International Organization for Standardization. Ergonomics of human system interaction - Part 210 (2009)
40. Human-centered design for interactive systems (formerly known as 13407). ISO F ± DIS 9241-210 (2009)
41. Law, E., Roto, V., Hassenzahl, M., Vermeeren, A., Kort, J.: Understanding, scoping and defining user experience: a survey approach (PDF). In: Proceedings of Human Factors in Computing Systems Conference CHI 2009, Boston, MA, USA, 4–9 April 2009 (2009)

42. Huang, T.C., Chen, C.C., Chou, Y.W.: Animating eco-education: to see, feel, and discover in an augmented reality-based experiential learning environment. Comput. Educ. **96**, 72–82 (2016)
43. Dunlap, J., Dobrovolny, J., Young, D.: Preparing e-Learning designers using Kolb's model of experiential learning. J. Online Educ. **4**(4), 1–6 (2008)
44. Fan, H., Scottpoole, M.: What is personalization? Perspectives on the design and implementation of personalization in information systems. J. Organ. Comput. **16**(3–4), 179–202 (2006)
45. Mayeku, B.: Enhancing personalization and learner engagement in context-aware learning environment - a pedagogical and technological perspective (2015)
46. Li, M., Ogata, H., Hou, B., Uosaki, N., Yano, Y.: Personalization in context-aware ubiquitous learning-log system. In: IEEE Seventh International Conference on Wireless, Mobile and Ubiquitous Technology in Education, vol. 16, pp. 41–48. IEEE (2012)
47. Kucirkova, N., Messer, D., Whitelock, D.: Parents reading with their toddlers: the role of personalization in book engagement. J. Early Child. Literacy **13**(4), 445–470 (2013)
48. Keller, J.M., Litchfield, B.C.: Motivation and performance. Trends Issues Instr. Des. Technol. **2**, 89–92 (2002)
49. Lidón, I., Rebollar, R., Møller, C.: A collaborative learning environment for management education based on experiential learning. Innov. Educ. Teach. Int. **48**(3), 301–312 (2011)
50. Roosta, F., Taghiyareh, F., Mosharraf, M.: Personalization of gamification-elements in an e-learning environment based on learners' motivation. In: International Symposium on Telecommunications, pp. 637–642. IEEE (2017)
51. Townsend, R.: A Handbook for Teaching and Learning in Higher Education: Enhancing Academic Practice, 3rd edn. Kogan Page, New York (2009)
52. Kwon, K., Kim, C.: How to design personalization in a context of customer retention: who personalizes what and to what extent? Electron. Commer. Res. Appl. **11**(2), 101–116 (2012)
53. Felicia, P.: Handbook of Research on Improving Learning and Motivation, p. 1003 (2011)
54. Hisatomi, K., Tomiyama, K., Katayama, M., Iwadate, Y.: Method of 3D reconstruction using graph cuts, and its application to preserving intangible cultural heritage. In: IEEE International Conference on Computer Vision Workshops, pp. 923–930. IEEE (2010)

VR: Time Machine

Doros Polydorou[1]([⊠]), Oded Ben-Tal[2], Atser Damsma[3],
and Nadine Schlichting[3]

[1] Cyprus University of Technology, Limassol, Cyprus
`dorosp@gmail.com`
[2] Kingston University, Kingston, UK
[3] University of Groningen, Groningen, The Netherlands

Abstract. Time Machine is an immersive Virtual Reality installation that explains – in simple terms – the Striatal Beat Frequency (SBF) model of time perception. The installation was created as a collaboration between neuroscientists within the field of time perception along with a team of digital designers and audio composers/engineers. This paper outlines the process, as well as the lessons learned, while designing the virtual reality experience that aims to simplify a complex idea to a novice audience. The authors describe in detail the process of creating the world, the user experience mechanics and the methods of placing information in the virtual place in order to enhance the learning experience. The work was showcased at the 4th International Conference on Time Perspective, where the authors collected feedback from the audience. The paper concludes with a reflection on the work and some suggestions for the next iteration of the project.

Keywords: Virtual Reality · Time perception · Installation · Immersion

1 Introduction and Background

We can hear, smell, taste and feel our environment – together forming a rich perception of the world. Neuroscientists have a pretty good idea how these senses are processed in the brain. We evidently also have an inner sense of time. One modern theory of time perception suggest that we can perceive time based on neural oscillatory activity in the cortex. VR:\\Time Machine is a virtual reality installation which explains the said neurobiologically plausible model of time perception. This work explores a number of different areas of investigations in the field of Virtual Reality. By using the immersive qualities of the medium, the experience builds upon the capabilities of the platform as a learning tool. Furthermore, it explores investigations of narrative structures in VR, using concepts such as localized sound sources, information placement in the 3d space and interactivity as mechanisms to aid learning.

1.1 Problem

For the modern scientist, it has become increasingly important to communicate their work and findings to an audience other than their respective field of research (Greenwood and Riordan 2001). While this is an important task, it is also a difficult one: One has to find the balance between simplification and scientific accuracy, identify

M. Kurosu (Ed.): HCII 2020, LNCS 12183, pp. 294–306, 2020.
https://doi.org/10.1007/978-3-030-49065-2_21

scientific jargon and tell an engaging story. VR experiences offer the unique opportunity to explain science in a multisensory way - listening to a narration, seeing visualisations of the concepts being told, and being able to interact and actively explore the thing that is explained. This work aims to frame a theoretical model of how time is encoded in the brain into an easily understandable audio-visual and ludic experience.

1.2 The SBF Model

Modern theories of time perception assume that the human brain can perceive temporal intervals, and therefore predict when a next instance of a regular event will happen (e.g., the next beep of an alarm clock), or whether a temporal interval will be long enough to perform a particular task within that interval (e.g., peek a quick look at a map while waiting at a red light). As we are able to estimate time even in the absence of any external information (e.g., in between two beeps of the alarm clock), the brain has to provide its own source of time. The brain consists of millions of neurons that communicate with each other through electrical signals. There are groups of neurons that fire these signals at a constant rate - like a regular drum beat. We call this phenomenon neural oscillations. Some groups oscillate faster than others, so that each group of neurons has its own unique speed. The striatal beat frequency (SBF) model proposes that when something interesting happens in the world, the oscillating neurons are reset and they synchronize with each other (Matell and Meck 2004). Because of their difference in firing speeds they quickly drift out of synch again. This creates different patterns over time. So, at any particular moment this pattern can tell us how much time

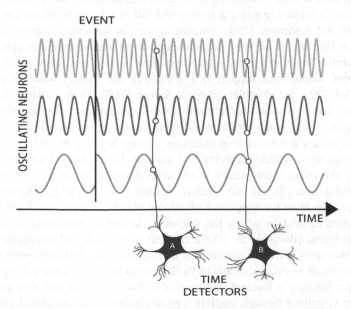

Fig. 1. Schematic depiction of the SBF model. Neurons oscillating at different speeds are synced or reset by an external or internal event. Time detector neurons located in the striatum react to different activation patterns that occur over time, allowing us to tell time.

has passed. Recent work, based on neuroscience studies, suggests that neurons in the striatum, a central part of the brain, react to specific oscillatory activation patterns of cortical neurons, making them "time detectors" (see Fig. 1) (Buhusi and Meck 2005; Gu et al. 2015). This way, we can predict events and anticipate actions, preventing us from looking at the map for too long.

Within the field of temporal cognition, the SBF model has been very influential because it aims to close the gap between theoretical psychological models and neuroscience. While the SBF model is not the last model to do so (see Merchant and de Lafuente 2014, for a review), it was one of the first.

The paper starts with a literature review on educational Virtual Reality experiences. It then continues by outlining the creation process, paying a special emphasis on the four immersion techniques followed by the team: Aesthetic choices, information placement, multi-mode experience, and audio. A first version of the experience has been presented on the 4th International Conference on Time Perspective, where the team manage to collect and reflect on audience feedback, which are outlined in the next section of the paper. Finally, in the concluding section, the authors identify certain elements of exploration for future work.

2 Literature Review

2.1 Serious Gaming

Science learning is generally considered to have an issue with engagement. Because the subject of science is often considered abstruse and challenging, many students actually cannot engage in science learning activities and fail to achieve better understanding of science (Lee and Anderson 1993). Student agency in simulated immersive environments is a credible way to allow students to experiment with science concepts and ideas – even theoretical ones and many researchers have argued that, even as an entertainment medium, videogames support rich discursive and inquiry-based practices (for example, Gee 2004; Steinkuehler 2006; or Squire 2006). Dede, talking about series games claims that it provides students with a subject impression of immersion that one feels like he/she is the avatar virtual world with a comprehensive, realistic experience, and research argues that immersion enhances science learning by at least authorizing multiple perspectives, situated learning and transfer (Dede 2009). Furthermore, Barab et all argue that using video games in science education has made learner centered science learning more efficient and effective. In their view, serious gaming can facilitate student science learning through transformational play by situating the learner within a rich interactive context in which the scientific content is embedded in a series of authentic problems (Barab et al. 2009). Student motivation and engagement can be potentially increased because pleasure and instructional materials are combined into a whole in the virtual world, which allows the learner to engage in a recursive game cycle so that deeper learning is fostered (Squire et al. 2004). Complex and abstract scientific concepts are visualized through tangible representations in the simulated game world, wherein one can generate hypotheses and test strategies iteratively without any need to worry about real-life consequences (Spires et al. 2011). Many natural phenomena – or in the context of this work, theoretical models - that cannot be produced in real-world situations, as well as many experiments and human behaviors that cannot be easily investigated, are allowed to be harmlessly simulated and evaluated in the game (Farrington 2011; Kobes et al. 2010).

2.2 Immersion

According to Brown and Cairns (2004), game immersion consists of three stages, with different barriers existing between the stages, such that a gamer cannot progress from one stage to the next until certain barriers are overcome. To get into the first stage, engagement, players must be satisfied with the game features and feel control over the game, as well as be willing to invest time and effort into the game. As players become further involved with the game, they enter the second stage, engrossment, in which their perceptions of their surroundings and physical needs decrease and their emotions are highly attached to the game. Finally, during the last stage, total immersion, individuals might feel like they are actually the avatars and thus empathize with their situations. When they have reached the stage of total immersion, players are entirely cut off from reality, and the game is all that matters to them. They are so absorbed in the game even to the extent as being in the game. However, total immersion is an intense experience that is relatively difficult to achieve.

Cheng et all conducted a number of studies to investigate how game immersion relates to learning. In their 2015 study, they employed construct validity approaches including exploratory and confirmatory factor analyses to confirm the three stages of game immersion experience and further verify its hierarchical structure. While all three stages of game immersion were positively correlated with student gaming performance (game scores, how students performed in the game) only the first stage, engagement, was positively correlated with students science learning outcomes (test scores, how students performed on science knowledge assessment). Furthermore, their results indicated that gaming performance partially mediates the effects of game immersion experiences on science learning through serious gaming. Furthermore, their cluster analysis results demonstrated that two core clusters presented meaningful patters: high gaming performance/high immersion and high science learning/low immersion (Cheng et al. 2015).

2.3 Sonification

Just as data can be visualised to aid understanding, it can also be mapped to audio or sonified. Sonification was utilised in a wide range of research fields including health (Cassidy et al. 2004; Poveda et al. 2017), astronomy (Tomlinson et al. 2017), Sports (Hummel and Hermann 2010, Du et al. 2018), or economics (Ben-Tal and Berger 2004, Chabot and Braasch 2017) to name just a few examples. Perhaps even more than the graphic representation of data, effective sonification benefits from a deeper understanding of sound and music. Arbitrary mapping of data to audio parameters can become confusing to the users (Du et al. 2018) and, as observed by Papachristodoulou et al. (2014) below, some of the choices regarding type of sounds have to be guided by aesthetics to make the result engaging to the user.

Neuroscience research often involves very large and complex data-sets that are difficult to navigate. Papachristodoulou et al. (2014) combined visualisation and sonification within an immersive 3D environment to represent simplified brain activation patterns. They mapped aspects of the data – number of nodes and connections, strength of the connections, hemispheric location – to sound. They utilised two types of sounds: a sustained, drone-like sound and brief bursts which they use in a manner akin to granular synthesis (Roads 2001). The data was used to modulate time, pitch, loudness, and stereo placement. They found that adding this sonification to the visual presentation enhanced users' understanding of the data.

Beyond making complex data comprehensible, sonification can also be an interface between science and artistic practice. Schmele and Gomez (2012) also applied sonification to neural activation patterns to sound but their ultimate aim was creative – the outcome was an immersive installation. The data, fMRI of people listening to sound-stimuli, was used as the basis for generating music. The first stage transformed the time-sequence of voxel activation into the frequency domain. The spectral peaks, expressed as frequencies in the hearing range, was treated as synthetic musical scales. In the next stage musical material composed within those scales were projected into a spatialisation system using virtual speaker location controlled by the fMRI data. Listeners were surrounded by rapidly changing patterns of sound derived from brain activation patterns. Unlike the previous example, the aim here was not to communicate specific knowledge about brain anatomy or function. Rather it engaged users through an illustration of the richness and complexity of information processing that underpin even mundane tasks such as listening to rhythmic patterns.

Another example illustrates the porous nature of science communication and creative endeavour in this field. Weinberg and Thatcher (2006) discusses two projects that allow participants to engage with neural activation patterns. The second iteration of their approach provided users with physical interfaces to activate neural pathways. The activation patterns in the network were visualised and sonified via an array of speakers. Similar to Shmele above our ability to perceive location through sound is a good match to the distributive pattern of activation in a spatial network. But Weinberg also observes that on its own the spatialisation did not communicate the activity in the network well enough. But at the same time, supplementing this with visual representation led many users to focus on that element at the expense of the sonic side.

3 Development

The development was made up of a number of different stages. Firstly, we decided that the experience was going to offer two different modes. The story mode and the game mode. Following on from there, we create a storyboard, a script and we had a voice actor record a narration for us. We then proceeded to build the world in Unity, identifying the assets we wanted to use and recording some motions through a kinect motion-capture system. Continuing on, we designed and prototyped the user experience in Unity for both story and game mode and did some basic user testing, In this section, we will look at the different stages of the development and analyze the main methods and considerations.

The aim of the project was to allow users to understand and experience the SBF model of time perception. To this end, we decided to let a narrator guide the user through the key components of the model in a simple way, while the narration is being enforced by visual and auditory experiences. The narration consisted of a short text explaining: 1) why time perception is something we all use in everyday life, as illustrated by an example, 2) that time perception is not easy to study, since there is no organ for time as there is for other senses, and 3) how the SBF model proposes that time perception could be achieved in the brain. In the process of developing this text, we aimed to make sure that the explanations were easily understandable for a broad audience of users. This was done by linking time perception to our everyday experience and by avoiding any technical terminology that could be unfamiliar to most users.

3.1 Overview of the Experience

When entering the experience, the viewer gets immersed into a VR world inhabited by neurons. The installation is made up of two parts. In part one, the viewer is guided through a narrated set piece that outlines the theoretical model. In part two the viewer assumes a more active role and becomes a player, trying out the model through a carefully designed ludic experience.

The experience is running in a loop. When a user is initially immersed, she will materialize in an ancient stone platform in a world of old ruins. Five groups of neurons will surround the user, pulsing at their own natural speeds. The user would be free to move around, approach the neurons and study them from up-close if they so wished. Looking beyond the platform, the user can see a portal where the same five pulses, appear from a top view perspective showcasing different patterns with each passing moment. The neurons are pulsating at specific intervals and a top down view of the same neurons can be seen through a stone portal. Even though it is not entirely evident at the once, the user can quickly identify that they are actually the same neurons by paying close attention between the visual and the audio cues. This is a way to train to the user to identify how the neurons are the pulses are actualized in the experience. As the user looks at the controller in their hands, they notice a subtle notification that asks them to press a button for the story mode to commence.

As soon as the button is pressed, the environment turns dark and a narrator, made of particles, appears in the scene. As the narrator explains each step of the model, different areas in the environment light up and visual illustrations are placed in different areas around the platform for future reference.

When the narration is finished, the environment returns back to its original state, completing the loop. The surroundings now make more sense and the user now has gained the ability to interact with certain elements of the scene. Interactions are performed by pressing the trigger button on the controllers.

3.2 Aesthetic Choices and World Building

As soon as the users put on the VR helmet, they can see around them a black starry night. In the background, they can identify statues and broken murals. Ruins have always been associated with the workings of time. As this association exists in many

peoples mind, we have decided to use the aesthetics as the background to our installations. Continuing with the transient theme, the narrator takes the form of a stream of
particles in order to avoid showings of gender or age. The minimal aesthetics are
complemented by an elevated black and white grid floor that that sets the boundaries of
an arena where the whole experience will take place. The experience is build with room
scale in mind, therefore the world is populated 360° around the arena (Fig. 2).

Fig. 2. The world as it is slowly unveiled to the users in story mode.

3.3 Information Placement

One of the main challenges of story-telling in VR is how to attract and keep the
attention of the user. For this experience, we decided to use the environment as a
method of structuring information and controlling the attention of the viewer. The user
is placed on an elevated platform in the center of the world and as the narrator is
talking, information appears around the user in a fixed space. As more details are
revealed about the model, the world gets more and more populated. By using spatial
dynamics, we hope to simplify the internal computations needed to process the
information. As the landscape is revealed, specific areas are "landmarked" through
certain mechanisms. For example, a big group of pillars in placed in the background, or
a distinct statue is revealed in a specific location. These specific landmarks were chosen
because they are at the optimal visual proximity from the user. As the experience
unfolds, the users identify those landmarks and uses them to create a mental image of
the space in their heads. Information, such as the timings of pulsating neurons are then
placed in front of those landmarks, making it easy for the user to make an association
(Fig. 3).

Fig. 3. Information placement around the space.

3.4   Multi-mode Experience

The VR experience is split into two modes. The story mode and the play mode. The experience begins in the play mode, where the user can trigger changes in the environment. By pressing the story button, the world is cleared, the narrator explains the concept of the time perception model and at the end of the story mode the experience returns back to the play mode. We decided to take this approach as we didn't want to add a menu system to the experience, nor force the user to sit through the story every time. Furthermore, briefly interactive with the world both before and after hearing the explanation can aid users to piece the story together more efficiently (Fig. 4).

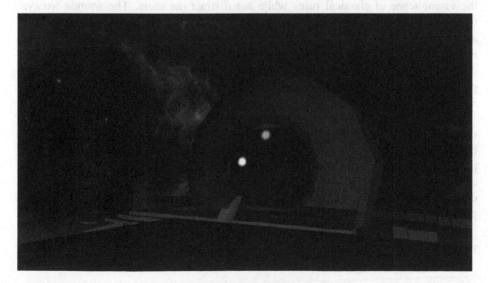

Fig. 4. Pulsating neurons in the play mode.

3.5 Sound

We used three types of sounds in the work: (1) a speaker narrating the scientific explanation (2) sounds synchronised with the visual pulsation of the neurons ('sound effect') (3) Sustained background sounds that echoed the visual design of the scene ('atmospheric').

A central aspect of the model of time perception we are illustrating is the phase patterns between different groups of neurons each group pulsating at a regular speed. This opened a simple and direct way of sonifying this effect. Though in our case we are working on a computational model not measurements of neural activity. While the model suggests a very large number of pulsed neurons are involved we simplify things and illustrate the principle using just five. Short pitched sounds, with different pitch for each neuron, are synchronised with the regular oscillation of that neuron. By linking each of these pulse rates to a different sounded pitch, time intervals are manifested as melodic patterns as well as visual patterns of firing neurons. Both are presented to the user to help illuminate how the combination of regular pulses can be used as an internal clock. The synthesised sound is based on the Karplus-Strong plucked string model (Karplus and Strong 1983). Both the pitch and the pulsation rate we chose through a process of experimentation. The changing relationship had to be visually and aurally clear as well as appealing, and work practically with the duration we expected users to engage with the work. The 'chord' we ended up using is not a standard major/minor chord of Western Tonal music but is a collection of five notes including microtonal pitches[1].

The sustained background sounds were used for purely aesthetic purposes in order to enrich the user experience of the VR environment. These were generated using granular synthesis (Roads 2001) where a source sound, singing in this case, is chopped into very short grains - 30 ms in this instance. The grains are then recombined to synthesise a novel sound. Granular synthesis is a very flexible method of generating new sounds. In this instance we were looking for background material that will match the visual scene of classical ruins while not distract the users. The sounds we synthesised were drone-like, though the parameter settings of the granular synthesis created sustained sounds with vague rather than sharp pitch definition. The narration explained the science we were trying to communicate to a wide audience. We developed the VR installation first using a recording we made ourselves. But we were able to get a better quality recording from a colleague who had experience producing audiobooks.

Sound in this project, therefore, follows cinematic conventions with dialogue as the most important element, and other sounds there to support the narrative and provide background. In this first iteration the sound was also presented in simple stereo. We plan to integrate sonic elements into the environment in the future. Sounds attached to objects and events in the scene can direct users to explore the space more. The main development we see for this project is in the interactive phase and there too sound can play a more significant and interesting role.

---

[1] Microtones are notes that fall between the regular semi-tones represented by the white and black keys of the standard piano keyboard.

3.6   Audience Feedback

The first evaluations were collected through informal interviews during the 4th International Conference on Time Perspective (France, August 2018). Overall, users responded positively to the VR experience. They complimented the aesthetic qualities of the visuals, the use of the avatar, the accessibility of the model explanation and the interactivity ("The world looks amazing and very immersive", "The avatar is really cool and it should appear more often", "The visuals and the sound helped me to understand how the pulses are linked to time". There were also some suggestions for improvement. Notably, some users had missed the ball-throwing example at the start of the narration, because they were still exploring the VR world ("The throwing scene could maybe be moved closer to the user, so that the ball also comes closer to the user or maybe the ball can have a more attention-grabbing color"). In addition, some noted that the sound and visuals of the pulsating neurons were slightly out of sync and that there could be more salient visual and auditory feedback when the neurons are 'reset' by the user. ("The sound seems to lack the visuals and be a bit out of synch". Finally, it was noted that the avatar was appealing and could appear more often ("Would be good if the avatar took a more substantial role, like a guide to the whole experience").

4   Conclusion and Future Work

With the VR:\\Time Machine project, we aimed to explain a scientific computational theory - the SBF model - to a diverse audience in an interactive, simple and enjoyable way. Using VR, the components of the model could be seen, as well as heard, in an immersive 3D environment. These components could also be manipulated by the user to enhance their understanding of the function of a particular component in the model.

During this work the authors build a virtual world by taking careful considerations of the user experience in virtual reality. The world was constructed in an aesthetic style with visual connotations to the ethereality of time. This has helped with the immersion qualities of the space as it situated the users into the right frame of mind. Continuing from there, an avatar was introduced to act as a guide to the experience and point to the user where to look and pay their attention during the experience. The user was situated in the center of the experience, in an elevated position, in order to be able to easily follow the narration around the circular space. The world was unveiled step by step, so the user could slowly absorb the information and as the narration was played out, notes appeared around the space creating a virtual learning canvas for the user to refer to. The visuals were complemented with sounds which played a very prominent role. The audio narration was driving the experience – complemented by the virtual avatar that appeared in various instances – and other sounds were there to support the visuals and to provide background.

Based on the audience feedback, several changes will be implemented in a subsequent version of the VR experience. We plan to develop the sonic aspect of the work to further enhance user engagement. The first aspect is to make use of spatialisation capabilities of VR environment. As noted above spatial cues are one of the interesting contributions of sound in this setting. We plan to integrate sounds into the virtual environment to encourage users to explore the environment more. In addition we plan to develop the interactive part of the installation more and here, again, audio can play a more significant role. Our aim is to demonstrate how the sural mechanism we describe can be used to estimate short durations. For instance, users can try to compare the duration of two time intervals. By varying relevant parameters in the model they can experience how those contribute to the measurement of time. Another option would be to illustrate what happens when the model is malfunctioning, as we believe is the case with some neurological disorders, and how this affects the accuracy of time estimations. Furthermore, we plan to use the avatar in even more parts of the experience as it seems the audience identified with it and it helped them to navigate in the virtual space. One more planned addition is to utilize the VR controllers a bit more. Currently, they are used to start or reset the experience but we aim to user them to offer supplementary information about the content to the user. As the narrator explains, the main points could appear in the form of bullet points in a virtual "notepad" attached to the controller. This mechanism can work in parallel with the information placement in the world space and it would allow the user to review – during the story mode – the main ideas of the model and afterwards – during interaction mode – have a reference to what each button on the controller does.

Credits. The theoretical model of time perception has been proposed by Neuroscientists Matthew S. Matell and Warren H. Meck [1] and it has been adapted by researchers Atser Damsma and Nadine Schlichting for this installation. The virtual environment has been created by Doros Polydorou. The sounds and the music have been composed by Oded Ben-Tal and the narration has been voiced by Nathan Ridley (Hermitage Works Studio).

References

Barab, S., Dede, C.: Games and immersive participatory simulations for science education: an emerging type of curricula. J. Sci. Educ. Technol. **16**(1), 1–3 (2007). https://doi.org/10.1007/s10956-007-9043-9

Barab, S.A., Cherkes-Julkowski, M., Swenson, R., Garrett, S., Shaw, R.E., Young, M.: Principles of selforganization: ecologizing the learner-facilitator system. J. Learn. Sci. **8**(3&4), 349–390 (1999)

Ben-Tal, O., Berger, J.: Creative aspects of sonification. Leonardo **37**(3), 229–233 (2004)

Brown, E., Cairns, P.: A grounded investigation of game immersion. In: CHI 2004 Extended Abstracts on Human Factors in Computing Systems, pp. 1297–1300. ACM Press, Vienna (2004)

Buhusi, C.V., Meck, W.H.: What makes us tick? Functional and neural mechanisms of interval timing. Nat. Rev. Neurosci. **6**(10), 755–765 (2005)

Chabot, S., Braasch, J.: High-density data sonification of stock market information in an immersive virtual environment. J. Acoust. Soc. Am. **141**(5), 3512 (2017)

Cheng, M.T., She, H.C., Annetta, L.A.: Game immersion experience: its hierarchical structure and impact on game-based science learning. J. Comput. Assist. Learn. **31**(3), 232–253 (2015). https://doi.org/10.1111/jcal.12066

Cheng, M.T., Lin, Y.W., She, H.C., Kuo, P.C.: Is immersion of any value? Whether, and to what extent, game immersion experience during serious gaming affects science learning. Br. J. Edu. Technol. **48**(2), 246–263 (2017)

Cassidy, R.J., Berger, J., Lee, K., Maggioni, M., Coifman, R.R.: Auditory display of hyperspectral colon tissue images using vocal synthesis models. In: Barrass, S., Vickers, P. (eds.) Proceedings of the 10th International Conference on Auditory Display, ICAD 2004, Sydney, Australia (2004)

Du, M., Chou, J.K., Ma, C., Chandrasegaran, S., Ma, K.L.: Exploring the role of sound in augmenting visualization to enhance user engagement. In: 2018 IEEE Pacific Visualization Symposium (PacificVis), pp. 225–229. IEEE, April 2018

Farrington, J.: From the research: myths worth dispelling: seriously, the game is up. Perform. Improv. Q. **24**, 105–110 (2011)

Gee, J.P.: Language, Learning, and Gaming. A Critique of Traditional Schooling. Routledge, New York (2004)

Gu, B.-M., Van Rijn, H., Meck, W.H.: Oscillatory multiplexing of neural population codes for interval timing and working memory. Neurosci. Biobehav. Rev. **48**, 160–185 (2015)

Hummel, J., Hermann, T., Frauenberger, C., Stockman, T.: Interactive sonification of German wheel sports. In: Proceedings of ISon 2010-Interactive Sonification Workshop: Human Interaction with Auditory Displays (2010)

Karplus, K., Strong, A.: Digital synthesis of plucked-string and drum timbres. Comput. Music J. **7**(2), 43–55 (1983)

Lesen, A.E., Rogan, A., Blum, M.J.: Science communication through art: objectives, challenges, and outcomes. Trends Ecol. Evol. **31**(9), 657–660 (2016)

Matell, M.S., Meck, W.H.: Cortico-striatal circuits and interval timing: coincidence detection of oscillatory processes. Cogn. Brain. Res. **21**, 139–170 (2004)

Merchant, H., de Lafuente, V.: Introduction to the neurobiology of interval timing. In: Merchant, H., de Lafuente, V. (eds.) Neurobiology of Interval Timing. AEMB, vol. 829, pp. 1–13. Springer, New York (2014). https://doi.org/10.1007/978-1-4939-1782-2_1

Papachristodoulou, P., Betella, A., Verschure, P.F.M.J.: Sonification of large datasets in a 3D immersive environment: A neuroscience case study. In: ACHI 2014: The Seventh International Conference on Advances in Computer-Human Interactions, pp. 35–40, March 2014

Poveda, J., O'Sullivan, M., Popovici, E., Temko, A.: Portable neonatal EEG monitoring and sonification on an Android device. In: 2017 39th Annual International Conference of the IEEE Engineering in Medicine and Biology Society (EMBC), pp. 2018–2021. IEEE (2017)

Roads, C.: Microsound. MIT Press, Cambridge (2001)

Kobes, M., Helsloot, I., de Vries, B., Post, J.: Exit choice, (pre-)movement time and (pre-) evacuation behaviour in hotel fire evacuation—Behavioural analysis and validation of the use of serious gaming in experimental research. Proc. Eng. **3**, 37–51 (2010). https://doi.org/10.1016/j.proeng.2010.07.006

Schmele, T., Gomez, I.: Exploring 3D audio for brain sonification. In: Proceedings of the 18th International Conference on Auditory Display, Atlanta, GA, USA, 18–21 June 2012 (2012)

Steinkuehler, C.A.: Massively multiplayer online video gaming as participation in a discourse. Mind Cult. Act. **13**(1), 38–52 (2006)

Spires, H.A., Rowe, J.P., Mott, B.W., Lester, J.C.: Problem solving and game-based learning: effect of middle grade students' hypothesis testing strategies on learning outcome. J. Educ. Comput. Res. **44**(4), 453–472 (2011)

Squire, K.: From content to context: Videogames as designed experiences. Educ. Res. **35**(8), 19–29 (2006)

Tomlinson, B.J., Winters, R.M., Latina, C., Bhat, S., Rane, M., Walker, B.N.: Solar system sonification: exploring earth and its neighbors through sound. In: The 23rd International Conference on Auditory Display (2017)

Weinberg, G., Thatcher, T.: Interactive sonification of neural activity. In: Proceedings of the 2006 conference on New interfaces for musical expression, pp. 246–249. IRCAM—Centre Pompidou, June 2006

Read Ahoy

A Playful Digital-Physical Viking Experience to Engage Children in Finding and Reading Books

Andrea Resmini[1(✉)] and Bertil Lindenfalk[2]

[1] Jönköping International Business School,
Jönköping University, Jönköping, Sweden
andrea.resmini@ju.se

[2] Jönköping Academy for Improvement of Health and Welfare,
School of Health and Welfare, Jönköping University, Jönköping, Sweden

Abstract. A digital/physical installation part a series of pilots developed for Habo Municipality, Sweden, in the context of a public co-design effort aimed at creating a shared understanding of the possibilities offered by digital transformation and the development of a connected city framework, "Read Ahoy!" provides children with a simple game-like challenge: find books randomly distributed in a number of locations by matching conceptual, spatial, aural, and verbal clues.

Built as an embodied experience for library spaces, "Read Ahoy!" is narratively centered on a Viking crew in need of help after they have lost much of their precious cargo of books in a storm, on their way back after a trade expedition. The story grounds the challenge in tropes familiar to Swedish culture and gives children a playful setup and well-defined goals as they search for books. "Read Ahoy!" explores how children entering the school system search and make sense of information in a blended space, structurally recreating the way they customarily mix action in digital and physical space.

Theoretically anchored in Benyon's conceptualization of blended spaces, in Bates' information seeking theory and information search tactics, and in Resmini and Lacerda's formalization of information-based experience ecosystems, "Read Ahoy!" was designed and implemented as a low-budget end-of-year project for the students in the Master's in Information Architecture and Innovation at Jönköping International Business School, Jönköping, Sweden, under the supervision of the authors. It was framed to meet the UN SDG4's sub-targets on "Early childhood development" and "Universal Youth Literacy" and installed in Habo Library from June through August 2019 where it was used extensively by local children under the supervision of librarians during the summer. A full description of the installation and preliminary post-mortem reflections are offered in the paper.

1 Introduction

Habo is one of the municipalities in Sweden with the highest percentage of residents under nineteen years of age, 29,1% of the total [12]. The United Nations (UN) have identified education as one of their top priorities among the 17 formulated sustainability goals. Within this space, "Read Ahoy!" was set up in cooperation with Habo municipality and Habo Public LIbrary to explore a design solution to address the UN SDG4's

© Springer Nature Switzerland AG 2020
M. Kurosu (Ed.): HCII 2020, LNCS 12183, pp. 307–325, 2020.
https://doi.org/10.1007/978-3-030-49065-2_22

sub-targets on "Early childhood development" and "Universal Youth Literacy" [20], as part of an ongoing series of joint initiatives and pilot projects involving academia, public bodies, and the local industry aimed at creating awareness of the challenges and opportunities of digital transformation and at laying the foundations of a connected city framework.

"Read Ahoy!" was developed in 2019 as an end-of-year project for the students in the Master's in Information Architecture and Innovation at Jönköping University. It was based on a brief called "La machine enchantée": an earlier, more complex concept for reinventing the children's library as a digital/physical experience and favor discovery, playfulness, and serendipity to "encourage children to interact with the space and content of libraries" [8]. The original concept was developed as a co-design information architecture exercise at UMIX 2014, a two-day student hackathon hosted by the École Normale Supérieure de Lyon, France. It was subsequently reimagined and repurposed as a design exercise called "The Enchanted Forest" and used as project work for students in both graduate and undergraduate courses at Jönköping University, Jönköping, Sweden, throughout 2016 and 2017.

1.1 The Early Brief and the Enchanted Forest Concept

The early brief insisted primarily on serendipity and intended to pay homage to Lyon as the "city of light" through its use of luminous paths that would light up to guide the children to boxes, and not shelves, containing the books (Fig. 1). A simple icon-only

Fig. 1. Prototyping La machine enchantée at ENS Lyon, 2014

interface sitting on top of a tag database would allow children to choose broad categories, such as "adventure".

The reimagined exercise of 2016 and 2017 reconceptualized the original "search" motif and immersed it in a fairytale-like experience: children would search for books in an enchanted forest where paths would light up to show them the way. This forest was imagined as a smaller space inside the library itself, a square deck roughly six meters by six meters and resting on a fifteen - twenty centimeters high deck to allow for cabling. The floor of this deck would be lined up with LED lights, and multiple boxes rigged with sensors and LEDs would be randomly arranged on its surface. A suggestion was also put forth that safe, child-friendly scenographic obstacles representing trees, roots, or rocks could be used to better suggest the labyrinthine space of a fairytale forest.

Just like in the original brief, children would use a kiosk with a touch interface to choose simple, broad pre-set categories such as "dragon", "car", or "forest", that could be joined in facet like fashion to obtain smaller result sets [17]. Once a choice had been made, the multi-colored LED lights would light up a temporary path, breadcrumb-like, from the kiosk to the box containing the most books tagged with the chosen category or categories. The path would stay lit up for a brief amount of time, and then go off.

The overall architecture rested on the individual tagging of the books, by means of RFID or similar technologies, and on the boxes tracking these tags through sensors connected to a central unit that also controlled the LED lights as books were moved around. At any given time this central unit would know what books, and hence categories, are in what boxes, and in what numbers. The boxes could then be ranked by category and, based on the choice of tags and on the instructions codified in the controlling algorithms, a certain path could light up in a certain color.

The way children were supposed to interact with the books created an emergent information architecture reflected in the constantly changing physical configuration of the experience: finding a book, picking it up, reading it, and then moving it to a different box would alter the distribution of the books in space over time and change the paths that would light up in response to identical future searches.

This conceptualization was used as the basis for a number of design exercises in two different courses in 2016 and 2017 and was then recast as the starting brief for the Habo installation.

2   Theoretical Foundations

The "Read Ahoy!" project was practically approached as a user experience design exercise and theoretically anchored to the curriculum of the Master's program, and specifically to Bates' information seeking theory and information search tactics [1, 2], to Benyon's conceptualization of blended spaces [3], and to Resmini and Lacerda's formalization of information-based experience ecosystems [18].

2.1 Information Seeking and Searching

In her 2002 paper "Toward An Integrated Model of Information Seeking and Searching", Bates introduces "a single model that incorporates both information seeking and searching" and that provides a way to "integrate the social and cultural with the underlying biological and physical anthropological layers of human experience" [2].

Bates considers the human experience to be describable as the stacking of seven layers that progressively move, discipline-wise, from the scientific to the humanistic: from "Chemical, physical, geological, astronomical" at the bottom, to "Social and historical (social sciences)" at the midpoint, to "Spiritual (religion, philosophy, quest for meaning)" at the top. "Complex interrelations" exist between these layers, and Bates "integrated model" is specifically aimed at understanding information seeking across them and at developing a model of "information seeking in relation to information searching" [2].

According to Bates such an approach is necessary since many aspects of human behavior are "neither totally biological nor totally social, but a complex mixture of both" and can be described as "complex mixes across the layers": any complete study of information seeking needs to "integrate the social levels with the underlying ones".

Her model describes information seeking and searching as four integrated but specific activities that can be described as being directed or undirected, and active or passive: searching and monitoring are directed and respectively active and passive, and represent the way "we find information that we know we need to know"; browsing, active, and being aware, passive, are undirected and represent the "ways we find information that we do not know we need to know". The two passive modalities, awareness and monitoring, "provide the vast majority of information for most people during their lives" (Fig. 2).

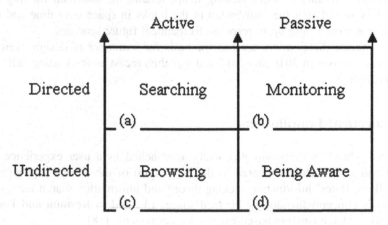

Fig. 2. Modes of information seeking. Image from Bates, 2002

Searching, active and directed, is a resource-intense activity, and when searching the principle of least effort plays an important role. According to Bates, this is why "we often arrange our physical and social environment so as to provide the information we need when we need it. From grocery lists to the arrangement of dials in airplane cockpits, to the physical placement of and organization of tools and offices, we make it possible to be reminded, when we need reminding, of next steps or appropriate behaviors". Offloading information into the environment allows us to "(cut) down on the need for active information seeking" [2].

In turn, environmental information produces "serendipitous encounters" that are the product of proximity and that rely on embodied activities such as "orientation, place-marking, comparison, resolution of anomalies" whose root can be identified in information foraging behavior and its subsequent exaptation to what Bates calls "sample and select".

Both the offloading of information into the environment and the chance of serendipitous encounters are connected to Bates' earlier concept of "berrypicking", identified as the "more common and natural way people actually engaged in active directed searching" [1]. Berrypicking is a sample and select behavior: Bates describes it as a form of meandering in which each step we take while we search provides us with a different vantage point, just like when we kneel to pick that elusive blueberry, that modifies our path and final destination.

Offloading information into artifacts and the environment, the idea of making serendipitous encounters, and the very concrete idea of a berrypicking path through boxes filled with books were direct influences for the "Read Ahoy!" project.

2.2 Blended Spaces

Benyon has introduced the notion of blended space as a space where "a physical space is deliberately integrated in a close-knit way with a digital space" [3]. Because of this integration, blended spaces possess entirely new properties, create a different sense of presence, and lead to new ways of interacting and novel user experiences. The idea of blended spaces has been applied to the domain of digital tourism [5] and to the design of meeting rooms [4].

The idea of blended spaces is anchored in conceptual blending or conceptual integration [9]. Conceptual blending is a theory of cognition that stipulates that elements and relationships belonging to different scenarios are blended in a continuous subconscious process which is ubiquitous to everyday thought. The blending creates new relationships and hence also new inputs to the space and experience that were previously not available. "Material anchors" [14], that is tangible artifacts to which relevant information is linked, have proven useful in helping actors in the formulation and comprehension of the new experience.

Blended spaces can be structured considering four generic characteristics: ontology, topology, volatility, and agency [3]. Ontology is concerned with what objects are present in the blended space; topology with their spatial relationships; volatility considers how quickly the objects in the space can change; and agency is concerned with what actors or agents can do in the space.

2.3 Information-Based Experience Ecosystems

Information-based experience ecosystems (IBEE) have been conceptually introduced in information architecture and user experience theory in a 2009 paper [19]. In response to the socio-technical changes brought along by convergence and pervasive and ubiquitous computing, Resmini and Rosati argued that the object of information architecture could not be identified in the individual, isolated artifact: as "every single artifact becomes an element in a larger ecosystem" [19], so information architecture should consider the set of relationships that constitutes the second-order structure [11] of said ecosystem.

The IBEE framework was formalized by Resmini and Lacerda [18] and identifies information-based ecosystems as the ecosystems "resulting from actor-driven choice, use, and coupling of touchpoints, either belonging to the same or to different systems, within the context of the strategic goals and desired future states actors intend to explicitly or implicitly achieve" [18]. They are "semantic constructs structured around the idea of 'experiences'" that "straddle physical and digital space, and include people, devices, locations, and software connected by information flows".

One of the primary constituents of the architecture of an IBEE is the idea of "path" as the linear description of an individual actor's experience, an extension of Bates' berrypicking and information seeking models to the non-contiguous spaces of digital/physical experiences (Fig. 3).

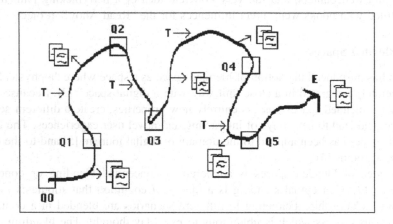

Fig. 3. A berrypicking, evolving search. Image from Bates, 1989.

Benyon and Resmini have further refined IBEEs by considering them a "superset of the blended space concept" and an instantiation of a blended space across non-contiguous physical spaces, shifting "the focus away from the individual interactions to a sustained user experience" and approaching "the many different interfaces, legacy systems, the constraints and opportunities afforded by physical locations, and the spatial and temporal variants strategically rather than tactically" [6].

This revised version of the framework has been applied to the Ambient Assisted Living domain to map the IBEE of home services [16], and was used to guide the design effort for the Habo installation. "Read Ahoy!" was designed to recreate a playful, fantastic equivalent of children's day-to-day experience with the non-continuous blended spaces they traverse as they interact with digital technology, with the aim to examine the weight of material anchors, investigate the interplay of the information architecture with the principles of offloading and berrypicking, and the impact of serendipitous encounters have on different seeking and searching strategies in digital/physical environments.

3   Design Process

The project ran for nine weeks in the spring of 2019 as an end-of-year project in the Master's in Information Architecture and Innovation at Jönköping International Business School (JIBS), Jönköping University, part of a course on "Digital transformation and renewal".

The entire project was set up to be student-driven and since the majority of the students were already familiar with Gray's game-inspired design process [13] from previous courses, his simple diverge-emerge-converge model was used as the implicit structure followed throughout development (Fig. 4). Gray compares the three phases to the way games play out and argues that "the first act opens the world": sets the stage, introduces the players, develops "the themes, ideas, and information that will populate (the) world". The second act allows us to "explore and experiment with the themes (…) develop(ed) in act one". The third act is where conclusions are drawn and solutions generated.

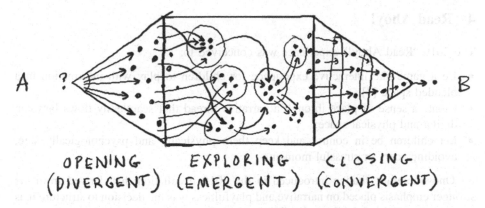

Fig. 4. Phases in the design process. Image from Gray et al., 2010.

After an initial two weeks of concept evaluation, idea generation, and collective discussion (opening phase), the students split up in self-organized teams to better tackle the different challenges presented by the installation in the course of the exploring and closing phases: the information architecture, the narrative and the user experience, the software and hardware parts including, once the story was finalized, the necessary props such as the story box and the ship. Students were free to move between teams at any time in accordance with their interests, skills, and current needs of the project: project management on the side of the teaching staff was kept to a minimum and mostly consisted of making sure that information was shared in-team and between different teams.

Most of the development and realization, including all of the necessary audio and video recording and editing, was done in-house at the creative studio at JIBS. The small budget, amounting to less than 700 EUR, was used to cover all software and hardware costs, to buy wood, primer, paint, sails and nails, and Viking attire.

During the opening phase the students explored a number of narratives and technical solutions. Consultations with external experts from the local industry, and specifically with a lighting company, suggested that use of LED lights or any other type of smart lighting would mean an increase in costs way beyond the allotted budget just to ensure the safety of the installation. Similarly, use of RFIDs, NFC, QR codes, or cameras for tracking the books resulted in architectures that were either too expensive, too fragile, or too cumbersome. In the end, a team decision was taken to radically simplify the final design.

Hardware- and software-wise, the most complex part of the installation was the "story box", the interactive initial touchpoint, which was built writing custom Java-script code for a browser-based interface using a Raspberry Pi 4, a Google Voice Kit, and a 24 inches screen encased in a purpose-made wooden box painted with an oak primer. The "salute screen", the end-of-experience touchpoint, was realized as a custom app running locally on an Android tablet also encased in a wooden box fastened to the box of the Viking ship prop.

4 Read Ahoy!

The 2019 "Read Ahoy!" experience was conceived to:

- Be a game-like interactive experience for children to play with information in a blended space [3];
- Create a sense of place through a narrative thread that seamlessly flows between digital and physical space;
- Let children be in control and keep them physically and psychologically safe, avoiding scary or stressful moments.

One important change introduced in the 2019 installation that derived from the stronger emphasis placed on narrative and playfulness was the decision to structure it as a game of sorts where children would play with the crew and against the environment (the storm and the water). Both the original envisioning and the 2016–2017 exercises had no "end status": children would just experience an ever-changing series of serendipitous paths as they searched, read, and moved the books between the different boxes or locations.

Starting from the definition of a game as "a closed formal system that engages players in structured conflict and resolves its uncertainties in unequal outcomes" [10], "Read Ahoy" was conceptualized to provide children resolution and a sense of achievement while maintaining a balanced challenge [7]. Structured conflict was introduced as a foundational part of the experience through the branching of the narrative into different successful and unsuccessful paths producing non-punishing unequal outcomes.

Correspondence between narrative flow and the space of the experience was one of the primary elements to be considered, and the installation was set up as a three-part, linear succession of clearly identifiable spaces that followed the open-explore-close playful model described by Gray [13]. The story box area offered the possibility to open the story; the book chests area offered exploration; the ship closure (Fig. 5). Conceptually, this structure, at once embodied physically in the space of the library and conceptually in the information architecture supporting the experience, helped the team to successfully recast what was originally an "enchanted machine" and then a simple backdrop for action, an "enchanted forest", into an actionable and meaningful narrative space.

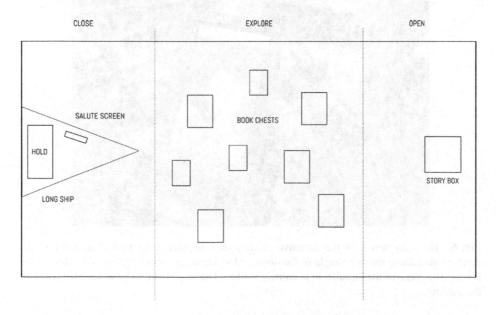

Fig. 5. Diagram illustrating the spatial structure of the Read Ahoy! installation

A number of changes were introduced to the physical architecture of the experience as well. As mentioned before, primarily because of the budget and time constraints that came with implementing "Read Ahoy!" as an end-of-year project, the more complex architecture of the 2014 brief, that would have necessarily involved some form of central processing and a network of sensors, was abandoned in favor of a simpler approach that favored narrative depth and play. A detailed script outlining the backstory of the Viking expedition was the result of this process, and from it a much richer "world" that allowed for more engaging storytelling. Individual crew members received names and occupations, a storm entered the picture, books were floating on the water, and Freja, a woman Viking and a leader of the expedition, emerged as the narrator.

In its final configuration, "Read Ahoy!" consisted of two digital touchpoints, the "story box" (Fig. 6) and the "salute screen" (Fig. 7), eight "book chests" marked by color-coded shields and containing 150 books in all (Fig. 8), and the scaled-down bow, hold, and sail of a Viking ship (Fig. 9). The "story box" and the Viking ship were entirely custom-built in pine and fir wood and painted a darker hue using a variety of oak primers; the "book chests" were bought at local stores in different sizes, also painted with primer, and decorated with printouts of the color-coded Viking shields glued on thick cardboard.

Fig. 6. The story box with the narrative running and displaying the topical moment in the narrative describing the ship caught in the storm and losing much of its cargo of chests filled with books. The space of the installation is entirely visible. The ship is still to be assembled (back of the picture).

Fig. 7. The "salute screen" on the ship. Kids were asked to say whether they had found any of the books or if they had not, and treated to a random selection of "success" or "try again" speeches from the various Viking crew members, played by students in the Master's in Information Architecture and Innovation at Jönköping University. The videos were shot in front of a green screen and then edited to include effects and backgrounds.

Fig. 8. The "book chests". The different colors, paired with those on the map, are visible on the shields.

Fig. 9. The ship awaiting the children at the end of their search. The encasing for the "salute screen" tablet is visible (port side of the ship).

The library was surveyed for an appropriate space and an area of approximately 30 square meters was identified with the help of the librarians on the side of the children's area. The narrow side facing towards the main entrance of the library was chosen for the story box, the point of entry into the narrative and the first visible element of the installation. Beyond it, the book chests were arranged in accordance with the digital map to be displayed on the story box, and laid on blue mats, representing water, connected by treasure map-like dotted curved paths created on the floor with blue tape (Fig. 10).

Keywords in Swedish had been previously associated with the 150 books through a collaborative labeling and open card sorting activity run by the students, using titles and covers as the seed. Seventy child-friendly terms were identified and then used to tag the books. Each book received a minimum of three tags and a maximum of six.

Fig. 10. An overview of the installation space from the side, with the "story box" right displaying the idle screen and the "book chests" left connected by the blue tape paths (Color figure online)

5   The Read Ahoy! Installation

The "story box", presenting itself as a bulky case of rough wood with a slanted upright part containing a large flat screen and a blue button as its only interface, marked the entrance to the installation space: it was the first physical element that children encountered and the one acting as a threshold to the space of the story. On idle, the screen displayed the white silhouette of a Viking ship as seen from the side on a black background, and the message "Tryck på knappen" ("press the button" in Swedish).

Pressing the button started a voice-and-image narrative told via six consecutive animated scenes drawn in cartoon style and using mostly vivid, flat colors: Freja, a female crew member voiced by a student, tells the tale of how the group left Birka, a famous Viking settlement on the island of Björkö near Stockholm, and journeyed long and far towards the East to acquire all sorts of precious goods, including chest upon chest filled with books (Fig. 11). On their way back, when they were no more than a couple of days away from home, the ship was caught in a storm and most of these chests of books were washed overboard.

At this point in her story, Freja asks the children for help: can they maybe recover some of these books? There were some that spoke of three important subjects and that came from three very specific chests: could they bring at least one back to the ship awaiting further on? This request leads to the final scene, showing a map that perfectly replicates the physical layout of the installation in the library: the ship, the boxes and their colors, and their relative positions as seen from the story box. The map highlights the three specific boxes Freja asks the children to search and the subjects (keywords) they should be looking for (Fig. 11). For example, search the boxes decorated with the blue, green, or red shields for books on "slott" (castle), "skatt" (treasure), and "stjärna" (star).

Fig. 11. The blue button has been pressed and the narrator, who identifies herself as Freja, starts to tell the story of the crew's journey (left). At the end of her recount, the map is shown, a few chests highlighted, and the set of three keywords (here "äventyr", "skog", and "stjärnor") is displayed. (Color figure online)

The map remained visible for 60 seconds, after which the story box resetted and the screen returned to its idle state, displaying the ship silhouette and the suggestion to press the button. A new press would generate another run of the story, with a new random combination of three boxes and three keywords.

No time limit was imposed on the search activity itself: children could spend as much time as they liked going from box to box and were free to sample any book they liked, stop to read something they found interesting, or drop out.

When children thought they found one of the books that matched Freja's request, they could keep looking for more or visit the ship, where they would find the "hold" lined up with a gunny sack for the books, and the "salute screen", a tablet encased in a wooden box bolted to the deck and running a custom local app. The idle screen of the app showed the cartoon crew waiting and offered children a choice between "yes, I found one or more books", or "no, I didn't" (Fig. 12).

Tapping either of these would show a video featuring a crew member saluting the children as heroes and, if they said they had been successful, inviting them to read the book(s), and then asking to leave them in the hold; if they said they had been unsuccessful, congratulating them for their efforts and telling them they could try again like a Viking would, if they wanted. Twentyfour short videos, twelve for the "yes" branch and twelve for the "no" branch, were shot in front of a green screen and post-edited to add effects and appropriate backgrounds. A number of male and female students, dressed in full Viking regalia, with male students also sporting a fake full Viking beard, played the role of crew members in the videos (Fig. 7).

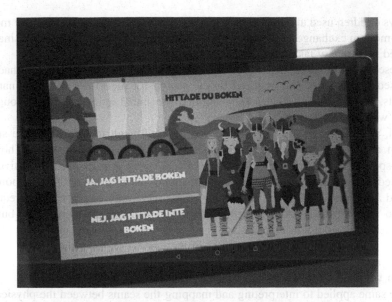

Fig. 12. The user interface for the salute screen

This marked the end of the experience: children were free to exit the space left and move to the main area of the children's library, or go back to the story box and start a new search. While the installation was primarily used in a structured way under the supervision of a librarian, unsupervised access was also possible at all times for the entirety of the residency.

Spatial, aural, and visual clues converged to structure the narrative, the digital map, and the library space into a blended space. Topologically, since the chests on the map occupied the same position the boxes occupied in physical space, children had to relate the map on the screen with the physical environment in which they were, correctly traversing the information seam between digital and physical space [18] to formulate an effective cognitive map of the area. The cognitive map could then be used to look for the books using active directed search strategies [2] within the blended space of the installation.

6   Testing and User Observations

No direct observation was carried out by students part of the design team or by the authors. This was by choice after considering the potential impact repeated observations could have on the day-to-day activities carried out in the children's library. The legal aspects of conducting research with minors also influenced the decision. Rather the authors asked the librarians, and specifically the staff working with the summer programs and the installation, to help. Being already a familiar presence specifically trained to work with children and to supervise them, they were trusted with observing the ways children used and interacted with "Read Ahoy!" throughout the three months. A post-mortem exchange in the fall of 2019, after the installation had been dismantled, provided preliminary take-aways.

These showed that the experience was engaging and well-liked: children had been engrossed by the story and engaged by the search for the lost books. The narrative elements, as told visually and aurally through the initial animation and through the videos, were openly lauded.

Still, some parts of the narrative proved to be difficult to follow for the smaller children and would have benefited from more clarity in the exposition. Choice of words, speed of enunciation, and the lack of a way to repeat parts of the narrative were suggested as possible improvements. Another sound- or voice-related friction point that received attention was the fact that the keywords were only displayed on screen with the map and not read aloud, something the team had initially considered but then abandoned because of time constraints. As a few keywords were deemed too specific or too "complex", because of their length or of their being unusual, the lack of a voice-over for them made the initial part of the experience something of a challenge for those children who had limited reading skills.

The same applied to interpreting and mapping the seams between the physical and digital elements of the experience, where most of the issues did not derive from spatial confusion or cognitive mapping mismatches. The material anchors provided to the narrative by the story box and the book chests proved extremely effective: most of the children could successfully relate the map and its physical embodiment in the space of the library, immersing themselves in direct search while going through the make-believe task of helping the crew. Problems were rather a consequence of language and literacy level slips, something that could be solved in future installations through better integrated, extended voice-overs to supplement the initial instructions, more attention to the enunciation and language aspects of the story, replay or slow down features and, when possible, a more user centered approach involving children early on in the design process.

Some of the physical props part of the installation did not manage to withstand the energetic approach of the children. Supervision only lessened the issue. While the "story box" and the boxes proved to be sturdy enough, the top of the stempost of the ship, the so called dragon head (in this case a carved curl) broke after a few days; more than once, throughout the summer, library staff had to reassemble the holder for the "salute screen" tablet that someone decided to disassemble from the ship. Additionally, even though the "salute screen" app prevented use of the tablet, some of the children understood that the wooden holder contained a device they knew and devoted their time to figure out whether they could play games with it or watch videos instead of participating in the Viking story.

The children using the demonstrator all showed signs of applying a directed active search strategy while interacting with the "Read Ahoy!" installation. They were looking for the specific books they were asked to find and although they could get sidetracked by other books encountered on the way and more to their personal liking, they continued until they found what they wanted. Not all children sat down to read the books they found: instead they wanted to repeat the experience and find the next "lost book" for the Viking crew. However, the proportion of children actually spending time reading or exploring the books themselves was considered to be fairly good by the librarians.

Library employees mentioned the fact that the installation itself was, in their opinion, extremely light in technology and heavy in narrative aspects and spatial engagement. This was not seen as a negative, but rather as a positive. Initial presentations, before "Read Ahoy!" was installed in the library, had led them to believe that managing the technical aspects of an installation of this sort required thorough "computer skills" they feared they did not possess. They were happy this proved not to be the case and that the basic instructions they received to restart or reset the "story box" and "salute screen" were effectively all they needed, so they could focus on the interactions they had with the children and that the children had with the narrative and the tasks it required them. This is an important lesson for digital/physical installations of this type and something important to consider whenever designing information-based experience ecosystems: the interplay of the different elements in the ecosystem and the environment itself, the topology of the blended space of action [3], should be used to create meaningful narrative pathways that support actors achieve their desired future state. In this process, all technology is a support layer, and its use is not a goal per se: quite the contrary, minimizing it creates a more inclusive experience.

7 Conclusions

The "Read Ahoy!" Project was framed to address the UN SDG4's sub-targets on "Early childhood development"and "Universal Youth Literacy". The installation was conceptually framed through the theories of information seeking, blended spaces, and information based experience ecosystems. The narrative structure was revised from its initial nondescript fairy tale forest settings and centered on a story more familiar to Swedish children, that of a Viking crew on their way back home from a trading journey. This generated changes in the physical and conceptual architecture of the experience, with the original luminous trails leading to books becoming a treasure map-like criss-crossing between chests of books floating on the water.

Children found the experience to be fun and engaging: the interactions with the Viking crew, through the story, the videos, and the physical props, were the primary motivation to go searching for the books. As a proof of concept, "Read Ahoy!" showed potential in assisting children to learn about the relationship between books, libraries, and categorization, in a structured manner conveyed through narrative and play. It did not provide reflections on the activities carried out, as this was left to the supervising libraries, but such an addition could be considered for situations where staff is not available, the children are slightly older, or a more reflective approach is desired.

In terms of its ontology and topology, "Read Ahoy!" provided a sound architecture whose elements were well-identifiable as individual constituents while clearly illustrating their relationships. Issues of robustness and solidity of the different physical parts of the installation as reported by the library staff, while always a concern in terms of safety, are mainly a consequence of the experimental nature of the project and, for possible future installations, to be addressed through appropriate budgeting and the employment of skilled craftsmen and builders.

On the other hand, crossing the seam connecting the map displayed on the "story box", the position of the boxes and the keywords, and their physical counterpart represented by the wooden boxes in the library proved to be a challenge in some cases because of reading- and language-related issues. Future installations will need to address this, structuring better seams between the digital and physical parts of the environment. More specific goals or user groups would help clarify what kind of modifications could be necessary. For example, a modification of the age group for whom the experience is being built would mean changes to the level of challenge provided by the search itself: narrowing it towards the higher limit considered so far would require raising it [7, 15], while broadening it down to even smaller children would require a reinforcement of the digital/physical seams leading from the story box to the ship via the boxes, and aural and visual aids, for example in the form or read-alouds and icons, to allow these younger children to play even when their reading skills are limited. As for the library staff, their experience has been a positive one, and happily unencumbered of feared technological issues. As they told the authors, "it has been fun to have the Viking story here. (…) It's (been) a positive experience for us to have been a part of this project and we're definitely open for more collaborations like this in the future."

References

1. Bates, M.J.: The design of browsing and berrypicking techniques for the online search interface. Online Rev. **13**(5), 407–424 (1989). https://doi.org/10.1108/eb024320
2. Bates, M.J.: Toward an integrated model of information seeking and searching. New Rev. Inf. Behav. Res. **3**(1), 1–15 (2002)
3. Benyon, D.: Spaces of Interaction, Places for Experience. Morgan & Claypool, San Rafael (2014)
4. Benyon, D., Mival, O.: Designing blended spaces. In: Proceedings of Designing Collaborative Interactive Spaces (2012). http://hci.uni-konstanz.de/dcis/
5. Benyon, D., Mival, O., O'Keefe, B.: Blended spaces and digital tourism. In: Proceedings of CHI 2013 Workshop on Blended Interaction Spaces (2013)
6. Benyon, D., Resmini, A.: User experience in cross-channel ecosystems. In: Proceedings of British HCI 2017 (2017)
7. Csikszentmihalyi, M.: Flow: The Psychology of Optimal Experience. Harper, New York City (2008)
8. ENS Lyon: Umix 2014 par les étudiants du master ArchInfo (2014). http://www.ens-lyon.fr/node/244855
9. Fauconnier, G., Turner, M.: The Way We Think: Conceptual Blending and the Mind's Hidden Complexities. Basic Books, New York City (2002)
10. Fullerton, T.: Game Design Workshop. Morgan Kaufmann, Burlington (2008)
11. Gharajedaghi, J.: Systems thinking: a case for second-order-learning. Learn. Organiz. **14**(6), 473–479 (2007). https://doi.org/10.1108/09696470710825088
12. Gitz, R.: Har näst yngst befolkning. SVT1 Rapport, 17 February. https://www.svtplay.se/video/25367619/rapport/rapport-17-feb-19-30-5

13. Gray, D., Brown, S., Macanufo, J.: Gamestorming. O'Reilly Media, Newton (2010)
14. Hutchins, E.: Material anchors for conceptual blends. J. Pragmat. **37**(10), 1555–1577 (2005). https://doi.org/10.1016/j.pragma.2004.06.008
15. Levin Gelman, D.: Designing for Kids. Rosenfeld Media, New York (2014)
16. Lindenfalk, B., Resmini, A.: Mapping an ambient assisted living service as a seamful cross-channel ecosystem. In: Pfannstiel, M., Rasche, C. (eds.) Service Design and Service Thinking in Healthcare and Hospital Management, pp. 289–314. Springer, Cham (2019). https://doi.org/10.1007/978-3-030-00749-2_17
17. Quintarelli, E., Resmini, A., Rosati, L.: The FaceTag engine. In: Zambelli, M., Janowiak, A., Neuckermans, H. (eds.) Browsing Architecture: Metadata and Beyond, pp. 204–217. Fraunhofer IRB Verlag (2008)
18. Resmini, A., Lacerda, F.: The architecture of cross-channel ecosystems. In: Proceedings of the 8th International ACM Conference on Management of Emergent Digital EcoSystems, MEDES 2016 (2016)
19. Resmini, A., Rosati, L.: Information architecture for ubiquitous ecologies. In: Proceedings of the International Conference on Management of Emergent Digital EcoSystems, MEDES 2009, pp. 196–199 (2009). https://doi.org/10.1145/1643823.1643859
20. United Nations: Sustainable Development Goals (2015). https://sustainabledevelopment.un.org/

Toward Inclusive Learning: Designing and Evaluating Tangible Programming Blocks for Visually Impaired Students

Zhiyi Rong, Ngo Fung Chan, Taizhou Chen, and Kening Zhu[✉]

City University of Hong Kong, Kowloon, Hong Kong
zingaiyung@hotmail.com, hugochan525@gmail.com,
taizhou.chen@my.cityu.edu.hk, keninzhu@cityu.edu.hk

Abstract. Tangible programming toolkits are widely used to nurture computational literacy in the young generation. However, novice learners with visual impairment have been neglected as these toolkits are primarily designed for sighted students, and mostly rely on visual cues in the whole manipulation process. To fill this gap, we present CodeRhythm (Fig. 1), a tangible programming toolkit for engaging blind and visually impaired (BVI) students to learn basic programming concepts by creating simple melodies. In this paper, we describe the design features of CodeRhythm and discuss the feedback and future improvement based on the preliminary user study.

Keywords: Accessibility · Tangible user interfaces · Computer-science education · Inclusive design

1 Introduction

Over the past decade, learning programming is no longer a priority of only a small group of people. Block-base programming language is becoming incrementally pervasive in schools, for example, Scratch [18] and Alice [14], empowering students to think creatively and systematically. Meanwhile, tangible user interfaces (TUIs) [11] have demonstrated their benefits to design iteration [5, 7], digital fabrication [19], and digital entertainment [21, 22]. Especially with the application of TUIs for Education, some new possibilities and definitions were added to block-based programming language, which provided effective and inviting pathways for programming constructs learning [4, 8–10, 23].

To realize the educational aim of supporting engagement and diversity, more and more effort has been made to engage students with special educational needs to learn basic programming knowledge. However, the early kids-coding toolkits did not pay specific consideration to novice learners with visual disability, since existing programming toolkits are primarily targeted for sighted students, who rely on visual cues to manipulate the system and experience the visual outcome. While some researchers started to develop programming-learning systems that are inclusive for learners with visual disability [2, 13], these systems are developed for BVI users with prior programming skills, which may result in barriers for novice BVI learners.

M. Kurosu (Ed.): HCII 2020, LNCS 12183, pp. 326–338, 2020.
https://doi.org/10.1007/978-3-030-49065-2_23

Fig. 1. CodeRhythm is a tangible programming toolkit for engaging blind and visually impaired (BVI) students to learn basic programming concepts by creating simple melodies.

To fill this gap, we present CodeRhythm, a tangible programming toolkit for engaging visually impaired students to learn fundamental programming concepts by creating a simple melody. We adopt the form factor of blocks as fundamental elements to represent codes. The whole toolkit contains a set of blocks comprising tangible syllables blocks - do, re, mi, fa, so, la, ti - and several distinctive function blocks, representing the programming concepts of execution, looping, conditional branching. In the rest of the paper, we will first discuss the background of tangible educational toolkits and accessible programming tools, describe the design features of CodeRhythm, and discuss the feedback and future improvement by the preliminary user study.

2 Background

2.1 Inclusive and Accessible Programming Tool

Researchers have started to explore different approached to introduce BVI students with programming. Bigham et al. [2] studied engaging students with personalized chatbots to study computer-programming language. Bonk enabled BVI users can create interactive and accessible audio games [14]. StructJumper [1] was created to help blind users quickly navigate the code with the assistant of audio cues and shortcuts. Another approach emphasizes on integrating digital fabrication, for example, 3D printing [13] into the instruction for BVI students by writing the Ruby program. These tools are beneficial to BVI users with programming skills and Braille literacy; however, they are too complicated and confusing for novice learners such as children.

2.2   Block-Based Graphical and Tangible Programming Tools

Scratch [18] is one of the most widely used block-based languages around the world, which aims at nurturing children with computational thinking through the Scratch Online Community [3]. Other educational tools such as Code.org [12] also provide a similar learning pathway using block-base language. However, these learning tools highly rely on visual properties and inaccessible for BVI users. Tangible tools have been paving an alternative and inviting pathway for learning computational constructs. Strawbies [10] utilized computer vision to capture the blocks assembled by children, and then control the game character in iPad. Tern [9] explored to control a moving robot by capturing the instruction of woodblocks. While BVI users can possibly distinguish the blocks by different shapes, these toolkits are still highly reliant on visual activities, for example, seeing feedback from the screen.

To address this issue, some effort has been made to address these tangible blocks to enable BVI children to learn basic programming literacy by connecting cables between blocks and creating audio feedback, such as Totino [17, 19]. While connecting cables and sockets may place challenges to young BVI users whose body and spatial awareness may be affected [6], CodeRhythm uses embedded magnets to connect the blocks rather than cables which make users confused about cable's direction and struggle to assemble. Our preliminary user study suggested that using magnets as the connection is helpful and preferred by BVI users. In addition, compared to existing musical programming blocks, which may only play the melody after full assembly, each syllable block of CodeRhythm can provide independent audio feedback as a complement to the tactile patterns, helping users distinguish syllable blocks. We also design the push-and-pull feature for adjusting the duration parameter of syllable, providing more variation on the sound-based programming. Lastly, CodeRhythm comprise more diverse functions, such as Switch function, which is not utilized in Torino, to provide a more inviting and diverse combination of tangible blocks. We address these features as complementary approaches to a similar challenge.

3   System Overview

CodeRhythm contains two categories of blocks: syllable blocks - do, re, mi, fa, so, la, ti, and distinctive function blocks – Start, Switch, Loop, Pause (Fig. 2). All of the blocks are connected by magnetic force. Each syllable block represents a specific note in the melody, and the user can directly control the parameter value of duration by pulling and pushing a protruding cube on the top of each syllable block (Fig. 3). The syllable block houses an Arduino Mini board and speaker module, which controls the block independently, enabling the user to experience the audio feedback immediately without connecting all sets of blocks. The Start block acts as an execution block, which locates on the left side of the overall sequence. The button on the top side allows users to initiate the program. Switch Block is designed to create the conditional branching function, which enables the user to choose different programming paths by controlling the knitter switch on the top of the block. The function of the Loop block is intended to repeat the syllable blocks attached to it. Pause block could be used with syllable blocks to set a duration of pause between them.

IMAGE OF BLOCK											
NAME OF BLOCK	Do	Re	Mi	Fa	So	La	Ti	Pause	Play	Switch	Loop
DESCRIPTION OF BLOCK	Represent Note - Do	Represent Note - Re	Represent Note - Mi	Represent Note - Fa	Represent Note - So	Represent Note - La	Represent Note - Ti	Represent Pause Between Notes	Act as Execution Function	Act as Conditional Branching Function	Act as Repetition Function

Fig. 2. CodeRhythm contains two categories of blocks: syllable blocks - do, re, mi, fa, so, la, ti, and distinctive function blocks – Start, Switch, Loop, Pause

Fig. 3. Each syllable block represents a specific note in the melody, and the user can directly control the parameter value of duration by pulling and pushing a protruding cube on the top of each syllable block

4 Inclusive Design Features

In our inclusive tangible learning system, each block represents one line of code. Since our toolkit is designed for BVI students, it is significant to lower the usability burden as much as possible. That is, make the identity of each block be distinguished easily and clearly, and make the assembly process as convenient as possible. In the following part, we will highlight and describe several inclusive design features of CodeRhythm.

4.1   Clear Embodiment of Block Character

We choose cubic block as a primary design metaphor because the flat interface of the cubic block can be combined quickly and adequately with the embed magnet. Also, this cubic metaphor can make the overall toolkit congruent in form factor. The Start block is a single cubic block, and the Syllable block has a protruding cube on the top, which can be pulled and push (Fig. 4). For the Switch Blocks, we use one block as an original block and two small blocks as end blocks, which connected with physical cables, to show the conditional branching action in a tangible way. For the Loop block, we use a cable to combine the start block and end block, indicating that the syllable blocks set between the two blocks would be manipulated to repeat. As a result, BVI users can distinguish the primary function of each type of block easily and quickly.

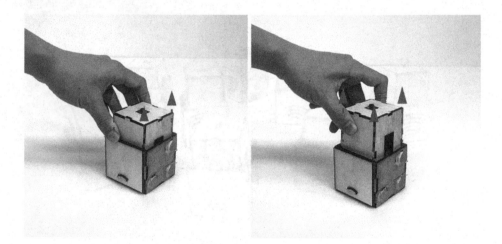

Fig. 4. Syllable block has a protruding cube on the top, which can be pulled and push.

4.2 Assistive Block Connection

Wire connection often causes BVI users to struggle to locate where they should plug the wire into sockets. It also disables them to distinguish if the direction of the wire is right. In contrast to using the wire as connection of blocks, each of the block in our system is connected by the embed magnet inside the interface. Regarding the signal transmission issue, we choose conductive tape as the medium. The conductive tape is attached to the block's surface, which performs well in transmitting the signal when we conduct experiments and user tests.

One of the essential advantages is that with the use of the magnet, we can decrease the difficulty of connection as much as possible (Fig. 5). In this way, the user can assemble two blocks if the direction of embedded magnets matches. The magnetic force also acts as an indication of the correct connection for BVI users. (Otherwise, two blocks with the wrong connection would repulse each other.)

Fig. 5. A figure caption is always placed below the illustration. Short captions are centered, while long ones are justified. The macro button chooses the correct format automatically.

Another advantage is that using magnet and conductive tape as a connection method can shorten the connection length compared to wire connection. In this way, the connected blocks would form a continuous interface, enabling BVI users to follow and trace the tactile patterns rapidly.

4.3 Identify Block's Function by Tactile and Audio Feedback

Touching and recognizing tactile patterns is one of the essential ways for BVI users to distinguish blocks. Since not all children learn to read Braille, we design the easily distinguish symbols as the tactile patterns and attach them to the surface of corresponding blocks. For instance, we use a triangle as the symbol of the Start function, and we use two arrows pointing to different directions to represent the Switch function.

Besides the tactile patterns, to create a more inviting and efficient interaction mechanism for the syllable block, we install an Arduino Mini board and speaker module into the block, which controls the block independently, enabling the user to experience the audio feedback immediately without connecting all set of blocks (Fig. 6). For example, the BVI user can pick up a syllable block, touch the tactile pattern on it and recognize which note it represents, and press the bottom on the top side to listen to the sound of the note immediately. At the same time, the user can also push or pull the protruding box to experience the duration of the note immediately. With the combination of tactile and audio sensation, CodeRhythm creates a more exciting and intuitive interaction mechanism, which provides a complementary approach to the blocks with only tactile function.

Fig. 6. We install an Arduino Mini board and speaker module into the block, which controls the block independently, enabling the user to experience the audio feedback immediately without connecting all set of blocks.

Fig. 7. We are developing and testing the recording block, which can record and replay sound that the user intent to customize. Engage Diverse Users for Collaboration

4.4 Possibility of Personalization and Customization

In addition to designing and developing syllable blocks whose duration can be adjustable, we also consider creating blocks that can provide a personalized and customized interaction experience. Currently, we are developing and testing the recording block (Fig. 7), which can record and replay sound that the user intent to customize. Mixing a recording block with syllable blocks can enable a more flexible interaction scenario and cultivate user's creativity.

Although CodeRhythm is designed for BVI students, we still want to make it as inclusive as possible, that is, engaging more diverse users in the learning process. Since the tactile symbols in our system are from ordinary and simple visual elements, they are also accessible for sighted students. Thus it provides an inclusive learning environment in which BVI students and sighted students can manipulate the toolkit collaboratively.

Fig. 8. The preliminary user study was conducted in a Special Education Needs Room of a University's library.

5 Preliminary User Feedback

5.1 Procedure

The initial prototype was demonstrated to a 30-year-old female with visual disability who was a BVI educator with a specialization in the music field and a female BVI student majoring in marketing. The preliminary user study was conducted in a Special Education Needs Room of a University's library (Fig. 8). The researchers first introduced the idea and goal of CodeRhythm and explained the function of each block. During this introduction session, researchers encouraged the participants to pick up each type of block, touch, and interact with it. Then the participants were told to connect Start Block and one of the syllable blocks, which enabled the users to create the first and basic program intuitively.

After the brief introduction, the researchers picked up one Start Block and two syllable blocks, connecting them with Switch and Loop Block, respectively. As a

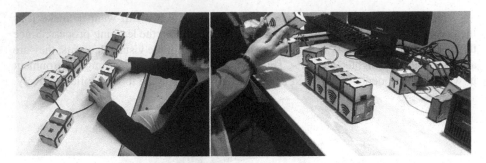

Fig. 9. The participants are using CodeRhythm to create melodies.

result, two different simple melodies were created, which introduced the participant how these two functions work in the program. In this process, the participants were told to touch and experience these two sequences of blocks.

In the next part, the researchers assemble a Start block, five syllable blocks, a Switch block, and a Loop block, to demonstrate a more diverse melody for participants. After experiencing and interacting with the overall effect of blocks, the participants were encouraged to create a personalized melody with assembling any types of blocks. In the end, we interviewed the participants about the usability challenge, the key advantages of the toolkit, and potential improvement in the future (Fig. 9).

5.2   Finding

In the experience process, the participants were able to assemble blocks to create a simple melody successfully. Also, the participants could connect blocks easily without much hesitation and exploration. When tracing the block sequence by touching, the participants were able to distinguish the different characteristics of each type of block clearly.

In the interview session, both of the participants commented that the experience was fun and inviting. Notably, they thought the audio feedback, which matched the tactile pattern on the syllable blocks, was surprising and helpful. Regarding the connection with magnet and conductive tape, the participants appraised that it was beneficial and eliminated the exploration time.

> *"The magnets help a lot. Now I can connect blocks without hesitation"* - Educator Participant
> *"It is so cool to connect blocks quickly."* – Student Participant

Also, the educator participant noted that we could also utilize the toolkit to help BVI students understand electric literacy since the connection was one of the significant parts of electric, and our method of using magnet and conductive tape performed well in decreasing the connection difficulties.

> *"Connecting blocks has the similar experience of connecting circuit. I think your toolkits could also be used for teaching BVI students the electric literacy."*

Regarding the tactile pattern design, the student participant suggested that we can develop different versions of the tactile patterns for BVI students with distinctive cognition ability.

"I think you could use English alphabet patterns for students who have learned English and music literacy, and adopt different numbers of curves to represent specific notes in melody for students with young ages."

The student participant also said that our toolkits reminded her of the experience of her childhood, in which she was the only BVI student in class. Regarding this learning experience, she pointed out that CodeRhythm had the potential to enable sighted students and BVI students to learn together and play together, which could help BVI students to integrate with society.

"More and more BVI students have been getting access to education. As a BVI student, I think it is necessary to learn everything about the world and integrate with society. Thus the ideal learning product is the one that could enable sighted students and BVI students to learn together and play together. I can see the great potential of CodeRhythm."

The participants mentioned that mastering all of the concepts and functions and manipulating them in a short time was challenging and difficult, which required high-level cognitive ability. Regarding this challenge, the participants suggested that it was better to design a well-structured and detailed curriculum and applied it to a workshop of multiple sessions.

"Since there are various functions of blocks, I think it is challenging for young students to learn so much content in a short time. You know, it requires a high cognition ability. Maybe some divided class would seem more reasonable."- Educator Participant
"I think you can design a well-structured curriculum, such as teaching how to use Syllable Blocks in the first class, then teaching Switch function in the next class, etc." - Student Participant

For the improvement of expressiveness, the educator participant suggested that we can add some more diverse and personalized tunes to provide a more compelling and exciting experience.

"Maybe you can add more possibilities to the blocks. More tunes seem better. And you can even design a recording blocks to record and replay various sounds."

Regarding the educational goal of CodeRhythm, the educator participant noted that it was useful and inviting to learn the basic and simple concept, but not proper enough for learning the advanced and traditional computational literacy.

"The toolkit is so interesting, and I think it is an inviting learning toys for young children. But it seems unnecessary for the BVI people who want to learn formal computer science."

Regarding the same question, the student participants said that our toolkit was so attractive that she would like to play with it and listen to the melodies, even though she did not intend to learn programming literacy.

"You know, it is satisfying enough for BVI people to build some toy blocks line by line because we cannot see what the blocks look like. However, when I play with your toolkit, I feel surprised, because the audio feedbacks of blocks create a new interaction experience for BVI people to play with blocks. I want to combine different blocks to get various audio feedbacks."

6 Conclusion and Future Work

We present CodeRhythm, a tangible programming toolkit for engaging blind and visually impaired (BVI) students to learn basic computational concepts by creating simple melodies. Our preliminary user study shows that CodeRhythm is an inviting and inclusive toolkit to learn computational concepts, which decreases the usability burden as much as possible. In the future, we will design and incorporate a well-structured and detailed curriculum into workshops of multiple sessions to teach BVI students computational thinking with CodeRhythm systematically. We will also develop blocks with more various tunes and blocks with recording and replaying functions to expand the expressiveness of CodeRhythm. Moreover, we will try to apply CodeRhythm in the inclusive learning environment where sighted students and BVI students can learn together and play together. While our toolkit is designed for learning computational thinking, we are pleased to see the potential for incorporating CodeRhythm into electric literacy teaching for BVI students.

Acknowledgement. This research was supported by the Young Scientists Scheme of the National Natural Science Foundation of China (Project No. 61907037), and the Centre for Applied Computing and Interactive Media (ACIM) of School of Creative Media, City University of Hong Kong. We thank the participants who took part in the user evaluation. We are also grateful for the help of Steve Ching and Shanshan Jiang.

References

1. Baker, C.M., Milne, L.R., Ladner, R.E.: StructJumper: a tool to help blind programmers navigate and understand the structure of code. In: Proceedings of the 33rd Annual ACM Conference on Human Factors in Computing Systems, CHI 2015, pp. 3043–3052 (2015). https://doi.org/10.1145/2702123.2702589
2. Bigham, J.P., Aller, M.B., Brudvik, J.T., Leung, J.O., Yazzolino, L.A., Ladner, R.E.: Inspiring blind high school students to pursue computer science with instant messaging chatbots. In: Proceedings of the 39th SIGCSE Technical Symposium on Computer Science Education, SIGCSE 2008, pp. 449–453 (2008). https://doi.org/10.1145/1352135.1352287
3. Brennan, K., Resnick, M.: New frameworks for studying and assessing the development of computational thinking. In: AERA 2012, pp. 1–25 (2012). http://scratched.gse.harvard.edu/ct/files/AERA2012.pdf. Accessed 18 Sept 2017
4. Buechley, L., Eisenberg, M., Catchen, J., Crockett, A.: The LilyPad Arduino: using computational textiles to investigate engagement, aesthetics, and diversity in computer science education. In: Proceedings of the SIGCHI Conference on Human Factors in Computing Systems, CHI 2009, pp. 423–432. ACM, New York (2009). https://doi.org/10.1145/1357054.1357123
5. Chen, T., Wu, Y.S., Zhu, K.: DupRobo: interactive robotic autocompletion of physical block-based repetitive structure. In: Lamas, D., Loizides, F., Nacke, L., Petrie, H., Winckler, M., Zaphiris, P. (eds.) INTERACT 2019. LNCS, vol. 11747, pp. 475–495. Springer, Cham (2019). https://doi.org/10.1007/978-3-030-29384-0_29
6. Coleman, J.M.: The use of music to promote purposeful movement in children with visual impairments. J. Vis. Impair. Blindness **111**(1), 73–77 (2017)

7. Dancu, A., et al.: Emergent interfaces: constructive assembly of identical units. In: Proceedings of the 33rd Annual ACM Conference Extended Abstracts on Human Factors in Computing Systems, CHI EA 2015, pp. 451–460. Association for Computing Machinery, New York (2015). https://doi.org/10.1145/2702613.2732509
8. Horn, M.S., Jacob, R.J.K.: Tangible programming in the classroom with Tern. In: CHI 2007 Extended Abstracts on Human Factors in Computing Systems, CHI EA 2007, pp. 1965–1970. ACM, New York (2007). https://doi.org/10.1145/1240866.1240933
9. Horn, M.S., Solovey, E.T., Crouser, R.J., Jacob, R.J.K.: Comparing the use of tangible and graphical programming languages for informal science education. In: Proceedings of the SIGCHI Conference on Human Factors in Computing Systems, CHI 2009, pp. 975–984. ACM, New York (2009). https://doi.org/10.1145/1518701.1518851
10. Hu, F., Zekelman, A., Horn, M., Judd, F.: Strawbies: explorations in tangible programming. In: Proceedings of the 14th International Conference on Interaction Design and Children, IDC 2015, pp. 410–413. ACM, New York, (2015). http://dx.doi.org/10.1145/2771839.2771866
11. Ishii, H.: The tangible user interface and its evolution. Commun. ACM 51(6), 32–36 (2008). https://doi.org/10.1145/1349026.1349034
12. Kalelioglu, F.: A new way of teaching programming skills to K-12 students: Code. org. Comput. Hum. Behav. 52, 200–210 (2015)
13. Kane, S.K., Bigham, J.P.: Tracking @Stemxcomet: teaching programming to blind students via 3D printing, crisis management, and all Twitter. In: Proceedings of the 45th ACM Technical Symposium on Computer Science Education, SIGCSE 2014, pp. 247–252 (2014). https://doi.org/10.1145/2538862.2538975
14. Kane, S.K., Koushik, V., Muehlbradt, A.: Bonk: accessible programming for accessible audio games. In: Proceedings of the 17th ACM Conference on Interaction Design and Children, IDC 2018, pp. 132–142. ACM, New York (2018). https://doi.org/10.1145/3202185.3202754
15. Kelleher, C., Pausch, R., Kiesler, S.: Storytelling Alice motivates middle school girls to learn computer programming. In: Proceedings of the SIGCHI Conference on Human Factors in Computing Systems, CHI 2007, pp. 1455–1464. ACM, New York (2007). https://doi.org/10.1145/1240624.1240844
16. Ladner, R.E.: Design for user empowerment. Interactions 22(2), 24–29 (2015). https://doi.org/10.1145/2723869
17. Morrison, C., et al.: Torino: a tangible programming language inclusive of children with visual disabilities. Hum.-Comput. Interact. (2018). https://doi.org/10.1080/07370024.2018.1512413
18. Resnick, M., et al.: Scratch: programming for all. Commun. ACM 52(11), 60–67 (2009). https://doi.org/10.1145/1592761.1592779
19. Thieme, A., Morrison, C., Villar, N., Grayson, M., Lindley, S.: Enabling collaboration in learning computer programming inclusive of children with vision impairments. In: Proceedings of the 2017 Conference on Designing Interactive Systems, DIS 2017, pp. 739–752. ACM, New York (2017). https://doi.org/10.1145/3064663.3064689
20. Zhu, K., Dancu, A., (Shen) Zhao, S.: FusePrint: a DIY 2.5D printing technique embracing everyday artifacts. In: Proceedings of the 2016 ACM Conference on Designing Interactive Systems, DIS 2016, pp. 146–157. Association for Computing Machinery, New York (2016). https://doi.org/10.1145/2901790.2901792

21. Zhu, K., Chen, T., Han, F., Wu, Y.-S.: HapTwist: creating interactive haptic proxies in virtual reality using low-cost twistable artefacts. In: Proceedings of the 2019 CHI Conference on Human Factors in Computing Systems, CHI 2019, pp. 1–13. Association for Computing Machinery, New York (2019). Paper 693. https://doi.org/10.1145/3290605.3300923

22. Zhu, K., Nii, H., Fernando, O.N.N., Cheok, A.D.: Selective inductive powering system for paper computing. In: Proceedings of the 8th International Conference on Advances in Computer Entertainment Technology, ACE 2011, pp. 1–7. Association for Computing Machinery, New York (2011). Article 59. https://doi.org/10.1145/2071423.2071497

23. Zhu, K., Ma, X., Wong, G.K.W., Huen, J.M.H.: How different input and output modalities support coding as a problem-solving process for children. In: Proceedings of the The 15th International Conference on Interaction Design and Children, IDC 2016, pp. 238–245. Association for Computing Machinery, New York (2016). https://doi.org/10.1145/2930674.2930697

Improvised Music for Computer and Augmented Guitar: Performance with Gen~ Plug-ins

Scott L. Simon[✉]

Adelaide, Australia

Abstract. This paper focuses on creating custom plug-ins for guitar augmentation with the Gen~ Max/MSP environment. The plug-ins are utilised in performance and compositional settings with electronic or electro-acoustic music. The author has programmed and used such plug-ins in various settings. Such plug-ins offer a unique and flexible aesthetic solution for music performances and studio recording.

Keywords: Max/MSP · Audio plug-ins · Electronic music · Improvisation

1 Introduction

The paper will describe an approach to music performances that combine traditional instruments with computer processes. In particular the focus will be on performances with the guitar. In the everyday practice of the author various strategies are used to achieve aesthetic goals, utilising software such as Gen~ (Max/MSP), SuperCollider, Processing and Open Frameworks. Some of those programs are specifically formed for music making, others are used to integrate diverse media into the performance process.

There are a multitude of performance options open to this type of artist, and within each option there are many components and functional aspects. In this paper I will focus on one particular component of a performance - the augmenting/effecting of the guitar signal. This is an interesting and important aspect of constructing a performance, and it has the quality of being vital to any particular performance for the present author.

We will describe the construction of sound palettes through augmenting and effecting the electric guitar. This will be formulated in relation to Gen~ (Max/MSP), a program that can be utilised within various software and hardware environments [1]. To name three such environments: (1) Ableton Live (a DAW that has customisable plug-ins produced as "Max for Live" devices); (2) Mod Devices "MOD Duo" (an audio processor/effects pedal that can be programmed using Gen~), and; (3) Rebel Technology's "OWL Pedal" (a guitar effect that can be programmed using Gen~).

I will mostly reference the first 2 environments as I am more familiar with them. In any case, using a particular environment does not change any of the Gen~

S. L. Simon—Freelance Creative Technologist.

M. Kurosu (Ed.): HCII 2020, LNCS 12183, pp. 339–349, 2020.
https://doi.org/10.1007/978-3-030-49065-2_24

programming, but each environment has pros and cons in relation to performance logistics. In what follows most of the discussion is focused upon Gen~ itself.

2 Electronic Music and Guitar

Using a traditional instrument in electronic and experimental music performances is a wide-spread practice, as many electronic artists continue to enjoy the control over gesture (in relation to musical expression) that a traditional instrument affords. There is a history of utilising different instruments within electronic music, often augmenting the sound of the instrument itself through some type of processing. A well known guitarist who works in this way is Robert Fripp [2]. Fripps "soundscapes" involve recording elements of live guitar and slowly augmenting the sounds through processing.

In the case of the present author the use of the guitar gives access to an improvisational tool with endless possibilities. The freedom of expression possible with the guitar is a vital aspect for a personal aesthetic in relation to composing, performing and recording. In some pieces I retain the un-effected guitar as a human element within the electronic world, in other pieces the guitar itself is deconstructed through processing. An example of both of these approaches within the same work is "Zonal" [3]. In that work the guitar is introduced and then decimated through multi-effects application - becoming a type of background feedback.

There is a need sometimes in performances to control the timbre of the guitar, and change its tone in some way. It is sometimes desirable to completely decimate the instrument's sound, or to have it "become" a synthesiser. In relation to synthesis: for artists that use a keyboard it is easy to use Midi as a way of unlocking new sounds. A guitar is slightly different beast - the tracking of plucked string and fretted note via Midi is often difficult. I have used some of the solutions offered by various technology companies and none has been entirely satisfactory. In general I have used signal processing to effect or augment the guitar signal rather than using it as a trigger for synthesis. In this paper a couple of concrete examples of plug-ins constructed by the author.

As noted the timbre and tone of the guitar can be manipulated through audio effects. However it is worth noting that the ultimate goal of the research also includes synthesised sound controlled by the guitar. In Sect. 4 of this paper a brief discussion of using audio buffers for real-time sound manipulation is presented. Utilising audio samples for granulation processes goes beyond a guitar effect and becomes a type of synthesis in its own right.

In relation to providing a personal "rationale" for the work, it is surely the "uniqueness" of the individual plug-ins. The use of Gen~ as the programming language - in relation to any of the hardware devices available - allows fine-grained control over the sound of the guitar, particularly in relation to timbre and envelope. Such control lends itself to the creation of "unique" sonic qualities - qualities that cannot be achieved with standard effects (pedals or DAW software).

3   Custom Plug-ins

I will dive straight into the creation of simple plug-ins here using Gen~. Some knowledge of Gen~ is an advantage here, and at the very least Max/MSP. However the signal processing aspects of the plug-ins and the general structure of the plug-ins, are of course not dependent on this environment.

Vanilla guitar effects are ones like phasing, chorus and flanging. These effects are both widely used and easy to understand. They also add a wealth of tonal variation to the sound that the artist is producing. In working with Gen~ I started on the path with effects like these. However I quickly moved to "hybrid" versions of these effects, versions in which some internal audio process or control process is used to manipulate or modulate the parameters of the effect.

In its basic form such dynamic modulation is like turning the knobs on a guitar effect pedal to create movement and introduce interaction. Some guitar effects (pedals) also allow such modulation to be controlled via Midi. Here, within the Gen~ environment, such modulation is achieved with different control signals (like a Phasor or Sine Oscillator). Note I did not write "control rate" signals here - everything in Gen~ happens in relation to single samples at audio rate. This fact makes using Gen~ slightly different from using Max/MSP.

In Max (as distinct from Gen~) one can send messages and use "counters" that run at different speeds in relation to Milliseconds (using a "metro" object). Audio elements and signals are processed in "blocks" of samples (64 samples is a popular block size). One can still have a counter in Gen~ but it is at audio rate, and thus it spits out a number 44100 times in a second (at a sample rate of 44100). This is not really a major issue but it requires a slight re-think when moving from Max to Gen~.

At this point we can move to some concrete examples. A first example is that of a modulated (process driven) flanger/chorus effect. I also added some waveshaping on some of the lines to introduce some distortion. An analysis of this hybrid effect will reveal some of the strategies required for constructing a Gen~ plug-in for the guitar.

First, if we take a look at a couple of wave scopes in the figure below (Fig. 1), we can clearly see signal shaping in action. A simple sawtooth wave has a modulated chorus/flanger and overdrive applied. Listening to the signal it has the typical "chorusing" sound, and in addition a modulated component - a motion process within the effect. The modulation is applied within the plug-in and compiled as part of it, in this case the "depth" and "speed" of the effect are modulated. A more detailed analysis of the code used will be provided in Sect. 3.1 below.

With this plug-in, tested in the Max environment first with the sawtooth wave, we then move the code to the hardware device. In this case the Mod Devices "Mod Duo". The translation of such effects to guitar might not always be ideal or successful (aesthetically speaking) - a bit of trial and error is involved. Some of the compiled plug-ins I tested on the Mod did not please aesthetically. It can also be quite time consuming testing different iterations. However: on a practical level one does not need to compile and load the patch onto the external hardware at every turn. Instead one can add a .wav file to a Max patch and pass that file into the Gen~ object for testing and debugging purposes. Once a "good" sound is achieved the next step is checking the plug-in with live guitar and hardware.

As we have noted not every effect achieved in Gen will translate well to the signal chain of the guitarist. Guitars are often plugged into amplifiers with valves and this requires a particular type of processing. The advantage of loading the plugins into hardware such as the Mod DUO is that the plug-in does its work in the guitarist's signal chain before hitting the amp (where one might then add reverb and eq). Adding plug-ins after this amplification (as one might do when micing the amplifier and mixing in the DAW) can often be problematic.

Therefore a definite plus of the Mod hardware is that it fits into a "true" signal chain for the guitarist. One is not applying the effect to an amplified signal. Rather the plug-in can be inserted into the chain before amplification (virtual or actual). This is one of the key aspects to such hardware, the artist able to build plugins that can be inserted in a chain with "traditional" pedals.

3.1   Gen~ Programming: Nuts and Bolts

On the following pages a Gen~ patch is provided in full, it depicts one aspect of our hybrid flanger/chorus (Figs. 2 and 3). It is one of the plug-ins that was loaded onto the Mod Device's MOD Duo and tested in a couple of ways. I used this patch on recordings and performance videos and it worked well in aesthetic terms.

A couple of points of interest in the patch diagram: (1) It has a "counter" that was modified from the C74 website. This counter is used as the heart of the control structure of the patch. The counter was originally designed by Gregory Taylor [4]. The counter itself is located in Fig. 1 (it is commented); (2) The counter then feeds some "scale" objects and phasors for our modulation structure. These scaled signals manipulate the delay times of the delay lines. The delayed signals are used in conjunction with the un-delayed signal to give us our chorus and flanger effects.

We use the counter to count up and back in order to create a specific effect. It allows us to keep the phasor frequency going between its end points smoothly without any major jumps. If the counter simply resets every time it hits its maximum it will make the phasor frequency jump back from maximum to minimum. This will in turn increase the likelihood of discontinuities entering into the soundscape.

I have modified the basic counter to do some of the work that we require. As noted the counter element from C74 is in the first diagram (Fig. 1). The C74 counter is scaled and manipulated in the main section of the patch (Fig. 2). Note that the phasor object outputs a normalised phase from its outlet (0–1), and the frequency of this phase is set through left inlet. That frequency is set through a scaled ramp from our counter. The phasor then drives a triangle wave of which we take the absolute value - giving us a positive signal-based envelope. This envelope is utilised to set a delay time. The guitar signal is passed into the delay, and the delayed signal is then mixed with our (un-processed) main signal. The mixture of the 2 signals gives us a chorus or flanger effect (depending on the amount of delay). The effect is constantly in motion as if we were turning the knobs of an effects pedal in real time.

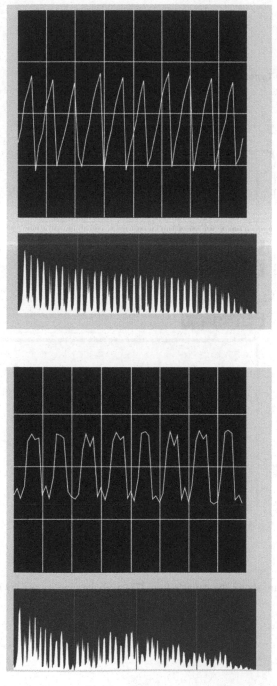

Fig. 1. A sawtooth wave in natural state and passed through Gen~ hybrid Chorus/Flanger.

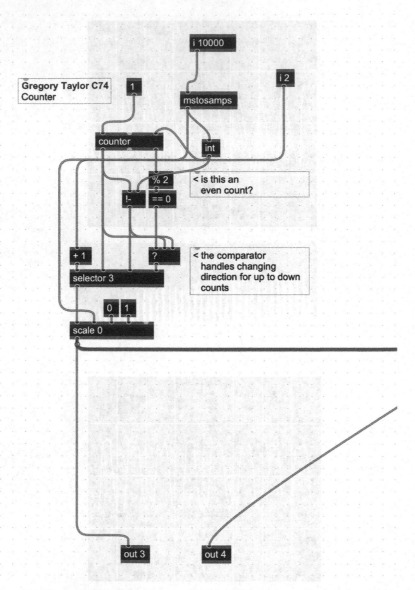

Fig. 2. This figure shows the counter from C74 website, constructed by Gregory Taylor.

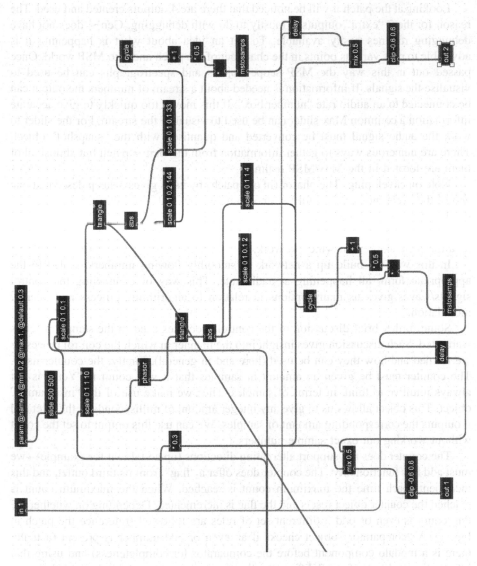

Fig. 3. Patch for process driven hybrid effect, constructed by Scott L. Simon.

Note also the "depth" of the effect is also modulated - this is achieved by multiplying the modulated sine signal (now oscillating between 0 and 1) with our triangle wave that is a ramp going from 0.1 to 2 on one side and 0.1 to 33 on the other. This set of oscillations controls our delay time and gives us the effect of flanging or chorusing (depending on the amount of delay at any given time). The "rate" of chorusing (on the other hand) refers to the speed with which our ramp moves (and if you refer to Fig. 3 it is clear that the red cables carry that [variable] speed).

Looking at the patch it will be noticed that there are 4 outputs created and used. The reason for the 2 "extra" outputs is mostly to do with debugging. Gen ~ does not have debugging routines easily available. To get an idea about what is happening it is advisable to pass various points in the chain out of the patch and into MSP world. Once passed out in this way the MSP scope objects and spectrographs can be used to visualise the signals. If information is needed about a stream of numbers the output can be connected to an audio rate "number box". If this moves too quickly to give accurate information a common Max slider can be used to visualise the stream. For the slider to work the audio signal must be converted and quantised with the "snapshot" object. There are numerous ways to gather information from the Gen ~ patch but almost all of them are located in the Max/MSP realm.

Note on enveloping: The phasor (in our patch) by itself gives a steep descent at one end of the cycle (not very useful for smooth transitions), also it only outputs the phase itself normalised between 0 and 1. We use this phase to feed the triangle object and then use the "abs" object to give us the positive value of the triangle wave. This gives us a ramp/envelope with which to work.

In this way we build up a network of smoothly flowing numbers, scaled to the appropriate form, all happening at audio rate. This way of channeling the control signals/waves gives us many options in relation to algorithmic process and internal modulation.

Some further brief discussion of the control processes used in the sample patch is warranted. Such discussion gives insight into the manner in which the control processes are formed and how they can be used (here and in general). Firstly, the counter itself. The counter must be given an amount in samples that it will count to. Yet it is not always intuitive to think in terms of samples. Thus we make use of the "mstosamps" object. This object allows us to give any integer amount of milliseconds in the inlet and it outputs the corresponding amount of samples. We can use this output to set the count without working out exact sample numbers.

The counter does not support alternating directions (up and down for example) - we must add this functionality. The counter does offer a "flag" from its third outlet, and this increments each time the maximum count is reached. When the maximum count is reached the counter object resets and the flag is incremented. Depending on whether the flag count is even or odd a different set of rules are followed (reference the patch in Fig. 1). A "comparator" object checks if an even or odd number is present (actually there is a modulo component before the comparator for completeness) and using that information it chooses from 2 different options in a selector. One option passes the count in its positive form (0 + 1 up to the maximum sample number) and the other option passes the count *subtracted* from the maximum samples (maximum samples −1 until 0 is reached). The patch switches from one process to the other as the flag changes.

Finally: sonically Gen ~ plugins can be very effective, and theoretically any pedal based effect can be cloned. However it is the control with internal modulation that is of particular interest. In addition to the modulation of delay times in our first example we could - for example - modulate the individual cutoff frequencies of all-pass filters inside a phaser. This allows more control over the motion of the phase dips that are characteristic of a phaser. I have created just such a phaser containing this kind of internal process control, and the singular nature of the resulting sound repays the work.

4 The Buffer Object and Sample Manipulation

Other directions that can be taken include utilising the buffer system in Gen $\sim$ to sample sections of the guitar signal. These buffers can then be used as the basis of granulation processes. Note that ideally this all takes place within the plug-in itself and therefore offers a clean profile in relation to the signal chain.

I have produced a couple of these type of devices in "Max for Live" - it is to be noted however they all use some objects outside of Gen $\sim$. Therefore they can only be said to be prototypes of a completely self sufficient (discrete) plug in. However it would not take too much more work to shift all of the processes into the Gen $\sim$ environment, so I will include some discussion of them here.

The basic idea in our next example is to sample the guitar signal into a buffer, and once captured, do some type of processing upon it. This processed signal can be mixed in with the real time improvisations of the performer. There are various ways to approach this, and one can end up with some type of "looped" effect, or one can use the buffer as a basis for granulation effects or sample-based triggering. In this next example the buffer is used as the basis of a real-time granulator.

In the prototype a basic Gen $\sim$ sampler triggers a random area from the buffer, and this area is multiplied with an envelope - a "window". The window allows for smooth transitions between each triggered sample. This is essential for eradicating clicks and discontinuities from the sounds. Another noteworthy element of the prototype is the fact that it has 4 outputs - each grain is triggered and pushed through a different output in a continuous circular motion. This allows different effects to be put on to different grains. It also has the potential for feeding multi-speaker arrays.

In the present case I made some recordings using different effects on the 4 outputs. The effects are simply added in Max for Live in this prototype, however adding separate effects for multiple outputs is trivial in the Mod Devices Hardware. Indeed with respect to the hardware, there is in fact no need to program each of the effects within a plug-in. The Gen $\sim$ plug-in can be programmed with 4 or 8 outputs and these can be run into any of the library of virtual pedals that the Mod Devices hardware has access to. A plug-in "mixer" then sums the different signals into one and the output of the sound is amplified. The plug-in layout (pictures and description) for the Mod Duo is available on the Mod Devices website [5].

In the present case I ran the outputs into MSP filters loaded into Ableton Live. This gives a good idea of how the system can be used, it is also a valid way to structure a performance in its own right.

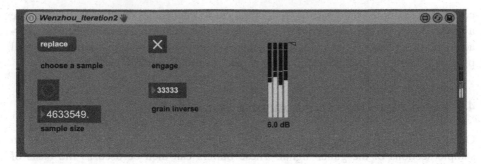

Fig. 4. The user interface for the multi-channel granulator prototype in "Max 4 Live".

Many such applications as the one shown in Fig. 4 can be produced in "Max 4 Live" (M4L) and distributed onto different channels in the DAW mixer. The sampled guitar can be distributed amongst the applications by naming the audio buffers identically. The sampled guitar then appears in each of the applications in the correct buffer awaiting processing or manipulation. Different effects and playback speeds of grains can be used, and one can mix these different channels together to create evolving soundscapes - quite removed from the original guitar sample. Naturally, the source of all the new sounds/textures is the original sample, and this constant aspect adds a continuity to the soundscapes. The artist can construct ambient soundscapes or industrial soundscapes in this way.

An example soundscape is provided as "soundscape 1" [3]. This piece highlights some of the potential directions the process affords. First, a guitar sound is recorded and sections of it are sampled into a buffer. The first manipulation is a random access trigger into the buffer. Each of the triggered grains (triggered slowly at this stage) are also effected and panned differently. The next step involves speeding up the grains and sending each grain to 4 outputs - the M4L application that does this is shown above in Fig. 4. The sound becomes more ambient and atmospheric. At this stage the sound can be treated as a type of drone, effects can be added within the mixer and real-time manipulations can be applied. This can all happen at the level of the DAW channels, with the approach allowing an endless stream of new paths radiating from the origin.

A note on the windowing of the grains: the windowing allows for smooth transitions and allows for very tightly packed, and fast grain triggering. This in turn creates textures that are not achievable through post-processing effects alone. Such textures are suggestive of different forms and spaces, and in "soundscape 1" we can hear the evolving textures becoming more abstract as grains are triggered more quickly and effects applied to some grains and not to others. The last texture in the example file has the quality of rushing air or white noise, and with (a final) additional resonance processing added to this white noise, the texture resonates like glass chimes.

5 Conclusion

We can make a list of the type of jobs that can be done in Gen~ environment in respect to the guitar.

1. Traditional effects (delays, flangers etc.).
2. Hybrid effects that blur the distinction between the different effects.
3. Self-modulating effects, algorithmic effects and process driven effects.
4. Sample based granulation using buffers.
5. Physical modelling within the plug-in's architecture.

In this paper we focused on the construction of hybrid effects in the Gen~ environment and installing these as plug-ins. I also looked at the possibilities of internal algorithmic and control processes that can be built into the plug-ins. Lastly a brief foray into buffer manipulation and granulation of source audio was provided. The augmentation of the guitar with the aid of computer languages and DSP is available to many practitioners through the new crop of hardware devices that will allow the installation of custom plug-ins. The combination of these custom effects with other standard effects can add a unique identifier to an artist's sound. Even without specific hardware, Ableton Live allows Gen~ devices to be built into its audio channels. While the Gen~ language is not easy to learn in some ways, it offers some very interesting possibilities. As Gen~ becomes more widely implemented on hardware it becomes more profitable to put time into acquiring some knowledge of building plug-ins therein.

References

1. Cycling 74. https://cycling74.com/. Accessed 22 Jan 2020
2. Fripp, R.: https://en.wikipedia.org/wiki/Soundscapes_by_Robert_Fripp. Accessed 22 Jan 2020
3. Simon, S.L.: https://sites.google.com/view/documenta-scott-simon/research-papers/media-content-hci-2020. Accessed 22 Jan 2020
4. Taylor, G.: Gen~ for beginners: a place to start. https://cycling74.com/tutorials/gen~-for-beginners-part-1-a-place-to-start. Accessed 22 Jan 2020
5. Mod Devices Plug-in Gallery. https://www.moddevices.com/gear-gallery. Accessed 22 Jan 2020

Product Design Model for E-Commerce Cantonese Porcelain Based on User Perceptual Image in China

Shengyang Zhong, Peng Tan, Tieming Fu, and Yi Ji[✉]

School of Art and Design, Guangdong University of Technology, Yuexiu
District of Dongfeng East Road No. 729, Guangzhou 510000, China
huisaqingchun1993@gmail.com, jiyi001@hotmail.com

Abstract. In recent years, more and more organizations and institutions sell the product of Intangible Cultural Heritage (ICH) to inherit ICH culture and promote local economy in E-commerce. Cantonese Porcelain (CP) is one of ICH in China, and it has gradually shifted sales channels from offline to online. However, it is found that the sales volume has been decreasing steadily through the previous research, which is a challenge for promoting CP's product design and extending CP's market. To address this question, this paper proposes a design model for CP's E-commerce products based on the model of user perceptual image, and proves a adaptive model with a cases study. Literature research of user perceptual image is useful with transferring ICH taxonomy to the related product design, which provide enterprises and designers with the development model and reference of product design. This paper is also conducive to the development and promotion of CP's E-commerce industry.

Keywords: Kansei Engineering · User perceptual image · E-commerce · Cantonese porcelain · Product design model

1 Previous Work

In 2003, UNESCO defined Intangible Cultural Heritage (ICH) as "practices, representations, expressions, knowledge, skills–as well as the instruments, objects, artefacts and cultural spaces associated therewith–that communities, groups, and individuals recognize as part of their cultural heritage" [1]. The safeguarding and promotion of ICH has been a trend in China. In this project, we investigate the design and market of Cantonese Porcelain, one of famous ICH in China, to better inherit and promote it. In our previous research, we have proposed that the CP's E-commerce platform is difficult to match the emotional needs of consumers through diversified products. A method based on Kansei Engineering is proposed to improve the visual presentation of CP's E-commerce platform, so as to increase the sales volume of CP's E-commerce [2].

We selected a popular type of Kansei Engineering called of Kansei Engineering Type I to translate emotional appeal into words that relates to design elements using item/category classification. 100 groups of Kansei words were collected and 15 groups were extracted as representative Kansei words. Then, 18 representative CP samples

© Springer Nature Switzerland AG 2020
M. Kurosu (Ed.): HCII 2020, LNCS 12183, pp. 350–364, 2020.
https://doi.org/10.1007/978-3-030-49065-2_25

were selected and classified according to their visual characteristics from 100 different forms of CP samples. In the experiment stage, 15 groups of selected Kansei words were combined with 18 CP samples, and questionnaires were made based on 5-point semantic differential (SD) scale. Twenty subjects were invited to score Kansei words. As for the results of the questionnaire survey, we obtained the data relationship between Kansei words and samples through the mean value algorithm. Finally, the score results of 15 groups Kansei words were calculated, as shown in Table 1. It can be concluded that the three most representative words of the CP's E-commerce product design are Concrete, Round and Tradition. The following Table 1 gives a summary of all heading levels.

Table 1. Summary of Kansei words group in samples.

Kansei words group	Mean
Modern & Tradition	0.70
Abstract & Concrete	1.01
Decorative & Utility	−0.54
Tech & Handmade	0.63
Round & Sharp	−0.79
Public & Selfhood	0.29
Nature & Man-made	0.33
Streamline & Tough	−0.63
Reason & Sensibility	0.35
Grace & Coarse	−0.54
Fashion & Simple	0.20
Coordinate & Abrupt	−0.30
Implicit & Publicity	0.09
Gorgeous & Frugal	−0.45
Lightweight & Bulky	−0.21

In the end, this study proposes CP's E-commerce selection list based on item/category classification list: Geometry form. Model: Plate, Bowl, Vase. Pattern: Animal, Flower, Landscape. Color: Blue, Cyan, Gold.

We selected all kinds of bottles, plates and bowls from the databases of CP for the modeling design direction of creative products based on the preliminary results. The shapes of different CP samples were extracted, and the results are shown in Table 2. In this table, the shape of the bottle is extracted from the elevation view, and the corresponding axisymmetric graph is finally obtained. The shapes of the plate and bowl are extracted from the top view and elevation view.

The key parts of the extracted shape were marked as deconstruction results of elements of CP's E-commerce product design, as shown in Table 3. In this table, A1–A7 represent the outer shape curve elements of the vise, and the key shape curves have been marked in red. B1–B4 represent the elements of the top view shape curve of the Plate or bowl. C1–C5 represents the shape curve elements of the plate or bowl, and the

Table 2. Extraction of the shape line of Cantonese Porcelain.

category	Model					
Vase						
Plate						
Bowl						

Table 3. Deconstruction table of design elements for CP's E-commerce products.

A1	A2	A3	A4	A5	A6	A7
B1	B2	B3	B4			
C1	C2	C3	C4	C5		
D1	D2	D3	D4			
E1	E2	E3	E4			

key shape curves are also marked in red. The above elements can be used for the overall linear design of CP's E-commerce products. In addition, for the design of the details of the shape of CP's E-commerce products, the typical elements of "Doufang" (a kind of composition element) and "Jindi" (a kind of background) are used to add or guide the details. The most commonly used elements of "Doufang" and "Jindi" are also shown in the table.

2 Situation of CP's E-Commerce Sales

Since the beginning of the 21st century, the development of cultural and creative industries and aesthetic economy have been prevailing all over the world [3]. Cultural and creative industries have fascinating prospects in promoting local trade and economy. It is the core industries in the new economic era, and it have great potential value for many countries or regions. Cultural and creative E-commerce industry is the product of Internet plus traditional cultural and creative industry, which is one of the important directions of cultural and creative industry transformation [4].

To support the inheritance of ICH, E-commerce products with ICH as cultural carrier are constantly being innovated and developed. For example, the design of cultural and creative products with paper-cutting culture as the carrier has deeply carried the visual elements, handicraft and cultural spirit of paper-cutting [5].

CP, also known as "Guangzhou Zhijin Ceramics", is a characteristic decorative porcelain art in Guangzhou. It has enjoyed a high reputation in domestic and abroad, and it was listed as a national intangible cultural heritage in 2008, which has been a significant breakthrough in the inheritance of CP. Emerging technologies have been added to the personalized learning and experience of CP handicraft [6–8]. The offline education classes of CP have also implemented new theories and practices [9]. However, the competition of traditional cultural products is extremely fierce, and the innovation and sales of CP have fallen into a dilemma.

We have collected 20 shops of CP and its cultural and creative products on the typical online sales platform Taobao. It can see that the maximum monthly sales volume did not exceed 10, and even the monthly sales volume of some stores was zero from the six online shops of CP (see Fig. 1). Meanwhile, it can be found that most of the CP cultural and creative products on the market are more decorative than practical products from the four shops of CP cultural and creative products (see Fig. 2), such as decorative paintings.

Product innovations of CP are also found in some public platforms of WeChat. The designers tried to extract the elements of CP and combine them into plane patterns. Then, they pasted these patterns on clothes, handbags, mobile phone shells and other items to design culture and creative products representing CP. The designer also refined the line features of CP to design the shape of the furniture. The surface of these furniture was decorated based on the composition characteristics of CP. Most of these

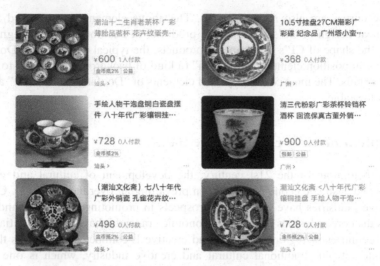

Fig. 1. Online shops of Cantonese Porcelain.

Fig. 2. Online shops of CP cultural and creative products

public platforms are creative attempts made by teachers, students or design enthusiasts in local universities in Guangzhou, which have expanded the development space of CP cultural and creative products. The young generation of designers have provided new opportunities for the development of the CP industry. The dissemination of traditional cultural products need the input of creative talents, and their sales also need a solid industrial foundation and a reliable development model [10]. However, there are still few opportunities for CP cultural and creative products to be put into the market, and there are no prominent advantages in its E-commerce sales. We can find the reasons for this situation through further research on the cultural characteristics of CP and its E-commerce sales. In a competitive market, user preferences and needs are the primary focus of product development [11]. The design of CP cultural and creative products fails to meet users' aesthetic preference and users' demand.

3 A Design Framework Based on User Perceptual Image

Consumers make some associations with products through precepting its forms to generate a series of images in their minds, and describe it with the form of perceptual image words in the era of perceptual consumption. Perceptual image is a kind of psychological reaction to things after information processing of various senses, including a sense of anticipation. Perceptual image is not a simple process of sensory organs producing sensation, but a psychological reaction produced by the brain after comprehensive processing of information. Its formation process includes the generation of perception and cognition and the generation and expression of emotion [12]. At present, the forms of perceptual image mainly include Kansei Engineering, image scale and design research based on user knowledge and design knowledge.

To make products succeed in the fierce market competition in the context of consumer orientation, designers must break through the black-box design mode. Users' subjective and objective needs and other tacit knowledge are transformed into products, which will help designers to design products that meet consumers' preferences and needs by analyzing user perceptual images [13].

In recent years, the application of perceptual images in the design of Chinese traditional cultural products has become more extensive and in-depth, from the research on the cultural characteristics of traditional culture itself to the development of its cultural creative design. S. Zhu et al. simplified the cultural image of Liangzhu artifacts into six recognition dimensions through Kansei Engineering and factor analysis. Secondly, the knowledge base and evaluation system of Liangzhu culture image were constructed, and the perceptual images of different user groups of Liangzhu artifacts were obtained. Finally, turn them into design elements. It provides a new way for computer aided cultural product design [14]. C. Chai et al. combined Jun porcelain elements extracted from perceptual images and visual communication and transformed 3d products into 2d patterns. Firstly, representative samples of Jun porcelain and sensitive words for Jun porcelain were screened out. Then, a 5-point SD scale was used for questionnaire survey. Then, through factor analysis, the sensitive characteristics of Jun porcelain were extracted. Through the analysis of Jun porcelain image, the color, texture and pattern of Jun porcelain were simplified. Then the analytic hierarchy process (APH) was used to analyze the perceptual characteristics of Jun porcelain. Finally, the most representative elements are combined to design a quadrilateral pattern [15]. R. T. Lin et al. drew elements from the lifestyle and cultural spirit of the indigenous people of Taiwan for product design. The representative samples were evaluated by the method of SD scale, and the Kansei words was cluster analyzed. Taking typical artistic features of Paiwan tribal culture as an example, new products containing Paiwan cultural elements are designed from a modern perspective [16].

In this research, the design framework of cultural and creative products was designed for CP's E-commerce products based on the Hybrid Kansei Engineering system (KES) model [17] (see Fig. 3). First, the Kansei words that conforms to consumers' preferences is transformed into design elements. Then, the design elements are transformed into CP's E-commerce products that meet consumers' aesthetic preferences and users' needs, so as to increase the sales volume of CP's E-commerce products. The goal is to enhance consumers' recognition and pursuit of Cantonese Porcelain culture.

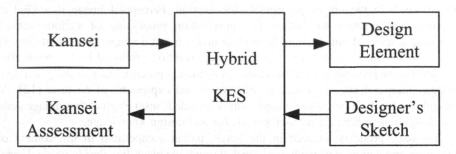

Fig. 3. A schema of hybrid Kansei Engineering system

The new design framework based on Hybrid KES model is carried out at the three levels of instinct, behavior and reflection. The framework of CP cultural and creative product design is proposed (see Fig. 4). This framework contains three parts. It also provides research method and overall design framework. The research methods include three processes. First, cultural features are extracted from the culture of CP by analyzing the user perceptual images. Second, cultural characteristics are translated into design elements, and design requirements are put forward. Third, based on these design elements and design requirements, CP culture and creative product will be designed. The overall design framework introduces the process from three culture levels to three layers of design characteristics [18], and then further applies the above research method to this process.

4   The Design Elements Extraction from Kansei Words

4.1   Design Elements and Requirements in Outer Level

The external level of CP culture focuses on visual effects, including colors, patterns, shapes, materials, themes and details. The Kansei words that conform to the user perceptual image are combined with the deconstructed Table 3, based on the previous work. Then we obtain the optimal representative elements B2 and C5 required for the design of outer level. These two elements are from the high foot plate in line with the Kansei words Round and Tradition, with a high degree of symmetry. These two elements can be used to modeling design of CP culture and creative products in outer level.

At the beginning of the 19th century, the painting of CP began to imitate the pattern of Chinese satin brocade as the decoration of ceramics. Thus the characteristics of "Zhijin Ceramics" of CP was formed. The use of gold to paint flowers, patterns or other

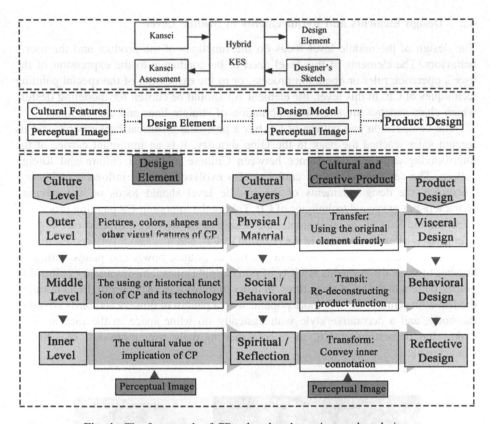

Fig. 4. The framework of CP cultural and creative product design.

Fig. 5. Representative pattern of Cantonese Porcelain.

details on porcelain is one of the most striking features of CP. In terms of patterns and themes, most of the CP was used to express the local culture. Later, the style was gradually fixed and became a commonly used pattern for CP painting, such as litchi, butterflies, goldfishes and flowers (see Fig. 5).

4.2 Design Elements and Requirements in Middle Level

The design of the middle level focus on the functions of the product and the user's behaviors. The elements of this level need to be conducive to the expression of the user's operation rules or operation process, or to the expression of the special painting techniques of CP. In this level, the element A3 should be chosen for modeling design, which characteristics are smooth combination of straight lines and curved lines.

The composition and pattern of CP has a profound historical background, and its foreign sales reached the peak in the Qing dynasty. It is an important carrier of the interweaving and mutual influence between Chinese traditional culture and foreign culture. The development of its craft has also evolved with the influence of history. Therefore, the design elements of the middle level should focus on the painting characteristics or special techniques of CP. Taking the important CP painting process of "Fengjin and Doucai" as an example, the design elements were extracted (see Fig. 6). "Fengjin" is often the last step in the painting of CP, and it is also a very representative step. The CP craftsmen need to paint the rim of bottles, bowls and plates with gold brushes to show the gorgeous nobility of porcelain. "Doucai" means adding colorful or golden pattern to the relief or pictures, in order to make it more beautiful. In addition, in the late 19th century, CP was more popular with a pattern of flowers and birds covering the body, and a decorative style with basically no white space in the picture. This makes the decoration of CP, as a container in daily use, more full of Chinese characteristics.

Fig. 6. "Fengjin and Doucai" (left) and The butterfly figure (right).

Therefore, based on the above two cultural characteristics of CP, it can be concluded that the middle design elements and design requirements should conform to the user perceptual image of special operation and special functions of CP. Then we need to select element B2 from Table 2 for behavioral design.

4.3 Design Elements and Requirements in Inner Level

The design of the inner level contains cultural connotations, emotional expressions or symbolic meanings. The extracted elements should be conducive to the shaping of the self-image of CP or the transmission of its cultural values. In terms of the cultural value of the painted elements, birds or flowers are often used in the painting of CP. "Da Huatou" is a common technique in painting CP, and "Huatou" is one of the most representative decorations in CP. Flowers in Chinese ceramics have the meaning of wealth, vitality and auspiciousness.

The more important cultural value of CP is that it carries the responsibility of spreading Chinese culture. CP was the very important carrier for the spread of Chinese culture, before the invention of photographic techniques. During the Qing dynasty, Europeans were very fond of CP, and tried to show the status of their countries or families by the painting on CP. So, "sample customization" gradually became one of the important factors influencing the composition characteristics of CP. "Doufang" is one of the important techniques of painting CP. The CP craftsman finished the composition with "Doufang" in advance, and then painted the required content on the porcelain after accepting the order. Thus formed a unique painting method (see Fig. 7).

Fig. 7. The technology of "Doufang".

5   Design of CP Culture and Creative Products Based on User Perceptual Image

5.1   Visceral Design Based on User Perceptual Image

The Visceral design focuses on the user's original response, and at this level, the visual effects of the products play an attractive role. Attention should be paid to the shape, color, composition, texture and pattern of CP at the outer level, for the cultural characteristics of CP. The elements extracted from the outer level can be directly combined to obtain the design of the visceral level, based on the perceptual image of the outer cultural level (see Fig. 8). They have round lines, but the lines are not disordered, and still have a certain symmetry. Goldfishes, flowers and other animal and plant elements are directly used in the curved product surface, and then gold lines are used to decoration. This is a desktop product and a candlestick design, involving people's daily necessities, and expressing blessings with the CP patterns.

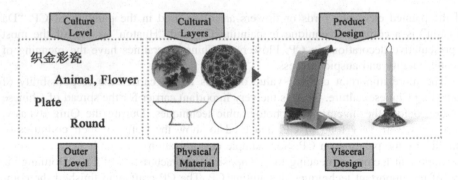

Fig. 8. Visceral design based on user perceptual image.

5.2 Behavioral Design Based on User Perceptual Image

The behavior design focuses on product function, operability and user experience. The design of CP cultural and creative products at the behavior level can be discussed from the functional and operational aspects. The behavioral design is shown in middle level, based on the transformation of middle level elements and the constraints of design requirements. This is a lamp design and a small bag design (see Fig. 9).

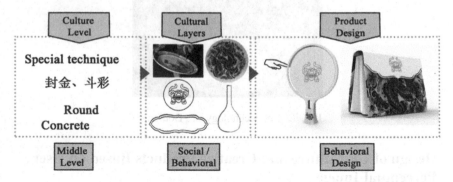

Fig. 9. Behavioral design based on user perceptual image.

CP not only has the function of appreciation and preservation, but also has great value of use, as a kind of porcelain. But today, daily porcelain tends to be a simple decorative style. CP is no longer in the mainstream aesthetic, covered with decorative patterns. The design of the small bag not only preserves the function of CP as a container, but also realizes this function with another product carrier.

According to the special technology of "Fengjin and Doucai", this lamp is designed to simulate the process of painting CP by the craftsmen. The operation process is shown in the figure below (see Fig. 10). The outer ring of the lamp is a touch switch. When the user's finger touches the outer ring for the first time, the LED light of the corresponding inner ring will light up. The user can make a circular motion on the outer ring of the lamp with his finger, and then in the form of lighting the lamp, the process of "Fengjin" of CP is copied. The hollow design in the middle of the lamp will become brighter with the increase of LED lights, which is the process reproduction of "Doucai".

Fig. 10. A sliding touch switch for the lamp design.

5.3   Reflective Design Based on User Perceptual Image

The reflective design is an expression of inner cultural meaning. In the CP cultural and creative product design, the reflective design contains the expression of cultural meaning of CP and good wishes conveyed by the porcelain itself. Based on the user perceptual image of the inner level of CP, the design elements and requirements in inner level are used to reflective design (see Fig. 11).

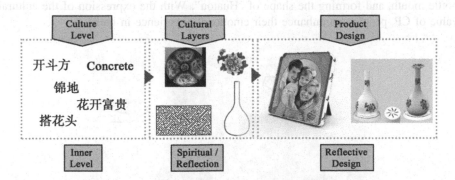

Fig. 11. Reflective design based on user perceptual image.

CP is an important carrier of cultural communication in the world. Many cultural information is recorded in the patterns of CP. In the history of "sample customization" of CP, its painting was mostly used by the combination of "Doufang" and "Jindi". In the photo frame design, the combination of "Doufang" and "Jindi" is used as the front part of the frame. Photos can be inserted from the side into the frame as expression of "sample customization" in the "Doufang" (see Fig. 12). This design conveys the cultural significance of the important historical value of CP.

Fig. 12. A picture frame design.

CP painting is rich in gold and colorful characteristics, and flowers, birds, fish and worms are usually used. It has a unique cultural nature, and has a very good blessing meaning. "Huatou" is a typical decoration in the painting of CP, which is also a skill that craftsmen must master. In the use of modern bath products, bath bubble can be used directly on the skin surface, with a certain affinity. The lotion bottle design directly uses the representative elements that most accord with Kansei words to design the body of bottle (see Fig. 13). The surface decoration has the characteristics of combining modern style with traditional style. In the bath, the users can press the switch on the top of the bottle to make the bath bubble squeezed from the gap in the bottle mouth, and forming the shape of "Huatou". With the expression of the cultural value of CP, people can enhance their emotional experience in bath.

Fig. 13. A bath bottle design.

These two cases start from the cultural value and blessing of CP, and finally complete the cultural and creative design. In the reflective design, it is necessary to grasp the user perceptual image at the inner level, combine the design elements that meet users' preferences, and translate the cultural values of CP that meet users' emotional needs.

6 Conclusion

A design framework based on user perceptual image is helpful to improve the consistency between production design and users' preferences. This study focuses on the extraction of design elements or the transformation of design requirements and realizes the final design. The main contents of the three levels of CP culture and the design methods of the three levels are clarified. An example is given to show the concrete flow of the design. Therefore, the frame proposed in this paper can be used to CP cultural and creative product design, to improve the sales volume of CP' E-commerce products. In the future research, we will continue to use Hybrid KES model to conduct perceptual evaluation on the final designed products. We will investigate the fit between the final design of CP's E-commerce products and Kansei words in the form of scale, so as to further prove the rationality of the design framework of CP products.

Acknowledgement. This research was supported by the 2018 Ministry of education production university cooperation education project. China (201802148006). 2018 school enterprise cooperative education project in Guangdong Province. China (PROJ1007206144650907648). Guangzhou University Innovation and Entrepreneurship Education Project. China (2019HD15). The completion of this study benefited from the tireless efforts of every teacher and classmate in the project team.

References

1. Convention for the safeguarding of the intangible cultural heritage. UNESCO (2003). https://doi.org/10.29171/azu_acku_pamphlet_ds353_c698_2003
2. Ji, Y., Tan, P., Chen, S.-C., Duh, H.B.-L.: Kansei engineering for E-commerce Cantonese Porcelain selection in China. In: Kurosu, M. (ed.) HCII 2019. LNCS, vol. 11566, pp. 463–474. Springer, Cham (2019). https://doi.org/10.1007/978-3-030-22646-6_34
3. Yeh, M.L., Lin, P.H.: Applying local culture features into creative craft products design. In: Rau, P.L.P. (ed.) IDGD 2011. LNCS, vol. 6775, pp. 114–122. Springer, Heidelberg (2011). https://doi.org/10.1007/978-3-642-21660-2_13
4. Zhang, R., Zhang, X.: Study on the factors affecting the development of cultural and creative E-commerce industries in Henan Province **32**, 283–289 (2017)
5. Chang, C., Huang, H.: A study on cultural and creative product design model from the perspective of paper, pp. 71–80 (2018)
6. Ji, Y., Tan, P., Duh, H.B.L.: Research on personalized learning pattern in traditional handicraft using augmented reality: a case study of Cantonese Porcelain. In: Kurosu, M. (ed.) HCI 2018. LNCS, vol. 10902, pp. 304–316. Springer, Cham (2018). https://doi.org/10.1007/978-3-319-91244-8_25

7. Tan, P., Ji, Y., Hills, D., Fu, T.: Bridging knowledge between craftsman and learner in Chinese intangible cultural heritage through WebAR, pp. 1–5 (2019). https://doi.org/10.1145/3354918.3361900

8. Ji, Y., Tan, P., Hills, D.: Chinese traditional handicraft education using AR content. Leonardo, 199–200 (2020). https://doi.org/10.1162/leon_a_01863

9. Ji, Y., Liu, Y., Sun, X., Tan, P., Fu, T., Feng, K.: Research on Chinese traditional handicraft education expansion model based on STEAM. In: Marcus, A., Wang, W. (eds.) HCII 2019. LNCS, vol. 11585, pp. 413–427. Springer, Cham (2019). https://doi.org/10.1007/978-3-030-23538-3_32

10. Xu, H.U.A.: Research on Development Mode of Ceramic Culture Creative Industry in Jingdezhen, pp. 1129–1134 (2017)

11. Hsu, S.H., Chuang, M.C., Chang, C.C.: A semantic differential study of designers' and users' product form perception. Int. J. Ind. Ergon. **25**, 375–391 (2000). https://doi.org/10.1016/S0169-8141(99)00026-8

12. Luo, S., Pan, Y.: Review of theory, key technologies and its application of perceptual image in product design. Chin. J. Mech. Eng. (2007). https://doi.org/10.3901/JME.2007.03.008. Jixie Gongcheng Xuebao

13. Su, J., Jiang, Y., Wang, P.: Research on product image styling design method based on neural network and genetic algorithm. In: Proceedings - 4th International Conference on Natural Computation, ICNC 2008 (2008). https://doi.org/10.1109/ICNC.2008.129

14. Zhu, S., Dong, Y.: Evaluation of Liangzhu cultural artifacts based on perceptual image. Appl. Mech. Mater. **268**, 1986–1992 (2013). https://doi.org/10.4028/www.scientific.net/AMM.268-270.1986

15. Chai, C., Li, D., Bian, M.: Research on innovative design of Jun Porcelain culture based on Kansei features. In: Proceedings - 2016 9th International Symposium on Computational Intelligence and Design, ISCID 2016, vol. 1, pp. 50–53 (2016). https://doi.org/10.1109/ISCID.2016.1020

16. Lin, R.T.: Transforming Taiwan aboriginal cultural features into modern product design: a case study of a cross-cultural product design model. Int. J. Des. **1**, 45–53 (2007)

17. Nagamachi, M.: Kansei engineering as a powerful consumer-oriented technology for product development. Appl. Ergon. **33**, 289 (2002)

18. Lin, C.L., Chen, S.J., Hsiao, W.H., Lin, R.: Cultural ergonomics in interactional and experiential design: conceptual framework and case study of the Taiwanese twin cup. Appl. Ergon. **52**, 242–252 (2016). https://doi.org/10.1016/j.apergo.2015.07.024

Human Values, Ethics, Transparency and Trust

Effects of Reputation, Organization, and Readability on Trustworthiness Perceptions of Computer Code

Gene M. Alarcon[1]($\boxtimes$), Anthony M. Gibson[2], Sarah A. Jessup[1],
August Capiola[1], Haider Raad[3], and Michael A. Lee[4]

[1] Air Force Research Laboratory, Wright-Patterson AFB, OH 45433, USA
gene.alarcon.1@us.af.mil
[2] Consortium of Universities, Washington D.C. 20036, USA
[3] Xavier University, Cincinnati, OH 45207, USA
[4] General Dynamics Information Technology, Dayton, OH 45434, USA

Abstract. Computer code has entered our society in contexts ranging from medical to manufacturing settings. The current study expanded previous literature by examining the effects of three between-subject factors (i.e., reputation, organization, and readability) on various trust-related outcomes. Participants ($N = 54$) were computer programmers recruited from Amazon's Mechanical Turk (MTurk). We used a 2 (reputable or non-reputable source) × 3 (high, medium, or low organization) × 3 (high, medium, or low readability) between-subjects design to examine how the independent variables interact to predict the trustworthiness perceptions of the code. The results show that programmers perceive code differently when coming from reputable sources. Thus, it is important to highlight whether or not any open source code comes from a reputable source and make this information readily available to programmers. Another trend we found is that programmers tend to prefer conspicuously high or low organization, particularly when readability is low. Thus, a medium level of organization could obfuscate the goals of the original programmer, which may undermine the programmer's intent and reduce code trustworthiness.

Keywords: Trust · Computer code · Trust in code

1 Introduction

Computer code, or simply code, has become ingrained in and inseparable from nearly all technology we use in modern times. Code facilitates everything from manufacturing to surgery to home entertainment centers. The ubiquity of code necessitates the production of safe and secure code in a timely manner. To facilitate these requirements, programmers reuse code from other sources, be it a fellow programmer they work with or online repositories such as Github or Stack Overflow. The decision to reuse code from one source and incorporate it into a separate architecture indicates trust, as the programmer is willing to be vulnerable [1]. That is, though the programmer may anticipate a positive outcome from reusing the code (e.g., saving time and money), the reused code may contain viruses, legacy issues, or other problems.

This is a U.S. government work and not under copyright protection in the U.S.;
foreign copyright protection may apply 2020
M. Kurosu (Ed.): HCII 2020, LNCS 12183, pp. 367–381, 2020.
https://doi.org/10.1007/978-3-030-49065-2_26

Recently, research has been conducted on the psychological perceptions of computer code from a programmer's perspective [1–5]. This research has illustrated that specific attributes of computer code affect one's trustworthiness perceptions towards that code, which in turn predicted decisions to reuse (i.e., trust behavior). The purpose of the current paper was replicate previous findings, and in some instances expand on gaps previously shown in the extant literature on trust in code.

1.1 Trust

With the advent of automation and autonomous systems, trust has become an important construct in the human factors field. Although the concept of trust originated in the interpersonal literature, the core foundation of the construct—accepting vulnerability from a referent [6]—has been applied to studies investigating trust towards automation [7], autonomous systems [8], and robots [9]. In the context of human-automation interactions, researchers describe the appropriateness of trust in terms of its calibration [10]. When a system or machine is over-trusted, the user trusts beyond the system's capabilities. Users may exhibit complacency or lackluster monitoring of the respective system. When a system or machine is under-trusted, the users' trust is lower than the systems actual capabilities. In these instances, users may not use the automation/machine when they should. Proper calibration describes the users relying on the system in accordance with the system's capabilities.

1.2 Code Reuse

Computer code is a compilation of commands executed by a computer, typically written in a programming language that humans can easily understand [11]. Reusing code from other programmers or websites facilitates the development of larger architectures in a timely manner. If the code is properly vetted, then reusing code can lead to more secure software as the reused code is assumed to have been assessed and repaired by several programmers in the past. Programmers may review the code, and based on their perceptions of the code, decide whether they want to reuse the code. This decision to reuse the code is a trust behavior, and trustworthiness perceptions should influence those trust behaviors [12].

Previous research in the computer science literature has defined code reuse as "the use of existing software or software knowledge to construct new software" [13, p. 529]. Reusing code indicates the programmer trusts the code, as s/he has decided to be vulnerable to the code [2]. If the code embedded in the larger architecture has bugs or vulnerabilities, this may cause issues in the new architecture. Indeed, [14] has estimated that 80–90% of code is reused. This is not surprising as much of the literature on code reuse in the computer science literature has focused on code reuse from a management perspective, espousing the time and effort saved in writing software [15]. Additionally, code that is reused may make the code more flexible and complex [16]. However, these benefits come with tradeoffs. It is estimated that most of the issues found in code are legacy issues that have patches, but the code was reused and the patches were not updated leading to a vulnerability [14]. Thus, reuse can lead to vulnerabilities and bugs in new software. In the section below, we describe a theoretical rationale for how programmers examine code to decide whether or not they will trust and reuse that code.

1.3   Heuristic-Systematic Processing Model of Trust in Code

The heuristic-systematic processing model (HSM) [17] of persuasion has been adapted to help understand how programmer's trust code [5]. The HSM posits two different processes for analyzing information: heuristic and systematic. Heuristic processing is characterized by the use of mental short cuts such as relying on biases, norms, and rules of thumb to reach a decision. In contrast, systematic processing is characterized by more in depth and effort driven strategies to reach a decision. There are tradeoffs to each type of processing. Heuristic processing is faster and more resource efficient, but it may come at a cost of decision accuracy. In contrast, systematic processing requires greater resource allocation and more time, but it results in greater decision accuracy. Realistically, cognitive processing is not discretized into one category of another, but differentiating the two processes in this way provides a greater understanding and ease of discussion concerning information processing characterized by different amounts of effort [18].

Recently, a cognitive task analysis (CTA) has delineated the factors that influence trust perceptions in code [1]. In their CTA, the authors found three factors that influence trust perceptions: reputation, transparency, and performance. Reputation pertains to the information that is obtained about the source of the code, typically through research and professional networks, and information provided on the website (e.g., reviews, number of users). Transparency describes the ability to read and ascertain the functionality of the code. This factor can include aspects such as readability, organization, style, and commenting of the code. Lastly, performance information is obtained by testing the code and client reports on the code. Performance characteristics pertain to the ability of the code to perform relevant necessary task.

Research on trust in code has demonstrated the reputation and transparency factors both exist and can be manipulated experimentally, which we outline below. Interestingly, the relationship between the variables is not as straightforward as one might think. In a study exploring trust in code, reputation and transparency were manipulated. Alarcon and colleagues [3] conducted an experiment where programmers evaluated 18 pieces of code that were degraded in reputation or transparency. Specifically, they manipulated organization and readability of the code for transparency. To manipulate reputation, they stated the code was either from a "reputable" or "unknown" source. The levels of manipulations were fixed across the 18 pieces of code and all code was presented in the same order. Findings indicated a three-way interaction such that for reputable code, trustworthiness increased as organization was degraded, regardless of the level of readability. They posited that participants performed more systematic processing and became more familiar with the code rather than abandoning the code. Indeed, analyses on the time spent on the code appeared to support this hypothesis, as participants spent more time on the code review as organization was degraded in the reputable conditions. However, these effects were not found in the unknown source condition, only in the high readability and unknown source condition did participants spend more time on the code if it was unorganized. In the medium and low readability conditions, participants abandoned the code relatively quickly.

Additional research using the same stimuli has demonstrated the effect is robust and replicable [2, 4]. However, a noted limitation of the studies conducted by the group is that the trustworthiness of the code is inherently tied to what the code does. Participants in their studies consistently noted they would not reuse server code that was from an unknown source due to the high-risk environment of servers [3]. As such, it remains unclear whether the trust perceptions are driven entirely by the manipulations or if they are inherent in the code itself.

Additional research by Alarcon and colleagues has tried to control for the effects of the code by showing the manipulations across two pieces of different code. As mentioned above, commenting is particularly important in code as it facilitates comprehension and helps to organize the code [19]. Alarcon and colleagues [20] explored the placement, validity, and style of comments on perceptions of code. They found valid comments led to higher trust assessments and more time spent on the code. In contrast, poorly placed comments led to greater trustworthiness perceptions. Again, this interaction must be viewed in the context of the HSM. Specifically, if the comments were valid and poorly placed participants trusted the code more as they spent more time on the code becoming more familiar with it. Additionally, participants spent more time on code with comments that were poorly placed but high in style, which the authors again interpreted as supporting the HSM of code.

The previous studies on trust in code have utilized a repeated measures design to explore their hypotheses. This is advantageous for most studies as it can reduce the number of participants needed as repeated measures are able to more accurately detect individual variations (e.g., high propensity to trust code). However, given the nature of the referent (i.e., computer code), a between-subjects design was necessary to fully understand the relationship of reputation, transparency, and performance on trust perceptions. As each piece of code is unique, it is analogous to changing participants for each trust interaction in an interpersonal context. As such, between-subjects studies are necessary to determine the true relationship of the CTA factors with trust, manipulating only one piece of code several times. Manipulating one piece of code for each condition will hold the referent constant so that any differences detected between cells are due solely to the manipulations of the code.

The current study sought to replicate the reputation and transparency findings of Alarcon et al. [3]. In addition, the previous studies only explored trustworthiness ratings with a single item. We expand on previous research by including additional trust items for reputation, transparency, performance, and maintainability. Including these additional items can help researchers understand what is driving the trust assessment. As such, we form the following hypotheses based on previous research:

Hypothesis 1: Reputable code will be perceived as more trustworthy than non-reputable code.
Hypothesis 2: Code higher in readability will be perceived as more trustworthy than code lower in readability.
Hypothesis 3: Code lower in organization will be perceived as more trustworthy than code higher in organization.

Although we have additional trust items (e.g., maintainability, performance) we do not make specific hypotheses concerning these items. Thus, all analyses were exploratory.

2 Method

2.1 Participants

Participants were recruited via the crowd-sourcing site Amazon Mechanical Turk (MTurk). In total, we collected data from 158 workers. We cleaned the data through a series of multiple steps. First, we removed participants who had duplicate or suspicious IP addresses (e.g., those with off-shore IP addresses). Next, in order to ensure participants exerted sufficient effort in the study, we removed participants who spent less than 120 s on the page that included both the computer code and the trustworthiness perceptions items. We also removed participants who failed to accurately identify the function of the computer code. Finally, we used the *dplyr* package [21] to randomly sample three participants per each experimental condition (i.e., the largest number of people that were present in all 18 conditions). After cleaning the data of insufficient responses, 54 participants were retained. Requirements to participate were at least three years of programming experience, and participants had to be able to read and understand JAVA code. Participants ranged 18–58 years of age ($M = 32.02$, $SD = 8.45$), 81% male, and 7.41% students. Total years of programming experience was 5–34 years, ($M = 10.50$, $SD = 6.16$), and 46.30% listed JAVA as their primary programming language.

2.2 Task

Participants viewed 6 pieces of computer code. Code 1 was a default properties parser, code 2 was an encryptor, code 3 comprised file operations, code 4 comprised basic annotation process, and code 5 was a bloom filter. Code 6 was an image filter that was low on all aspects of the manipulations to see if programmers at the end of the experiment were still attending to what was happening (i.e., all participants should choose to discard this piece of code). All participants viewed the same code 1, code 2, code 4, code 5, and code 6. Code 3 was presented to participants randomly as the original version or versions that were manipulated eight different ways (see Data Analysis section below), for a total of nine versions of the file operations code. Participants were also provided with information as to whether the code came from either a reputable or unknown source. Code 1, 2, 4, and 5 were all described as reputable and code 6 was from an unknown source. Code version manipulations and source information provided 18 different conditions.

2.3 Measures

Code Ratings. Participants were asked to answer the following questions about each code piece using a 7-point scale: "How reputable is the code?" (1 = *Not at all* *reputable* to 7 = *Very reputable*), "How maintainable is this code?" (1 = *Not at all maintainable* to 7 = *Very maintainable*), "How transparent is this code?" (1 = *Not at all transparent* to 7 = *Very transparent*), "How well do you think this code will perform?" (1 = *Not at all well* to 7 = *Very well*), and "How trustworthy is the code?" (1 = *Not at all trustworthy* to 7 = *Very trustworthy*).

Code Description. At the end of each page containing the code piece, participants were asked to describe what each piece of code does with the following prompt, "To the best of your knowledge, please describe what this code does in the text box below."

2.4 Procedure

The task and surveys were presented to participants using Qualtrics. To obtain consent and attempt to reduce attrition rates [22], the following information was presented to each participant prior to the start of the task. "This is a survey consisting of multiple questions. Most questions are self-report questions where you will need to select an answer on a scale ranging from 1–7 (such as from strongly disagree to strongly agree). Many MTurk workers do not like answering self-report questions and tend to quit a survey once they see such questions. If a sizeable number of people quit a survey halfway, the data quality of that survey would be compromised. However, our research depends on good quality data. Thus, please make sure you do not mind self-report questions before taking this survey. Would you like to continue?" If participants selected "Yes, I would like to continue," then they were presented with a text box and the following instructions, "Please type this short sentence to indicate you are willing to answer self-report questions: "I will answer self-report questions." After consenting, background, demographic, and experience surveys were completed, followed by personality surveys, which do not pertain to the present research and will not be mentioned further.

After the surveys and prior to the task, participants were shown the following information, "**Please read the following information carefully:** On the following pages, you will be shown a total of 6 Java classes as images. Please examine the **6 pieces of code** to determine if you would use the code without changes. **All comments have been removed from the code. All packages have been modified to remove original sources. All code compiles. Above each code artifact there is information about the code.** For each code artifact, you will be asked a series of questions about the code. The response options range from 1 to 7. Please select the value that most closely represents your opinions about each piece of code you have examined." After clicking the next button, participants saw the first piece of code and then evaluated the code using the code ratings and code descriptions. These evaluations were completed for each of the code pieces participants viewed. Only one code piece was viewed and evaluated at a time. Note that this procedure was nearly identical to [3], as we attempted to replicate their findings using a between-subjects design. After the task was complete, we reviewed participant descriptions of code pieces within 5 days of completion. Workers were compensated with $10 USD if their work was accepted. Participants who incorrectly described 3 or more code pieces, had a suspicious or duplicate IP address, or spent less them 120 s on the page were rejected (see description in the Participants section above).

2.5 Data Analysis

In order to test whether those assigned to different levels of reputation, organization, and readability reported different perceptions of code trustworthiness, we ran a series of 2 (Reputation: reputable, non-reputable) × 3 (Organization: high, medium, low) × 3 (Readability: high, medium, low) ANOVAs. We ran all models in R [23] using the *afex* package [24]. We then tested any significant Omnibus tests with post-hoc comparisons using the *emmeans* package [25] and plotted significant effects using *ggplot2* [26].

3 Results

The means, standard deviations, and zero-order correlations between the dependent variables are shown in Table 1.

Table 1. Means, standard deviations, and correlations of dependent variables at time point three

Variable	M	SD	1	2	3	4	5
1. Reputability	4.59	1.56	–				
2. Maintainability	4.65	1.57	.74*	–			
3. Transparency	4.96	1.44	.56*	.65*	–		
4. Performance	4.69	1.36	.76*	.72*	.63*	–	
5. Trustworthiness	4.52	1.45	.85*	.75*	.67*	.81*	–

*Note. N = 54. *p < .01.*

We found a significant main effect of Reputation on perceptions of code reputability, $F(1, 36) = 8.90$, $p < .01$, $\eta_p^2 = .20$ (see Table 2), which provides evidence that participants considered whether the code was written by a reputable or non-reputable source (see Fig. 1). No other main effects or interactions were significant for reputability perceptions.

Table 2. The effect of reputation, organization, and readability manipulations on perceived reputability of code

Manipulation	df	MSE	F	η_p^2
1. Reputation	1, 36	2.13	8.90*	.20
2. Organization	2, 36	2.13	2.23	.11
3. Readability	2, 36	2.13	0.79	.04
4. Reputation × Organization	2, 36	2.13	0.14	.01
5. Reputation × Readability	2, 36	2.13	0.53	.03
6. Organization × Readability	4, 36	2.13	1.43	.14
7. Reputation × Organization × Readability	4, 36	2.13	0.65	.07

*Note. N = 54. *p < .01.*

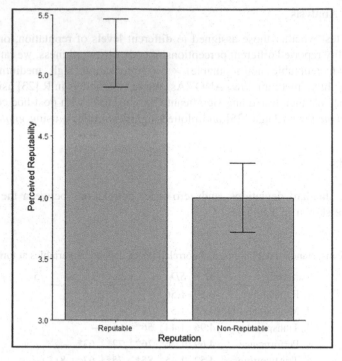

Fig. 1. Main effect of reputation manipulation on perceived code reputability.

We found a significant Organization × Readability interaction, $F(4, 36) = 3.18$, $p < .05$, $\eta_p^2 = .26$ on perceptions of code maintainability (see Table 3). However, we observed no other significant effects for the Maintainability dependent variable. Additionally, although there was a significant Organization × Readability interaction, the simple main effects failed to reach significance across either of the factors (see Fig. 2).

Table 3. The effect of reputation, organization, and readability manipulations on perceived maintainability of code

Manipulation	df	MSE	F	η_p^2
1. Reputation	1, 36	2.00	2.08	.05
2. Organization	2, 36	2.00	1.81	.09
3. Readability	2, 36	2.00	0.29	.02
4. Reputation × Organization	2, 36	2.00	0.44	.02
5. Reputation × Readability	2, 36	2.00	1.75	.09
6. Organization × Readability	4, 36	2.00	3.18*	.26
7. Reputation × Organization × Readability	4, 36	2.00	1.44	.14

Note. $N = 54$. *$p < .05$.

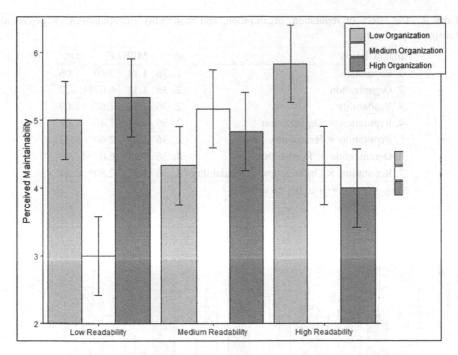

Fig. 2. Organization × Readability interaction on perceived code maintainability.

We found a significant main effect for Organization, $F(2, 36) = 6.67$, $p < .01$, $\eta_p^2 = .27$, on perceived code transparency (see Table 4). The main effect of Organization was qualified by both an Organization × Readability interaction, $F(4, 36) = 6.07$, $p < .01$, $\eta_p^2 = .40$, as well as a significant Reputable × Organization × Readability interaction, $F(4, 36) = 2.80$, $p < .05$, $\eta_p^2 = .24$ (see Fig. 3). We found that participants assigned to a reputable source condition (*EMMean* = 6.00, *SE* = 0.61) reported higher levels of transparency when the organization was medium and the readability was high compared to those in the low reputable condition (*EMMean* = 3.33, *SE* = 0.61), $t(36) = 3.10$, $p < .01$. When organization was low and readability was medium, participants assigned to the reputable condition also reported higher levels of perceived transparency (*EMMean* = 6.00, *SE* = 0.61) than when participants were assigned to the non-reputable condition (*EMMean* = 4.00, *SE* = 0.61), $t(36) = 2.32$, $p < .05$.

For the performance perceptions outcome, we found no significant effects for any independent variables or interaction terms (see Table 5).

Finally, there was a significant main effect for reputation, $F(1, 36) = 6.13$, $p < .05$, $\eta_p^2 = .15$, on perceived trustworthiness (see Table 6). In addition, there was a significant Organization × Readability interaction, $F(4, 36) = 2.69$, $p < .05$, $\eta_p^2 = .23$. When readability was low, we found a significant difference in trustworthiness perceptions when organization was high (*EMMean* = 5.33, *SE* = 0.54) compared to when organization was medium (*EMMean* = 2.83, *SE* = 0.54), $t(36) = 3.28$,

376   G. M. Alarcon et al.

Table 4. The effect of reputation, organization, and readability manipulations on perceived transparency of code

Manipulation	df	MSE	F	η_p^2
1. Reputation	1, 36	1.11	2.40	.06
2. Organization	2, 36	1.11	6.67**	.27
3. Readability	2, 36	1.11	1.87	.09
4. Reputation × Organization	2, 36	1.11	1.40	.07
5. Reputation × Readability	2, 36	1.11	2.60	.13
6. Organization × Readability	4, 36	1.11	6.07**	.40
7. Reputation × Organization × Readability	4, 36	1.11	2.80*	.24

Note. $N = 54$. **$p < .01$, *$p < .05$.

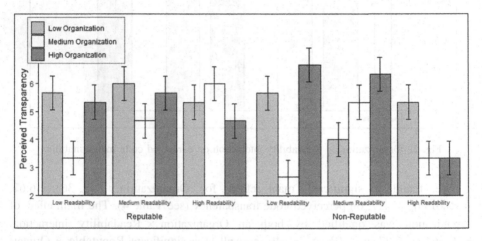

Fig. 3. Reputation × Organization × Readability interaction on perceived code transparency.

Table 5. The effect of reputation, organization, and readability manipulations on perceived performance of code

Manipulation	df	MSE	F	η_p^2
1. Reputation	1, 36	1.87	1.20	.03
2. Organization	2, 36	1.87	1.26	.07
3. Readability	2, 36	1.87	0.25	.01
4. Reputation × Organization	2, 36	1.87	0.31	.02
5. Reputation × Readability	2, 36	1.87	0.49	.03
6. Organization × Readability	4, 36	1.87	1.76	.16
7. Reputation × Organization × Readability	4, 36	1.87	0.84	.09

Note. $N = 54$.

$p < .01$. Similarly, when reliability was low, there were significant differences in perceived trustworthiness when organizational was low ($EMMean = 5.33$, $SE = 0.54$) than when organization was medium ($EMMean = 2.83$, $SE = 0.54$), $t(36) = 3.28$, $p < .01$ (see Fig. 4).

Table 6. The effect of reputation, organization, and readability manipulations on perceived trustworthiness of code

Manipulation	df	MSE	F	η_p^2
1. Reputation	1, 36	1.74	6.13*	.15
2. Organization	2, 36	1.74	3.07	.15
3. Readability	2, 36	1.74	0.01	.00
4. Reputation × Organization	2, 36	1.74	0.03	.00
5. Reputation × Readability	2, 36	1.74	0.61	.03
6. Organization × Readability	4, 36	1.74	2.69*	.23
7. Reputation × Organization × Readability	4, 36	1.74	0.93	.09

Note. $N = 54$. *$p < .05$.

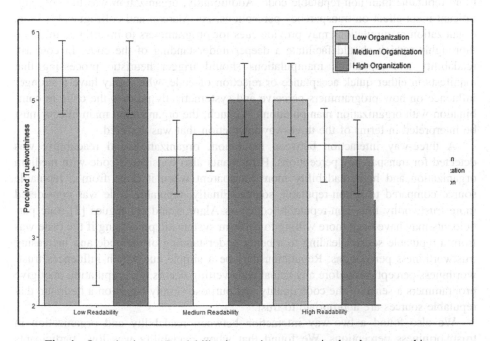

Fig. 4. Organization × Readability interaction on perceived code trustworthiness.

4 Discussion

The present study investigated the effects of reputation, organization, and readability code manipulations on programmers' perceptions of code. This research replicated past research investigating these manipulations on trust in code in term of the importance of code reputation and its effect on perceptions of the code [3]. However, we failed to replicate some of the interactions in previous research, as outlined below. Additionally, the present study expanded the scope of past research in having three separate manipulations in a between-subjects design to better isolate the effect of each manipulation without the nuisance of order or stimuli effects (see [27]).

In the current study we separated the constructs of reputation, transparency, performance, and maintainability from overall trustworthiness, leading to a clearer understanding of how the reputation, organization, and readability manipulations affect each aspect of trustworthiness. Several findings from the present study point to the importance of code reputation on programmers' perceptions. That is, when programmers evaluate code for potential incorporation into a more overarching architecture, they consider the reputation of the code. Reputation perceptions could be attributed to the author of the code or the organization from which the code was obtained. We observed an intuitive pattern of results, such that participants rated reputable code as more reputable than non-reputable code. Additionally, organization was the only significant main effect on transparency perceptions. As Alarcon and colleagues [3] state, organization manipulations may provide cues for programmers to investigate the code thoroughly, which should facilitate a deeper understanding of the code. In contrast, readability and reputation manipulations should trigger heuristic processing that manifests in either quick acceptance or rejection of code, which may have a stronger influence on how programmers perceive and systematically process the code in combination with organization manipulations. As such, the organization main effects must be interpreted in terms of the three-way interaction that was detected.

A three-way interaction between reputation, organization and readability was detected for transparency perceptions. Participants also considered code with medium organization and high readability more transparent when it came from a reputable source compared to a non-reputable source. Finally, reputable code was considered more trustworthy than non-reputable code. As Alarcon and colleagues [3] state participants may have been more willing to perform systematic processing if the code was from a reputable source, leading to a better understanding of the code and increasing trustworthiness perceptions. Reputation may be a simple cue which influences trustworthiness perceptions before any actual code vetting occurs. The reputation may give programmers a sense of the code quality and purpose simply based on a heuristic that reputable sources are appropriate to trust.

We also found a two-way interaction between readability and organization in trustworthiness perceptions. We found that when readability was low, participants perceived the code as more trustworthy when organization was high compared to when it was medium. Similarly, when reliability was low, there were significant differences in perceived trustworthiness when organization was low than when organization was medium. It may be that some factor being low—in this case, readability—may influence more scrutiny of the code, particularly organization. We struggle to interpret this finding, as it does not coincide with any a priori hypotheses or align with past findings observed in trust in code research. Additionally, in low readability conditions, perceived trustworthiness was the same when organization was both high and low. Together, these findings do not support our hypotheses that code perceived as more readable and less organized will be perceived as more trustworthy than code that is less readable and more organized. However, in the high readability condition the fact that trustworthiness increased as organization decreased is similar to the findings of Alarcon and colleagues [3] and we may be underpowered in the current study. Related to the power, our study did not find a three-way interaction as Alarcon and colleagues did, as such the effects of reputation are mixed across the two-way interaction. A larger sample may find reputation has an influence and that the results may make more sense.

4.1   Limitations

With 18 conditions and only 54 participants, the current study is underpowered to find significant interactions without interpreting with caution. As such, an effect such as the aforementioned interactions should be replicated with a larger sample size to determine if this effect is simply an artifact. Another limitation of the present research is that we had to jettison 48 participants for not spending a minimum amount of time each code trial, in which we determined a-priori using best practices. That is, a large portion of the data had to be removed from the present study, because participants did not allocate the minimum amount of time on the task to actually comprehend what each code stimuli was written to execute. We attributed this to careless responding on MTurk. However, Alarcon et al. [3] explored time spent on the code and found certain factors influence processing, leading to more or less time spent on the code. In the current study, we were unable to differentiate careless responding from heuristic processing though. Future studies investigating trust in code may want to avoid uploading code studies to MTurk, expecting careful participation in the study. Though we took care to ensure participants were attending to the task (see [27]), future iterations of this experimental design should conduct the code review task in person to ensure participants are attending adequately.

4.2   Implications

The major finding from this study was that the perceived reputation of code matters. Information pertaining to the code reputation has an influence on the code's perceived transparency and trustworthiness, with the latter perception having an influence on subsequent code reuse [2, 4]. This consistent finding from the present and past research shows that programmers do consider reputation as a factor which influences their reuse of code, and organizations may want to ensure developers have this information when they receive code for vetting and deciding whether or not to implement code into larger architectures. Future research may wish to investigate what aspects of reputation matter and influence code reuse. For instance, does the individual author of the code matter more or less for decisions to reuse than the team or business in which the individual works? Questions like these should be investigated.

Acknowledgements. DISTRIBUTION STATEMENT A. Approved for public release: 88ABW-2020-0095;

Cleared 13 Jan 2020. This research was supported in part by an appointment to the Post-graduate Research Participant Program at the U.S. Air Force Research Laboratory, 711th Human Performance Wing, Airman Systems Directorate, Warfighter Interface Division, Collaborative Interfaces and Teaming Branch, Collaborative Teaming Section administered by the Oak Ridge Institute for Science and Education through an interagency agreement between the U.S. Department of Energy and USAFRL.

References

1. Alarcon, G.M., Millitello, L.G., Ryan, P., Jessup, S.A., Calhoun, C.S., Lyons, J.B.: A descriptive model of computer code trustworthiness. J. Cogn. Eng. Decis. Making **11**(2), 107–121 (2017)
2. Ryan, T.J., et al.: Trust in automated software repair. In: Moallem, A. (ed.) HCII 2019. LNCS, vol. 11594, pp. 452–470. Springer, Cham (2019). https://doi.org/10.1007/978-3-030-22351-9_31
3. Alarcon, G.M., Gamble, R.F., Jessup, S.A., Walters, C., Ryan, T.J., Wood, D.W.: The influence of reputation and transparency on trustworthiness perceptions and reuse of computer code. Cogent Psychol. **4**(1), 1–22 (2017)
4. Ryan, T.J., Walter, C., Alarcon, G.M., Gamble, R., Jessup, S.A., Capiola, A.: The influence of personality on code reuse. In: 52nd Hawaii International Conference on Systems Sciences Proceedings, pp. 5805–5814. IEEE Computer Society Press, Los Alamitos (2019)
5. Alarcon, G., Ryan, T.: Trustworthiness perceptions of computer code: a heuristic-systematic processing model. In: 51st Hawaii International Conference on System Sciences Proceedings, pp. 5384–5393. IEEE Computer Society Press, Los Alamitos (2018)
6. Mayer, R.C., Davis, J.H., Schoorman, F.D.: An integrative model of organizational trust. Acad. Manag. Rev. **20**(3), 709–734 (1995)
7. Hoff, K.A., Bashir, M.: Trust in automation: integrating empirical evidence on factors that influence trust. Hum. Factors **57**(3), 407–434 (2015)
8. de Visser, E.J., Pak, R., Shaw, T.H.: From 'automation' to 'autonomy': the importance of trust repair in human–machine interaction. Ergonomics **61**(10), 1409–1427 (2018)
9. Oleson, K.E., Billings, D.R., Kocsis, V., Chen, J.Y., Hancock, P.A.: Antecedents of trust in human-robot collaborations. In: 1st IEEE International Multi-Disciplinary Conference on Cognitive Methods in Situation Awareness and Decision Support Proceedings, pp. 175–178. IEEE, Piscataway (2011)
10. Lee, J.D., See, K.A.: Trust in automation: designing for appropriate reliance. Hum. Factors **46**(1), 50–80 (2004)
11. Harman, M.: Why source code analysis and manipulation will always be important. In: 10th IEEE Working Conference on Source Code Analysis and Manipulation Proceedings, pp. 7–9. IEEE Computer Society Press, Los Alamitos (2010)
12. Ryan, T.J., Walter, C., Alarcon, G.M., Gamble, R., Jessup, S.A., Capiola, A.: The influence of personality on code reuse. In: 52nd Annual Proceedings of the Hawaii International Conference on Systems Sciences, pp. 5805–5814 (2019)
13. Frakes, W.B., Kang, K.: Software reuse research: status and future. IEEE Trans. Softw. Eng. **31**(7), 529–536 (2005)

14. Hautala, L.: Programmers are copying security flaws into your software, researchers warn. CNET. https://www.cnet.com/news/programmers-are-copying-security-flaws-into-your-soft ware-researchers-warn/. Accessed 23 Oct 2019

15. Banker, R.D., Kauffman, R.J.: Reuse and productivity in integrated computer-aided software engineering: an empirical study. MIS Q. **15**(3), 375–401 (1991)

16. Babar, M.A., Zhu, L., Jeffery, R.: A framework for classifying and comparing software architecture evaluation methods. In: 15th IEEE Australian Software Engineering Conference Proceedings, pp. 309–318. IEEE Computer Society Press, Los Alamitos (2004)

17. Chaiken, S.: Heuristic versus systematic information processing and the use of source versus message cues in persuasion. J. Personal. Soc. Psychol. **39**(5), 752–766 (1980)

18. Kahneman, D.: Thinking, Fast and Slow. Macmillan, New York (2011)

19. Tenny, T.: Program readability: procedures versus comments. IEEE Trans. Softw. Eng. **14** (9), 1271–1279 (1988)

20. Alarcon, G.M., et al.: The influence of commenting validity, placement, and style on perceptions of computer code trustworthiness: a heuristic-systematic processing approach. Appl. Ergon. **70**, 182–193 (2018)

21. Wickham, H., François, R., Henry, L., Müller, K.: dplyr: A Grammar of Data Manipulation. R package version 0.8.3. https://CRAN.R-project.org/package=dplyr. Accessed 5 Dec 2019

22. Zhou, H., Fishbach, A.: The pitfall of experimenting on the web: How unattended selective attrition leads to surprising (yet false) research conclusions. J. Pers. Soc. Psychol. **111**(4), 493–504 (2016)

23. R Core Team: R: A language and environment for statistical computing. R Foundation for Statistical Computing. https://www.R-project.org/. Accessed 14 Nov 2019

24. Singmann, H., Bolker, B., Westfall, J., Aust, F., Ben-Shachar, M.S.: afex: Analysis of Factorial Experiments. R package version 0.25-1. https://CRAN.R-project.org/package=afex. Accessed 14 Nov 2019

25. Lenth, R.: emmeans: Estimated Marginal Means, aka Least-Squares Means. R package version 1.4.2, https://CRAN.R-project.org/package=emmeans. Accessed 14 Nov 2019

26. Wickham, H.: ggplot2: Elegant Graphics for Data Analysis. Springer, New York (2016). https://doi.org/10.1007/978-3-319-24277-4

27. Tabachnick, B.G., Fidell, L.S.: Experimental Designs Using ANOVA. Thomson Brooks/Cole, New York (2006)

User Trust and Understanding of Explainable AI: Exploring Algorithm Visualisations and User Biases

Dawn Branley-Bell[1](✉) ⓘ, Rebecca Whitworth[2] ⓘ,
and Lynne Coventry[1] ⓘ

[1] Northumbria University, Newcastle upon Tyne NE1 8ST, UK
{dawn.branley-bell,lynne.coventry}@northumbria.ac.uk
[2] Red Hat, The Catalyst, Newcastle upon Tyne NE4 5TG, UK
rsimmond@redhat.com

Abstract. Artificial intelligence (AI) is increasingly being integrated into different areas of our lives. AI has the potential to increase productivity and relieve workload on staff in high-pressure jobs such as healthcare. However, most AI healthcare tools have failed. For AI to be effective, it is vital that users can understand how the system is processing data. Explainable AI (XAI) moves away from the traditional 'black box' approach, aiming to make the processes behind the system more transparent. This experimental study uses real healthcare data – and combines a computer science and psychological approach – to investigate user trust and understanding of three popular XAI algorithms (Decision Trees, Logistic Regression and Neural Networks). The results question the contribution of understanding towards user trust; Suggesting that understanding and explainability are not the only factors contributing to trust in AI. Users also show biases in trust and understanding – with a particular bias towards malignant results. This raises important issues around how humans can be encouraged to make more accurate judgements when using XAI systems. These findings have implications in relation to ethics, future XAI design, healthcare and further research.

Keywords: Explainable AI · Artificial intelligence · Machine Learning · Health · Trust · Understanding · Healthcare · Medical diagnoses · Cognitive biases

1 Introduction

Artificial intelligence (AI) has the potential to increase productivity and relieve workload on staff in high-pressure jobs such as healthcare; where staff report high levels of exhaustion detrimental to their own wellbeing and patient safety [1]. AI based healthcare tools have generally failed, and research suggests that a lack of HCI considerations are a key reason for failure [2, 3].

Artificial intelligence (AI) is a broad concept of machines that can carry out tasks in a manner that we could consider as 'smart'. Machine learning (ML) is the application of AI based upon the premise of giving the machine access to data and the machine

© Springer Nature Switzerland AG 2020
M. Kurosu (Ed.): HCII 2020, LNCS 12183, pp. 382–399, 2020.
https://doi.org/10.1007/978-3-030-49065-2_27

'learning for itself' [4]. By 2022, one in five workers engaged in mostly non-routine tasks will rely on AI to do their jobs [5]. There are many healthcare applications for AI, particularly in relation to clinical decision support tools (DSTs) [2]. However, as aforementioned AI based healthcare tools have generally failed, due to a suggested lack of HCI considerations [2, 3]. Traditionally, AI has involved a 'black box' approach, where the user inputs some raw data, and then receives the machine-generated output/result – without any information around the reasoning or processes leading to this outcome. However, for AI to be effective, it is vital that users can understand how the system is processing data. AI reasoning must be more transparent when it is used in domains that could have a critical impact upon individuals. In healthcare, inaccurate results could be detrimental to patient wellbeing, and in the worst cases potentially fatal [6, 7]. It is vital that systems are open to human understanding. Only through understanding the processes involved within the system, can users evaluate and identify how the data is being used and whether the outcome is correct. The need for understanding may feed into clinicians' current lack of motivation to use AI based DSTs [2].

Explainability of AI also has important security implications. For example, healthcare can be victim to cyber risk, such as the malicious manipulation of connected medical devices including insulin pumps, MRI scanners and other diagnostic equipment [8]. Without insights into the processing of data, inconsistencies in the system are much harder to detect.

In order to address this need for greater explainability and user understanding, there is a transition towards explainable AI (XAI) [9]. XAI encompasses a move towards a 'glass box' approach where human-friendly explanations of AI reasoning are provided [10]. To help achieve this, XAI uses algorithm visualisations.

Current XAI work focuses on explainability and user interface (UI) design but tends to overlook the influence of a key psychological factor - user trust [11]. Transparency is vital to trust formation, therefore XAI has the potential to significantly impact on human-computer synergy [10]. As with all collaborative relationships, good communication, trust, clarity and understanding are key [10]. However, it is also vital that we establish whether users are making accurate choices when their decisions are aided by XAI, as inaccurate decisions (e.g., due to cognitive biases) could be detrimental to patient wellbeing.

This study expands upon the existing literature by applying a multidisciplinary, experimental approach and empirical analysis using real healthcare data [12]. To address three key questions:

1. How is user understanding related to user trust of an XAI system?
2. How does the type of algorithm visualisation affect users' perceived understanding and/or trust?
3. Do users make accurate decisions based upon an XAI system, or do they show any biases?

The paper contributions are threefold:

- Firstly, we believe that this is the first paper to investigate both user understandability *and* trust in relation to three different XAI algorithms (decision tree, logistic regression, neural network) – including how understanding and trust may interact to contribute to users' overall perceptions of a healthcare system.

- Secondly, we use real-world healthcare data to provide empirical testing of the effectiveness of these algorithms.
- Finally, we show how user bias(es) may influence perceptions of understanding and/or trust in an XAI system.

2   Related Work

In this section we summarize the current XAI literature, including research into explaining algorithms, user trust and the legalities of XAI.

2.1   XAI Algorithms

Various solutions have been proposed to help XAI explain the processes behind the system – each relying on a different algorithm and accompanying visual aid/output. Three of the most popular are: Decision Trees (DT), Logistic Regression (LR) and neural networks (NN).

ML has the potential to support the medical industry and make healthcare more efficient. Mena and colleagues [13] tested different algorithms used to train a model to help predict medical prognoses. The algorithms were compared for *accuracy* and *performance*. Salama et al. [14] also tested the *accuracy* of different ML algorithms, in relation to the diagnosis of breast cancer. They focused primarily upon how *accuracy* of ML training can be improved using different algorithms (Fig. 1).

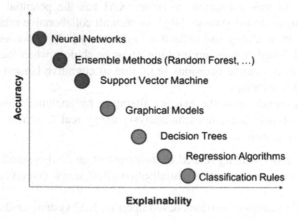

Fig. 1.   Accuracy vs explainability [14]

However, *performance* (i.e., predictive accuracy of the algorithm) is only one part of the XAI puzzle. It is also vital that users can understand and interpret the outcome of such systems. Without *understanding* there is no way to progress towards *user evaluation* of the accuracy of predictions. Therefore algorithms need to be both accurate *and* understandable. This is particularly important given that Salama et al.'s [14] findings suggest that more accurate algorithms are harder to explain. Currently there is a lack of data available regarding whether XAI algorithms actually do increase user understanding. The current study addresses this gap in the current knowledge by empirically testing user perceptions of different algorithms.

2.2 The Importance of User Trust

"There is probably no area in which the information asymmetry is greater and the need for trust more vital than in health care" [15].

Human trust involves making oneself vulnerable to the actions of others based on our expectations about the trustee's likely actions, intentions, or capabilities (see [16] for an overview of trust). The challenge of AI is to effectively balance and manage the collaboration between humans and agents during decision-making tasks. A basic level of trust must be achieved in order for the AI system to be utilized however too much trust can lead to over reliance on AI (misuse). Trust in AI is therefore a vital influence on the collaborative decision-making process, yet current work on XAI tends to overlook its importance.

AI cannot reach its full potential unless humans (in this instance, doctors and patients) can trust the accuracy of the system [17]. This is significant as the benefits of AI in healthcare could be lifesaving in many ways, for example through enabling quicker surgeries, reducing waiting list times, and/or reducing surgeon fatigue. Therefore, a measure of trust is included in the current study, enabling us to investigate two key areas: Firstly, whether people may be comfortable using AI systems within critical environments such as healthcare; and secondly, whether understanding and trust may interact.

Trust between a doctor and patient is also vital, and when things go wrong, trust is easily lost [18]. We now live in a world where many activities are being supported by AI, including complicated medical procedures and diagnostics. This adds further dimensions of trust: Trust in the AI system by the doctor (and potentially by the patient if they are made aware of its uses during their diagnosis/treatment) as well as potentially impacting upon the patient-doctor trust relationship [19].

Trust can be grounded and driven by different factors. Firstly, people differ in their *natural predisposition to trust*, i.e., some individuals will have a stronger natural tendency to trust in AI regardless of any experience or knowledge with the technology. In some cases, this could lead to blind faith, i.e., accepting the systems decision without hesitation or questioning of the reasoning involved [20]. A tendency to over trust automation is known as automation bias. Research suggests that an effective way to reduce automation bias could be to increase user understanding of AI algorithms (and their limitations) [21].

Secondly, *trust can be grounded in experience*, this is known as 'behavioural trust' and it develops over time as experience is gained and reliability is proven [22]. This trust can be reduced by negative experiences, such as unreliability or inaccuracy in a technology. For example, a recent decision tool made by IBM Watson incorrectly predicted cancer prescriptions that would have aggravated the symptoms experienced by the patient [23]. This could have resulted in a catastrophic impact upon patient health. Luckily, in this instance, the system error was identified, and the tool was not implemented. However, this does demonstrate the criticality of healthcare XAI systems and the link to patient and societal behavioural trust.

Thirdly, *trust can be grounded in understanding* of the way in which a decision was made. This is linked to adequate communication between the system and the user. A recent study investigating implicit communication between AI agents and humans, showed that the ability to communicate with a system could have a significant impact on AI use [24]. This communication requires understanding between both human and AI – otherwise, the system will fail to offer correct and/or helpful support. Within this study we aim to investigate user understanding of ML algorithms systems, which could support design enhancements for improved human-computer communication.

2.3   XAI and Data Legislation

The introduction of legislation around data usage provides another driving factor behind XAI. For example, in the UK the recent introduction of the General Data Protection Regulation (GDPR) imposes the legal requirement for a "right to explanation" about algorithm-derived decisions [25]. This means that AI must be able to not only explain its decision-making process but be able to explain this in a way that is easily open to human interpretation and evaluation. GDPR has generated an increase in XAI research (from two papers in 2009, to eighteen papers in 2018, [26]). However, current literature is still limited and further investigation is warranted. The current study addresses this through experimental methodology and empirical results based upon real world healthcare data.

3   Methodology

This section provides details of the study sample and procedure. It then leads on to explaining the three chosen algorithms.

3.1   Analysis

A-priori power analysis was conducted using G*Power 3.1. The results indicated that a minimum sample size of 66 participants would provide sufficient power to detect a medium effect size (based upon Cohen's suggestion of 0.5 for a medium effect size [27], and given the planned analysis). The final sample ($N = 70$) provides enough power to detect an effect size of 0.48.

Data was analyzed using SPSS v24. Correlational analysis was used to explore the relationship between user understanding and trust, and repeated measures ANOVAs were applied to test for differences in understanding and trust between the algorithms. Multiple comparisons were controlled for by applying the Bonferroni correction.

Prior to conducting the main analyses, an ANOVA was conducted to test for differences in understanding and trust, between participants with – and without -

experience of working within healthcare. No significant differences were found. Therefore, all reported results relate to the complete dataset.

3.2 Sample

The final sample consists of 70 participants, between 18 and 65 years of age (M = 30.06 years, SD = 9.60 years). 44 (62.9%) participants were female, and 26 (37.1%) were male. Most participants were based in the UK (57.1%), followed by Australia, Italy and Netherlands (5.7% respectively), United States of America (4.3%) and 14 other countries making up <2% each. All participants were fluent English speakers. Of those recruited, 21 (30%) indicated that they had experience of working in a healthcare environment.

3.3 Procedure

Data was collected using an online Qualtrics survey. During the study, 70 international participants, age 18–65 years, were presented with biopsy results (predicted by the ML models mentioned above) for three hospital patients being tested for the presence of breast cancer. The results for each patient were presented using a different XAI-driven visualisation of each model (DT, LR or NN). Each participant was presented with all three visualisations but the order of presentation was randomised to prevent order effects.

In addition to the visual output, participants were presented with the suggested diagnosis, e.g., "The tool suggests the following diagnosis: [Benign, i.e., non-cancerous *or* Malignant, i.e., cancerous]". The diagnosis provided for each algorithm was counterbalanced. This was to control for any potential influence of the nature of diagnosis (i.e., malignant or benign) upon users' understanding and/or trust of the system. Counterbalancing means that – for each algorithm condition (DT, LR or NN) – half of the participants received a malignant result, and the other half received a benign result; enabling the researchers to identify any biases driven by the nature of diagnosis.

For each of the three algorithm visualisations, participants were asked to rate the degree to which they trusted the accuracy of the diagnosis, and the degree to which they understood how the system had arrived at this diagnosis.

Real breast cancer medical data was used for this study. This data was obtained using Weka, a ML tool which has many datasets available for research use. This is accessed using scikit-learn, a Python library (https://scikit-learn.org/stable/modules/generated/sklearn.datasets.load_breast_cancer.html).

The three algorithms tested in this paper are explained in more detail below. These are *supervised learning* algorithms. Supervised learning is a function which maps input X to output Y, where, within the training data set the actual values for X and Y are known [28]. These label the data so when predictions are made a probability of accuracy can be given (usually using a cost function).

3.4   Algorithms

Three types of algorithm were used in the current study: decision tree, logistic regression and neural network. Each are described briefly below:

Decision Tree

A decision tree is a basic tree structure that can be used to make probabilistic decisions (Fig. 2). The trees used in the current study are standard binary trees; they allow models to output discrete and continuous values. Continuous values use a regression algorithm whereas discrete values use *classification*. Classification is a function where the output Y is binary, in the case of this study either malignant or benign. A decision tree can also use cost functions, the cost function used in this paper is the Gini index. This cost function gives a probability for the accuracy of the output Y, the higher the index the greater the chance of inaccuracy [29].

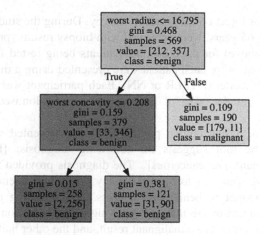

Fig. 2. Example of a decision tree output

Logistic Regression

Logistic regression is used to classify a binary model (in this case malignant or benign). The function allows predictive analysis using features and relationships in the data set [30]. The results are displayed in a bar chart (Fig. 3) showing training and test data.

The training data is the actual data labelled by medical professionals, i.e., this data shows actual real-world diagnoses. Typically, when using logistic regression 20% of the sample data will be used for training and then predictions are made from this. Therefore, the current study also follows this procedure. The predictions give a diagnosis on whether a mass is likely to be malignant or benign.

Neural Networks

A neural network is a network or circuit of neurons. It has an algorithm that is weighted across each layer of these neurons (Fig. 4). The system calculates the most accurate answer at each layer until it produces an output.

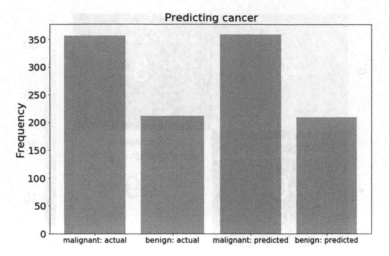

Fig. 3. Example of logistic regression output

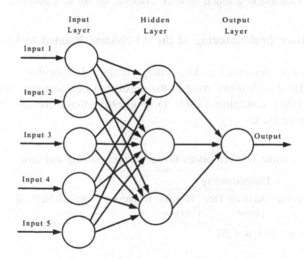

Fig. 4. Visual representation of a neural network

The results from the neural network algorithm are displayed in the form of a confusion matrix (Fig. 5). A confusion matrix is a table that is often used to describe the performance of a classification model (or "classifier") on a set of test data for which the true values are known.

4   Results

In this section we display the results of the study in relation to each of the three research questions.

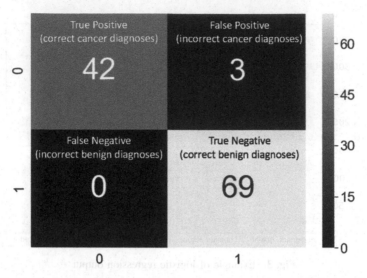

Fig. 5. Example of a neural network's output, known as a confusion matrix

RQ1. How is User *Understanding* of the AI System Related to User *Trust* of an XAI System?

As predicted, users' perceived understanding of the AI algorithm was significantly, positively correlated with users' trust in the algorithm decision (i.e., the patient diagnosis), across all three conditions (Table 1). Suggesting that increased understanding is related to increased trust.

Table 1. Correlations between understanding and trust

Trust	Understanding		
	Decision Tree	Logistic Regression	Neural Network
	.332**	.338**	.400**

Note: ** = p < .01

However, the correlations are moderate at best, suggesting that there are other factors playing a role in user's trust of the system.

RQ2. How Does Type of Algorithm Visualisation Affect Users' Perceived *Understanding* and/or *Trust*?

The results show no significant effect of algorithm type on user understanding, $F(2, 138) = 1.377$, $p = .256$ (Fig. 6).

This is in direct contrast to previous research [14], which suggests that as the algorithm becomes less accurate it will become more explainable/understandable (and vice versa, as the algorithm becomes more accurate, explainability will decrease). This previous research would list the algorithms in order of explainability (from most

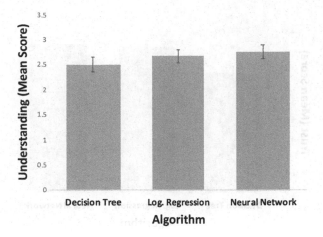

Fig. 6. Mean understanding score for each algorithm (bars represent standard error)

explainable to least explainable) as: 1). Logistic regression 2). Decision tree then 3). Neural network. However, our results show no significant differences in understanding between the algorithms (Fig. 7).

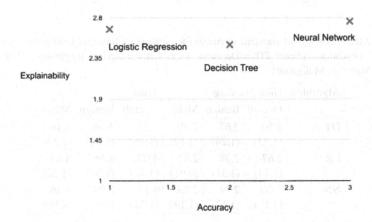

Fig. 7. Mean explainability score and accuracy score for each algorithm

Interestingly, the results do show a significant effect of algorithm type on user trust, $F(2, 133.93) = 7.978, p = .001$ (Greenhouse-Geisser correction applied). Post hoc tests revealed that the decision tree algorithm ($M = 3.33, SD = 1.55$) resulted in a significant decrease in user trust compared to logistic regression ($M = 4.07, SD = 1.42, p = .002$) and neural network ($M = 4.14, SD = 1.31, p = .002$). There was no significant difference in trust between the logistic regression and neural network algorithms (Fig. 8).

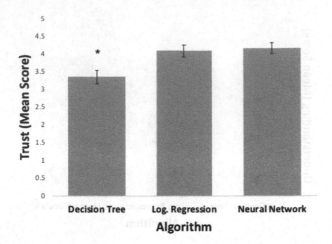

Fig. 8. Mean trust score for each algorithm (bars represent standard error, * = $p < .05$)

RQ3. Do Users Make Accurate Decisions Based Upon an XAI System, or Do They Show Any Biases?

Interestingly, there were some differences in both user understanding and trust, based upon whether the diagnosis provided by the system was malignant or benign (Table 2).

Table 2. Mean scores (and standard deviation) for understanding and trust across the different diagnoses' conditions (*Note*: DT = Decision Tree, LR = Logistic Regression, NN = Neural Network, Malig. = Malignant)

Algorithm	Understanding			Trust		
	Overall	Benign	Malig.	Overall	Benign	Malig.
DT	2.50	2.67	2.29	3.33	3.46	3.16
	(1.22)	(1.24)	(1.19)	(1.55)	(1.57)	(1.53)
LR	2.67	2.38	2.92	4.07	3.66	4.42
	(1.14)	(1.31)	(0.91)	(1.42)	(1.54)	(1.22)
NN	2.76	2.79	2.73	4.14	3.79	4.46
	(1.17)	(1.17)	(1.19)	(1.31)	(1.60)	(0.90)

A significant difference was found for understanding in the LR group ($p < .05$; Fig. 9), with users more likely to indicate *greater* understanding of the system when the diagnosis provided was malignant ($M = 2.92$) compared to benign ($M = 2.38$).

Diagnosis also significantly influenced users' trust in the system. Significant differences ($p < .05$) were found for two of the three algorithms: LR and NN (Fig. 10). In both of these conditions, users are *more* likely to trust the accuracy of the system if the diagnosis provided was malignant, compared to when the diagnosis provided was benign (Table 2). Suggesting a bias towards a malignant diagnosis.

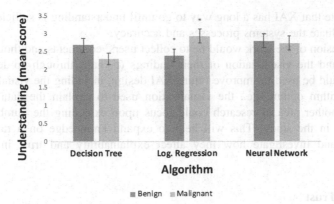

Fig. 9. Mean understanding score for each algorithm, for both diagnosis conditions (Bars represent standard error, * = $p < .05$)

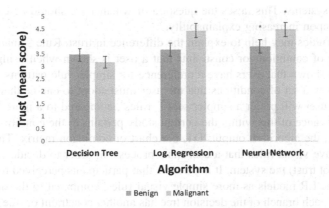

Fig. 10. Mean trust score for each algorithm, for both diagnosis conditions. (Bars represent standard error, * = $p < .05$)

5 Discussion

In this section we discuss the findings of the study, derive explanations for each of the results and suggest further work and design considerations.

5.1 User Understanding

Our findings are in direct conflict to previous non-experimental research which has suggested that the algorithms would differ in the level of user understanding [14]. It has been suggested that more accurate algorithms (usually NN and others that tend to apply more 'black box' approaches) would be less understood by a human user. Whereas we found no difference. This may suggest that users need more interaction with systems to have a higher or changed level of understanding [31]. Alternatively, these findings could indicate that XAI has a long way to go until understanding is sufficient to allow users to evaluate the systems processes and accuracy.

An extension of the work would be to collect users' comments and thoughts on the algorithms and the visualization of their findings (perhaps through co-design). This feedback could be used to improve future XAI design, including the visual generation of the algorithm output (i.e., the visualization used to explain the data processing method). Another area of research could focus upon extending the number of algorithms used in the study. This will help to expand knowledge on a range of ML techniques and investigate how they affect explainability and trust in automated systems.

5.2   User Trust

Surprisingly despite the lack of difference in user understanding, the results do show significant differences in trust between the algorithms. This is particularly interesting as it suggests that other factor(s) outside of user understanding are playing a role in user trust of XAI systems. This raises the question of whether we should be careful not to focus solely upon increasing explainability.

Rule semantics may help to explain the difference in trust. Rule semantics refer to 'the meaning of conditions or constraints that a user is shown when using a system'. Research has shown that users have a preference for simpler rule patterns. This means that when given a set of conditions that the user must adopt to enable them to make a decision, the user will prefer a simpler set of 'rules', compared to a more complex set [32]. The relevance of this within the current study pertains to the conditions shown to the users, i.e., the algorithm output: DT, bar chart or confusion matrix. The algorithm outputs all have visual rules that a user must process, in order to decide whether they trust (or do not trust) the system. It is possible that participants perceived the confusion matrix and the LR models as more simple visual rules, compared to the decision tree. For example, each branch of the decision tree has another constraint or rule whereas the confusion matrix and bar chart have one constraint. So, although users may understand the basic premise of the decision tree (i.e., that it uses multiple stages - or branches - to reach its decision) they may not trust the algorithm due to the apparent complexity of the calculations leading to the decision at each of these stages/branches.

The findings fit with previous research, which suggests that, in general, humans have a lack of trust in DSTs [16] (with the exception of those individuals that may show an automation bias [21]). The DT may have appeared more automated, as users can see the sequential actions taken for each step of the decision process. This is interesting given that previous non-experimental research would predict that the decision tree would be the most understandable of the three algorithms [14]; and raises questions over whether showing the stages of automation may actually help or hinder user understanding and trust.

5.3   Designing for Trust

Trust is important when designing AI-based DSTs for healthcare, but designing for trust alone is not enough, accuracy and performance must also be taken into account.

At the moment users appear to be depending upon mental heuristics (i.e., 'rules of thumb') to reach a decision of trust, rather than making a deliberated assessment based upon explicit understanding. Established economic research shows that there are two distinct modes of human decision making, often referred to as System 1 (automatic and fast) and System 2 (slow and considered). System 1 relies upon heuristics to provide an efficient system for quick decision making. Whilst System 1 is less effortful for the individual, it can be more prone to error and biases [9, 33]. Giving our findings and the criticality of XAI in healthcare, developers may wish to consider ways to encourage users to make decisions based more upon System 2.

Potential design considerations include providing users with ongoing feedback concerning the accuracy of the system. Other factors that affect trust include the occurrence – and regularity – of false alarms (known as a Type I error) and incorrect benign diagnoses (Type II error) [34].

Designers should also be aware of the influence that design can have upon trust. For instance, anthropomorphism – the attribution of human characteristics or behavior – can promote greater trust. De Visser et al. [35] ran three studies where participants received advice that deteriorated gradually in reliability from a computer, avatar, or human agent. Their results showed (a) that anthropomorphic agents were associated with greater trust resilience, i.e. a higher resistance to breakdowns in trust. AI anthropomorphism is therefore a critical variable that should be carefully incorporated into any general theory of human–agent trust as well as AI design. However, as aforementioned, it is critical that design facilitates an appropriate level of trust that is reflective of the system capabilities, limitations and accuracy. Design must avoid promoting blind trust and overreliance [20].

5.4 User Bias

Another fascinating finding is that users show bias in their trust (and to a limited degree their understanding) of the system, depending upon the nature of the diagnosis that the system suggests. Participants showed a negative bias, i.e., a bias towards malignant results. This may initially seem surprising given that this result represents the non-desirable outcome, i.e., the presence of cancerous cells. Again, possible reasons for this bias could relate to users making decisions based upon mental rules or heuristics. Some existing research suggests that humans show a negativity bias when it comes to making assessments of health-risks [36]. However, this has been contested by research on unrealistic optimism and positivity-bias, i.e., that people show a tendency to under-estimate their own health risk compared to others [37]. Optimism bias has been shown in relation to breast cancer screening [38]. Based upon the conflicting literature, and the current findings, the authors suggest that this bias may depend upon the situation or context. Individuals may be more likely to assume that cancer will not occur, until there is a tangible sign they associate with the disease (i.e., the presence of a lump). This notion is supported by research suggesting that people form health-risk assessments on the basis of idiosyncratic *case-risk information*, including whether a patient possesses symptoms of an illness. Therefore, it is possible that individuals will show a tendency to assume the worst when there is a tangible sign associated with a disease. In this instance, being more likely to trust a malignant diagnosis as accurate when a lump is present. Dunning et al. [19] describe this as the *symmetry rule* – the heuristic that people believe symptoms to denote illness. The symmetry rule would predict that individuals would be more likely to accept a positive test result when a symptom is present (such as a malignant diagnosis of a lump); and conversely be more skeptical of a negative test result.

Future research should aim to further investigate the underpinnings of this bias towards negative health results (including whether it is dependent upon the situation or context, e.g., presence of symptoms) and its implication upon XAI design considerations.

The current study strengthens the existing literature by applying a multidisciplinary, experimental approach and empirical analysis of user trust and understanding. The authors acknowledge two limitations: firstly, although the sample size was sufficient to detect a medium effect size it is possible that a larger sample may have been able to detect more differences in understandability between the algorithms. Therefore, future research should seek to increase the sample size to increase statistical power. Secondly, the study did not involve any participant interaction with the XAI systems, the authors suggest that future research includes participant interactivity to identify the effect that this may have on aiding user understanding and trust [18]. This could include allowing participants to manipulate different values of the system and enabling them to ask the system questions.

6   Conclusion

In summary, this study addresses an important gap in the current body of knowledge by highlighting three key findings:

1. Level of user understanding was not significantly different between the algorithm visualisations – contradictory to previous non-experimental research which suggests that more accurate (but typically more 'black box' approaches such as NN) would be less understood.
2. Despite no significant difference in user understanding, user trust between the different algorithm visualisations was significantly different. This suggests that understanding and explainability are not the only factors contributing to user trust in AI; and raises concerns over research and design focusing solely upon explainability.
3. Users display biases in trust – and to a lesser degree, understanding – depending upon the nature of the XAI diagnosis (benign or malignant). Specifically, participants show a negative bias, i.e., a bias towards malignant results. This raises important issues around how humans can be encouraged to make more accurate judgements of XAI outcomes. Whilst trust is important when designing XAI-based systems for healthcare, accuracy and performance must also be taken into account – particularly if users do not appear to be reaching their decisions based upon deliberated assessment and explicit understanding.

These findings have implications in relation to ethical AI use, precise human assessment of AI accuracy, future XAI design, and healthcare. There is clearly still a long way to go for XAI research and the goal of obtaining a truly trusted and explainable system. This is especially critical when being used in a medical scenario where people's lives and wellbeing are at stake. It is critical that design facilitates an appropriate level of trust that is reflective of the system capabilities, limitations and accuracy. Design must avoid promoting blind trust and over-reliance [20]. Ongoing research in this area is vital to work towards systems that can accurately and efficiently support healthcare staff to deliver effective and timely patient care. This has the potential to positively impact upon the wellbeing of staff, patients and broader society due to the wider application of XAI systems.

References

1. Hall, L.H., Johnson, J., Watt, I., et al.: Healthcare staff wellbeing, burnout, and patient safety: a systematic review. PLoS One **11**, e0159015 (2016). https://doi.org/10.1371/journal.pone.0159015
2. Yang, Q., Steinfeld, A., Zimmerman, J.: Unremarkable AI: fitting intelligent decision support into critical, clinical decision-making processes. In: CHI Conference on Human Factors in Computing Systems Proceedings (CHI 2019) (2019)
3. Musen, M.A., Middleton, B., Greenes, R.A.: Clinical decision-support systems. In: Shortliffe, E.H., Cimino, J.J. (eds.) Biomedical Informatics, pp. 643–674. Springer, London (2014). https://doi.org/10.1007/978-1-4471-4474-8_22
4. Marr, B.: What is the difference between artificial intelligence and machine learning? In: Forbes (2016). https://www.forbes.com/sites/bernardmarr/2016/12/06/what-is-the-difference-between-artificial-intelligence-and-machine-learning/#404d18732742. Accessed 3 Apr 2019
5. Dunie, R., Miers, D., Wong, J., et al.: Magic quadrant for intelligent business process management suites. In: Gartner (2019). https://www.gartner.com/doc/reprints?id=1-66KPV4X&ct=190201&st=sb. Accessed 3 Apr 2019
6. Szolovitz, P.: AI for the M.D. Science **80**(363), 1402 (2019). https://doi.org/10.1126/science.aaw4041
7. Ting, D.S.W., Liu, Y., Burlina, P., et al.: AI for medical imaging goes deep. Nat. Med. **24**, 539–540 (2018). https://doi.org/10.1038/s41591-018-0029-3
8. Coventry, L., Branley, D.: Cybersecurity in healthcare: a narrative review of trends, threats and ways forward. Maturitas **113**, 48–52 (2018). https://doi.org/10.1016/j.maturitas.2018.04.008
9. Wang, D., Yang, Q., Abdul, A., Lim, B.Y.: Designing theory-driven user-centric explainable AI. In: Proceedings of the 2019 CHI Conference on Human Factors in Computing Systems - CHI 2019, pp. 1–15. ACM Press, New York (2019)
10. Accenture. Explainable AI: The Next Stage of Human-machine Collaboration (2018)
11. Amershi, S., Inkpen, K., Teevan, J., et al.: Guidelines for human-AI interaction. In: Proceedings of the 2019 CHI Conference on Human Factors in Computing Systems - CHI 2019, pp. 1–13. ACM Press, New York (2019)
12. Scikit-Learn Wisconsin Breast Cancer Database. https://scikit-learn.org/stable/modules/generated/sklearn.datasets.load_breast_cancer.html. Accessed 14 Jan 2020
13. Mena, L.J., Orozco, E.E., Felix, V.G., et al.: Machine learning approach to extract diagnostic and prognostic thresholds: Application in prognosis of cardiovascular mortality. Comput. Math. Methods Med. (2012). https://doi.org/10.1155/2012/750151

14. Salama, G.I., Salama, G.I., Abdelhalim, M.B., Zeid, M.A.: Breast cancer diagnosis on three different datasets using multi-classifiers. Int. J. Comput. Inform. Technol. 2277 (2012)
15. Graham, J.L., Giordano, T.P., Grimes, R.M., et al.: Influence of trust on HIV diagnosis and care practices: a literature review. J. Int. Assoc. Phys. AIDS Care **9**, 346–352. https://doi.org/10.1177/1545109710380461
16. Lewicki, R.J., Tomlinson, E.C., Gillespie, N.: Models of interpersonal trust development: theoretical approaches, empirical evidence, and future directions. J. Manag. (2006). https://doi.org/10.1177/0149206306294405
17. Parasuraman, R., Riley, V.: Humans and automation: use, misuse, disuse, abuse. Hum. Factors (1997). https://doi.org/10.1518/001872097778543886
18. Skirbekk, H., Middelthon, A.L., Hjortdahl, P., Finset, A.: Mandates of trust in the doctor-patient relationship. Qual. Health Res. (2011). https://doi.org/10.1177/1049732311405685
19. Larosa, E., Danks, D.: Impacts on trust of healthcare. In: Proceedings of the 2018 AAAI/ACM Conference on AI, Ethics, and Society, December 2018, AIAIES 2018, pp. 210–215 (2018). https://doi.org/10.1145/3278721.3278771
20. Clare, A.S., Cummings, M.L., Repenning, N.P.: Influencing trust for human-automation collaborative scheduling of multiple unmanned vehicles. Hum. Factors (2015). https://doi.org/10.1177/0018720815587803
21. Osoba, O.A., Welser IV, W.: An Intelligence in Our Image: The Risks of Bias and Errors in Artificial Intelligence. RAND Corporation, Santa Monica (2017). https://www.rand.org/pubs/research_reports/RR1744.html
22. Ahmed, A.M., Salas, O.: The relationship between behavioral and attitudinal trust: a cross-cultural study. Rev. Soc. Econ. **67**, 457–482 (2009). https://doi.org/10.1080/00346760902908625
23. Chen, A.: IBM's Watson gave unsafe recommendations for treating cancer - The Verge. The Verge (2018)
24. Liang, C., Proft, J., Andersen, E., Knepper, R.A.: Implicit communication of actionable information in human-AI teams. In: Proceedings of the 2019 CHI Conference on Human Factors in Computing Systems - CHI 2019, pp. 1–13. ACM Press, New York (2019)
25. EU GDPR. Key Changes with the General Data Protection Regulation (2018). https://eugdpr.org/the-regulation/. Accessed 3 Apr 2019
26. Intersoft Consulting General Data Protection Regulation (GDPR) – Official Legal Text
27. Cohen, J.: Statistical Power Analysis of the Behavioral Sciences (1988)
28. Chandrayan, P.: Supervised Machine Learning For Dummies: Part 1 Overview. In: codeburst.io (2018). https://codeburst.io/supervised-machine-learning-for-dummies-part-1-overview-15c18f2269ba. Accessed 19 Sept 2019
29. Gini coefficient and Lorenz curve explained - Towards Data Science. In: Towar. Data Sci. (2019). https://towardsdatascience.com/gini-coefficient-and-lorenz-curve-f19bb8f46d66. Accessed 19 Sept 2019
30. Brownlee, J.: Logistic Regression for Machine Learning. In: Mach. Learn. Mastery (2016). https://machinelearningmastery.com/logistic-regression-for-machine-learning/. Accessed 22 Aug 2019
31. Track, R., Anjomshoae, S., Najjar, A., et al.: Explainable agents and robots: results from a systematic literature review. In: Proceedings of the 18th International Conference on Autonomous Agents and MultiAgent Systems (AAMAS 2019) (2019)
32. Fürnkranz, J., Kliegr, T., Paulheim, H.: On Cognitive Preferences and the Plausibility of Rule-based Models (2018)
33. Kahneman, D.: Thinking, Fast and Slow. Penguin, London (2011)
34. Banerjee, A., Chitnis, U.B., Jadhav, S.L., et al.: Hypothesis testing, type I and type II errors. Ind. Psychiatry J. **18**, 127–131 (2009). https://doi.org/10.4103/0972-6748.62274

35. de Visser, E.J., Monfort, S.S., McKendrick, R., et al.: Almost human: anthropomorphism increases trust resilience in cognitive agents. J. Exp. Psychol. Appl. (2016). https://doi.org/10.1037/xap0000092

36. Siegrist, M., Cousin, M.-E., Frei, M.: Biased confidence in risk assessment studies. Hum. Ecol. Risk Assess. Int. J. **14**, 1226–1234 (2008). https://doi.org/10.1080/108070308 02494527

37. Hoorens, V., Buunk, B.P.: Social comparison of health risks: locus of control, the person-positivity bias, and unrealistic optimism1. J. Appl. Soc. Psychol. **23**, 291–302 (1993). https://doi.org/10.1111/j.1559-1816.1993.tb01088.x

38. Clarke, V.A., Lovegrove, H., Williams, A., Machperson, M.: Unrealistic optimism and the health belief model. J. Behav. Med. **23**, 367–376 (2000). https://doi.org/10.1023/A:1005500917875

Inclusive Design – Go Beyond Accessibility

Roland Buß[✉]

SAP SE, Dietmar-Hopp-Allee 16, 69190 Walldorf, Germany
roland.buss@sap.com

Abstract. Inclusion pays off, but how to make that happen? Inclusive design describes a widely acknowledged approach combining user centered design principles and accessibility demands. Recent studies show a strong positive impact of accessibility on the overall user experience. This article provides a brief overview on accessibility regulations and requirements. We will go beyond these regulations to achieve design recommendations that enable efficient product design. Also, we will introduce prerequisites for a large-scale adoption of these principles.

Keywords: Accessibility · Inclusion · Standard adoption · Scaling

1 Accessibility Regulations in the Context of Inclusive Design

Since almost 20 years several Design for All concepts are in discussion. Common for these concepts is a mindset that is aimed at designs which are accessible to and usable by as many people as possible. Every concept comes with a set of principles which are recommended to designers and developers to bear in mind. Principles are for instance technical robustness, error tolerance, understandability, flexibility, and more. However, it is hard to judge whether these principles are fulfilled by a product unless having an expert background or by applying empirical methods. A translation is required how to express these principles into real software features and characteristics. This is the clear advantage of accessibility guidelines like Web Content Accessibility Guidelines (WCAG). The WCAG in its current version 2.1 comes with 78 clear technical success criteria which are comparatively easy to test whether accessibility requirements are fulfilled or not.

Regarding the adoption of inclusion principles, it seems to be a good start to be compliant to regulations like WCAG. They provide an anchor or a minimal scope of inclusion aspects that need to be implemented in software products. But how do accessibility features harmonize with other inclusion principles like usability or user experience? Often, we are faced with statements like: "Why should I invest in some people with disabilities and let all others suffer i.e. by not using the latest technology?" Fortunately, latest research proofs these statements wrong. Schmutz et al. (2016) conducted a study that investigates the effect of applying accessibility principles on the overall user experience of a web service. Following WCAG 2.0 categories three versions of a web service were designed and tested either with people having disabilities but also with people not having disabilities. The results show that a higher level of accessibility compliance leads to better task completion time and better completion rate

M. Kurosu (Ed.): HCII 2020, LNCS 12183, pp. 400–407, 2020.
https://doi.org/10.1007/978-3-030-49065-2_28

also for people that do not have disabilities. But not only objective data improved significantly. Also, subjective ratings for usability, aesthetics, workload and trust-worthiness increased with higher WCAG compliance.

2 Inclusive Design Aspects Beyond Accessibility Standards

Having heard about the positive effect of accessibility on the user experience, can we already call our product "inclusive" if accessibility standards are fulfilled? Unfortunately, this is not the case. Accessibility guidelines are more aimed at enabling users to accomplish a task. Thus, they focus more on the effectiveness of a product. Efficiency as defined in the ISO usability definition is not covered to that extend. Buß et al. (2016) investigated which aspects are underrepresented or simply missing in current accessibility standards. Data were derived from in-depth interviews with blind and people with low vision and from a metanalysis of 582 accessibility test reports

Data revealed that problems of efficiency reduction occur more often than problems of loss of effectiveness. In the following, results are presented as examples, which show that a loss of efficiency has a significant impact for users with impairments. Some of the findings are well covered by Accessibility regulations, i.e. the need for descriptive link texts, issues related to low contrast or missing text alternatives for graphical content. Therefore, we will only introduce those results from the study, which are not or not fully covered by WCAG.

2.1 Conventions, Guidelines and Expectations

Conventions: Users with impaired vision are particularly dependent on their memory or on interaction patterns they already learned, respectively. If these patterns are bro-ken, orientation and understanding problems arise. Violations of design guidelines or conventions, deviations from the design guidelines of the underlying operating system or changes from one version to the next were mentioned by users as particularly critical in the interviews. Changes to keyboard shortcuts are particularly mentioned by blind users, while changes in the arrangement of standard operating elements are mentioned by visually impaired users.

Technology Breaks: Technology breaks are also critical if different technologies are used within an application or if products have been embedded that behave differently. Depending on the nature of the technology mix several design recommendations apply. First, let us look at classical embeds such as embedded documents, videos, maps, etc.

Embeds usually come along with interaction inconsistencies. Thus, the design of your product should really show, that in this section another technology is used. This is that users can anticipate a different behavior in this section and are not surprised by it. However, this is not true for Mashups. Mashups are seamless combinations of two or more sources in order to create something new. The interaction design should follow the service which is the dominant one from the UI perspective as much as possible. At moment, there is no requirement for this in WCAG.

Interaction Inconsistencies: Keyboard users are often faced with different keyboard controls for the same user interface elements. Navigation elements such as tabs and tree navigation are affected, but also form controls such as group selections and list controls also sometimes come with different keyboard operating concepts. Keyboard users such as blind and motor impaired users have to learn how to use them every time and the efficiency in the operability of the application drops. The WCAG just partly covers these requirements.

2.2   Text Sizes

Different Text Sizes: With regard to fonts of different sizes that diverge when enlarged, the degree of enlargement must be constantly readjusted. WCAG 2.1 comes with requirements related to font enlargement, but it does not address this specific problem.

2.3   Keyboard Operation

Aspects of keyboard operability can make it difficult or impossible for blind users to perform a task independently.

Missing Filter Functions: For instance, the lack of filter functions in selection lists with a large number of entries is experienced as very lengthy and time-consuming because each individual entry must be read out. WCAG does not provide a suitable efficiency-increasing requirement for this problem.

PopUps: Separate dialog windows or popups were mentioned several times in the interviews as a problem. Sometimes they are overlooked, they may not be accessible using the keyboard, cannot be exited or only the title is read aloud by the screen reader. WCAG does not contain sufficient requirements for this problem.

Updated Information: The focus of the screen reader for blind users usually follows the keyboard focus. If changing areas of the page are not focused during dynamic updates, blind users will not notice the changes. So often users don't know what to do after the update. In this context, the accessibility tests also identified the problem that the focus is shifted to the beginning of the page or the structural element when the page is updated. Blind users lose their sense of where they are in the dialog. The loss of focus is also confusing for users with motor impairments. Since the expected element is not or will not remain focused, you have to search the dialog surface for the current focus in order to reorient yourself.

2.4   Settings

Persistence of Settings: Visually impaired users complain about the lack of setting options or double work on settings. This is especially the case if an application does not take over the settings of the operating system (i.e. color themes) or if already made adjustments are not persistent. If the application itself does not have sufficient customization options, it makes task processing difficult.

2.5 Help

Version Changes: Autonomy is a very important aspect for the surveyed users. Therefore, help systems are very important. In particular this is true, if the interaction changes from one version to another and familiar operating steps or key combinations are no longer offered or are offered in another way, the help system is the first approach for a solution. The help system must be designed in such a way that it provides both contextual and generally goal-oriented information.

Access Keys: Access keys are usually conveyed by screen readers via the structural information. Also, short information is often displayed to mouse users when the element is passed over with the mouse. Motor- impaired users often do not receive this context-specific hint because the keyboard interface is not addressed. These users are forced to look up the program documentation. This is seen by the authors of the article as a slight decrease in efficiency.

2.6 Conclusion

The data show, that many problems are not covered or only partly covered by accessibility standards. This applies to aspects like

- Deviations from design guidelines
- Guidelines how to deal with media- and technology changes within an application
- Setting of suitable default values

All these aspects are not new and are all related to a good usability of a product. Everybody would profit from avoiding these issues. Again, this underlines the strong relationship of usability and accessibility and the evidence of an inclusive design approach.

3 Inclusive Design - Adoption and Scaling

We will now focus on measures how to adopt inclusive design in products and how to scale inclusive design principles for many products.

3.1 Scaling via Technology

As learned from the studies mentioned above a huge amount of considerations have to be taken into account for designing inclusive products. Leaving all these considerations to the individual application development would not scale and led to applications that might be usable and accessible in itself, but might be not consistently designed towards each other. A design system and an underlaying technology is required, that is supports application development by means of having inclusive design requirements already built-in.

The design system for SAP Fiori together with SAPUI5 was developed to accelerate the entire development process starting from the first concept to the ready-to-use application. It forms a coherent framework of different design languages, which were designed from scratch for a native user experience. With SAP Fiori, SAP Fiori for iOS and SAP Fiori for Android, every design language offers great flexibility in developing visually appealing business applications for every screen size.

First, we will introduce how the technological platform can support inclusive design for the development of individual applications. i.e. with already implemented descriptions for icon libraries, consistent floorplans, consistent interaction behavior for individual UI elements, etc. and in the next section we will show some examples, that still have to be considered by the development teams (Fig. 1).

Fig. 1. SAP Fiori default theme and high-contrast theme taken from sap.com

Minimum Contrast: Following the requirements from WCAG 2.1 much attention was spend on contrasts for individual UI elements and the floorplan graphics. SAPUI5 UI elements support various themes. SAP Fiori's default theme fulfills the requirements for text-background contrast of 4.5:1. But also there is a high-contrast theme in place following the demand of a contrast ratio of 7:1. Among other themes it is accessible via personal settings. The individual choice of a theme will be stored as preference until the user changes it again.

Consistency for Icons. In order to meet user expectations SAP Fiori and SAPUI5 come with a comprehensive Icon library. This is to ensure a product internal and product external consistency of icon usage. The icon library comes along with predefined descriptions. This enables the development teams not only to use consistent icons, but also produce consistent descriptions for tooltips as a textual alternative for the graphical representation (Fig. 2).

Keyboard Focus Visualization Design: Focus visualization is very important for user's efficiency. SAP Fiori defines this visualization in a contrast ratio that it is easily to perceive in the various themes.

Fig. 2. Sample of icons from SAP Fiori guideline

Base Font Sizes Readable on all Devices: Since SAP Fiori is aimed to be applied for various devices it comes with default font sizes that are adapted to the display resolutions parameters of the individual device.

Support for Text Resizing: Although already adapted the font size can be easily adapted by users. The layout adopts to these adjustments without the loss of content.

Keyboard Navigation and Control Interaction: All standard UI elements and controls are keyboard enabled. This is implemented in a way, that all suitable input channels (i.e. mouse, keyboard or touch) are treated equally according to the capabilities of the device or the individual preferences of the user.

Tab Order of Controls: According to the placement of controls on the screen there is a predefined tab order sequence helping users to access the intended control using the keyboard. This includes the tab order for the floorplan but also the sequence of accessing individual applications.

Standard Messaging Patterns (Busy, Errors, Notifications): In SAP Fiori a message system is implemented. This ensures, that system messages appear at predefined locations with a consistent design.

As mentioned above, many requirements are covered by the technological framework. However, there are still a number of things to do by the individual development teams. This applies basically to design aspects related to the individual purpose of the application. In the following some examples of individual development efforts are listed.

Initial Focus Position: Depending on the task an initial focus has to be set. This is very important to enable an efficient task accomplishment. The focus should be set at the UI element which is either logically the first interaction element or if known to that element, which is very likely to be the first one in the task sequence.

Text Size and Fonts: Although SAP Fiori comes with suitable fonts it is still up to the development team to make sure, that font sizes do not differ that much that users using a screen magnifier have to adjust too often.

Error Handling: Although the shape and appearance of system messages is predefined the actual content of these messages needs to be entered in an understandable manner.

Fast Navigation: The navigation within an application needs to be designed in a sufficient und logical manner following the task structure of the intended purpose.

Screen Reader Support: Although screen reader support is technically granted it is still at the development side to arrange the individual UI elements in relationships that are needed for a screen reader. Also, alternative texts for application specific graphical content have to be defined and implemented by the development team.

3.2   The Organizational Setup for Inclusive Products

We will now focus on organizational aspects, that enable a large-scale adoption of inclusive design principles. First, we will introduce the newly released standard EN 17161 and then will show how SAP incorporates accessibility and inclusive design in its organizational setup.

In 2010 the European Commission published in 2010 Mandate 437. It strives to implement the "inclusive design" approach in all relevant standardization initiatives of the EU. The standard, which is based on the mandate, is the EN 17161: Accessibility of products, goods and services based on a "design for all "approach - expansion of the user group. EN 17161 was released in November 2019. The standard covers actions to be taken by organizations in order to being enabled to deliver design for all products and also suggests organizational setups supporting these actions. Topics, that are covered are:

- Leadership and leadership commitment including the corresponding company policy for design for all.
- Definition of organizational roles, responsibilities and authorities.
- The planning of an inclusive design approach including actions to address risks and opportunities, objectives and the planning of a change management.
- Supportive measures such as resource allocations, competences needed, the raise of awareness, communications and documentation of the design for all activities.
- The operation for design and development, the identification of the intended users including their skills, preferences and corresponding requirements up to the evaluation of these efforts. This includes also the involvement of users.
- Also, the standard covers the control of and the communication with external suppliers.
- Performance evaluation including monitoring, measurement, analysis and evaluation.

At SAP, Accessibility is defined by internal development guidelines basically following WCAG 2.1 Level AA. These guidelines are embedded into SAP's development framework (Fig. 3).

The central accessibility unit defines SAPs internal accessibility development guidelines including development tasks and test criteria and conducts trainings and consulting regarding Accessibility.

Each line of business has appointed accessibility experts which act as multipliers across SAP. Product teams plan accessibility in accordance with their market demand and use case.

In internal accessibility testing, violations to accessibility conformance are detected and internal incidents are opened. The product team will work on those incidents in accordance with their internal roadmap.

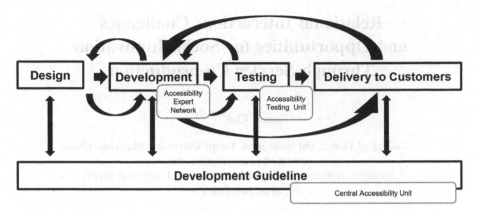

Fig. 3. General overview on SAP's development process including allocated accessibility units

Additionally, new cross-unit programmes are in place fostering inclusive design principles and raising awareness for the benefits of a design for all approach.

Newly released products such as SAP Fiori and SAPUI5 come with characteristics of modern technologies and UIs. Examples for that are modern UI themes that fulfil accessibility requirements or multichannel input (i.e. touch, mouse, keyboard). Also, conversational interfaces are in place depending on the product and its purpose.

References

Schmutz, S., Sonderegger, A., Sauer, J.: Implementing recommendations from web accessibility guidelines: would they also provide benefits to nondisabled users. Hum. Factors **58**(4), 611–629 (2016)

Buß, R., Kreichgauer, U., Meixner, C., Rangott, A.-M.: Barrierefreiheit effizient gestalten. In: Proceedings of Mensch und Computer Conference (2016)

EN 17161: Design for All - Accessibility following a Design for All approach in products, goods and services - Extending the range of users, Beuth (2019)

EN 301 549 V2.1.2 (2018-08): Accessibility requirements for ICT products and services. European Telecommunications Standards Institute (ETSI) (2018)

Fiori Design Guidelines. https://experience.sap.com/fiori-design-web/. Accessed 1 Mar 2020

Web Content Accessibility Guidelines (WCAG). https://www.w3.org/TR/WCAG21/. Accessed 1 Mar 2020

Relational Interaction: Challenges and Opportunities for Social Innovation Through Service Co-production

Eun Ji Cho[1,2(✉)]

[1] College of Design and Innovation, Tongji University, Shanghai, China
ej.cho@tongji.edu.cn
[2] Shanghai Institute of Design and Innovation, Tongji University,
Shanghai, China

Abstract. The significant role of the interaction between a service provider and a user in service production has been pointed out by a number of studies. While interpersonal service interaction has been studied mostly from the perspective of traditional services, based on the dichotomy of a service provider who plays a more active role in service production and a user who is viewed as a recipient of a service. This paper explores interpersonal service interaction from the perspective of service 'co-production' that has drawn attention as a potential strategy for public service innovation and social innovation. In particular, this study pays attention to relational interaction as a pillar and object of a collaborative service tackling social challenges. The nature and characteristics of interpersonal interaction in the production of a collaborative service, and the implication for service design are discussed based on literature review, and a case study of a service design project aiming at connecting people who temporarily move to Niguarda in Milan for medical treatment of their sick family member at the Niguarda Hospital and the locals who will be their 'neighborhood friends' is presented.

Keywords: Human-to-human interaction · Relational interaction · Service co-production · Collaborative service · Social innovation

1 Introduction

1.1 Service Co-production: Users as Service Co-producers

The 'inseparability' of production and consumption has been pointed out as one of the distinctive characteristics of services, different from tangible goods [1]. Unlike products, which can be produced before consumption, most services are produced and consumed simultaneously ([1], p. 33), and "the customer must be present during the production of many services" ([1], p. 34). In many services, customers have vital roles to play in producing service outcomes, but the level of customers' participation in creating the service varies across different types of services ([2], p.193). Some services require a low level of participation from a customer. In such services, all that is required to the customer is his/her physical presence, and service production work is

© Springer Nature Switzerland AG 2020
M. Kurosu (Ed.): HCII 2020, LNCS 12183, pp. 408–419, 2020.
https://doi.org/10.1007/978-3-030-49065-2_29

mostly done by the employees of the service firm. Bitner et al. [2] take an example of a concert: "Symphony-goers must be present to receive the entertainment service, but little else is required once they are seated" (p. 194). On the other hand, some services require a high level of participation and contribution from a customer during the production of a service: "All forms of education, training and health maintenance fit this profile. Unless the customer does something (e.g. studies, exercises, eats the right foods), the service provider cannot effectively deliver the service outcome" (p. 195). In such services, customers have 'essential production roles' that affect the service outcome (p. 195).

It has been pointed out that a customer of a service is "always a coproducer" ([3], p. 10) rather than a "recipient", but the term 'co-producer' or 'co-production' has been used in different studies with different meanings and implications. Some studies viewed customers as co-producers in the sense that they participate in producing a service - regardless of the level of participation - and some actions from a consumer's side are needed to produce a service. For instance, Lovelock and Gummesson [4] used the term 'co-production' in the narrow sense of "a transfer of work from the provider to the customer" (p. 29). Some studies (e.g. [5–7]) even viewed service customers 'partial' employees whose work during service production can contribute to increasing productivity [8]. Customers are also considered as 'productive resources' [2] that impact productivity and the quality of service output. As an example, if a customer of healthcare service - a patient - provides "accurate information in a timely fashion, physicians will be more efficient and accurate in their diagnoses. Thus, the quality of the information patients provides can ultimately affect the quality of the outcome" (p. 197).

1.2 Co-production as an Innovation Strategy

While many studies from the perspective of service management and marketing - especially in the 80's and 90's - used the term 'co-production' to articulate the distinctive nature of services different from tangible goods, and its implication for marketing and management, another stream of studies - especially in the last decade - that have paid strong attention on the notion of 'co-production' are studies related to public service innovation and social innovation. In those studies, the notion of co-production is discussed as a promising approach to innovate public services and also to promote more sustainable ways of living. For instance, Boyle and Harris [9] argued "co-production as a new way of thinking about public services has the potential to deliver a major shift in the way we provide health, education, policing and other services, in ways that make them much more effective, more efficient, and so more sustainable" (p. 3). Examples include programs such as the 'Expert Patient' scheme in the UK where patients with long-term health conditions teach others about the experience (p. 14), and the 'Shared Lives' scheme that pair up disabled people and those with long-term problems with families (p. 14). The meaning of 'co-production' in those studies has some common denominators with the ones mentioned above, such as viewing service users as active 'actors' - not passive 'recipients' - and recognizing them as 'resources' involved in the value creation process, yet differs in the sense that a strong emphasis is put on the 'shift in attitude to the users of services' – viewing them as people who have capabilities, not as people who have needs or problems - and an 'equal and reciprocal partnership' between service providers and users. In this sense, Boyle and Harris [9] pointed out "co-production is certainly about effectiveness, but it is also about humanizing services" (p. 14). Similarly, Nesta's report [10] underlined "Co-production can also tackle the lack of trust between some users and professionals, a dependency culture where people look to the state to solve their problems and a culture of expertise where professionals are trained to be the sole source of solutions. At its best, co-production can build people's capacity to live the life they want, in the community where they live" (p. 2).

The notion of co-production in the studies of social innovation design also underlines its innovative potential to address societal issues and the proactive role of 'ordinary people' (i.e. citizens) in it. In particular, Jégou and Manzini [11] paid attention to the innovative potential of 'collaborative services' which are produced by end-users who use their own resources and capabilities for mutually beneficial outcomes, based on peer-to-peer and collaborative relationship. Different from traditional services, collaborative services are co-produced through collaboration among participants who cannot be defined as either 'the server' or 'the served' as the boundary is blurred in collaborative services. Examples of collaborative services, ranging from peer-to-peer sharing services to community-based mutual help, may not seem particularly innovative as many of them have already existed long before the term was coined, but the notion of collaborative services and its implication for social innovation have sparked discourse (e.g. [12–16]) about new approaches to service design and the object of service design.

2 Collaborative Services for Social Innovation

2.1 Interpersonal Dimension in Collaborative Services

As collaborative services are co-produced by end-users for themselves by using their own resources and capability, Selloni [12] compared collaborative services to 'Fab-lab' and 'Maker' activities and described them as self-produced services (p. 156). Due to the nature and characteristics of collaborative services different from traditional services, a number of studies have sought new design knowledge and approaches for collaborative services. As an example, Cipolla [17] explored two dimensions in a service: operational dimension and interpersonal dimension. According to Cipolla, the operational dimension of a service is its manner of functioning, whereas the interpersonal dimension is related to the evaluation and definition of the qualities embedded in the face-to-face encounters between the participants of a service. These two dimensions are intrinsically related, and any service - whether it is a traditional service or a collaborative service - has the two dimensions. Yet, Cipolla pointed out the form of interpersonal interactions in the production of collaborative services is different from that in traditional services. Cipolla described the form of interpersonal interactions in collaborative services by using a 'circular' interaction model where a group of participants interacts with each other, while describing the form of interpersonal interactions in traditional services as a dyadic interaction between a service provider and a customer. Similarly, Manzini [18] described interactions between participants of a collaborative service as 'symmetrical' interactions, by comparing 'asymmetrical' interactions between a service provider and a user in traditional services where a service provider plays more active role than a user.

Based on case studies, Cipolla [17] highlighted the critical role of the interpersonal dimension and 'relational qualities' such as trust and friendship in the production of collaborative services. Yet, she argued the interpersonal dimension of a service and human-to-human interactions cannot be directly designed. Instead, she argued they need to be 'meta-designed' by creating conditions that enable people to enter into interpersonal relations and subsequently create their own service autonomously (p. 175). In this sense, the role of a service designer is to design an 'enabling system' that enables the participants to build their interpersonal relations autonomously. According to her, service designers can offer some tools to direct the interpersonal relations among participants towards solving a common problem (p. 149) but need to be open to the unpredictability of human-to-human interaction (p. 178).

2.2   Relational Interaction as a Pillar of a Service

The influential role of interpersonal interaction in service quality or user experience has been pointed out by a number of studies. Solomon et al. [19] argued that the interaction between a service provider and a customer is "an important determinant of the customer's global satisfaction with the service" (p. 99), and Lehtinen and Lehtinen [20] claimed 'interactive quality' - which includes the quality of interaction between a service personnel and a customer, as well as the quality of interaction between the customer and other customers - is one of the three dimensions of service qualities. Similarly, Berry et al. [21] identified a number of determinants of service quality related to interaction between a service employee and a consumer, such as 'courtesy (politeness, respect, consideration, and friendliness of contact personnel)' and 'credibility' (trustworthiness, believability, honesty which are partly contributed by personal characteristics of the service personnel).

While much research has examined interpersonal service interaction as a factor influencing service quality and user experience, this study pays attention to interpersonal interaction - more specifically, relational interaction - as a pillar and object of a collaborative service. In general, interpersonal service interaction refers to all sorts of human-to-human interactions during service production and consumption, which is not necessarily relational. Some interactions can be transactional, while some can be relational. In this study, relational interaction refers to the type of interaction that is oriented to human relationship, whether they are short-term relationship or long-term relationship, as the main purpose of interaction.

3   Case Study: T.Ospito

3.1   Project Description

The project 'T.Ospito' was developed in October 2018 as an outcome of a postgraduate course in PSSD (Product Service System Design) at Politecnico di Milano in Italy, which aimed to develop innovative services to revitalize Niguarda district in Milan. Niguarda is located in the northern outskirts of Milan and known mainly for the hospital 'ASST Grande Ospedale Niguarda' which is one of the major public hospitals in Italy. The hospital is famous for transplants, and every year around 6000 patients from other cities are admitted to the Niguarda hospital for surgery or medical treatment [22].

The project paid attention to the fact that not only the patients but also at least one family member of the patients come to Niguarda to accompany them (ibid., p.13). According to a study, the life span of a caregiver can be shortened by 17 years than the normal population, because of the stress and lack of institutional assistance (cited in [22], p. 3). The project team carried out interviews with the family members of patients staying in Niguarda to take care of the patients in order to better understand their life in Niguarda and to identify the needs of them. As illustrated in the personas (Fig. 1) developed based on the common characteristics and needs found among the 6 interviewees, the caregivers undergo stressful times in a new environment they are not familiar with. (e.g. "I wasn't prepared, I don't even know where I am" "I rushed to arrive here, I didn't even bring anything" "Most of all, I miss the sea and my friends…". [22], pp. 35–39). The interviews revealed that the support the caregivers need includes not only practical support such as information about affordable accommodation, local shops, restaurants, transportation, but also social support as they do not have any social network in Niguarda.

Based on the findings from the interviews, the project T.Ospito (which can be translated as "I host you", or "Be my guest" in English) aims to create a more welcoming environment for the caregivers. The main service concept is a system of 'Amico di Quartiere' (which can be translated as a "neighborhood friend"), a local resident who is willing to be a 'neighborhood friend' for a caregiver who is not familiar with the neighborhood. A 'neighborhood friend' can provide practical or social support

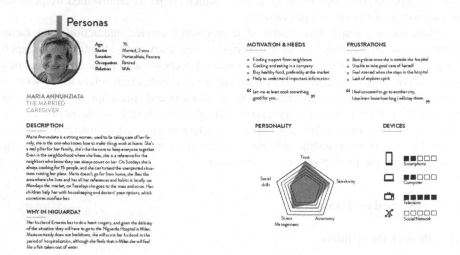

Fig. 1. One of the personas of caregivers who temporarily live in Niguarda to take care of their family members hospitalized at the Niguarda Hospital. (Image by T.Ospito project team)

a caregiver needs by personally interacting with him/her. The type, frequency, and duration of support provided by a 'neighborhood friend' are up to him/her, based on his/her availability and willingness. For instance, a 'neighborhood friend' can give a tour of the neighborhood to a caregiver, and introduce good markets and restaurants. Or s/he may give a hand with daily chores such as grocery shopping and laundry. More importantly, a 'neighborhood friend' plays the role of a local buddy that a caregiver can hang out when s/he wants to have a break outside the hospital, and socialize. When there is an interesting event or social activities in the neighborhood, a 'neighborhood friend' may invite a caregiver and go together.

To introduce the service concept to local residents in the Niguarda district, and to see their interest in joining the project as 'neighborhood friends', an informal meeting at a local shop was organized by the project team on 14 May 2019 (Fig. 2). The meeting participated by twelve local residents (Fig. 3) revealed their interest and willingness to become 'neighborhood friends'. The participants were asked about their availability (e.g. how many hours per week) and types of activities they can provide as 'neighborhood friends' for caregivers (Fig. 4). Eight people among the twelve participants showed a willingness to dedicate 3–4 h per week, and some participants answered they can be available every day. Six of them can be available during weekdays as they are either retired or housewives, while six of them answered they are available only weekends or evenings of weekdays as they have a full-time job. Various indoor and outdoor activities such as 'taking a walk in the park' to 'dining together' were mentioned as their preferred activities with caregivers. ([22], p. 25).

Fig. 2. A poster inviting local residents to become 'neighborhood friends' and join the meeting/social drinks (Photo by T.Ospito project team. Address in the poster blurred by the author)

3.2   Autonomous Approach to Relational Interactions

The project development is still in progress, and service prototyping is planned to be carried out in spring 2020. Further studies after prototyping and implementation will be needed in the future to examine the effect of the service more thoroughly. Yet, a feasibility study carried out by the project team from March to May in 2019 provides some points to discuss from the perspective of service design. The feasibility study, funded by the DESIGNSCAPES (Building Capacity for Design enabled Innovation in Urban Environments) project that financially supported around 50 pilot projects addressing urban challenges, aimed to check the interest of the locals, the value for them to be part of the service, and the types of activities and offering the locals would like to provide to caregivers. The feasibility study also investigated the interest of local shops in participating in the service as local partners that will offer some benefits (e.g. discounts) to caregivers. At the present moment, 15 residents joined as 'neighborhood friends' and 16 local shops and organizations, ranging from a community garden to an ice cream shop, showed interest in joining as local partners. Interested locals and caregivers can sign up any time through the online platform of T.Ospito (Fig. 4).

Fig. 3. Local residents who joined the meeting. Some people came with friends, but most of them were unacquainted with each other (Photo by T.Ospito project team. Faces of the participants blurred by the author)

One of the challenges of collaborative services is the fact that they cannot be produced unless there is a critical mass of participants (Fig. 5). In the case of T.Ospito, the participation of the locals is of critical importance to make the service work. As briefly mentioned above, the first group of 'neighborhood friends' showed a high level of interest and willingness to participate in the service, despite the fact that the benefit

T.Ospito   **CHE AMICO DI QUARTIERE VORRESTI ESSERE?**

Nome
Cognome _____   **età** _____   **professione** _____

◢

SCRIVI IL TUO NOME E UN SOSTANTIVO/
AGGETTIVO CHE TI RAPPRESENTA
Es. "Paolo il pizzaiolo", "Giulia la chiacchierona"

◢

SCEGLI TRE ATTIVITA' CHE POTRESTI
FARE COME AMICO DI QUARTIERE

◢

QUANTO TEMPO POTRESTI DEDICARE A
FARE L'AMICO DI QUARTIERE? QUANDO?

☐ ore/settimana   ☐ nel weekend
☐ ore/settimana   ☐ in settimana

Fig. 4. A form given to the participants at the meeting to check their availability as 'neighborhood friends' (e.g. how many hours per week), and types of activities they can offer to caregivers (Image by T.Ospito project team)

for them is not as obvious as the one for caregivers. The activities they would like to offer to caregivers range from practical support (e.g. *"I'll do your laundry" "You can sleep at my place" "I'll lend you a bicycle" "I'll recommend the best shops in the neighborhood"*) to social support and friendship in a very personal manner (e.g. *"I'll listen to you" "I'll invite you for dinner" "I'll come with you for a drink" "I'll share my friends" "I'll organize a surprise for you" "We watch TV shows together" "We go running in Parco Nord every week"* ([22], p. 27).

The response from the potential 'neighborhood friends' seems very promising, but how to facilitate relational interaction between caregivers and 'neighborhood friends' still remains as a design challenge. For instance, a small-scale co-design activity the T. Ospito team organized to envision possible interactions between a 'neighborhood friend' and a caregiver revealed that the locals feel empathy with caregivers and are willing to interact with them, but do not know how to start an interaction with them. Also, it was found the locals do not want to go to the hospital to meet caregivers. Instead, they prefer to meet and interact with them in more casual environment.

Human-to-human interaction cannot be fully designed nor controlled, but still, how to design – or at least guide – the interaction between service providers and users has been widely explored by studies over decades especially from the perspective of service marketing and user experience. However, as Cipolla [17] pointed out, collaborative services require approaches different from the ones developed for traditional services in which a service provider and a user have different roles that can be pre-defined to a considerable extent. As collaborative services are co-produced by participants who are not service employees, the nature and dynamics of their interaction are

Fig. 5. The online platform of T.Ospito. Local residents of Niguarda can join as 'Amico di Quartiere (neighborhood friend)'. Screenshot from https://tospito.wixsite.com/tospito (accessed on 25 January 2020)

different from the interaction between a service employee and a user in the traditional sense. More importantly, the case of T.Ospito exemplifies that interpersonal interaction can be the main object and outcome of some services, not a means or a factor for efficient service production. In this sense, Cipolla's meta-design approach [17] shows one potential approach to interpersonal interaction different from traditional approaches. The 'meta-design' approach advocates autonomous and creative interactions among people and embraces the unpredictability of human-to-human interaction. Thus, instead of design guidelines or tools, the 'meta-design' approach focuses on facilitating 'meta-dynamics'. The 'meta-dynamics' consists of three stages - from 'acceptance' to 'affirmation', then to 'confirmation' - illustrating the evolving process of relational construction between people ([17], pp. 151–152).

Similarly, T.Ospito favors autonomous interaction between participants, and lets their relationship evolve through interactions. Yet, the difference lies in the fact that the interaction between 'neighborhood friends' and caregivers of T.Ospito does not aim at producing long-term relationships, while the meta-design approach fosters long-term relationships among people who interact repetitively over time (e.g. interaction between residents of a co-housing). In the case of T.Ospito, caregivers temporarily stay in Niguarda to take care of their hospitalized family members. Thus, when the medical treatment at the Niguarda hospital is no longer needed, they leave Niguarda and return to their home in another city. Depending on the condition of the patients, they may stay in Niguarda for weeks or months, but not for years. They may keep the friendship with their 'neighborhood friends' after they go back to their home, but it is out of the scope of T.Ospito. Once a caregiver leaves Niguarda, the 'neighborhood friend' of the caregiver will become a friend for another caregiver newly arrived in Niguarda.

While T.Ospito plans to employ some tactics such as matchmaking based on profiles of caregivers and potential 'neighborhood friends' (e.g. age, hobby, occupation), and teambuilding activities, the main strategy of T.Ospito is 'prototyping' events where the locals and caregivers will be invited to participate. Plans include 'Collaboration Week' during which 'neighborhood friends' are encouraged to invite caregivers to their home and cook together. The 'Collaboration Week' is expected to create an opportunity for 'neighborhood friends' and caregivers to meet up and interact in their own way, and catalyze initial social interaction. Although T.Ospito intends not to predefine nor directly design interaction between caregivers and 'neighborhood friends', what the project intends to facilitate is manifested in an anecdote that one of the project team members described as a "WOW moment": In December 2018, the project team tried out a role-playing game with four 'neighborhood friends' to observe how interaction between a caregiver and a 'neighborhood friend' would go when they first meet. Based on fictional profiles made by the project team, two participants played the role of caregivers, and the other two played the role of 'neighborhood friends'. They started a conversation in pairs - one neighborhood friend, and one caregiver – as if they were the people illustrated in the profiles they were given. During the role-play, a 'neighborhood friend' recommended a couple of nice places in the neighborhood to a caregiver, but the caregiver - who was characterized as an introvert person - reacted negatively as s/he was afraid of going to new places s/he is not familiar with. Then, the 'neighborhood friend' proposed *"I can come with you. Let's go together!"*

4   Conclusion

The concept of T.Ospito is deeply rooted in the local context of Niguarda in Milan, but its relevance and applicability are not limited to Niguarda. As an example, loneliness and isolation have become big challenges to tackle in many countries nowadays [24], which are difficult to be addressed by approaches of traditional public services (e.g. short visits of paid service workers on a regular basis). The models of 'people helping people' [23] or 'collaborative services' [11], which have drawn attention as promising alternatives, underline the potential of service co-production - not in the sense of transferring the work of a service employee to a user, but in the sense of mobilizing capabilities and resources of users and empowering them as service co-producers - and genuine human-to-human relationship. However, "making human relations integral to the way in which public services are designed and delivered" ([24], p. 6) is not an easy task, and there is still a lack of design knowledge and tools.

By studying a case of T.Ospito, this paper discussed approaches to design a service that takes relational interaction among participants as a pillar of a service, and the potential of such approaches. The feasibility study of T.Ospito and a number of activities experimented with local residents of Niguarda show great potential of T.Ospito, but yet there are still challenges from an operational perspective (e.g. managing the balance between the number of caregivers and 'neighborhood friends', so every caregiver can have a 'neighborhood friend') and from a quality perspective (e.g. preventing or mediating any conflicts or problems between a caregiver and a 'neighborhood friend'). As this study was carried out at the early stage of the project development, further observation and analysis will be needed after implementation of the service to validate the design strategy and tools employed in the service.

Acknowledgments. The author thanks T.Ospito project team - HousingLab and the PSSD students of Politecnico di Milano (N. Cervinscaia, A. Cislagi, Y. Hou, M. Monelli, N. Orlando, S. Padannappurath, A. Puppini, G. Romagnoli, S. Shrivastava) - for allowing to use images and photos presented in this paper. The author is particularly grateful to Nadejda Cervinscaia for all the help with the case study.

References

1. Zeithaml, V., Parasuraman, A., Berry, L.L.: Problems and strategies in services marketing. J. Market. **49**(Spring 1985), 33–46 (1985)
2. Bitner, M.J., Faranda, W.T., Hubbert, A.R., Zeithaml, V.A.: Customer contributions and roles in service delivery. Int. J. Serv. Ind. Manag. **8**(3), 193–205 (1997)
3. Vargo, S.L., Lusch, R.: Evolving to a new dominant logic. J. Market. **68**(January 2004), 1–17 (2004)
4. Lovelock, C., Gummesson, E.: Whither services marketing? In search of a new paradigm and fresh perspectives. J. Serv. Res. **7**(1), 20–41 (2004)
5. Mills, P.K., Chase, R.B., Margulies, N.: Motivating the client/employee system as a service production strategy. Acad. Manag. Rev. **8**(2), 301–310 (1983)
6. Mills, P.K., Morris, J.H.: Clients as 'partial' employees: role development in client participation. Acad. Manag. Rev. **11**(4), 726–735 (1986)
7. Larsson, R., Bowen, D.E.: Organization and customer: managing design and coordination of services. Acad. Manag. Rev. **14**(2), 213–233 (1989)
8. Lovelock, C.H., Young, R.F.: Look to consumers to increase productivity. Harvard Bus. Rev. **57**(Summer), 9–20 (1979)
9. Boyle, D., Harris, M.: The Challenge of Co-production: How equal partnerships between professionals and the public are crucial to improving public services. Discussion paper by Nef, Nesta and The Lab, publications (2009). http://b.3cdn.net/nefoundation/312ac8ce93a00d5973_3im6i6t0e.pdf. Accessed 25 Jan 2020
10. Penny, J., Slay, J., Stephens, L.: People Powered Health Co-production Catalogue. Nesta, London (2012)
11. Jégou, F., Manzini, E.: Collaborative services: Social Innovation and Design for Sustainability. Edizioni Polidesign, Milano (2008)
12. Selloni, D.: CoDesign for Public-Interest Services. Springer, Heidelberg (2017). https://doi.org/10.1007/978-3-319-53243-1
13. Bason, C.: Designing co-production: discovering new business models for public services. In: Proceedings of 18th DMI: Academic Design Management Conference, 8–9 August 2012. Boston, MA, USA (2012)
14. Botero, A., Paterson, A.G., Saad-Sulonen, J. (eds.): Towards Peer-Production in Public Services: Cases from Finland. Aalto University, Helsinki (2012)
15. Bauwens, M.: People as assets: towards the co-production of people-powered public services (2012). https://blog.p2pfoundation.net/people-as-assets-towards-the-co-production-of-people-powered-public-services/2012/07/14. Accessed 25 Jan 2020
16. Manzini, E., Staszowski, E. (eds.): Public and Collaborative. Exploring the Intersection of Design, Social Innovation and Public Policy. DESIS Network (2013)

17. Cipolla, C.: Designing for interpersonal relational qualities in services: a model for service design theory and practice. Unpublished Ph.D. thesis, Politecnico Di Milano (2007)
18. Manzini, E.: Service design in the age of networks and sustainability. In: Miettinen, S. (ed.) Designing Services with Innovative Methods, pp. 44–57. TAIK Publications/University of Art and Design Helsinki, Helsinki (2009)
19. Solomon, M.R., Surprenant, C., Czepiel, J.A., Gutman, E.G.: A role theory perspective on dyadic interactions: the service encounter. J. Market. **49**, 99–111 (1985)
20. Lehtinen, U., Lehtinen, J.R.: Two approaches to service quality dimensions. Serv. Ind. J. **11** (3), 287–303 (1991)
21. Berry, L., Zeithaml, V.A., Parasuraman, A.: Quality counts in services, too. Bus. Horiz. **28** (3), 44–52 (1985)
22. HousingLab (2019). T.Ospito Feasibility study report. (unpublished internal report)
23. Sellick, V.: People Helping People: Lessons Learned from Three Years Supporting Social Action Innovations to Scale. Nesta, London (2016)
24. Clarence, E., Gabriel, M.: People Helping People: The Future of Public Services. Nesta, London (2014)

An Examination of Dispositional Trust in Human and Autonomous System Interactions

Priscilla Ferronato[1(✉)] and Masooda Bashir[2]

[1] Illinois Informatics Institute, University of Illinois at Urbana-Champaign,
Champaign, IL, USA
pf4@illinois.edu
[2] School of Information Science, University of Illinois at Urbana-Champaign,
Champaign, IL, USA
mnb@illinois.edu

Abstract. The rapid advancement of technology has changed the human and AS interactions, blurring the boundaries of what must be a human or automation action. The successfully implementation of human-in-the-loop is essential for the new relationship between humans and AS, in which control is shared and a team-mate collaboration arises. We believe that only through the best understanding of human factors and individual differences it will be possible to work towards the formation and calibration of trust in human and AS interactions. Therefore, this study conducted an online questionnaire to investigate the influence of personality traits, culture orientation, and individual differences on dispositional trust, as an effort to map out humans' baseline trust in autonomous systems. We found that while some factors presented significant relation with trust in autonomous systems when analyzed as an isolated variable, such as agreeableness trait, they do not have significant results when investigated concomitantly to other factors. Thus, we were able to identify that some individual differences – cultural values, extrovertion trait, and age – presented stronger influence on the dispositional trust in automation. Thus, our study provides valuable information about human factors that mediate trust, which supports the optimization and improvement of the overall interaction between humans and autonomous systems.

Keywords: Trust · Autonomous systems · Personality · Cultural orientation

1 Introduction

Autonomous Systems (AS) plays an essential role in our daily lives, having significant potential to extend human capabilities and adapt to different demands in complex environments, particularly the ones in which safety-critical situations

© Springer Nature Switzerland AG 2020
M. Kurosu (Ed.): HCII 2020, LNCS 12183, pp. 420–435, 2020.
https://doi.org/10.1007/978-3-030-49065-2_30

endanger human lives—such as disaster rescue missions. While our specific interactions with AS may vary, the frequency is certainly increasing and we are going to depend on these systems in many more aspects of our life [23].

AS has dramatically changed with the rapid advent of computing technologies in recent years. Human and AS interactions are becoming more intricate, independent and even human-like [23], changing some human tasks towards minimal or no human intervention or into a collaborative process with the AS. The decrease of the need for humans to be in direct and manual control of AS alters some of these systems from 'object-based' to 'agent-based' systems. As consequence, it becomes progressively more difficult to distinguish the causes and effects in human and AS interactions [23]. In other words, human operators are no longer just controllers, rather they are teammates sharing the control with AS.

As these new collaborative interactions between humans and AS increase and become more critical and complex in their nature, the design of AS and underlying human tendencies, such as trust in these systems, become a vital area of study. Human-centered computing becomes essential as we move towards a scenario in which we will respond to the behavior of machines and machines will respond to our behaviors. While there are sophisticated efforts into enhancing the capabilities of AS, human factors and how individuals interact with AS have not been adequately researched or considered.

When introducing autonomy into human-dominated fields, for example autonomous vehicles, integrating humans is crucial to reaching successful aspirations, particularly in cases where a human is in the loop and is monitoring the performance of the system [9]. Most AS used in daily life require human input, and how this interaction is understood and designed from the humans' trust point of view will have a profound impact on their continued use and adaptation [27]. In addition, the teammate relationship between human and non-human agents raise an essential but challenging question: How do humans develop and maintain trust in AS interactions?

Just as it does in interpersonal relationships, trust is crucial in determining and guiding human–automation reliance in order to avoid the misuse, disuse, or abuse of automation [16]. A poor trust calibration in automation often degrades the system performance in safety or efficiency. Thus, users' trust and system capabilities should be carefully balanced. Hoff and Bashir [16]proposed that interpersonal trust and trust in AS are two different constructs and should be investigated as such. They developed a theoretical and dynamic model of trust in automation based on three different dimensions, previously identified by Marsh and Dibben [28] - dispositional trust, situational trust, and learned trust. Each dimension reflects the main sources of variability in human–automation trust, which are the human operator, the environment, and AS itself.

Prior to any interaction with automation, humans have an inherent baseline degree of dispositional trust toward AS, which is based on personal characteristics, individual differences, and the reputation of the system [16,27]. However, when it comes to secondary and recurrent trust in AS, in other words the calibration of trust after initial interactions, previous research found no significant influence of personal factors. The only impacting factor was the initial trust, and therefore, individuals may use the baseline of primary trust to calibrate their secondary trust in AS after more interactions with it [19]. Since it is until unclear what exact human factors affect human trust in AS and how, the focus of this paper is on the dispositional trust dimension as an effort to initially map out the baseline trust in AS.

Dispositional human factors that interfere in the process of trust formation, like personality traits, cultural orientation, and individual differences must be carefully studied and understood in order to optimize performance and unlock the potential of interactive AS. Therefore, through an online questionnaire this paper aims to answer the following research question: Do individual personality traits, cultural orientation, and demographics influence their dispositional trust in AS? Drawing from Huang and Bashir's study [20], we investigate the relationship between trust in AS with personality traits and cultural orientation concomitantly. Understanding the influences of human factors and individual differences on trust formation and calibration allows for the optimization and improvement of the overall interaction between humans and AS through the development of personalized systems that can be adjusted to better suit human factors and preferences.

2   Research Background

Trust between humans and AS have various definitions and we adopt the most widely employed one, in which trust is defined as 'the attitude that an agent will help achieve an individual's goals in a situation characterized by uncertainty and vulnerability' [25]. Prior research shows that people often exhibit a positive bias in trusting a novel AS [10]. Therefore, users' initial trust is based on faith. However, this initial trust rapidly dissolves following system errors or situational features, and as relationships with AS progress, dependability and predictability replace faith as the basis of trust [27]. Therefore, trust in AS can be considered a dynamic and evolving process.

Different studies have identified several individual factors that affect users' trust in AS, including propensity to trust, personality traits, age, gender, culture, portrait ethics, and values [19,20,35]. Although these studies have acknowledged the impact of human factors on trust formation, there is still a lack of empirical evidence on how they influence users' dispositional trust in AS.

As previously mentioned, by adopting Hoff and Bashir's model [16], we understand trust in AS as a dynamic process and intrinsically correlated with three broad sources of variability in human-automation trust: the human operator, the environment, and the automated system itself. Thus, we concentrate our study on the understanding of dispositional trust and the human operator, as an effort to initially identify and map the baseline trust in AS, as shown in Fig. 1 [16].

In this model, dispositional trust represents an individual's enduring tendency to trust in automation, while situational trust depends on the specific

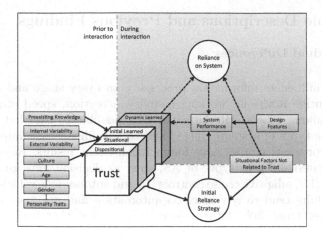

Fig. 1. Full model of factors that influence the dynamic trust in automation developed by Hoff and Bashir [16].

context of an interaction. Hoff and Bashir [16] suggest two broad sources of variability in situational trust: the external environment and the internal, which are context-dependent characteristics of the operator. The environment exerts a strong influence on situational trust, but context-dependent variations in an operator's mental state can also alter situational trust. The final dimension, learned trust, is based on past experiences relevant to a specific AS. Learned trust is closely related to situational trust, since both are guided by past experience [16,20].

Although this theoretical model [16] is one of the most compelling models that acknowledge the importance of human factors for the development, calibration, and understanding of trust in AS, it is to the best of our knowledge that no previous research has adopted the entire model and simultaneously explored its three dimensions. We believe that an in-depth investigation of each dimension is necessary to validate the role and influence of each human factor and individual differences that comprise the dispositional trust dimension. Therefore, in this paper we concentrate our efforts on dispositional trust, as the representation of an individual's overall tendency to trust in AS, independently of context, situation, or type of AS. Moreover, it refers to long-term tendencies arising from both psychological and environmental influences. Although it can change gradually over time (e.g., cultural values, age, and personality traits), it is generally stable within the course of a single interaction [9]. In the next section we present a brief review of relevant studies that examine the different components of dispositional trust in AS.

3 Variable Descriptions and Previous Findings

3.1 Individual Differences

Age: Aging influences information processing on every stage and component, such as executive functions, working memory, attention, speed of information processing, among others [44]. Although it is possible to say that age has an impact on the types of systems trusted and the likelihood that automation will be adopted, previous studies have found inconsistent results. Researches who have investigated different types of AS, such as decision aids for medication management [15], adaptive cruise controls [7], and autonomous vehicles [34] claim that older adults tend to rely more on automation and are more complacent, leading to over trust [30]. Rather, some later studies, that have not explored the direct correlation between age and trust in AS, found that younger adults are generally more comfortable and receptive with the idea of automation when compared to older adults [6]. A major hypothesis to explain the tendency of older adults for over-reliance and complacency is that age-related cognition changes in working memory, making it more difficult to detect automation faults [15]. Therefore, we hypothesize that younger participants present higher scores on trust in AS.

Gender: The influence of gender on trust in AS has been explored as a demographic variable in academic and market surveys. Although earlier explorations found no gender influence on trust in automation development [33, 40], many recent surveys have explored humans' acceptance and perception of specific types of AS, like driverless cars. These studies found that men are more likely to have a positive attitude towards automation and are less concerned about functionality or possible failures [6,14,22,24]. Moreover, males are more comfortable with higher levels of automation than women [24]. Thus, we hypothesize that our data will follow the same pattern and men will present a higher level of trust in AS when compared to women.

3.2 Personality Traits

Different theories have been applied to understand human personality and how it might reflect and shape behaviors and social attitudes [32]. In the dispositional theory, traits are defined as enduring dispositions, being relatively consistent over situations and influencing behaviors. Traits can be considered as contrary to states, which are more transitory dispositions [5].

The Big Five Model describes five broad dimensions of human personality, namely openness to experience, conscientiousness, extraversion, agreeableness, and neuroticism. It has been subject to substantial amount of research and validated by various works across different contexts and cultures [32].

Neuroticism is defined as a tendency to experience the world as threatening and distressing. High scores on neuroticism describe individuals who are anxious, vulnerable to stress, depressed, insecure in relationships, moody, and easily frustrated [3]. We expect that participants with high scores on this trait will have lower propensity to trust.

Extraversion. This term generally describes the tendency toward highly active behavior, positive emotional feelings, assertiveness, and being out-going [43]. We expect that participants with high scores on this trait will trust more in AS.

Conscientiousness refers to differences in volitional control of an individual's behavior and cognition. People who score high on this dimension are described as responsible, playful, attentive, careful and orderly. Moreover, these trait is related with a high need for individual achievement and high commitment to work [5]. Our hypothesis is that people with higher conscientiousness will present higher trust in AS.

Agreeableness refers to the quality of interpersonal behaviors. Individuals with higher scores on agreeableness are empathic, considerate, generous, polite, warm, and harmonious in relationships with others [5]. We expect that participants with higher scores on agreeableness will exhibit higher trust in AS.

Openness refers to a general propensity toward new experiences, creativity, intellectual curiosity, and aesthetic sensitivity [32]. This factor is the least understood of the Big Five and the only one not mapped onto the temperament substrate [3]; therefore, we hypothesize that those with higher scores in this trait will trust more in AS.

While the 44-item Big Five Personality Inventory Questionnaire [13] is the most adopted measure to identify the five personality traits, the shorter version of the questionnaire Mini-IPI [8]has gained much popularity due to its validity. Previous research that have employed the 44-item version have not found statistical significance to claim that personality traits are correlated to trust in AS. However, Chien and colleagues [4], showed that only two dimensions, agreeableness and conscientiousness, are significantly correlated to an individual's initial trust, and higher values in an individual's personality traits will result in higher initial trust in AS.

3.3   Cultural Orientation

Cultural orientation is considered to be the patterns and inclinations of thinking, feeling, and behaving in a way that is culturally determined by people across different cultures. It defines the basis of differences among cultures such as self-identity, interpersonal relationships, communication, and resolving conflict [17, 18]. Therefore, these cultural patterns lead people to view their world through different lenses, attaching different meanings to life events, which is considered one of the reasons why societies are different [41]. One of the most important dimensions of cultural difference in social behaviour is the relative emphasis on individualism and collectivism. Independently of their culture, humans have access to both individualism and collectivism cognitive structures; however, what differs is the accessibility of these structures [42].

In collectivist cultures, people are mainly motivated by the norms and duties imposed by the collective entity. They are closely linked individuals who view themselves primarily as parts of a whole, be it a family, a network of co-workers, a tribe, or a nation, and their social behavior is largely determined by goals, attitudes, and values that are shared with some collectively [18,41]. While in individualist cultures people are motivated by their own preferences, needs, and rights. In other words, they give priority to personal rather than to group goals [18,41].

Although prior research has indicated that individualism is positively related to general trust in automation, it is uncertain whether collectivism has a similar impact [27]. Huang and Bashir [20] found that both horizontal individualism and collectivism are significantly positive predictors of trust in automation, suggesting that people holding more horizontal values are more inclined to have higher trust in automation, regardless of their collectivism or individualism orientation.

Horizontal individualism and collectivism emphasize equality, while vertical values regardless of collectivist or individualist orientation emphasize hierarchy [41,42]. Thus, drawing from Huang and Bashirs' findings, we also adopt Triandis' perspective [41], examining the relationship between the four dimensions of collectivism-individualism: horizontal collectivism, horizontal individualism, vertical collectivism, and vertical individualism. According to this perspective, vertical values relate to achievement and power, and horizontal values relate to universalism and benevolence. Therefore, we hypothesize that (H3) our results are going to follow the same previous results and participants with horizontal values will have higher trust in AS, and there will be no significant relation between trust and collectivism versus individualism.

4   Method

This study is an investigation to validate and better understand the human factors and individual differences related to the human dispositional trust in AS. To answer the research question and validate the previously mentioned hypotheses we conducted an online survey with three hundred and forty-four participants in the United States (N = 344). Since there is no standardized and validated measurement for dispositional trust in automation, we adopted the 12 items from Singh et al. [39], which we believe is an adequate measurement available to assess trust propensity in automation. To explore individual differences, we adopted the 16-item scale developed by Triandis and Gelfland [41] to assess the four cultural dimensions of collectivism and individualism, and the interpersonal propensity to trust assessment developed by Mayer and Davis [29]. Regarding the examination of personality traits, we decided to employ the Mini-IPI Scale [8], which is a shorter alternative to Goldberg's questionnaire. In addition, we assessed individual differences such as gender, age, education, household income, and occupation.

Participants were recruited on Amazon MTurk and received $1 US dollar for their participation after completing the study. Regarding the demographic distribution, 48.58% of the respondents were female and 54.06% were between 23 and 38 years old. For education, 59.29% of participants held a bachelor degree or higher. To better analyze the age groups, we classified the participants as Gen Z (up to 22 years old), Millennials (23–38), GenX (39–54), Boomers(55–73), and the Silent Generation (74–91) adapted from Howe and Strauss [15].

5   Results

5.1   Preliminary Analysis

We began our analyses by examining the relationship between participants' trust in AS and their personality traits (see Table 1) and cultural orientation (see Table 2), by performing independent linear regressions. In addition, we investigated if age and gender presented significant relationships with both cultural orientation and personality traits.

We found a relationship pattern between personality traits and trust in AS, and neuroticism is the only trait that has not showed a significantly relationship ($p = 0.9052$). Extroversion presented a negative relation (std $= -0.2337$, p $= 0.0249$), while openness, conscientiousness and agreeableness have a positive relation with trust in AS.

Regarding individual differences, we observed that gender presents a significant and negative relation with openness ($p = 0.0163$), agreeableness ($p = 1.487 * 10\text{-}05$), and conscientiousness ($p = 00622$), meaning that males tend to have lower scores when compared to females. Rather, gender did not present a significant relationship to explain the scores on extroversion and neuroticism. When examining the relationship between personality traits and age, we found significant results on neuroticism ($p = 0.001608$), agreeableness ($p = 0.00227$), and conscientiousness ($p = 1.18 * 10\text{-}05$). Younger participants (GenZ, Millenials, and GenX) have higher scores in neuroticism, and lower scores on agreeableness and conscientiousness than baby boomers and older adults. No significant relationship was found between extroversion and openness traits.

Table 1. Results of the linear regression of trust in AS and personality traits

Variable	Std	p-value	Adjusted R-square
Neuroticism	−0.01391	0.9052	−0028
Extroversion	−0.2337	0.02498	0.01173
Openness	0.4466	3.887 * $10\text{-}05$	0.04557
Conscientiousness	0.3536	0.003491	0.02182
Agreeableness	0.4215	0.0006144	0.03094

Next, we examined the relationship between trust in AS and cultural orientation. As shown in Table 2, our linear regression analyses found a strong, positive, and significant relationship with horizontal values (p = 6.99 * 10^-06) and trust in AS, corroborating with results from previous studies. While these preliminary results related to vertical values and trust in AS demand further investigation (p = 0.01 and adjusted R- squared = 0.01), with perhaps more advanced statistical methods, the overall collectivism and individualism orientation show similar trends, as can be seen in Fig. 2. Interestingly, individual factors shows a significant relationship with cultural orientation values. Gender is related to individualism (p = 0.00069) and vertical values (p = 4.128 * 10^-05) and males tend to demonstrate higher scores than females. Concerning the relation between age and cultural orientation, our results show that Millennials tend to have higher scores in individualism (p = 0.024), while GenZ has lower collectivism scores (p = 0.025) when both are compared against boomers. In other words, younger participants are more orientated to individualism, and this result confirms our study's hypothesis. Furthermore, cultural values showed similar trends. Younger participants presented lower scores for horizontal values (p = 0.0352) and higher scores for vertical values (p = 0.0279).

Table 2. Summary of linear regression results from trust in AS and cultural orientation

Variable	Std	pvalue	Adjusted R-Squared
Collectivism	0.1225	0.0021	0.0243
Individualism	0.1401	0.0014	0.0266
Horizontal values	0.2288	6.99*10^-06	0.0546
Vertical values	0.0090	0.0172	0.0236

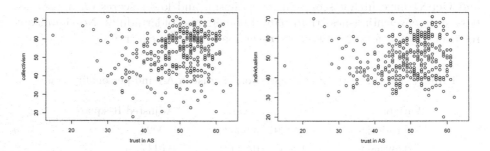

Fig. 2. The spread of trust in AS score across cultural orientation.

Our statistical analyses did not reveal any significant correlation between gender and propensity to trust in AS (p = 0.649), while surprisingly both male and female followed a similar pattern regarding their trust scores.

5.2   Exploratory Analysis

In the preliminary analysis above, personality traits and cultural orientation were investigated as individual variables. However, we believe that these factors are not isolated and they are mutually influenced by each other as well as other individual differences. Therefore, the goal of this exploratory analysis is to investigate the possible changes in the relationship of human factors and individual differences with dispositional trust in AS, when they are simultaneously analysed. This exploratory investigation was conducted in two phases as follows.

During phase one, we identified how personality traits are related to cultural values using linear regression. Our results show that agreeableness (p = $5.98*10^{-}$ 14) is the personality trait with the strongest relation with horizontal values, followed by conscientiousness. While, extroversion (p = $2.514 * 10^{-}12$) has the strongest relationship with vertical values, followed by openness.

In the second phase we analysed two different combinations of individual factors, including age, gender, personality traits, and cultural values. The first combination investigated horizontal values, agreeableness trait, age, and gender with trust in AS. The results of the multiple linear regression show that horizontal values have a positive relationship with trust in AS even when other individual variables are added to the analysis. Although agreeableness has a highly significant relation with trust in AS (p = 0.0006144), when analysed with the other variables, no significant results were found (std = 0.20720 and p = 0.133074). In this same variable combination, gender did not show significant results, while GenX (participants between 40 and 54 years old) was negatively related to trust in AS. No other age group presented any significant results.

The second combination investigated vertical values, extroversion trait, age, and gender with trust in AS. Through the multiple linear regression, we observed that vertical values have a very strong relationship with trust in AS (p = 0.000113). Independently, if its investigated isolated or with other variables, extroversion remains significant and negatively related with trust in AS (p = 0.000440). As seen in the previous combination, gender did not present significant results. Moreover, GenX has a negative relationship with trust in AS and it is the only age group presenting significant results.

6   Discussion

In this study, we present the results of an online survey assessing the influence of human factors and individual differences on dispositional trust in human and AS interactions. When analysing individualism versus collectivism, through the linear regression model, our results show no significance in terms of values nor in distribution to support the understanding of the effects of cultural orientation on dispositional trust in AS. We believe that cultural orientation should not be investigated as excluding or opposing factors, since one individual might have scores for both types of cultural orientation depending on the situation. Because our data was collected only in the United States, and as previous studies have shown, there is no significance results between cultural orientation factors and trust in AS. Drawing from Huang and Bashir's findings, the study of cultural orientation must be investigated with the inclusion of cultural value dimensions - vertical and horizontal values.

Our results show a strong and significant relationship between horizontal values and trust in AS. Thus, participants who exhibited more horizontal values, such as benevolence and universalism, tend to have higher trust in AS, regardless of whether they are oriented towards collectivism or individualism. This sustains previous findings suggesting that people holding more horizontal values may also have more positive bias toward automation [27]. This relation can be better understood by closely examining world view versus a vertically oriented world view. According to Shavitt [36,37], vertical values emphasize hierarchy, thus one's self is different from others, as opposed to horizontal values, where one's self is more or less like others. Moreover, horizontal values may relate to the benefits of automation, regardless if it will enhance personal autonomy for each individual in society, as in horizontal individualism, or if it will advance the whole community or society, as in horizontal collectivism [20].

As previously explained in the methods section, we employed the Mini-IPI scale, which is a smaller version of the Big Five personality traits assessment. Since previous studies verified its efficiency, we believed that a shorter questionnaire would have a positive impact on the overall performance of participants in their response to the survey. Different from previous studies [1], our results did not show a significant relationship between trust in AS and neuroticism. Although we adopted a different questionnaire, some of this research has not analysed the direct relationship between personality traits and trust in AS, rather they analyze the compliance of a specific type of AS, and the perception of risk related to automation, among others indicators. Furthermore, the use of specific types of automation to contextualize the survey, such as autonomous vehicles or robots, might also exert influence on the results. Despite no statistically significant correlation, it was possible to observe that participants with higher neuroticism scores tend to have lower scores on trust in AS. This might be related to the perception of risk related to unknown situations or even to possible system's failure.

The negative relationship between trust in AS and extraversion opposes results from Merritt and Ilgen [33], that people who have a more extroverted personality show higher levels of trust in AS. However, it corroborates with the negative trend found by Huang and Bahsir's study [21]. Extraversion is highly related to socialization and people who seek stimulating activities [31]. Therefore, further investigation must be done regarding their perceptions on socialization with machines, and how it might affect their social relationship with other human beings. In addition, with participants associating AS to specific contexts, such as autonomous vehicles, their current understanding of socialization might change regarding the situation, lowering the scores of trust in AS.

By presenting a weak but positive relationship, participants who are more agreeable tend to trust more in AS. This result stands previous findings [1,21], where the same result was found independently of the level of automation or

the degree of congruence. Agreeableness is linked to compassion and cooperation, and important facets of this trait are trust and altruism [13], representing
an initial bias towards the higher scores of trust in AS. Furthermore, conscientiousness also demonstrated a weak and positive relationship with trust in
AS. People scoring high on conscientiousness tend to be less spontaneous, more
self-disciplined, goal-oriented, an rational [13], thus, AS might be seen as a supporting tool for the accomplishment of these individuals' goals.

Openness presented the strongest relationship with trust in AS, which has
also been observed in a previous investigation of trust in robot interactions
[11]. Since this trait is associated with intellectual curiosity, coupled with a
general disposition toward new experiences and intellectual curiosity [13], we
speculate this relationship is a consequence of the novelty of working with AS,
especially on primary interactions. Therefore, further investigation must be done
to understand this relation throughout time and constant interactions.

Most researchers argue that personality influences outcomes in life not in
a direct way, but rather by affecting someone's general tendencies to act. For
instance, in a risky context where all parameters are known to the subjects, personality traits other than risk attitude do not have predictive power; conversely,
in an uncertain setting, personality parameters do play a direct and indirect role
in determining decisions [12] (2017). Hence, the influence of personality traits is
essential during initial interaction with AS. After that, when further experience
is achieved, openness, agreeableness, and neuroticism must be further studied to
understand how the behavior related to these personality traits will endure over
time.

Although there are significant and important findings regarding the individual relationship between the presented human factors and trust in AS, we
believe that some of them might have a stronger influence than others. Moreover, as previously mentioned, these factors and individual differences might
change their influence when combined with other variables. The isolated and
individual investigation of their relationship with trust in AS might not present
an accurate result. The exploratory analysis shows that while extroversion is
negatively related to trust in AS regardless the other factors presented in the
analysis, agreeableness did not present influence on trust when investigated with
other variables. However, this is not a trend with all the factors analysed. Cultural values, for instance, showed significant results, both when analysed isolated
or with other variables.

Although cultural orientation is a complex human factor and must be further
investigated, our results show that cultural values - horizontal and vertical - are
stronger related to trust in AS than collectivism and individualism. Furthermore,
cultural values are also more constant than personality traits. Therefore, it is necessary to investigate how the five personality traits might change their influence
on trust when other factors, like age and value orientation, are present. One reason why we believe that personality does not present a constant and significant
influence on trust in AS is the fact that personality traits are accentuated when

individuals seek to transform novel, ambiguous, and uncertain circumstances into familiar, clear, and expectable social encounters [2].

Finally, based on our results, gender does not have a significant relationship with trust in AS, which means that other factors like individual personality for example, might exert more influence as one individual has more or less dispositional trust in AS. Notwithstanding, age presents significant results, and it must be analysed in terms of age groups. GenX is the only age group that was related to trust in AS, regardless of the type of analysis, isolated or concomitantly with other variables.

7   Limitations and Further Research

Despite the contribution of this study, this topic presents unique challenges like the difficulty of manipulating different experiences with different types of AS in a laboratory environment. Completely autonomous technology, for example autonomous vehicles with no human inputs, does not yet exist and research on how people behave towards certain AS is nearly absent or simulated [26]. Moreover, all our participants were recruited on Amazon Mturk, which brings an initial bias regarding adoption of technology and lack of diversity to our data and does not allow for any type of generalization. Although we found significant relation between specific cultural orientation and personality traits, further qualitative research must be done in order to empirically understand these individual behaviors.

The next steps of this research will narrow the investigation to only one type of automation. By adopting mixed methods – survey, in-depth interview and heuristic analysis – we believe that we will be able to fill the research gaps found in this paper.

8   Final Considerations

The rapid advancement of technology has changed human and AS interactions, blurring the boundaries of what is a human action versus what is an AS action. The successful implementation of human-in-the-loop is essential for the new relationship between humans and AS, in which control is shared and a teammate collaboration arises. We believe that only through the best understanding of human factors and individual differences will it be possible to work towards the formation and calibration of trust in human and AS interactions.

In this research, we aimed to investigate the influence of personality traits and culture orientation on dispositional trust in AS, as an effort to map out humans' baseline trust in AS. In sum, we do not expect to be able to explain trust in AS by only one personality factor. We believe that since personality has an influence on human behavior, it should at least contribute to the understanding of smaller interactions and user actions in the same way that analysis of cultural orientation will offer "several sources of value – as a predictor of new user psychology phenomena and as a basis for refining the understanding of known phenomena" [38]. Therefore, considering that individual personality traits and cultural orientation influence humans' trust on AS, we suggest designers and developers to allow the customization of AS systems to meet different users' tendencies according to their personal and cultural dispositions through the full integration of human-in-the-loop.

References

1. Alarcon, G.M., Lyons, J.B., Christensen, J.C., Bowers, M.A., Klosterman, S.L., Capiola, A.: The role of propensity to trust and the five factor model across the trust process. J. Res. Pers. **75**, 69–82 (2018)
2. Caspi, A., Moffitt, T.E.: When do individual differences matter? A paradoxical theory of personality coherence. Psychol. Inquiry **4**(4), 247–271 (1993)
3. Caspi, A., Roberts, B.W., Shiner, R.L.: Personality development: stability and change. Annu. Rev. Psychol. **50**, 453–484 (2005)
4. Chien, S.Y., Sycara, K., Liu, J.S., Kumru, A.: Relation between trust attitudes toward automation, Hofstede's cultural dimensions, and big five personality traits. In: Proceedings of the Human Factors and Ergonomics Society Annual Meeting, vol. 60, pp. 841–845. SAGE Publications, Los Angeles (2016)
5. Costa Jr., P.T., McCrae, R.R.: Four ways five factors are basic. Pers. Individ. Differ. **13**(6), 653–665 (1992)
6. Deb, S., Strawderman, L., Carruth, D.W., DuBien, J., Smith, B., Garrison, T.M.: Development and validation of a questionnaire to assess pedestrian receptivity toward fully autonomous vehicles. Transp. Res. Part C: Emerg. Technol. **84**, 178–195 (2017)
7. Donmez, B., Boyle, L.N., Lee, J.D., McGehee, D.V.: Drivers' attitudes toward imperfect distraction mitigation strategies. Transp. Res. Part F: Traffic Psychol. Behav. **9**(6), 387–398 (2006)
8. Donnellan, M.B., Oswald, F.L., Baird, B.M., Lucas, R.E.: The mini-IPIP scales: tiny-yet-effective measures of the big five factors of personality. Psychol. Assess. **18**(2), 192 (2006)
9. Driggs-Campbell, K., Shia, V., Bajcsy, R.: Improved driver modeling for human-in-the-loop vehicular control. In: 2015 IEEE International Conference on Robotics and Automation (ICRA), pp. 1654–1661. IEEE (2015)
10. Dzindolet, M.T., Peterson, S.A., Pomranky, R.A., Pierce, L.G., Beck, H.P.: The role of trust in automation reliance. Int. J. Hum.-Comput. Stud. **58**(6), 697–718 (2003)
11. Elson, J., Derrick, D., Ligon, G.: Trusting a humanoid robot: exploring personality and trusting effects in a human-robot partnership. In: Proceedings of the 53rd Hawaii International Conference on System Sciences (2020)
12. Fréchette, G.R., Schotter, A., Trevino, I.: Personality, information acquisition, and choice under uncertainty: an experimental study. Econ. Inquiry **55**(3), 1468–1488 (2017)
13. Goldberg, L.R.: The development of markers for the big-five factor structure. Psychol. Assess. **4**(1), 26 (1992)
14. Hillesheim, A.J., Rusnock, C.F., Bindewald, J.M., Miller, M.E.: Relationships between user demographics and user trust in an autonomous agent. In: Proceedings of the Human Factors and Ergonomics Society Annual Meeting, vol. 61, pp. 314–318. SAGE Publications, Los Angeles (2017)

15. Ho, G., Wheatley, D., Scialfa, C.T.: Age differences in trust and reliance of a medication management system. Interact. Comput. **17**(6), 690–710 (2005)
16. Hoff, K.A., Bashir, M.: Trust in automation: Integrating empirical evidence on factors that influence trust. Hum. Factors **57**(3), 407–434 (2015)
17. Hofstede, G.: Culture's Consequences: Comparing Values, Behaviors, Institutions and Organizations Across Nations. Sage Publications (2001)
18. Hofstede, G., Hofstede, G.J., Minkov, M.: Cultures and Organizations: Software of the Mind, Revised and Expanded 3rd edn. McGraw-Hill, New York (2010)
19. Huang, H.Y., Bashir, M.: Personal influences on dynamic trust formation in human-agent interaction. In: Proceedings of the 5th International Conference on Human Agent Interaction, pp. 233–243. ACM (2017)
20. Huang, H.Y., Bashir, M.: Users' trust in automation: a cultural perspective. In: Chen, J. (ed.) AHFE 2017, vol. 595, pp. 282–289. Springer, Heidelberg (2017). https://doi.org/10.1007/978-3-319-60384-1_27
21. Huang, H.-Y., Twidale, M., Bashir, M.: 'If you agree with me, do i trust you?': an examination of human-agent trust from a psychological perspective. In: Bi, Y., Bhatia, R., Kapoor, S. (eds.) IntelliSys 2019. AISC, vol. 1038, pp. 994–1013. Springer, Cham (2020). https://doi.org/10.1007/978-3-030-29513-4_73
22. Hulse, L.M., Xie, H., Galea, E.R.: Perceptions of autonomous vehicles: relationships with road users, risk, gender and age. Saf. Sci. **102**, 1–13 (2018)
23. Jennings, N.R.: On agent-based software engineering. Artif. Intell. **117**(2), 277–296 (2000)
24. Kyriakidis, M., Happee, R., de Winter, J.C.: Public opinion on automated driving: results of an international questionnaire among 5000 respondents. Transp. Res. Part F: Traffic Psychol. Behav. **32**, 127–140 (2015)
25. Lee, J.D., See, K.A.: Trust in automation: designing for appropriate reliance. Hum. Factors **46**(1), 50–80 (2004)
26. Linkov, V., Zámečník, P., Havlíčková, D., Pai, C.W.: Human factors in the cybersecurity of autonomous cars: trends in current research. Front. Psychol. **10**, 995 (2019)
27. Madhavan, P., Wiegmann, D.A.: Similarities and differences between human-human and human-automation trust: an integrative review. Theoret. Issues Ergon. Sci. **8**(4), 277–301 (2007)
28. Marsh, S., Dibben, M.R.: The role of trust in information science and technology. Ann. Rev. Inf. Sci. Technol. **37**(1), 465–498 (2003)
29. Mayer, R.C., Davis, J.H.: The effect of the performance appraisal system on trust for management: a field quasi-experiment. J. Appl. Psychol. **84**(1), 123 (1999)
30. McBride, S.E., Rogers, W.A., Fisk, A.D.: Understanding human management of automation errors. Theoret. Issues Ergon. Sci. **15**(6), 545–577 (2014)
31. McCrae, R.R., Terracciano, A.: Personality profiles of cultures: aggregate personality traits. J. Pers. Soc. Psychol. **89**(3), 407 (2005)
32. McCrae, R.R., et al.: The validity and structure of culture-level personality scores: data from ratings of young adolescents. J. Pers. **78**(3), 815–838 (2010)
33. Merritt, S.M., Ilgen, D.R.: Not all trust is created equal: dispositional and history-based trust in human-automation interactions. Hum. Factors **50**(2), 194–210 (2008)
34. Payre, W., Cestac, J., Delhomme, P.: Intention to use a fully automated car: attitudes and a priori acceptability. Transp. Res. Part F: Traffic Psychol. Behav. **27**, 252–263 (2014)
35. Schaefer, K.E., Chen, J.Y., Szalma, J.L., Hancock, P.A.: A meta-analysis of factors influencing the development of trust in automation: implications for understanding autonomy in future systems. Hum. Factors **58**(3), 377–400 (2016)

36. Shavitt, S., Cho, H.: Culture and consumer behavior: the role of horizontal and vertical cultural factors. Curr. Opin. Psychol. **8**, 149–154 (2016)
37. Shavitt, S., Johnson, T.P., Zhang, J.: Horizontal and vertical cultural differences in the content of advertising appeals. J. Int. Consumer Market. **23**(3–4), 297–310 (2011)
38. Shavitt, S., Lalwani, A.K., Zhang, J., Torelli, C.J.: The horizontal/vertical distinction in cross-cultural consumer research. J. Consumer Psychol. **16**(4), 325–342 (2006)
39. Singh, I.L., Molloy, R., Parasuraman, R.: Automation-induced "complacency": development of the complacency-potential rating scale. Int. J. Aviat. Psychol. **3**(2), 111–122 (1993)
40. Stedmon, A.W., Sharples, S., Littlewood, R., Cox, G., Patel, H., Wilson, J.R.: Datalink in air traffic management: human factors issues in communications. Appl. Ergon. **38**(4), 473–480 (2007)
41. Triandis, H.C., Gelfand, M.J.: Converging measurement of horizontal and vertical individualism and collectivism. J. Pers. Soc. Psychol. **74**(1), 118 (1998)
42. Triandis, H.C., Suh, E.M.: Cultural influences on personality. Ann. Rev. Psychol. **53**(1), 133–160 (2002)
43. Vazsonyi, A.T., Ksinan, A., Mikuška, J., Jiskrova, G.: The big five and adolescent adjustment: an empirical test across six cultures. Pers. Individ. Differ. **83**, 234–244 (2015)
44. Wickens, C.D., Hollands, J.G., Banbury, S., Parasuraman, R.: Engineering Psychology and Human Performance. Psychology Press, New York (2015)

Are All Perfect Automation Schemas Equal? Testing Differential Item Functioning in Programmers Versus the General Public

Anthony M. Gibson[1], Tyler J. Ryan[2], Gene M. Alarcon[3($\boxtimes$)],
Sarah A. Jessup[3], Izz Aldin Hamdan[2], and August Capiola[3]

[1] Consortium of Universities, Washington DC 20036, USA
anthony.gibson.9.ctr@us.af.mil
[2] General Dynamics Information Technology, Dayton, OH 45431, USA
[3] Air Force Research Laboratory, Wright-Patterson AFB, OH 45433, USA

Abstract. Humans routinely overestimate the reliability of automated systems. Given people's different experiences in using automated systems, their schemas regarding the performance of those systems may be more or less developed. Extant research has assessed people's automation schema using the Perfect Automation Schema (PAS) scale, a self-report scale comprising two facets (i.e., high expectations and all-or-none thinking). We used item response theory to determine the extent to which two populations (the public versus computer programmers) responded to self-report items similarly. Computer programmers ($n = 245$) and members of the public ($n = 285$) completed the PAS scale in the laboratory and Amazon's Mechanical Turk, respectively. Results showed that items of the high expectations facet functioned differently across the two subgroups. In addition, we observed that the high expectations facet as a whole functioned differently across the two groups. Theoretical and practical implications are discussed.

Keywords: Automated systems · Perfect automation schemas · Item response theory

1 Introduction

The degree to which comparisons across groups can be made using self-reported scales assumes that two different groups respond similarly to the items. Thus, any self-report measures that will be compared across two different populations must function similarly across the two groups. Prior research has used item response theory (IRT) to test differential item functioning (DIF) using various self-report measures including perceived stress [1] personality [2], and aptitudes tests [3]. The use of IRT analyses, however, remains absent throughout much of the human factors research. The purpose of the current study was to examine the extent to which the test items from the Perfect Automation Schema scale (PAS) [4] showed the same item properties across programmers and the public.

M. Kurosu (Ed.): HCII 2020, LNCS 12183, pp. 436–447, 2020.
https://doi.org/10.1007/978-3-030-49065-2_31

1.1 Automation Bias and Perfect Automation Schema

Humans often overestimate the efficacy and reliability of automation, which has been referred to as automation bias [5]. Automation bias can influence the extent to which people use automation following system errors. Specifically, when people encounter automation errors (especially those that accompany easy tasks), they will be less likely to use automation in subsequent tasks (i.e., automation disuse; [5–7]). For example, failure to use a visual aid was more common with automated aids compared to human aids after errors were attributed to both [6]. Given that automated systems can reduce user mental effort and can save lives [8], it is important that researchers consider the extent to which automation bias violations lead to disuse. One important factor in automation disuse is the extent to which people perceive automation to function perfectly (i.e., perfect automation schema; [4]). Below, we describe schemas generally and then link them to the perfect automation schema (PAS) specifically.

In general, schemas are mental representations people use to filter the information they acquire throughout everyday life experiences [9]. People also use schemas to understand current information and predict future events [10]. In essence, schemas are *heuristics* people use to exert less mental effort in day-to-day tasks, which are usually correct and aid cognitive functioning [10]. Although schemas allow us to allocate more resources to urgent stimuli in our environment, they can also cause errors [11]. When schemas are violated, people respond in predictable patterns following those violations.

According to findings in cognitive psychology, people are more likely to recall events or information that align with their cognitive schema [12]. Furthermore, people are more likely to falsely recall details that align with cognitive schemas. In the context of PAS, people may create false memories of automation working perfectly, which may cause a false perception of machine reliability. In contrast, research has demonstrated people were more likely to recall information inconsistent with their schemas when that information was surprising and intense [13, 14]. Thus, because automation typically aids humans with important, sensitive tasks (e.g., monetary or online purchases, navigation systems), automation errors should be particularly evident and surprising. As such, people likely recall events when automation errors and may thus disuse automation after few errors [6]. Given the negative effects of violations to the PAS on future reliance behaviors, researchers have begun examining the best approach to measure PAS.

1.2 Measurement of the Perfect Automation Schema

Similar to other attitudinal variables, PAS has mainly been measured using self-report scales. The most common self-report scale used to measure PAS is the Perfect Automation Schema scale [4]. As stated in the scale development article [4], PAS was theorized as a cognitive schema represented as the extent to which people perceive automated systems to be perfectly reliable. According to Merritt and colleagues, the PAS construct comprises two facets, high expectations and all-or-none-thinking. High expectations corresponds to the perception that automation is perfectly reliable, and all-or-none thinking involves the belief that inaccurate automation is useless. Although personality and attitudinal constructs may both be measured using self-report scales, these constructs have different properties and thus may function differently over time. Specifically, attitudes are subjective, evaluative mental representations of some referent person or object [15]. Researchers have conventionally assumed attitudes to change more frequently than personality traits, as within-person attitudes towards a referent can change and develop with experience. In contrast, personality traits are more consistent across time and show smaller rank-order changes over the lifetime than attitudes [15]. Although the theoretical argument of PAS as a personality or attitudinal construct is beyond the scope of the current paper, it is important that researchers consider the extent to which changes in schemas affect how people respond to the self-report items used to measure the given construct(s) of interest. In the section below, we discuss how item response theory can be used to test differences in item responses across groups.

1.3 Item Response Theory

The goal of item response theory (IRT) is to model person parameters that are independent of the item parameters [16]. The common item parameters in dichotomous IRT models are item ability (α) and item difficulty (β). The ability parameter denotes the extent to which the item differentiates between people scoring low and high on the construct of interest. The item difficulty corresponds to the theta level required for a fifty percent probability of endorsing the item for dichotomous items [16]. Finally, the theta parameter (θ) corresponds to the location of a particular person on the construct of interest and typically has a mean of zero and standard deviation of one. The graded response model (GRM) [17] is an extension of the dichotomous IRT models and can be used to model Likert-type scales with more than two response options (i.e., polytomous items). Rather than having one difficulty parameter, GRM models produce multiple threshold values corresponding to one less than the number of response options. The probability of endorsing each of the response option can be computed indirectly based on these threshold values (for more information, we refer readers to [16], Chapter 8).

IRT parameters can then be used to test whether the item parameters are invariant across different samples. At its most basic, item invariance occurs when the item difficulty and/or discrimination parameters are different across samples [18]. Violations to item invariance is typically referred to as differential item functions (DIF), which indicates that the item does not function the same across different groups. Furthermore, differential test functioning (DTF) occurs when people with the same theta level respond differently to the items across different groups. Because group membership may cause spurious findings when using a scale associated with DIF/DTF, it is important to test for these differences to make any subsequent group comparisons meaningful. Thus, in the current study, we tested whether or not DIF and/or DTF were present in the PAS scale [4] between programmers and the public, and we describe this further below.

1.4 The Current Study

The current study examined the extent to which specific items (and scale generally) showed DIF and/or DTF when comparing programmers versus the public. As stated earlier, researchers have conceptualized PAS a schema that people use when interacting with automation [4]. People create and refine these schemas by gaining experience with instances of similar events [10]. As programmers receive training and education in the functioning of automation, we propose that programmers have more well-developed schemas in general compared to the public. Thus, we expect to observe both DIF and DTF in the PAS scale between the two groups. Note that the all-or-none thinking facet of PAS has only three items, and three items are insufficient to establish model fit indices for IRT models in the package *mirt*. Additionally, the all-or-none thinking facet showed a poor internal consistency estimate, which can cause model convergence issues [16]. Thus, we tested our expectations with the high expectations facet only.

2 Method

2.1 Participants

Participants were recruited from two different populations, across two separate studies. The overall sample ($N = 530$) had an average age of 35.83 ($SD = 11.31$) years, and 68% were male. One sample was recruited on Amazon Mechanical Turk (MTurk), and the other sample was collected on computer programmers in a laboratory setting. Both samples were recruited as part of larger studies that, for the purpose of this paper, will not be discussed further. In the sample from the public ($n = 285$), the average age was 38.61 years ($SD = 10.36$), and 50% were female. In the sample from the programmers ($n = 245$), the average age was 32.59 years ($SD = 11.54$), and 78% of workers were male.

2.2 Measures

Perfect Automation Schema. Perfect automation schema comprises two facets (i.e., high expectations and all-or-none thinking). As noted above, the all-or-none thinking facet has only three items, and therefore we could not confidently model the data using IRT. Thus, the results will focus on the high expectations facet. Note, however, that we describe the all-or-none thinking facet in the subsection below for the sake of completeness.

High Expectations. The high expectations facet is defined as the perception that automation will perform perfectly [4, 6]. People with high expectations also believe that automation should perform tasks better than humans. We measure high expectations facet using Merritt and colleagues' 4-item High Expectation scale. Items included: 1) Automated systems have 100% perfect performance, 2) Automated systems rarely make mistakes, 3) Automated systems can always be counted on to make accurate decisions, and 4) People have NO reason to question the decisions automated systems make. Participants were asked to rate their agreement to each item on a 5-point response scale ranging from one (*strongly disagree*) to five (*strongly agree*). Cronbach's alpha in the current study was .75.

All-or-None Thinking. All-or-none thinking is the belief that automated systems must either perform perfectly every time, or else the automation is useless and should be discarded [4, 6]. We used Merritt and colleagues' 3-item All-or-none thinking scale to measure the construct. Items included: 1) If an automated system makes an error, then it is broken, 2), If an automated system makes a mistake, then it is completely useless, and 3) Only faulty automated systems provide imperfect results. Participants were asked to rate their agreement to each item on a 5-point response scale one (*strongly disagree*) to five (*strongly agree*). Cronbach's alpha in the current study was .60.

2.3   Analyses

As the PAS scale [4] comprises polytomous, ordinal response options, we modeled the data using the GRM [17]. The GRM is a general model that relaxes the assumptions that the response options have equal distances across items and models Likert-type data reasonably well [17]. Before testing for DIF or DTF, it is first important to show that the model provides an adequate fit to the data. In the current study, we tested fit using the C_2 statistic and the Root Mean Square Error of Approximation (RMSEA). We used the *mirt* package [19] in the R programming language [20] to run all analyses. A model shows adequate fit if the C_2 statistic as the corresponding p-value is less than .05 and when RMSEA values are ≤ 0.08 [21]. Finally, we tested whether DIF and DTF were present in the scale.

3   Results

The four-item high expectations facet [4] showed inadequate fit, $C_{2(2)} = 20.62, p < .05$, RMSEA = .13. Additionally, the high expectations facet showed poor model fit for both the programmers [$C_{2(2)} = 9.31$, $p < .05$, RMSEA = .11] and the public sample [$C_{2(2)} = 9.91, p < .05$, RMSEA = .13]. The inadequate model fit may be due to the scale only have four items or from the low internal consistency estimate. We then tested the DIF and DTF across two samples (i.e., programmer versus the public) to examine whether programmers answered the items differently than the public. In order to test for DIF, we followed the instructions provided by [22]. Although other methods for testing DIF are available, we adopted this method due to its simplicity and availability of pdf tutorials online. Thus, the interested reader can use the document provided by [22] to explore testing for DIF further. Specifically, we used the constrained baseline model approach to determine which variables to use as anchor items. The results showed that the fourth item on the high expectations facet showed no DIF, [$\chi^2_{(4)} = 6.73, p > .05$], so we used that item as an anchor item (see Table 1). We found significant DIF for item 1, [$\chi^2_{(5)} = 22.52$, $p < .01$], for item 2, [$\chi^2_{(5)} = 70.22, p < .01$], and item 3, [$\chi^2_{(5)} = 22.14, p < .01$], see Fig. 1. Table 1 shows the item stems for the high expectations facet items.

Table 1. High expectations IRT parameters across samples.

Item # and Item Stem	α	b1	b2	b3	b4
Public Sample					
1. Automated systems have perfect performance	1.60	0.09	1.95	2.24	NA
2. Automated systems rarely make mistakes	2.39	−1.11	−0.11	0.28	2.28
3. Automated systems can always be counted on to make accurate decisions	3.38	−0.91	0.26	1.13	2.78
4. Automated systems make more mistakes than people realize (R)	1.61	−0.06	2.24	3.10	NA
Programmer Sample					
1. Automated systems have perfect performance	3.08	−0.17	0.77	1.34	2.06
2. Automated systems rarely make mistakes	0.72	−3.62	−0.68	1.01	3.32
3. Automated systems can always be counted on to make accurate decisions	2.18	−1.24	0.49	1.08	2.76
4. Automated systems make more mistakes than people realize (R)	2.48	−0.12	1.42	2.59	NA

Note. (R) = Reverse-scored item.

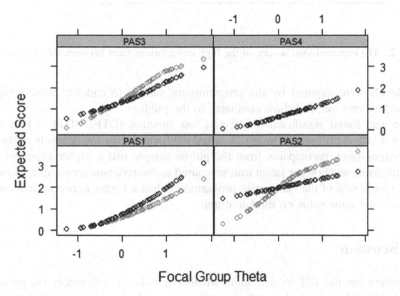

Fig. 1. Expected item scores on the high expectations facet between the two groups. Programmers are shown in red. (Color figure online)

There was significant DIF in the discrimination (α) parameters for item 2 [$\chi^2_{(1)} = 35.34, p < .01$] and for item 3 [$\chi^2_{(1)} = 7.81, p < .01$]. Specifically, these two items showed greater discrimination for the programmer sample compared to the public. The results showed significant DIF in the difficulty parameters (β) for item 1 [$\chi^2(4) = 18.57, p < .01$] and item 3 [$\chi^2(4) = 17.66, p < .01$]. Specifically, lower

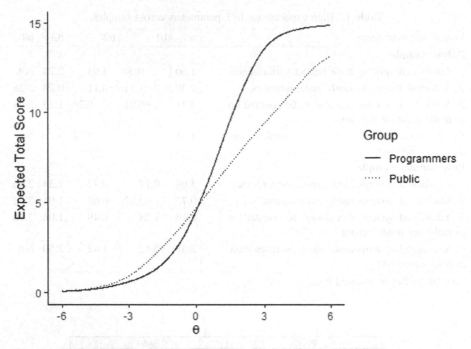

Fig. 2. The expected total scores on the high expectations facet between the two groups.

theta levels were required by the programming sample to endorse higher response options for items one and three compared to the public.

We also found significant differential test function (DTF), sDTF = 1.16 [0.69, 1.64], $p < .05$. As illustrated in Fig. 2, when we focus on the lower levels of the high expectations facet, participants from the public sample had a higher expected score given the same level on the latent trait compared to the programmer sample. However, on the higher side of the latent trait, programmers had a higher expected score on the test given the same value on the latent trait.

4 Discussion

Researchers can use IRT to determine whether population differences are present in how respondents answer Likert-type scales. As such, the purpose of the present research was to investigate whether or not items from the PAS scale [4] functioned differently across two samples (i.e., the public versus computer programmers). Programmers receive training and education in the functioning of automation. Therefore, it seemed plausible that programmers—who may spend more time working with (dys)-functional software comprising underlying autonomous systems compared to the public —may have different automation schemas and thus respond differently to PAS scale items [4]. Specifically, we hypothesized that programmers have more well-developed schemas regarding the reliability of automated systems compared to the public, leading to DIF and DTF in the PAS scale.

In the present research, items 1, 2, and 3 of the high expectations facet had significant DIF. Specifically, items two and three showed significant DIF in the alpha parameter, whereas items one and three showed significant DIF in the beta parameter. In addition, there was significant DTF for the high expectations facet as a whole, meaning responders with identical perceptions of automation high expectations respond differently to the scale depending on whether they came from the programmer versus the public sample. We also found that respondents from the public failed to endorse the highest response option for items one and four. Similarly, respondents from the computer programmer sample failed to endorse the highest response option for item four. In the section below, we describe the implications of the current findings.

4.1   Theoretical and Practical Implications

The current findings have implications for the PAS construct. First, items two and three from the high expectations facet had higher discrimination parameters for the programmer sample compared to the public. Stated simply, these items were better able to distinguish programmers who were high versus low in high expectations compared to those people in the public. The item stems described the number of mistakes automated systems make and the degree to which automated systems are reliable. Programmers may interact with technology (and automated systems) more often compared to the general public, which may result in programmers having better developed schemas regarding automation errors. Indeed, people adapt and solidify schemas with new experiences [10]. As such, the better developed schemas may result in programmers being able to more accurately report their attitudes toward the reliability of automated systems. Researchers could clarify the high expectations items for the public samples by providing examples of automated systems in the survey directions. Automation is becoming common throughout all parts of society (e.g., ATMs), and the general public may be unsure about which machines qualify as "automated systems." If researchers wish to measure attitudes toward referents (in this case automated systems), they should ensure all respondents have an understanding of the objects being evaluated. An alternative approach could be providing specific examples of automated systems in the items. This approach, however, may have several limitations. First, the scale would need to include many items, including different automated systems, to assess general perceptions of automated systems. Second, this would call for construction of a new scale, which would be less parsimonious given the popularity of the current scale.

In addition, we observed significant differences in difficulty parameters for items one and three for computer programmers versus the public. Specifically, there was evidence that items one and three were easier for the programming group versus the public. Stated simply, respondents with equal high expectations perceptions would be more likely to choose higher response options if they were in the programmer group compared to the public. Based on the item content, these findings suggest that programmers were more likely to endorse the statements that described automated systems as performing perfectly. Similar to the argument in the preceding paragraph, programmers may have a more established schema of automated systems with which to assess using the PAS scale. The more clearly defined construct to the test taker will lead to more accurate response option thresholds and better overall assessment. Another possibility could be that the items measure more than one construct, and programmers differ from the general public in their relative locations on this unknown second dimension [for a full description, see 16]. Note that we found that the unidimensional model showed poor model fit for the high expectations facet. Thus, future research should explore whether this four-item facet is truly unidimensional. Finally, the programmers may have had an increased tendency to choose the extreme response options than the general public sample independent of the item content [23]. Measuring the extent to which respondents were more or less likely to endorse the extreme response options was beyond the scope of the current paper. Thus, future research should investigate whether these two groups respond to Likert-type scales differently independent of the construct being assessed.

Another noteworthy finding in the current study was that some response options were never endorsed. Specifically, respondents failed to endorse the highest response option for two high expectations items in the public sample and one item in the programmer sample. Respondents in neither group strongly endorsed the perception that automated systems make more mistakes than people realized. As such, this item may need to be re-worded or replaced to ensure all response options are being endorsed across the typical levels of theta (i.e., three standard deviations above and below the mean). Additionally, the lack of endorsement in the highest response option may have resulted in poor parameter estimates in the IRT models, as previous researchers have noted the importance of sufficient frequency distribution across all response options [16]. These findings highlight the importance of writing items that capture the entire distribution of normal theta values.

The findings of the current study have important implications for much of the research on PAS. People that work in the technology sector may have more established schemas than participants from the public. This can be problematic as much of the research using the PAS scale has been conducted on students in an experimental setting, and the available instructions for the PAS scale have been scant or non-existent [4]. The PAS has also demonstrated mixed ability to predict criterion. This may be in part because participants are typically students that may not have fully formed schemas about automation, coinciding with the lack of established instructions for these items. It remains to be seen whether these are a limitation of the scale, the construct in question, or the samples used in the current study. Indeed, as mentioned in the limitations below, these differences may be representative of the MTurk sample and not necessarily the scale itself.

In summary, the present research shows that programmers and the public respond differently to the PAS scale items [4]. This suggests that those with different life experiences may interpret these items differently. In practice, researchers should be cautious when comparing the current PAS items across samples, as differential item functioning can lead to inaccurate conclusions being drawn from the data. Furthermore, researchers should use caution when comparing programmers to other groups using the High Expectations facet of the PAS scale. These findings contribute to the extant literature by utilizing the IRT methodology to tease apart item from sample characteristics in order to find a purer assessment of individual differences in PAS.

4.2   Limitations and Future Research

An obvious limitation of the present research is that we omitted DIF and DTF tests for the all-or-none thinking facet of PAS. As Merritt et al. [4] theorized PAS to comprise both high expectations and all-or-none thinking, the latter should be investigated in order to explicate PAS differences between programmers and the public using the IRT framework. We omitted these tests in the current study because the all-or-nothing facet of PAS has only three items, and three items are insufficient to obtain measures of model fit using the *mirt* package. Future research could create additional, validated items that assess this facet of the PAS in order to assess DIF and DTF in the all-or-none thinking facet. In this way, researchers will more fully understand the differences in PAS between samples of interest. Relatedly, there was inadequate model fit of the high expectations facet. As such, we recommend the findings be interpreted with caution, as we would prefer the models show good fit for each group when testing DIF/DTF.

One less obvious limitation of this research concerns uncovering the impetus by which programmers have different automation schemas than the public. People are more likely to recall information that aligns with their cognitive schema [12]. However, people are also more likely to recall information inconsistent with their schemas when that information was surprising and intense [13, 14]. The present research does demonstrate that items assessing PAS function differently for programmers and the public. However, this research cannot determine the impetus for establishing PAS (e.g., many "expected" experiences using automation versus one "surprising" unexpected experience), or whether *development* of this schema differs between programmers and the public. Future research should investigate the impetus for which these two populations form their differential PASs and potentially how this might be augmented to establish more calibrated expectations of automation.

Finally, the MTurk sample we used may not be representative of the public at large [24]. In theory, any person can create an MTurk account and complete surveys on the website. Indeed, we found a variety of different occupations and geographic regions represented in the MTurk sample. MTurk respondents, however, may differ from the general population in personality and general attitudes. Although we used the MTurk sample to represent the public, people who are attracted to completing HITs on MTurk may differ from the public in their item responses, their interaction with automation, or their personality types [24]. Furthermore, some respondents from the MTurk sample also worked in technology-related fields (e.g., Information Technology). As such, those respondents might have similar experiences with automation compared to the programmer sample. Future research should replicate the findings of the current study with samples that may be more representative of the public at large, as well as other samples that may have more experiences with automation (e.g., information technologist, data analyst).

Acknowledgements. This research has been approved for public release: 88ABW Cleared 1/13/20; 88ABW-2020-0077. This research was supported in part by an appointment to the Postgraduate Research Participant Program at the U.S. Air Force Research Laboratory, 711th Human Performance Wing, Airman Systems Directorate, Warfighter Interface Division, Collaborative Interfaces and Teaming Branch, Collaborative Teaming Section administered by the

Oak Ridge Institute for Science and Education through an interagency agreement between the U. S. Department of Energy and USAFRL.

References

1. Cole, S.: Assessment of differential item functioning in the Perceived Stress Scale-10. J. Epidemiol. Commun. Health **53**(5), 319 (1999)
2. Huang, C., Church, A., Katigbak, M.: Identifying cultural differences in items and traits: differential item functioning in the NEO Personality Inventory. J. Cross-Cult. Psychol. **28**(2), 192–218 (1997)
3. Sehmitt, A., Dorans, N.: Differential item functioning for minority examinees on the SAT. J. Educ. Measur. **27**(1), 67–81 (1990)
4. Merritt, S., Unnerstall, J., Lee, D., Huber, K.: Measuring individual differences in the perfect automation schema. Hum. Factors **57**(5), 740–753 (2015)
5. Dzindolet, M., Pierce, L., Beck, H., Dawe, L., Anderson, B.: Predicting misuse and disuse of combat identification systems. Mil. Psychol. **13**, 147–164 (2001)
6. Dzindolet, M., Pierce, L., Beck, H., Dawe, L.: The perceived utility of human and automated aids in a visual detection task. Hum. Factors **44**, 79–94 (2002)
7. Parasuraman, R., Riley, V.: Humans and automation: use, misuse, dis-use, abuse. Hum. Factors **39**, 230–253 (1997)
8. Lyons, J., et al.: Comparing trust in Auto-GCAS between experienced and novice Air Force pilots. Ergon. Des. **25**, 4–9 (2017)
9. Markus, H.: Self-schemata and processing information about the self. J. Pers. Soc. Psychol. **35**, 63–78 (1977)
10. Matlin, M.: Cognition, 8th edn. Wiley, New Jersey (2013)
11. Davis, D., Loftus, E.: Internal and external sources of misinformation in adult witness memory. In: Toglia, M., Read, J., Ross, D., Lindsay, R. (eds.) The Handbook of Eyewitness Psychology, vol. I, pp. 195–238. Psychology Press, New York (2017)
12. Brewer, W., Treyens, J.: Role of schemata in memory for places. Cogn. Psychol. **13**, 207–230 (1981)
13. Brewer, W.: Bartlett's concept of the schema and its impact on theories of knowledge representation in contemporary cognitive psychology. In: Saito, A. (ed.) Bartlett, Culture, and Cognition, pp. 69–89. Psychology Press. East Sussex (2000)
14. Davidson, D.: Recognition and recall of irrelevant and interruptive atypical actions in script-based stories. J. Memory Lang. **33**, 757–775 (1994)
15. Ajzen, I.: Attitudes, Personality, and Behavior. McGraw-Hill Education, New York (2005)
16. De Ayala, R.: The theory and practice of item response theory. The Guilford Press, New York (2009)
17. Samejima, F.: Estimation of latent ability using a response pattern of graded scores. Psychometrika Monograph **17**, (1969)
18. Bond, T., Fox, C.: Applying the Rasch Model: Fundamental Measurement in the Human Sciences, 3rd edn. Routledge, London (2015)
19. Chalmers, R.: mirt: a multidimensional item response theory package for the R environment. J. Stat. Softw. **48**, 1–29 (2012)
20. R Core Team R: A language and environment for statistical computing. R Foundation for Statistical Computing (2018). https://www.R-project.org/
21. Toland, M., Sulis, I., Giambona, F., Porcu, M., Campbell, J.: Introduction to bifactor polytomous item response theory analysis. J. Sch. Psychol. **60**, 41–63 (2017)

22. Mead, A.: Guide to IRT invariance using the MIRT package in R. Department of Psychology, North Carolina State University (2016). https://www.ncsu.edu/search/global. php?search-submit=&q=Guide+to+IRT+Invariance+Tests+in+R+-+Adam+W. +Meade&cx=
23. Böckenholt, U.: Measuring response styles in Likert items. Psychol. Methods **22**, 69–83 (2017)
24. Paolacci, G., Chandler, J.: Inside the turk: understanding mechanical turk as a participant pool. Curr. Dir. Psychol. Sci. **23**, 184–188 (2014)

Gaps in Neuroethics in Relation to Brain Computer Interfaces: Systematic Literature Review

Negar Hosseini[✉] and Praveen Kumar[✉]

The University of Sydney, Sydney, NSW 2006, Australia
{negar.hosseini,praveen.kumar}@sydney.edu.au

Abstract. With the advent of novel neurotechnologies, existing ethical frameworks run the risk of falling behind. It is important to identify these shortcomings and address them in a manner that will stand the test of time. We help address this problem by identifying ethical issues that are relevant to the industry and subjecting them to existing prominent frameworks to illuminate the gaps for further ethical discussion and to help structure a more robust ethical framework. In our systematic literature review, we explain the selection criteria for both the ethical issues and frameworks obtained from multiple other papers. In total, 25 ethical issues are treated to 7 frameworks and gaps are identified where current research is lacking. The goal of this paper is to inform future development in the area and provide a springboard for further research. To that end, we hope to raise awareness of the need for the spotlight on ethics to keep up with BCI advancements.

Keywords: Brain Computer Interaction (BCI) · Neuroethics · Ethical frameworks · BCI application

1 Introduction

Brain computer interface (BCI) refers to interactive applications between the human brain and computer. This paper discusses the ethical issues that arise from BCI applications and extract valuable insights from neuroethical discussions of issues encountered in BCI. All BCI-based communications follow a series of ethical principles to allow an individual to interact with the system. An ethical framework in BCI includes a common set of methods that helps with unifying the BCI community. Ethical standardization introduces clarity among BCI applications and increases interoperability. This is beneficial for both users and developers of the system as it raises control and agency amongst environmental and communicational interactions. There are several studies in this field such as the Belmont Report, James Giordano's 'Six W's, Six C's', Nuffield Council's ethical framework, and many more. These existing proposals suggest ethical guidelines for BCI development but there is no aggregated source which would be applicable across all brain-computer applications [1].

© Springer Nature Switzerland AG 2020
M. Kurosu (Ed.): HCII 2020, LNCS 12183, pp. 448–474, 2020.
https://doi.org/10.1007/978-3-030-49065-2_32

There is a need to address gaps in ethics that are organically occurring as progress in BCI overtakes the corresponding ethical discussions and framework development. BCI devices are being developed while evidence in the literature about their impact on the patient experience is inadequate. For instance, questions regarding self-image, autonomy, and identity are raised across a spectrum of BCI applications - in areas of communication, movement control, environmental control, and neuro-rehab [2]. If these questions are not addressed, this may have severe neuroethical repercussions on society which will be exponentially problematic in the future. Studies of ethics in BCI has spiked in recent years. As a research space, it is still not mature and there are areas that have yet to be addressed [3]. Any BCI study ethically has to have a justified rationale and a comprehensive course of action. This is not always the case and a reason being that there are too many areas and specialties with different ethical requirements. We hope to address that by providing a comprehensive outlook at BCI ethics and isolating gaps where there is a dearth of exploration.

2 Methodology

To accomplish our goal towards a systematic literature review, first we searched for relevant studies by accessing 3 databases, namely: (1) Springerlink, (2) ScienceDirect, and (3) Web of Science. These databases were chosen to cover a wide range of literature specifically on BCI applications and their ethical issues. We applied a nesting strategy to filter published studies related to our research topic. Used nesting strategies on all 3 databases are listed in Table 1.

Table 1. Nesting strategies

Code	Applied nesting strategies	Keywords
NS1	(TS* = (BCI AND Neuroethics)) AND LANGUAGE: (English)	BCI, Neuroethics
NS2	(TS = (BCI Application AND ethical issues)) AND LANGUAGE: (English)	BCI Application, Ethical issues
NS3	(TS = (BCI Application AND ethical issues) OR TS = (BCI AND Neuroethics)) AND LANGUAGE: (English)	BCI Application, Ethical issues, BCI, Neuroethics
NS4	(TS = (BCI AND Neuroethics) OR TS = (Brain computer interaction AND ethical issues)) AND LANGUAGE: (English)	BCI, Neuroethics, Brain computer interaction, Ethical issues

The results of each nesting strategy were manually filtered by their average yearly citations to collect more-referenced papers (Average citations per year > 1). Further, to avoid duplications, remaining papers were reviewed by researchers individually. The result of our systematic review and applied filters are shown in Table 2.

Next step was to form an inclusive list of raised ethical concerns. We conducted an issue-oriented approach to categorise ethical issues in a taxonomic classification

(Table 3). To serve the goal of the research and identify gaps in existing neuroethical frameworks, we reviewed existing/suggested frameworks and highlighted ethical issues which were covered/uncovered in each framework. Figure 1 visualises our research approach.

2.1 Systematic Literature Review

To conduct our research we followed information systems (IS) systematic literature review guidelines by Vom Brocke et al. that contains the following steps: (1) Topic and scope definition, (2) Search for related literature, (3) Found literature analysis, and (4) Add reviewer's insights to the research [4].

As discussed in our problem statement, the topic and the main goal of this research is to collectively review general neuroethical issues related to BCI applications and

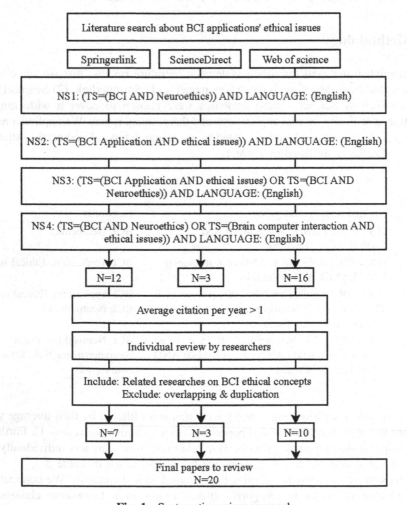

Fig. 1. Systematic review approach

Table 2. Research result

Database	NS[a]	Filtering	Article	Journal	ACY[b]	Incl.
Springerlink	NS1 n = 82	ACY > 1 && ! duplication, n = 11	A Four-part Working Bibliography of Neuroethics: Part 1: Overview and Reviews - Defining and Describing the Field and Its Practices	Philosophy Ethics and Humanities in Medicine	2.33	Yes
			A Four-part Working Bibliography of Neuroethics: Part 2: Neuroscientific Studies of Morality and Ethics	Philosophy Ethics and Humanities in Medicine	1.4	Yes
			A Four-part Working Bibliography of Neuroethics: Part 3: "Second Tradition Neuroethics" - Ethical Issues in Neuroscience	Philosophy Ethics and Humanities in Medicine	1.5	Yes
			A Four-part Working Bibliography of Neuroethics: Part 4: Ethical Issues in Clinical and Social Applications of Neuroscience	Philosophy Ethics and Humanities in Medicine	1.67	Yes
			Psychosocial and Ethical Aspects in Non-Invasive EEG-Based BCI Research-A Survey Among BCI Users and BCI Professionals	Neuroethics	2.33	Yes
			Ethical Challenges Associated with the Development and Deployment of Brain Computer Interface Technology	Neuroethics	2.33	Yes
			Ethical Aspects of Brain Computer Interfaces: A Scoping Review	BMC Medical Ethics	3.33	Yes
			Informed Consent in Implantable BCI Research: Identifying Risks and Exploring Meaning	Science and Engineering Ethics	1.5	No
			Brain to Computer Communication: Ethical Perspectives on Interaction Models	Neuroethics	1.5	No
			An Analysis of the Impact of Brain-Computer Interfaces on Autonomy	Neuroethics	1	No
			Ethical Considerations in the Use of Brain-Computer Interfaces	Central European Journal of Medicine	1.43	No
	NS2 n = 154	ACY > 1 && ! duplication, n = 1	Wired Emotions: Ethical Issues of Affective Brain–Computer Interfaces	Science and Engineering Ethics	1	No

(continued)

Table 2. (*continued*)

Database	NS[a]	Filtering	Article	Journal	ACY[b]	Incl.
Web of science	NS1 n = 21	ACY > 1 && ! duplication, n = 8	Using Brain-Computer Interfaces: A Scoping Review of Studies Employing Social Research Methods	BMC Medical Ethics	1	Yes
			Beyond 'Communication and Control': Towards Ethically Complete Rationales for Brain-Computer Interface Research	Brain-Computer Interfaces	0.5	Yes
			Ethics in Published Brain-Computer Interface Research	Journal of Neural Engineering	1	Yes
			Informed Consent in Implantable BCI Research: Identifying Risks and Exploring Meaning	Science and Engineering Ethics	1.5	Yes
			Ethical Challenges Associated with the Development and Deployment of Brain Computer Interface Technology	Neuroethics	2.33	Yes
			The Asilomar Survey: Stakeholders' Opinions on Ethical Issues Related to Brain-Computer Interfacing	Neuroethics	6	Yes
			Ethical Issues in Brain-Computer Interface Research, Development, and Dissemination	Journal of Neurologic Physical Therapy	3.25	Yes
			A Note on Ethical Aspects of BCI	Neural Networks	2.73	Yes
			Brain-computer Interfaces in Neurological Rehabilitation	LANCET Neurology	43.83	Yes
			Brain-Computer Interface Technology: A Review of the Second International Meeting	IEEE	12.71	Yes
			Embodiment and Estrangement: Results from a First-in-Human "Intelligent BCI" Trial	Science and Engineering Ethics	43.83	No
			BCI2000: A General-Purpose, Brain-Computer Interface (BCI) System	IEEE Transactions on Biomedical Engineering	71.75	No
			Empirical Neuroethics - Can Brain Imaging Visualize Human Thought? Why is Neuroethics Interested in Such a Possibility?	EMBO Reports	1.8	No
			Systematic Review and Meta-Analysis: A Primer	INT J Sports Phys Therapy	6.8	No

(*continued*)

Table 2. (*continued*)

Database	NS[a]	Filtering	Article	Journal	ACY[b]	Incl.
			BCI Meeting 2005 - Workshop on Clinical Issues and Applications	IEEE	5.36	No
			Clinical Applications of Brain-Computer Interfaces: Current State and Future Prospects	IEEE	39	No
	NS2 n = 10	ACY > 1, n = 5 ACY > 1 && ! duplication, n = 0	N/A	N/A	N/A	N/A
	NS3 n = 26	ACY > 1, n = 9 ACY > 1 && ! duplication, n = 0	N/A	N/A	N/A	N/A
	NS4 n = 26	ACY > 1, n = 9 ACY > 1 && ! duplication, n = 0	N/A	N/A	N/A	N/A
ScienceDirect	NS1 n = 24	ACY > 1 && ! duplication, n = 2	Neuroethics Questions to Guide Ethical Research in the International Brain Initiatives	Neuron	5.5	Yes
			On the Necessity of Ethical Guidelines for Novel Neurotechnologies	Cell	2.25	Yes
	NS2 n = 92	ACY > 1 && ! duplication, n = 1	An Ethics Toolbox for Neurotechnology	Neuron	1.4	Yes

[a]NS: Nesting Strategy
[b]ACY: Average Citations per Year

highlight current gaps in proposed ethical frameworks. The scope of this research primarily focuses on ethical issues within health-related BCI applications. We review the impact of BCI application's usage on both user and producer/researcher from research phase to post-research and public access. The second step of IS guideline is to search for related literature. We used customized search algorithms to query the aforementioned databases; carried out search strategies that filtered publications which: (1) used keywords of the paper and (2) contributed in BCI-related studies. Table 2 presents information about the search results and all the studies included in the review. The results of steps 3 and 4 are provided in the Result and Analysis section. The total number of reviewed papers are 20, within 3 databases and 12 journals.

3 Result

Here, we categorise all the identified ethical issues and concerns about BCI applications in a taxonomic classification. Further, we analyse proposed ethical frameworks and guidelines to identify gaps (ethical issues which are not addressed in existing frameworks) to help structure a more comprehensive framework. These are represented via 2 main tables: (1) Taxonomic classification of ethical concerns in BCI in Table 3, and (2) Existing ethical frameworks in Table 4.

3.1 Taxonomy

BCI terminologies used by researchers vary upon the target of the study. In the following classification, we draw similarities where possible and use one terminology for all similar terms.

3.2 Frameworks

As a result of the systematic overview, in total we found 13 guidelines addressing ethical concerns in both medical and neuroethical fields. We applied a thematic analysis of the research result and ended up with 2 main categories: (1) Framework Validators and (2) Frameworks. Validators generally propose must-have characteristics for a framework, such as inclusivity and flexibility, while frameworks contain specific guidelines required in an ethical framework. Out of 13 guidelines, 7 of them are evaluated as Frameworks that are presented in Table 4 followed by a brief definition. The remaining 6 are considered as Framework Validators.

Framework Validators

Neuroethics Questions. "Neuroethics Questions" [5] presents a framework via a series of challenging questions. By ultimately answering them, one can expect to cover the most significant bases in neuroethics. Here are the proposed questions:

1. Can you identify the main social consequences of BCI?
    1a. What are the Social Stigma and Self Stigma consequences?
    1b. Have all social/cultural biases through the process been addressed?
2. Can we standardise local processes with global collaborators?
    2a. How do we protect users' data and preserve privacy?
    2b. Brain tissue presents unique challenges due to its source and its past - How do we resolve that?
3. How are we future proofing ethics to keep up for neuroscience development?
    3a. What attributes surrounding a BCI research or project can widely be considered to trigger ethical questions?
    3b. Are current ethical practices and standards sufficiently handling the rapidly developing neuroethical industry?
4. What is the autonomy impact of BCI interventions on the brain?
    4a. What safeguarding measures may be implemented for the user to preserve autonomy and agency?

4b. Who will be assuming responsibility (in all meanings of the word)?
5. Have we done as much contextual research before deployment of BCI technologies?
   5a. Can we identify all potential abusive use cases beyond a supervised setting?
   5b. How is the issue of equity: among stakeholders, dissemination, and other applications handled?

This framework presents valid questions, targeting multiple ethical, cultural concerns [6], but due to different interpretations, there is no guarantee of addressing those concerns by only answering the questions. Instead, researchers will benefit from validating how robust a framework is with these proposed questions rather than solely relying on them for answers.

Anticipatory Governance. Anticipatory governance with relation to BCI relies on foresight and predictive behaviours to develop more efficient ways to address problems and tackle issues within the integration, production and engagement aspects of emerging technology [1, 7]. It serves as a general guideline that focuses mainly on four aspects: (1) Future simulations, (2) Geography of decision-making, (3) New constituencies, (4) Transparency.

While this is presented as a framework, it might better serve researchers as a validatory tool, checking if a framework is actually future proof by taking into account anticipatory governance.

Consequentialism and Deontology. Consequentialist ethics is an outcome-based approach to determine if an action is ethically viable - they primarily deal with risk-benefit ratios to help evaluate actions. However this is not a binary utilitarian approach, the common example afforded is: it would still be unethical to sacrifice a healthy being to save multiple unhealthy beings. Where consequentialist ethics shines is when it is applied on top of other ethical discussions as a means to provide some positional clarity where there is confusion present.

Deontological ethics refers to a rule-based ethical system wherein an action is not determined to be ethical from its consequences but instead, from its premise. In essence, even if the benefits of a research study massively outweigh the risks, it would be unethical from a deontology perspective to snare in participants without complete informed consent [8].

These approaches when carefully weighed can provide researchers clarity to definitions of moral/ethical dilemmas from a philosophical perspective. Much like "Neuroethical Questions", they are better used to validate frameworks rather than BCI ethical concerns.

Table 3. Taxonomic classification of ethical concerns in BCI

Ethical issue	Concept	Cluster	Author
Responsibility of thoughts	Moral and legal responsibility come into question when users are able to control or project via thought through BCI devices	Accountability Ethics	[12, 20]
Responsibility	There are 2 branches to responsibility: • BCI application researchers and producers responsibilities, providing a risk-free, secure and helpful BCI application to users. • User's responsibilities over actions and their interaction with machine. Discussions deal with whether BCI's distinctions may be cause for changes that are both moral and legal in nature and if so, under whose purview they should fall under. Identifying nodes of failure along the BCI process and noting liability in relation to the subject versus the technology	Accountability Ethics	[1, 11, 12]
Modesty	False promises and overoptimistic painting of the future with respect to BCI should be eschewed. Progress for progress's sake should be avoided: prioritising the simpler solution whether or not it involves BCI, to address the problems that BCI is attempting to solve	Accountability Ethics/Data Ethics	[1]
Privacy	The extent of data which is being drawn from the user could be under-represented by providers and/or system. Concerns about mind reading and information privacy. Concerns of discrimination and stratification based off of BCI data	Data Ethics	[11, 14, 16, 20]

(continued)

Table 3. (*continued*)

Ethical issue	Concept	Cluster	Author
Informed consent	Users need to understand what they are signing up for: a matter of education and data accuracy. Obtaining consent needs to be able to account for all answers between yes and no To resolve idiosyncrasies and eccentricities among patients with regards to communication, to increase interpretive accuracy by BCI professionals Diseases such as the locked in syndrome (LIS) render patients unable to communicate. Proxy decision makers must also be educated to provide informed consent. If they do use barebone BCI devices to perform simple binary tasks, the complexity of consent may not be accurately reflected in their answers	Data Ethics/Accountability Ethics/Participation Ethics	[11–14, 19]
Legal systems	Many consequences of BCI technologies are inherent and unique to the industry. These may necessitate a case-by-case approach regarding security, responsibility, privacy, etc. • Case 1: Can logical BCI devices handle emotional flare ups? If they receive the necessary signals, they could trigger actions. This is a tricky matter when dealing with matters of the subconscious and throw away thoughts • Case 2: Hacking: third party access to devices could cause issues when ascribing liability legally	Data Ethics	[11]
Data ownership	Data ownership is also an important point of consideration. Who owns the data during and after the experiment?	Data Ethics	[11]
Data security	A need for institutional protocols safeguarding against external interference and third party exploitation	Data Ethics	[11]

(*continued*)

Table 3. (*continued*)

Ethical issue	Concept	Cluster	Author
Risk-Benefit analyses	When merging different industries, the integration will have to take into account all stakeholders and benefit them equally. Decision making regarding allocation of resources with regards to BCI, the need to balance priorities with respect to looking out for the individual versus the greater good of the public Balancing decision making from a user perspective: are the risks worth the reward?	Data Ethics	[12, 16, 19]
Education	Flawed coverage among BCI professionals in the field of ethics, and consequently neuroethics. There is a need for greater education in neuroethics globally This is incumbent upon the BCI professionals to not only educate themselves about the ethics, but also to educate prospective users about the technology and risks involved so users fully understand what they are signing up for	Participation Ethics/Accountability Ethics/Data Ethics	[5]
Care of subject	Discussions about customized care for different kinds of subjects during and post study, ranging from animals and humans to stem cells and in vitro experiments Concerns about the well being of patients post study and providing the opportunity to back out at any time during the process	Participation Ethics	[1, 8, 9]
BCI communication control	Communication channels for incapacitated users need to be calibrated for potential malfunctioning devices to prevent miscommunication and harmful consequences	Participation Ethics	[14]
User safety	Burden during and post study/treatment on the user and their relations from multiple	Participation Ethics	[11, 14]

(*continued*)

Table 3. (*continued*)

Ethical issue	Concept	Cluster	Author
	perspectives: physical, emotional, mental, financial, etc. Subsequently, a need for measuring discomfort and measuring interference from BCI across the posited spectrum Concerns about user interaction strain: mental strain in trying to control BCI devices over a prolonged period can have debilitating consequences in the long term		
Personhood & social identity	Existential dilemma caused by extended capabilities brought on by machines; separation of ego, what it means to be a person. Considerations about changes in the concept of self: Agency in consciousness could be challenged as neurotechnologies develop Profound changes to "individuality" and irredeemable changes to identity socially and further. Consideration to "plastic" changes in the brain	Psychological Aspects	[1, 11, 20]
Post-research concerns	The intensive nature of BCI research may lead to post-research fatigue emotionally and mentally, manifesting as cases of mental illness. Consideration to whether the user gets to keep the device post research needs to be addressed How the caregiver and user's family will cope with the post-research situation is also paramount	Psychological Aspects/Participation Ethics/Social Aspects	[11, 12, 14]
Autonomy	The concept of autonomy as is, covers the BCI sphere as well. It essentially measuring agency - a human's capability to self-determine. Will BCI devices infringe upon people's fundamental right for self determination?	Psychological Aspects	[1, 11, 12]

(*continued*)

Table 3. (*continued*)

Ethical issue	Concept	Cluster	Author
	Other concepts of responsibility and liability tie in with autonomy as well, especially when viewing it at an institutional scale. Who owns a thought and an action bore of those thoughts is a necessary discussion		
Culture	Cross-cultural approaches to the same issues in the scientific sphere often result in gaps which unless resolved have ramifications in the form of missed opportunities toward further advancements and an inability to identify risks and hazards in either the short or long term at a global scale	Social Aspects	[5]
BCI applications misusage	Lack of global code of conduct for BCI applications usage which results in an unpredictable future impact while public access is provided. Which applications might be considered misuse beyond the laboratory?	Social Aspects/Accountability Ethics	[5]
Public policy & communication	Where does BCI advancement place in a nation's list of priorities? Can a nation draw from precedence in other fields or learn from other countries? These are policy decisions that a nation makes that will have repercussions as it pertains to managing resources, updating legal systems, etc. There is also the underlying assumption that governments exist to execute its citizens' wills faithfully which is not always the case in practice	Social Aspects	[1, 5]
Negative stereotypes	When BCI technologies adopt self-learning algorithms to help facilitate decision making, might biases surface or negative stereotypes be reinforced from a racial perspective?	Social Aspects	[20]
Social division	A stratification concern, a dissemination bias: the need for	Social Aspects	[1, 11, 20]

(*continued*)

Table 3. (continued)

Ethical issue	Concept	Cluster	Author
	fair access could be compromised by user's affordability, technology and nationality, among others		
Unrealistic expectations & motivations	BCI carries a vogue clout in the media, leading to unreasonable expectations and motivations among prospective study participants, users, their carers and care-givers	Social Aspects	[11–14]
Stigma and normality	Association of certain BCI devices with disability could dissuade a prospective user base from seeking them for fear of discrimination and judgement from the public Issues of normalcy: what is considered a "treatment vs enhancement" and how we define normality in society	Social Aspects	[11]
Study participants selection	Diverse selection of recruited participants where possible to account for the full demographic Discussion about vulnerable users and where the line should be drawn regarding their scouting and participation. The subsequent balancing of exercising caution in recruiting vulnerable participants versus mass on-boarding in an urgency to push out the BCI product	Social Aspects	[12]
Gender equality	BCI technologies are developed with the entire population in mind, and the gender breakdown among all parties in the R&D process should likewise reflect the balance	Social Aspects	[18]

Table 4. Review of existing neuroethical frameworks

Name	Framework	Author

Belmont Report	The Belmont principles, much like the Declaration of Helsinki, offer viable starting positions in a discussion of neuroethics, but fall short with respect to some of the more essential issues surrounding the subject. Belmont Principles:
	•Boundaries Between Practice and Research
	•Basic Ethical Principles
	  ◦ Respect for Persons
	  ◦ Beneficence
	  ◦ Justice
	•Applications
	  ◦ Informed Consent
	  ◦ Assessment of Risks and Benefits
	•Selection of Subjects
		[1]

Emanuel, E. J., Wendler, D., & Grady, C. (2000)	Relying on Emanuel et al.'s clinical research ethical framework, medical research with human subjects must address the following: (1) Value of research, (2) Scientific validity of methods, (3) Fair subject selection, (4) Favorable risk-benefit ratio, (5) Independent review, (6) Informed consent, (7) Respect for subject	[15]
"Responsible Research and Innovation (RRI)"	RRI offers a process wherein all participants share accountability and have a say in both the creation and application of technology. It deals with five different actors: (1) Researchers, (2) Policy Makers, (3) Educators, (4) Business & Industry Innovators, (5) Civil Society Organisations. Including 6 different agendas: (1) Ethics, (2) Gender Equality, (3) Governance, (4) Open Access, (5) Public Engagement, (6) Science Education	[1, 18]
"Six Ws/Six Cs"	James Giordano's methodology involves applying the 6'W's (what, why, when, where, who, which) to the 6'C's (capacities, consequences, character, continuity of clinical care, consent, context). This treatment is applied to all ethical elements in a conversation to demarcate and provide insights. Summarising this process reveals a typical formula in 6 steps: (1) Establishing the circumstances surrounding the case, (2) Pinpointing the involved agents and their specific roles, (3) Isolating the problem statement of an ethical issue and applying the 6'C's where applicable, (4) Brainstorming solutions and providing rational justifications for each, (5) Identify and extrapolate the effects of	[1]

(continued)

Table 4. (*continued*)

Name	Framework	Author
	each solution above, (6) Determine the course of action and final justification	
"The Four Canons", Principles of Biomedical Ethics	The four canons introduced 30 years ago still form a strong basis for ethical discussion in the biomedical field. A lot of those sentiments may be carried forward when contemplating ethics in the neuroethical field The Four canons are: (1) Autonomy: • Personal Autonomy deals with self governance • Voluntariness relates to performing an action without third party influences ◦ Coercion refers to credible and severe harm threatening to force and control actions. Automatically voids voluntariness ◦ Persuasion is when beliefs are adopted via appealing to reason. Voluntariness can still exist under persuasion ◦ Manipulation is an influence that's neither coercion or persuasion. Voluntariness can still exist under manipulation • Information & Informed consent. • Competency refers to the ability behind decision making (2) Non-maleficence: • Do not harm (3) Beneficence: • Do good and stop others from harming • Paternalism is when beneficence overrules autonomy (4) Justice: • Distribution of benefits and risks.	[1, 21]
"The Nuffield Council's Ethical Framework"	The Nuffield Council provides a fleshed out set of guidelines for neurotechnologies. While broadly designed for neurotechnologies, BCI technologies can also gain takeaways from this framework. It identifies the following points of interest with relative subdivisions: (1) Safety, (2) Autonomy, (3) Autonomy and decision making, (4) Privacy, (5) Equity, (6) Trust, (7) Humility, (8) Responsibility	[1, 12, 22]
"WMA Declaration of Helsinki"	The BCI arena and the medical field share many of the same ethical problems: reason being that both fields essentially meddle with the human body. Technology utility in Medicine was always driven	[17, 19, 20]

(*continued*)

Table 4. (*continued*)

Name	Framework	Author
	with the positive goal of preserving and improving the health of all beings, and since neuroscience shares the same goal, a lot of the ethical issues and solutions are also interchangeable. Helsinki's ethical principles include 35 terms in the following categories: (1) General Principles, (2) Risks, Burdens, Benefits, (3) Vulnerable groups and Individuals, (4) Scientific Requirements and Research Protocols, (5) Research Ethics Committees, (6) Privacy and Confidentiality, (7) Informed Consent, (8) Use of Placebo, (9) Post-Trial Provisions, (10) Research Registration and Publication and Dissemination of Results, (11) Unproven Interventions in Clinical Practice	

Specker Sullivan & Illes. Ethically robust rationales that fuel research allow for a more transparent and open process, leading to easier resolutions when snags are encountered. This paper proposes the following four methods in order to create well-thought out rationales: (1) Identify subject choice, (2) Risk benefit analysis statement, (3) Background research justifying claims about target populace, (4) Multiple citations behind target's needs, values, fears, desires, etc. [9].

Specker et al. suggest critically thinking through all use cases of the BCI device, and noting complementary opportunities or exceptions. This addresses the pre-study phase, helping drive rationale, and might not serve as an inclusive framework for the rest of the BCI process.

Klein. To suggest a framework of safety for informed consent, Klein identifies six types of safety risks of implantable BCI components. Risks related to BCI technologies (including both device safety, BCI research and subject decision-making) are as follows: (1) Cognitive and communicative impairment, (2) Inappropriate expectations, (3) Vulnerability, (4) Affective impairment, (5) Privacy and security, (6) Identity disruption. Suggested approaches are: (1) Multidisciplinary, (2) Systemic, (3) Transparent, (4) Iterative, (5) Relational, (6) Exploratory [10].

Klein's framework is one tailored for informed consent. It raises important approaches but we cannot use them for our other ethical concerns as the framework is too specific.

4 Analysis

Overall, we classified the 25 ethical issues from Table 3 into 5 main clusters: (1) Accountability ethics, (2) Data ethics, (3) Participation ethics, (4) Psychological aspects, and (5) Social aspects as shown in Fig. 2.

To analyse these classified ethical concerns in Table 3 and the aforementioned frameworks in Table 4, we merged the information into one integrated table (Table 5) and applied a qualitative analysis on each element. Table 5 essentially tests frameworks to discover if it provides enough guidelines to address raised ethical concerns. The shared ethical issues across multiple clusters, such as informed consent or post-research concerns are mentioned only once to avoid duplication. We consider their impact on other clusters in our analysis as well. Each ethical concern is evaluated by three terms: (1) Covered, (2) Partially covered, and (3) Not covered. If the issue is covered, we state which section of the corresponding publishing it appears in. We do make assumptions in our analysis that are discussed further on. Measuring the extent of its coverage is out of the scope of this study.

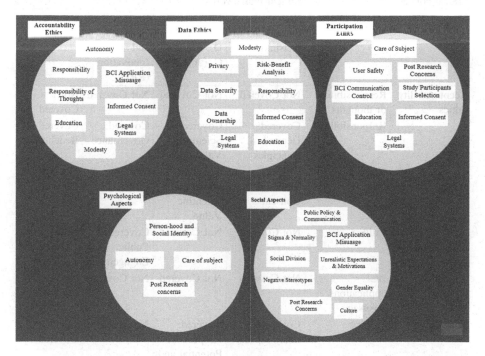

Fig. 2. Clustering classification of ethical issues

4.1 Gaps

Identifying gaps in the field of neuroethics is obviously not a straight-forward exercise - complex judgement calls frequently have to be made and a blind following of rules should be eschewed. The expansive range of actors in this field mandates a dynamic, versatile approach as it pertains to appropriating gaps.

Disclaimer: Not all of our identified ethical concerns carry the same weightage, and as a result, it is not possible to do a quantitative ranking of our frameworks by how many concerns each of them address. For example, Legal Systems as an ethical concern carries a tangible effect on stakeholders, requiring immediate concern, as compared to Negative Stereotypes, whose concerns are felt in the long-term and more passive in nature. In this part, we highlight the ethical clusters that are mainly uncovered in each of the frameworks. Provided in Table 5 is a specific breakdown of gaps in each cluster/framework for reference. Our interpretation of the frameworks' coverage is also restricted by our definitions of our ethical issues arising from our research and may not be what the framework authors intended exactly. Our table also treats issues that appear in multiple clusters as a single entity, so this also changes the scope of the ethical issues.

Table 5. Qualitative analysis on BCI ethical frameworks

Ethical concerns		Ethical Frameworks			
Cluster	Ethical Concern	WMA Declaration of Helsinki	Emanuel, E. J., Wendler, D., & Grady, C. (2000)	Responsible Research and Innovation (RRI)	Belmont Report
Accountability Ethics	Responsibility of thoughts	Not Covered	Not Covered	Not Covered	Not Covered
	Responsibility	Covered: General Principles	Covered: Scientific Validity	Covered: Governance	Covered: Beneficence
	Modesty	Covered: Informed Consent	Covered: Social and Scientific Value	Covered: Ethics	Not Covered
	Culture	Not Covered	Not Covered	Covered: Public Engagement	Not Covered
	BCI applications misusage	Not Covered	Not Covered	Not Covered	Not Covered
Data Ethics	Privacy	Covered: many aspects	Covered: Respect for Potential and Enrolled Subjects	Not Covered	Not Covered
	Informed consent	Covered: many aspects	Covered: Informed Consent	Covered: Science Education	Covered: Informed Consent
	Legal systems	Partially Covered: International vs Local	Partially Covered: Respect for Potential and Enrolled Subjects	Covered: Governance	Not Covered

(continued)

Table 5. (*continued*)

Ethical concerns		Ethical Frameworks			
Cluster	Ethical Concern	WMA Declaration of Helsinki	Emanuel, E. J., Wendler, D., & Grady, C. (2000)	Responsible Research and Innovation (RRI)	Belmont Report
	Data ownership	Not Covered	Not Covered	Not Covered	Not Covered
	Data security	Partially Covered: Privacy & Confidentiality	Not Covered	Not Covered	Not Covered
	Risk Benefit analyses	Covered: many aspects	Covered. Favorable Risk-Benefit Ratio	Not Covered	Covered: Assessment of Risks and Benefits
Participation Ethics	Education	Covered: General Principles	Covered: many aspects	Covered: Open Access	Not Covered
	Care of subject	Covered: many aspects	Not Covered	Not Covered	Covered: Boundaries Between Practice and Research
	BCI communication control	Not Covered	Not Covered	Not Covered	Not Covered
	Study participants selection	Covered: General Principles	Covered: Fair Subject Selection	Not Covered	Covered: Selection of Subjects
	User safety	Covered: General Principles	Covered: Respect for Potential and Enrolled Subjects	Not Covered	Covered: Beneficence
Psychological Aspects	Personhood & social Identity	Not Covered	Not Covered	Not Covered	Not Covered
	Post-research concerns	Partially Covered: Post-Trial Provisions	Not Covered	Not Covered	Covered: Respect for Persons
	Autonomy	Covered: General Principles	Covered: Informed Consent	Not Covered	Covered: Respect for Persons

(*continued*)

Table 5. (*continued*)

Ethical concerns		Ethical Frameworks			
Cluster	Ethical Concern	WMA Declaration of Helsinki	Emanuel, E. J., Wendler, D., & Grady, C. (2000)	Responsible Research and Innovation (RRI)	Belmont Report
Social Aspects	Public policy & communication	Not Covered	Covered: Independent Review	Covered: Public Engagement	Covered: Justice
	Negative stereotypes	Not Covered	Not Covered	Not Covered	Not Covered
	Social division	Not Covered	Covered as: Fair Subject Selection	Not Covered	Covered: Justice
	Unrealistic expectations & motivations	Not Covered	Covered: Favorable Risk-Benefit Ratio	Not Covered	Covered: Respect for Persons
	Stigma and normality	Not Covered	Not Covered	Not Covered	Not Covered
	Gender equality	Partially Covered: General Principles	Not Covered	Covered: Gender Equality	Covered: Justice
Ethical concerns		Ethical Frameworks			
Cluster	Ethical Concern	Six 'W's/Six 'C's	The Nuffield Council's Ethical Framework	"The Four Canons", Principles of Biomedical Ethics	
Accountability Ethics	Responsibility of thoughts	Not Covered	Not Covered	Not Covered	
	Responsibility	Not Covered	Covered: Trust	Not Covered	
	Modesty	Partially Covered: consequences	Covered: Trust	Not Covered	
	Culture	Partially Covered: context	Not Covered	Not Covered	
	BCI applications misusage	Partially Covered: Capacities	Not Covered	Partially Covered: Non-maleficence	

(*continued*)

Table 5. (*continued*)

Ethical concerns		Ethical Frameworks			
Cluster	Ethical Concern	WMA Declaration of Helsinki	Emanuel, E. J., Wendler, D., & Grady, C. (2000)	Responsible Research and Innovation (RRI)	Belmont Report
Data Ethics	Privacy	Not Covered	Covered: Privacy		
	Informed consent	Covered: Consent	Covered: Autonomy and Decision-making	Covered: Autonomy	
	Legal systems	Not Covered	Partially Covered: Autonomy and Decision-making	Partially Covered: Beneficence	
	Data ownership	Not Covered	Covered: Data Protection	Not Covered	
	Data security	Not Covered	Covered: Privacy	Not Covered	
	Risk-Benefit analyses	Covered: Consequences	Covered: Autonomy and Decision-making	Partially Covered: Many Aspects	
Participation Ethics	Education	Not Covered	Not Covered	Not Covered	
	Care of subject	Covered: many aspects	Not Covered	Partially Covered: Beneficence	
	BCI communication control	Partially Covered: Capacities	Covered: Privacy	Not Covered	
	Study participants selection	Not Covered	Covered: Equity	Partially Covered: Justice	
	User safety	Covered: many aspects	Covered: Safety	Partially Covered: Beneficence	
Psychological Aspects	Personhood & social Identity	Partially Covered	Covered: Autonomy and Identity	Not Covered	

(*continued*)

Table 5. *(continued)*

Ethical concerns		Ethical Frameworks			
Cluster	Ethical Concern	WMA Declaration of Helsinki	Emanuel, E. J., Wendler, D., & Grady, C. (2000)	Responsible Research and Innovation (RRI)	Belmont Report
	Post-research concerns	Covered: Consequences	Not Covered	Not Covered	
	Autonomy	Not Covered	Covered: Autonomy	Covered: Autonomy	
Social Aspects	Public policy & communication	Not Covered	Covered: Equity	Not Covered	
	Negative stereotypes	Partially Covered: Consequences	Not Covered	Not Covered	
	Social division	Partially Covered: Consequences	Covered: Equity	Not Covered	
	Unrealistic expectations & motivations	Not Covered	Covered: Autonomy and Decision-making	Not Covered	
	Stigma and normality	Partially Covered: Consequences	Covered: Equity	Not Covered	
	Gender equality	Not Covered	Partially covered: Equity	Not Covered	

WMA Declaration of Helsinki. Social Aspects receives very little coverage in this framework. This is followed by Accountability Ethics, although the main tenet, Responsibility, is covered by General Principles in the article. The other three clusters receive major coverage.

Emanuel, E. J., Wendler, D., & Grady, C. (2000). 13 guidelines on biomedical ethics shaped this framework which addresses all five clusters of ethical issues to an extent. The sentiment behind the paper's Respect of Potential and Enrolled Subjects largely covers the cluster of Data and Participation Ethics topics. Accountability Ethics and Psychological Aspects are fairly untouched, although Informed Consent as a highly weighted concern is addressed.

Responsible Research and Innovation (RRI). RRI largely emphasises an active, iterative procedure involving all actors. We have found that as it stands, it largely leaves gaps in all the clusters other than accountability ethics. Data Ethics receives attention in the important aspects of Informed Consent and Legal Systems, although we specifically feel Risk-Benefit Analysis area deserves attention. Participation ethics, Psychological Aspects and Social Aspects are sparsely covered.

Belmont Report. Belmont Report leaves gaps in Accountability Ethics and partially in Data Ethics & Participation Ethics. It has comprehensive coverage in Psychological and Social Aspects. Notably, Privacy does not receive detailed attention and Responsibility in general is largely covered by Beneficence, which is quite large in scope.

Six 'W's/Six 'C's. James Giordano's "Six Ws/Six Cs" offers an interesting contribution to framing ethics. It is more open and exploratory in nature, offering a procedural outlook at issues rather than providing specific direction. Thus, it is best handled case-by-case and our interpretation of its comprehensiveness is limited. As is, this framework largely does not cover Data Ethics - Informed Consent and Risk-Benefit Analysis are two commendable inclusions although Legal Systems is a glaring omission. Psychological Aspects and Social Aspects are both partially covered - Autonomy is a largely relevant exclusion and Study Participant Selection could stand to be acknowledged.

The Nuffield Council's Ethical Framework. Nuffield's framework is one specifically focused on ethical issues raised from the use of novel neurotechnologies. Keeping that in mind, all 5 clusters are mainly covered by provided recommendations for research, policy, governance and public engagement. Data Ethics is fully covered under Privacy and Autonomy terms in the framework. Followed by Social Aspects which is addressed by Equity. The only remaining clusters with less inclusivity are: Accountability and Participation Ethics, lacking attention on terms such as Care of Subject and Education.

"The Four Canons", Principles of Biomedical Ethics. The broad umbrella nature of the "four canons" lends itself to extensive coverage, if abstract. The tenets of Beneficence and Nonmaleficence essentially address positive and negative actions at large and philosophically cover everything! Finding gaps, as a result, becomes a function of specificity, and we feel we cannot make a judgement call on what the four canons encapsulate. As a result, unless we can find a very transparent match of tenet to ethical issue, or if the issue is specifically listed as an example in the source, we have conservatively chosen to list most issues as gaps. Thus, the "Four Canons" only cover parts of clusters in Data Ethics and Participation Ethics.

To summarize, Informed Consent is covered across all frameworks, standing out as the most important ethical issue. Responsibility, Modesty, Risk-Benefit Analysis, Study Participant Selection, Autonomy and User Safety are represented by most frameworks. Conversely, Responsibility of Thoughts is not covered by any of the frameworks and sticks out as the predominant gap. However, we can largely attribute this to our definition for this issue. It otherwise falls under the umbrella of Responsibility, which is adequately covered.

BCI Communication Control, BCI Application Misusage, Data Security, Data Ownership, Culture, Personhood, Social Identity, Stigma and Normality are only covered by one or two frameworks, and could for our intent be considered gaps to be addressed. As expected, a common theme across would be the highly BCI specific nature of the ethical issues.

4.2 Further Research

As a result of our systematic review, we identified a set of suggestions which can be added individually to the existing or proposed ethical frameworks for better inclusivity. Suggestions are not framed guidelines but practical enhancements to current ethical evaluation system, namely:

- **Legal adjustments**: Considering both user liability and manufacturer's responsibility [11],
- **Governance structure**: By pairing a partner and a third party advisor, an advisory board may be created wherein the deciding vote goes to the third party advisor in case of an internal dispute regarding ethical impact.
- **The consent process**: A viable consent process, accounting for user expectations, communicated to both user and their representation.
- **Knowledge transfer**: Training for all parties involved behind BCI setup is not only useful but necessary.
- **Experimental issues**: Standardizing non-invasive EEG issues other than the well developed electrical safety and infection dissuasion protocols is necessary when considering public dissemination. This involves time to set up, user control and aesthetics, motivation factors, return on investment issues among others.
- **Consequences of success or failure**: Success in the experiment can have a negative effect on the user if the technology is not made available post study. Likewise, failure may lead to great levels of frustration and even lead to depression. Developing and committing to guidelines that determine the success benchmark and managing of halting measures.
- **Mitigation of risk**: Establish conservative behaviours in order to mitigate risks when it comes to interaction with modal entities via BCI devices [12].

Relying on the provided analysis in this research, we consider below possible paths for further studies: (1) Extending the systematic review by investigating through more databases, to conduct a grasp understanding of other existing gaps (2) Extending the scope of the study and considering a wider range of BCI applications for analysis, and (3) Suggesting a comprehensive ethical framework considering impactful ethical issues mentioned in this paper.

Due to the defined scope of this study, we followed a structured methodology that impacted the findings of the research and applied limitations that were used to focus on a specific aspect of neuroethical frameworks. Below are the limitations throughout the study:

- We reviewed a limited number of databases and a selective number of papers.
- We relied on each framework's code of conduct to capture ethical gaps that were not addressed in those frameworks.
- We didn't analyse how stakeholders apply each of the frameworks to their BCI applications.

Further studies are required on the evaluation of applied frameworks on BCI applications, to grasp an overall understanding on the practicality of frameworks.

5 Conclusion

This research reviewed main arguments about neuroethics in BCI to provide an aggregated set of common ethical issues encountered in the BCI sphere that are not addressed in neuroethical frameworks. We conducted a systematic literature review on 20 papers within 3 databases. As a result, 25 ethical issues were clustered in 5 main clusters. We reviewed 13 ethical guidelines under 2 main categories: (1) Framework Validators and (2) Frameworks. Further on, we analysed each framework and identified 8 common ethical issues considered as gaps to be addressed. Applied methodology and limited number of reviewed papers had implications on the result which demand further studies.

References

1. Pham, M., Goering, S., Sample, M., Huggins, J.E., Klein, E.: Asilomar survey: researcher perspectives on ethical principles and guidelines for BCI research. Brain-Comput. Interfaces **5**(4), 97–111 (2018)
2. Gilbert, F., Cook, M., O'Brien, T., Illes, J.: Embodiment and estrangement: results from a first-in-human "intelligent BCI" trial. Sci. Eng. Ethics **25**(1), 83–96 (2019)
3. Sullivan, L.S., Illes, J.: Ethics in published brain-computer interface research. J. Neural Eng. **15**(1), 013001 (2018)
4. Vom Brocke, J., Simons, A., Niehaves, B., Riemer, K., Plattfaut, R., Cleven, A.: Reconstructing the giant: on the importance of rigour in documenting the literature search process. In: ECIS, vol. 9, pp. 2206–2217 (2009)
5. Amadio, J., et al.: Neuroethics questions to guide ethical research in the international brain initiatives. Neuron **100**(1), 19–36 (2018)
6. Garden, H., Winickoff, D.E., Frahm, N.M., Pfotenhauer, S.: Responsible Innovation in Neurotechnology Enterprises (2019)
7. IFTF Homepage. http://www.iftf.org/uploads/media/SR-1272_anticip_govern-1.pdf. Accessed 20 Dec 2019
8. Farah, M.J.: An ethics toolbox for neurotechnology. Neuron **86**(1), 34–37 (2015)
9. Sullivan, L.S., Illes, J.: Beyond 'communication and control': towards ethically complete rationales for brain-computer interface research. Brain-Comput. Interfaces **3**(3), 156–163 (2016)
10. Klein, E.: Informed consent in implantable BCI research: identifying risks and exploring meaning. Sci. Eng. Ethics **22**(5), 1299–1317 (2015)
11. Burwell, S., Sample, M., Racine, E.: Ethical aspects of brain computer interfaces: a scoping review. BMC Med. Ethics **18**(1), 60 (2017)
12. McCullagh, P., Lightbody, G., Zygierewicz, J., Kernohan, W.G.: Ethical challenges associated with the development and deployment of brain computer interface technology. Neuroethics **7**(2), 109–122 (2014)
13. Kögel, J., Schmid, J.R., Jox, R.J., et al.: Using brain-computer interfaces: a scoping review of studies employing social research methods. BMC Med. Ethics **20**, 18 (2019)

14. Grübler, G., et al.: Psychosocial and ethical aspects in non-invasive EEG-based BCI research—a survey among BCI users and BCI professionals. Neuroethics **7**(1), 29–41 (2014)
15. Emanuel, E.J., Wendler, D., Grady, C.: What makes clinical research ethical? Jama **283**(20), 2701–2711 (2000)
16. Vlek, R.J., et al.: Ethical issues in brain-computer interface research, development, and dissemination. JNPT **36**, 94–98 (2012)
17. Adopted by the 18th WMA General Assembly, Helsinki, Finland, June 1964. https://www.wma.net/policies-post/wma-declaration-of-helsinki-ethical-principles-for-medical-research-involving-human-subjects/. Accessed 20 Dec 2019
18. RRI-Tools Homepage. https://www.rri-tools.eu/about-rri. Accessed 20 Dec 2019
19. Haselager, W.F.G., Vlek, R.J., Hill, J., Nijboer, F.: A note on ethical aspects of BCI. Neural Netw. **22**(9), 1352–1357 (2009)
20. Goering, S., Yuste, R.: On the necessity of ethical guidelines for novel neurotechnologies. Cell **167**(4), 882–885 (2016)
21. Principles of biomedical ethics Homepage. https://www.researchgate.net/publication/12869379_Principles_of_biomedical_ethics. Accessed 20 Dec 2019
22. Novel neurotechnologies: intervening in the brain. Nuffield Council on Bioethics. http://nuffieldbioethics.org/wp-content/uploads/2013/06/Novel_neurotechnologies_report_PDF_web_0.pdf. Accessed 20 Dec 2019

TRUE – Transparency of Recommended User Experiences

Sparshad Kasote[✉] and Krishnan Vijayaraghavan

SAP Labs, #138, Sap Labs Road, EPIP Zone, Whitefield, Bangalore 560066,
Karnataka, India
sparshad501@gmail.com, krishvj@gmail.com

Abstract. One of the fundamental goals of user recommendations is to drive higher user engagement with applications and ecosystems. However, there is a lack of clarity for the user on how end user data is used to create these recommendations. This paper explores a framework that explains and gives control to a user, on how their usage data was utilized to generate recommendations. It will shed light on how a system recommendation could be more transparent from the user's perspective. The framework aims to expose the relationship between recommendations and contextual user activity, thereby leading to transparency. This framework would also allow users to finetune how usage data from their activity, can be better utilized to generate recommendations. The adoption of this framework could lead to higher user engagement with the application and a better user experience for the user.

Keywords: Recommendation systems · Privacy · Transparency · Explainable UX · Trust · Instructional design

1 Introduction

With the rise in technology utilizing ML and AI, recommendations have started to drive aspects of user centric preferences with systems. These recommendation systems use a combination of complex algorithms that rely on passive and active user data to ultimately generate relevant content [1]. This relevancy being targeted for higher user engagement, leads to more transactions for the service provider and better preferences for the user. However, the use of targeted recommendations generated from user data can lead to a lack of trust from the users, if the reasoning behind it is not explained. Catering to this, the explanations for a recommendation process have been attempted in various forms that provide a visual clue for the user, and an ability to interact with it [3]. This ability to give feedback in the form of visual manipulations and interactions, have proven to give results that show higher accuracy in recommendations and an enhanced user experience [3, 4]. There have been efforts made to curate guidelines for personalized content by enabling users to interact with their respective suggestions [2]. Additionally, the intent behind giving a visualization of a recommendation process, is to give a sense of satisfaction to the user, which arises from the transparent nature of the explanations [5]. Users tend to have a decision-making process which is more confident in nature, when the recommended suggestions are explained [6]. It has also

© Springer Nature Switzerland AG 2020
M. Kurosu (Ed.): HCII 2020, LNCS 12183, pp. 475–483, 2020.
https://doi.org/10.1007/978-3-030-49065-2_33

been contrived that the giving of control to the user in the form of filtering out data, can end up being constructive both for the user and the service provider [7].

The explanation visualizations and interactions of current solutions do give transparency in their own manner by giving the ability to filter and specify preferences [6, 7]. Users have been also given the ability to manipulate with their neighborhood's preferences to vary their requirements [4]. However, in all the current day explanations, there is no direct relation of the user activity shown to the user. TRUE (Transparency of Recommended User Experiences) is a solution that intends to give a similar range of explanation and control to the user about their respective suggestions but aims to perform this by associating the recommendations directly to user activity. It provides a framework in which the user can understand the relationship between the recommendation and the user activities that contributed to that recommendation It uniquely strives to increase transparency by showing all aspects of the user activity that were utilized for a recommendation.

2 Approach

The premise to describing TRUE, apprehends that current day recommender systems apply their own complex algorithms to user data for generating curations. For understanding TRUE, the recommendation process has been layered (See Fig. 1). Its approach consists of layers that are involved between the user activity and the recommendation. These segregated layers are used to give users an explanative link between the recommendation and the activity that contributed to that recommendation. The layers consist of the following:

2.1 User Activity Layer

User activity layer is the ultimate layer of the TRUE framework which consists of all the user's actions and conducts that are the source, leading to recommendations. These activities could include location details, content consumed, interactions with content, content shared, voice recorded, or any aspect of the user's daily timeline that contributed to a particular recommendation.

2.2 Recommendation System Layer

Recommendation system layer is an intermediate layer for establishing a relation between the user activity and the recommendation. The user activities tracked by the system are categorized as data sets using the complex algorithms implemented by the respective recommender system. Different combinations of these data sets would be used to generate relevant recommendations.

2.3 Recommendation Layer

Recommendation layer consists of all the recommendations and suggestions displayed to the user. This is the surface layer through which the user can choose to explore the explanative link to all its related activities.

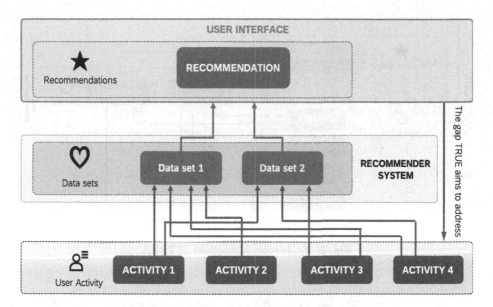

Fig. 1. Understanding TRUE with layers

Explainable Interactivity. The first interactive ability TRUE provides to the user is an explanation of the recommendation into its respective user activities. The framework provides a path for different systems on how to guide the user to the recommendation's respective user activity. The explanation given to the user is directly into the user activity layer (See Fig. 2). The recommender system layer as shown in Fig. 1 is dependent on every respective technology used by various service providers. This layer need not be explained to the user as it is a collection of different sets of data and user activity that were combined based on any computing algorithm respective to the recommender system. The TRUE framework intends to bring transparency by directly revealing the user activity layer related to the recommendation being investigated. The user activity layer which is chosen to be disclosed is displayed in the form of a timeline (See Fig. 3B) which contains all the recorded activity within the journey of the user.

Control. TRUE also gives the interactive ability to the user for fine tuning the way in which user activity is consumed for ultimately altering the recommendation. This arises from the fact that some recommendations may be triggered by unsolicited user activity, and it would be of help if the user is explicitly involved in making an amendment. In some contemporary recommender systems, the user is given the ability to choose for not being provided with a kind of suggestion. With TRUE, the user can backtrack such unwanted suggestions right up to the user activity that generated it. After investigating the set of activities that triggered an undesirable recommendation, TRUE enables the user to choose and take appropriate action on the same in the following three ways:

Deleting Activity from Context. This feature allows the user to remove the undesired activity from the particular recommendation being investigated. This control is provided if the user wishes that a particular activity should not be contributing to a

478   S. Kasote and K. Vijayaraghavan

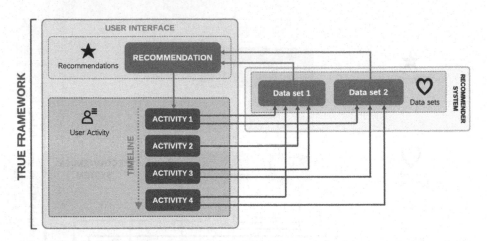

Fig. 2. Explainable interactivity of TRUE

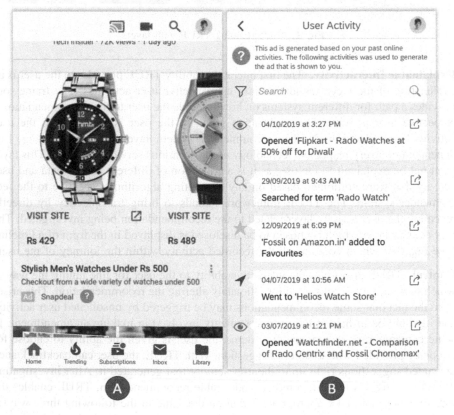

Fig. 3. Explanative interface showing (A) Recommendations, (B) User activities

respective recommendation. However, the same activity will still be consumed by other data sets that generate other recommendations.

Deleting Activity from Context. This feature allows the user to remove a particular activity from all the recommender system data sets consuming it. There are various unintended activities that are monitored by the system that in turn generate undesired recommendations. There could be activities that the user wouldn't want to be revealed to the system like passive activities sensed by the system. These could be the map location sensed, speech recognition tag words recorded, etc.

Where Used. The 'where used' control is provided to the user for viewing the association of a particular activity with the different recommendations it has been used in. This explains how one specific activity is correlated with its respective recommendations. Occurrences in which users have an activity which is desired only in some recommendations but not in all, give rise to this control. For example, if a location history activity generates desired recommendations for places to visit, but also generates unwanted recommendations in preferred food, then the user can choose to remove the activity only from a specific recommendation.

Figure 4 shows the explorative interface prototype which provides these controls to the user. The list of user activities shown in a timeline can be chosen to be deleted either from the entire system or just from the recommendation which is being investigated. The user can trigger the menu options for a particular activity by clicking on its respective menu icon as shown in Fig. 4A. The 'delete from this recommendation' removes the activity from context. The 'delete from system' removes the activity from all the recommendations and data sets it has been used in. The 'where used' option takes the user to a list of all the recommendations that the particular activity has been used in. Figure 4B shows the list of all the recommendations for the selected activity. The user can choose to remove this particular activity from the unwanted recommendations in this list as well. This control is similar to the 'delete activity from context' but it enables the removal of the activity from multiple recommendations.

3   Evaluation

The evaluation of TRUE was conducted with 20 users. The users varied from heavy users of applications using recommendation engines (Amazon, YouTube, Instagram, Facebook etc.) to light users. The age groups of the participants varied from 20 to 50 years.

3.1   Scope

The tests were done to understand the following:

1. Users current experience with recommendation systems and how relevant are their recommendations.
2. The sense of transparency TRUE achieves by exposing their own online activity that was used to generate the recommendation.

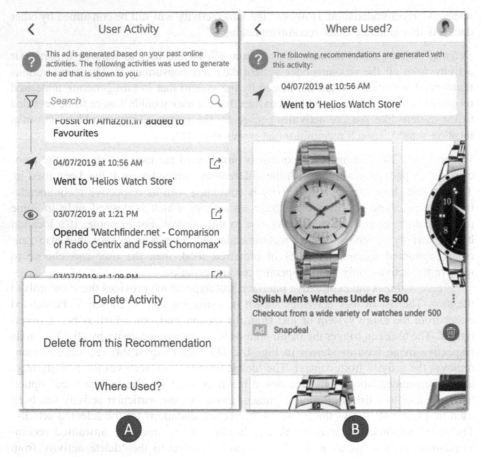

Fig. 4. User control showing (A) Menu options on user activity, (B) 'Where used' functionality

3. The change in user's behavior with systems because of the transparency.
4. The effect of giving access to control on the efficiency and relevancy of future recommendations.

3.2 Test

Each user was given two tasks and eight questions related to the tasks. The users were given a prototype of a long scrolling feed of videos (YouTube) with recommendations inserted between the list of videos. Their first task was to understand why a recommendation was shown to them by checking what data was used to generate it. Once this was done, the second task was to take action on irrelevant data activities that were used to generate that recommendation, so that it is not used for future recommendations.

4   Results

To evaluate the effects of TRUE on the user's experience, a pre and post questionnaire was answered by the users which revolved around the scope. They were asked to rate the questions based on a 5-point scale where 1 was the least (Strongly Disagree) and 5 was the highest (Strongly Agree). Figure 5 shows the aggregated results of the study in the form of a bar chart. The highest agreed upon score was for the increase in transparency after the advent of using TRUE. The least score of 3.7 was still a somewhat agreed upon opinion for the fact that users would change their behavior with

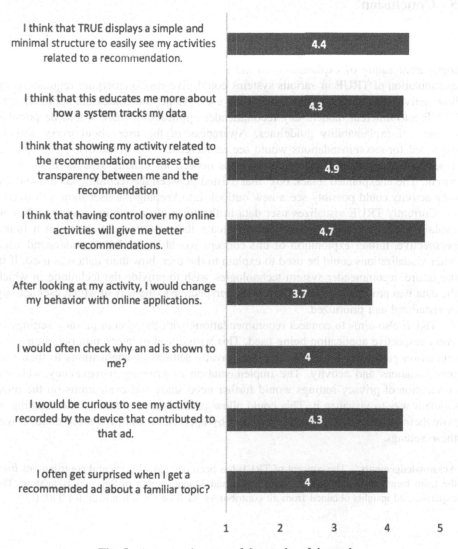

Fig. 5. Aggregated scores of the results of the study

applications after seeing their activity being monitored for it. 55% strongly agreed that TRUE had a simple structure to explain how their activity was related to a recommendation. Before introducing TRUE, 66% agreed that were curious to see their activity recorded for a recommendation. Majority of the participants thought that they would change their behavior with online applications after seeing their data being recorded. Conversely, 11% of them strongly disagreed with this and mentioned that they would continue using applications without any conscious behavioral change. As far as giving control over recorded activity is concerned, 100% of the participants were above the agreeing mark, for believing that it would give them better recommendations.

5 Conclusion

The introduction of explainable recommendations has taken its course in current day applications. With the advent of TRUE, users could see a new perspective to the transparent nature of explanations in the form of their respective user activity. The extrapolation of TRUE in various systems could give rise to emerging regulations on how activity data could be put forth to the user. As per the contextual application of TRUE into different modern-day recommender applications, there would be possible advents of explainability guidelines. Awareness of the user about every activity exploited for recommendations would see an increase. This would also shed light on aspects of data privacy and regulatory steps needed for making systems more transparent. The unexplained 'black box' that existed between the recommendation and the user activity could possibly see a new outlook into keeping the user more informed.

Currently TRUE visualizes user data in the form of an activity based timeline to explain to users what data was used to create the recommendation. From a future perspective, further exploration of this concept would be needed to understand what other visualizations could be used to explain to the user, how their data was used. If in the future, recommender system technologies wish to provide the technique in which the data was processed, it would add more perspective to the way in which user activity is visualized and prioritized.

TRUE also aims to connect recommendations with the system privacy settings of every respective application being used. This would lead to interaction paradigms and regulation guidelines for associating the privacy settings of applications to their recommendations and activity. The implementation of bringing transparency with the connection of privacy settings would further need study and evaluations on the most efficient way to visualize it. This could allow users to have a better understanding of how their system privacy settings are used by apps and could give more control over these settings.

Acknowledgements. The concept of TRUE has been devised with integral contributions from the team members of the Digital supply chain and Manufacturing in Sap labs Bangalore. The expertise and insights obtained from all contributors, facilitated the headway for TRUE.

References

1. Naren, K.: How Can We 'Design' An Intelligent Recommendation Engine. https://uxplanet. org/how-can-we-design-an-intelligent-recommendation-engine-b9bb1db4d050. Accessed 18 Dec 2019
2. Aurora, H.: UX Guidelines for Recommended Content. https://www.nngroup.com/articles/ recommendation-guidelines. Accessed 14 Dec 2019
3. Svetlin, B., John, O., Tobias, H.: Taste weights: a visual interactive hybrid recommender system. In: Proceedings of RecSys 2012, pp. 35–42. ACM (2012)
4. John, O., Barry, S., Brynjar, G., Svetlin, B., Tobias, H.: PeerChooser: visual interactive recommendation. In: Proceedings of the SIGCHI Conference on Human Factors in Computing Systems, pp. 1085–1088. ACM (2008)
5. Brynjar, G., John, O., Svetlin, B., Christopher, H., Tobias, H.: SmallWorlds: visualizing social recommendations. Comput. Graph. Forum **29**, 833–842 (2010)
6. Martijn, M., Nyi Nyi, H., Cristina, C., Katrien, V.: To explain or not to explain: the effects of personal characteristics when explaining music recommendations. In: Proceedings of the Conference on Intelligent User Interface (2019)
7. Hongyi, W., Longqi, Y., Michael, S., Deborah, E.: Exploring recommendations under user-controlled data filtering. In: Twelfth ACM Conference on Recommender Systems (RecSys 2018), Vancouver, BC, Canada, 2–7 October. ACM, New York (2018)

Ideal Election Method by Adopting
the Interval Scale Instead of the Ordinal Scale

Masaaki Kurosu[1]([✉]) and Ayako Hashizume[2]

[1] The Open University of Japan, 6-20-5 Kokuryo,
Chofu, Tokyo 182-0022, Japan
nigrumamet-s23@mbr.nifty.com
[2] Hosei University, 4342 Aihara-cho, Machida, Tokyo 194-0298, Japan
hashiaya@gmail.com

Abstract. Today, most democratic countries adopt the election system based on the notion of *"one vote for one voter"*. The winner will be determined by the total number of votes that s/he obtained. But will it be the optimal voting method considering the occurrence of the cracked vote? If there are two opposite sides and there are only two candidates one for each side, it would be adequate. But if there is only one candidate on one side and more than one candidate on other side, the latter votes will be cracked, thus the former side may win. Because of this phenomenon, each side strives to coordinate the candidate just to one.

This paper proposes another way of voting method based on the rating method where the basic notion is *"onetime ratings for one voter"*. In this method, each voter gives ratings to all candidates, for example, from 1 to 5 where 1 is negligible and 5 is the most preferable. The default rating value for each candidate is 1 and voters can change the point for the preferable candidate to 5 or 4. After the vote, all the rating points will be summed up and the candidate who won the maximum summative rating point will win.

Keywords: Democracy · Voting system · Rating method

1 Introduction

1.1 Voting as a Basis for a Democratic Society

Today, in such democratic societies as Japan, the US, the UK, etc. where the election is guaranteed by the constitution, the election by equal voting is held. The fundamental idea adopted in the election is *"one vote for one voter"*. This means, every people living in a specific organizational system (nation, state, local government, etc.) will have the right to vote equally disregard to the ethnic group, gender, disability, economic strength, etc. Even a millionaire does not have the right for many votes but just one.

This way of voting, however, is said to have a possibility to fall into the mobocracy as Plato and Aristotle pointed out. Concepts of equality and equity should be discussed in relation to this issue. Another crucial issue is the treatment for the minority opinion, especially when the voting result is split into, for example, 51 points vs 49 points. But, in this article, authors will not focus on these aspects.

© Springer Nature Switzerland AG 2020
M. Kurosu (Ed.): HCII 2020, LNCS 12183, pp. 484–493, 2020.
https://doi.org/10.1007/978-3-030-49065-2_34

What authors would like to point out here is that the election based on "*one vote for one voter*" is apt to bring about the cracked vote or the vote splitting. An example is that in some situation where there is a big issue to which two candidates A and B are supporting pro and con respectively, there will be no cracked vote and the voting result could be accepted by voters on both sides. But if there is another candidate C whose major claim is similar to B with small differences only for minor issues, a part of potential voters for B will change their support from B to C, thus decreasing the possible vote for B. The result may be that A will win the race.

1.2   An Example – 2000 United States Presidential Election

The United States presidential election that was held on October 11, 2000 was a typical case where the cracked vote might have happened.

The result of election is summarized in Table 1. After the close fight, Bush won the election by 271 votes and Gore lost by 266 votes although the popular count was 50,456,002 for Bush and 50,999,897 for Gore.

Table 1. Electoral results of 2000 US presidential election (from Wikipedia)

Presidential candidate	Party	Home state	Popular vote		Electoral vote
			Count	Percentage	
George Walker Bush	Republican	Texas	50,456,002	47.87%	271
Albert Arnold Gore, Jr.	Democratic	Tennessee	50,999,897	48.38%	266
Ralph Nader	Green	Connecticut	2,882,955	2.74%	0
Pat Buchanan	Reform	Virginia	448,895	0.43%	0
Harry Browne	Libertarian	Tennessee	384,431	0.36%	0
Howard Phillips	Constitution	Virginia	98,020	0.09%	0
John Hagelin	Natural Law	Iowa	83,714	0.08%	0
Other			51,186	0.05%	—
(*abstention*) [a]	—	—	—	—	1
Total			105,421,423	100%	538
Needed to win					270

An interesting fact is that there were Nader at the third and Buchanan at the fourth. Nader was thought to get some part of votes from Gore and Buchanan from Bush. If Nader and Buchanan did not stand as the candidates and some part, say 50%, of the votes for them went to Gore and Bush, the result would have been as in Fig. 1, Fig. 2. Votes for Bush + 0.5*Buchanan is 50,680,450 and Gore + 0.5*Nader is 52,441,375. Of course, the history cannot be changed. But something different might have happened if the cracked vote had not occurred.

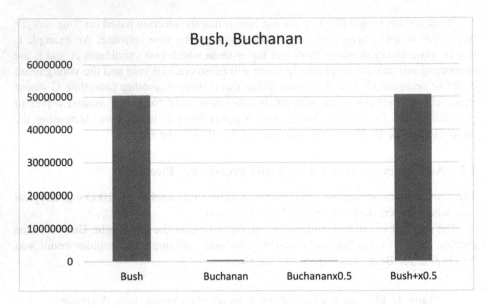

Fig. 1. Bush + 0.5*Buchanan (at the far right)

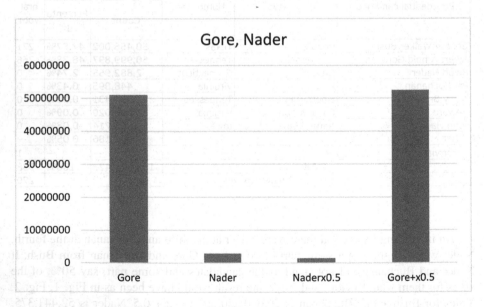

Fig. 2. Gore + 0.5*Nader (at the far right)

2   Cracked Vote and Ordinal Scale

2.1   Scale Degradation

The reason why the cracked vote can occur is because of the discipline "*one vote for one voter*" although this discipline is regarded as the basis for the democracy. It seems to be paradoxical. But the discipline can correctly be stated as "*only one vote is allowed for one voter*". Furthermore, the accumulated vote, though it actually is at the level of ratio scale, is only treated at the level of ordinal scale.

The same is true for the medal system at Olympics. Gold medal is the top, Silver medal is the second and Bronze medal is the third. The original score, for example, the time to reach the goal is at the level of ratio scale. But the medal awarding is at the level of ordinal scale. There is a degrading of the scale level from the ratio scale to the ordinal scale. As a result, in the case of Fig. 3, Fig. 4, athletes A, B, and C will be awarded Gold, Silver and Bronze regardless of the actual time difference.

In sports games, we get used to seeing such situations and we applaud the athlete A without regard to the actual score (time) between A and B. But can it be validated in the politics? The result is far more important compared to the sports competition. Because there are cases where the number of votes for the second candidate is close to that for the top candidate caused by the cracked vote, we should consider the better way of voting that will not be influenced by the vote splitting.

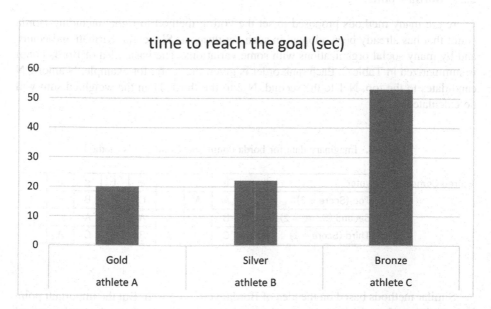

Fig. 3. Result of the time race where athlete A and B are close, but the former wins the Gold medal while the latter wins the Silver medal

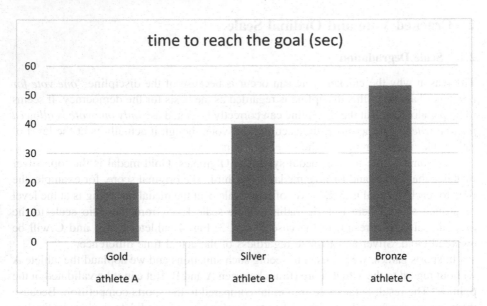

Fig. 4. Result of the time race where athlete A and B are far away, and the former wins the Gold medal while the latter wins the Silver medal

2.2 Borda Count

There are many methods proposed to set the voting method to rights including Borda count that has already been adopted in such countries as Slovenija, Kiribati and Nauru and by many social organizations with some variations. The basic idea of Borda count is summarized in Table 2. Each rank order is given the score, for example, N among N candidates to the top, N-1 to the second, N-2 to the third. Then the weighted sum will be calculated.

Table 2. Imaginary data for borda count and Condorcet's method

Paired Comparison	voter	a	b	c	d	e	f	g	h	i
	Top (Score = 3)	A	A	A	C	C	B	B	B	B
	Second (Score = 2)	B	B	B	A	A	A	A	C	C
	Third (Score = 1)	C	C	C	B	B	C	C	A	A

Similar methods based on the idea of Borda were proposed. But the important point is that it is based on the judgement at the level of ordinal scale, then convert the ordinal data to the level of interval scale.

Furthermore, voters will have to give the rank order to all of the candidates even if there were 20 or more of them. Of course, the lower ordered candidates may not be influential and could have been neglected. It is tiresome for voters to make the comparison of each specific candidate to all other candidates (Table 3).

Table 3. Borda count for the imaginary data

Sum of Comparison	sum of voter	3	2	2	2
	Top (Score = 3)	A	C	B	B
	Second (Score = 2)	B	A	A	C
	Third (Score = 1)	C	B	C	A

Borda Count	Total score for A	19 (3x3+2x2+2x2+2x1)
	Total score for B	20 (3x2+2x1+2x3+2x3)
	Total score for C	15 (3x1+2x3+2x1+2x2)

B is the Winner

2.3   Condorcet's Method

This method is also known as "Condorcet-Young Maximum Likelihood Estimation" or Kemeny-Young Method that aimed to improve the Borda Count. The procedure is shown in Table 4. Every paired comparison is calculated and summed up to decide the final winner.

Table 4. Condorcet's method for the imaginary data

Sum of Comparison	sum of voter	3	2	2	2
	Top	A	C	B	B
	Second	B	A	A	C
	Third	C	B	C	A

Condorcet's Method	A>B	3	2				A=5	A wins B for 5 times while B wins A only for 4
	B>A			2	2		B=4	times
	A>C	3		2			A=5	A wins C for 5 times while C wins A only for 4
	C>A		2		2		C=4	times
	B>C	3		2	2		B=7	B wins C for 7 times while C wins B only for 2
	C>B		2				C=2	times

Thus, A is the winner (A wins two times while B wins only once)

But Condorcet's method as well as Borda Count is based on the paired comparison and has a difficulty in the actual situation. For example, at 2016 Tokyo gubernatorial election, there were 21 candidates for one position. That is, every voter had to make

$_{21}C_2 = 21 * 20/2 = 210$ times of comparison if Condorcet's method was adopted. Nobody would agree that it is realistic to adopt this method considering the length of voting time, the decrease of motivation of voters, hence, the decrease of reliability of vote during the comparative judgments.

3   Proposed Method

3.1   General Description

The method that we propose here is not based on the judgment at the ordinal level but on the judgement at the interval level (or the ratio level). It directly gives the rating score to each candidate from 0 to 10 or 0 to 100 or whatever. In addition, the default value for every candidate is set to 0 and voters will need only to give the adequate point to those whom they are concerned.

The processing of rating score is straight-forward. Because the Likert scale value obtained from the calculation using the normal distribution is similar to the simple average score, we can simply calculate the average score for each candidate.

If this method were applied to 2000 United States presidential election, Gore, for example, will get the same score if Nader stood as a candidate or not. The fact that each vote can be made independently with each other is based on the notion "*onetime ratings for one voter*". One voter will give all the rating at one time voting but the vote is not just once. When the total number of candidates is N and the total ratings that a voter will make is n, the voter can neglect N-n candidates and leave the rating to the default value of 0. The voter will make only n time ratings as shown in the right half of Fig. 5.

In this figure, the result of one imaginary voter is shown. Be focused that on the left-hand side only candidate E get the vote and all the others get nothing, but on the right-hand side candidate E gets the 10 rating while candidate B gets 9 and candidate I gets 8 that were neglected in the conventional voting method.

If the claim of candidate B was similar to candidate E, vote for E in the conventional method might have been affected by the vote for B. But that will not happen in the proposed method because each rating is independent.

For M voters, total of M voting data will be accumulated, then the average of rating will be calculated by dividing the sum by M (but it's not a necessary step because the sum of ratings will be proportional to the average). Furthermore, because the proposed method is based on the interval (or ratio) level, there is no need to transform the ordinal data to the interval (or ratio) level. Hence, the situation described in Fig. 2, Fig. 3 will not happen.

Conventional Method
Before the voting

candidate A	
candidate B	
candidate C	
candidate D	
candidate E	
candidate F	
candidate G	
candidate H	
candidate I	

After the voting

candidate A	no
candidate B	no
candidate C	no
candidate D	no
candidate E	Vote
candidate F	no
candidate G	no
candidate H	no
candidate I	no

One vote for one voter

Proposed Method
Before the voting

candidate A	0 (default)
candidate B	0 (default)
candidate C	0 (default)
candidate D	0 (default)
candidate E	0 (default)
candidate F	0 (default)
candidate G	0 (default)
candidate H	0 (default)
candidate I	0 (default)

After the voting

candidate A	0 (default)
candidate B	9
candidate C	0 (default)
candidate D	0 (default)
candidate E	10
candidate F	0 (default)
candidate G	0 (default)
candidate H	0 (default)
candidate I	8

One time ratings for one voter

Fig. 5. Comparison of the conventional voting (left) and the proposed voting (right) for an imaginary data

3.2   Restriction

The crucial point for the proposed method is that it can only be applied to the election for one winner, for example, the election of a representative, president or to the vote for yes or no, acceptance or denial or to the court decision for guilty or not guilty.

But it is not adequate to apply this method to the situation where more than or equal to two candidates will win if there is an organized vote, in other words, if there is a party where every member gives the maximum ratings to candidates who belong to that party. This is the extreme case as described in Fig. 6. In such cases, the party with the maximum number of voters can monopolize all the seats.

Before the vote

candidate A	party X	0 (default)
candidate B	party X	0 (default)
candidate C	party X	0 (default)
candidate D	party X	0 (default)
candidate E	party Y	0 (default)
candidate F	party Y	0 (default)
candidate G	party Y	0 (default)
candidate H	party Y	0 (default)
candidate I	party Z	0 (default)

A vote by one voter who support the party X

candidate A	party X	10
candidate B	party X	10
candidate C	party X	10
candidate D	party X	10
candidate E	party Y	0 (default)
candidate F	party Y	0 (default)
candidate G	party Y	0 (default)
candidate H	party Y	0 (default)
candidate I	party Z	0 (default)

A vote by one voter who support the party Y

candidate A	party X	0 (default)
candidate B	party X	0 (default)
candidate C	party X	0 (default)
candidate D	party X	0 (default)
candidate E	party Y	10
candidate F	party Y	10
candidate G	party Y	10
candidate H	party Y	10
candidate I	party Z	0 (default)

Fig. 6. A biased vote based on the supporting party. Two cases are shown where the left is by a supporter of party X and the right is by a supporter of party Y. If the total number of supporters of party X was larger than any other parties, all candidates from party X will get the full score of 10 while all other candidates will get the minimum score of 0 (default).

4   Conclusion

As has been criticized, the simple voting method that is prevalent worldwide has many problems including the cracked vote and a better method for the majority decision is expected to appear. Borda, Condorcet and others proposed their new methods but they were based on the paired-comparison and is almost impossible to be adopted in the real situation even though they have a good theoretical background.

Authors proposed a new method using the rating method that directly brings the interval (or ratio) scale value and is better to any other previous method considering the nature of psychophysical scale. Although it has a disadvantage in the case of two or more seats if there is a biased vote by party(ies), it is considered to be the best solution, especially, for selecting one candidate (person, opinion, etc.) from among many candidates.

References

1. Stevens, S.S.: Problems and methods of psychophysics. Psychol. Bull. **55**(4), 177–196 (1958)
2. De Borda, J.-C.: Memoire sur les elections au scrutiny. Histoire de l'Academie Royale des Sciences (1781)
3. de Condorcet, M., de Caritat, N.: Essai sur l'application de l'analyse à la probabilité des décisions rendues à la pluralité des voix (1785)
4. Young, H.P., Levenglick, A.: A sosistent extension of condorcet's election principle. SIAM J. Appl. Math. **35**(2), 285–300 (1978)
5. Young, H.P.: Condorcet's theory of voting. Am. Polit. Sci. Rev. **82** (1988)
6. Likert, R.: A technique for the measurement of attitudes. Arch. Psychol. **140**(55) (1932)
7. Sakai, T.: Questioning the Majority Decision, (in Japanese). Iwanami Books (2015)

Using Blink Rate to Detect Deception: A Study to Validate an Automatic Blink Detector and a New Dataset of Videos from Liars and Truth-Tellers

Merylin Monaro[1]([✉]), Pasquale Capuozzo[1], Federica Ragucci[1],
Antonio Maffei[1], Antonietta Curci[2], Cristina Scarpazza[1],
Alessandro Angrilli[1], and Giuseppe Sartori[1]

[1] University of Padova, Via Venezia 8, 35131 Padua, Italy
merylin.monaro@unipd.it
[2] Università degli Studi di Bari Aldo Moro,
Via Scipione Crisanzio, 42, 70122 Bari, Italy

Abstract. Eye-blink is a sensitive index of cognitive load and some studies have reported that it can be a useful cue for detecting deception. However, it is difficult to apply in the real forensic scenario as very complex techniques to record eye blinking are usually needed (e.g., electrooculography, eye tracker technology). In this paper, we propose a new approach to automatically detect eye blinking based on a computer vision algorithm, which does not require any expensive technology to record data. Results demonstrated that the automatic blink detector reached an accuracy similar to the electrooculogram in detecting the blink rate. Moreover, the automatic blink detector was applied to 68 videos of people who were lying or telling the truth about a past holiday, testing the difference between the two groups in terms of blink rate and response timing. Training machine learning classification models on these features, an accuracy up to 70% in identifying liars and truth-tellers was obtained.

Keywords: Eye-blink · Lie detection · Deception · Cognitive load · Automatic blink detector

1 Introduction

1.1 The Cognitive Load Approach in Detecting Deception

Many studies in the literature have demonstrated that lying is cognitively more complex than truth-telling and that this higher cognitive complexity is reflected in a number of indices of cognitive effort, which are useful to distinguish liars from truth-tellers [1]. The theoretical framework that best developed and demonstrated this phenomenon is the "imposing cognitive load approach" [2], where the cognitive load is defined as the mental effort requested for completing a mental process [3].

According to this approach, the cognitive load can be manipulated by some interviewing strategies that have the effect to increase the mental effort of the liars but

© Springer Nature Switzerland AG 2020
M. Kurosu (Ed.): HCII 2020, LNCS 12183, pp. 494–509, 2020.
https://doi.org/10.1007/978-3-030-49065-2_35

leaving intact the cognitive effort of the truth-tellers [4]. Examples of the proposed interviewing strategies are asking the examinee to perform a second task at the same time as the interview (dual task), imposing time restrictions to respond to questions, recall the events in reverse order, asking the examinees to continuously switch between two tasks. One of the most effective strategies is asking unexpected questions, that is questions that cannot be foreseen and to which the interviewees cannot prepare their response in advance [5].

The technique of asking unexpected questions was originally applied to investigative interviews [6] and different studies have tested its efficacy in detecting deception, reaching high accuracy rates [7, 8]. The procedure commonly provides that the examiner initially asks anticipated questions and then switches to unanticipated questions. Such questions may be related to spatial or temporal details of the recalled event. For example, Vrij et al. [5] interrogated liars and truth-tellers about a lunch that they had at the restaurant (truth-tellers really ate at the restaurant, whereas liars were instructed to pretend to had done it). During the interview the examiner asked questions about temporal and spatial features of the lunch-event (e.g., who finished to eat first? Where was your table located?). Comparing the responses to unexpected questions of liars and truth-tellers, the former were identified with an accuracy of 80%. In a second experiment [7], the authors observed that liars, with respect to truth-tellers, reported many more details to the expected questions versus the unexpected questions, and participants could be classified based on this difference with a good classification rate (78% for truth-tellers and 83% for liars). Moreover, Monaro et al. [9] reported that liars are much slower and inaccurate than truth-tellers when they are asked to respond to unexpected questions. This is because liars need to fabricate the fake response in real-time, checking the congruency of the response with the other faked information and maintaining credibility and consistency in front of the examiner. This mental process results in an increment of cognitive load and, consequently, in an increment of response time and number of errors. Using the error rate and the response time, the authors were able to identify liars with an accuracy up to 95% [8].

In general, a recent meta-analysis [2] demonstrated that the lie detection approaches based on imposing cognitive load produce higher accuracy rates compared to standard approaches in spotting deception.

1.2 Using Eye-Blink Rate to Detect Deception

The effect of cognitive overload due to deception can be assessed and measured by different behavioural and physiological indices. As mentioned above, one of the simplest cues of deception related to an increment of the cognitive load is the reaction time (RT). A recent meta-analysis argues that RTs are able to spot the cognitive cost of deception, although they are susceptible to countermeasures [10]. Other behavioural and physiological indices that recently demonstrated their utility in spotting the cognitive cost of deception are the keystroke dynamics [11], the kinematic analysis of mouse movements [12], the verbal indices, such as the number of details and complications provided [13], and the eye-blink rate.

The eye-blink is a physiological index, defined as a rapid, synchronized and joined movement which consists of a quick closing and re-opening of the lower and upper eyelids [14]. Since the scientific research have largely proved that eye-blink is an index sensitive to cognitive load [15], some studies have suggested that it could be a cue to detect deception [16, 17]. The first attempt in this direction was made by Fukuda [17]. The paradigm used was a variation of the Guilty Knowledge Test (GKT) where participants were asked to choose a card from a deck and then to deny having chosen that specific card. During the experimental task, a video camera was placed on a helmet on the participant's head for recording the eye-blink pattern. Counting the number of eye-blinks, the author found lower blink rates for relevant cards than irrelevant ones and observed that the eye-blinks were delayed after the relevant cards offset.

In a subsequent study, Leal and Vrij [16] have measured the eye-blink activity in a mock crime paradigm in which half of the participants were instructed to steal a paper from an office and then to deny that during an interview, while the other participants were asked to talk about their normal business. The results revealed that liars showed both a decrease in the eye-blink rate at the moment of the lie production – that the authors hypothesized was due to the cognitive effort requested by the deceptive task, and an increase in the eye-blink rate immediately after the lie production (called by authors compensatory effect) compared to truth-tellers. The authors conducted a second experiment [18] following the same mock crime paradigm but using the GKT as a task. Again, results showed a decrease in the eye-blink rate in liars' group to key items compared to control items, while in the truth-tellers' group no differences were observed between key and control items.

A step further was done by Marchak [19] who tried to verify if eye-blink can be diagnostic of deception not only for past action but also for future intentions. Using a mock crime paradigm modified for detecting false intents, the author found fewer numbers of blinks and shorter maximum blink duration for subjects who had a false future intent compared to those who had not.

These results strengthen Fukuda's intuition and support the hypothesis that eye-blink activity can be a useful cue of deception. Specifically, it seems confirmed that the blink rate decreases during the lie production, due to the cognitive effort request by the deceptive task, and increases immediately after [16, 17].

However, this index of deception is difficult to be measured in the real forensic scenario (e.g., during investigative interviews) as very complex techniques to record eye blinking are usually used (e.g., electrooculography, eye tracker technology). Of the four studies mentioned above [16–19], in one the blink count was made by the experimenters manually, two studies derived the blink rate recording the electroencephalographic (EEG) activity, whereas one study collected the number of blinks through the eye tracker. Although these techniques are able to capture the eye-blink with great accuracy, they require a high level of expertise to collect and interpret data. Moreover, the cost of the equipment makes its application impossible on a large scale for screening purposes.

1.3 Aim of the Study

In this paper, we propose a new approach to automatically detect eye blinking based on a computer vision algorithm, which does not require any expensive technology and any expertise to record and portray data. Then, the automatic blink detector was applied to videos of people who were lying or telling the truth testing the difference between the two groups in terms of blink rate.

In more detail, two different experiments are reported. In the first experiment, we validated an automatic eye-blink detection system based on the algorithm proposed by Soukupová and Cech [20]. In the second experiment, we collected a dataset of 60 videos from participants randomly assigned to the truth-teller or liar condition and we tried to classify them based on the eye-blink rate and the response time to unexpected questions.

The added value of the second experiment mainly consists of the dataset. Indeed, few multimodal (video) dataset of liars and truth-tellers are currently available in the literature. We identified just eight scientific papers that attempted to detect deception by analyzing videos of liars and truth-tellers, extracting different indices, such as verbal cues, voice stress, facial micro-expressions, and blinking [21–28]. Four of them described experiments conducted in the laboratory environment, one collected the data through crowdsourcing platforms, and three have assembled videos from real court trials. However, just two out of the eight works follow the best practice to guarantee the replicability of the results allowing access to the dataset. Finally, in none of these studies, the examiner introduced interviewing strategies to increase the mental effort of the respondents. Given these limitations, here we propose a new dataset of videos from liars and truth-tellers that will be made available to the scientific community (upon request), and where the interviews are conducted imposing cognitive load through the technique of asking unexpected questions.

2   Automatic Blink Detector Validation

2.1   The Eye-Blink Automatic Detection Algorithm

The goal of the first experiment was to validated an automatic eye-blink detector to verify whether a system based on machine vision could reach the same accuracy of traditional physiological methods (e.g., eye tracking, EEG, electrooculogram) in detecting eye blinking.

The automatic eye-blink detection system we validated is based on the algorithm developed by Cech and Soukupová [20], which identifies the eye-blinks using facial landmarks as input. The algorithm was developed by using Python 3.6 programming language, through the OpenCV [29] and dlib [30] libraries for the acquisition of the facial landmarks. The algorithm calculates the eye-blink according to the eye-opening state during each frame of the video it receives as input. Specifically, it estimates the Eye Aspect Ratio (EAR), determined by the ratio between the height and the width of the eye. The algorithm calculates the average EAR value across both eyes for each frame of the video using the following formula (1):

$$EAR = \frac{||p2 - p6|| + ||p3 - p5||}{2||p1 - p4||} \tag{1}$$

where *p1 ... p6* are the corresponding six eye landmark locations, shown in Fig. 1, and $\|p2 - p6\|$ is the Euclidean distance between the locations *p2* and *p6*.

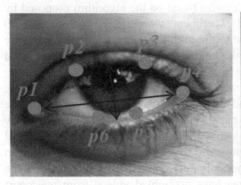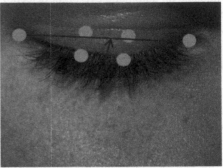

Fig. 1. The figure reports the six landmarks identified by the algorithm and used to calculate the EAR.

The EAR is mostly constant when the eyes are open and is getting close to zero while closing the eyes. Nonetheless, low EAR values can be observed not only during a blink but also when the subject is turning his head, looking down, smiling and yawning. In order to minimize this kind of errors, a Support Vector Machine (SVM) classifier was trained to establish if an eye-blink effectively occurred or not, searching for the features that best described the eye-blink behaviour. The final algorithm detected a blink only if the EAR dropped below a certain threshold (EAR = 0.28) for a certain number of consecutive frames (n = 2).

2.2 Participants

Eight participants were recruited for this study among the students of Padova University. The sample consisted of 1 male and 7 females, with age ranging from 22 to 25 years (M = 24, SD = 0.9). All participants voluntarily agreed to take part in the research and provided informed consent before the experiment began.

The experiment took place in the laboratories of the Department of General Psychology of the University of Padua. The experimental procedure was approved by the local ethics committee for psychological research of the University of Padova, in accordance with the Declaration of Helsinki.

2.3 Experimental Procedure

An adapted version of Mackworth Clock Test (MCT) was administered to the ten subjects as attentional task [31]. The MCT stimuli consisted in 100 white dots (radius = 2.6 mm) arranged to form a circle (radius = 105 mm) displayed at the centre of a computer screen. In each trial, a red dot was displayed moving across the circle, advancing from one position to the following at a constant rate. The task for the subject consisted in detecting when the red dot jumped a position (i.e., a white dot) by pressing the space button on the computer keyboard. The task difficulty was manipulated by changing the red dot speed moving across the circle, which could be 200 ms (Hard condition), 350 ms (Medium condition) or 500 ms (Easy condition). Target events (jumps) occurred at random positions and represented the 1% of total dot moves [32].

Stimuli were presented on the computer screen placed in front of the participants. Each participant underwent three Mackworth tasks of 7 min duration each (21 min overall), with a brief break between each session; the presentation order of the three MCT tasks was randomized and balanced for difficulty (Easy, Medium, Hard) across participants. Each session was preceded by a 3-min resting phase (baseline).

For the entire duration of the experimental task, the face of the participant was videotaped with a C920 Logitech HD Pro webcam (720p/30fps) placed on the computer screen in front of the subject. Moreover, spontaneous eye-blinks were collected through a vertical electrooculogram (EOG) recorded by two electrodes placed above and below the participant's right eye. Signal was amplified with a gain of 4000 and online filtered with a time constant of 10 s and a low pass filter set at 80 Hz. A high pass filter set at 0.5 Hz was applied offline in order to remove slow oscillations due to movement artifacts. The EOG was chosen between other physiological techniques (EEG, eye tracking) as it has been demonstrated to be a gold standard measure to catch eye blinking [33].

Afterward, the number of eye-blinks that occurred during the experimental task was derived through three different measures:

- manual count: for each subject an external observer counted the number of blinks caught 'by eye' watching the videos;
- EOG analysis: eye-blinks were defined as a peak of positive voltage change exceeding the threshold of 100 microvolts in a time window of 500 ms;
- automatic detection by machine vision algorithm: the videos recorded during the experiment were processed by the algorithm; the system returned the blink timing list and the list of the EAR values.

2.4   Analysis and Results

The number of blinks detected by the computer vision algorithm was compared with both the number of blinks recorded by the EOG and the number of blinks caught "by eye" from an external observer. The difference between the three measures was tested in both the 3-min resting phase (baseline) and the 21-min MCT task. In Fig. 2 the difference in the number of eye-blinks counted by three measures (external oberver, EOG and algorithm) for each subject are reported.

The Pearson's correlation coefficient (r) highlighted a positive, linear and strong association between EOG-observer ($r = .998$), EOG-algorithm ($r = .985$) and algorithm-observer ($r = .981$) as concerns the MCT task. Similar results were obtained also in the baseline scenario: EOG-observer ($r = .970$), EOG-algorithm ($r = .973$) and algorithm-observer ($r = .947$).

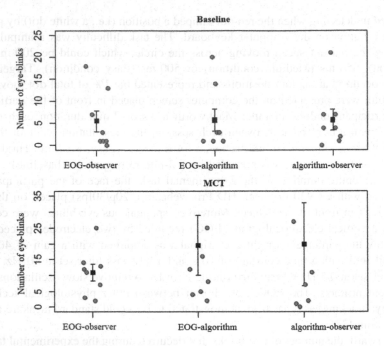

Fig. 2. The figure reports the difference in the number of eye-blinks between the three measures (external oberver, EOG and algorithm), respectively for the baseline and the MCT task.

The inter-rater reliability analysis showed a percentage of agreement between the three measures that varies from 89.8% to 92.8% (see Table 1), with a lower rate of agreement for the comparisons of the baseline phase involving the external observer. The Intraclass Correlation Coefficient (ICC) was calculated to assess the inter-rater correlations statistical significance. In general, ICC values less than 0.5 are indicative of poor reliability, values between 0.5 and 0.75 indicate moderate reliability, values between 0.75 and 0.9 indicate good reliability and values greater than 0.90 indicate excellent reliability [34]. Analyses were computed using the "irr" package in the R software. Results showed high reliability both in the baseline (ICC = 0.946, $F_{(7,14)}$ = 65, p < 0.01) and the MCT task (ICC = 0.952, $F_{(7,14)}$ = 67, p < 0.01), see Table 2.

Table 1. Results from the inter-rater reliability analysis.

	EOG-observer	EOG-algorithm	algorithm-observer
Baseline	89.8%	91.4%	89.8%
MCT	92.8%	91.6%	91.3%

Table 2. Intraclass Correlation Coefficient (ICC)

	Type	ICC	95% Confidence Interval		F test			
			Lower bound	Upper bound	F	df1	df2	p
Baseline	ICC2	0.946	0.827	0.988	65	7	14	<0.01*
MCT	ICC2	0.952	0.853	0.989	67	7	14	<0.01*

3   Dataset of Videos from Liars and Truth-Tellers

3.1   Participants

In the second experiment, we collected a dataset of videos from 60 participants who were asked to lie or tell the truth about a past holiday.

Forty-three females and 17 males took part in the study. All participants were volunteers recruited among the students of Padova University. The age ranged from 20 to 29 years (M = 24, SD = 1.8). The experiment took place in the laboratories of the Department of General Psychology of the University of Padua. Each participant provided consent form for both participation in the study and video-recording.

The experimental procedure was approved by the local ethics committee for psychological research of the University of Padova, in accordance with the Declaration of Helsinki.

3.2   Experimental Procedure

The experimental procedure was divided into two different phases: recruitment and interview. An observer-blind experimental design was adopted, as the first phase of the experiment (recruitment) and the second phase (interview) were carried out by two different experimenters.

During the recruitment phase, the first experimenter randomly assigned participants to the truth-teller or liar condition based on a matched-pairs experimental design. Participants assigned to the truth-teller condition were asked to recall a holiday experience that happened in the last 12–18 months and lasted a minimum of 1 day and a maximum of 7 days. They were instructed to fill in an empty form asking for some information about their holidays: where they went, how they traveled, how long they stayed there, with whom they went, how was the weather like and a daily activity plan. Participants were suggested to omit details if unable to remember them. Furthermore, they were suggested to help the memory with tools, such as photographs and videos, just to be sure that what they remembered was correct. On the other hand, participants assigned to liar condition were provided with a partially pre-compiled form with some information about a holiday they have never experienced before. In order to maintain the liars' narration as much comparable as possible in terms of length and content with the truth-tellers' one, each precompiled form was drafted by the first experimenter based on the form compiled by a matched truth-teller. Consequently, before assigning a travel destination to a liar, the experimenter had to make sure that the participant never visited that specific place before. Starting from the provided information (where they went, how they traveled, how long they stayed there, with whom they went), liars were asked to compile the form's empty sections (how was the weather like and the daily activity plan) with faked details. The experimenter encouraged liars in using the internet to find information about the unknown destination, in order to make the lie as truthful as possible. Finally, liars were asked to learn the faked holiday and to pretend that it really happened during the second phase of the experiment. Indeed, liars were informed by the first experimenter that the second experimenter would have been unaware of their experimental condition, so they had to make the lie as truthful as possible.

The day after the recruitment phase, the second experimenter invited the participants to the laboratory for a brief individual interview about the vacation. It should be noted that the second experiment was blinded about the experimental condition to which each subject belonged to. During the interview, the experimenter was sitting in front of the participants to keep eye contact; a C920 Logitech HD Pro webcam (720p/30fps) installed on a PC video-recorded the participants' faces.

In the first interview phase, participants were sitting in front of the video camera for 60 s without any specific task (baseline period); then the interviewer collected their autobiographical data. Afterward, they were encouraged to freely recall their holiday for approximately 2 min. Finally, the experimenter asked a number of unexpected questions about the vacation. The unexpected questions were equal in amount and contents for both truth-tellers and liars. As reported above, asking unexpecting questions is an interview strategy aimed to increase the liars' cognitive load [35]. Previous studies demonstrated that using unexpected questions technique significantly increases the accuracy in detecting deception [9].

In order to asses whether the interviewees perceived the examiner's questions as unexpected or not, at the end of the interview all participants were asked to fill in a 7-point Likert-scale questionnaire (1 = "totally expected", 7 = "totally unexpected"). The questionnaire consisted of five items: the first item assessed the perceived "expectancy" or "unexpectedness" as regards to the vacation recalling request (expected), whereas the remaining items investigated how the participants perceived the questions asked by the experimenter in the last part of the interview (unexpected questions).

For each participant, the entire experimental session was video recorded. The dataset (60 videos) is freely available upon reasonable request to the corresponding author. Then, the number of eye-blink for each interview phase (baseline, free recall, unexpected questions) was computed by the automatic eye-blink detection algorithm. The number of blinks was counted also for the 10 s immediately after the interview to test the presence of the compensatory effect, as observed by Leal and Vrij [16]. The duration of the speech for each phase (free recall and unexpected questions) was also calculated. In this way, we obtained the following features:

- time duration (duration): it is the time length (expressed in seconds) of each phase of the interview (free recall and unexpected questions). Note that the baseline had a standard duration of 60 s;
- raw number of blinks (blink raw): it is the raw number of eye-blinks counted during each phase (free recall and unexpected questions);

– blink per minute (bpm): it is the eye-blink frequency computed by dividing the raw number of blinks for the time duration (in seconds) of the respective phase, and then multiplying it for 60. The bpm has been calculated for each interview phase (baseline, free recall, unexpected questions, last 10 s);
– normalized blink per minute (bpm norm): the normalization was performed by dividing the number of blink per minute, respectively for the free recall, the unexpected questions phase and the last 10 s, by the number of blinks occurred in the baseline period.

3.3   Analysis and Results

To test the difference between liars and truth-tellers and within-subjects in the different phases of the interview (baseline, free recall, unexpected questions, last 10 s), a mixed ANOVA was run for each variable (duration, blink raw, bpm and bpm norm). With respect to the ANOVA magnitude, $\eta_G^2 = 0.02$ was considered indicative of a small effect, $\eta_G^2 = 0.13$ a medium effect, and $\eta_G^2 = 0.26$ a large effect [36]. The analyses were performed using JASP software [37].

Moreover, machine learning (ML) models were built using a 10-fold cross-validation procedure, to estimate the accuracy of classification of liars and truth-tellers based on the above-mentioned features (duration, blink raw, bpm and bpm norm). The classification models were implemented using the data mining software WEKA 3.9 [38].

Time Duration. As concerns the duration of the free recall phase and the unexpected questions phase, the ANOVA revealed a main effect of the interview phase on the time duration ($F_{(1,58)} = 51.99$, $p < 0.01$, $\eta_G^2 = 0.202$). Indeed, the post hoc analysis suggested that the free recall phase has a lower duration compared to the unexpected questions phase both for liars and truth-tellers ($t = 7.10$, $p_{holm} < 0.01$, $d = 0.917$). This result is not surprising, as it probably simply reflects the organization of the interview (participants were asked to recall their holidays for approximately 2 min).

Moreover, a significant effect was found for the experimental condition (liar vs. truth-teller) on the time duration ($F_{(1,58)} = 10.98$, $p < 0.01$, $\eta_G^2 = 0.120$). The post hoc test ($t = 3.31$, $p_{holm} < 0.01$, $d = 0.428$) highlighted that truth-tellers took more time than liars to free recall their holiday (liars M = 136.30, SD = 60.45; truth-tellers M = 174.47, SD = 80.38) and to respond to unexpected questions (liars M = 194.97, SD = 60.45; truth-tellers M = 268.97, SD = 100.95).

Finally, no statistically significant results were generated by the interaction between the interview phase and experimental condition $F_{(1,58)} = 2.85$, $p = 0.097$, $\eta_G^2 = 0.014$).

Raw Number of Blinks. The ANOVA uncovered a significant effect of the interview phase on the raw number of blinks ($F_{(1,58)} = 16.04$, $p < 0.01$, $\eta_G^2 = 0.061$), as the post hoc test showed that a higher number of eye-blinks was counted in the unexpected questions phase, compared to the free recall phase ($t = 4.01$, $p_{holm} < 0.01$, $d = 0.517$). However, this result is not interesting as it probably just reflects the higher time duration of the unexpected questions phase compared to the free recall phase for the participants in both conditions.

Furthermore, the raw number of eye-blinks significantly suffered from the main effect of the experimental condition (liars vs. truth-tellers), $(F_{(1,58)} = 6.30, p < 0.05, \eta_G^2 = 0.077)$. Indeed, the post hoc analysis $(t = 2.51, p_{holm} < 0.05, d = 0.324)$ highlighted that truth-tellers showed a greater raw number of eye-blinks compared to liars both in the free recall phase (liars M = 72.57, SD = 29.33; truth-tellers M = 91.20, SD = 46.59) and in the unexpected questions phase (liars M = 88.54, SD = 38.66; truth-tellers M = 117.34, SD = 49.91). Again, this result could simply reflect the observations about time duration, that is truth-tellers took more time than liars to respond to unexpected questions and to free recall the vacation.

The interaction between the interview phase and the experimental condition did not show any statistically significant result $(F_{(1,58)} = 0.94, p = 0.337, \eta_G^2 = 0.004)$.

Blink per Minute. To eliminate the effect of the duration of each interview phase on the number of blinks observed, the eye-blink frequency per minute (bpm) was calculated. The mixed ANOVA indicated that there was a significant effect of the interview phase on the bpm $(F_{(1,58)} = 18.63, p < 0.01, \eta_G^2 = 0.129)$. The post hoc analysis reported a higher bpm in the free recall phase $(t = 6.67, p_{holm} < 0.01, d = 0.861)$ and in the unexpected questions phase $(t = 4.20, p_{holm} < 0.01, d = 0.542)$ compared to the baseline. No statistically significant difference in bpm was found between the baseline and last 10 s of the interview $(t = 0.75, p_{holm} = 0.455, d = 0.097)$. As concerns the difference between the free recall and the unexpected questions phase, participants showed a lower number of bpm when they respond to unexpected questions $(t = 5.70, p_{holm} < 0.01, d = 0.736)$ and in the last 10 s after the interview $(t = 5.38, p_{holm} < 0.01, d = 0.695)$ compared to free recall. Finally, a lower number of bpm was found in the last 10 s of the interview compared to the unexpected questions phase $(t = 2.32, p_{holm} < 0.05, d = 0.300)$. Temporally speaking, during the free recall phase there was an increase in eye-blink frequency respect to the baseline, followed by a decrease during the phase of the unexpected questions, to return then to the baseline level in the last 10 s after the interview (bpm baseline M = 21.25 SD = 11.98; bpm free recall M = 32.54, SD = 9.84; bpm unexpected questions M = 27.08, SD = 8.68; bpm last 10 s M = 22.70, SD = 14.58).

As concerns the difference between liars and truth-tellers, the ANOVA highlighted that there was no significant effect of the experimental condition on the bpm $(F_{(1,58)} = 0.15, p = 0.701, \eta_G^2 = 0.001)$.

Similarly, no statistically significant results were generated by the interaction between the interview phase and the experimental condition $(F_{(1,58)} = 0.03, p = 0.992, \eta_G^2 < 0.001)$.

Normalized Blink per Minute. Analyzing the normalized bpm, we got similar results to that obtained by the bpm analysis. Indeed, it emerged a main effect of the interview phase $(F_{(1,58)} = 11.52, p < 0.01, \eta_G^2 = 0.055)$ on the bpm norm, whereas there was no main effect of the experimental condition on the bpm norm $(F_{(1,58)} = 0.06, p = 0.814, \eta_G^2 = < 0.001)$ and no significant interactions between interview phase and experimental condition $(F_{(1,58)} = 1.32, p = 0.272, \eta_G^2 = 0.007)$. The post hoc test revealed that participants showed a lower bpm nom in the unexpected questions phase $(t = 3.73, p_{holm} < 0.01, d = 0.481)$ and during the 10 s after the interview $(t = 4.18, p_{holm} < 0.01,$

d = 0.539) compared to the free recall phase. However, they did not show any significant difference in bpm nom when they responded to unexpected questions compared to the 10 last seconds after the interview (t = 1.94, p_{holm}= 0.057, d = 0.250).

ML Classification Model. To investigate the possibility to detect liars according to the collected features (duration, blink raw, bpm and bpm norm), different ML models were trained and validated through a 10-fold cross-validation procedure. The ML approach is useful when the focus of the analysis is prediction instead of explanation [39]. Moreover, learning algorithms allow to find patterns in highly complex datasets: they can be effective also in the presence of complicated non-linear interactions [40]. Furthermore, model evaluation techniques (e.g., k-fold cross-validation) are intended to guarantee that the reported results are not overly optimistic. The 10-fold cross-validation procedure [41] consisted of repeatedly partitioning the original sample into a training set and a validation set. For this study, the original sample of 60 participants was randomly partitioned into 10 equal-size subsamples, or folds (10 folds of 6 participants each). Of the 10 subsamples, data from a single subsample was retained as validation data for testing the model, and the remaining 9 subsamples were used to generate training data. This process was repeated 10 times, with each of the 10 folds used exactly once as validation data. The results of the 10 folds were then averaged to produce a single estimation of prediction accuracy.

The results of four different ML classifiers (logistic [42], random forest [43], RBF Network [44] and Support Vector Machine [45]) are presented in Table 3. For each model, accuracy, recall, precision, F-measure, and ROC area were reported. The classification accuracy is stable across all classifiers, ranging from 66% to 71%, with RBF network demonstrating the best performance (71.67%).

Table 3. Results from the 10-fold cross-validation of four different ML classifiers.

	Accuracy	Precision	Recall	F-measure	ROC area
Logistic	66.67%	0.67	0.67	0.67	0.73
Random forest	70%	0.70	0.70	0.70	0.68
SVM (c = 100)	66.67%	0.67	0.67	0.67	0.67
RBF network	71.67%	0.71	0.71	0.71	0.68

Finally, the weight of each predictor was examined by measuring the correlation (r_{pb}) between each feature and the outcome (liar vs. truth-teller). This analysis confirmed that the most important predictor was the duration of the unexpected questions phase (r_{pb}= 0.41), followed by the raw number of eye-blinks in the unexpected questions phase (r_{pb}= 0.31), the time duration of the free recall phase (r_{pb}= 0.26) and the raw number of blinks in the free recall phase (r_{pb}= 0.24). For all other variables, r_{pb} value was less than 0.2.

Analysis of the Unexpectedness Questionnaire. At the end of the interview, a 7-point Likert scale questionnaire was administered to each participant to investigate how much the unexpected questions and the request to free recall the vacation were perceived as unexpected (1 = "totally expected", 7 = "totally unexpected").

Results suggested that both liar and truth-tellers perceived as more "unexpected" the questions about planning (*"Which was/were the most difficult thing(s) to plan?"*, *"Was there anything that didn't go to plan during this trip?"*). This result is in line with the previous literature that found that questions about planning are those more difficult to foresee [13], so much so that liars usually report few planning details in their stories.

4   Discussion and Conclusion

In this paper, we reported the results of two different experiments. The first experiment was aimed to validate an automated blink detector based on the computer vision algorithm developed by Soukupová and Cech [20]. The performance of the algorithm was compared with the accuracy of the EOG recording and the manual count of the eye-blinks made by an external observer. The number of blinks made by eight participants, who were engaged in three MCT tasks, were counted using the three measures (algorithm, EOG, external observer). The results demonstrated that the machine vision algorithm has an accuracy comparable to that of the EOG (a gold standard measure to catch eye blinking) in detecting the single eye-blink. The implications of this result are very important, as it demonstrates that the eye-blink recording does not necessarily require expensive technologies, such as the EEG and the eye-tracking, or high expertise. Consequently, the eye-blink measure could be applied also at the screening level on a large scale, making it a useful tool for security purposes.

The second experiment was aimed to collect a new dataset of videos from liars and truth-tellers, overcoming the limitations of the few datasets currently available in the literature. Indeed, only two datasets of liars and truth-tellers' videos are open-access. Moreover, during the participants' interview, we introduced the technique of asking unexpected questions, as previous studies demonstrated that this technique significantly increases the accuracy in detecting deception [9]. The final dataset consisted of 60 videos obtained from 30 truth-tellers and 30 liars: the former told a truly lived vacation and responded honestly to the unexpected questions of the examiner; the latter reported a faked holiday and responded to the unexpected questions giving false information. The interview was video-recorded and divided into four phases: baseline, free recall, unexpected questions and 10 s immediately after the interview. The number of eye-blinks and the time length of each phase were calculated.

The between-subject analysis revealed that liars and truth-tellers differed mainly for the duration of the free recall phase and the unexpected questions phase. Indeed, truth-tellers took more time than liars both to recover the vacation and to respond to the unexpected questions of the examiner. As a consequence, truth-tellers showed a greater raw number of eye-blinks during these two phases (free recall and unexpected questions) compared to liars. However, the higher raw number of eye-blinks of the truth-tellers was just the effect of the time, as comparing the two groups for the frequency of blink per minute (bpm) they showed similar performance. To conclude, according to our experiment, the eye-blink is not a good measure to differentiate liars from truth-tellers. On the contrary, the duration of the response (holiday recall or response to unexpected questions) is a more useful index, as it allowed to detect liars with an accuracy up to 71%. This result supports the evidence that liars have generally less to say than the truth-tellers [46].

The within-subjects analysis gave more interesting results. Indeed, it demonstrated that both liars and truth-tellers showed a higher blink rate (bpm) in the free recall phase and in the unexpected question phase compared to the baseline, with a decrease in the bpm during the response to unexpected questions compared to the free recall. This result could be interpreted as the confirmation of the fact that the unexpected questions are efficient in increasing the cognitive load of the interviewee, which is reflected in a lower frequency of eye-blinks. Finally, no compensatory effect was found in the 10 s after the interview, contrary to what is reported by Leal and Vrij [16].

To conclude, the present study found discrepant results compared to previous researches [16, 17] on the possibility to record the eye-blink as a cue of deception. Thus, further investigations are needed in this field. The possibility to apply computer vision algorithms to detect eye-blinks with the same accuracy of other physiological measures can facilitate future research.

References

1. Vrij, A., Fisher, R., Mann, S., Leal, S.: A cognitive load approach to lie detection. Investig. Psychol. Offender Profiling **5**, 39–43 (2008)
2. Vrij, A., Fisher, R.P., Blank, H.: A cognitive approach to lie detection: a meta-analysis. Leg. Criminol. Psychol. **22**, 1–21 (2017). https://doi.org/10.1111/lcrp.12088
3. Paas, F., Renkl, A., Sweller, J.: Cognitive load theory and instructional design: recent developments. Educ. Psychol. **38**, 1–4 (2003). https://doi.org/10.1207/S15326985EP3801_1
4. Walczyk, J.J., Igou, F.P., Dixon, A.P., Tcholakian, T.: Advancing lie detection by inducing cognitive load on liars: a review of relevant theories and techniques guided by lessons from polygraph-Based approaches. Front. Psychol. **4**, 14 (2013). https://doi.org/10.3389/fpsyg.2013.00014
5. Vrij, A., Leal, S., Granhag, P.A., Mann, S., Fisher, R.P., Hillman, J., Sperry, K.: Outsmarting the liars: the benefit of asking unanticipated questions. Law Hum Behav. **33**, 159–166 (2009). https://doi.org/10.1007/s10979-008-9143-y
6. Hartwig, M., Granhag, P.A., Strçmwall, L.: Guilty and innocent suspects' strategies during interrogations. Psychol. Crime Law Law **13**, 213–227 (2007)
7. Lancaster, G.L.J., Vrij, A., Hope, L., Waller, B.: Sorting the liars from the truth tellers: the benefits of asking unanticipated questions on lie detection. Appl. Cogn. Psychol. **27**, 107–114 (2013). https://doi.org/10.1002/acp.2879
8. Monaro, M., Galante, C., Spolaor, R., Li, Q.Q., Gamberini, L., Conti, M., Sartori, G.: Covert lie detection using keyboard dynamics. Sci. Rep. **8**, 1976 (2018). https://doi.org/10.1038/s41598-018-20462-6
9. Monaro, M., Gamberini, L., Sartori, G.: The detection of faked identity using unexpected questions and mouse dynamics. PLoS ONE **12**, e0177851 (2017). https://doi.org/10.1371/journal.pone.0177851
10. Suchotzki, K., Verschuere, B., Van Bockstaele, B., Ben-Shakhar, G., Crombez, G.: Lying takes time: a meta-analysis on reaction time measures of deception. Psychol. Bull. **143**, 428–453 (2017). https://doi.org/10.1037/bul0000087

11. Monaro, M., Spolaor, R., QianQian, L., Conti, M., Gamberini, L., Sartori, G.: Type me the truth!: Detecting deceitful users via keystroke dynamics. In: Proceedings of the 12th International Conference on Availability, Reliability and Security, ARES 2017, Reggio Calabria, Italy (2017). https://doi.org/10.1145/3098954.3104047

12. Monaro, M., Gamberini, L., Sartori, G.: Identity verification using a kinematic memory detection technique. In: Hale, K., Stanney, K. (eds.) Advances in Neuroergonomics and Cognitive Engineering. Advances in Intelligent Systems and Computing, vol. 488, pp. 123–132. Springer, Cham (2017). https://doi.org/10.1007/978-3-319-41691-5_11

13. Vrij, A.: Deception and truth detection when analyzing nonverbal and verbal cues. Appl. Cogn. Psychol. 33, 160–167 (2019). https://doi.org/10.1002/acp.3457

14. Rucker, J.C.: Normal and abnormal lid function. In: Kennard, C., Leigh, R.J. (eds.) Handbook of Clinical Neurology, vol. 102, pp. 403–424. Elsevier (2011)

15. Nourbakhsh, N., Wang, Y., Chen, F.: GSR and blink features for cognitive load classification. In: Kotzé, P., Marsden, G., Lindgaard, G., Wesson, J., Winckler, M. (eds.) INTERACT 2013. LNCS, vol. 8117, pp. 159–166. Springer, Heidelberg (2013). https://doi.org/10.1007/978-3-642-40483-2_11

16. Leal, S., Vrij, A.: Blinking during and after lying. J. Nonverbal Behav. 32, 187–194 (2008). https://doi.org/10.1007/s10919-008-0051-0

17. Fukuda, K.: Eye blinks: new indices for the detection of deception. Int. J. Psychophysiol. 40, 239–245 (2001). https://doi.org/10.1016/S0167-8760(00)00192-6

18. Leal, S., Vrij, A.: The occurrence of eye blinks during a guilty knowledge test. Psychol. Crime Law 16, 349–357 (2010). https://doi.org/10.1080/10683160902776843

19. Marchak, F.M.: Detecting false intent using eye blink measures. Front. Psychol. 4 (2013). https://doi.org/10.3389/fpsyg.2013.00736

20. Soukupová, T., Cech, J.: Real-time eye blink detection using facial landmarks. In: 21st Computer Vision Winter Workshop (CVWW 2016), pp. 1–8 (2016)

21. Mihalcea, R., Burzo, M.: Towards multimodal deception detection – step 1. In: Proceedings of the 14th ACM International Conference on Multimodal Interaction - ICMI 2012, p. 189. ACM Press, New York (2012)

22. Pérez-Rosas, V., Abouelenien, M., Mihalcea, R., Burzo, M.: Deception detection using real-life trial data. In: Proceedings of the 2015 ACM on International Conference on Multimodal Interaction - ICMI 2015, pp. 59–66. ACM Press, New York (2015)

23. Pérez-Rosas, V., Mihalcea, R., Narvaez, A., Burzo, M.: A multimodal dataset for deception detection. In: Proceedings of the Ninth International Conference on Language Resources and Evaluation (LREC 2014), pp. 3118–3122. European Language Resources Association (ELRA) (2014)

24. Yu, X., et al.: Is interactional dissynchrony a clue to deception? Insights from automated analysis of nonverbal visual cues. IEEE Trans. Cybern. 45, 492–506 (2015). https://doi.org/10.1109/tcyb.2014.2329673

25. Pérez-Rosas, V., Abouelenien, M., Mihalcea, R., Xiao, Y., Linton, C., Burzo, M.: Verbal and nonverbal clues for real-life deception detection. In: Proceedings of the 2015 Conference on Empirical Methods in Natural Language Processing, pp. 2336–2346. Association for Computational Linguistics, Stroudsburg (2015)

26. Su, L., Levine, M.: Does "lie to me" lie to you? An evaluation of facial clues to high-stakes deception. Comput. Vis. Image Underst. 147, 52–68 (2016). https://doi.org/10.1016/j.cviu.2016.01.009

27. Yap, M.H., Ugail, H., Zwiggelaar, R.: A database for facial behavioural analysis. In: 2013 10th IEEE International Conference and Workshops on Automatic Face and Gesture Recognition (FG), pp. 1–6. IEEE (2013)

28. Michael, N., Dilsizian, M., Metaxas, D., Burgoon, J.K.: Motion profiles for deception detection using visual cues. In: Daniilidis, K., Maragos, P., Paragios, N. (eds.) ECCV 2010. LNCS, vol. 6316, pp. 462–475. Springer, Heidelberg (2010). https://doi.org/10.1007/978-3-642-15567-3_34

29. Bradski, G.: The OpenCV Library. Dr. Dobbs J. (2000)

30. King, D.E.: Dlib-ml: a machine learning toolkit. J. Mach. Learn. Res. **10**, (2009)

31. Maffei, A., Angrilli, A.: Spontaneous eye blink rate: an index of dopaminergic component of sustained attention and fatigue. Int. J. Psychophysiol. **123**, 58–63 (2018). https://doi.org/10.1016/j.ijpsycho.2017.11.009

32. Mackworth, N.H.: The breakdown of vigilance during prolonged visual search. Q. J. Exp. Psychol. **1**, 6–21 (1948). https://doi.org/10.1080/17470214808416738

33. Denney, D., Denney, C.: The eye blink electro-oculogram. Br. J. Ophthalmol. **68**, 225–228 (1984). https://doi.org/10.1136/bjo.68.4.225

34. Koo, T.K., Li, M.Y.: A guideline of selecting and reporting intraclass correlation coefficients for reliability research. J. Chiropr. Med. **15**, 155–163 (2016). https://doi.org/10.1016/j.jcm.2016.02.012

35. Warmelink, L., Vrij, A., Mann, S., Leal, S., Poletiek, F.H.: The effects of unexpected questions on detecting familiar and unfamiliar lies. Psychiatry Psychol. Law **20**, 29–35 (2013). https://doi.org/10.1080/13218719.2011.619058

36. Cohen, J.: Statistical Power Analysis for the Behavioral Sciences. Routledge, Hillsdale (1988)

37. JASP Team: JASP (Version 0.11.1) (2019). https://jasp-stats.org/

38. Hall, M.A., Frank, E., Holmes, G., Pfahringer, B., Reutemann, P., Witten, I.H.: The WEKA data mining software: an update. ACM SIGKDD Explor. Newsl. **11**, 10–18 (2009). https://doi.org/10.1145/1656274.1656278

39. Yarkoni, T., Westfall, J.: Choosing prediction over explanation in psychology: lessons from machine learning. Perspect. Psychol. Sci. **12**, 1100–1122 (2017). https://doi.org/10.1177/1745691617693393

40. Orrù, G., Monaro, M., Conversano, C., Gemignani, A., Sartori, G.: Machine learning in psychometrics and psychological research. Front. Psychol. **10**, (2020). https://doi.org/10.3389/fpsyg.2019.02970

41. Kohavi, R.: A study of cross-validation and bootstrap for accuracy estimation and model selection. In: Proceedings of the 14th International Joint Conference on Artificial Intelligence. pp. 1137–1143. Morgan Kaufmann, San Mateo (1995)

42. le Cessie, S., van Houwelingen, J.C.: Ridge estimators in logistic regression. Appl. Stat. **41**, 191–201 (1992)

43. Breiman, L.: Random forest. Mach. Learn. **45**, 5–32 (2001)

44. Broomhead, D.S., Lowe, D.: Radial basis functions, multi-variable functional interpolation and adaptive networks. Royals Signals & Radar Establishment (1988)

45. Keerthi, S.S., Shevade, S.K., Bhattacharyya, C., Murthy, K.R.K.: Improvements to platt's SMO algorithm for SVM classifier design. Neural Comput. **13**, 637–649 (2001)

46. Hauch, V., Blandón-Gitlin, I., Masip, J., Sporer, S.L.: Are computers effective lie detectors? A meta-analysis of linguistic cues to deception. Personal. Soc. Psychol. Rev. **19**, 307–342 (2015). https://doi.org/10.1177/1088868314556539

Pathway to a Human-Values Based Approach to Tackle Misinformation Online

Lara S. G. Piccolo[1]([⊠])(iD), Alisson Puska[2](iD), Roberto Pereira[2](iD), and Tracie Farrell[1](iD)

[1] Knowledge Media Institute, The Open University, Milton Keynes MK7 6AA, UK
{lara.piccolo,tracie.farrell}@open.ac.uk
[2] Department of Computer Science, Federal University of Paraná, Curitiba, Brazil
alisson.puska@gmail.com, rpereira@inf.ufpr.br

Abstract. Echoing what matters to us, our values pervade the criteria we apply in the judgment of the information we receive on social media when assigning to it a degree of relevance. In this era of "fakenews", understanding how the values of a social group influence perception and intentions for sharing pieces of (mis)information can reveal critical aspects for socio-technical solutions to mitigate misinformation spreading. This particular study contrasts the reasoning of a group in the United Kingdom and another in Brazil when judging and valuating the same set of headlines. The results confirm the influence of dominant values in the group in the interpretation of the headlines and potential motivations for sharing them, pointing out directions to advance with the human values-based approach to fight misinformation.

Keywords: Human values · Misinformation · Disinformation · Fake news

1 Introduction

With more and more people around the world relying on social media as a source of information and actively promoting what they judge as relevant, distinguishing whether the information received is reliable, accurate and shared in good faith is becoming increasingly harder. In this global scenario, false or manipulated information has commonly played a role in challenging or distorting values that shape the public opinion in different sectors of the society, such as health, science, politics, etc.

The information intentionally created to trigger, mislead, generate decision errors, manipulate beliefs or deceive is characterised as *disinformation* [34]. Illustrating that, persuasive strategies similar to those used in cyber attacks exploring cognitive hacking [6], which persuades people to fall into spear phishing and malware installation [4,20] have been applied in the creation and dissemination of false and manipulative news and hoaxes [1].

M. Kurosu (Ed.): HCII 2020, LNCS 12183, pp. 510–522, 2020.
https://doi.org/10.1007/978-3-030-49065-2_36

Misinformation, in turn, can be defined as misrepresented information that causes confusion and is not always intentionally created [34]. Despite the difference in intention, misinformation can be equally harmful and challenging both for human judgement and computational detection. As a matter of simplification, in this paper we refer to *misinformation* as any type of false information, which includes disinformation.

Events worldwide notably influenced by the power of social media, as the results Brexit referendum in the UK and 2016 presidential elections in the US [3,7], have alarmed the world about the need to review practices and regulation on information spreading online, and better prepare the society to deal with eventual manipulation. Beyond the political arena, the spread of misinformation against vaccines in the form of myths and conspiracy theories reinforced by individuals' beliefs have undermined public health programs to immunise citizens. As a consequence, some diseases such as yellow fever, measles and poliomyelitis, which have been under control for decades, are infecting and causing deaths again [11]. Similarly, cancer treatments which have been proven ineffective keep being promoted online [11], usually with good will.

We argue that the problem of misinformation spreading can not be understood from a single perspective. In different countries, regions or even social groups, communication is established in different ways, including meta-factors in the communication process, how they perceive and appropriate received messages [14]. Social media mediated communication is not apart from the sociocultural influence [3]. People's judgement on whether a piece of information is relevant and how it should be communicated is influenced by several conditions, such as social and economic factors, education, cultural traits [31] and human values [9].

Expanding the view presented by Piccolo et al. [22], we understand the problem of misinformation spreading in three different layers that coexist and interact with each other as a social information system. Figure 1 illustrates this view by applying the metaphor of an 'onion' [30]. The *technical* layer is where computational solutions and platforms are situated; the *formal* layer with policies and regulation in place, which also influences ethics, an aspect with formal elements. Motivations, beliefs and human values are mainly in the *informal* layer of the society.

Although computational advances are essential to deal with misinformation spreading online, focusing on technical aspects alone captures a minimal perspective of this information system. A lack of a comprehensive understanding on how people perceive and deal with misinformation online can potentially lead to limited or inefficient solutions, and the risk to produce non-desired impacts to the society; therefore, it is not a responsible way to tackle a social issue [21].

In this paper, we present the first steps towards informing with human values technical solutions for tackling misinformation spreading on social media. We argue that understanding values embedded in some pieces of information and the possible impact of this information upon some cultural groups (i.e. potential to trigger fear, violence, altruism) can inform automated detection of

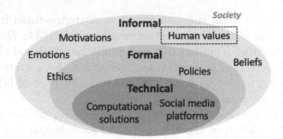

Fig. 1. Three layers of misinformation in a social system

misinformation online in early stages of dissemination, providing an opportunity to social media platforms to prioritise the credibility check or to nudge users before they actually share [9].

We build this study on the results of a survey in the UK that investigated how people interpreted a set of news headlines in terms of veracity and potential to be shared [9]. To this end, we analyse and contrast results of similar tasks with a group of participants in Brazil, evidencing that dominant values according to the Schwartz's theory [25] influence judgment, perception and possible intentions for sharing. Therefore, considering social values embedded in pieces of information should not be a one-size-fits-all approach.

In the next section, the literature review is organised as approaches focused on technical, formal and informal levels and then human values are discussed from a theoretical perspective. In the sequence, the value-based study is described followed by the discussion of the findings using socio-technical lenses. After that, the paper is concluded pointing to future works.

2   Background

At the *technical level*, most popular approaches to fight misinformation support credibility assessment [13] or target the detection of misinforming content [10]. This content include claims, statements containing information/facts that can potentially be assessed; clickbaits, persuasive content leading people to click on particular links [18]; bots, agents that communicate on social media promoting specific information [19], naming a few. Other studies seek to understand the dynamics of misinformation online as echo chambers and filter bubbles [7]. Detection of human values has been addressed by Chen et al. [5], where Reddit posts were analysed to identify a number of word categories that are associated with values. Drawing on Schwartz's basic values theory [26], the research confirmed word-use in social media as a potential predictor of people's values.

At the *formal level*, policies and regulation substitute meaning and intention. According to [16], there are no clear policies regulating misinformation spreading on social media and no guidance towards legal frameworks or ethical issues to be considered. Criticism and public accusations of contributing to the spread of misinformation led big social media players to invest in solutions to tackle it. Like Facebook, many platforms created internal policies for communities and users' content management to deal with content considered not adequate. However, for [15], these policies are the result of centralised policy-making by small groups of experts, platform managers, and developers, failing to include and empower platform users. Another formal and crucial approach to fight misinformation is fact-checking, journalistic practices determined by a shared code of principles to verify information [17]. However, as a laborious work performed by groups of experts, existing fact-checking initiatives struggle to cope with the speed, broadness and volume of information spread on social media.

At the *informal level*, Thorson [32] investigated people's beliefs and evidenced that only informing that the information they believed was incorrect is not enough. Exposing explanations or demographic similarity of the opposing group are some possible strategies to potentially influence changes in opinion. Understanding sharing behaviour is another typical approach. Researches with this objective typically know very little about the characteristics of users, especially regarding subjective aspects. Few studies have considered the social and demographic contexts and their influence on misinformation consumption and spreading. Bedard et al. [2] found that age, education, sex, and political affiliation predict distinguishing "fake news" and satire, and Goyanes [12] applied demographic and situational factors like perception of responsibility, for example, to predict the probability of sharing misinformation. Trilling et al. [33] and Vousoughi et al. [36] investigate characteristics of pieces of news that can suggest its potential for dissemination. Subjective aspects like an emotional language, as well as positivity or negativity, were found to have an influence. Current approaches to detect emotions are mainly based on patterns referring to a small set of basic human emotions [36], limited when referring to emotions as a social construct, culturally built [23].

Human values were addressed by Verma et al. (2019) [35] with demographic information to understand individuals' trust behaviour online. Their findings shed light on the potential role values play in shaping people's interaction with hyperlinks (and potentially other features) on social media posts.

2.1   Human Values

Values reflect what is important to people in life; as a concept, they have been used in the social sciences and psychology literature to characterise social groups, individuals, to trace changes over time, and to explain the motivational bases of attitudes and behavior [29]. For Schwartz [26], human values are "the criteria people use to select and justify actions, to evaluate people (including the self) and events". His theory is based on ten basic personal values shared universally [29]:

– *Self-direction*: Independent thought and action;
– *Stimulation*: Excitement, novelty and challenge in life;
– *Hedonism*: Pleasure or sensuous gratification for oneself;

- *Achievement*: Personal success, demonstrating competence;
- *Power*: Social status, control or dominance over people and resources;
- *Security*: Safety, national security, family security, social order;
- *Conformity*: Obedience, self-discipline, politeness;
- *Tradition*: respect, commitment, and acceptance of customs and ideas;
- *Benevolence*: preserving and enhancing the welfare of the 'in-group';
- *Universalism*: Understanding, appreciation and protection for the welfare of all people and for nature.

This set of values are represented in a circular structure that illustrates conflicts and compatibility among them. Self-direction, Stimulation and Hedonism are values related to *Openness to change*, which contrasts the *Conservation* values of Conformity, Tradition and Security. Similarly, *Self-transcendence* values of Universalism and Benevolence refer to the importance of enhancing others, beyond selfish interests, opposing to *Self-enhancement* of Hedonism, Achievement and Power.

Judging the veracity of a piece of information, according to this theory, is related to personal beliefs. Values come into play by adding feelings to this judgment, setting it a level of importance and, possibly influencing people's decision to share it with others or not. Typically, people consider possible consequences for their most important values as a criteria to decide what is good or bad, justified or illegitimate. This decision, though, is often not conscious [29].

As the basic values are understood as universal with varying degrees of influence over human understanding and behaviour [24], previous knowledge acquired on priority values for specific social groups could point directions on how specific pieces of information will be judged and potentially shared. As an example, the European Social Survey[1] systematically assesses the priority values in several European Countries along the years. This approach can help to understand or predict, in a situated context, underlying motivations for sharing and potential social impact due to triggered emotions.

3   Values-Based Study

As fully described in [9], an online survey in the UK recruited 97 library professionals to analyse how they judge a piece of information they see online. This particular group of participants was targeted for sharing a similar background on information literacy.

As part of the survey, without consulting any other source of information, the participants were asked to: (i) judge whether ten headlines were true or false; (ii) select three of the headlines to be shared and justify why; (iii) if they could verify the information before sharing, select three of them and justify the choices. No additional data beyond the headlines was presented, simulating a typical social media behaviour where people quickly browse only the headlines. The ten headlines presented to the participants did not address political issues

---

[1] www.europeansocialsurvey.org.

but touched on themes related to national security, natural world, etc. [9]. They were selected from a commercial card game[2], as described below:

1. Bearded London hipster mistaken for a member of ISIS and assaulted by nationalists. FALSE. *The Sunday*
2. Man high on drugs rescues dog from imaginary house on fire. TRUE. *The Telegraph*
3. Nigerian restaurant serves human flesh. FALSE. *BBC News*
4. Fish survives six months without half its body. TRUE. *The Independent*
5. Neighbour from hell eats girl's guinea pig. FALSE. *USA Today*
6. Man allowed to board plane after bomb found in his baggage. TRUE. *CTV News*
7. NHS purchases Gluten-free bread for £32.27 per loaf. FALSE. *The Express, the Sun and the Telegraph*
8. In Switzerland, it is illegal to own only one guinea pig. TRUE. *The Mirror*
9. The Bluegill fish is one of the most dangerous fish in North America. When the bluegill are feeding in a school, they can completely dismantle a human body in less than 15 min. FALSE. *Facebook*
10. Britain has the highest rate of cocaine use among young adults in Europe, their consumption being almost double that of other nations on the continent. TRUE. *The Times*

The justifications were analysed qualitatively by a group of independent researchers and associated with Schwartz's basic values. Declared interest in the topic and avoidance of risk of consequences were the dominant reasons for choosing what to be shared. Therefore, the headlines (8) 'Guinea pig in Switzerland', (4) 'Fish survives' and (2) 'Rescue dog', which are mainly associated to the values of Stimulation and Universalism, were top-ranked for sharing. While those headlines related to close values of Security and Power (1) 'Hipster', (7) 'NHS bread', and (6) 'Bomb' had the strongest demand for fact-checking, but a low intention for sharing. The results of the study also suggest that, in some cases, the values associated to the headlines are even more critical in the decision of sharing than the judgment of it is true or false.

The analysis of priority human values according to Schwartz's theory [27] on the data collected by the European Social Survey in 2018[3] [8] supports participants' expressed rationale. Power was found the predominant value in the UK, followed by Achievement and Stimulation.

Avoiding headlines that challenge Power can be seen as a strategy to avoid risks on triggering negative social impact, and also, for the sender, to be perceived by the social network as someone that challenges dominant societal values. Favourite headlines to be shared support Stimulation or Self-enhancement, also dominant aspects of the social group.

---

[2] Fake News Card Game by The Takeover Game.
[3] European Social Survey Round 9 Data (2018). Data file edition 1.2. NSD - Norwegian Centre for Research Data, Norway - Data Archive and distributor of ESS data for ESS ERIC.

Relative priority of basic values in the UK (data 2018)

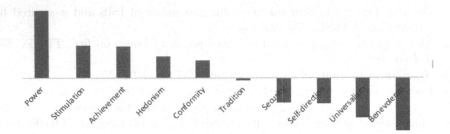

Fig. 2. Relative priority values in the UK in 2018

3.1 Survey in Brazil

A group of 15 media literacy postgraduate students in Brazil were invited to: (i) complete the short version of Schwartz' Portrait Values Questionnaire (PVQ) [29], the same one used by the European Social Survey (ESS) to capture and compare priority values in different countries [8,27]; (ii) point out which values they believe are priority among their social network online; (iii) judge the same ten headlines used in the UK-based survey whether they are true or false; (iv) associate headlines with predominant value(s); (v) select three headlines they would share if they had to; (vi) select which ones they would fact-check before sharing; (vii) select those they would never share. They were asked to justify the choices in the last three tasks.

Participants had a brief introduction to Schwartz's theory of Human Values before completing the online survey. Eventual questions about values or the headlines were answered as the survey was applied in English, a second language for the participants. Headline (7) 'NHS' was briefly explained to make it clear that it refers to a national-health entity in the UK.

Results. The group of students in Brazil had Universalism as the primary value, followed by Benevolence and Self-direction. Power and Tradition were the least significant values, as illustrated in Fig. 3. This resulting ranking is very similar to the 'dominant values they perceived in their social network', with the only distinction that Power is perceived as slightly more important than assessed via questionnaire.

Results obtained for the headlines classifications are described in Table 1 below. For each headline, the percentage of participants that correctly classified the headline as true or false and the values most frequently associated with the headlines are presented.

Six out of the ten headlines had a very similar percentage of people that judged it correctly. Other four had the true or false judgment notoriously distinct,

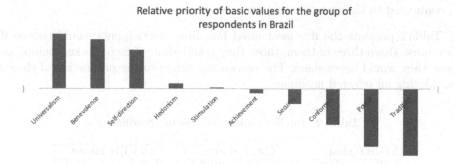

Relative priority of basic values for the group of respondents in Brazil

Fig. 3. Relative priority of values as calculated from PVQ survey

Table 1. Results of data collected in the survey

	Headline	T or F	Values associated
1	Hipster	7%	Security; Power
2	Rescue dog	80%	Stimulation; Benevolence
3	Nigerian	87%	Security; Tradition
4	Fish survives	40%	Universalism
5	Neighbour	67%	Security
6	Bomb	27%	Security; Power/Universalism
7	NHS	53%	Power; Benevolence
8	Guinea pig	13%	Universalism; Tradition
9	Bluegill	60%	Universalism; Security
10	Cocaine	67%	Security; Power/Hedonism

as described below. These and a few other headlines also differ in the way they have been connected to values:

- (8) 'Guinea pig' was correctly judged as true by 13% of the Brazilian participants and by 61% in the UK, where it has been associated mostly to Power instead of Universalism in Brazil;
- (1) 'Hipster' was judged correctly as false only by 7% and associated to Security and Power, while in the UK 48.5% got it right and connected mostly to Universalism;
- (2) 'Rescue dog' correctly judged as true by 80% of the Brazilian participants which understood it as Stimulation, and the 50.5% in the UK that connected it to Conformity.
- (4) 'Fish survives' and (9) 'Bluegill' were both associated to Stimulation due to the learning element in the UK. They were understood as Universalism due to the connection with the natural environment. In Brazil, 40% understood the 'Fish survives' headlines as true, while 72% in the UK.

– (6) 'Bomb' was related to Security and Power in Brazil, while in the UK was connected to Universalism as a social concern.

Table 2 presents the five most cited headlines participants would choose if they must share three of them, those they could share if fact-checked before, or those they would never share. The percentage refers to the proportion of choice considering all selected headlines.

Table 2. Top-five ranking of selected headlines

MUST share	CAN share	NEVER share
1 Hipster (18%)	1 Hipster (20%)	5 Neighbour (25%)
10 Cocaine (18%)	10 Cocaine (20%)	3 Nigerian (18%)
3 Rescue dog (18%)	3 Nigerian (13%)	8 Guinea pig (16%)
9 Bluegill (11%)	7 NHS (11%)	7 NHS (11%)
7 NHS (11%)	9 Bluegill (11%)	6 Bomb (9%)

The majority of justifications for choosing headlines to be shared refers first to their perceived plausibility, relevance to society, or humour 'because it sounds funny'. Interestingly, headlines (1) 'Hipster', (10) 'Cocaine', and (3) 'Rescue dog' had multiple justifications based on Universalism 'a way to prevent drugs consumption', 'an alert about intolerance', 'expression of solidarity' or 'to be used as a comparison, evidencing that developed countries have similar problems to ours', or as example of protecting the nature or welfare.

Social relevance, personal interest and the suspicious it is a false news due to the text style led the decisions on the headlines to be fact-checked before sharing. Headlines associated with Security and Power were the most consensual ones regarding the need for fact-checking as a way to prevent a negative societal impact. The lack of relevance for the society dominated decisions to never share some specific news. The 'bad news' tone of some headlines, for example (3) 'Nigerian flesh', was also considered a reason for not sharing.

Similar to the rationale applied by UK-based participants, the decision for sharing seems to be more influenced by the perception of the social network in terms of interest and impact. For this particular public with a degree of information literacy, plausibility is a significant criterion in both scenarios. The concern to avoid societal harm by spreading challenging headlines associated with Security is also present, especially as a principle to never share negative news. Part of Brazilian respondents introduced a new perspective in the way to judge and value some headlines, different from the results found in [9]. The stories that were somehow challenging important values were seen as a way to alert, raise awareness or compare realities, and not necessarily as a risk or threat.

As Schwartz explains [29], Self-transcendence values (Universalism and Benevolence), which are dominant in this group, are more focused on the social than personal aspects, with motivation to preserve and enhance the welfare of others [27,28], a characteristic that can explain these results.

4   Discussion

Contrasting results obtained in the UK and Brazil illustrates the role of values in adding feelings or setting the level of importance to the headlines, as per Schwartz's theory [29]. Therefore, the perceived 'shareworthyness' seems to be tuned to the values (and interest) of the participants' social network.

Headlines considered 'neutral', with no potential to assert any societal harm, as (4) 'Fish survives' and (9) 'Bluegill' were associated with Stimulation in the UK and with Universalism in Brazil. Although it sounds similar, Schwartz [28] details the drives behind these values: while Stimulation is related to learning (know, understand, by exercising curiosity...), Universalism refers to 'connecting plus learning', where connecting means to build social relationships and develop mutual commitment, suggesting that people may be still prone to share things that are not necessarily connected to their individual values, but to communicate with their 'audience'.

For Schwartz [29], Self-transcendence values (Universalism and Benevolence) lead to motivation for preserving and enhancing the welfare of others. They are opposed to Self-Enhancement values (Achievement and Power) which justify self-serving behaviour instead. For the participants with dominant Self-transcendence values, even headlines challenging societal values as Security and Power were many times seen through the lenses of Universalism, as an expression of solidarity, or as an example to (not) be followed.

Both in the UK and in Brazil, the intention to avoid triggering a negative societal impact by sharing potential risky headlines was evident. In fact, *risk of harm* has been a credibility signal considered in assessing credibility of online information in the Web[4].

Building on the idea of how informal, formal and technical layers in Fig. 1 can be connected for providing solutions to tackle misinformation on line, we argue that the notion of human values could inform the characterisation of potential societal harm as a credibility signal, and applied as a way to prioritise assessment by fact-checkers or the social platform or to nudge users about the potential to assert risks.

4.1   Limitations

As limitations for this study, it is acknowledged in the literature that researches that ask people how likely it is that they would share some stimulus hardly mimics a real-life situation [33]. For the survey, participants received instruction that they had to share three headlines and should select which ones. Yet, the headlines not necessarily match their personal interests. Then, the most important point for the analysis is how they perceived the headlines, their reasoning, and not the real intention of sharing them or not.

---

[4] *Credibility Signals*: a live document by the W3C Credible Web Community. https://credweb.org/signals-beta/#claim-risk-of-harm.

For the Brazilian survey, the group size ($n = 15$) limited the range of statistical analysis that could be performed like correlations or trends. This sample size is not enough either to compare relative priority values across countries. For this reason, the PVQ results presented here must NOT be understood as representative of the Brazilian population, referring only to the group of participants in the study. Cross-national studies within Europe could rely on the ESS data for comparisons, which was not the case for Brazil.

For ensuring compatibility in terms of information literacy, this study restricted the participation to groups of people with a known background. On the one hand, a broader audience could lead to different results, for example, on the importance of plausibility. But on the other hand, it would add extra variables related to the understanding and objectives of the survey.

As a preliminary study, results can be applied to inform the setup for broader comparative analysis, suggesting what needs to be taken into account to understand better and predict the role of human values in perceived 'shareworthyness', and to consider these factors when designing technical solutions to mitigate misinformation spreading.

5   Conclusion

This research explored the role of human values in perceiving and judging a set of headlines, simulating pieces of news accessed through social media. Groups with different cultural background perceived and valuated headlines in different ways, evidencing the influence of dominant values in this subjective process. This study points direction to broader research across nations where dominant values have been periodically assessed. Future work comprises analysing real social media data, especially on how similar topics have been perceived and spread across countries to build a more systematic knowledge on how human-values can inform existing pipelines for fact-checking or contextual strategies to nudge social media users.

Acknowledgment. This paper has been supported by the EC within the Horizon 2020 programme under grant agreement 770302 - Co-Inform.

References

1. Bazan, S.: A new way to win the war. IEEE Internet Comput. **21**(4), 92–97 (2017). https://doi.org/10.1109/MIC.2017.2911419
2. Bedard, M., Schoenthaler, C.: Satire or fake news: social media consumers' socio-demographics decide. In: Companion Proceedings of the The Web Conference 2018, pp. 613–619 (2018)
3. Bond, R.M., et al.: A 61-million-person experiment in social influence and political mobilization. Nature **489**(7415), 295–298 (2012)
4. Caputo, D.D., Pfleeger, S., Freeman, J.D., Johnson, M.: Going spear phishing: exploring embedded training and awareness. IEEE Secur. Priv. **12**(01), 28–38 (2014). https://doi.org/10.1109/MSP.2013.106

5. Chen, J., Hsieh, G., Mahmud, J.U., Nichols, J.: Understanding individuals' personal values from social media word use. In: Proceedings of the 17th ACM CSCW & Social Computing, pp. 405–414 (2014)
6. Cybenko, G., Giani, A., Thompson, P.: Cognitive hacking: a battle for the mind. Computer **35**(8), 50–56 (2002). https://doi.org/10.1109/MC.2002.1023788
7. DiFranzo, D., Gloria-Garcia, K.: Filter bubbles and fake news. XRDS **23**(3), 32–35 (2017). https://doi.org/10.1145/3055153
8. ESS Round 9: European Social Survey Round 9 Data. Data file edition 1.2. NSD - Norwegian Centre for Research Data, Norway – Data Archive and distributor of ESS data for ESS ERIC (2018). https://doi.org/10.21338/NSD-ESS9-2018
9. Farrell, T., Piccolo, L., Perfumi, S.C., Alani, H.: Understanding the role of human values in the spread of misinformation. In: Proceedings of Truth and Trust Online (2019)
10. Garrett, R.K., Weeks, B.E.: The promise and peril of real-time corrections to political misperceptions. In: Proceedings of CSCW 2013, pp. 1047–1058. ACM (2013)
11. Ghenai, A., Mejova, Y.: Fake cures: user-centric modeling of health misinformation in social media. Proc. ACM Hum.-Comput. Interact. **2**(CSCW), 1–20 (2018)
12. Goyanes, M.: The sociology of fake news: factors affecting the probability of sharing political fake news online. LSE Working Paper Series, June 2018
13. Gupta, A., Kumaraguru, P., Castillo, C., Meier, P.: TweetCred: real-time credibility assessment of content on Twitter. In: Aiello, L.M., McFarland, D. (eds.) SocInfo 2014. LNCS, vol. 8851, pp. 228–243. Springer, Cham (2014). https://doi.org/10.1007/978-3-319-13734-6_16
14. Hall, E.T.: The Silent Language, vol. 1, p. 959. Fawcett Publications. Inc., Greenwich (1959)
15. Han, O., Baris, I., de Nigris, S., Staab, S.: Democratic policy-making for misinformation detection platforms by git-based principles. In: Workshop Exploring the Limits of Misinformation at INTERACT 2019, Paphos. https://coinform.eu/wp-content/uploads/2019/11/Democratic_platform_policy_deliberation_through_git_based_principles.pdf
16. Hosseini, A.: Content Management Policies for Combating Misinformation (2020). https://coinform.eu/content-management-policies-for-combating-misinformation/
17. Ireton, E.C., Posetti, J.: Journalism, 'Fake News' & Disinformation Handbook for Journalism Education and Training. United Nations Educational, Scientific and Cultural Organization - UNESCO (2018)
18. Karadzhov, G., Gencheva, P., Nakov, P., Koychev, I.: We built a fake news & click-bait filter: what happened next will blow your mind! arXiv preprint arXiv:1803.03786 (2018)
19. Kudugunta, S., Ferrara, E.: Deep neural networks for bot detection. Inf. Sci. **467**, 312–322 (2018)
20. Nguyen-Vu, L., Park, J., Chau, N.T., Jung, S.: Signing key leak detection in Google Play Store. In: Proceedings of the 2016 International Conference on Information Networking (ICOIN), pp. 13–16. IEEE Computer Society, USA (2016)
21. Pereira, R., Baranauskas, M.C.C.: A value-oriented and culturally informed approach to the design of interactive systems. Int. J. Hum Comput Stud. **80**, 66–82 (2015)

22. Piccolo, L.S.G., Joshi, S., Karapanos, E., Farrell, T.: Challenging misinformation: exploring limits and approaches. In: Lamas, D., Loizides, F., Nacke, L., Petrie, H., Winckler, M., Zaphiris, P. (eds.) INTERACT 2019. LNCS, vol. 11749, pp. 713–718. Springer, Cham (2019). https://doi.org/10.1007/978-3-030-29390-1_68. http://oro.open.ac.uk/68822/
23. Richerson, P.J., Boyd, R.: Not by Genes Alone: How Culture Transformed Human Evolution. University of Chicago press, Wiley (2008)
24. Rokeach, M.: The Nature of Human Values. Free Press, New York (1973)
25. Schwartz, M.: Guidelines for Bias-Free Writing. ERIC, Bloomington (1995)
26. Schwartz, S.H.: Universals in the content and structure of values: theoretical advances and empirical tests in 20 countries. Adv. Exp. Soc. Psychol. **25**, 1–65 (1992). Academic Press
27. Schwartz, S.H.: A proposal for measuring value orientations across nations. Quest. Packag. Eur. Soc. Surv. **259**(290), 261 (2003)
28. Schwartz, S.H.: Les valeurs de base de la personne: théorie, mesures et applications. Revue française de sociologie **47**(4), 929–968 (2006)
29. Schwartz, S.H.: An overview of the schwartz theory of basic values. Online Read. Psychol. Cult. **2**(1), 0919–2307 (2012)
30. Stamper, R., Liu, K., Hafkamp, M., Ades, Y.: Understanding the roles of signs and norms in organizations-a semiotic approach to information systems design. Behav. Inf. Technol. **19**(1), 15–27 (2000)
31. Theng, Y.L., Goh, L.Y.Q., Lwin, M.O., Shou-Boon, S.F.: Dispelling myths and misinformation using social media: a three-countries comparison using the case of tuberculosis. In: 2013 IEEE International Conference on Healthcare Informatics, pp. 147–152. IEEE (2013)
32. Thorson, E.: Belief echoes: the persistent effects of corrected misinformation. Polit. Commun. **33**(3), 460–480 (2016)
33. Trilling, D., Tolochko, P., Burscher, B.: From newsworthiness to shareworthiness: how to predict news sharing based on article characteristics. J. Mass Commun. Q. **94**(1), 38–60 (2017)
34. Tudjman, M., Mikelic, N.: Information science: science about information, misinformation and disinformation. Proc. Inform. Sci.+ Inf. Technol. Educ. **3**, 1513–1527 (2003)
35. Verma, N., Fleischmann, K.R., Koltai, K.S.: Understanding online trust and information behavior using demographics and human values. In: Taylor, N.G., Christian-Lamb, C., Martin, M.H., Nardi, B. (eds.) iConference 2019. LNCS, vol. 11420, pp. 654–665. Springer, Cham (2019). https://doi.org/10.1007/978-3-030-15742-5_62
36. Vosoughi, S., Roy, D., Aral, S.: The spread of true and false news online. Science **359**(6380), 1146–1151 (2018). https://doi.org/10.1126/science.aap9559

Using Inclusive Research to Promote Inclusive Design: Possibilities and Limitations in a Corporate Environment

Gregory Weinstein[✉]

Pittsburgh, PA, USA

Abstract. In this paper, I address the challenges of doing research into the experiences of disabled participants in a corporate context where disability is not often considered. I conducted research into the experiences of blind and visually impaired riders for Uber, and I discovered a number of transportation challenges these individuals face. However, I argue that making a product such as Uber's more inclusive is not simply about fixing the many surface-level design flaws I discovered, but about making the service more broadly useful and promoting accessibility within the corporate culture. This paper is a reflection on my attempt to conduct inclusive research as a means to promoting inclusive app and service design, and the obstacles to inclusivity I encountered along the way.

Keywords: Accessibility · Inclusive design · Disability

1   Introduction: The Alley

A woman named Vera (not her real name) waits in an alley a block away from San Francisco's busy Market Street. She is waiting for a car she ordered through a ridesharing app to arrive and take her home. She has been waiting for about 10 min, even though when she ordered the ride the app told her it would only take three or four minutes for the car to reach her location. Vera is getting worried; where is the car?

She tried calling the driver who had been assigned to her trip, but the call went to voicemail. Vera hands me her phone and asks me if I can find the problem, and I spot it immediately: the driver has gone past the alley and is now heading away from our location. I know this because I can see the car's location in real time on the map of our area, and I observe that it is traveling away from us. However, Vera couldn't see this problem for herself because she is blind, and the ridesharing app does not provide any information about distance or relative location between the car and the rider. At this point, without any further contact with Vera, the driver cancels the ride, and Vera is stranded in the alley.

Vera knows the alley well, as do many of her friends. The building houses an organization that serves people with visual disabilities, and Vera and many others come regularly to events there. They often use ridesharing services to get to and from the building, but because drop-offs and pick-ups are not allowed in front on Market Street, they are forced to wait in the alley behind it. Everyone who travels from there with any regularity has a story of ordering a ride that never came. The pick-up point is infamous

© Springer Nature Switzerland AG 2020
M. Kurosu (Ed.): HCII 2020, LNCS 12183, pp. 523–536, 2020.
https://doi.org/10.1007/978-3-030-49065-2_37

among blind people who try to get rides from the building, but rideshare companies and their drivers seem oblivious to its existence.

There are many reasons why Vera and others with disabilities have difficulty accessing services like ridesharing, but one major reason is that they are largely invisible to the companies. Human-centered design revolves around the experiences and pain points of real people trying to accomplish a task or use a product. Because it relies on knowledge of users, it is only as inclusive as the user base a company chooses to research and test with. Uber, like many companies large and small, has historically not conducted very much research with people with disabilities, so it is unsurprising that these groups have difficulty using Uber's services.

In this paper, I reflect on the research I conducted at Uber in 2019 into the transportation and mobility experiences of people with visual disabilities. I attempted to incorporate inclusive research methods into my work, with the ultimate goal of making Uber's app and overall service more inclusively designed. In the course of my research, I encountered the structural barriers to inclusive design that often exist in companies, from established business priorities to design and development processes that neglect to make accessibility a regular consideration. Inclusive research is a way of pushing back against the standard operating procedures and drawing more diverse participants into the research process. Like inclusive design, inclusive research is difficult to implement in a corporate setting, but it is essential that user research becomes more inclusive if we want more people to be able to use the products and services that companies create.

2   Separate, Not Equal

During my research blind users repeatedly told me that the Uber app does not provide useful information to them. One research participant even told me of her anger when she learned that sighted users get a full map of their area on which they can track the progress of the car on its way to them and then on their trip. In contrast, blind riders using the app with VoiceOver or another screen reader are given only an estimated time of arrival and no real-time tracking information. The lack of appropriate, useful information was one of the most frequent complaints I heard.

Uber's pick-up screen (Fig. 1) is a case-in-point of the app's information disparity. This screen is one of Uber's most iconic, and a deceptively simple design. The screen presents information about the car's route and position relative to the user (users can see the position of the car and themselves on a map of the area, and can track the progress of the car in real time); the driver (their name, rating, and photograph); the car (make, model, license plate, and often a photograph); and an estimated time of arrival. This wealth of information is the product of extensive and interative design, development, and research, and is intended to provide the user with the most necessary information in a layout that is intuitive to use.

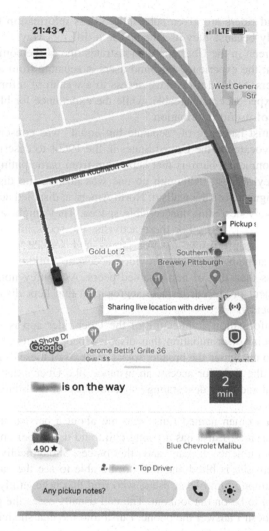

Fig. 1. The Uber pick-up screen. VoiceOver reads out the information displayed on the screen, but does not add information that a blind user would find useful. Screenshot from the author's account, 8 February 2020.

Intuitive for a *sighted* user, that is, because the screen assumes that the user can see it. For an Uber user who can't see the screen and who uses the app with an assistive technology, the experience of the pick-up screen is much less robust. Swiping onto the ETA box will read out only the estimated time of arrival of the car. Swiping further to the car and driver information will read out that text—although, as was repeatedly pointed out to me in interviews, much of that information is only useful to people who can *see* the car and driver in order to match them to the app. The VoiceOver experience of the pick-up screen does not include information such as the distance of the car from the rider or the direction from which the rider can expect the car to arrive.

Consequently, blind riders are given substantially less information than their sighted counterparts, simply because they use the app in a different way.

The pick-up screen in the Uber app demonstrates one of the common accessibility problems in design: the experience for blind users is separate from and inferior to the one for sighted users. Sighted users have access to a wealth of information curated to make a complex experience manageable, while the experience for blind users is made worse by the lack of useful information.

The segregationist language of "separate but equal" was consciously adopted by disability rights advocates in the United States in the 1960s to describe their lives in a world full of environmental barriers that kept them from participating fully in society. As Elizabeth Guffey argues, "Although no one was posting 'no disabled' or 'handicapped keep out' signs across the walls of North America, disabled activists argued that builders were actively designing inaccessible spaces. They might as well be posting such signs" (Guffey 2018: 97). For these activists, the accessible workarounds were almost as bad: makeshift (often unsafe) ramps and service entrances that could accommodate wheelchairs may have provided access to buildings, but it was a distinctly lesser access than that of non-disabled peers. As Guffey notes, barriers in the designed environment produced de facto segregation that kept disabled people apart from the rest of society.

The unequal information architecture of the Uber rider app is yet another of the many forms of social discrimination that disabled people routinely face. While we should be careful to recognize the broader social contexts of these different moments of inaccessibility and the fight for access, an instance like Uber's disparate experiences nonetheless has real and often devastating consequences for the blind people who try to use rideshare services.

For instance, a woman named Luisa told me about a persistent problem she has with ridesharing services. Luisa has a young child and uses Uber and Lyft to take her child to doctor appointments, daycare, and other places. She typically calls the driver in advance to tell them she is blind and will not be able to see the car arrive. This is a common practice among blind Uber users, who find that it generally helps to alert the driver and ask *them* to be on the lookout. The call usually eases the pick-up process—unless the driver doesn't answer the phone. Luisa told me that she has sometimes been stranded by an incommunicative driver:

> We've had people not answer their phones, and it's taken us a while to find them... Sometimes they even cancel because they're tired of looking or tired of waiting... I've reported it. I felt discriminated against because I couldn't see my driver and they weren't answering their phones and I got charged with a no-show fee because I couldn't see them. That's not fair.

Transportation is a substantial obstacle for many blind people, and in principle ridesharing represents a substantial improvement over other options. Blind people use diverse modes of transportation, including fixed-route public transit, paratransit services provided by local governments, rides from friends and family, and, increasingly, ridesharing. Each of these forms of transportation has barriers. Fixed-route public transit, for instance, is cheap, but it requires the user to wayfind to and from the set stops, which can be a substantial challenge, particularly when the person is not familiar with the area. Paratransit services operate door-to-door and are affordable, but they are very time-consuming and unreliable: they typically have pick-up windows of 30 min, make multiple stops en route, and can take as much as two hours for a journey that a car can make in 20 min.

Against these options, ridesharing has obvious appeal: the ease and reliability of ordering a ride from your phone, the ability to travel directly from one point to another without unnecessary delay. A large proportion of the blind people I met operate with substantial financial restriction (a reported 70% of blind working-age adults are un- or under-employed) that prevents them from using ridesharing services as much as they want, but for blind riders who can afford to use these services extensively, Lyft and Uber have indeed been revelatory.

However, even for these users, rideshare services contain barriers to use that make them unappealing or impossible. For example, a man named Chuck told me about his experiences using Uber, and generally they were positive. Chuck is blind since birth and he is extremely mobile and skilled at getting around using assistive technologies and remarkably route hearing. He is able to afford Uber by taking shared rides, which are cheaper than rides when you have the car to yourself. He is also a savvy Uber user, making sure the driver says Chuck's name so that he knows he is getting into the correct car.

Still, when I shadowed Chuck on a ride, the difficulties with the app became immediately evident. First, he had difficulty finding his destination in the app. He dictated the name of the store and scrolled through a list of options using the Voice-Over gestures. None of the options was correct, though, and he couldn't figure out how to modify the search to get the correct location. As a workaround, he used the name of a store next to the one he wanted to go to. Second, the app was not correctly detecting Chuck's location, putting him not in his home, but instead on an adjacent street. Fortunately, he realized this problem before requesting his ride and was able to dictate his home address so that the driver would come to the correct place to pick us up.

We went outside to wait for the car in front of Chuck's house. Chuck double-checked the information in the Uber app, and it's a good thing he did: despite all of his efforts to input the correct destination, the app had it wrong and had arranged a much longer trip than he anticipated. Chuck did not know how to fix the problem, so he canceled that trip and went through the process again, finally finding his desired destination (and likely incurring a penalty for canceling the trip). Ultimately, from the time Chuck began using the app to when he had correctly ordered his ride, almost ten minutes had elapsed—and all to accomplish a task that typically takes sighted people well under one minute.

Finding the correct destination can be difficult for all Uber riders, particularly when one knows the name of the destination but not its address. For example, use the Uber app (or any map program) to search for your local chain supermarket by name and it will come up with a list of options with only street addresses to differentiate them (Fig. 2). But the difficulty is exaggerated for blind users, because they have the double difficulty of not knowing which street address is correct *and* being unable to visually verify that they have chosen the correct location once they have selected from the list. There is no alternative means to verify a destination or starting point for blind users, placing an additional burden on them to know information that is not expected of sighted users, and thus making their experience distinctly more stressful and unpleasant.

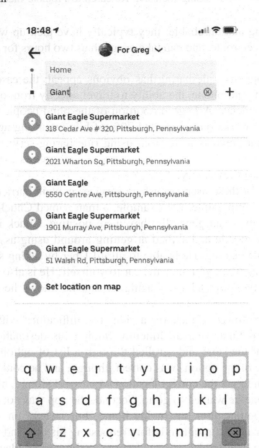

Fig. 2. A list of suggested destinations. Only street addresses differentiate between the different options. Blind users get no additional information (such as distance) to help them determine which destination they want to select. Screenshot from the author's account, 23 February 2020.

3 Inclusive Design: Ensuring *All* Users Can Participate

There is a long-held perception that while accessible design might be necessary, it is not good business because there are not enough consumers of accessible products and services to justify the investment. Steinfeld and Maisel argue that thinking only in terms of "accessibility" leads designers to believe that there is only a small "niche market" in serving people with disabilities (2012: 68). However, accessibility advocates counter that designing for people at the extremes makes *everyone's* experience better.

The curb cut is the classic example of a design innovation that had impact far beyond its initial use case. These sloping transitions between sidewalk and street came into prominent use to aid the mobility of veterans in wheelchairs after World War II, but they are also valuable for people pushing babies in prams, workers wheeling equipment, people with luggage, skateboarders, cyclists, and many others.

Perhaps more relevant, though, are innovations that have become foundational for experiences many of us take for granted today, like turn-by-turn directions, which was developed largely because of their accessible features. Kat Holmes makes a powerful case that "inclusion drives innovation," with such examples as the typewriter and the touch screen to demonstrate how an assistive technology can find broad appeal. (The typewriter was developed by a blind countess and her lover to enable her to write her own letters, and thus maintain their privacy, while the touchscreen that became the central innovation of the iPhone began as a gesture-based computer controller for people who could not type because of carpal tunnel syndrome.)

Holmes suggests that the reason people don't often view accessible designs as drivers of innovation is because they are used to seeing accessibility as a necessary and onerous add-on, rather than a critical element of the design process. She argues, "When a solution is treated as 'for disability' or 'for accessibility,' there's often little or no attention paid to the design. A solution might meet all of its functional requirements but still lead to emotional or aesthetic mismatches that can be equally alienating" (Holmes 2018, 117). In this mindset, the accessible design is thought of entirely separately from the "normal" one, and this separation allows the designers to maintain the fiction that these really are separate domains.

Considering accessible design separate from "normal" design can only happen if one ignores the social dimensions of disability. The social model of disability, which is widely accepted among accessibility advocates and theorists, distinguishes between "impairment" and "disability": "the terms *impairment* and *disability* distinguish between bodily states or conditions taken to be impaired, and the social process of disablement that gives meaning and consequences to those impairments in the world" (Garland-Thomson 2011: 591). As a group, a given company's users will have a wide variety of abilities and impairments—but only some of these will functionally be disabilities based on the ways in which the company's designs include or exclude them from using their product or service. For instance, a user might have the impairment of no sight, but this becomes a disability in relation to a particular service when that service can only be performed by sighted people (such as if you need to visually identify a button on a screen in order to tap it).

In other words, disability is substantially produced through inaccessible design. Holmes describes this as a "mismatch," a design that requires particular abilities to use and that therefore excludes anyone who does not possess those particular abilities. She draws this concept from Garland-Thomson, who describes these situations as "misfits," in that they are the product of a person not fitting a particular context, and vice versa. Garland-Thomson emphasizes that misfits are material and unstable because they result from real conditions in the world, and those conditions are always shifting. Moreover, "the concept of the misfit…lodges injustice and discrimination in the materiality of the world more than in social attitudes or representational practices" (Garland-Thomson 2011: 593). Thus, while recognizing the importance of changing social attitudes towards disability, Garland-Thomson suggests that the key to ensuring everyone can participate equally in society lies in producing better fits between people and the built environment—essentially, inclusive design.

Inclusive design is often seen as a remedy to the mismatches between impairments and the built environment. Ron Mace, a designer and disability rights advocate, coined the term "universal design" (often used synonymously with "inclusive design"), which he defined as "the design of products and environments to be usable by all people, to the greatest extent possible, without the need for adaptation or specialized design" (Center for Universal Design website). The Center for Universal Design, founded by Ron Mace at North Carolina State University, developed seven principles to elaborate on the general definition. These included ideas such as equitable use, flexibility to "accommodate a wide range of individual preferences and abilities," and tolerance for error to minimize the negative impacts of mistakes that users make.

It is easy to see in a system like Uber's how little the principles of universal design have been applied. As an example, take Chuck's experience, described above. At a minimum, his lengthy attempt to order a ride in the Uber app points to a lack of equitable use (principle one) arising from a lack of consideration to the design of the VoiceOver experience; a lack of flexibility (principle two), particularly "facilitate[ing] the user's accuracy and precision" with information input, seen in Chuck's inability to find and confirm the correct destination; and a lack of simple and intuitive use (principle three). Further, the Uber app showed little tolerance for error: when Chuck discovered he had ordered a ride to the wrong location, he could not figure out how to fix his error other than to cancel the ride (and incur a penalty) and then order a new ride.

At the same time, where there are exclusive designs such as Uber's, there are also opportunities to innovate something inclusive. I argued earlier that Uber's pick-up screen (Fig. 1) creates a disparity of information—and, thus, ease of use—for sighted and blind users. The solution to such a problem is dictated by the principles of universal design: create an experience for screen reader users that provides useful information, such as distance and direction. Doing so need not alter anything about the existing design, since it is only in the VoiceOver readouts that users would notice the difference. It would simply make the experience of that screen more flexible, allowing more users to access relevant information in a way that fit their needs and preferences.

4 Inclusive Research: Value and Barriers

But how can a company achieve the goal of creating more inclusive design? I argue that in order to achieve truly inclusive design, companies must promote inclusive research that goes well beyond what is typically done by in-house and external researchers.

Melanie Nind has written extensively about inclusive research, arguing that it is less a method and more of a philosophy of how to conduct research. She suggests that participants ought to have control over how the research is conducted, input into the meanings and outputs generated by the research, and a greater degree of ownership over the entire research process (Nind 2014).

By giving greater control to participant-researchers, Nind believes, professional researchers can combat the power dynamics inherent in much human-centered research. She observes, "most qualitative research…retains the status quo of the researcher being the person who defines the questions, handles and controls the interpretation of the data, and makes and communicates the conclusions" (Nind 2014: 4). Inclusive research, in contrast, disrupts the usual relationship between researcher and participants by shifting control to the people most directly affected by the research, the participants themselves. By disrupting those relationships, inclusive research can combat the biases and assumptions of researchers, including very foundational assumptions about the capabilities of their users. Nind describes inclusive research as "research *with, by* or sometimes *for* them…in contrast to research *on* them" (*ibid.*: 3).

Inclusive research has been a particularly powerful tool for empowering people with disabilities to represent themselves in various contexts. Indeed, much of Nind's inclusive research has been oriented towards putting the tools of inquiry and repre-sentation into the hands of people with learning disabilities (see, for instance, Nind et al. 2016). While there is debate about how much and what sort of training participant-researchers need in order to take control of research, these methods invariably decenter the power hierarchies present when professional researchers lead the research. As Booth and Booth observe, "too often the potential problems of interviewing inarticulate subjects are seen in terms of *their* deficits rather than the limitations of *our* methods" (1996: 67, emphasis added). Participant-researchers, who are not professionals, are not bound by the histories and training of professional research.

4.1 Inclusive Research and Corporate Ethics

Advocates of inclusive research often frame their advocacy in ethical terms: by empowering participants to take control of the research and shape is objectives and methods, the people most impacted by the research can also have the most central voice in the process and outcomes. The alternative, for these advocates, is coopting the voices of their participants, potentially misrepresenting them and failing to help them through the research.

For this reason, inclusive research has largely found its home in academic contexts and in non-profit, public, and community organizations. Academics researchers are strongly bound by professional and institutional codes of ethics and they possess an acute awareness of structural power dynamics. Sam Ladner observes, "University-based researchers have privilege, and ethnographic research brings that privilege into stark relief, particularly when the study focuses on some facet of inequality itself" (Ladner 2014: 90). Thus the ethical drive to empower participants can be highly motivating in academic contexts. Research, for instance, was often a tool of colonial oppression, and consequently, "inclusive research has developed as the antidote to the bulk of research *done to* people which is experienced as oppressive" (Nind 2014: 17). Relatedly, Nind suggests that the rise of inclusive research in public and non-profit contexts has been driven by concerns with inclusion, democracy, and empowerment: "Concerns with social reform and community development have driven the more critical action research and emancipatory research. Grass roots organizations have been major drivers informing the development of ideas about collaborative, co-produced knowledge for change" (*ibid.*: 19).

In contrast, private sector ethnographers have to contend with the ethics of doing research in a setting where their work is intended to generate profit for a company. While Ladner rightly insists that the profit motivations of companies sponsoring ethnographic research are not inherently corrupting, researchers must still give careful consideration to the moral implications of their work—such as whether insights derived from research with people will be used in a way that benefits or exploits those people. It is important, for instance, that participants know who is sponsoring the research because "deceit does nothing to improve the outcomes and simply serves to corrode the relationship between ethnographer and participant" (Ladner 2014: 93).

Private sector researchers have substantial power to conduct their research ethically —as Ladner says, by being as truthful as possible with participants—but at the same time, they are limited in how *inclusive* they can make their work. Corporate approaches to research, no matter how ethical, are almost always fundamentally at odds with the principles of inclusive research. Inclusive research requires participants to have ownership over research processes and outputs to a substantial degree. But in corporate user research, participants invariably sign non-disclosure agreements in advance that stipulate that anything said during their interview is property of the company. Legal departments exert substantial control over how research participants are recruited and treated. Inclusive research's challenge to power hierarchies, as well as more radical attempts to shift ownership of research, are inherently discordant with corporate procedures.

Nonetheless, there are things researchers can do to be more inclusive in their research practices.

4.2 Recruiting Inclusively

As a result of this dissonance between private sector research and inclusive methodologies, it can be difficult to even do the most fundamental part of research, the recruiting of participants. When I was beginning my research into the experiences of blind users at Uber, I needed to recruit a pool of blind users who would be willing to participate in interviews and be shadowed on trips. However, the first challenge arose immediately: Uber does not track information on disabilities, so there was no way to derive a list of potential participants from Uber's internal database. While you can obtain a list of riders who have taken so many trips in the past month or who have traveled a certain distance, there is no way to find the riders who are blind.

Since internal methods were not available, I worked with a colleague in research operations to find a way to recruit outside the company. Our proposed solution was to approach organizations in the Bay Area who serve people with visual disabilities and ask them to pass on our screener to their constituencies. The next hurdle was convincing the legal department to allow this approach. Their concerns were twofold: one, that the information gathered through the screener would be available to the organizations as well; and two, that we would be gathering data about blind riders who were already in Uber's system. The first concern was easy to address, since the external organizations would email our screener out to their members, but all of the responses would come directly and only to us. The second concern was more substantial, due to concerns about potential bias claims, but we addressed this by agreeing to anonymize participants and not keep personal data longer than needed for the project—which are good ethnographic practices anyhow.

Partnering with local organizations presented ethical as well as pragmatic challenges. Because the organizations were not approved vendors, we were not able to hire them as third-party recruiters (which is a service that they all provide to Bay Area companies). Instead, I was in the rather uncomfortable position of coming from a large corporation and asking these local non-profits to essentially do us a favor—which they did, because they understood the potential value of the research to their members. I was fortunate that they saw the situation in this way, because needing to approach these organizations emphasized the difference in power between the large for-profit corporation and the smaller non-profits that helped to further my research.

This leads to another ethical consideration in corporate research. Participants are interested in the company and the research they are conducting, and they derive sometimes unrealistic expectations about what will come of it. I experienced this regularly when I met with research participants. They took my presence as a sign that Uber as a company cared about their experiences and wanted to improve the services they provided. This is a fair inference based on what I told them about my project and the sorts of questions I asked, but of course it is not reasonable when one thinks about how long it takes for research to filter up through an organization and bring about noticeable results. Trying to be as truthful as possible with participants, I tempered expectations somewhat without being discouraging. However, since participants cannot have greater ownership of the research—the research cannot be truly inclusive—some have likely been disappointed by the lack of quick and appreciable improvements to their experiences of Uber's services.

5 Participant Phonography: An Inclusive Methodology

In order to make my research at Uber more inclusive, I attempted to implement a research method I call participant phonography. The method is analogous to the more widely known participatory visual methods such as photovoice, in which research participants are empowered to represent themselves through photographs. However, I adapted the visual method to an acoustic one, in order to access insights about sound that could help design for people with visual disabilities.

Participatory photographic methods combine elements of inclusive research with the affective representations of photography to produce evidence and analysis that might otherwise be inaccessible to researchers. By arming participants with cameras and guidelines to capture a particular experience in photographs, those participants "acquire great power to represent the personal, cultural, and economic influences that shape their lives and present obstacles to their vitality" (Ozanne et al. 2013: 46).

Although researchers often still exercise considerable control over the form of participatory photographic research, these methods encourage participants to take greater ownership over the research process. Tabitha Steager aims to empower participants even further in a slightly different method she calls "participant photography":

Participatory to me implies an active role on the part of the research participant, which is not always the case with photo voice. Rather than imposing my presuppositions on the experience and telling my participants what photos they should make, I wanted participants to lead the process, not only in what and how they chose to photograph but also within the interview process itself when we discussed their photos, so that they were working with me to build a shared understanding, of a shared experience, of place (Steager 2018: 163).

In conceptualizing my sound recording method, I followed Steager's lead in prioritizing the ability of research participants to control the form of the recording research. I initially intended to equip participants with small microphones that plug into their phones and leave them to make recordings on their own, thus substantially removing myself from much of the research process. However, I discovered that the microphones I wanted to use are not accessible—they turn off VoiceOver readouts when plugged into the iPhone, and thus are completely unusable for blind participants —and I had to revise the method.

In the revised approach, I retained the objective of letting participants pick the focus of the recordings, but I went with them and we made the recordings together using my more complicated set-up of digital recorder, wired microphone, and headphones. As I anticipated, participants felt constricted in this method, because my presence inhibited them from experimenting with the recording equipment. Nonetheless, they were generally intrigued by the different perspective they heard through microphones and headphones, and after some initial uncertainty, most participants found the recording process interesting.

5.1 Participatory Phonography and Disability Research

The rise of inclusive research, as noted earlier, has been substantially driven by research into disability and the social structures that produce it. However, remarkably few participatory methods use multimedia approaches. Of the examples Nind analyzes, only two involve participants creating in a medium other than spoken or printed words. This seems to me a remarkable shortcoming, since inclusive research is concerned with ensuring that participants are able to control how their experiences are represented, and quite obviously, not everyone prefers or is able to represent themselves in words.

There are some reasons why multimedia methods may be absent from inclusive disability research. First, inclusive multimedia methods such as participant photography raise pragmatic and ethical questions. Pragmatically, participants need to understand how to use technologies to capture experiences in any given medium. With the rapid advances in smartphone technology, though, this is less of a barrier than before.

But a bigger challenge is that inclusive multimedia research demands more time and investment from participants. In the case of my participatory phonography project, I simply did not have time within the fairly rigid boundaries of an interview to train participants to use my recording equipment (which is not particularly accessible), and the smartphone-based version of the research was not possible because the microphones were not accessible. Moreover, this research would ideally consist of a recording portion and then a subsequent interview, but it would not have been appropriate to ask participants to commit that much time without being able to promise a greater sense of ownership over the results.

As a result, the insights generated directly from my participant phonography were limited. I did gain some knowledge that was otherwise inaccessible, though, such as the subtle sonic cues that some of my participants use to navigate public spaces. I had not realized before how silent the Uber app is. Certainly, blind users have VoiceOver turned on, and that is a sonic experience. But it is not an experience designed by Uber, and overall, Uber had not conceived of their service as having a sonic dimension. With some further research and development, the sorts of subtle sonic cues I learned about could be used to make the app more inclusive and flexible, allowing people who prefer sound and those who rely on it to make better use of Uber's services.

6   Conclusions

I regret that I was not able to make my research at Uber even more inclusive. Limited severely by the length of my own contract and the institutional research practices that constrain research session lengths, I could not develop the participatory dimension of my work as much as I wanted. However, my research did point to a few practices that can make research more inclusive, even in a restrictive corporate environment.

First, adapting research methods to the context and needs of participants. By this, I mean not only the difference between surveys and semi-structured interviews, but rather, being willing to make changes to the form and medium of research as a situation dictates. Participant photography works very well for some projects; for people who can't see, but who rely on sound for navigation, a sonic research method would clearly be preferable.

Second let participants shape the focus of the research. This is a good practice for human-centered research anyhow, but to make research inclusive, participants need to be able to direct the research in directions that haven't been considered before. Participants have questions and needs that a researcher can't anticipate. For instance, I went into my research expecting that finding the car would be a central problem to solve. However, while that was indeed a challenge that participants noted, it was rarely the most important pain point. Rather, participants themselves directed me towards parts of the Uber experience outside the bounds of what the company usually thinks about, such as wayfinding *after* being dropped off, and thus, I adjusted my research beyond the goals I initially set.

Finally, let participants represent their own experiences as much as possible. Again, this sounds like a routine part of human-centered design and research. But it is surprisingly easy to coopt the voices of participants, editing not only their words but also their identities to fit neatly into a slide or make a particular point. But the more power people have to represent themselves directly—whether through photographs, words, or sound recordings—the more inclusive the research can be.

None of these points made my research as radically inclusive as many inclusive research practitioners advocate, or that I wanted. Participants did not get any sort of ownership in the research and subsequent design and development that came out of it, and there was no opportunity for them to take on the role of the researcher and guide the project from a position of leadership and power. In short, I view my research as a partial, though still important, step in making Uber's products and services more inclusive. The culture of thinking about accessibility as "niche" is deeply embedded, and the institutional barriers to inclusive research and design are strong. But if researchers can make the process more transparent and inclusive for participants, we can begin to make inclusive research a more constant feature in corporate contexts, and thus, can make inclusion a real priority.

References

The Center for Universal Design Website. https://projects.ncsu.edu/ncsu/design/cud/about_ud/about_ud.htm. Accessed 24 February 2020

Garland-Thomson, R.: Misfits: a feminist materialist disability concept. Hypatia **26**(3), 591–609 (2011)

Guffey, E.: Designing Disability: Symbols, Space, and Society. Bloomsbury, London (2018)

Holmes, K.: Mismatch: How Inclusion Shapes Design. The MIT Press, Cambridge (2018)

Ladner, S.: Practical Ethnography: A Guide to Doing Ethnography in the Private Sector. Routledge, London (2014)

Nind, M.: What Is Inclusive Research?. Bloomsbury, London (2014)

Nind, M., Chapman, R., Seale, J., Tilley, L.: The conundrum of training and capacity building for people with learning disabilities doing research. J. Appl. Res. Intellect. Disabil. **29**, 542–551 (2016)

Ozanne, J.L., Moscato, M.M., Kunkel, D.R.: Transformative photography: evaluation and best practices for eliciting social changes. J. Public Policy Mark. **32**(1), 45–65 (2013)

Steager, T.: Evidence outside the frame: interpreting participants' "framing" of information when using participant photography. In: Ethnographic Praxis in Industry Conference Proceedings, pp. 159–178. Wiley, London (2018)

Steinfeld, E., Maisel, J.L.: Universal Design: Creating Inclusive Environments. Wiley, Hoboken (2012)

HCI in Complex Environments

Stability Maintenance of Depth-Depth Matching of Steepest Descent Method Using an Incision Shape of an Occluded Organ

Miho Asano[1]([⊠]), Tomohiro Kuroda[2,3], Satoshi Numata[4], Tsuneo Jozen[4], Tomoki Yoshikawa[5], and Hiroshi Noborio[5]

[1] Preemptive Medicine and Lifestyle-Related Disease Research Center, Kyoto University Hospital, 54 Shogoinkawahara-cho, Sakyo-ku, Kyoto-shi, Kyoto 606-8507, Japan
masano@kuhp.kyoto-u.ac.jp

[2] Department of Social Informatics, Graduate School of Informatics, Kyoto University, Yoshida-honmachi, Sakyo-ku, Kyoto-shi, Kyoto 606-8501, Japan

[3] Division of Medical Information Technology and Administration Planning, Kyoto University Hospital, 54 Shogoinkawahara-cho, Sakyo-ku, Kyoto-shi, Kyoto 606-8507, Japan

[4] Department of Digital Games, Osaka Electro-Communication University, Kiyotaki 1130-70, Shijo-Nawate, Osaka 575-0063, Japan

[5] Department of Computer Science, Osaka Electro-Communication University, Kiyotaki 1130-70, Shijo-Nawate, Osaka 575-0063, Japan

Abstract. Liver surgery is typically performed to dissect part of the liver to remove a malignant tumor. The role of technology is to assist the surgeon to swiftly navigate to the area of interest. Our work involved the development of a liver surgery navigation system in which a steepest descent liver tracking algorithm is used to accurately track the real liver with a virtual liver. We recently demonstrated that our digital potential function was globally stable at the point at which the virtual liver coincided with its real counterpart. The same stability was achieved for several actual surgeries using 3D printed viscoelastic liver in an operating room with two light-emitting diode (LED) shadowless lamps. Increasing the number of lamps improved the stability of depth-depth matching in the steepest descent algorithm because the lamps did not emit in the infrared wavelength region unlike the depth cameras. Furthermore, the use of the characteristic uneven shape of the liver has greatly improved liver tracking accuracy. The complex and asymmetric shape of the upper part of the liver during surgery plays a key role in the liver in depth and depth matching. In this study, we experimentally investigated the stability of a virtual liver dissection configuration following a real liver in an operating room equipped with two LED shadowless lamps. As a result, deeply incised livers have superior depth-depth matching stability. In addition, even when using occlusion to simulate actual surgery, the convergence stability of the experimental performance is improved.

Keywords: Steepest descent method · Incision shape of virtual liver · Incision shape of actual liver · Occlusion · Triangular polyhedron STL · Liver surgery navigator · Shadowless light-emitting diode lamp

1 Introduction

The liver is an organ, which is made up of small blood vessels, and which resembles a mass of blood. Even small resections can cause major bleeding. In liver surgery, accurate resection of the area containing the tumor is crucial for maintaining postoperative liver function in the short term and for curing the cancer in the long term. The ongoing development and spread of technology to navigate to liver surgery areas with complex anatomical characteristics is important to perform safe and accurate operations.

Surgical navigation systems have been spreading rapidly in recent years [1–7]. Many surgical navigators use ultrasonic sensors with 3D mechanical or 2D non-mechanical probes. However, in general, because the image resolution of the ultrasonic sensor is low, it is impossible to accurately detect the actual liver shape, position, and direction during surgical navigation [8]. Indocyanine Green (ICG) fluorescence images require frequent eye movement between the surgical field and the monitor to view the images presented on the monitor. In addition, it is necessary to turn the surgical light off to prevent interference with this light, and this causes the operating field to become dark, which is problematic. Real-time navigation using projection mapping technology projects ICG emission in real time onto the liver transection plane. A projection image is generated from the ICG image taken by the camera on the operation field, and the projector projects the image directly onto the organ under surgery. As a result, although real-time navigation is possible, projection into deep surgical fields is not achievable [9]. Few studies have focused on capturing the actual translation and rotation of the liver and also liver transformation using marker or markerless 3D camera stereo vision. Positioning artificial markers on a real liver during surgery, gives accurate detection of the shape, location, and orientation of the liver; however, this approach damages the liver after surgery. Furthermore, calculating the shape, position, and orientation of a large number of points can be time-consuming [10–16].

Our work was motivated by the need to address the aforementioned problems. First, the 3D-CG virtual environment, controlled using OpenGL on the graphics processing unit (GPU), is theoretically tuned to the 3D real-camera environment, controlled by Kinect SDK and Kinect Studio API. Next, a real liver is overlaid with a virtual liver using the initial position, orientation and the shape adjustment system [17]. This algorithm uses matching depth-depth images in the same Camera and CG coordinate systems. In this system, we recognize the difference between the depth images, which capture real and virtual livers in 3D real and virtual environments with several types of colors, based on Kinect v1.

Concurrently, we design several motion transcription algorithms by matching real and virtual 2D depth images and also search the space defined by three parallel and rotational degrees of freedom (df), based on depth differences [18–21]. The real liver depth image is captured by Kinect v1 and v2 and the STL-format polyhedral virtual liver depth image is also obtained by GPU z-buffering. Based on the Kinect v1 and v2 depth cameras, we evaluated the performances (motion accuracy and computational time) of many algorithms proposed in several types of experiments.

In our recent paper [22], we theoretically showed that our digital potential function of depth-depth matching based on the steepest descendent method is globally stable. In another study [23], we experimentally investigated whether the same stability is maintained for several real operations using a 3D printed visco-elastic liver in a surgical room with two shadowless light-emitting diode (LED) lamps. If the real liver is not occluded by any part of the human body at all, in other words, if the entire shape of the liver is used for depth-depth matching, the difference is always variable and consequently the subsequent stability is completely maintained. Otherwise, especially if only the top of the liver, which is quite flat, can be measured by a depth camera because of body occlusion, the difference is always invariable and consequently the subsequent stability is frequently disrupted. However, the purpose of surgery is to incise the liver to remove a malignant tumor from a non-occluded area. Therefore, during surgery, the top of the liver takes on a complicated shape. The complex and asymmetric shape has the key role of liver following in our depth-depth matching.

In this study, we experimentally investigate the stability of an algorithm in which an incision-shaped virtual liver swiftly tracks an incision-shaped real liver in an operating room equipped with two LED shadowless lamps. In depth–depth-matching, the incision-shaped virtual liver is constantly moved to minimize the difference between the depth images obtained from the incision-shaped virtual liver and the incision-shaped real liver. Real images can be captured with a depth camera such as that of Kinect v2. Virtual images can be automatically transmitted from virtual liver z-buffers formed by segmented triangular polyhedra (STL) from the patient database Digital Imaging and Communications in Medicine (DICOM) captured by CT/MRI. In this study, an STL polyhedron is formed of the dissected liver based on actual surgical videos to use the dissected liver. Using this STL, the corresponding incised liver is printed on a 3D printer. The tracking performance of the incision-shaped virtual liver is evaluated when the incision-shaped real liver is rotated at different speeds. Next, we evaluate the tracking performance of the incision-shaped virtual liver when the incision-shaped real liver is translated using occlusion assuming the actual incision operation site.

Section 2 presents the experimental elements. Section 3 describes the operating room and some of the experiments performed there, and presents the results. Section 4 explains the significance of the key findings. Finally, Sect. 5 summarizes the key findings and their significance, draws conclusions, and uses the findings to guide future research.

2   Experimental Components

This section presents the experimental components used in this study.

2.1   Virtual Liver

A virtual liver with an STL-polyhedron segmented from a tomographic image of a patient (obtained from DICOM) is used. In this study, we create a dissected virtual liver with the original segmented STL-polyhedron, with reference to a real surgery video, to set up some dissected livers. STL virtual liver models of a liver before incision, a liver with a shallow incision shape, and a liver with a deep incision shape as controls are shown (Fig. 1 (a)–(c)). In this study, the STL virtual liver model before and after the incision is used as the virtual liver.

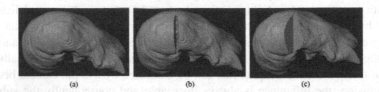

Fig. 1. STL virtual liver model. (a) Liver before incision as control and (b) liver with a shallow incision shape and (c) liver with a deep incision shape.

2.2   Actual Liver

The STL data of the virtual liver before and after the incision in Fig. 1 (a)–(c) was printed with a 3D printer to fabricate a model of a real liver from plastic, and it was colored with acrylic paint. This model is shown in Fig. 2 (a)–(c) and was used as the real liver.

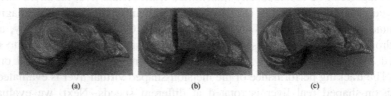

Fig. 2. Model of a real liver fabricated from plastic. (a) Liver before incision as control and (b) liver with a shallow incision shape and (c) liver with a deep incision shape.

2.3   Liver Surgery Navigator Using the Steepest Descent Method

Figure 3 shows the various windows that control the liver surgery navigator we created. The window in Fig. 3(a) is a real-time color image taken with the Kinect v2. This image enables researchers to monitor the movement of the real liver. The window in Fig. 3(b) is the depth image of Fig. 3(a), and the range of the initial position can be set. The STL virtual liver is displayed in the window of Fig. 3 (c), and the corresponding depth image is displayed in the window of Fig. 6 (d). The window in Fig. 3(e) displays the different depth images of a real liver and a polyhedral STL virtual liver in such a way that the difference between Fig. 3(b) and Fig. 3(d) can be easily determined visually. The score displayed in Fig. 3(b) is the sum of the squares of the differences between the depth values of all pixels, superimposing the depth images of the real liver and the polyhedral STL virtual liver; i.e., the residual sum of squares (Fig. 4). The smaller the score, the higher the overlap rate.

We use a steepest descent algorithm to assess the performance of real-time tracking of the liver. Steepest descent is a well-known algorithm that enables 3D models to be tracked in real time. This method allows the first-order derivative $f'(x)$ of the function $f(x)$ to be optimized and viewed, updated to a more optimal point, and finally converged to the best point. Because of its simplicity, the characteristics of depth image matching of the liver can be clearly understood. The depth image of the incision-shaped real liver is compared with the depth image of the incision-shaped virtual liver to find the exact position and orientation of the liver. The accuracy of this comparison is important for tracking the state of the liver and displaying navigation information on the virtual liver. Improving the accuracy would require an investigation of the extent to which the depth image of the incision-shaped virtual liver differs from the depth image of the incision-shaped real liver, and to evaluate the performance of tracking the position and orientation [18, 19].

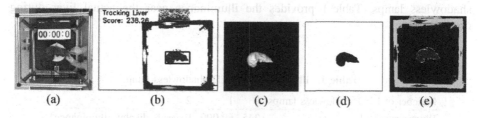

Fig. 3. Liver surgery navigation system windows.

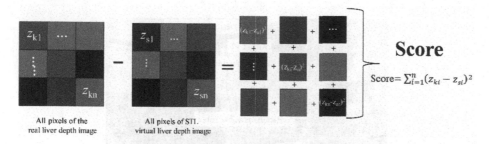

$$Score = \sum_{i=1}^{n}(z_{ki} - z_{si})^2$$

All pixels of the real liver depth image

All pixels of STL virtual liver depth image

Score

Fig. 4. Score to evaluate the accuracy of liver surgery navigator.

3   Experiments in the Operating Room

Experiments were performed in the surgical operating room to create an environment similar to actual surgery. Figure 5 shows the layout of the entire experiment. As shown in Fig. 5, an incision-shaped real liver was placed on a turntable set on the operating table, and the turntable was moved. The Kinect v2 was fastened to a metal rod and attached to a vertically movable robot. The distance from the bottom of the incised liver to Kinect v2 is 0.9 m.

The experimental procedure entailed first capturing photographic images of the incision-shaped real liver with Kinect v2, after which the incision-shaped STL virtual liver of the liver surgery navigator was moved, and the initial positions of the incision-shaped real liver and virtual liver depth images were aligned. Based on actual surgical videos, the rotational movement of the real liver in the incision shape was manually rotated by ±30° at 6°/s or 30°/s about the z-axis. Furthermore, assuming the actual incision surgery site, using a black plastic board cut out of a circle with a diameter of 0.1 m or 0.09 m as an occlusion, the incised real liver was translated in the x-axis direction at ±0.01 m/s. Figure 5 shows each coordinate axis. Then, the tracking performance of the incision-shaped virtual liver was evaluated when the incision-shaped real liver was translated and rotated using occlusion. The accuracy was evaluated by using the score from the adjustment from the initial position to after rotation and translation. The liver before incision was used as a control.

In the next section, rotation and translation using occlusion are described when using an LED shadowless lamp, specifically one LED shadowless lamp, and two LED shadowless lamps. Table 1 provides the illuminance near the actual liver during observation.

Table 1. Illuminance of LED shadowless lamp.

Number of LED shadowless lamps	0	1	2
Illuminance [lx]	245	69,000	Exceeds display illuminance[a]

[a]Display illuminance: 0–99,000.

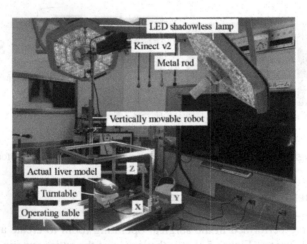

Fig. 5. Experimental layout in the surgical operating room.

3.1   Surgical Observation of Rotational Movement Using an Incised Real Liver

The entire liver was used to adjust the initial position of the incision-shaped real and virtual liver depth images. The rotation speed of the real liver in the incision shape was rotated by ±30° at 6 or 30°/s. The depth image was captured in real time with Kinect v2. Our steepest descent algorithm based on depth-depth-matching showed that the incision-shaped virtual liver automatically follows the real counterpart based on the acquired depth image data.

The first experiment was executed in a surgical operating room in which the LED shadowless lamps were turned off. When the incised real liver was manually rotated by ±30° at 6°/s or 30°/s, the incised real and virtual livers rotated side by side (Fig. 6). The second experiment was conducted in a surgical operating room in which only one LED shadowless lamp was turned on. When the incision-shaped real liver was manually rotated by ±30°at 6°/s or 30°/s, it was confirmed that the incision shaped virtual liver also rotated and moved in the same way (Fig. 7). The third experiment was performed in a surgical operating room in which two LED shadowless lamps were turned on. When the incision-shaped real liver was rotated by ±30° at 6°/s or 30°/s, the incision-shaped real and virtual livers rotated in conjunction (Fig. 8).

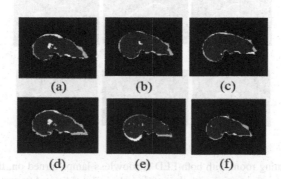

(a)   (b)   (c)

(d)   (e)   (f)

Fig. 6. In the operating room with the LED shadowless lamp turned off, the incision-shaped virtual liver rotated in conjunction with the incision-shaped real liver. After rotation, the real liver depth image (white) and the virtual liver depth image (black) overlap. Superimposed depth images of the real and virtual liver: (a) control liver after rotation at 6°/s, liver with (b) shallow and (c) deep incision shape after rotation at 6°/s, (d) control liver after rotation at 30°/s, liver with (e) shallow and (f) deep incision shape after rotation at 30°/s.

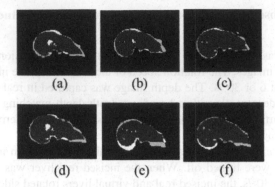

Fig. 7. In an operating room with only one LED shadowless lamp turned on, the incision-shaped virtual liver rotated in conjunction with the incision-shaped real liver. After rotation, the depth images of the real (white) and virtual (black) livers overlap. Super-imposed depth images of the real and virtual liver: (a) control liver after rotation at 6°/s, liver with (b) shallow and (c) deep incision shape after rotation at 6°/s, (d) control liver after rotation at 30°/s, liver with (e) shallow and (f) deep incision shape after rotation at 30°/s.

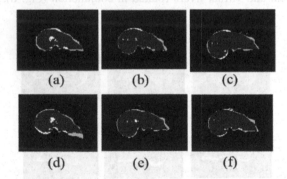

Fig. 8. In an operating room with both LED shadowless lamps turned on, the incision-shaped virtual liver rotated in conjunction with the incision-shaped real liver. After rotation, the real liver depth image (white) and the virtual liver depth image (black) overlap. Superimposed depth images of the real and virtual liver: (a) control liver after rotation at 6°/s, liver with (b) shallow and (c) deep incision shape after rotation at 6°/s, (d) control liver after rotation at 30°/s, liver with (e) shallow and (f) deep incision shape after rotation at 30°/s.

The results showed that our steepest descent algorithm based on depth–depth-matching ensured that the incision-shaped virtual liver automatically followed the real counterpart based on the acquired depth image data.

In the operating room with the LED shadowless lamp turned off, the overlap rate when rotated at 6°/s averaged approximately 440, reaching a value as high as 550 in the liver before the control incision. For the liver with the shallow incision, the average was approximately 420 and the maximum was 500, whereas for the deep-cut liver, the average was approximately 340 and the maximum was 450. In addition, the overlap rate when spun at 30°/s averaged approximately 890 with a maximum of 1050 in the pre-dissection liver of the control. In the case of the shallow incised liver, the average was approximately 780 and the maximum was 990. The average overlap rate of the liver with the deep incision was approximately 730 and up to 950. Therefore, as shown in Fig. 9(a) and Fig. 9(b), as the angular velocity increased, the overlap ratio deteriorated during the simulation operation. In addition, compared to the control liver before the incision, the overlap ratio of the incised liver was lower on average. The overlap ratios of deeply incised liver were lower than those of shallow incised liver.

In the operating room where only one LED shadowless lamp was turned on, the overlap rate when rotated at 6°/s averaged approximately 410, reaching a maximum of 470 in the control liver without an incision. For the liver with the shallow incision, the approximate average and maximum were 400 and 480, respectively. For the deeply cut liver, the approximate average and maximum overlap rates were 330 and 400, respectively. In addition, the overlap rate when spun at 30°/s averaged approximately 800 and reached 1000 for the control liver without the incision. In the case of the shallow incised liver, the average was approximately 540 and the maximum was 730. For the deeply cut liver, the average was approximately 450 and the maximum was 720. Therefore, as shown in Fig. 9(c) and Fig. 9(d), as the angular velocity increased, the overlap ratio deteriorated during the simulation operation. In addition, compared to the control liver before the incision, the overlap ratio of the incised liver is lower on average. The overlap ratio of deeply incised liver is lower than that of shallow incised liver.

In the operating room where both LED shadowless lamps were turned on, the overlap rate when the control liver without incision was rotated at 6°/s averaged approximately 400 with a maximum of 470. For the shallow incised liver, the average was approximately 360 and the maximum 440. For the deep-cut liver, the approximate average and maximum were 270 and 340, respectively. In addition, the overlap rate when spun at 30°/s averaged approximately 620, reaching 920 in the control liver before incision. In the case of the liver with the shallow incision, the overlap rate averaged approximately 500 with a maximum of 910. For the deeply cut liver, the average was approximately 420 and the maximum 670. Therefore, as shown in Fig. 9 (e) and Fig. 9(f), as the angular velocity increased, the overlap ratio deteriorated during the simulation operation. In addition, compared to the control liver before the incision, the overlap ratio of the incised liver was lower on average. The overlap ratio of deeply incised liver was lower than that of shallow incised liver.

A comparison of the depth images displayed in Fig. 7(b), (c), (e), and (f) with the corresponding depth images displayed in Fig. 8(b), (c), (e), and (f) reveals that the convergence obtained using two LED lamps was significantly superior to that obtained using only one lamp.

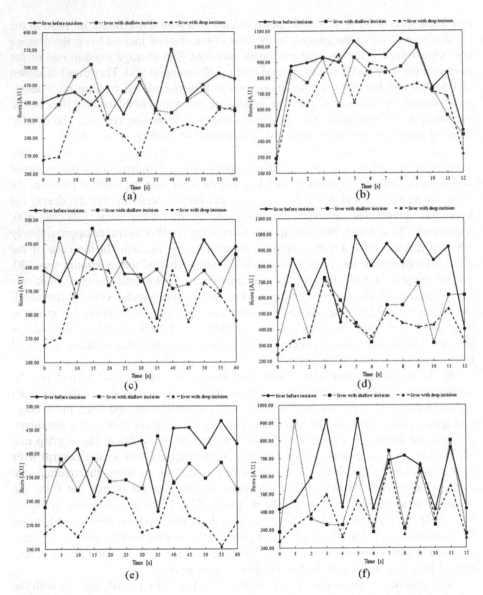

Fig. 9. Extent to which the virtual liver with incision followed the actual counterpart rotated at 6°/s and 30°/s in an operating room where the LED shadowless lamps were (a), (b) turned off; (c), (d) only one LED shadowless lamp was turned on; (e), (f) two LED shadowless lamps were turned on.

3.2   Surgical Observation of Translation of the Real Liver with Incision Using Occlusion

Figure 10(a) shows the experimental apparatus used to conduct the occlusion experiments. A video of an actual operation indicated that the height from the highest part of the liver to the occlusion was 0.02 m (Fig. 10(b)). The occluding object was fabricated from black plastic board with a circle of 0.1 m or 0.09 m in diameter, and the initial position of the depth image of the incised real and virtual livers was adjusted using the rectangle drawn within the occlusion circle (Fig. 10(c)). Figure 11 shows strobe shots from a video of an actual operation. The incised real liver is translated in the x-axis direction at ±0.01 m/s, and its depth image is captured in real time with Kinect v2. Using the acquired data, the steepest descent algorithm is employed to enable the virtual liver to follow the movement of the real liver.

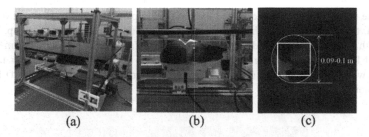

(a)   (b)   (c)

Fig. 10. Experimental setup for occlusion experiments: (a) experimental apparatus, (b) side view (close-up) of the experimental apparatus. The distance from the highest part of the liver to the occlusion is 0.02 m. (c) view of the experimental apparatus from directly above. The occlusion was achieved using an object fabricated from a black plastic board cut out from a circle with a diameter of 0.1 m or 0.09 m, and the initial position of the depth images of the incised real and virtual livers was adjusted using the rectangle within the occlusion circle.

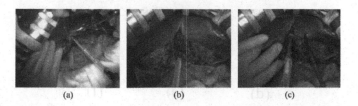

(a)   (b)   (c)

Fig. 11.   (a), (b), (c) Strobe shot of actual liver surgery video.

The first experiment was executed in a surgical operating room in which the LED shadowless lamps were turned off. The incised real and virtual livers moved in parallel (Fig. 12(a)–(f)). The second experiment was conducted in a surgical operating room in which only one LED shadowless lamp was turned on. The results confirmed that the incised real and virtual livers move in parallel (Fig. 13(a)–(f)). The third experiment was performed in a surgical operating room in which both of the two LED shadowless

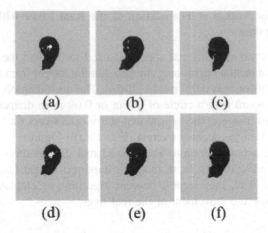

Fig. 12. Results of occlusion experiments in an operating room where the LED shadowless lamps were turned off. The incised virtual liver moved in parallel to the incised real liver. After translation, the depth images of the real (white) and the virtual (black) liver overlap. Superimposed depth images of the real and virtual liver: after translation combined with 0.1 m occlusion (a) control liver (b) shallow liver with incision, (c) deep liver with incision; after translation combined with 0.09 m occlusion (d) control liver, (e) liver with shallow incision, (f) liver with deep incision.

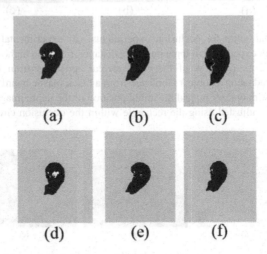

Fig. 13. Results of occlusion experiments in an operating room where one of the LED shadowless lamps was turned on. The incised virtual and real livers underwent parallel translational movement, after which the depth images of the real (white) and virtual (black) livers overlap. Superimposed depth images of the real and virtual liver: after translation combined with 0.1 m occlusion (a) control liver (b) shallow liver with incision, (c) deep liver with incision; after translation combined with 0.09 m occlusion (d) control liver, (e) liver with shallow incision, (f) liver with deep incision.

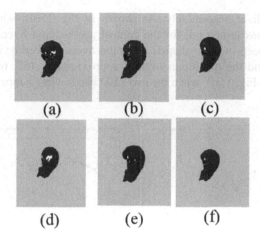

Fig. 14. Results of occlusion experiments in an operating room in which both of the two LED shadowless lamps were turned on. The incised virtual and real livers underwent parallel translational movement, after which the depth images of the real (white) and virtual (black) livers overlap. Superimposed depth images of the real and virtual liver: after translation combined with 0.1 m occlusion (a) control liver (b) shallow liver with incision, (c) deep liver with incision; after translation combined with 0.09 m occlusion (d) control liver, (e) liver with shallow incision, (f) liver with deep incision.

lamps were turned on. Again, we were able to confirm that the incised real and virtual livers moved in parallel with each other (Fig. 14(a)–(f)).

As a result, our steepest descent algorithm based on depth–depth matching showed that the virtual liver with an incision shape automatically followed its real counter-part based on the acquired depth image data.

Figure 15(a), (c), and (e) show the score transition for an occlusion of 0.1 m when 0, 1, or 2 LED shadowless lamps were turned on, and Fig. 15(b), (d), and (f) show the transition of the score for an occlusion of 0.09 m when 0, 1, or 2 LED shadowless lamps were turned on.

As shown in Fig. 15(a), when the LED shadowless lamps were turned off, the average superimposition rate approximated 154, 72, and 60, and the maximum superimposition rate was approximately 183, 96, and 80, for the control pre-incision liver, shallow incision liver, and deep incision liver, respectively. As shown in Fig. 15 (c), when only one LED shadowless lamp was turned on, the average overlay was approximately 130, 66, and 56, and the maximum overlay approximately 157, 89, and 78 for the control pre-incision liver, shallow incision-shaped liver, and deep incision-shaped liver, respectively. As shown in Fig. 15(e), when both of the two LED shadowless lamps were turned on, the average overlay was about 128, 64, and 52, and the maximum overlay was about 156, 84, and 66, for the control pre-incision liver, shallow incision shaped liver, and deep incision shaped liver, respectively. As shown in Fig. 15 (b), when the LED shadowless lamps were turned off, the average superimposition rate was approximately 156, 58, and 45, and the maximum superimposition rate was approximately 170, 70, and 63 in the control pre-incision liver, shallow incision liver, and deep incision liver, respectively. As shown in Fig. 15(d), when only one LED shadowless lamp was turned on, for the control pre-incision liver, shallow incision-shaped liver, and deep incision-shaped liver, the average overlay was approximately 140, 56, and 39, and the maximum overlay approximately 157, 69, and 48, respectively. As shown in Fig. 15(f), when the two LED shadowless lamps were turned on, in

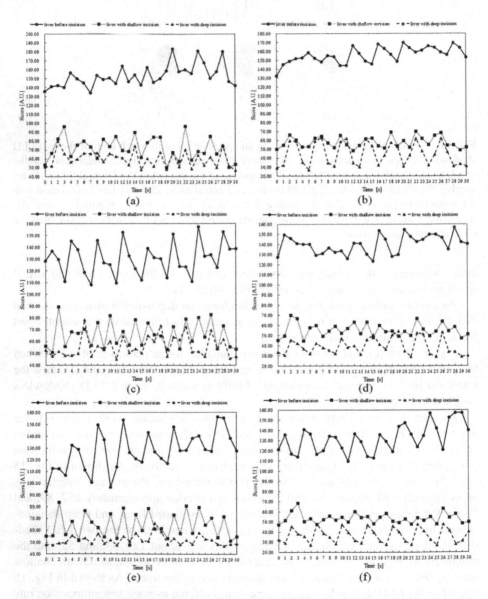

Fig. 15. Extent to which the virtual liver with incision followed the actual counterpart (score). Using 0.1 m occlusion, (a) zero, (c) one, or (e) two LED shadowless lamps were turned on. Using 0.09 m occlusion, (b) zero, (d) one, or (f) two shadowless lamps were turned on.

the control pre-incision liver and the livers with shallow and deep incisions, the average overlay was approximately 132, 54, and 37, and the maximum overlay approximately 157, 69, and 48, respectively.

These results suggest that increasing the number of LED lamps improved the accuracy with which the virtual liver followed the translational movement of the real liver. In addition, the improvement was significantly more pronounced for incised livers with complex, asymmetrical shapes than for the control pre-incision livers.

4 Discussion

This study employed the steepest descent method to determine the tracking performance and convergence stability when the depth image of a virtual liver with an incision shape tracks the depth image of a real liver with an incision shape. The results were acquired by the depth sensor of Kinect v2 and were confirmed by using an experimental setup that closely approximates an operating theater during surgery. The experiment had the following five outcomes.

(1) In our recent paper [23], we reported that the performance of tracking the real liver by the virtual liver increased as the number of lamps increased in both rotational and translational relocation. However, in the experiment described in the current paper the accuracy we obtained for the virtual and real livers with incisions was similar.

(2) In our recent work [23], it was found that focusing on a region in which the depth difference of the real liver is large improves the tracking performance compared to using a flat part of the liver. As reported, the difference between the depth images of the real and virtual livers with an incision was always smaller because the depth of the deeply incised liver was larger than that of the liver with a shallow incised shape. This suggested that complex and asymmetric shapes are particularly advantageous for depth and depth matching.

(3) In the experiment using occlusion, when the initial alignment was performed with an occlusion of 0.08 m in diameter, the orientation of the incised virtual liver was not normal. In the case of an occlusion with a diameter of 0.09 m, the real liver with the incision behaved irregularly, and tracking was possible with two LED shadowless lamps.

(4) A video of the actual operation confirmed that the liver did not rotate and translate significantly when the speed, angle, and distance of the rotation and movement of the incised real liver were adjusted. However, the tracking performance was generally accurate, and the score was low on average.

(5) Even when the rotation and translation speed were high, the tracking performance did not decrease if the distance of movement was small.

5 Conclusion

This study carefully evaluated the steepest descent liver tracking algorithm during liver surgery using LED shadowless lamps in the surgical operating room. Because the depth image of the real liver with an incision shape is not affected by the LED shadowless lamp, the greater the number of LED shadowless lamps, the more depth-depth matching with the steepest descent algorithm stabilized. Therefore, by increasing the number of LED shadowless lamps, the tracking performance of the incised real liver by the incised virtual liver is greatly improved. This suggests that our liver surgery navigation system is highly effective, considering that it is necessary to turn off the operating light in the fluorescent navigation system using ICG. In addition, the surface of the liver is not particularly flat, and the shape of the liver is greatly deformed by excision, etc., which is particularly advantageous for adjusting an incision of a section of the liver that is occluded during actual surgery. In addition, even if the speed of movement of a real liver with an incision were to increase, provided the movement is limited, this suggests that the incision-shaped virtual liver sufficiently follows the incision-shaped real liver if the movement of the liver is similar to that during actual surgery. These results suggest that the liver surgery navigator we propose is feasible for use in actual surgery. In the future, it is urgently necessary to evaluate the accuracy of the liver surgery navigator by replicating the conditions of an actual operation, such as when the liver is complicatedly deformed during the operation or when the surgeon's hand is reflected.

Acknowledgment. This study was supported in part by 2014 Grants-in-Aid for Scientific Research (No. 26289069) from the Ministry of Education, Culture, Sports, Science, and Technology, Japan. Further support was provided by the 2014 Cooperation Research Fund from the Graduate School at Osaka Electro-Communication University. We would like to thank Editage (www.editage.com) for English language editing.

References

1. Peterhans, M., et al.: A navigation system for open liver surgery: design, workflow and first clinical applications. Int. J. Med. Robot. **7**(1), 7–16 (2011)
2. Nicolas, C.B., et al.: Augmented environments for the targeting of hepatic lesions during image-guided robotic liver surgery. J. Surg. Res. **184**(2), 825–831 (2013)
3. Satou, S., et al.: Initial experience of intraoperative three-dimensional navigation for liver resection using real-time virtual sonography. Surgery **155**(2), 255–262 (2014)
4. Pessaux, P., et al.: Towards cybernetic surgery: robotic and augmented reality-assisted liver segmentectomy. Langenbecks Arch. Surg. **400**(3), 381–385 (2015)
5. Morita, Y., Takanishi, K., Matsumoto, J.: A new simple navigation for anatomic liver resection under intraoperative real-time ultrasound guidance. Hepatogastroenterology **61**(34), 1734–1738 (2014)
6. Mahmud, N., et al.: Computer vision and augmented reality in gastrointestinal endoscopy. Gastroenterol. Rep. (Oxf.) **3**(3), 179–184 (2015)
7. Chen, X.-P., et al.: Image classification of liver cancer surrounding right hepatic pedicle and its guide to precise liver resection. Int. J. Clin. Exp. Med. **8**(7), 11093–11100 (2015)

8. Souzaki, R., et al.: Navigation surgery using indocyanine green fluorescent imaging for hepatoblastoma patients. Pediatr. Surg. Int. **35**(5), 551–557 (2019). https://doi.org/10.1007/s00383-019-04458-5

9. Nishino, H., et al.: Real-time navigation for liver surgery using projection mapping with indocyanine green fluorescence: development of the novel medical imaging projection system. Ann. Surg. **267**(6), 1134–1140 (2018). https://doi.org/10.1097/SLA.0000000000002172

10. Besl, P.J., McKay, N.D.: A method for registration of 3-D shapes. IEEE Trans. Pattern Anal. Mach. Intell. **14**(2), 239–256 (1992)

11. Zhang, Z.: Iterative point matching for registration of free-form surfaces. Int. J. Comput. Vis. **13**(2), 119–152 (1994)

12. Granger, S., Pennec, X.: Multi-scale EM-ICP: a fast and robust approach for surface registration. In: Heyden, A., Sparr, G., Nielsen, M., Johansen, P. (eds.) ECCV 2002. LNCS, vol. 2353, pp. 418–432. Springer, Heidelberg (2002). https://doi.org/10.1007/3-540-47979-1_28

13. Liu, Y.: Automatic registration of overlapping 3D point clouds using closest points. J. Image Vis. Comput. **24**(7), 762–778 (2006)

14. Salvi, J., et al.: A review of recent range image registration methods with accuracy evaluation. J. Image Vis.-Comput. **25**, 578–596 (2007)

15. Rusu, R.B., Cousins, S.: 3D is here: point cloud library (PCL). In: Proceedings of IEEE International Conference on Robotics and Automation, pp. 1–4 (2011)

16. Wu, Y.F., Wang, W., Lu, K.Q., Wei, Y.D., Chen, Z.C.: A new method for registration of 3D point sets with low overlapping ratios. In: 13th CIRP Conference on Computer Aided Tolerancing, pp. 202–206 (2015)

17. Noborio, H., et al.: Image-based initial position/orientation adjustment system between real and virtual livers. J. Teknologi Med. Eng. **77**(6), 41–45 (2015). https://doi.org/10.11113/jt.v77.6225

18. Noborio, H., et al.: Motion transcription algorithm by matching corresponding depth image and Z-buffer. In: Proceedings of the 10th Anniversary Asian Conference on Computer Aided Surgery, pp. 60–61 (2014)

19. Watanabe, K., et al.: Parameter identification of depth–depth–matching algorithm for liver following. J. Teknologi Med. Eng. **77**(6), 35–39 (2015). https://doi.org/10.11113/jt.v77.6224

20. Watanabe, K., et al.: A new 2D depth–depth matching algorithm whose translation and rotation freedoms are separated. In: Proceedings of International Conference on Intelligent Informatics and Biomedical Sciences (ICIIBMS 2015), Track 3: Bioinformatics, Medical Imaging and Neuroscience, Okinawa, Japan, 28–30 November 2015, pp. 271–278 (2015)

21. Noborio, H., et al.: Experimental results of 2D depth-depth matching algorithm based on depth camera Kinect v1. J. Bioinf. Neurosci. **1**(1), 38–44 (2015)

22. Numata, S., Koeda, M., Onishi, K., Watanabe, K., Noborio, H.: Performance and accuracy analysis of 3D model tracking for liver surgery. In: Kurosu, M. (ed.) HCII 2019. LNCS, vol. 11567, pp. 524–533. Springer, Cham (2019). https://doi.org/10.1007/978-3-030-22643-5_41

23. Asano, M., et al.: Convergence stability of depth-depth matching of steepest descent method in really imitated surgery. In: Proceedings of the 2nd International Conference on BioMedical Technology (ICBMT 2020), Hanoi, Vietnam, 19–22 February 2020 (2020, to appear)

BeaCON - A Research Framework Towards an Optimal Navigation

Arun Balakrishna[1(✉)] and Tom Gross[2(✉)]

[1] Automotive Software Development Services, HERE Technologies,
Frankfurt, Germany
arun.balakrishna@here.com
[2] Human Computer Interaction Group, University of Bamberg,
Bamberg, Germany
tom.gross@uni-bamberg.de

Abstract. In an optimally integrated HMS (Human Machine System), human must understand the machine as well as the machine must understand the human user. Same principle applies for car NS (Navigation System) which is a human-in-the-loop system. An ideally integrated NS knows how, when and what navigation information must be provided for the user and create minimal interruption for the primary task. To do the same, NS must hold the behavioral models of the user for providing the guidance information in an effective way. A research framework which uses these principles, is needed to create such models as well as for conducting further analysis for the research problem of "Giving the driver adequate navigation information with minimal interruption". Until now no such research framework exists and because of that further analysis of the mentioned research problem cannot be conducted. In this paper we present the research framework BeaCON: Behavior-and Context-Based Optimal Navigation that enables detailed analysis of this research problem.

Keywords: Navigation system · HMS · Entity of Interest · Cognitive load · Machine learning · GUI · OEM

1 Introduction

A car navigation system is used to provide navigation information which guides the user to reach a destination. Identified research gaps in the area of optimum integration of HMS where human and machine learns together which is applicable for modern day NS is listed in [1]. NS shows a user the current location on the map and gives both audio and visual information for efficient travel from one location to another such as the path to be taken which is calculated based on graph theory as well as the dynamic information i.e. Traffic [3]. The main research problem of "Giving the driver adequate navigation information with minimal interruption" can be divided into following sub problems

1. Given a set of route and map information, what is an optimal guidance information for a user?

M. Kurosu (Ed.): HCII 2020, LNCS 12183, pp. 556–574, 2020.
https://doi.org/10.1007/978-3-030-49065-2_39

2. How to find optimal guidance information for a user, provided set of inputs to create the same is given?
3. How to find when, how and what guidance information must be given to the user?

These research questions must be addressed for achieving the optimal human NS integration which is needed to avoid driver distraction [4] created by NS as well as to reduce the cognitive load associated with navigation task. This paper introduces BeaCON (Behaviour-and Context-Based Optimal Navigation) - a research framework for enabling research in the mentioned problems. The driving context and the driver behavioral aspects must be considered to decide when, how and what guidance information must be given to the user [2]. Natural guidance as well as mobility graph addresses a very minimal aspect of this problem but with tailored solutions [5]. As an initial step to understand the research problems better, [2] conducts a survey to identify the scenarios where optimal integration between the human user and NS is not achieved. The critical survey questions addressed in [2] are regarding.

1. Driver distraction by NS
2. The extent to which NS understands the user intentions
3. Optimal integration of NS with the user

Based on the responses from users, behavioral models are created for these critical survey questions [2], which is also used in BeaCON. Since these models are created only once and will not change, the same can be called static behavioral models. An example of static behavior model created by using the data collected as a part of [2] is given in Fig. 1. Also BeaCON holds dynamic behavioral models created using WEKA machine learning suite [6] for different navigation specific user contexts, created per user. Static and dynamic models are created based on decision tree algorithm C4.5 in order to achieve high interpretability. The navigation specific user contexts created while conducting experiments using BeaCON is abstracted in a concept called Entity Of Interest (EOI) [2]. EOI can be visualized as the context which influence the cognitive load. EOI is currently created for junctions, roundabout and manoeuvres. Whenever a new behavior is identified for the user, the dynamic behavioral models will be recreated or modified using the machine learning algorithms. These models along with other components of BeaCON enables analysis of the research problems mentioned above.

2 Related Work

For designing intelligent navigation systems, a deeper understanding of their effects on human navigation behavior is necessary [7]. The dynamic behavioral models in Bea-CON incorporate the effects of navigation system on human driver along with other characteristics. Classification of driver's cognitive state to improve the in-vehicle information by using the drivers cognitive load and driving situation is conducted in [8]. But the classification approach given by [8] is not connecting the driving situation to the real-world map entities (Maneuvers, Roundabout etc.) as well as to the environmental factors (fog, rain etc.), by making the same also as a part of the behavioral models, which is addressed by BeaCON. Also [8] uses support vector machine (SVM) based machine learning models and for driver behavioral models while Bea-CON uses decision tree-based driver behavioral models and conditional interconnection between them for enhancing the interpretability of the same [9]. A framework for automated driving testable scenarios including failure mitigation strategies is given in [10]. The list of behavioral competency scenarios mentioned in [10] for automated driving benchmarking is applicable for human driver-based scenarios also. But [10] focuses only on automated driving system as a whole and the optimization steps involved in human based and automated agent-based driving scenarios are different.

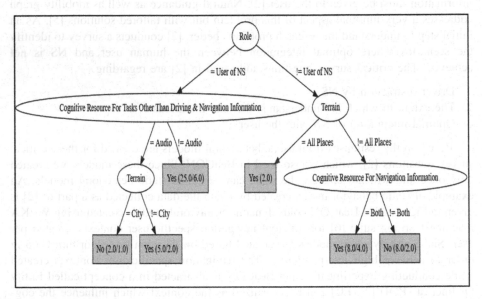

Fig. 1. An example of a static behavioral model (created for the extent by which NS understanding the user intentions)

3   BeaCON and Its Components

The research framework BeaCON: Behaviour-and Context-Based Optimal Navigation enables to conduct experiments using human-in-the-loop systems, create behavioral data and based on that find user cognitive load points, optimize the machine learning behavioral models, which are the models used by the system to understand the user. The components of BeaCON which also shows the interconnection between different components is given in Fig. 2. Many steps related to BeaCON i.e. start, stop, create cognitive load report etc., are currently automated as well as near real time performance is achieved while conducting experiments. BeaCON consists of 5 main components which are

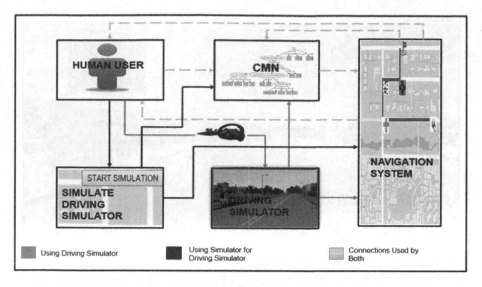

Fig. 2. BeaCON and its components

1 Driving Simulator (DS)
2 Navigation System (NS)
3 Cognitive Models for Navigation (CMN)
4 Simulator for DS
5 Human User (HU), The description of these components is given below

3.1 Driving Simulator (DS)

CARLA open source simulator for autonomous driving research [11] is used in Bea-CON with extensive adaptations. Since CARLA simulator is primarily designed for testing autonomous driving agents, extensive enhancements for existing interfaces are done to support the same for human driver interface using Logitech G920 driving hardware. CARLA provides extensive configuration support for creating different environments for experiments. For example, it is possible to control weather, number of pedestrians, state of different objects etc. in the simulator. Using these facilities, BeaCON supports conducting experiments for different cognitive load environments. A DS screen for conducting experiments in environments which induce heavy cognitive load is given in Fig. 3.

3.2 Navigation System (NS)

A custom-made NS is created and integrated to BeaCON. Currently the image from city 1 from CARLA is used for the NS. Navigation system tracks the car position in the route as well as highlights the path to be taken by the human user while conducting experiments. In the NS different images are used to represent different entities like junction, roundabout or a maneuver. Different symbols are used to indicate the start and end points of the test path in the map. GUI for NS is shown in Fig. 4.

Fig. 3. Sample GUI for the DS from CARLA

The path taken in the map while conducting the experiment is configurable. Once a specific path from the map is configured, the same will be highlighted in the map. Different entities are represented using different images and the semantic of each entity must be informed to the candidate before conducting experiments. Different entities and their semantics are given in Table 1. Another functionality of NS is to give guidance information for the user based on the current behavior models.

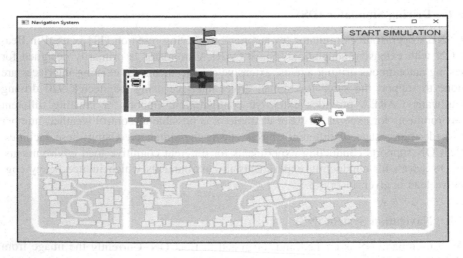

Fig. 4. GUI of NS process

Table 1. Images used for different NS entities

Entity	Image used for marking the entity in the map	Semantic
Start point		The location where bench marking data collection starts
Destination		Location planned as destination for experiment. Bench marking tool stops running once user reaches the destination
Maneuver		Curve in the road, defined by shape points in the road, which needs attention from the driver
Roundabout		Locations with circular intersection of the road with predefined rules for traffic flow, which needs attention from the driver
Junction		Locations where the road intersects and typically the traffic flow is controlled by signals, which needs attention from the driver

3.3   Cognitive Models for Navigation (CMN)

CMN holds the static and dynamic behavioral models and using the same the cognitive load values of the user for different driving context (EOI) are generated. The models in CMN are created using C4.5 algorithm. The static behavior models are created based on a statistical survey from 77 candidates from different countries [2]. Dynamic behavior models are created for different entities per user. A basic model for different entities is supplied to the system and reconfiguration of the same will be conducted at later point. When a new driver behavior is observed the dynamic behavioral models are updated accordingly. Static and dynamic behavior together create the complete behavior model for the user. It is possible to see the result of cognitive load calculation for all the questionnaires which was a part of the static analysis. An example GUI for one of the static analysis questions for NS creating distraction while driving is given in Fig. 5.

Similarly, it is possible to view the results for other static behavior models based on different input. Different dynamic contexts which occur during the navigation which is represented by EOI is represented by different dynamic models. For example, a very basic dynamic model created for roundabout is given in Fig. 6. User behavioral aspects are applied on the basic dynamic models to create user specific dynamic models for different EOIs.

A generic dynamic factor attribute is currently used as a placeholder for different traffic flow related factors. It is also possible to see the configuration of different EOI for a user in the system. For example, for a selected user the current value of cognitive load for a junction for a context can be identified by a GUI given in Fig. 7. Similarly, it is possible to identify the cognitive load values for different contexts for different users. It is also possible to make the system learn for a different cognitive load value for an EOI for a user manually by using the similar GUI.

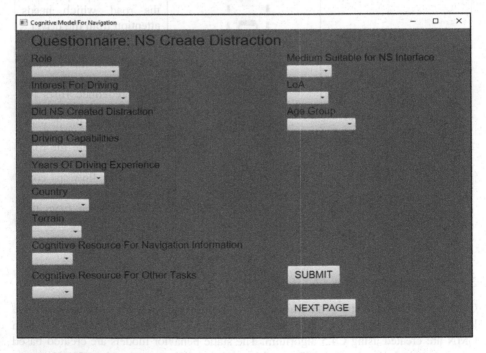

Fig. 5. An example of interface to static behavior models of BeaCON

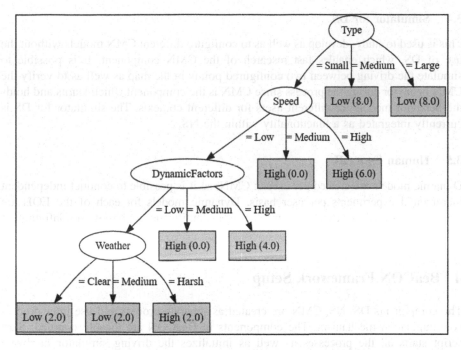

Fig. 6. Basic dynamic model created for Roundabout

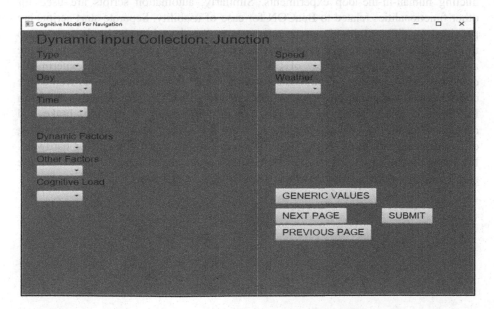

Fig. 7. Interface for dynamic model for junction for a user

3.4   Simulator for DS

This is used to study, develop as well as to configure different CMN models without the use of DS, which enables fast research of the CMN component. It is possible to simulate the driving between two configured points in the map as well as to verify the CMN behavior during the process since CMN is the component which learns and holds the behavior models for different users for different contexts. The simulator for DS is currently integrated as a functionality within the NS.

3.5   Human User (HU)

Dynamic models are created per user in CMN, so it is possible to conduct independent incremental experiments per user basis. Dynamic models for each of the EOIs are created and stored per user basis and the user identification is based on configuration values.

4   BeaCON Framework Setup

The components DS, NS, CMN are created as separate process and use inter process communication mechanism. The components in BeaCON are loosely coupled. Start script starts all the processes as well as initializes the driving simulator hardware setup. Preloaded configuration decides the path to be highlighted in the map for conducting human-in-the-loop experiments. Similarly, automation scripts are used for other functionalities related to BeaCON for ease of usability. Separate start scripts are provided for different driving environments as well as based on the hardware used to run BeaCON. For example, it is possible to run BeaCON on a less powerful hardware at the cost of rendering quality of DS. The generated report from the experiments contains x and y position, throttle, acceleration, brake, POI information, as well as the cognitive load values corresponding to each position. BeaCON set up used is shown in Fig. 8. It is also possible to configure the responsiveness of steering, brake and accelerator using the Logitech gaming software application as well as by controlling different parameters in the script used for interfacing the driving simulator hardware. For integrating other cities supported by CARLA necessary changes are needed for the map configuration which is used for highlighting the test route.

Fig. 8. BeaCON framework setup

5 Conducting Human in Loop Experiments

Presently three different environments are supported for conducting experiments which are low cognitive load (50 Pedestrians, clear weather), medium Cognitive Load (50 Pedestrians, Soft rain noon) and high Cognitive Load (300 Pedestrians, Hard rain sunset). The algorithm for conducting human in loop experiments are given below, the steps for conducting experiments using BeaCON is given in Fig. 9.

```
//Input: Candidate choose and drive between two points on the map using a
selected configuration
//Output: Performance evaluation of the driver behavior, CMN models are
re-created based on new behavior observed
Step 1: Two points in the map and configuration are selected for conducting
experiment
Step 2: Candidate drives between the selected points, collect the behav-
ioral data
Step 3: Once user reached the destination, stop collecting behavioral data
Step 4: Give the behavioral data input to the custom bench marking tool
Step 5: Custom bench marking tool creates necessary logs for driving
behavior
Step 6: Measure cognitive load at different contexts of driving, create
report
Step 7: Replay the driving behavior to re-verify the findings from report
with the user
```

Step 8: Cognitive load values at different points are used to recreate the dynamic behavioral models for EOI

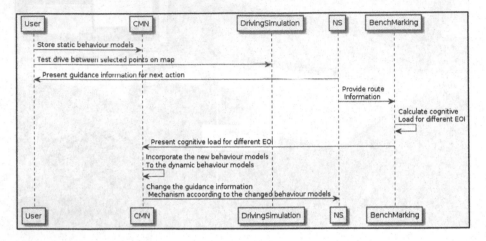

Fig. 9. Conducting experiments in BeaCON

Individual measurements from the test (steering, brake, throttle values etc.) are getting logged in separate files so that the same can be easily used in different data analysis tasks. Using a replay mechanism, it is possible to show different scenarios to the candidate which occurred during the test and to understand why the candidate has a certain behavior at certain EOIs. Replay mechanism helps to confirm the assumptions regarding the root cause of cognitive load with the user. Once the root cause is identified the same information can be used for configuring the dynamic models in the CMN, so that optimal guidance information for the subsequent tests might be generated. The following parameters of the guidance information in the navigation system varies based on the corresponding cognitive load

- Distance to the entity at which the guidance information must be triggered beforehand.
- The symbols used for indicating the entity in the NS display, different symbols for low, medium and high cognitive load contexts

It is also possible to configure other parameters of the NS in scenarios with different cognitive load values. The methodology used for cognitive load measurement, which is the step 6 given above in the algorithm for conducting human in loop experiments is explained in Sect. 6. The result of different experiments by following the steps mentioned in Fig. 9 is given in Sect. 7.

6   Cognitive Load Measurements

Steering entropy method [12] with custom enhancements are used for measuring the cognitive load. The principle of steering entropy method is that when user can assess the actions needed in an effective way, the steering angle motion is in a smoother and predictive way. When driver is distracted vehicle deviates from the planned position and user must apply more corrective measures. These corrective measures decrease steering angle predictability. One of the main advantages of this method is that driver is not interrupted by the process of collecting the steering entropy data. The data is collected every 150 ms which is a justifiable best human response time. The error is calculated based on the predicted and observed values as shown in Fig. 10.

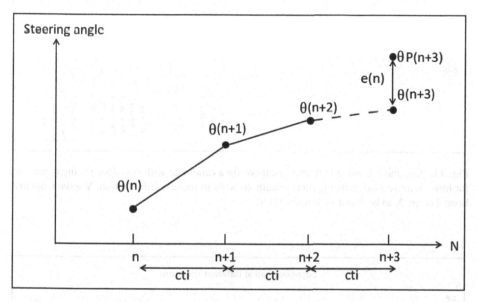

Fig. 10. Steering entropy method visualized. **X axis:** Increment, **Y axis:** Steering Angle

Where configurable time interval (cti) is 150 ms by default. The entities corresponding to the EOIs are configured in the framework, so the report generated contain the cognitive load for the corresponding EOIs. A configurable radius around the EOIs is used for recognizing the entities which created the cognitive load. A custom-made location mapping tool is used to map the cognitive load points to the location on the map. Cognitive load can be calculated as f(e(n)) + f(u(n)) where u(n) is a user specific value for the increment n for a user in a context and e(n) is the steering entropy value calculated for the increment n. The user specific values mainly use the static models. It is also possible to enhance u(n) with behavior models deducted from previous experiments.

7   Experimental Results

Multiple experiments are conducted with candidates of different driving experience and different age group. BeaCON enables to calculate the cognitive load for different EOIs, different instantaneous speed as well as for different accelerations. Patterns as well as root cause deductions are possible from the analysis data. One of the cognitive load measurement results from an experiment conduced with a candidate with very less driving experience is given in Fig. 11, Fig. 12, Fig. 13. The spikes indicate the locations where the candidate experiences more cognitive load than normal.

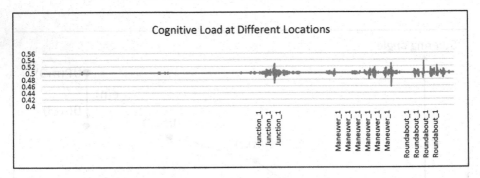

Fig. 11. Cognitive Load at Different Locations for a candidate with very less driving experience for low cognitive load inducing route conditions without route familiarization. **Y axis:** Cognitive Load Points, **X axis:** Point of Interest (POI)

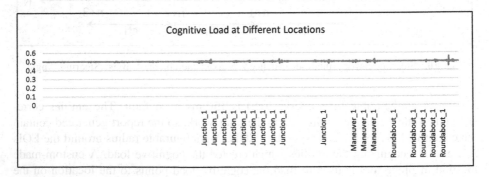

Fig. 12. Cognitive Load at Different Locations for a candidate with very less driving experience for medium cognitive load inducing route conditions, once the candidate is familiarized with the route. **X axis:** Cognitive Load Points, **Y axis:** Point of Interest (POI)

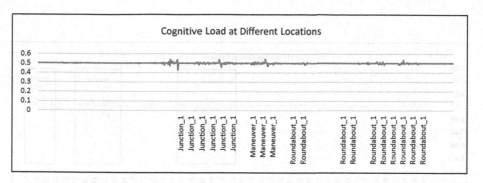

Fig. 13. Cognitive Load at Different Locations for a candidate with very less driving experience for high cognitive load inducing route conditions, once the candidate is familiarized with the route. **Y axis:** Cognitive Load Points, **X axis:** Point of Interest (POI)

Along with instantaneous cognitive load, it is also possible to calculate the cumulated value of the cognitive load value introduced by a specific EOI. This is done by aggregating the high cognitive load values observed, where measurement starting from a configured point before the user reaches the EOI. It can be observed that the more the candidate is familiarized with the route the cognitive load is reduced independent of harsh driving conditions as well as independent of less driving experience.

For example, the variation of cognitive load for different instantaneous speed and different accelerations for a candidate with very less driving experience is given in Fig. 14 and Fig. 15 respectively. The high cognitive load is experienced at the points with high instantaneous speed when the user drives through different EOIs as shown in Fig. 14.

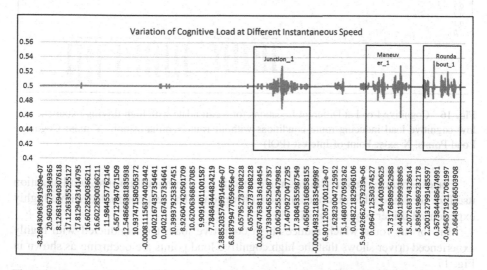

Fig. 14. Cognitive Load at Different Instantaneous Forward Speed for a candidate with very less driving experience for high cognitive load inducing route conditions without route familiarization. **X axis:** Cognitive Load Points, **Y axis:** Instantaneous Forward Speed in m/s

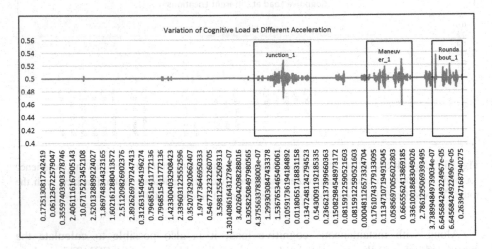

Fig. 15. Cognitive Load at Different Acceleration for a candidate with very less driving experience for high cognitive load inducing route conditions without route familiarization. **X axis:** Cognitive Load Points, **Y axis:** Acceleration in m/s^2

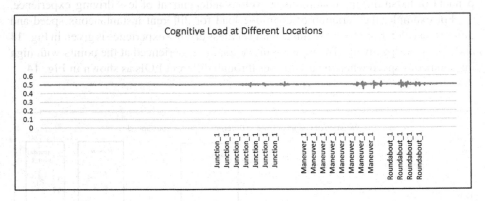

Fig. 16. Cognitive Load at Different Locations for a candidate with high driving experience for low cognitive load inducing route conditions without route familiarization. **Y axis:** Cognitive Load Points, **X axis:** Point of Interest (POI)

For experienced driver, the cognitive load is less without the route familiarization itself for the route which induces low cognitive load. The test conducted with a highly experienced driver is given in Fig. 16.

But for the route which induces high cognitive load, test conducted with highly experienced driver shows that the high cognitive load points are occurring as shown in Fig. 17.

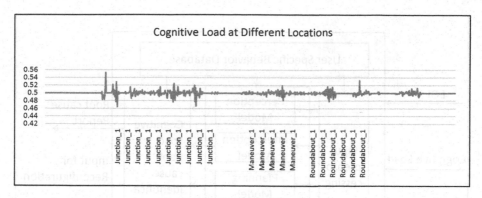

Fig. 17. Cognitive Load at Different Locations for a candidate with high driving experience for high cognitive load inducing route conditions without route familiarization. **Y axis:** Cognitive Load Points. **X axis:** Point of Interest (POI)

Analysis of the results deduct some of the information regarding cognitive load of the candidates. They are given below

- The familiarization of the route reduces the cognitive load significantly independent of the weather conditions for candidate with very less driving experience
- High speed contributes to high cognitive load points during the test
- A sudden deceleration is followed by a high cognitive load peak
- The timely guidance information from NS reduces the cognitive load related to maneuvers especially with harsh weather conditions
- Years of driving experience lead to less cognitive load values for low inducing cognitive load environments
- High cognitive load instances are less during low speed driving

Similarly, it is possible to conduct other similar experiments and measure the cognitive load values with different combinations in terms of behavioral aspects and technology aspects of the contexts.

8 Future Work

A fusion with other cognitive load measurement techniques can be done and is in progress for better analysis of the root cause of cognitive load. For example, steering entropy together with eye tracking mechanism can be used to understand the reason for cognitive load in more granular way. The contribution of cognitive load at each stage of human cognition can be analyzed for identification of the root cause.

The root cause identification can also make use of interpretable algorithms like LIME [13]. This enables more automation of the root cause identification task which is currently more manual in nature with the help of replay mechanism. Once the context which is creating the cognitive load is identified from all the collected data, the semantics must be identified for finding the root cause. A model which include human

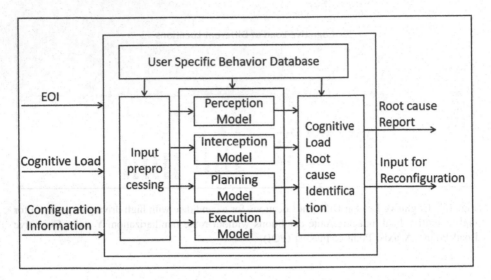

Fig. 18. Detailed analysis for cognitive load root cause with reduced manual work

cognitive constraint is needed for automatic identification of this semantics which is shown in Fig. 18. Integration of this model, which is in the road map for BeaCON enable identification of the root cause of cognitive load with less manual work.

Mixed reality environment [14] can be integrated to the research framework for avoiding the creations of stubs as well as to get more close realistic driving environments with a 3D view. Also, mixed reality environment will give more provision for identification of the root cause, for example identification of where the user is looking at a moment of time as well as where the user must be looking ideally based on the context. Brake, accelerator and the steering can be from the real environment and the other entities of the driving simulator can be presented via virtual environment. The NS screen can be projected as a head up display in the virtual environment.

The behavior of CMN can adapt the rules suggested by [15] for human AI interaction. Especially CMN must update and adapt cautiously as well as to what is the reconfiguration occurred, why the same occurred, and inform the same to the user. Also integrating enhanced interpretability should not compromise the human centered nature of the system.

9 Conclusion

The research problem "Giving the driver adequate navigation information with minimal interruption" and its relevance is presented. Introduced BeaCON for analyzing this research problem as well as the importance of this is justified. Comparison with the state of the art is done as well as value addition by BeaCON is presented. The experimental results confirm that the cognitive load of the user can be measured quantitatively as well as the reason for cognitive load can be analyzed with the same.

The roadmap of BeaCON for deducting more granular root cause information which can be used for effective reconfiguration of the behavioral models using machine learning algorithms are presented. BeaCON enables state of the art research for providing optimal guidance information by integrating with best suited machine learning algorithms as well as with modern driving simulators.

The design of BeaCON is aligned with the research in the area of connected vehicles and infrastructure conducted by many OEMs [16] for future vehicles. This design enables to incorporate new features to BeaCON based on connected vehicles and infrastructure which lead to more optimal navigation solutions, which can be easily accepted by the automotive industry. Also, the result produced by BeaCON can be used to enhance the connected vehicles and infrastructure.

References

1. Balakrishna, A., Gross, T.: Towards optimum automation of human machine systems for maximum performance. In: Proceedings of the Fifth International Conference on Multimedia, Scientific Information and Visualization for Information Systems and Metrics - MSIVISM 2018, 29–31 January, Las Palmas de Gran Canaria, Spain, pp. 1–14. Blue Herons Editions, Bergamo (2018). ISBN 978.88.96.471.65.4
2. Balakrishna, A., Gross, T.: Towards optimum integration of human and car navigation system. In: 2019 Proceedings of the Third IEEE International Conference on Electrical, Computer, and Communication Technologies - ICECCT 2019, Coimbatore, India, pp. 189–197. IEEE Computer Society Press, Los Alamitos (2019). ISBN: 978-1-5386-8158-2
3. Skog, I., Händel, P.: In-car positioning and navigation technologies. IEEE Trans. Intell. Transp. Syst. **10**(1), 4–21 (2009)
4. Driver Distraction Summary, published by European Road Safety Observatory (ERSO) (2018). www.erso.eu
5. HERE Maps for Life product catalogue, published by HERE Technologies (2015). www.here.com
6. Witten, I.H., Frank, E., Hall, M.A., Pal, C.J.: Data Mining: Practical Machine Learning Tools and Techniques, 4th edn. Morgan Kaufmann, Burlington (2016)
7. Brügger, A., Richter, K.-F., Fabrikant, S.I.: How does navigation system behavior influence human behavior? Cogn. Res.: Princ. Implic. **4**(1), 5 (2019)
8. Yoshida, Y., Ohwada, H., Mizoguchi, F., Iwasaki, H.: Classifying cognitive load and driving situation with machine learning. Int. J. Mach. Learn. Comput. **4**(3), 210 (2014)
9. Molnar, C.: Interpretable Machine Learning: A Guide for Making Black Box Models Explainable, 1st edn. GitHub, Lulu, 24 March 2019, eBook, 19 June 2019
10. National Highway Traffic Safety Administration (NHTSA): A framework for automated driving system testable cases and scenarios, September 2018
11. Dosovitskiy, A., Ros, G., Codevilla, F., López, A., Koltun, V.: CARLA: An Open Urban Driving Simulator CoRL (2017)
12. Nakayama, O., Boer, E.R, Nakamura, T., Futami, T.: Development of a steering entropy method for evaluating driver workload, pp. 39–48. Human Factors in Audio Interior Systems, Driving, and Vehicle Seating (SAE-SP-1426). Warrendale (1999)
13. Ribeiro, M.T., Guestrin, C., Singh, S.: Why should I trust you?: Explaining the predictions of any classifier. In: 22nd ACM SIGKDD International Conference (2016)

14. Costanza, E., Kunz, A., Fjeld, M.: Mixed reality: a survey. In: Lalanne, D., Kohlas, J. (eds.) Human Machine Interaction. LNCS, vol. 5440, pp. 47–68. Springer, Heidelberg (2009). https://doi.org/10.1007/978-3-642-00437-7_3

15. Amershi, S., et al.: Guidelines for human-AI interaction. In: Proceedings of the SIGCHI Conference on Human Factors in Computing Systems (CHI 1919), Glasgow, U.K., 4–9 May 2019, pp. 1–13 (2019)

16. Bagloee, S.A., Tavana, M., Asadi, M., Oliver, T.: Autonomous vehicles: challenges, opportunities, and future implications for transportation policies. J. Mod. Transp. **24**(4), 284–303 (2016)

Computational Design for Complexity-Related Issues. Strategies to Foresee Emergent Behavior and Social Conflict in the 'Organic' Tirana

Sotir Dhamo[1,2], Ledian Bregasi[1,2], and Valerio Perna[1,2(✉)]

[1] Faculty of Architecture and Design (FAD), POLIS University,
Tirana, Albania
valerio_perna@universitetipolis.edu.al
[2] INNOVATION_Factory Unit (IF), Tirana, Albania

Abstract. After the fall of the Communist regime, the city of Tirana has been facing a series of social/spatial issues related to a top-down decisional system that could not take into account the new needs of a society shifting from a centralized system to a new one based on private property. The result of this phenomenon is the growth of a series of urban areas, where the poorest citizens have used informal settlements has a way to reclaim their portion of private land. In this paper, starting from original research (Dhamo [20]), we present Tirana as a paradigmatic case of 'organic city' (derived from the former Ottoman architecture) and we analyze a peculiar model of urban settlements that are able to grow following complex and fractal structures. The study here presented, structured as an academic class at POLIS University, will be developed through computational design and interactive engaging technologies, with the main aim of creating an interdisciplinary study framework to tackle complexity and evolutionary issues in contemporary urban fabrics. The process will be explained through three didactic cycles where interactive technologies, such as artificial intelligence and engaging human-based tools, can play to set the debate for a deeper understanding of the informal areas reality and foster co-design processes from the perspective that a collective interest is a key to let professionals, institutions, and citizens, work together in a more informed process of city-making.

Keywords: Complexity · Parametricism · Emergence behavior · Urban fabric · Social conflict

1 Introduction | The City of Tirana. Towards Clashing Mentalities in the Urban Environment

In the following paragraphs, we will describe Tirana as a city that stratifies/embodies opposing or sometimes even clashing mentalities, which are reflected in the social and physical structure of the city. All that happened in a relatively short life span of only four centuries, from Tirana's geneses at the beginning of the 17th century, (1614),

© Springer Nature Switzerland AG 2020
M. Kurosu (Ed.): HCII 2020, LNCS 12183, pp. 575–585, 2020.
https://doi.org/10.1007/978-3-030-49065-2_40

when this territory was part of the Ottoman Empire. The first nucleus emerged in the middle of Tirana Valley, in a fertile territory pervaded by a series of river neckless, gently curbed, and oriented towards the North West. Further mushrooming of urban nuclei and the first organic layer that knitted the space between them, represent the combined nature of spontaneous urbanization processes, with a premeditated strategy based on religious practices nourished by the Ottoman culture of that period based on the system of "Imarets" [1].

The organic network continued to gradually grow very slowly, up to the beginning of the last century, when Tirana was proclaimed the capital of Albania in 1920. King's Zog "Grand Travaux" inspired from the European renaissance to stretch and enlarge the main organic radials of the city, or to open new boulevards, are the first layer of disturbance piercing the organic fabric of Tirana. Some years later, after the Italian Fascist occupation, other important transformations happened in Tirana, this time according to a "new" interpretation of the historicist tradition, the so-called "Stile Littorio". These operations represent the first move from the organic system of "Imarets" [1] rooted in the Ottoman culture, to serious attempts for Europeanization of Tirana; from labyrinth structure of the city and dead ends to the stretched and open perspectives avenues. These interventions that continued up the end of the Second World War, were the first layer of "disturbance" imposed on the continuity of organic urban fabric.

Most importantly, at the end of this period Two Tirana(s) were created: one rooted and nourished in the organic radials of the origin and the other one rooted in the symmetric axis of the boulevard. Despite serious attempts to decrease the ottoman influence, this remained strong because it was niched in the hidden visceral parts of the city and was sleeping there for centuries.

The interventions after the war, during the dictatorship that lasted from 1944 to 1991 were even more violent against the pre-existing city fabric. During this period Albania moved from the strong influence of the Eastern Block to a total self-isolation. The entire country was engaged in a social experiment to forge new humankind and the appropriate physical environment for this "pure" prodigious being. The most tangible result of this social experiment was the creation of the ghost city, deprived of any spirit and personal identity from where everybody wanted to leave. The new collective housing blocs in the center and in the periphery were supposed to bring a new model of life that was never born. In fact, they created the condition of emptiness. A triple collage collision constituted the urban morphology: organic fabric pierced by monumental/orthogonal axis and hollowed by frames of emptiness. Important to mention that architects and urban planners during this period more than ever became an ideological arm manipulated by political power.

The collapse of the dictatorship in 1991 was associated with the release of unexpected and uncontrollable human energy that highly affected the urbanization processes in the entire country, Tirana especially. It was a kind of return to the bottom-up self-organized organic processes, or an interfering pattern emerging from its origin, but on an exponential scale. Tirana lost the compactness and continuity of its shape and transformed into an advanced state of dissolution. The massive influx of people into the city took place without any concern from the authorities. As Portugali [2] argues about self-organized processes, it is a "... phenomena by which a system self-organizes its internal structure independent of external causes ...". Because of this, Tirana changed from within through infill densification and from without extending in shapeless tentacles, and peripheral sprawling. The tentative to study and reshape the city was moving from Tirana to Greater Tirana, to Parallel Tirana and Durana [3].

In conclusion of this part, we can distinguish three important phases in the morphological stratification of Tirana. First, the city started as a self-organized spontaneous urbanization process organically knitted around the first nucleus of the old bazaar and the mosque. Second, the organic urban fabric was pierced by centrally planned geometric axes during the monarchy period and fascist occupation. However, the spontaneous-organic logic that started with the origin of the city resisted. Third, the massive invasion of the city by spontaneous urbanization tides after the collapse of the dictatorship. The last stage affected not only the periphery but pervaded also the central areas through fill-ins and parasite structures, in the erupted residential areas during the dictatorship.

What described so far shows the specifics of Tirana as a complex system embodying characteristics of bottom-up self-organized processes, combined with elements of centrally controlled planning. As such, Tirana represents a condition of a blurred dichotomy between planned and unplanned. The advanced status of osmoses between these two categories creates difficulties to distinguish in many cases the differences between planned and unplanned, and give to Tirana the aspect of a natural/real city. The discrepancy between the real city and the order understood in simplistic logic often is not accepted by controlling authorities that tend to automatically exclude and sterilize the natural phenomena in the city, which emerges organically and reflects the interaction between human properties. This process is often stigmatized as informal.

At this point, it would be with interest to discuss the position of the architect in relation to this kind of natural/spontaneous/informal phenomenon in the city? Even though the architects already have a long tradition of their approach to the so-called informality that began with Turner in the 1960s in the informal settlements of Lima, still many of them underestimate or contemn the phenomena as something that has nothing to do with the profession. This position reflects the lack of in-depth knowledge and limitations in relation to the paradigms they see and analyze the reality. However, while Turner was convinced that people have a better understanding of their own situations, and supported the idea of the self-help community-driven projects, which was typical for the participatory processes during the 60s and 70s, normally in an already built and post-factum situation, nowadays this may not be enough. The architect may understand the natural properties of the city and use the data as inputs in a modeling process.

Can we as architects and urban planners learn from the intelligent adaptability of cities in general and particularly from Tirana as a specific reality seen as a complex system? A city that harbored the clash between Ottoman and western civilization, between extreme orthodox/puritan/Franciscan communism, and anarchic/chaotic/oligarchic capitalism.

A city that sensitively activated the blurring devise/tides to process the differences between centralized planning and spontaneous or informal developments? A city where urban conflicts emerge and disappear cyclically between government and urban neighborhoods because of large-scale land speculation/corrupted urban projects? Can we recreate interactive processes where successful urban patterns, are self-organized and self-recognized in a more conscious self-generated development?

2   Aims and Objectives

In this paper, we argue about our position related to the specific role of the architect related to these issues.

To do so, we will present our work at POLIS University in Tirana, where all of us involved are currently involved as professors in different roles and subjects. Our main aim was to develop a joint academic format where the criticalities of the Albanian urban patterns (and complex behavioral mentalities) could be explored together with the students through an interactive-based approach oriented towards three main objectives: the first one is to analyze the existing situations through the modeling [4] of previously gathered data that could be transformed into meaningful pattern and cluster to shape a morphological city pattern. The aim is to extract from the actual reality tangible – and intangible – patterns that could help us to understand the reasons why the urban environment has been developing itself through the decades with specific criticalities and the rise of settlements not only in the peripheral areas but also in the premise of the historical city.

As a second step, we will use the clusters in classwork with our students to start to identify which one of the study models developed will contain specific enzymes that will define its capability of surviving and – eventually – evolve through time and continuous environmental changes. The main insight behind this chapter is that, if the city can be seen as an evolutionary system [5], it is then possible to have access to its inner structure to orientate the further development towards the ideas of resiliency and positive self-organization [2]. The critical lens under which this would be done is our shared conviction that cities are complex systems ruled by relationships based on nonlinearity, emergence, spontaneous order, adaptation, and feedback loops [6–8].

In the end, last didactic cycle will concentrate on the idea of machine learning and artificial intelligence [9] training neural networks to learn from the model and generate improved models that learn from their environment and from their past to open new possibilities about the role of the architects to affect the evolution. Specifically, we will speculate on how to integrate GAN (General Adversarial Network) strategies on architectural and space design to trigger new reflections on how interactive responsive system can foster interdisciplinary step forwards in our discipline.

This work must be intended as a bootstrap to shift the implementation of such technology and procedures in architectural design from a mere descriptive practice to a prescriptive tool.

3   Advanced Architecture and IT Studio – Computational Strategies for a New Reality

The Advanced Architecture and IT studio[1] (ASA&IT) is part of the IV year program of the Integrated Master in Architecture and Urban Design at POLIS University[2]. The class aims for discussing the presence of Information Technology in contemporary design practice and how these cultural debates have been changing several dimensions both at a technical and a philosophical level, provoking the paradox of further fragmentation of the design experience unity. The course, therefore, wants to analyze and criticize such tendencies, making students aware, that rather than creating sub-branches of architecture and design experience, Information Technology (IT), should constitute a means of interactive connection between things [10].

The cultural framework, to which this course relies upon, links to the idea regarding the historical modifications that are changing our world, and architecture and design themselves, in relation to the widespread development of IT and how the world, since the end of the WWII, has been fastly shifting to a new kind of society where the main value is not the industrial power but the possession of Data and Information [11]. If then, Information Technology, could be conceived as a new paradigm [4], the course wants to explore and analyze the meaning of this assumption in both the architecture and design fields, by focusing on their most emerging phenomenon: the production of form, whereas the presence of IT through computer technology played a crucial role during the last decades, and how this tools can be used either to understand the inner structure of the existing reality and to offer new generative models to achieve a further evolution of them through IT and ICT technologies.

The class is composed of students from different fields: not from architecture but also from the MA Degree in Applied Design. This choice was driven by the will of having more design methodologies at hand and, at the same time, to foster a multi-disciplinary Research through Design (RtD)[3] processes.

Indeed, the objectives of the course are the following:

- Enrich the students with a critical awareness of the impact of Information Technology and Interactive Computational Tools in the contemporary world and culture;
- To provide critically advanced specific tools, like contemporary popular software (McNeel Rhinoceros, Autodesk 3dsMax, Grasshopper), through a base of scripting techniques. In any case, this course, since being held at the end of a formative

---

[1] The ASA&IT studio has been founded by the former dean of POLIS University Antonino di Raimo. Through the years, the class have been speculating on several topics dealing with contemporary crisis (such as ecology issues; the IT revolution in Architecture; future interplanetary scenarios) in order to offer a new perspective for the architectura discipline. Currently, the studio is conducted by Professors Ledian Bregasi, Sotir Dhamo, Valerio Perna, and PhD Candidate Gerdi Papa.

[2] http://www.universitetipolis.edu.al/.

[3] Research Through Design (RtD) aims for generating new knowledge by understanding the current state and then suggesting new possibilities future state in the form of a design. It usually The process involves the developing of a series of cycles of research insights to broaden the research possibilities of a topic [12, 13].

academic cycle, should be intended as based on software learning and related functions to foster cultural debate and ideas;

- General awareness of the technical and practical features regarding Computer-Aided Design (CAD);
- Direct and in-depth knowledge of specific areas of design information used in support of advanced experimentation. Moreover, the course aims to introduce students to 'Parametric Design'.

Until the first semester of 2019, the studio was organized on a series of thematic cycles that could conduct the students step-by-step towards a deeper understanding on the final objectives, enriching them with a methodology characterized by the use of some tools that could give the students to the possibility explore some topics like simulation of swarm behaviors in urban fabric [14] the knowledge on how to build parametrize and responsive geometrical path through minimal path systems [15]; the capacity to create a correspondence within the computational design diagrams and the composition of an architecture form through operations of simplification and adaptation.

Briefly, we will present these already existing three modules, together with some of the best scripting achievements by some of the students participating in the class. We will try in every description to highlight their relation to urban spaces and their generative potentialities when it comes to the design discipline.

3.1 Minimal Path – Scripting to Optimize the Space

With minimal path, we refer to a spatial construction that can show us the shortest connections between sets of nodes. For example, in the physical world soap films behave in a precise way to minimize its surface area in relation to a given boundary. The theorization of this model was made by Frei Otto [15] where he underlined the phenomena of urban networks as self-organized systems, path and surface occupation, and territorial expansion. What he pointed out is that all the natural and humanized occupations of spaces are linked to two concepts: occupation and connection.

In a city like Tirana, these specific behavior are more than just a mere supposition. As we pointed out in the first part, after the fall of the Communist dictatorship, there has been strong territorial aggression by the citizens that started to – independently and without rules – occupy and connecting parcel of territories. The result is a dense and chaotic urban sprawl where nothing is certain and where emergent behaviors [16, 17] are still conforming and undefined and under on-going transformation urban space.

The task for the students was to try to 'give the order' within this spatial complexity through an optimization of the occupation system underneath the existing urban pattern. According to the topic of their final project – proposed by them after brainstorming on some strong concepts they choose during the first two lessons – they set two lists of point: the principal ones, that were the one where the urban weave would have been generated from; and the strong ones, that would have distorted the system through the simulation of space occupations in the new urban palimpsest.

The outcome consisted of 10 different diagrams. Among them, the one that would be recognized more 'generative-oriented' would then be used to design a new masterplan for the urban sector and to simulate the swarm behavior (Fig. 1).

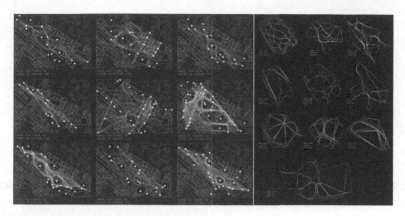

Fig. 1. Minimal path networks. a) Students: Avrili Meshi, Eni Gjoka, Xhesjan Cela; b) Students: Teuta Daxha, Rixhers Dengo, Enkeleda Lika

3.2   Swarm Pattern Simulation – Foreseeing Emergent Behavior in the City

After having defined their masterplan proposal in the chosen urban sector of the city of Tirana, the students will develop a further investigation through the interactive computational tool. In this step, the class will challenge itself with simulating swarm behavior, a collective attitude demonstrated by entities such as animals or, in a more abstract definition, the collective motion of a large number of self-propelled entities. What we are interested in, and that we can refer to an evolutionary generative model for urban solutions, are two specific qualities of the swarms: the emergence [18] and the stigmergy [19]. The first one is intended as the properties and functions visible at a hierarchical level, and that are not present and are irrelevant at the lower levels, and which is linked to the system of self-organizing models. The second one deals with indirect coordination between agents or actions. Briefly, we can define as the trace left in the environment by one action that subsequently leads to the performance of the next one by the same agent or a different one.

Through a script made through Grasshopper to simulate this behavior in real-time, the students will define another layer that will overlap the existing masterplan and will be used to implement other elements in the design process (such for example, the presence of unexpected paths or spaces suggested by the simulation done by the system), that tackle also possible conflicts due to human presence in the city (Fig. 2).

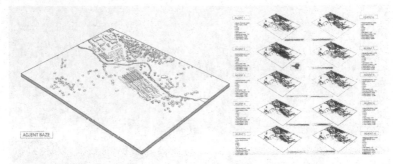

Fig. 2. Agent base models. Students: Kostandino Pirko, Gerald Thoma, Raxhino Bicaku

3.3   Design Through Diagrams. Iterative Steps for Design

The last part of the studio deals concretely with the architectural design space. All the diagrams, and inputs, taken by the interactive simulations done during the semester will be used to realize an original design network of possibilities for the city of Tirana.

What is important to the students to understand is that their final product will be just one of the many possibilities that could be generated by the process. The fascinating thing about these tools is that the proposed is just a 'moment' among the many iterations calculated by the digital tools. Changing specific parameters will generate other emergent paths that can be followed or discarded by the designers, after considering their adherence to the boundary conditions previously set.

Even though the years of application of this structure has demonstrated the effectiveness of these process we have outlined, we still think that there are some unexplored possibilities that could help us to reach a further level towards the comprehension of complex matters and their translation into 'architectural design material'. For these reasons, we have started a transformation process for the studio thanks to the presence of new tools that might be implemented in new didactic cycles (Fig. 3).

Fig. 3. Proposed masterplan and Vertical Farm by the students: Teuta Daxha, Rixhers Dengo, Enkeleda Lika

4 Urban Morphologies and Specific Realities. Towards New Research Questions

The work described up to this moment is meant to serve as a base for the research and a second and deepened course organized with the same students achieving the result explained in the previous paragraphs. Intentionally and for practical reasons, the research and the course will be organized in three subsequent stages. The first part of the course will focus on the analysis of an urban case study located in the historical center of Tirana and on the definition of a morphogenetic model based on this analysis. The analysis will have a double nature, formal and social. In this way, it will be possible to relate social needs to the spatial configuration of the examined settlement. The social context of the area under examination is complex considering the heterogeneous background of the inhabitants and historical layering of the sample. From the other side, the morphological analysis will produce quantitative data related to formal aspects of the area being studied.

The hypothesis to be verified is that the urban tissue shows a fractal nature and this nature can be used as a tool for understanding reality and design new urban tissues. The successive hypothesis is that the urban settlements created following such criteria can perform better and are fitter in some specific conditions. This quantitative data collected in the settlement will inform a statistical model that will be able to simulate an unlimited number of urban models that share the same probabilities of certain phenomena to happen. A preliminary example will be the creation of an urban model were starting from the main vector, different paths bend, branch and rotate following the same probability with which these actions happen in the tested urban sample.

4.1 Performance, Evolution, and Optimization

A large number of such urban design models can be created following an iterative process based on fractal properties of the organization observed in the historical center of Tirana. It is possible to measure how these models perform in solving different kinds of organizational problems. Once we can have a quantitative indicator of the performance, some basic principles of evolution can be applied to the model in order to increase have ever better-performing solutions. Genetic algorithms, in particular Galapagos components of Grasshopper 3D modeling software, will copy, combine and mutate a very large number of urban design models evaluating their performance in offering privacy for the settlers. The need for visual privacy was observed to be one of the common characteristics of the historical settlements in Tirana so through the genetic algorithm the generations of urban design models will undergo a survive of the fittest process that will allow the emergence of new models of settlement that continue to have the same probabilities of the observed phenomena to happen but at the same time will perform better in delivering, in this case, the right to visual privacy.

The genetic mechanisms in this procedure are three. The first is the selection of individuals who demonstrate better characteristics than the average population and their reproduction in the next generation. The second genetic mechanism is a crossover resulting from the random combination of characteristics present in two-parent models.

As in sexual reproduction, the individuals of the new generation demonstrate traits present in the two parents but are not identical copies neither of them nor of their siblings. The third genetic mechanism is the mutation, which, by choosing the best individuals, randomly changes parts of the model creating a new generation that inherits most of the characteristics from its predecessors but which also demonstrates new characters.

The new population made up of three categories of descendants undergoes the same process of evaluating fitness and evolution and thus, from generation to generation, individuals with ever better characteristics and inclined to solve complex and non-linear problems emerge. The result of this phase of the process will most probably generate a number of segment models composed by the different hierarchies of roads and paths and the division the plots where to settle.

4.2 Towards a Learning System

The last step of the process will try to propose the generation of building footprints and plans deriving from the shape of the plots. The relation of the footprints to the plots is supposed to be the same that links the shape of the houses in the historical center to their property plot. Due to a large number of very diverse footprint/plot combinations, this relation is expected to be very complex and not easily graspable by traditional statistical models. A generative adversarial network (GAN) which is a class of machine learning systems is proposed to be used and trained in recognizing patterns and regularities in the existing situation. The so trained GAN will successively be used to place the footprints of the houses in the plots generated through the genetic algorithm. The same procedure will be used for generating from the footprint of the pant of the house. In this way, the students will be able to guide a process that starting form the understanding of the specific spatial qualities of a historical settlement will later develop in designing new settlements that are not copies of the existing ones but learning from history could propose novel models of settling.

5 Conclusion and Further Discussions

As we stated at the beginning of this contribution, this paper is for us a positioning paper. It reflects a completely different way to deal with the topics of interactivity and intelligence in architecture and space and, mostly, on how to communicate it to our students and insert it in a didactic cycle within an academic class.

From the get-go, we didn't want to frame the issue under a narrow/specialistic point of view; we are aware that young architects are not in need of mind-bending tools but to develop a sense of agency in the real world through their actions. All of us share the certainty that the students, not only in Albania but in any other place and with any kind of background, have to understand the importance of the IT instruments always in relationship with their impact in the urban fabric and on the society that inhabits those spaces. If this doesn't not happen, the risk is to merely equip them with powerful tools that can be used only for academic purposes while losing the importance of the research as a way to engage and empower people through technological advancements.

For this reason, the upcoming class will be based on practical applications of the theory here presented, where for every action there will be a reaction analyzed and explored altogether. The aim will be to have, for Autumn 2020 the first set of experiments completed that can be a confirmation for us of the validity of our theory and, at the same time, a moment of self-reflection and analysis for more improvements.

References

1. Ingersoll, R., Kostof, S.: World Architecture: A Cross-Cultural History. Oxford University Press, Oxford (2012)
2. Portugali, J.: Self-Organization and the City. Springer, Berlin (2000). https://doi.org/10. 1007/978-0-387-30440-3_471
3. Declerck, J., Zenghelis, E., Aureli, P.V.: Tirana Metropolis. Berlage Institute, Rotterdam (2004)
4. Saggio, A.: Introduzione alla rivoluzione informatica in architettura. Carocci, Roma (2007)
5. MVRDV/DSD: Space Fighter: The Evolutionary City (game). Actar, Barcelona (2007)
6. Bertanlaffy, L.: General System Theory. Foundation, Development, Application. George Braziller, New York (1968)
7. Bocchi, G., Ceruti, M.: La sfida della complessità. Mondadori, Milano (1985)
8. Bregasi, L.: Proprietà Emergenti come Strumento per la Gestione della Complessità in Architettura Simulatori e Generatori per la Guida di Progetti Autoregolati, Ph.D. thesis, Sapienza - Università di Roma, Roma (2016)
9. Zheng, H., Huang, W.: Architectural Drawings Recognition and Generation through Machine Learning. ACADIA, Cambridge (2018)
10. Capra, F.: The Web of Life. Anchor Books, New York (1996)
11. Toffler, A.: The Third Wave. Bantam Books, New York (1980)
12. Zimmerman, J., Forlizzi, J., Evenson, S.: Research through design as a method for interaction design research in HCI. In: Proceedings of the 2007 Conference on Human Factors in Computing Systems, CHI 2007, San Jose, California, USA (2007). https://doi.org/ 10.1145/1240624.1240704
13. Forlizzi, J., Zimmerman, J., Stolterman, E.: From design research to theory: evidence of a maturing field. In: Conference: International Association of Societies of Design Research Conference (2009)
14. Hildebrandt, H., Carere, C., Hemelrijk, C.K.: Self-organized aerial displays of thousands of starlings: a model. Behav. Ecol. 21(6), 1349–1359 (2010). https://doi.org/10.1093/beheco/ arq149
15. Otto, F.: Occupying and Connecting: Thoughts on Territories and Spheres of Influence With Particular Reference to Human Settlement. Axel Menges, Felibach (DE) (2008)
16. Bateson, G.: Steps to an Ecology of Mind. University of Chicago Press, Chicago (1972)
17. Fromm, J.: The Emergence of Complexity. Kassel University Press, Kassel (2004)
18. Van Dyke Parunak, H.: Making swarming happen. In: Proceedings of Conference on Swarming and Network Enabled Command, Control, Communications, Computers, Intelligence, Surveillance and Reconnaissance (C4ISR), McLean, Virginia, USA (2003)
19. Marsh, L., Onof, C.: Stigmergic epistemology, stigmergic cognition. Cogn. Syst. Res. 9(1), 136–149 (2008). https://doi.org/10.1016/j.cogsys.2007.06.009
20. Dhamo, S.: Specific realities and new hypotheses for urban analyses and urban design - Tirana as a case study, developed in the framework of the PhD program in architecture and urban planning between POLIS and Ferrara Universities (2018)

Research on Service Design of Real-Time Translation Based on Scenario Analysis

Yingying Miao, Shaolun Zhang, and Bin Jiang[✉]

Nanjing University of Science and Technology, Xiaolingwei 200,
Nanjing, Jiangsu, China
398991222@qq.com, 2353820164@qq.com, jb508@163.com

Abstract. With the acceleration of the process of globalization, the increase of global online conferences, cross-border tourism, telephone paging services, video communication services, global shopping and so on will correspondingly promote the demand of the translation industry. As one of the traditional industries, the combination of the translation industry and the mobile Internet will usher in a new opportunity for development. How to change the traditional service mode of manual translation and build a new service system to better serve the public is the focus of this paper. First of all, this paper studies the current situation of the translation market, explores the market demand, investigates both translators and translation demanders, establishes a feature user model, and obtains the key elements needed to construct the situation. Secondly, the user usage scenario is constructed, and the invisible needs of users are obtained through the analysis and research of users' scenarios in the future. Through the construction of the application scenario of the instant translation service, the interaction flow and operation mode of the user under the specific tasks of each function are obtained in the scenario expectation, and a multi-scenario real-time translation service system is formed. In addition, the KJ method is used to sort out and classify the requirement items to make them more organized and independent. Finally, through the AHP analytic hierarchy process, we let professionals compare and evaluate the demand items, use the analytic hierarchy process to express the structure and calculate the weight of the demand items, construct the demand hierarchy model of users, and put forward the overall design strategy from the global perspective of service design.

Keywords: Real-time translation · Scenario analysis · Service design

1 Introduction

More and more traditional industries get new development opportunities by combining with the Internet, such as MOOC provides large-scale open online courses, Uber provides online taxi service and so on. The new e-commerce model not only changes the operation mode of the traditional industry, but also greatly improves the convenience of life. Today, with more and more frequent foreign exchanges, the importance of the translation industry is self-evident, and for the general public, how to find a suitable translation to solve the translation needs of users has become an urgent problem to be solved. The introduction of Internet model can provide a new way for users to find

© Springer Nature Switzerland AG 2020
M. Kurosu (Ed.): HCII 2020, LNCS 12183, pp. 586–603, 2020.
https://doi.org/10.1007/978-3-030-49065-2_41

translation. Based on this, this paper classifies the translation needs of users, establishes different user roles and usage scenarios to analyze the translation needs of users, and puts forward design strategies combined with the concept of service design. To provide a reliable basis for the design of real-time translation services in the future.

2 Current Status of Instant Translation Service

2.1 The Present Situation of the Translation Industry

The trend of globalization is becoming more and more obvious, and the prospect of the translation industry must be gratifying. Chinese people leaving the country, foreigners entering the country, global online conferences, telephone paging services, video exchange services, global shopping and so on will correspondingly boost the demand of the translation industry. The scale of mobile translation users is also getting larger and larger. According to the iMedia consulting, it is estimated that the number of mobile translation users in China will reach 490 million by 2020.

In the face of the translation needs of such a large scale of mobile translation users. Machine translation is one of the technologies that have attracted much attention. Machine translation is fast, convenient and practical, and has high cost-effectiveness. However, there are many existing problems in machine translation. first of all, machine translation is not culturally sensitive and prone to translation errors; secondly, machine translation can not understand contextual connections, translation is stiff and lack of emotion. Third, almost all machine translation requires manual post-editing. In view of the shortcomings mentioned above, there is still a lot of room for improvement in machine translation. At present, it can not replace manual translation.

2.2 Current Status of Instant Translation Service

At present, there are two main kinds of instant translation services, one is manual translation, and the other is manual translation, which is a handheld device, such as the translation stick launched by iFLYTEK, which can translate daily conversations. When in use, press and hold the recording key to input the translated voice into the device for machine translation, and then play the translated voice through the loudspeaker. In order to achieve the purpose of communication between different languages. The other is that APP, on mobile devices, such as Google Translation APP, can also achieve the same functions as translation sticks. Another kind of real-time translation service is manual translation, which is also divided into two categories, one is online manual translation, the other is offline manual translation. At present, the online manual translation mainly carries on the text translation through the website and mobile application, and the offline manual translation service is mainly the service mode provided by most translation companies. These two service methods have their own advantages and disadvantages, the former is convenient and fast, and is suitable for people who do not have high requirements for translation. The latter has the advantages of high price and low convenience, so it is suitable for people who have higher requirements for translation.

3 Scenario Analysis Theory

Scenario analysis is based on the hypothesis of "situation", which is a research method to describe the development trend of things. Situational analysis was first used in human-computer interaction design, paying attention to the interaction between people and things. In the process of research, scenario analysis can further analyze and compare the phased research results and get a variety of different understandings so as to mix into a comprehensive system. This is an effective way to improve software usability based on the idea of situational design in the field of human-computer interaction.

Usually, the research process of using scenarios to predict is as follows: first, to investigate the historical scenarios, secondly, to make reasonable assumptions about the possible future development direction, and finally, to take corresponding solutions to the results of the assumptions, (see Fig. 1). The situational method combines quantitative and qualitative analysis, obtains historical scenarios to guide the process of quantitative analysis, and conceives future scenarios through qualitative analysis. The research of instant translation product service system is divided into the following research steps: defining customer decision points, identifying key factors that affect customer selection and decision, exporting scenario cards (or storyboards), scenario analysis, and so on.

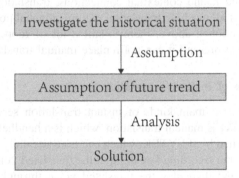

Fig. 1. Research process of situational method

4 Service Design

Service design is to integrate the design concept into the whole service system, and in this process, the designer must participate in the service link in order to understand the problems in the service link, and use the design knowledge to improve each link. Solve the problems, so as to provide users with a better experience. The essence of service design is to design a reasonable service model to plan the relationship among people, products and environment in the whole service system, so as to improve service quality and user experience.

The theory, method and characteristics of service design determine that it is suitable for solving the problem of real-time translation product service system, (see Fig. 2). Service design is a people-centered design, which interprets the relationship between the system and user contact points. This paper chooses the concept and method of service design to interpret real-time translation products, and discusses how to better meet the translation needs of users in the new social environment, business environment and technical environment.

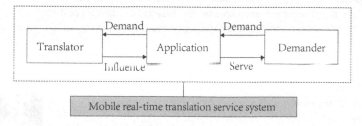

Fig. 2. Mobile real-time translation service system

5 Construction of Translation Requirement Model Based on Scenario Analysis

5.1 Scenario Establishment Based on User Role

In order to understand the translation needs of users, this paper uses the questionnaire method to identify 10 subjects, including 3 undergraduates, 3 graduate students, 2 company executives, a doctor and a university teacher. Therefore, all the subjects have the experience of paying for translation, and look forward to a simpler way to find translation. Therefore, an in-depth interview was conducted for these 10 users, and the relevant information was recorded. The interview outline is shown in the Table 1:

Table 1. Interview outline

Serial number	Question
1	What is your occupation?
2	Under what circumstances do you need to translate?
3	In what ways do you find translation?
4	Do you think these ways are convenient? Or can you solve your problem well?
5	What do you think are the bad experiences in the whole process of translation service?
6	If there is a APP that provides reservation translation service, what functions would you like to have?

According to the analysis of interviews with 10 subjects, typical users are classified and persona is established. According to the types of translation needs and preferences of users looking for translation approaches, four types of users are identified, (see Fig. 3).

No. 1 user

Name: Gao Xiaohan

Gender. Female

Age: 24

Occupation: Master graduate student

Introduction: non-English majors, class cadres, often publish papers, like to participate in various activities, and often communicate with students from different countries.

The characteristics of translation demand: higher requirements for literature translation, less use of translation, and low price.

No. 2 user

Name: Zheng Huaxin

Gender: Male

Age: 45

Occupation: University teacher

Introduce: He often reads the literature in foreign professional fields, write chemical professional papers, and publish them on the relevant academic websites. at the same time, they often receive teachers and students from foreign schools and conduct academic exchanges. The characteristics of translation demand: higher requirements for literature translation, less use of translation, more types of translation, in the price.

No. 3 user

Name: Xiong Yu

Gender: Male

Age: 40

Occupation: Doctor

Introduce: a doctor in Nanjing, often have foreign students to see a doctor, at the same time, often participate in academic exchanges.

The characteristics of translation demand: irregular, low price.

No. 4 user

Name: Wang Jianhua

Gender: Male

Age: 39

Occupation: Senior executive of a biotechnology company in Nanjing

Introduction: responsible for external sales of company equipment, receiving foreign experts, responsible for enterprise training, etc.

The characteristics of translation demand: manual translation, accompanying translation, high price.

Fig. 3. Typical user portrait

5.2   Scenario Construction

Based on the classification of situations by users, a typical scenario is established. In service design, the composition of the situation includes five dimensions: role, environment, purpose, activity and contact. Starting from the lives of the four typical users, combined with the five dimensions of situations, sort out the situations that each user often encounter that need to be translated, and use vivid language to describe the user's situational stories. Through a comprehensive analysis of the scenarios of all different users, 13 typical user scenarios are summarized, as shown in the Table 2, 3, 4, 5.

Table 2. Gao Xiaohan's situation of translation needs

Situation	Scenario description
Thesis translation situation	Gao Xiaohan recently finished a paper, and her tutor asked her to submit it to a foreign journal, but Gao Xiaohan found that there were only two days left to submit Li's paper. First of all, she wanted to translate with the help of some mobile translation APP, so she tried to type the abstract into APP, and sure enough, an English abstract was translated in a few seconds. But when Gao Xiaohan looked carefully, she found that there were translation errors in several places, and there was nothing she could do about it. She spent hundreds of yuan to help a website that could provide manual translation
Exchange situations with foreigners	During the summer vacation, Gao Xiaohan attended a summer camp for the exchange of multinational students, and she met a foreign friend. One day, she took the foreign friend to visit the local museum. The foreign friend was very interested in some cultural relics and asked Gao Xiaohan several questions about the local culture. However, Gao Xiaohan did not know how to express it accurately. Even if she compared hands and feet, it was impossible for foreign friends to understand. Gao Xiaohan hoped that a classmate who could speak a foreign language would help her at the moment
Subtitle translation of American TV dramas	Gao Xiaohan recently fell in love with an American TV series, but for some reason, there are no Chinese subtitles in the last few episodes of the show. This frustrated Gao Xiaohan, who hopes to translate the subtitles of the final episodes

Table 3. Zheng Huaxin's situation of translation needs

Situation	Scenario description
Foreigners see a doctor	As there are many colleges and universities around Zheng Huaxin's hospital, students from all over the world often come to see him, but he only speaks English and knows nothing about other foreign languages, so he has no way to communicate with foreign patients. usually at this time, he will take out his mobile phone and use the machine translation on the mobile phone APP for simple voice communication. In this way, a lot of time is wasted and other patients are affected to see a doctor

(continued)

Table 3. (*continued*)

Situation	Scenario description
Visit abroad	The hospital organized an activity to exchange abroad, and Zheng Huaxin, as one of the representatives of the Chinese side, was also sent abroad for exchange. in a hospital in the United States, he found that the outpatient rooms of the hospital were all equipped with equipment to provide manual translation. patients from different countries can communicate without barriers through this equipment

Table 4. Xiong Yu's situation of Translation needs

Situation	Scenario description
Thesis translation situation	Similar to Gao Xiaohan, Xiong Yu often needs to read a lot of literature. because of his special specialty, there are many professional words in the paper that need him to translate one by one. in order to save time, he had to look for translation on Taobao, even manual translation. there is also a translation deviation because he does not understand Xiong Yu's professional knowledge, which gives Xiong Yu a great headache
Academic exchanges with foreign teachers	Whenever a foreign teacher came to the school to communicate, Xiong Yu went to the translation company in advance to find a temporary translator, and asked the translator to have relevant field knowledge background. The search process was not very smooth, and many translators could not meet Xiong Yu's requirements. He had to go to more companies to look for it
Chinese and foreign distance classes	The school has some cooperative courses with foreign schools. Xiong Yu often works as a teacher in Chinese and foreign distance classes because of his major, but he also finds that it is difficult for students to fully understand his courses because of the language barrier

Table 5. Wang Jianhua's situation of translation needs

Situation	Scenario description
Receive foreign experts	Generally speaking, when foreign experts come to the company to communicate, he will call the translation company and ask them to send an interpreter. The translator will arrive at the agreed place on time, but the cost is high

(*continued*)

Table 5. *(continued)*

Situation	Scenario description
Draw up foreign trade orders and contracts	In this case, the translator will be contacted in advance and the drawn up foreign trade orders and contracts will be sent to the translator
Foreign experts come to the company for training	Every year, the company will have some staff training, training on imported equipment, etc., usually the training cycle is about a week. In the same way, Wang Jianhua contacted the translation company in advance and asked the company to send translators for short-term work

5.3 Demand Analysis of Human Translation Service

The situational stories of the above users vividly and intuitively reflect the process of different types of people looking for translation, and in this process, many problems are exposed, which directly affect the user's experience. it makes users hesitate or even reject in the process of choosing translation. Through the comparative analysis of these processes, find the problems, and explore the corresponding user needs. As shown in the Table 6.

Table 6. Scenario requirement extraction

Translation situation	Problems in the context	Extracted requirement item
1. Translated text (papers, resumes, instructions, e-mails, etc.)	1. Whether the translation of papers and other documents is accurate or not	1. Manual inspection service can be provided for problematic translated texts
2. Voice content needs to be translated into text.	2. How to find a professional translator	2. The professional information of translators should be transparent and public
3. Video subtitles need to be translated	3. What is the quality of translation by translators?	3. Each order will be scored and evaluated at the end of each order
4. Communicate with foreign friends (cultural introduction, academic exchanges, etc.)	4. How to determine the translation time	4. Provide date and working hours selection service
5. Communication situations such as foreigners seeing a doctor	5. Communication situations such as foreigners seeing a doctor	5. Provide text translation and file transfer interface
6. Translation of cross-border e-commerce websites and advertising languages	6. How to realize online communication	6. Provide audio translation and file transfer interface
7. A brief meeting	7. How to quickly match to the right translator	7. Provide video subtitle translation and file transfer interface

(continued)

Table 6. (*continued*)

Translation situation	Problems in the context	Extracted requirement item
8. Remote voice and video translation	8. What is the medium of online communication?	8. Provide online voice and video service for translators
9. Travel, study and exchange abroad	9. How to use it by foreigners	9. There is a quick entrance to translation classification.
10. On-site exchange and translation of foreign experts	10. How to translate in a video conversation	10. Mobile devices and external devices (headphones, microphones, etc.)
11. Short-term employment or long-term translation	11. Whether services can be provided abroad	11. Intelligently recommend translation according to user information
12. Business exchanges between foreign customers	12. How to book the door-to-door service of a translator	12. Provide the same translation service for foreigners
13. Training guidance for foreign experts	13. Training guidance for foreign experts	13. Provide multi-window video translation service
	14. How to negotiate the working time and place of the translator	14. Simplified door-to-door reservation service process
	15. What if the translator's ability level is not up to the required level?	15. Work agreement signed to protect the interests of both parties
	16. How to protect confidential documents, privacy, etc.	16. Provide order grabbing mode
	17. How to agree on the price of different services	17. Price comparison
	18. Is it possible to provide short-term or long-term translation services?	18. Can provide short-term and long-term translation services
	19. What is the method of payment?	19. Small language translation
	20. The operation of related websites is tedious.	20. Order after-sales service
		21. A simple and humanized interface

5.4   Collation of User Demand Items Based on KJ Method

The requirements analyzed above are simplified and sorted out by KJ method, and the similar requirements are classified into one category. The KJ method is a scheme obtained by improving the intellectual incentive method. It is a non-quantitative tool, which classifies messy materials and qualitative words on small cards to organize thoughts, carry out creative thinking, and find ways to solve problems. The process is as follows:

(1) Dentify personnel

The selected team members are highly relevant to the topic and have some knowledge of the field, including 3 teachers, 3 industrial designers and 3 translators.

(2) Make demand cards

The requirements will be written on 20 cards, a total of 9 points, one for each member of the team, (see Fig. 4).

1.Provide manual inspection service	2.The professional information of translators should be transparent and public.	3.Each order will be scored and evaluated at the end of each order.	4.Provide date and working hours selection service
5.Provide text translation and file transfer interface	6.Provide audio translation and file transfer interface	7.Provide video subtitle translation and file transfer interface	8.Provide online voice and video service for translators
9.There is a quick entrance to translation classification.	10.Mobile devices and external devices (headphones, microphones,	11.Intelligently recommend translation according to user information)	12.Provide the same translation service for foreigners
13.Provide multi-window video translation service	14.Simplified door-to-door reservation service process	15.Work agreement signed to protect the interests of both parties	16.Provide order grabbing mode
17.Price comparison	18.Can provide short-term and long-term translation	19.Small language translation	20.Order after-sales service
21.A simple and humanized interface			

Fig. 4. Demand cards

(3) Sort out the cards

Each member of the team classifies 20 cards, the cards of the same nature are classified into a group, and each group draws up a title, and the extra cards are grouped into a group, and then the grouped cards and redundant cards are classified into a large group and draw up a title for this large group, and remove the duplicate cards. Finally, we get the cards sorted, (see Fig. 5).

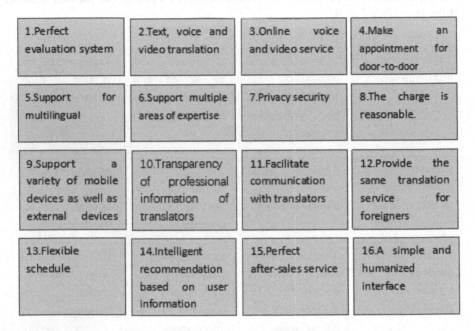

1.Perfect evaluation system	2.Text, voice and video translation	3.Online voice and video service	4.Make an appointment for door-to-door
5.Support for multilingual	6.Support multiple areas of expertise	7.Privacy security	8.The charge is reasonable.
9.Support a variety of mobile devices as well as external devices	10.Transparency of professional information of translators	11.Facilitate communication with translators	12.Provide the same translation service for foreigners
13.Flexible schedule	14.Intelligent recommendation based on user information	15.Perfect after-sales service	16.A simple and humanized interface

Fig. 5. Screened demand cards

5.5   Establish a Hierarchical Structure Model of User Requirements

The above 16 requirements are summarized into a first-level demand index according to their corresponding attributes, which are: convenience, professionalism, reliability and aesthetics, as shown in the Table 7.

Table 7. Hierarchical structure model of user requirements

Target	First-level demand	SECOND-level demand
A Provide translation services	A1 Convenience	A11 Text, voice and video translation
		A12 Online voice and video service
		A13 Make an appointment for door-to-door service
		A14 Support a variety of mobile devices as well as external devices
		A15 Flexible schedule
	A2 Professionalism	A21 Support for multilingual
		A22 Support multiple areas of expertise
		A23 Provide the same translation service for foreigners
	A3 Reliability	A31 Perfect evaluation system
		A32 Privacy security
		A33 The charge is reasonable.
		A34 Intelligent recommendation based on user information
		A35 Facilitate communication with translators
		A36 Transparency of professional information of translators
		A37 Perfect after-sales service
	A4 Aesthetics	A41 A simple and humanized interface

6 Determination of Importance of User Demand Items Based on ANP Analytic Hierarchy Process

The analytic hierarchy process decomposes the decision-making problem into different hierarchical structures in the order of general objectives, sub-objectives of each layer, evaluation criteria and specific alternative investment schemes, and then uses the method of solving the eigenvector of the judgment matrix. the priority weight of each element of each level to an element of the upper level is obtained, and finally the final weight of each alternative to the total goal is merged step by step by the method of weighted sum. The one with the largest final weight is the optimal scheme.

6.1 The Tester Determined

The testers are three categories of people who are closely related to this topic, namely, college students (b1), teachers (b2) and senior executives of foreign companies (b3).

There are 7 people in each category, with a total of 21 testers.

6.2   Construct Contrast Matrix

In the first step, 21 testers scored the convenience, professionalism, reliability and aesthetics of the first-level demand items, and the integer in the middle of 1–9 was graded. The larger the number, the greater the weight of the demand item. Then the average score of the three types of testers was calculated as B (b1), B (b2), B (b3). In the second step, according to the same method, three types of evaluators score 16 items of the second-level demand item A11–A41 respectively, and calculate the average value, which is counted as C (b1), C (b2), C (b3).

The average scores of the four items of the first-level requirement item A1–A4 by the three categories of evaluators are as follows:

$$B(b1) = (7.2, 8.7, 8.2, 6.1), B(b2) = (8.8, 8.2, 8.5, 6.9),$$
$$B(b3) = (7.1, 8.9, 8.8, 5.3)$$

The average scores of the 16 items of the level 2 requirement item A11–A41 by the three categories of evaluators are as follows:

$C(b1) = (7.8, 7.8, 6.7, 7.9, 7.8, 7.0, 7.9, 8.6, 7.1, 7.2, 6.2, 7.8, 7.7, 7.0, 7.3, 7.6)$
$C(b2) = (8.5, 7.1, 7.8, 7.8, 8.5, 8.3, 8.2, 8.3, 7.1, 7.8, 8.6, 5.5, 8.0, 8.2, 7.8, 7.1)$
$C(b3) = (5.2, 5.9, 8.3, 6.1, 6.8, 7.5, 7.5, 3.3, 7.0, 8.1, 6.9, 5.5, 7.8, 6.9, 8.2, 5.8)$

This paper makes a pairwise comparison of the first-level demand project A1 ~ A4 to judge their contribution to the overall goal (providing translation services), that is, the contribution of A1 and A2 to the overall goal, A2 and A3 to the overall goal, A3 and A4 to the overall goal, A1 and A3 to the overall goal, A1 and A4 to the overall goal, A2 and A4 to the overall goal, and score according to the following scale xi/xj. The scale of relative importance evaluation is shown in the Table 8.

Table 8. Relative importance evaluation table

Serial number	Comparison value	Description
1	xi/xj = 1	Xi and xj contribute to the same degree
2	xi/xj = 3	The contribution of xi is slightly greater than that of xj
3	xi/xj = 5	The contribution of xi is greater than that of xj
4	xi/xj = 7	The contribution of xi is much greater than that of xj
5	xi/xj = 9	The xi is very large
6	2,4,6,8	The median of the above importance

The comparison matrix of the first type tester b1 to the first-level item requirements is:

$$B(b1) = \begin{bmatrix} 1 & 0.83 & 0.88 & 1.18 \\ 1.21 & 1 & 1.06 & 1.43 \\ 1.14 & 0.92 & 1 & 1.31 \\ 0.85 & 0.70 & 0.74 & 1 \end{bmatrix}$$

By the same token, the comparison matrix of the first type tester b1 to the second-level requirement items is:

$$B'(b1) = \begin{bmatrix} 1 & 1 & 1.16 & \cdots & 1.03 \\ 1 & 1 & 1.16 & \cdots & 1.03 \\ 0.86 & 0.86 & 1 & \cdots & 0.88 \\ \vdots & \vdots & \vdots & \vdots & \vdots \\ 0.97 & 0.97 & 1.13 & \cdots & 1 \end{bmatrix}$$

Using the same method, the comparison matrix of other types of testers for first-level requirements and second-level requirements can be obtained. Write it down as B (b2), B' (b2), B (b3), B' (b3), respectively, as shown below:

$$B(b2) = \begin{bmatrix} 1 & 0.83 & 0.88 & 1.18 \\ 1.21 & 1 & 1.06 & 1.43 \\ 1.14 & 0.92 & 1 & 1.31 \\ 0.85 & 0.70 & 0.74 & 1 \end{bmatrix}, B'(b2) = \begin{bmatrix} 1 & 1 & 1.16 & \cdots & 1.03 \\ 1 & 1 & 1.16 & \cdots & 1.03 \\ 0.86 & 0.86 & 1 & \cdots & 0.88 \\ \vdots & \vdots & \vdots & \vdots & \vdots \\ 0.97 & 0.97 & 1.13 & \cdots & 1 \end{bmatrix}$$

$$B(b3) = \begin{bmatrix} 1 & 0.83 & 0.88 & 1.18 \\ 1.21 & 1 & 1.06 & 1.43 \\ 1.14 & 0.92 & 1 & 1.31 \\ 0.85 & 0.70 & 0.74 & 1 \end{bmatrix}, B'(b3) = \begin{bmatrix} 1 & 1 & 1.16 & \cdots & 1.03 \\ 1 & 1 & 1.16 & \cdots & 1.03 \\ 0.86 & 0.86 & 1 & \cdots & 0.88 \\ \vdots & \vdots & \vdots & \vdots & \vdots \\ 0.97 & 0.97 & 1.13 & \cdots & 1 \end{bmatrix}$$

6.3 Constructing the Weight Matrix of User Demand

Calculate the weight coefficient of each user demand index according to the following formula:

$$wi = \frac{\overline{wi}}{\sum_{i=1}^{n} \overline{wi}}, i = 1, 2, \ldots, n \tag{1}$$

Of which $\overline{wi} = \sqrt[m]{\prod_{k=1}^{m} a_{ijk}}$

The k in the formula represents the type k tester, of which k = 1, 2, ..., m.ai is the k-bit tester's assignment to xi/xj, of whichi, j = 1, 2, ..., n, Taking the comparison matrix of three types of testers to four first-level user demand items as an example, the user demand index (1) is calculated, and the result. $w_1^1 = 0.27$, By the same token,$w_1^2 = 0.33$, $w_1^3 = 0.17$, $w_1^4 = 0.23$. Therefore, the subjective weight vector of tester b1 to the four first-level demand evaluation indicators is $w1 = (0.27, 0.33, 0.17, 0.23)^T$

By the same token, the subjective weight vectors of other testers for the four first-level demand indicators are sorted out.:

$$w = \begin{bmatrix} 0.27 & 0.33 & 0.17 & 0.23 \\ 0.27 & 0.25 & 0.27 & 0.21 \\ 0.24 & 0.30 & 0.29 & 0.17 \end{bmatrix}$$

By the same token, the subjective weight vectors of three types of testers for 16 secondary demand indicators are obtained.:

$$w2 = \begin{bmatrix} 0.065 & 0.065 & 0.056 & \dots & 0.063 \\ 0.068 & 0.057 & 0.063 & \dots & 0.057 \\ 0.049 & 0.055 & 0.076 & \dots & 0.054 \end{bmatrix}$$

6.4 Demand Weight Results

Now the final weight value is calculated by using the formula (5-2) through the weight coefficient method.:

$$w = \frac{1}{k} \sum_{k=1}^{4} w_k^j \text{(k is the k tester, j is the evaluation index)} \tag{2}$$

Through the above formula, the first-order demand weight is calculated to be: A1 = 0.26, A2 = 0.29, A3 = 0.24, A4 = 0.21.

The second level demand weight is: A11 = 0.061, A12 = 0.059, A13 = 0.065, A14 = 0.062, A15 = 0.066, A21 = 0.065, A22 = 0.067, A23 = 0.057, A31 = 0.060, A32 = 0.066, A33 = 0.062, A34 = 0.053, A35 = 0.067, A36 = 0.063, A37 = 0.068, A41 = 0.058.

6.5 Build a User Demand Model

According to the weight values calculated above, the following user demand structure model can be obtained., shown in the Table 9.

Table 9. User demand structure model

Target	First-level demand	Weight	SECOND-level demand	Weight
A Provide translation services	A1 Convenience	0.26	A11 Text, voice and video translation	0.061
			A12 Online voice and video service	0.058
			A13 Make an appointment for door-to-door service	0.065
			A14 Support a variety of mobile devices as well as external devices	0.062
			A15 Flexible schedule	0.066
	A2 Professionalism	0.29	A21 Support for multilingual	0.065
			A22 Support multiple areas of expertise	0.067
			A23 Provide the same translation service for foreigners	0.057
	A3 Reliability	0.24	A31 Perfect evaluation system	0.060
			A32 Privacy security	0.066
			A33 The charge is reasonable.	0.062
			A34 Intelligent recommendation based on user information	0.053
			A35 Facilitate communication with translators	0.067
			A36 Transparency of professional information of translators	0.063
			A37 Perfect after-sales service	0.068
	A4 Aesthetics	0.21	A41 A simple and humanized interface	0.058

7 Service Design Strategy Based on Scenario Analysis

Through the above user demand weight analysis, summed up the service design strategy:

(1) user experience optimization strategy

Nowadays, many traditional industries have taken advantage of the development of the Internet, and in order to stand out in the fierce competition, a good user experience is the key. Real-time translation service needs to understand the actual needs of users. from the analysis, we can know that professionalism and convenience are the two factors that users care about most. Users encounter a variety of translation problems. Being able to find a suitable translation in the shortest possible time can often affect the user's experience. At the same time, the translation provider in the instant translation service system needs to have qualified professional qualifications, such as the grade certification of translators and the areas of expertise they are good at, so as to solve the needs of users. In case of disputes and other problems in the service process, the system can have effective means to ensure the interests of both sides of the service. This strategy pays attention to the differences of users' needs without changing the service content itself, so as to improve the user experience.

(2) **Strategy of high integration of resources**
The construction of this service requires a large number of translation providers and can adopt a business model similar to Uber, and translators can provide translation services after passing the professional qualification examination. in this way, the work of many translators is not limited to their own work, but also to expand the scope of work by participating in online services, while generating additional income. This way can give full play to the initiative of the translator and gain a sense of participation at the same time. Make use of the co-created business model to achieve innovation and maintain competitiveness.

(3) **The strategy of full-coverage translation service with high accessibility**
The instant translation service system provides diversified, flexible and translation services. In the previous research, most of the translations of college students are papers, resumes and other text translation. People who travel abroad need voice or video services, and for some foreign trade company executives, they may need to be accompanied by an interpreter to participate in the whole communication. In the face of the diversified needs of users, the online real-time translation system should have a variety of service modules, such as online voice or video communication module, text translation module, translator door-to-door service module, etc., to cover as many situations encountered in life as much as possible, ensure the comprehensiveness and efficiency of the service, and improve the stickiness of users at the same time.

8   Conclusion

Starting from the existing real-time translation problems, combined with the general trend of industrial development, this study investigates the translation situation of users, assumes a series of scenarios and tells vivid user stories. The problems that affect the user experience are found in the whole process, and the translation needs of users are explored according to the problems. The demand is sorted out by the KJ method, and the user demand model is established, and then through the AHP analytic hierarchy process, the weight of the user's demand is analyzed, and the user's demand preference is obtained. Finally, combined with the concept of service design, the paper puts forward the design strategy of instant translation service. This paper studies the service mode of instant translation, hoping to provide some reference for other related industries to integrate the Internet model.

References

1. Dan, X.: Research on Innovation Design of Walking assistant device Based on Situations. Chang'an University (2019)
2. Liang, J., Wu, J., Qu, J., Yin, H., Qu, X., Gao, Z.: Robust bus bridging service design under rail transit system disruptions. Transp. Res. Part E **132**, 97–116 (2019)
3. Vasconcelos, P., Furtado, E.S., Pinheiro, P., Furtado, L.: Multidisciplinary criteria for the quality of e-learning services design. Comput. Hum. Behav. (2019)
4. Alves, T., Natálio, J., Henriques-Calado, J., Gama, S.: Incorporating personality in user interface design: a review. Pers. Individ. Differ. **155** (2020)

Deadlock-Free and Collision-Free Liver Surgical Navigation by Switching Potential-Based and Sensor-Based Functions

Hiroshi Noborio[1,2,3,4(✉)], Kiyomi Kawai[1,2,3,4], Kaoru Watanabe[1],
Katsunori Tachibana[2], Takahiro Kunii[3], and Kiminori Mizushino[4]

[1] Department of Computer Science, Osaka Electro-Communication University,
Kiyotaki 1130-70, Shijyo-Nawate, Osaka 572-0063, Japan
nobori@osakac.ac.jp
[2] Department of Biomedical Engineering, Osaka Electro-Communication
University, Kiyotaki 1130-70, Shijyo-Nawate, Osaka 572-0063, Japan
[3] Kashina System Co., Hirata-Cho 116-22, Hikone, Shiga 522-0041, Japan
[4] Embedded Wings Co., Ine 5-2-3, Minoh, Osaka 562-0015, Japan

Abstract. In this study, we developed a deadlock-free and collision-free liver surgical navigation method by switching potential-based and sensor-based approaches. The potential-based approach selects a near-optimal route from a scalpel tip to an arbitrary neighbor position around a tumor in a 3D organ map converted from digital imaging and communications in medicine (DICOM) data captured by magnetic resonance imaging or computed tomography. However, among complex-shaped blood vessels, the approach sometimes loses the route. To overcome this drawback, we switch to the sensor-based approach. This approach always finds a route near a tumor. However, the path becomes longer. Therefore, when the potential-based approach recovers to find another path, we switch the sensor-based approach back to the potential-based approach. The usefulness of this switching method was carefully ascertained in several kinds of allocations of tumor and blood vessels.

Keywords: Potential-based navigation · Sensor-based navigation · Triangular polyhedron stereolithography · Liver surgery navigator · Deadlock-free property · Local minima

1 Introduction and History of Our Research

In the past decade, development of xR mixing virtual reality (VR), mixed reality (MR), and augmented reality (AR) has been intensely pursued around the world [1]. In the medical field, many techniques working in xR are aggressively used. Since the 1970s, many basic techniques and system have been developed in biomedical engineering, such as computed tomography (CT), magnetic resonance imaging (MRI), and digital imaging and communications in medicine (DICOM), as well as the da Vinci surgical robot (Si). Among them, we focus here on many surgical navigation systems based on the abovementioned imaging and robotics systems [2–7].

© Springer Nature Switzerland AG 2020
M. Kurosu (Ed.): HCII 2020, LNCS 12183, pp. 604–622, 2020.
https://doi.org/10.1007/978-3-030-49065-2_42

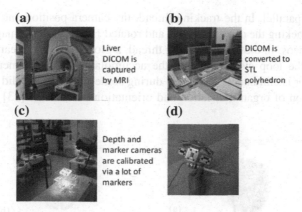

Fig. 1. (a) Pig liver captured by MRI, (b) STL polyhedron converted from DICOM of pig liver, (c) calibrated depth cameras by many active markers, (d) our scalpel with many markers. This pig experiment was performed at the Kobe Medical Device Development Center (MEDDEC).

Almost all surgical navigators involve the use of a 3D mechanical or 2D non-mechanical probe with ultrasonic sensors. However, because of the insufficient image resolution of ultrasonic sensors, the system cannot detect position, orientation, and shape when manipulating a real liver precisely in surgical navigation. Instead, a system can capture translation and rotation motions of a real liver and deformation of the real liver by stereo vision of a 3D camera with real markers. However, the system cannot locate any artificial markers on a real liver because of damage left in the liver after the surgical operation (Figs. 1 and 2).

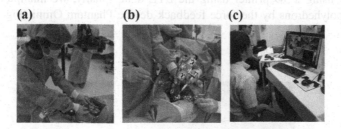

Fig. 2. (a) Many active landmarks on a pig liver, (b) scalpel with many landmarks, (c) overlapping check in real and virtual livers of pig experiment. This pig experiment was performed at the Kobe Medical Device Development Center (MEDDEC).

Therefore, we chose the simultaneous localization and mapping (SLAM) technique to identify the position, orientation, and shape of a real liver precisely by using artificially selected markers [8–10] in place of real markers. The SLAM method grasps the shape of the surrounding environment and estimates its own position and orientation using the shape data. In our system, we used partially modified ORB-SLAM2 [11] as the SLAM library. In ORB-SLAM2, three threads of tracking, local mapping, and loop closing run in parallel. In the tracking thread, the camera position and orientation are estimated by tracking the oriented FAST and rotated BRIEF (ORB) image features [12] in the input videos. In the local mapping thread, a global map and a camera position is displayed. In the loop closing thread, the accumulation of the camera position and orientation error is eliminated. However, during some surgeries, we did not sufficiently test the precision of organ translation and orientation movements [13] (Fig. 3).

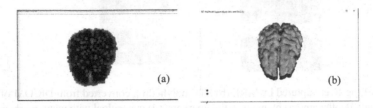

(a)   (b)

Fig. 3. (a) Many passive landmarks selected by SLAM on the real brain. (b) A real brain (colored red) is traced by its virtual brain (colored pink) by using movements of passive landmarks. (Color figure online)

Using the algorithms described herein, we initially capture the patient's liver, its blood vessels, and tumors by DICOM data by MRI or CT. Then, we convert the volumes of the liver, its blood vessels, and tumors into several stereolithography (STL) polyhedrons by using 3D Slicer software (Slicer). This software is a free and open-source software package for image analysis [14] and scientific visualization. STL is employed to maintain the visual quality and to rapidly calculate a depth image using the Z-buffer of the graphical processing unit (GPU). We constructed a plastic replica of a real liver using a 3D printer using the STL data. Finally, we manipulate the STL formatted polyhedrons by the force feedback device Phantom Omni (Fig. 4).

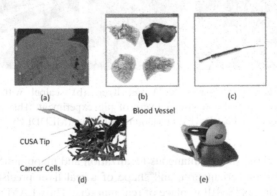

(a)   (b)   (c)

Blood Vessel

CUSA Tip

Cancer Cells

(d)   (e)

Fig. 4. (a) Liver DICOM data; (b) whole liver, arteries, veins, and portal vein STL; (c) scalpel CUSA; (d) Simulator screen; (e) Phantom Omni [29].

Moreover, we built a tracking system such that a virtual liver (organ) follows its real liver (organ). For this purpose, we proposed depth-depth matching (DDM) of virtual and real depth images among the narrow part [15–17] (Fig. 5). For this purpose, we use a smart depth camera to precisely capture a depth image of a manipulated real liver. The merit of using the depth image for a real liver is that it is easy to compare the virtual depth image efficiently calculated by GPU Z-buffering against its virtual liver. Furthermore, in order for a virtual liver image to coincide with a real liver image, we investigated the position and orientation of a virtual liver in six-degrees-of-freedom space using 3D Euclidean coordinates. In the search, we prepare a large number of neighbor directions for moving the virtual liver to check the coincidence. For this reason, depth-depth matching should not be time consuming. The depth image of a virtual liver comes from the GPU Z-buffer for a virtual liver modeled by STL data. On the other hand, the depth image of a real liver comes from a depth image by an arbitrary depth camera. Thus, in our depth-depth matching, we need only $K \times L$ subtractions between virtual and real depths in $K \times L$ image pixels (K and L are selected for some depth camera; both values are usually near 1,000).

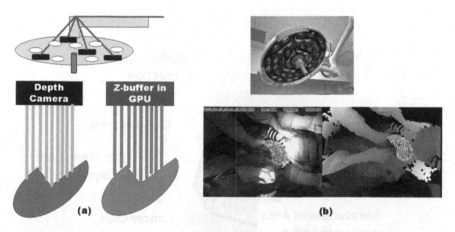

Fig. 5. By minimizing the sum of square differences between real and virtual depths in all the pixels, we seek overlapping position and orientation between real and virtual livers.

This calculation is much faster than using the popular iterative closest point (ICP) algorithm in the Point Cloud Library (PCL) for checking the coincidence of two kinds of point clouds of whole objects [18–24]. The ICP is quite time consuming because it needs $M \times N$ combinatorial calculations of 3D Euclidean distances (M and N are usually near 100,000). Addition and subtraction of 2D depths is thus much faster than the Euclidean distance calculation of 3D cloud points.

This paper is organized as follows. Section 2 describes the GPU-based fast calculation of the Euclidean distance between two position. Section 3 shows the two types of navigation algorithms, sensor-based and potential-based. Then, we show how to switch both algorithms for maintaining the deadlock-free property and near-optimal property. In Sect. 4, we describe simulation results in several different 3D environments with blood vessels and tumors. Finally, Sect. 5 briefly summarizes our research.

2 Calculation of the Euclidean Distance from a Scalpel Tip to a Tumor or Blood Vessels

As an intelligent system for supporting surgeons, we have already developed software that calculates the shortest Euclidean distance from the tip of the scalpel to a blood vessel or malignant tumor [25, 26] (Fig. 6). However, if multiple pieces of such distance information are provided to a physician simultaneously, the act of attempting to interpret all this information during surgery causes stress to the physician and triggers confusion during surgery.

In order to address this challenge, this study used a haptic feedback device, Phantom Omni, to change the approach from visually displaying multiple pieces of distance information to providing a single tactile presentation of optimum navigation force, thus enabling physicians to manipulate the scalpel in an optimum manner. The grip of the Phantom Omni has approximately the same size as the grip of a real scalpel, albeit somewhat thicker; therefore, it is possible to perform simulated surgical operations in a manner that feels similar to a real operation (Fig. 4).

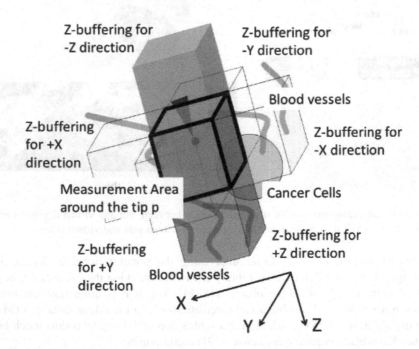

Fig. 6. Area in which it is possible to measure the smallest Euclidean distance to vascular networks or cancerous cells where the following six Z-buffering areas overlap: the +X direction, −X direction, +Y direction, −Y direction, +Z direction, and −Z direction [25]. (Color figure online)

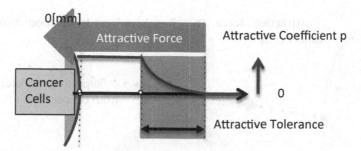

Fig. 7. Cancerous tissue attraction at point p.

3   Potential-Based and Sensor-Based Approaches and Their Switching

In this section, we explain potential-based and sensor-based approaches. Then, we explain how to switch the approaches among a 3D environment with complicated blood vessels and tumors.

The potential method, a type of motion programming, is often used for obstacle avoidance in robots; numerous reports related to this method have been published [27, 28]. The potential method uses environment information obtained in advance to establish two types of potential functions. The first function generates the attraction toward a target point (Fig. 7). The second function generates the repulsion from an obstacle (Fig. 8). The superposition of these functions on each other creates a potential field for the entire space and generates the appropriate amount of force to guide the robot to any location in that space (Fig. 9). Further, recent studies have explored the scenario in which this force is displayed to the robot operator during robotic surgery [26, 27].

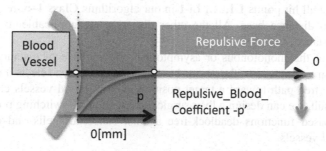

Fig. 8. Cancerous tissue repulsion at point p.

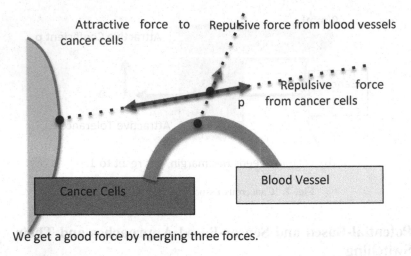

Fig. 9. Combination of repulsion vector and attraction vector at point p

In a surgical navigation, the first function generates the attractive force near cancerous cells. The second function generates the repulsive force from blood vessels. By using this navigation system, the scalpel tip can be automatically guided around cancerous cells without cutting any blood vessels [29]. Using the potential approach, we can easily select a near-shortest route from the tip of the scalpel around the malignant tumor. However, if shape and location of blood vessels are complicated, it is difficult to find a deadlock-free and collision-free route near the malignant tumor. The reason is that the repulsive and attractive forces are completely balanced.

In order to overcome this obstacle, we use sensor-based navigation using local geometrical information. In this, we selected our algorithms **Class 1–5** [30, 31] among many other algorithms [32]. The algorithms are distinguished as follows: A present position (scalpel in surgery or mobile robot in navigation) always leaves a point **Li** whose distance toward the target point is closer than the closest point **C**; the previous hit point **Hi**; the previous leave point **Li-1**; the average of all hit points **H1, …, Hi**; and the average of all hit points **L1, …, Li-1** in our algorithms **Class 1–5**, respectively, on the Euclidean distance base. All the other distances are applicable in place of the Euclidean distance.

Because of the monotonous or asymptotical convergence of distance toward the target position near a tumor, the sensor-based approach always selects a collision-free and deadlock-free path toward a target position even in blood vessels cluttered in an organ. As result, we can design a liver surgical navigation by switching potential-based and sensor-based functions deadlock-free against cancerous cells and collision-free against blood vessels.

```
[Navi]
atractionCoefficient=1.0000
repulsionCoefficient=2.0000
repulsionBloodCoefficient=1.0000
atractionTolerance=0.0050
repulsionTolerance=0.0050
margin=0.0100
maxBloodVesselDistance=0.0050
[Cut]
firePower=0.0050
fireRadius=0.0020
[SensorNavi]
step=0.0200
sensorMargin=5.0000
radius=1.0000
sensorDpmm=10.0000
sensorWidth=5.0000
sensorHeight=5.0000
sensorAlgorithm=1.0000
sensorType=4.0000
sensorStepCount=1500.0000
area=2
fovDegree=90.0000
[ColorTumor]
r=0.0
g=1.0
b=0.0
a=1.0
[ColorNavi]
r=0.0
g=1.0
b=0.0
a=0.7
```

Fig. 10. All the selected parameters in our potential-based approach.

The potential functions (parameters) set in this study are as follows (Fig. 10):

- The distance that specifies the location of the start of excision: Attractive_Coefficient
- The function that specifies the distance at which attraction to cancerous cells begins to be returned to the physician: Attractive_Tolerance
- The function that sets the size of the repulsion from cancerous cells: Repulsive_Coefficient
- The function that specifies the distance at which repulsion from cancerous cells is generated: Repulsive_Tolerance
- The function that specifies the distance at which repulsion from blood vessels is generated: Repulsive_Blood_Vessel_Coefficient
- The function that sets the distance at which repulsion from blood vessels begins to be returned to the physician: Max_Blood_Vessel_Distance

```
[SensorNavi]
step=0.0200
sensorMargin=5.0000
radius=1.0000
sensorDpmm=10.0000
sensorWidth=5.0000
sensorHeight=5.0000
sensorAlgorithm=1.0000
sensorType=3.0000
sensorStepCount=1500.0000
area=1
fovDegree=90.0000
```

Fig. 11. All the selected parameters in our sensor-based approach.

In addition to cancerous cells, the surroundings of these cells are also excised according to the potential functions because there is a strong possibility of the existence of metastases in the surrounding cells. In this section, figures are used to explain the amount of force generated in the scalpel tip by each function. In Figs. 7 and 8, **p** denotes the location of the scalpel tip, **d** and **dv** represent the smallest value of the positive Euclidean distance from cancerous cells or blood vessel groups to the CUSA (Cavitron ultrasonic surgical aspirator) scalpel tip, and **dmar** and **dvmar** represent the distance margin used for the generation of the attraction to or the repulsion from cancerous cells or blood vessel groups. We measure **dmar** and **dvmar** as positive Euclidean distances from cancerous cells or blood vessel groups to the CUSA tip.

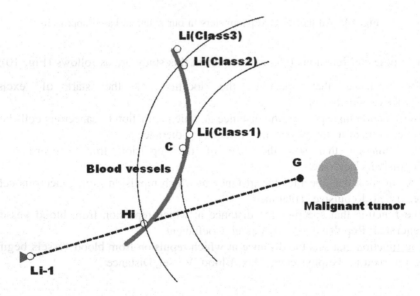

Fig. 12. Monotonous convergence of the leave point in the sensor-based approaches Class 1–3 (Const.).

In our study, the smallest value for the Euclidean distance from the scalpel tip to a blood vessel group or from the scalpel tip to cancerous cells determined the measurement range for the shortest distance calculation algorithm [25, 26] from scalpel to blood vessel group using the general-purpose graphics processing unit (GPGPU) that we proposed previously, and established the area (the area contained within the dotted line) for the measurement of d and dv (the smallest value of the positive Euclidean distance from cancerous cells or blood vessel groups to the CUSA scalpel tip) in all directions (360°) in a space by superimposing the range for the six directions of Z-buffering (the light purple, light blue, and light yellow-colored areas in Fig. 6): the +X direction, −X direction, +Y direction, −Y direction, +Z direction, and −Z direction.

- Cancerous tissue attraction at point **p**: **n = max(0, min(d − dmar, Attractive_Tolerance))/Attractive_Tolerance** (note that n is always normalized within [0, 1]), **p = Attractive_Coefficient × (1 − n)²**
- Cancerous tissue repulsion at point **p**: **n = max(0, min(dmar − d, Repulsive_Tolerance))/Repulsive_Tolerance** (n is normalized within [0, 1]), **p = Repulsive_Coefficient × n²**
- Blood vessel repulsion at point **p**: **n = max(0, min(dvmar − dv, dvmar))/dvmar** (n is within [0, 1]), **p = Repulsive_Blood_Vessel_Coefficient × (1 − n)²**

These three formulas are used to combine the repulsion vector and the attraction vector generated at the scalpel tip location **p** to yield a merged vector.

As contrasted with this, in the sensor-based algorithm, we use a depth map to calculate the Euclidean minimum distance [25, 26] from a scalpel to three kinds of blood vessels or bad tumors. The depth map is usually defined as the following parameters (Fig. 11):

- Step: The movement distance (mm) of the scalpel per sampling time in our simulation
- sensorMargin: The closest Euclidean distance (mm) from the scalpel to some blood vessels
- radius: The acceptable margin which a scalpel collides with a blood vessel (mm)
- sensorDpmm: The pixel number per depth map of 1 mm
- sensorWidth: The width of the depth map (mm)
- sensorHeight: The height of the depth map (mm)
- sensorAlgorithm: The five types of sensor-based approaches, Class 1–5
- sensorType: The five kinds of projective methods (from the perspective to the parallel projection) in the Z-buffer of the GPU
- sensorStepCount: The upper bound of Step number
- Area: The area for averaging pixels
- fovDegree: The upper and lower angle against the X axis defined as the moving direction of the scalpel, where we get tumor or blood vessels.

3.1   The Algorithms Class 1 (Const.) and Class 1 (Alter.)

In this section, we explain details of a classic algorithm **Class 1 (const.)** and its revised algorithm **Class 1 (alter.)** (Fig. 12).

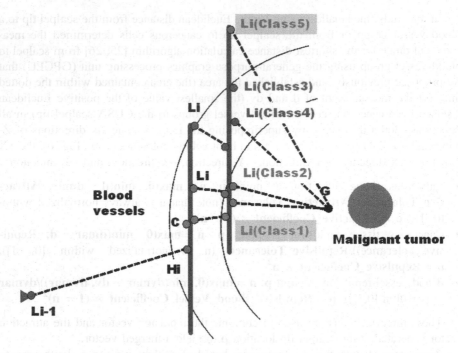

Fig. 13. Asymptotical convergence of the leave point in the sensor-based approaches Class 1–5 (Const.).

[Step 1] Set j = 1, a scalpel position *np* and a leave position *lj-1*, and a closest position *cj-1* by a start position *ns*.

[Step 2] Move a neighbor position *ni* of *np* by the step along the segment between centers of *np* and an arbitrary goal position *ng* around a tumor.

[Step 2(a)] If *ni* is an arbitrary goal position *ng* near a tumor, exit with success.

[Step 2(b)] If *ni* is a *Free* position that is outside the safety area around blood vessels, set *np* by *ni* and then continue; otherwise, set a hit position *hj* and a closest position *cj (j = j + 1)* by *np* and go to step 3.

[Step 3] Select a neighbor Free position *ni* of *np* by one of the clockwise and counter-clockwise orders, which is adjacent to a neighbor *Obs* position that is inside the safety area around blood vessels until one of the following occurs.

The following order is fixed in advance in **Class 1 (const.)**; on the other hand, it is alternatively changed in **Class 1 (alter.)**.

[Step 3(a)] If *ni* is a goal position *ng* near a tumor, exit with success.

[Step 3(a)] If *ni* is closer to *ng* than the closest position *cj*, reset *cj* by *ni* only in the algorithm **Class 1**. Then, if *ni* is closer to *ng* than the closest position *cj* in the algorithm **Class 1**, the previous hit point *hj* in the algorithm **Class 2**, the previous leave point *lj-1* in the algorithm **Class 3**, the average of all the previous hit points in the algorithm **Class 4**, the average of all the previous leave points in the algorithm **Class 5** and simultaneously the direction from *ni* to ng is *Free* position (that is, a few positions from *ni* to *ng* are *Free* position), regard *ni* as a leave position *lj* and return to step 2 (Fig. 13).

[Step 3(c)] If *ni* equals to the last hit position *hj*, exit with failure.

In both algorithms **Class 1 (const.)** and **Class 1 (alter.)**, leave and hit positions (*lj* and *hj*) monotonically approach *ng*, and consequently np arrives at *ng* finally if a path (a sequence of *Free* positions) between *ns* and *ng* exists in a given map. Otherwise, a point scalpel *np* automatically recognizes no solution (path) between ns and ng in an unknown map by returning the last hit position *hj* without finding a leave point *lj*.

3.2   How to Switch the Potential-Based and Sensor-Based Approaches

First, the potential-based approach automatically leads a scalpel near a tumor while avoiding blood vessels. However, if the potential-based approach cannot move the scalpel because of the balance of attractive and reactive forces, we switch the potential-based approach into the sensor-based approach (Figs. 14, 15, 16).

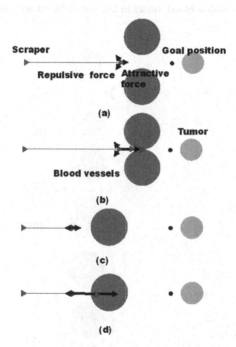

Fig. 14. (a) and (b) Deadlock around a concave obstacle. (c) and (d) Deadlock around a convex obstacle.

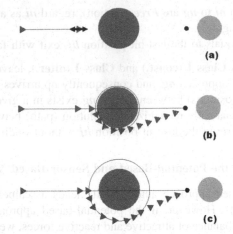

Fig. 15. (a) Deadlock occurring around multiple obstacles by the potential-based approach. (b) and (c) Deadlock-free path toward a goal position around two types of acceptable margins, where a scalpel collides with a blood vessel in the sensor-based approach.

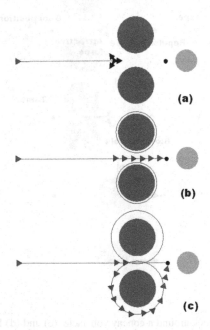

Fig. 16. (a) Deadlock occurring around a single obstacle by the potential-based approach. (b) and (c) Deadlock-free path toward a goal position around two types of acceptable margins where a scalpel collides with a blood vessel in the sensor-based approach.

The sensor-based approach leads the scalpel to trace around blood vessels. The sensor-based approach always finds some leave point around blood vessels to go near the tumor without any deadlock. The leave point is selected under three conditions: (1) It is monotonously or asymptotically closer than the closest position *cj* in the algorithm Class 1, the previous hit point *hj* in the algorithm **Class 2**, the previous leave point *lj-1* in the algorithm **Class 3**, the average of all the previous hit points in the algorithm **Class 4**, and the average of all the previous leave points in the algorithm **Class 5**. (2) At the leave point, the direction toward the tumor is not obstructed by any blood vessels. (3) At the leave point, a force merging the attractive and reactive forces is active.

4 Simulation Results

In this section, we describe three different surgical scenarios with different tumor positions. In all cases, switching potential-based and sensor-based approaches is successively achieved, and consequently a reasonable surgical route near a tumor is recommended for the surgeon in real time.

4.1 First Allocation of Tumor and Blood Vessels

In this simulation, we allocated a tumor in the right side of blood vessels (Fig. 17). In this result, the switching between potential and sensor-based approaches always selects a near-optimal path from the left side near a tumor, which is colored light blue.

4.2 Second Allocation of Tumor and Blood Vessels

In this simulation, we allocated a tumor in the middle of blood vessels (Fig. 18). In this result, the switching between potential and sensor-based approaches always selects a near-optimal path from the left side near a tumor, which is colored light blue.

4.3 Third Allocation of Tumor and Brood Vessels

In this simulation, we allocated a tumor in the left side of blood vessels (Fig. 19). In this result, the switching between potential and sensor-based approaches always selects a near-optimal path from the left side near a tumor, which is colored light blue.

Fig. 17. Near-optimal route toward a right-side tumor colored by light blue is selected by our switching navigation algorithm: (a) Front view, (b) side view, (c) focusing view, (d) total view. (Color figure online)

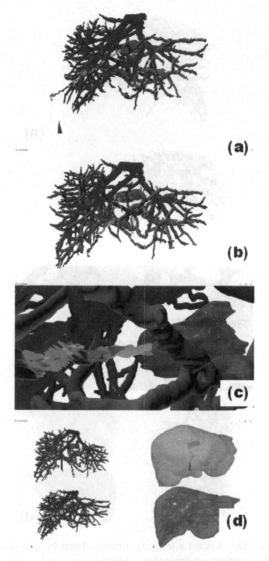

Fig. 18. Near-optimal route toward a middle tumor colored by light blue is selected by our switching navigation algorithm: (a) Front view, (b) side view, (c) focusing view, (d) total view. (Color figure online)

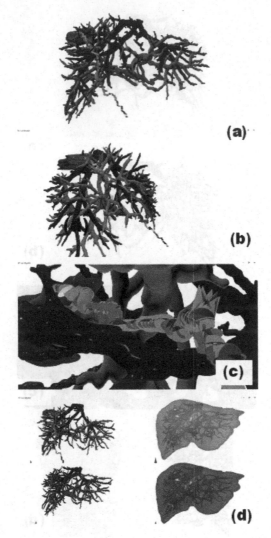

Fig. 19. Near-optimal route toward a left-side tumor colored by light blue is selected by our switching navigation algorithm: (a) Front view, (b) side view, (c) focusing view, (d) total view. (Color figure online)

5   Conclusion

In this study, we developed a switching method between potential-based and sensor-based approaches in a virtual organ with a complex-shaped tumor and blood vessels. Using the switching, a surgeon always knows a near-optimal route near a bad tumor while avoiding all the blood vessels. In a cluttered 3D environment with complex-shaped blood vessels, this route is quite useful for a surgeon. In future, as a total system for liver surgical navigation, we will use the switching between potential-based and sensor-based approaches during a real surgery.

Acknowledgment. This study was supported partly by 2014 Grants-in-Aid for Scientific Research (B) (No. 26289069) and 2017 Grants-in-Aid for Scientific Research (C) (No. 17K00420) from the Ministry of Education, Culture, Sports, Science, and Technology, Japan. Further support was provided by the 2014 Cooperation Research Fund from the Graduate School at Osaka Electro-Communication University. We would like to thank Editage (www. editage.com) for English language editing.

References

1. World Forum for Medicine. https://www.medica-tradefair.com/
2. Peterhans, M., et al.: A navigation system for open liver surgery: design, workflow and first clinical applications. Int. J. Med. Robot. **7**(1), 7 16 (2011)
3. Nicolas, C.B., et al.: Augmented environments for the targeting of hepatic lesions during image-guided robotic liver surgery. J. Surg. Res. **184**(2), 825–831 (2013)
4. Satou, S., et al.: Initial experience of intraoperative three-dimensional navigation for liver resection using real-time virtual sonography. J. Surg. **155**(2), 255–262 (2014)
5. Pessaux, P., Diana, M., Soler, L., Piardi, T., Mutter, D., Marescaux, J.: Towards cybernetic surgery: robotic and augmented reality-assisted liver segmentectomy. Langenbecks Arch. Surg. **400**(3), 381–385 (2015)
6. Morita, Y., Takanishi, K., Matsumoto, J.: A new simple navigation for anatomic liver resection under intraoperative real-time ultrasound guidance. Hepatogastroenterology **61** (34), 1734–1738 (2014)
7. Mahmud, N., Cohen, J., Tsourides, K., Berzin, T.M.: Computer vision and augmented reality in gastrointestinal endoscopy. Gastroenterol. Rep. (Oxf.) **3**(3), 179–184 (2015)
8. Smith, R., Cheeseman, P.: On the representation and estimation of spatial uncertainty. Int. J. Robot. Res. **5**(4), 56–68 (1986)
9. Brooks, R.A.: Visual map making for a mobile robot. In: Proceedings of the IEEE International Conference Robotics and Automation, pp. 824–829. IEEE, St. Louis (1985)
10. Chatila, R., Laumond, J-P.: Position referencing and consistent world modeling for mobile robots. In: Proceedings of the IEEE International Conference on Robotics and Automation, pp. 138–145. IEEE, St. Louis (1985)
11. Mur-Artal, R., Tardós, J.D.: ORB-SLAM2: an open-source SLAM system for monocular, stereo and RGB-D cameras. IEEE Trans. Robot. **33**(5), 1255–1262 (2017)
12. Konolige K., Bradski, G.R.: ORB: an efficient alternative to SIFT or SURF. In: Proceedings of the 2011 International Conference on Computer Vision, pp. 2564–2571 (2011)
13. Koeda, M., Nishimoto, S., Noborio, H., Watanabe, K.: Proposal and evaluation of AR-based microscopic brain surgery support system. In: Kurosu, M. (ed.) HCII 2019. LNCS, vol. 11567, pp. 458–468. Springer, Cham (2019). https://doi.org/10.1007/978-3-030-22643-5_36
14. Pieper, S., Halle, M., Kikinis, R.: 3D slicer. In: Proceedings of the 1st IEEE International Symposium on Biomedical Imaging: From Nano to Macro, pp. 632–635 (2004)
15. Noborio, H., et al.: Motion transcription algorithm by matching corresponding depth image and Z-buffer. In: Proceedings of the 10th Anniversary Asian Conference on Computer Aided Surgery, pp. 60–61, Kyusyu University, Fukuoka (2014)
16. Noborio, H., et al.: Experimental results of 2D depth-depth matching algorithm based on depth camera Kinect v1. J. Bioinf. Neurosci. **1**(1), 38–44 (2015). ISSN: 2188-8116

17. Watanabe, K., et al.: Parameter identification of depth-depth-matching algorithm for liver following. J. Teknologi Med. Eng. **77**(6), 35–39 (2015). https://doi.org/10.11113/jt.v77.6224. Penerbit UTM Press, E-ISSN 2180-3722

18. Besl, P.J., McKay, N.D.: A method for registration of 3-D shapes. IEEE Trans. Pattern Anal. Mach. Intell. **14**(2), 239–256 (1992)

19. Zhang, Z.: Iterative point matching for registration of free-form surfaces. Int. J. Comput. Vis. **13**(2), 119–152 (1994)

20. Granger, S., Pennec, X.: Multi-scale EM-ICP: a fast and robust approach for surface registration. In: Heyden, A., Sparr, G., Nielsen, M., Johansen, P. (eds.) ECCV 2002. LNCS, vol. 2353, pp. 418–432. Springer, Heidelberg (2002). https://doi.org/10.1007/3-540-47979-1_28

21. Liu, Y.: Automatic registration of overlapping 3D point clouds using closest points. J. Image Vis. Comput. **24**(7), 762–778 (2006)

22. Salvi, J., Matabosch, C., Fofi, D., Forest, J.: A review of recent range image registration methods with accuracy evaluation. J. Image Vis.-Comput. **25**, 578–596 (2007)

23. Rusu, R.B., Cousins, S.: 3D is here: point cloud library (PCL). In: Proceedings of IEEE International Conference Robotics and Automation, pp. 1 – 4 (2011)

24. Wu, Y.F., Wang, W., Lu, K.Q., Wei, Y.D., Chen, Z.C.: A new method for registration of 3D point sets with low overlapping ratios. In: Proceedings of 13th CIRP Conference on Computer Aided Tolerancing, pp. 202 – 206 (2015)

25. Noborio, H., Kunii, T., Mizushino, K.: Omni-directional shortest distance algorithm by complete parallel-processing based on GPU cores. Int. J. Biosci. Biochem. Bioinf. **8**(2), 79–88 (2018). https://doi.org/10.17706/ijbbb.2018.8.2.79-88. ISSN: 2010-3638

26. Noborio, H., Kunii, T., Mizushino, K.: GPU-based shortest distance algorithm for liver surgery navigation. In: Proceedings of 10th Anniversary Asian Conference Computer Aided Surgery, pp. 42–43 (2014)

27. Khatib, O.: Real-time obstacle avoidance for manipulators and mobile robots. Int. J. Robot. Res. **5**(1), 90–98 (1986). https://doi.org/10.1177/027836498600500106

28. Schulman, J., et al.: Motion planning with sequential convex optimization and convex collision checking. Int. J. Robot. Res. **33**(9), 1251–1270 (2014)

29. Noborio, H., Aoki, K., Kunii, T., Mizushino, K.: A potential function-based scalpel navigation method that avoids blood vessel groups during excision of cancerous tissue. In: Proceedings of the 38th Annual International Conference of the IEEE Engineering in Medicine and Biology Society (EMBC 2016), pp. 6106–6112 (2016)

30. Noborio, H.: A sufficient condition for designing a family of sensor-based deadlock-free path-planning algorithms. J. Adv. Robot. **7**(5), 413–433 (1993)

31. Noborio, H.: On a sensor-based navigation for a mobile robot. J. Robot. Mechatron. **8**(1), 2–14 (1996)

32. McGuire, K., Croon, G., Tuyls, K.: A comparative study of bug algorithms for robot navigation. J. Robot. Auton. Syst. **121** (2019). https://doi.org/10.1016/j.robot.2019.103261

Study on the Development of Augmented-Reality Navigation System for Transsphenoidal Surgery

Katsuhiko Onishi[1]([⊠]), Seiyu Fumiyama[1], Yohei Miki[1],
Masahiro Nonaka[2], Masanao Koeda[1], and Hiroshi Noborio[1]

[1] Osaka Electro-Communication University, Shijonawate, Japan
onishi@oecu.jp
[2] Kansai Medical University, Hirakata, Japan

Abstract. In this study, we developed an augmented-reality (AR) navigation system that can assist surgeons during transsphenoidal surgery, including identification of the tumor site. Since transsphenoidal surgery is performed by looking at an endoscopic image, thus requiring situational judgment on the image, transsphenoidal surgery poses greater challenges with regard to grasping the positional relationships between the tumor and the organs compared with normal operations. The proposed system is expected to help surgeons understand the conditions surrounding the operating field, by intraoperatively displaying a real-time overlaid 3D model based on preoperative MRI images of the patient.

Markers were used to obtain the data necessary to view the overlaid images, which were attached to the operating table and to the end of the endoscope. The patient's head was held in a fixed position during the surgery. The relative positions of the maker on the operating table and the feature point on the patient's head were captured by a camera mounted on top of the operating table. Then, using this information, the positions of the tumor and the organs were estimated, and a 3D model was created using the patient's MRI scans. Further, by obtaining the relative position of the markers attached to the end and tip of the endoscope, the position of the tip of the endoscope was estimated from the marker at the end even if it could not be seen from outside after inserting it into the patient's body during surgery. The relative positions of the tip of the endoscope and the tumor site were calculated, and a 3D model was displayed using the MRI images in conjunction with the current endoscopic image. By constantly updating the positional information in accordance with the behavior of the endoscope, the overlaid image of the tumor and the organs could be viewed. In this study, we developed a prototype of the proposed system, and discussed the accuracy of its results.

Keywords: Camera position and orientation estimation · Marker-based augmented reality · Surgical navigation system · Transsphenoidal surgery

M. Kurosu (Ed.): HCII 2020, LNCS 12183, pp. 623–638, 2020.
https://doi.org/10.1007/978-3-030-49065-2_43

1 Introduction

Transsphenoidal surgery is an operation that removes tumors (pituitary adenomas) developed in the part of the brain called the pituitary gland. The pituitary gland is involved in hormone production, with a size of approximately 1 cm, and connected to the base of the brain through a thin tube. It is located in the depression (sella turcica) at the center of the skull, and is seated further inside the nasal cavity behind the nose. The enlargement of pituitary adenomas broadly produces two symptoms: visual-field defects and abnormal hormone secretion. Visual-field defects include bitemporal hemianopsia, which means loss of vision on the temporal side triggered by the oppression on the optic chiasm, as well as tunnel vision. As for abnormal hormone secretion, since pituitary adenomas can affect various hormones, symptoms can also vary.

In transsphenoidal surgery, surgeons approach the brain from the nostrils to remove tumors. In general, an endoscope is inserted from the left nostril and a dissecting instrument from the right nostril. As the bone inside the nose is resected, the instrument reaches a cavity called the sphenoidal sinus. From there, the bottom part of the bone called sella turcica, which contains the pituitary gland, can be observed. As this bone is shaved, a white membrane (dura mater) appears. As the dura mater is incised, the pituitary gland can be seen; this is where the tumor is located. The incision of the intranasal membrane and tumorectomy must be carried out by looking at the endoscopic image. Drilling the smallest possible hole in the skull must be done in close proximity to the tumor. Thus, the surgeon needs to determine the location of the incision by comparing the endoscopic image and the MRI images of the patient, which requires deep knowledge and skills.

Currently, assisting systems for transsphenoidal surgery include the simulation systems for surgical training and the navigation systems for grasping circumstances surrounding the operating field during surgery. With regard to simulation systems, many researchers have proposed endoscopic surgery training systems that utilize a 3D model, which helps surgeons to locate the tumor position in three dimensions intuitively [1–4]. Meanwhile, dominant navigation systems display the current position of the endoscope in a separate screen from that of the two-dimensional endoscopic image.

Accordingly, in this study we examined an assistance navigation system based on AR that allows us to view information close to the affected site overlaid on the operating field image, to reduce the load on the surgeon. It seeks to assist the surgeon ascertain the circumstances surrounding the operating field, by viewing a 3D model overlaid on the endoscopic image using the navigation system. Specifically, we considered a technique to estimate the position and orientation of the endoscopic camera, and developed a method of viewing an overlaid 3D model at a preferred location using these measured data. We have hitherto carried out a basic study on the position and orientation of the endoscopic camera [5]. In this study, we developed a prototype that improved on the previous device, and therefore we discussed the results of measurement of the position and orientation of the endoscopic camera, measurement accuracy assessment, and the image overlay method in this article.

2 Proposed System

The proposed system provides an image of the tumor and the organs to be overlaid on the endoscopic image during surgery. The image overlay consists of two algorithms. The first is the position and orientation estimation system, which estimates the position and orientation from the coordinates of markers necessary for image overlay. The second is the image overlay system, for matching the actual positional relationships with the positional relationships of the 3D model in the virtual space (Fig. 1).

The position and orientation estimation system estimates the position and orientation of the tip of the endoscope and the position and orientation of the tumors and organs [5 7] by reading the markers. To read markers, a camera (external camera) is placed on top of the operating table. The relative vector from the marker from the end to the tip of the endoscope is obtained for estimating the position and orientation of the tip of the endoscope (Fig. 2). The position and orientation of the tip of the endoscope can always be obtained from the position and orientation and the relative vector of the marker at the end. As for estimating the position and orientation of the tumor and the organs, a 3D model based on the patient's MRI images was used. The vector from the marker attached to the operating table to the feature point on the head was obtained. Using the position and orientation of the feature point on the head and the corresponding feature point on the 3D model created from MRI images, the positions of the tumor and the organs were estimated. Since the endoscope is rigid, the relative positional relationship with the marker at the end does not change. Furthermore, since the operation is conducted by fixing the patient's head on the operating table, the positional relationship between the marker on the operating table and the head also does not change. Thus, these relative vectors allow constant estimations of the positions of the tip of the endoscope and the tumor using marker information.

The image overlay system must match data retrieved from the external camera with the coordinate system in virtual space to view the 3D model. The tip of the endoscope was determined as the reference point in the virtual space coordinate system. The position and orientation of the tip of the endoscope, as well as the position and orientation of the tumor and the organs in the external camera coordinate system, were converted into those in the virtual space coordinate system. Then, the tumor and the organs were displayed on the endoscopic screen based on converted data.

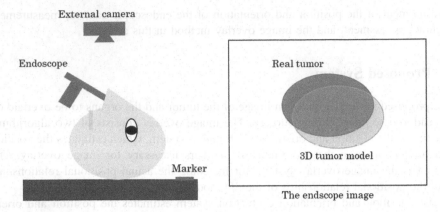

Fig. 1. System operation diagram.

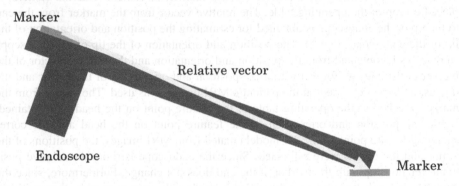

Fig. 2. Estimating the tip of the endoscope.

3 Prototype System

3.1 System Overview

The overall view of the system created for this study is shown in Fig. 3. Markers were read from the external top-mounted camera. ArUco markers were used (Fig. 4) [8, 9], which can be downsized to a minimum of 22 mm. Downsizing the markers reduces their effect on the surgery. The position of the tip was estimated using the relative vector from the marker from the end to the tip of the endoscope. The position and orientation of the tumor and the organs were estimated by using the relative vector from the marker attached to the operating table to the feature point and matching the feature point with the feature point on the 3D model. The estimated positional relationships were converted from the external camera coordinate system to the virtual space coordinate system, and the 3D model was viewed in conjunction with the endoscopic image. The positional relationships in the real space and in the virtual space shift in the similar way, which enables image overlay. In this study, we could not estimate the position or orientation of the tumor or the organs. We checked the shift using a 3D model of the kidney, as we did not have a 3D model of the pituitary adenoma.

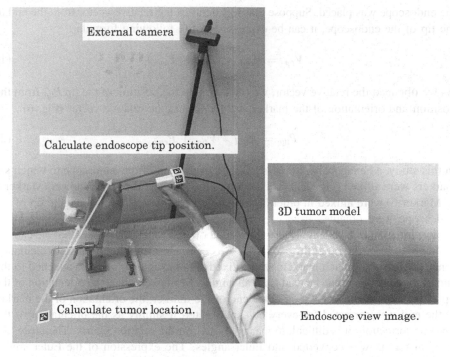

Fig. 3. Image of system implementation.

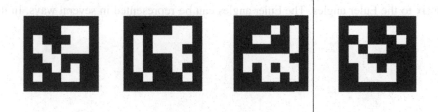

Fig. 4. ArUco markers.

3.2 Estimating the Position and Orientation of the Tip of the Endoscope

The position and orientation estimation system estimates the position and orientation of the tip of the endoscope and the position and orientation of the tumor and the organs. Both of these two estimation techniques use relative vectors. In estimating the position and orientation of the tip of the endoscope, the relative vector from the end to the tip of the endoscopic camera was calculated before surgery (Fig. 5). To calculate the relative vector from the end to the tip of the endoscopic camera, the tip was placed on the marker. Let P_{end}, denote the position of the marker at the end, let R_{end} denote the rotation matrix R_{end}, and let P_{tip}. Denote the position of the marker on which the tip of the endoscope was placed. Suppose that V_{tip} denotes the relative vector from the end to the tip of the endoscope, it can be expressed in the following formula:

$$V_{tip} = R_{end} * (P_{tip} - P_{end}) \tag{1}$$

As we obtained the relative vector, we can estimate the position of the tip P_{tip} from the position and orientation of the marker at the end and the relative vector (Fig. 6).

$$P_{tip} = R_{end} * V_{tip} + P_{end} \tag{2}$$

In this study, a hexagonal prism was attached to the end of the endoscope to which six markers were affixed (Fig. 7). From the top to the side, six different markers (Marker 1 to Marker 6) were affixed in order. The relative vectors used to estimate the tip of the endoscope were obtained from each marker. Since the external camera reads information from the top, six markers can be read at once. From each marker that the camera was able to read, the tip of the endoscope was estimated, and the mean was calculated. Since the prism to which markers were affixed was hexagonal, markers attached to the end of the endoscope can be read from all angles. Moreover, since the orientation of the tip is the same as the orientation of the end of the marker, the orientation of the marker at the end was corrected for every 60° and treated it simply as the orientation of the tip. For correction, it is difficult to manage based on the rotation matrix. Therefore, the rotation matrix was converted into Euler angles. The expression of the Euler angles carries the problem of gimbal lock. The gimbal lock problem occurs when a system is rotated multiple times using the Euler angles and the system loses rotation axes due to parallel alignment of two axes. However, in this study, gimbal lock does not occur because the correction applies only once to the rotation after converting the rotational matrix to the Euler angles. The Euler angles can be represented in several ways. In this

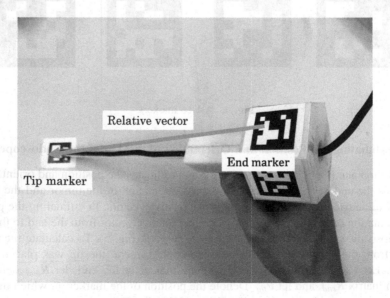

Fig. 5. Relative vector image.

study, we used the z-y-x rotation. To represent the z-y-x rotation uniquely, exception handling must be made.

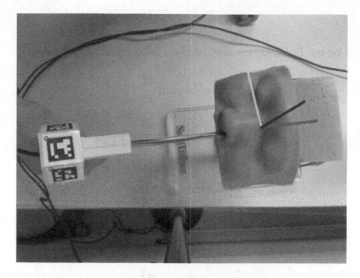

Fig. 6. Estimating the tip position of the endoscope.

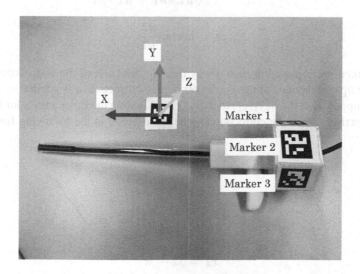

Fig. 7. Endoscope replica.

The rotation matrix is represented in the following formula.

$$R_{mat} = \begin{pmatrix} n1 & n2 & n3 \\ n4 & n5 & n6 \\ n7 & n8 & n9 \end{pmatrix} \quad (3)$$

To check for exceptions, the conversion formula shifts between cases where the exception approximates to zero and cases where it does not.

$$\text{exception} = \sqrt{n1^2 + n2^2} \tag{4}$$

Let $\theta(x, y, z)$ be the Euler angles, and in cases where exception $\fallingdotseq 0$,

$$x = \arctan\frac{n8}{n5} \tag{5}$$

$$y = \arctan\frac{n3}{\sqrt{n1 * n1 + n2 * n2}} \tag{6}$$

$$z = 0 \tag{7}$$

And in other cases,

$$x = \arctan\frac{n6}{n9} \tag{8}$$

$$y = \arctan\frac{n3}{\sqrt{n1 * n1 + n2 * n2}} \tag{9}$$

$$z = \arctan\frac{n2}{n1} \tag{10}$$

Since markers were placed in such a way that the direction of the endoscope from the end to the tip corresponds to the x-axis, 60-degree correction was applied to x for each marker. Suppose that $\theta_1(x_1, y_1, z_1)$ to $\theta_6(x_6, y_6, z_6)$ denote the Euler angles for Markers 1 to 6, respectively, then the correction can be represented in the following formula.

$$x_1 = x_1 \tag{11}$$

$$x_2 = x_2 + \frac{\pi}{3} \tag{12}$$

$$x_3 = x_3 + \frac{2\pi}{3} \tag{13}$$

$$x_4 = x_4 - \pi \tag{14}$$

$$x_5 = x_5 - \frac{2\pi}{3} \tag{15}$$

$$x_6 = x_6 - \frac{\pi}{3} \tag{16}$$

With respect to the position and orientation of the tip as represented by these Euler angles, an estimated value cannot be calculated as intended by simply adding these and calculating the mean because positive and negative values are mixed. Therefore, the corrected estimated orientation must be converted back to the rotation matrix before calculating the mean. The conversion formula is shown below.

$$
R_{mat} = \begin{pmatrix} \cos(\theta.z) & \sin(\theta.z) & 0 \\ -\sin(\theta.z) & \cos(\theta.z) & 0 \\ 0 & 0 & 1 \end{pmatrix} \times \begin{pmatrix} \cos(\theta.y) & 0 & -\sin(\theta.y) \\ 0 & 1 & 0 \\ \sin(\theta.y) & 0 & \cos(\theta.y) \end{pmatrix}
$$
$$
\times \begin{pmatrix} 1 & 0 & 0 \\ 0 & \cos(\theta.x) & \sin(\theta.x) \\ 0 & -\sin(\theta.x) & \cos(\theta.x) \end{pmatrix} \tag{17}
$$

Euler angles for markers that the camera was able to read were all converted to the rotation matrix using the formula (17). Suppose that R_1 to R_6 denote the rotation matrix for each marker, the mean R_{ave} can be calculated by the following formula.

$$
R_{ave} = \frac{\sum_{n=1}^{6} R_n}{6} \tag{18}
$$

The position of the tip P_{tip} can be calculated by the formula (2), and the orientation of the tip R_{ave} can be calculated by the formula (18).

3.3 Estimation of Position and Orientation of Tumor

The relative vectors between the marker on the operating table and several feature points on the head of the patient were calculated (Fig. 8. Estimating the position and orientation of the tumor, etc.). Let P_f be the position of the feature point, R_f be the orientation of the feature point, and P_{table} be the marker of the operating table. Then, the relative vector V_f can be represented by the following formula.

$$
V_f = R_f * (P_f - P_{table}) \tag{19}
$$

By matching the feature point on the head and the corresponding feature point on the 3D model of the patient's head created from MRI images, we hypothesize that the position and orientation of the tumor can be estimated from the marker on the operating table. However, in this study, we could not implement the feature point detection technique and the technique for matching 3-dimensional multiple points.

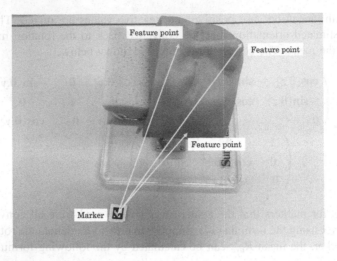

Fig. 8. Estimating the position and orientation of the tumor, etc.

3.4   Image Overlay

In the image overlay system, the position and orientation of the tip of the endoscope and the position and orientation of the tumor and the organs estimated from markers read by the external camera undergo a conversion from the external camera coordinate system to the virtual space coordinate system. Then, a 3D model of the patient is displayed in conjunction with the endoscopic image. The tip of the endoscope is determined as the reference point of the virtual space coordinate system. Suppose that P_{tip}^{cam} denotes the tip position of the endoscope in the external camera coordinate system, R_{tip}^{cam} denotes the tip orientation of the endoscope, P_{model}^{cam} denotes the position of the 3D model, and R_{model}^{cam} denotes the orientation of the 3D model. Then, the position of the 3D model in the virtual space coordinate system as represented by P_{model}^{vr} and the orientation of the 3D model in the virtual space coordinate system as represented by R_{model}^{vr} can be calculated by formula (20) and (21), respectively.

$$P_{model}^{vr} = R_{tip}^{cam} * (P_{model}^{cam} - P_{tip}^{cam}) \tag{20}$$

$$R_{model}^{vr} = R_{tip}^{cam} * R_{model}^{cam} \tag{21}$$

Suppose that the position of the camera in the virtual space is the origin, then by displaying the image from the endoscope in the background and the 3D model in the position of P_{model}^{vr}, the 3D model can be viewed as overlaid on the real image. The 3D model has been color coded and permeabilized before being displayed on the screen (Fig. 9).

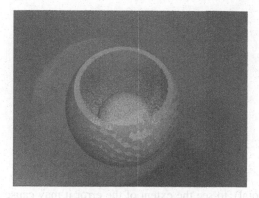

Fig. 9. Image overlay.

4 Basic Experiment

4.1 Experimental Environment

We evaluated the accuracy of the endoscope position estimation method. In the experiment, we confirm whether the same operation is performed in virtual space coordinates when the endoscope is translated. For this purpose, Logitech BRIO c1000e is used as an external camera (Fig. 10). And PROXXON cross table is used as a device to translate the endoscope (Fig. 11). The cross table is an instrument for allowing translation of an object by shifting the stage by as little as 0.1 mm by turning the handle on the side of the instrument.

4.2 Assessment Experiment

The tip of the endoscope was translated 6 times from the adequate reference point in the external camera coordinate system at 5 mm intervals with respect to the x-, y-, and

Fig. 10. Logitech BRIO c1000e.

Fig. 11. PROXXON cross table.

z-axes (30 mm in total), to see the extent of the error it may cause from the real space coordinates. The translation of the x- and y-axes was carried out while fixing the external camera at the position approximately 500 mm above the cross table (Fig. 12). The translation of the z-axis was carried out while fixing the camera approximately 500 mm to the side of the cross table (Fig. 13).

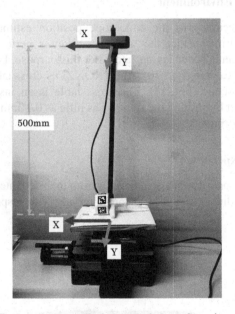

Fig. 12. Experiment overall view (translation of x-axis and y-axis).

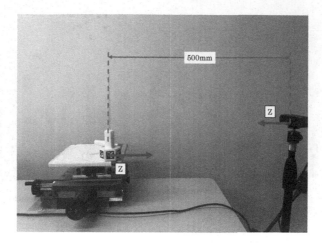

Fig. 13. Experiment overall view (translation of z-axis).

Two errors were calculated: the mean error derived from the 5 mm displacement for each round (error in displaced coordinates), and the mean error derived from the displaced magnitude from the reference point (reference point error). Two markers (Markers 1 and 2) were recorded by the camera. The results of the experiments are shown in the following tables and graphs with respect to each axis translation (Tables 1, 2, 3 and Figs. 14, 15).

Table 1. Amount of displacement and mean error when translated with respect to x-axis.

Real coordinates displacement (mm)	5	10	15	20	25	30
Error in displaced coordinates (mm)	0.71	0.64	0.67	2.01	1.66	1.62
Reference point error (mm)	0.71	0.97	1.61	0.95	1.69	1.53

Table 2. Amount of displacement and mean error when translated with respect to y-axis.

Real coordinates displacement (mm)	5	10	15	20	25	30
Error in displaced coordinates (mm)	0.67	2.4	1.67	1.87	1.62	2.71
Reference point error (mm)	0.67	2.7	2.41	2.14	2.4	3.19

Table 3. Amount of displacement and mean error when translated with respect to z-axis.

Real coordinates displacement (mm)	5	10	15	20	25	30
Error in displaced coordinates (mm)	16.5	36	3.43	38.49	18.19	25.81
Reference point error (mm)	16.5	21.95	22.8	14.21	24.2	15.24

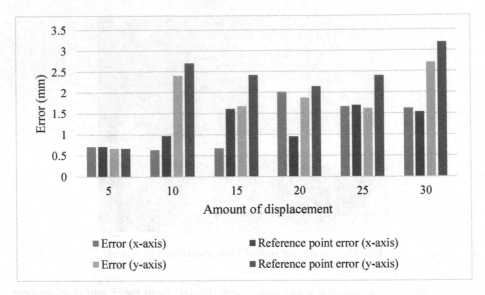

Fig. 14. Error in displacement with respect to x-axis and y-axis.

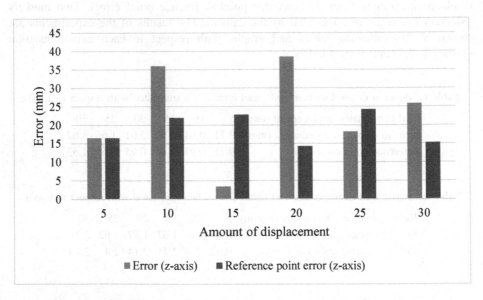

Fig. 15. Error in displacement with respect to z-axis.

4.3 Discussion

In the estimation of the tip of the endoscope replica, translation with respect to the x-axis and y-axis by 5 mm in each round demonstrated an error ranging from 0.6 to 2.4 mm. An error of 2.4 mm for a 5 mm displacement is a significant error. The error of displacement from the reference point was 3.4 mm (maximum) with respect to the x-axis and y-axis combined. This is relative to a shift of 30 mm, demonstrating that the system can display positional relationships with a modest degree of reliability. As for the experiments in relation to the z-axis, extremely large errors occurred. As a procedure, the same displacement was made as experiments with other two axes, and the only difference was the position of the camera. Therefore, such large errors were unexpected. There are two possible explanations for these errors. First, errors might be generated when the external camera is fixed in a direction parallel or perpendicular to the cross table. Second, when reading markers, some orientations of markers might be easy to read while other orientations might be difficult to read. Some spots might have larger errors than others in each round of experiment. Since the margin of error in the overall displacement did not differ considerably from the margin of error in each displacement, objects were viewed in positions that were modestly reliable. However, it is likely that large errors with respect to the z-axis generate errors in the image overlay in the vertical direction. As an improvement measure for this second problem, although the estimated mean of all markers relevant to the tip position estimation was calculated and used, it might be better to use the marker with an orientation that was most accurately read. Furthermore, with respect to the z-axis, markers can be read by more than one camera from various angles, rather than by one camera from the front angle. This is expected to enhance the accuracy of the estimated position and orientation of the markers, and to enhance the accuracy of the tip estimation system itself.

A more accurate image overlay method for the 3D model is yet another point of improvement. We considered applying markers to feature points on the head and defining the default position of the 3D model based on relative vectors between these markers and the marker on the operating table. However, errors may arise between feature points and markers. Thus, we need to consider an approach of obtaining positions of the feature points externally, by using an algorithm that allows us to detect feature points on the head without using markers and matching it with the 3D model.

5   Conclusion

In this study, we considered the development of an AR navigation system for transsphenoidal surgery as a system to help surgeons ascertain the circumstances surrounding the operating field. The proposed system consists of a position and orientation estimation system and an image overlay system. By using ArUco markers and reading them with an external camera, the position and orientation estimation system was able to estimate the position and orientation of the endoscope tip and the tumor in real time. The image overlay system converted the coordinates obtained from the external camera in the external camera coordinate system into coordinates in the virtual space coordinate system, and displayed the 3D model created from the patient's MRI images as defined in the virtual space coordinate system in conjunction with the endoscopic image. The 3D model was color-coded and permeabilized before being viewed, ensuring the surgeon could obtain information from the endoscope, such as the site of the section. The accuracy assessment for the position and orientation estimation system revealed that a small displacement with respect to the x-axis and y-axis produced a large error, while the margin of error between a small displacement and long displacement remained almost the same. However, large errors were observed with respect to the z-axis. For future research, improvement on the marker recognition technique as well as the measurement accuracy using filtering of the measurement data, and the better coordination with the image overlay system can be considered.

References

1. Qian, K., Bai, J., Yang, X., Pan, J., Zhang, J.: Virtual reality based laparoscopic surgery simulation. In: Proceedings of the 21st ACM Symposium on Virtual Reality Software and Technology, pp. 69–78 (2015). http://doi.org/10.1145/2821592.2821599
2. Coles, T.R., Meglan, D., John, N.W.: The role of haptics in medical training simulators: a survey of the state of the art. IEEE Trans. Haptics 4(1), 51–66 (2011). https://doi.org/10.1109/TOH.2010.19
3. Shousen, W., Jun-Feng, L., Shang-Ming, Z., Jun-Jie, J., Liang, X.: A virtual reality model of the clivus and surgical simulation via transoral or transnasal route. Int. J. Clin. Exp. Med. 7, 3270–3279 (2014)
4. Li, L., et al.: A novel augmented reality navigation system for endoscopic sinus and skull base surgery: a feasibility study. PLoS One 11(1), e0146996 (2016). https://doi.org/10.1371/journal.pone.0146996
5. Onishi, K., Fumiyama, S., Miki, Y., Nonaka, M., Koeda, M., Noborio, H.: A study of camera tip position estimating methods in transnasal endoscopic surgery. In: Kurosu, M. (ed.) HCII 2019. LNCS, vol. 11567, pp. 534–543. Springer, Cham (2019). https://doi.org/10.1007/978-3-030-22643-5_42
6. Yano, D., et al.: Accuracy verification of knife tip positioning with position and orientation estimation of the actual liver for liver surgery support system. J. Bioinf. Neurosci. (JBINS) 3 (3), 79–84 (2017)
7. Koeda, M., Yano, D., Doi, M., Onishi, K., Noborio, H.: Calibration of surgical knife-tip position with marker-based optical tracking camera and precise evaluation of its measurement accuracy. J. Bioinf. Neurosci. (JBINS) 4(1), 155–159 (2018)
8. Garrido-Jurado, S., Muñoz-Salinas, R., Madrid-Cuevas, F., Medina-Carnicer, R.: Generation of fiducial marker dictionaries using mixed integer linear programming. Pattern Recognit. 51, 481–491 (2015). https://doi.org/10.1016/j.patcog.2015.09.023
9. Romero Ramirez, F., Muñoz-Salinas, R., Medina-Carnicer, R.: Speeded up detection of squared fiducial markers. Image Vis. Comput. 76, 38–47 (2018). https://doi.org/10.1016/j.imavis.2018.05.004

Conception and Development of a Support System for Assembly Technology

Bernhard Rupprecht[1]([✉]) [iD], Emanuel Trunzer[1] [iD], Jozsef Kovac[2],
and Birgit Vogel-Heuser[1] [iD]

[1] Institute of Automation and Information Systems,
Technical University of Munich, Garching, Germany
{bernhard.rupprecht,emanuel.trunzer,vogel-heuser}@tum.de
[2] HAWE Hydraulik SE, Munich, Germany
j.kovac@hawe.de

Abstract. Due to the digitization of industry and the adaption of Industry 4.0, manufactures have to face considerable challenges. Industrial assembly processes must be as flexible as possible to react to fast-changing customer demands. Today, this is mostly achieved by the use of personnel manually executing the assembly tasks. However, assuring a constant quality of the produced goods is a problem under these circumstances. A possible solution to reduce human errors could be the introduction of assistance systems for highlighting important information and guidance during the assembly process. However, most of the available systems cannot adequately provide the required flexibility and restrict assembly workers. Hence, new and innovative assistance systems for industrial assembly are needed that can overcome these limitations and that allow greater flexibility. This contribution compares different basic concepts for the realization of such an innovative assistance system. It proposes a Pick-by-Local-Light system as a suitable approach to meet industrial requirements. The concept foresees small modules mounted directly to the front side of the individual load carriers. These modules visually highlight the respective carriers. The conceptual work is evaluated with a prototypical proof-of-concept. Also, a questionnaire with industrial experts and assembly workers for hydraulic valve assembly processes verified the suitability of the proof-of-concept assistance system. In summary, the developed assistance system has received widespread approval. This work thus laid the foundation for the implementation of a novel assistance system in industrial assembly.

1 Industrie 4.0 and Industrial Assembly

The transformation of industry induced by the concept of Industry 4.0 and the need for higher degrees of flexibility confronts industry with considerable challenges. Today, significant parts of the production process are still manually executed by personnel. Especially in the field of product assembly, the human factor still plays a crucial role. This fact will also remain valid in the future as

© Springer Nature Switzerland AG 2020
M. Kurosu (Ed.): HCII 2020, LNCS 12183, pp. 639–657, 2020.
https://doi.org/10.1007/978-3-030-49065-2_44

assembly steps often require enormous flexibility. Nevertheless, the performance of employees is always subject to variations, which can lead to errors and losses during assembly. At the same time, a constant product and assembly quality have to be guaranteed to customers. Additionally, assembly quality greatly depends on the experience of the assembly workers and is challenged by the increasing shortage of skilled personnel and demographic change. As a result, employees working in assembly often can no longer draw on the same wealth of experience as in the past. In parallel, the tasks to be mastered are becoming increasingly complex as more and more information has to be processed by the employees. Therefore, assistance systems for highlighting important information and guidance during the assembly are an effective way to optimize the assembly process and to support human workers [11,23,25].

Despite the increasing demand for assistance systems in industrial assembly, most of the available systems cannot adequately provide the required flexibility and hence restrict the assembly process. Existing systems depend on the knowledge of the actual position of the small load carriers (SLCs), which contain the assembly components. This circumstance leads to storage shelves with rigid layouts and requires the SLCs to be placed inside a fixed rail system that significantly limits the flexibility of the system. As a consequence, load carriers need to follow strict sizing rules and can only be placed in the related channels of the rail system that correspond to the carrier size. Therefore, the random placement of the carriers is impossible. This random placement leads to inefficient use of the shelves, restrictions of the carrier sizes as well as an inflexible assembly process that requires great efforts in case of reconfiguration [4,20].

Hence, new and innovative assistance systems for industrial assembly are needed that can overcome these limitations. This contribution compares different basic concepts for the realization of such an innovative assistance system. It proposes a Pick-by-Local-Light system as a suitable approach to meet the industrial requirements. The concept foresees small modules mounted at the front sides of the individual load carriers. These battery-powered modules are controlled by a central computer via a wireless communication link and can be individually activated to highlight the respective load carriers visually. Therefore, relevant Internet-of-Things wireless communication technologies are surveyed and compared for their suitability.

The remainder of this paper is structured as follows: The next section will discuss the requirements for an assistance system applied in industrial assembly processes. Afterward, state-of-the-art approaches are described and compared to the requirements. The section "Prototypical Implementation" discusses the aspects of the proposed assistance system, including a high-level concept as well as a detailed discussion of the selected technologies for its realization. The following evaluation section presents the results of a battery lifetime estimation, as well as the findings of an expert questionnaire. The last section concludes this paper and provides an outlook on future research.

2   Requirements for an Assistance System in Industrial Assembly Processes

For an industrial application of the assistance system, several requirements must be met. These include the general goals for the introduction of assistance systems, additional functional requirements as well as requirements dedicated to the overall assembly process and the user interaction.

2.1   General Aims

In this contribution, the assembly process includes the picking of components provided employing the Kanban principle [16]. An assistance system should target to reduce dead times between picks ($Z1$) and to avoid picking errors ($Z2$). Both aspects ultimately lead to increased picking performance and productivity. Also, the focus is on reducing the workload of employees through a suitable information display ($Z3$), which also enables less experienced employees to carry out the assembly process safely and efficiently.

2.2   Functional Requirements

In functional terms, the assistance system should provide visual worker guidance ($F1$) and therefore highlight the relevant boxes with parts to be removed. Furthermore, visualizing the number of parts to be removed directly to the employee would be beneficial ($F2$). Once the component(s) has/have been removed, the successful removal needs to be registered by the system for continuing the assembly process and for verifying its correctness ($F3$).

2.3   User and Process Requirements

The ability of the assistance system to react flexibly to changes at the assembly workplace is of crucial importance. Employees often set up the workplace according to their preferences. This is done, for example, by manually rearranging SLCs. For parts that are required very frequently during an assembly process, employees may also remove an SLC from the shelf and place it on the worktop. It is then returned to the shelf, but not necessarily to the same position as before. The assistance system should, therefore, react flexibly to position changes of the SLCs and maintain its functionality ($N1$).

Since the assembly worker needs both hands to carry out his work, the assistance system must not contain any components that have to be carried in hand. A theoretically possible depositing of these components after the removal and before the assembly process is not considered due to additional gripping distances and slowing down of the entire process ($N2$).

Furthermore, a modular design ($N3$) is crucial to ensure future industrial use of the assistance system. The assistance system should not only be designed for a specific assembly station. It must be ensured that the system functions reliably at assembly stations of different types. The parallel operation of the assistance system at several workstations of an assembly line should also be possible.

3   State-of-the-Art in Industrial Assistance Systems

The section provides an overview of actual assembly and picking assistance systems and compares them to the requirements stated in the previous section.

3.1   Projection-Based Systems

If relevant information is displayed using a projector, this can be referred to as projection-supported assembly assistance. The worker is supported by multimedia content projected onto the work surface. Besides, the system offers Pick-to-Light functionality. Inputs can be made using buttons, speech, and gesture recognition as well as touch screens. Therefore, the functional requirements (F1–F3) can be realized. As the system is not able to recognize the provided boxes, the desired flexibility (N1) cannot be guaranteed. Therefore, the system depends on the correct positioning of the SLCs at all times. After changing an SLC position, this change must be manually stored in the system [2].

3.2   Pick-by-Vision Systems

Pick-by-Vision (PbV) refers to Augmented Reality (AR) supported picking using so-called Head-Mounted Displays (HMD) [12]. PbV systems are able to meet all functional requirements (F1–F3). HMDs need to be tracked in order to highlight the corresponding SLCs correctly. Additional information, such as the quantity to pick, can easily be projected into the user's field of vision (FOV). The acknowledgment of the removal is possible via gestures or additional input devices. The required flexibility (N1) can also be covered by continuous tracking of the SLC over i.e., barcodes or QR codes attached to them. Nevertheless, an undisturbed line-of-sight between SLC and HMD is required. As the HMD is mounted on the head of the employee, both hands are free for assembly (N2). A PbV system can be used at several assembly stations and applies to different scenarios. Thus (N3) is fulfilled.

Unfortunately, the use of PbV inevitably results in additional burdens for the user. For example, AR can lead to dizziness and nausea [2]. In addition, the user's FOV is restricted because data glasses still have a smaller field of vision than the human eye [3]. Moreover, HMDs darken the environment, even when switched off, because ambient light does not fully penetrate the semitransparent displays [5]. This darkening is particularly disadvantageous in industrial assembly processes. In this case, even a switched off HMD would mean an unacceptable restriction for the employee.

Günthner et al. [12] also advise against a full-shift operation due to the comparatively high weight, the low wearing comfort, and the heat generation during operation. Furthermore, data glasses are usually unsuitable for spectacle wearers, which severely limits the circle of users. In summary, it can be stated that PbV systems represent a very interesting field with lively research activity. However, due to the mentioned disadvantages, it cannot be used for the assistance system to be developed.

3.3 Pick-by-Light Systems

Pick-by-Light (PbL) Systems are increasingly finding their way into order picking. Signal lights are mounted above or below each SLC. If a component is to be removed from a container, the corresponding light is illuminated. Additionally, depending on the system, the quantity to be picked can also be displayed using display elements. After the removal of the components, the process is acknowledged either automatically by a sensor that detects the employee's intervention or manually by pressing a button. Classically, the individual display elements are built into the shelf, which requires technical installations at each storage location [13,18].

The functional requirements *(F1–F3)* can be fulfilled by a PbL system. However, it must be ensured that the signal unit contains functionality for displaying the quantity. The information is also displayed ergonomically, and the employee has both hands available for work *(N2)*. Problems arise concerning flexibility [17]. A classical PbL system is not able to react to changes at the assembly workplace *(N1)*. If an SLC is moved to another location, this cannot be recognized automatically. Although various assembly stations can be equipped with the system, first installation of the system causes high costs and is complex, since conversions of shelving and assembly stations are necessary [13] *(N3)*.

Therefore, a PbL system is a sensible way of supporting order pickers with a non-changing assortment and a fixed warehouse structure. However, it is particularly unsuitable for assistance systems in industrial assembly due to its low flexibility.

3.4 Pick-by-Local-Light Systems

A modification of the classical PbL principle is a so-called Pick-by-Local-Light (PbLL) system. PbLL systems aim to mitigate the disadvantages of classical PbL systems. Therefore, the display elements (modules) are battery powered and equipped with a wireless communication link so that no cabling is required. These modules are directly mounted on the shelf or the SLCs, thus reducing the installation effort to a minimum. Moreover, the quantity to be picked is shown on a display and lights installed in the module indicate the picking position. Furthermore, a button is used for manual acknowledgment [6].

In Fig. 1 a PbLL system is shown. If energy-saving hardware components and radio technology are used, battery lifetimes of up to one year are possible [14]. Due to its similar construction to a classical PbL system, a PbLL system fulfills the same requirements that a PbLL system does.

However, in contrast to classical PbL guidance, PbLL systems can offer the desired flexibility. If the display modules are installed directly on the SLCs, the system retains its function if the containers are repositioned. Even the temporary positioning of an SLC on the worktop poses no problem *(N1)*. Due to the elimination of the need for cabling, integration into existing assembly systems is simple. Thus, a PbLL system is very modular and adaptable to various picking scenarios *(N3)*. If new SLCs are placed on the shelves, only the display modules

Fig. 1. Module of a PbLL system. LEDs indicate the removal position, a display shows the quantity, buttons can be pressed to acknowledge part removal (Hölczli et al. [14]).

have to be repositioned. Hence, the basic principle of a PbLL system is very suitable for an assistance system for industrial assembly.

3.5   Selection of a Concept for the Assembly Assistance System

A summary of all presented systems and the requirements they meet is provided in Table 1. PbV and PbLL systems can meet all requirements. Still, a PbV system is not considered as a suitable approach due to the limitations for the user stated in Subsect. 3.2. Therefore, a PbLL-based assistance system will be developed in this contribution.

Table 1. Summarized assessment of the assistance systems under consideration of the requirements (adapted from Wölfle [24]). Symbols: x fulfills, - does not fulfill and/not considered.

			Projection-based	Pick-by-Vision	Pick-to-Light	Pick-by-Local-Light
Requirements	F1	Worker guidance	x	x	x	x
	F2	Display Picking quantity	x	x	x	x
	F3	Acknowledgment of picking	x	x	x	x
	N1	Flexibility	–	x	–	x
	N2	Free use of hands	/	x	x	x
	N3	Modular design	/	x	–	x

4   Use-Case: Assembly of Hydraulic Valves

The developed prototype was evaluated in cooperation with a hydraulic valve manufacturing company in Germany. Small lot-sizes and high variance of manufactured hydraulic valves characterize the underlying assembly process. The developed system should be used at an assembly station inside this assembly process. The parts are provided in SLCs (80 SLCs maximum per shelf) that are stored on shelves using the Kanban principle. The station is equipped with an assembly control systems which specifies the assembly process. Ideally, this external system contains the part numbers and quantities for the assembly process. The stored data can, therefore, be forwarded to an assistance system. Additionally, any acknowledgment of a successful picking process needs to be sent back to the assembly control system.

5   Prototypical Implementation of the Support System

This section introduces the concept of the prototypical implementation based on the PbLL principle as well as the selection of suitable technologies for wireless connectivity, part quantity display, and the other components of the system.

5.1   High-Level Concept

The modules should be directly attached to the SLCs to provide the necessary flexibility *(N1)*. To highlight the respective SLC and to show the quantity to pick, each module needs a display. Moreover, as successful part removal has to be tracked, a button is installed in each module. This button is pressed by the employee to end the respective picking process. As the modules are not part of the SLCs but only mounted to them, their removal has to be detected. If a module is removed from an SLC, it should not react to external signals and mislead the employee until it is reinitialized. Therefore, an additional sensor is necessary, that ensures a correct assignment between module and SLC. Each module includes a printed-on barcode with its ID on its backside, which allows a simple assignment to an SLC using a barcode scanner standard in industrial assembly. Figure 2 shows a schematic representation of a shelf equipped with the PbLL assistance system and a close-up of the so-called "module disconnected" sensor.

As coordinator of all installed modules, a central host application is foreseen. This host application takes the input (part to pick and quantity) from the assembly control system that organizes the assembly process. The modules are installed locally on each SLC so that there is no necessity of wiring them up. Therefore, each module should be powered by its battery. A wireless communication link is necessary to decouple communication between the host application and the modules. Each module, as well as the computer that runs the host application, need a component for wireless connectivity. A local microcontroller unit (MCU) in each module provides the possibility to communicate with the

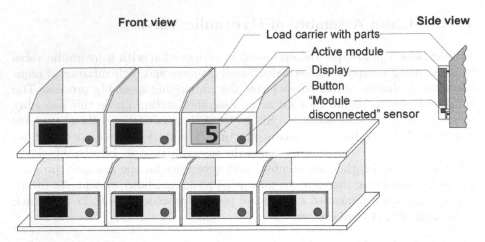

Fig. 2. Schematic representation of a shelf with the PbLL assistance system and detail of its components.

central host application, to process the incoming data as well as to interface the display, the button, and the "module disconnected" sensor. Figure 3 provides an overview of the structural composition of a module. If an SLC is empty after several picking processes, the module is removed from the SLC. The SLC goes back to logistics for refilling, while the module stays at all times at the assembly station (where it is recharged if required).

Although the PbLL system presented in the state-of-the-art [6] is based on the same principle as the conceptualized assistance system, it is not suitable for industrial assembly. The original solution focuses on the domain of logistics with large picking zones, while in assembly, the picking zones are very compact. Furthermore, the proprietary wireless network "S-Net" used in the original

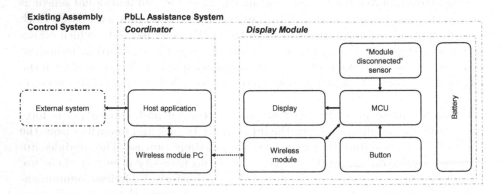

Fig. 3. Overview of the main components used for the prototypical implementation of the PbLL system. The communication with the host application is wireless. The host application is also the interface of the assistance system to external systems.

approach is problematic. This wireless technology is currently not widely available on the free market. Currently, the required components can only be obtained from a single source. This circumstance is unacceptable for widespread industrial application.

5.2   Wireless Technology

Before the decision for a specific radio module can be made, a suitable wireless communication technology must first be selected. For IoT (Internet-of-Things) applications, the aspects of energy consumption, range, radiofrequency, transmission speed, standardization, communication security, distribution in the industry, and failure susceptibility should be taken into account [22]. For the given application, energy consumption is a decisive criterion, since a battery supply is intended. The radio frequency used should also be selected so that there is no interference with other wireless systems used in production. Moreover, a strong standardization of technology ensures the availability of hardware components from various suppliers (no lock-in). The transmission speed is less relevant for the given application since only small amounts of data have to be transmitted. It should also be possible to exchange data via encrypted communication channels to prevent unauthorized access to the system. The IoT communication technologies Bluetooth Low Energy (BLE), LoRa, MiWi, Thread, Wireless HART, Wi-SUN, Wi-Fi, ZigBee, NB-IoT and Z-Wave are compared and considered for their suitability [8,9].

A standardized wireless technology is WLAN (Wireless Local Area Network) [15]. This very widespread technology provides high data rates and ranges. WLAN can use two different radio frequencies. Encryption of the communication is also specified in the standard. Concerning susceptibility to interference, obstacles (e.g., walls) can weaken the signal and limit the range, but the range is sufficient for the given application. Yet, WLAN has a high energy consumption, which is why it is unsuitable for the required application [22].

A very energy-saving communication is possible via Bluetooth Low Energy (BLE). This extension of the Bluetooth standard exists since the specification version 4.0. Version 5.0 improves the range and data throughput compared to the previous versions. Interference can be reduced by the ability to change the transmission frequency within a given band, resulting in BLE having a low susceptibility to interference. Encryption ensures secure communication. Also, BLE is widely available technology. This facilitates the development as well as the later interaction with the assistance system [19,24].

The LoRaWAN (Long Range Wide Area Network) radio protocol is characterized by low energy consumption and the transmission of small amounts of data over long distances. Encrypted communication is guaranteed. The LoRa Alliance certifies available products. Also, LoRWAN is relatively robust against interference, but component availability is limited as only a few manufacturers currently produce components. Furthermore, LoRaWAN is not yet a widely used technology. Therefore, LoRaWAN is not chosen as radio standard for the PbLL system, but may become an alternative in the future [22].

Another promising technology is the Narrowband Internet of Things (NB-IoT). The primary focus of this technology is the networking of IoT devices with high radio coverage and low energy consumption. A high level of safety and reliability is also ensured. For the use of this technology, network availability at the place of use is an absolute prerequisite. The difference to locally built networks is that, as it is based on conventional cellular networks, the availability of NB-IoT depends on a service provider. It is not possible to set up local NB-IoT infrastructure. Therefore, its provision at the site of use by a provider is a mandatory prerequisite [7]. However, the implementation of NB-IoT is still in its infancy, and in Germany, there are no comprehensive infrastructure available today [1]. Currently, the availability of NB-IoT is not necessarily guaranteed at all locations, and the latency is relatively high. Therefore, NB-IoT is not used as radio technology for the PbLL system to be developed. With the implementation of the next-generation 5G mobile radio standard, significant improvements compared to current NB-IoT, such as a massive reduction in latency and a response to requests in quasi-real-time, can be achieved. Hence, with the area-wide availability of the 5G mobile radio standard, the use of this technology can be considered.

If real-time communication is required, a Wireless HART architecture can be used. The focus of this technology is to design wireless systems based on traditional fieldbuses. In addition to real-time capability, very high reliability and communication security are crucial, but the costs of such a network are very high. Since the conceptualized assistance system is not time-critical nor a safety-critical system, Wireless HART is not selected [19,21].

The ZigBee specification describes an energy-efficient radio standard. Zigbee is particularly suitable for use in wireless sensor networks. Due to the low data rates provided, this standard is only suitable for the transmission of small data volumes. Parallel operation with other wireless networks such as Wi-Fi is possible, but data rate and communication reliability may decrease due to interference. Communication security is ensured by encryption [9,24].

Components for other popular technologies, such as Thread, MiWi, Z-Wave, and Wi-SUN, are not widely available. The reader is referred to Cheng et al. [8] for further details.

Table 2 summarizes the characteristics of the discussed technologies. Functionally, ZigBee meets all requirements for the PbLL system. However, the current prevalence of ZigBee is still low, which is why ZigBee is not selected. Since BLE has significant advantages over other technologies in terms of availability of components and fulfills all functional requirements, it is selected for the prototype of the assistance system.

5.3 Display Technology

The display unit showing the number of parts to be removed is a central component of the conceptualized PbLL system. As the modules should be battery-powered, their energy consumption is a crucial aspect when selecting an appropriate display technology. Additionally, the display must be readable under all

Table 2. Quantitative and qualitative overview of the considered radio technologies with their relevant characteristics. Symbols: + very suitable, o conditionally suitable, − unsuitable and ? no information.

Wireless technology	Data rate	Range	Frequency	Standardization	Energy consumption	Security	Susceptibility to faults	Distribution in the industry
BLE 4	max. 1 Mbps	10 − 100 m	2,4 GHz	IEEE 802.15.1/ SIG	+	+	+	+
BLE 5	max. 2 Mbps	40 − 400 m	2,4 GHz	IEEE 802.15.1/ SIG	+	+	+	+
LoRaWAN	0.3 − 50 kbps	3 − 15 km	868 MHz	Lora Alliance	+	+	+	−
MiWi	?	?	2,4 GHz	IEEE 802.15.4	?	?	?	−
NB-IoT	max. 250 kbps	1 − 8 km	compare 4G	3GPP	+	+	−	
Thread	?	?	2,4 GHz	IEEE 802.15.4	+	?	+	−
Wireless HART	?	?	2,4 GHz	HART Protocoll	?	+	+	o
Wi-SUN	50 − 150 kbps	0.1 − 2 km	800/900 MHz	IEEE 802.15.4g/ Wi-SUN Alliance	?	?	?	−
WLAN	54 − 1300 Mbps	15 − 150 m	2,4/5 GHz	IEEE 802.11	−	+	o	+
ZigBee	max. 250 kbps	10 − 100 m	868/2,4 MHz/GHz	IEEE 802.15.4/ Zigbee Alliance	+	+	o	−
Z-Wave	40 − 200 kbps	15 − 150 m	868/915/2,4 MHz/GHz	Z-Wave Alliance	+	o	−	−

ambient conditions (e.g., ambient lighting). The maximum viewing angle under which the display can still be read should also be as large as possible for flexible use. The aspects price and availability of the display components should also be taken into account for industrial applicability. From a functional point of view, the display should be capable of showing two-digit numbers as, during the underlying assembly processes, more than 99 parts are never necessary. Other assembly processes may require an adaption here. In the following, the display technologies LCD, E-Paper, OLED, as well as LED segment displays are considered. All technologies considered are characterized by moderate power consumption, which makes them suitable for the given application.

The Liquid Crystal Display (LCD) technology is currently the most widely used display technology. LCDs employ a backlight to illuminate the display. In general, power consumption is higher than that of E-paper and OLED displays. The viewing angle of classic LCDs is also relatively low at about 45° [10].

OLED (Organic Light Emitting Diodes) displays are characterized by high contrast, high brightness, fast response time, and a wide viewing angle of about 160°. Energy consumption depends on the displayed content, as only non-black pixels are illuminated, but is relatively low. The price of OLED displays is still significantly higher than that of LCDs. The availability is partly limited depending on the display size [10].

E-Paper Displays (EPD) aims to achieve a representation similar to that of printed paper. Ambient light is reflected, and no backlight is used. An advantage of EPD is their bi-stable characteristic. Therefore, they only need the energy to change the displayed content but not to display it. Readability and viewing angle are similar to printed paper and can be considered reasonable. Still, a sufficiently bright environment is required to ensure proper readability. A significant disadvantage is the long latency of about 500 ms when refreshing the display content. EPD displays are still expensive, and component availability of suitable drivers and displays is limited. Another problem is the superposition of the previously displayed image with the current image, known as "ghosting" [10].

LED segment displays depend on individual segments illuminated by LEDs. Seven-segment displays allow the representation of single decimals and a limited set of characters. Several displays can be combined for multi-digit displays. LED segment displays exhibit good readability, large viewing angles, low prices as well as good component availability. Disadvantageous is permanent power consumption while the display is active.

A qualitative summary of the discussed technologies is provided in Table 3. As can be seen, LED segment displays are best suited when the active time of the display is low. This is the case in the given use-case, as the displays should only be displaying a quantity when a pick from the respective SLC is necessary. Therefore, the displays will be inactive most of the time. By combining two single seven-segment displays, quantities of up to 99 parts can be shown with good readability and at a low cost.

Table 3. Qualitative overview of the considered display technologies with their relevant characteristics. Symbols: + very suitable, o conditionally suitable and − unsuitable

	Energy use	Readability	Point of view	Price	Availability
LCD	o	o	−	o	+
OLED	+	+	+	−	o
EPD	+	+	+	−	−
LED segment display	o	+	+	+	+

5.4 Hardware Selection and Additional Components

For the prototypical realization of a module, the Microchip/Atmel SAMB11-ZR Xplained Pro Evaluation Kit is used. This kit is based on the BLE 5 module Microchip/Atmel ATSAMB11-ZR with an internal ARM Cortex-M0 MCU. For the prototype, a two-digit seven-segment display DC08-11SRWA from Kingbright is selected. Furthermore, a photodiode of type SFH 213 from OSRAM

Opto Semiconductors is used as a "module disconnected" sensor. It measures the ambient light as the backside of the module to detect a removal. Therefore, it sits recessed to prevent the detection of ambient light in the mounted position. An additional tactile push-button serves to acknowledge part removal. The prototype does not contain a battery and is supplied over a USB connection. A practical realization would encompass a battery module and possibly a charging circuit, depending on the realization of a recharging procedure. Furthermore, the components are assembled on a breadboard and are not soldered onto a Printed Circuit Board (PCB) and packed into a casing. A practical realization would include a custom PCB and housing unit.

The host application runs on a standard Windows 10 laptop that is equipped with a BLE module. The application is programmed with C#, provides a defined interface between the assembly control system and the modules of the assistance system, and coordinates all connected modules. A barcode scanner connected to the laptop serves to couple of modules and SLC. The test setup can be seen in Fig. 4.

Fig. 4. Illustration of the test setup used for demonstration purposes. The PC simulates the assembly control system which integrates the host application.

6 Evaluation of the Developed Prototype

In the following section, the evaluation of the prototype will be presented. At first, a battery lifetime estimation is given. Afterward, the results of a questionnaire with industrial experts from the domain are summarized. Both evaluations are discussed under consideration of the hydraulic valve assembly use-case.

6.1   Battery Lifetime Estimation

TTo ensure the uninterrupted operation of the assistance system, the battery life of the wireless modules is of central importance. The two largest energy consumers of the selected hardware components are the MCU and the seven-segment display. All other components of the system have a negligible contribution to energy consumption and are not considered further. For the battery lifetime calculation, it is assumed that the worker needs 45 s to remove a part from an SLC and acknowledge the removal process over the button. A module's display is powered only during this period. In one hour of operation, ten partial withdrawals from the SLC under consideration are assumed. The module is foreseen to be powered by three standard AAA (Micro) NiMH rechargeable batteries connected in series. NiMH batteries have the benefit of high robustness and good discharge characteristics with relatively stable voltage levels. Through the combination of three batteries in series, each with 1.2 V, the 3.3 V needed for the components can be supplied over a long time.

Each battery under consideration here has a capacity of 1000 mA h, which is a typical value for NiMH batteries. Thus the battery pack has a total energy content of 3600 mW h.

With the energy consumption data provided by the manufacturers of the seven-segment display and the BLE module, it can be seen that the power dissipation of the display contributes about 87% to the total energy consumption. In contrast, only 13% is accounted for by the MCU. The possible operating time with the selected batteries is about 333 h, which corresponds to the use of almost 42 eight-hour shifts (assumed that the module is completely switched off outside of the shifts). To guarantee a seamless assembly process with the assistance system and reduce the workload of the assembly workers for recharging the modules, it should function at least one complete shift without interruption. The estimated battery life is, therefore, considered more than sufficient.

6.2   Expert Questionnaire

In order to obtain an independent opinion on the developed assistance system, a questionnaire with industrial experts was conducted. The expert group includes a total of 16 persons familiar with the use-case. They originate from different groups, including assembly workers, assembly planners, project managers, and other employees. The course of the survey included a presentation of the assistance system for about ten minutes. The prototype was then practically demonstrated, and the respondents were able to interact with the system themselves. After the experts were finished with trying out the prototype, a questionnaire was filled out by each expert individually.

The assistance system should highlight the SLC with the parts to be removed. Since the respondents rated the display of the containers consistently positive, the functional requirement *(F1)* can be regarded as fulfilled. According to the comments of the respondents, an additional signal should be added to highlight the SLCs if the luminosity of the LED segment display is not sufficient.

The respondents agreed that the number of items to be removed is adequately visualized. Therefore, requirement *(F2)* can also be regarded as fulfilled. However, the readability of the display under real operating conditions should be validated again in a test field. Within this test, it can also be examined whether an additional highlighting signal besides the display is essential.

Concerning the acknowledgment of part removal, a majority of the respondents confirmed that an acknowledgement of withdrawals is possible. However, the manual acknowledgment through a button was viewed rather critically. The assemblers, in particular, fear that the acknowledgment process will restrict the workflow, as a large number of different parts are needed for the assembly. Another employee remarks that manual confirmation is complicated and costs much time. The requirement *(F3)* is thus functionally fulfilled. However, for successful industrial use of the assistance system, an automatic acknowledgment (e.g., using a sensor attached to the display module) should be provided.

Furthermore, the reduction of search times is evaluated positively by the interviewees. To which extent the search times will be reduced, however, cannot be judged at this time. Additional tests of the system with employees who have different working experience could provide information. Since a reduction of search times and thus, also of dead times seems probable, the basic concept of the assistance system can be considered to fulfill objective *(Z1)*.

To evaluate the fulfillment of objective *(Z2)*, the participants were asked whether incorrect component withdrawals could be avoided. For the most part, the persons questioned affirmed this question. However, it was noted that the current concept still allows for mistakes to be made, although the probability is reduced to a minimum. Theoretically, the components can be removed from an incorrect SLC, and then the removal can be acknowledged on another SLC by pressing the button. Automatic acknowledgment also provides a remedy here. However, this does not entirely prevent deliberate mistaken removals. Since the employees are willing to manufacture a fault-free product, and the components to be removed are not safety-critical, the assistance system developed offers a suitable approach to prevent incorrect removals. Thus a reduction of picking errors can be assumed in real use.

Since flexibility is a decisive criterion for the development of the assistance system, respondents were asked to assess whether the assistance system can react flexibly to changes in the position of the SLCs. Only the assemblers were partly critical of this aspect, as they feared that the system would restrict their flexibility. All other persons were unanimous of the opinion that the system offers sufficient flexibility for the application. In summary, the user requirement *(N1)* can be regarded as fulfilled.

In order for the assistance system to be widely accepted by employees, the users should not experience any additional stress from the use of the system. The workers do not see any problems with the use of the system, whereas other employees have expressed concerns. These included the fact that the use of additional hardware and technology creates an increased burden for the employees since they have to operate and maintain the assistance system, as well as assigning modules to SLCs. Also, the modules have to be charged at the assembly station, and the employees are bound to step-by-step processing in a rigid order. However, the latter can also be advantageous for process stability. The assignment process can also be further simplified by using NFC technology instead of a barcode for automatic assignment. The requirement *(Z3)* should be re-evaluated in the course of a field test, since the loads or restrictions occurring in real operation depend on the final design of the system and loads are perceived differently depending on the employee. At the current stage of development, it cannot yet be determined beyond doubt whether the users experience overall cognitive relief.

For the assembly process, the assembly worker must have both hands available. This is also the case with the assistance system, but only after the worker has completed the removal process. Here, the manual acknowledgment process was once again criticized, especially by the assembly workers. If an automatic confirmation were used, there would be no difference between the picking process and picking without an assistance system. Nevertheless, the majority of respondents confirmed that the worker can assemble the components without any problems using both hands after manual acknowledgment. Therefore, *(N2)* is fulfilled.

All participants widely accepted the flexibility of the system concerning the place of deployment. All persons recognized the advantages of the system compared to the already available assistance systems. Due to the chosen concept, a wide variety of workplaces can be equipped, whereby it is not necessary to limit oneself exclusively to assembly.

Challenges in the modularity were seen for the integration of the system into the existing IT landscape. In the given use-case, not all material numbers and quantities to pick are yet stored in the superordinate IT system. Before the assistance system can be introduced practically, this information needs to be inserted into the system and therefore requires modifications to the external system. However, this is essential and applies to every other assistance system as well. Also, the hardware expenditure was partly estimated high, since many SLCs must be equipped with modules. Furthermore, the prototype system is not yet ready for production and requires additional development effort. Therefore, the process requirement *(N3)* is considered to be only partially fulfilled.

Table 4 summarizes the results. In summary, the prototype of the developed assistance system proved to be a promising concept. Nevertheless, additional development and evaluation studies are needed before an industrial application is feasible.

Table 4. Summary of the evaluation of the formulated objectives and requirements. Symbols: + fulfilled, o further tests required, / additional development needed.

Requirement	Description	Evaluation
Z1	Reduction of dead times	+
Z2	Reduction of picking errors	+
Z3	Cognitive relief	o
F1	Worker guidance	+
F2	Display picking quantity	+
F3	Picking confirmation	/
N1	Flexibility	+
N2	Free use of hands	+
N3	Modular design	o

7   Conclusion

In order to remain competitive in today's globalized market economy, continuous development and constant optimization of assembly processes are essential. A central challenge is to achieve a high quality of the produced goods, greater flexibility in assembly, and high productivity in the assembly process simultaneously. Assistance systems offer an approach to solve this problem because they act as an interface between human and technology, and thus combine the advantages of these two production factors.

Within the scope of this work, an assistance system for the industrial assembly was designed and developed. For the selection of a suitable basic concept, different assistance systems from the field of assembly, as well as order picking, were compared. Finally, the basic principle of a PbLL system has been chosen for a prototypical realization of the assistance system for industrial assembly. Based on this prototype, an evaluation was carried out through a survey with industrial experts. All respondents have widely accepted the system. Due to the predominantly positive feedback, further development of the system up to series production is being considered.

In order to be able to use the developed assistance system in a real industrial environment, the existing prototype has to be scaled down (miniaturized). Besides, an automatic acknowledgment of the removal process employing a sensor instead of the previously used push-button is preferable, as this increases employee acceptance and simplifies the removal process considerably. At the same time, this makes the system more robust due to the elimination of mechanical components.

Finally, as part of a field test, a complete assembly station has to be equipped with modules in order to assess the functionality of the system in a real industrial environment and its scalability. In particular, the reaction time of the system, the stress that occurs for the assembly staff, and the robustness of the assistance system should be carefully examined. The knowledge gained from the tests about weak points of the system then forms a basis for further development.

After implementation in the assembly process, the assistance system can contribute to the competitiveness. This work thus has laid the foundation for the industrial application of a novel assistance system in the areas of order picking and assembly.

References

1. NB-IoT: Vodafone und Telekom kämpfen um die Vorherrschaft für das Maschinennetz, 15 October 2018. https://www.elektronikpraxis.vogel.de/nb-iot-vodafone-und-telekom-kaempfen-um-die-vorherrschaft-fuer-das-maschinennetz-a-766228/
2. Apt, W., Bovenschulte, M., Priesack, K., Weiß, C., Hartmann, E.A.: Forschungsbericht 502: Einsatz von digitalen Assistenzsystemen im Betrieb (2018)
3. Blattgerste, J., Strenge, B., Renner, P., Pfeiffer, T., Essig, K.: Comparing conventional and augmented reality instructions for manual assembly tasks. In: PETRA 2017, pp. 75–82. ICPS, ACM, New York (2017). https://doi.org/10.1145/3056540.3056547
4. Bornewasser, M., Bläsing, D., Hinrichsen, S.: Informatorische Assistenzsysteme in der manuellen Montage: Ein nützliches Werkzeug zur Reduktion mentaler Beanspruchung? Zeitschrift für Arbeitswissenschaft **72**(4), 264–275 (2018). https://doi.org/10.1007/s41449-018-0123-x
5. Bundesanstalt für Arbeitsschutz und Arbeitsmedizin: Head Mounted Displays - Arbeitshilfen der Zukunft. https://doi.org/10.21934/baua:praxis20160809
6. Chair of Materials Handling, Material Flow, Logistics: Schlussbericht zu dem IGF-Vorhaben 18139N Pick-by-Local-Light (2016). http://www.fml.mw.tum.de/fml/images/Forschung/Pick-by-Local-Light/Forschungsbericht_PbLL.pdf
7. Chen, J., Hu, K., Wang, Q., Sun, Y., Shi, Z., He, S.: Narrowband internet of things: implementations and applications. IEEE Internet Things J. **4**(6), 2309–2314 (2017). https://doi.org/10.1109/JIOT.2017.2764475
8. Cheng, Y., Zhang, H., Huang, Y.: Overview of communication protocols in internet of things: architecture, development and future trends. In: IEEE/WIC/ACM International Conference on Web Intelligence (WI), pp. 627–630. IEEE (2018). https://doi.org/10.1109/WI.2018.00-25
9. Devalal, S., Karthikeyan, A.: Lora technology - an overview. In: Second International Conference on Electronics, Communication and Aerospace Technology (ICECA), pp. 284–290. IEEE (2018). https://doi.org/10.1109/ICECA.2018.8474715
10. Fernández, M., Casanova, E., Alonso, I.: Review of display technologies focusing on power consumption. Sustainability **7**(8), 10854–10875 (2015). https://doi.org/10.3390/su70810854
11. Ferreira, L., Lopes, N., Silva, J. (eds.): Technological Development in Industry 4.0 for Business Applications. Advances in Logistics, Operations, and Management Science (ALOMS) Book Series. IGI Global, Business Science Reference, Hershey (2019)
12. Günthner, W.A., Blomeyer, N., Reif, R., Schedlbauer, M.: Pick-by-Vision: Augmented Reality unterstützte Kommissionierung. Chair of Materials Handling, Material Flow, Logistics, Technical University of Munich, Garching (2009)

13. Guo, A., Wu, X., Shen, Z., Starner, T., Baumann, H., Gilliland, S.: Order picking with head-up displays. Computer **48**(6), 16–24 (2015). https://doi.org/10.1109/MC.2015.166
14. Hölczli, A., Lang, A., Evers, F.: Knoten sind auch eine Lösung: Drahtlose Kommissioniertechnik erschließt neue Potenziale in der Intralogistik. Hebezeuge Fördermittel **2016**(01–02), 28–30 (2016)
15. IEEE: 802.11-IEEE standard for information technology–telecommunications and information exchange between systems LANs–specific requirements - part 11: MAC and PHY specifications. https://doi.org/10.1109/IEEESTD.2016.7786995
16. Institut für Produktionssysteme- Technical University Dortmund: Schluss-bericht zum IGF-Forschungsvorhaben 17159 N/1 (2013). http://www.gvb-ev.de/fileadmin/pdfs/Schlussbericht_17159.pdf
17. Klaus, P., Krieger, W.: Gabler Lexikon Logistik: Management logistischer Netzwerke und Flüsse, 4 Auflage edn. Gabler, Wiesbaden (2009). https://doi.org/10.1007/978-3-8349-8772-3
18. Mulcahy, D.E., Sydow, J.: A Supply Chain Logistics Program for Warehouse Management. Auerbach Publications, New York (2008)
19. Nikoukar, A., Raza, S., Poole, A., Gunes, M., Dezfouli, B.: Low-power wireless for the internet of things: standards and applications. IEEE Access **6**, 67893–67926 (2018). https://doi.org/10.1109/ACCESS.2018.2879189
20. Hirsch-Kreinsen, H., et al.: Key themes of Industrie 4.0. Research Council of the Plattform Industrie 4.0 (2019). https://en.acatech.de/wp-content/uploads/sites/6/2019/10/Forschungsbeirat_Key-Themes-to-Industrie-4.0.pdf
21. Song, J., et al.: WirelessHART: applying wireless technology in real-time industrial process control. In: IEEE Real-Time and Embedded Technology and Applications Symposium, pp. 377–386. IEEE (2008). https://doi.org/10.1109/RTAS.2008.15
22. Vannieuwenborg, F., Verbrugge, S., Colle, D.: Choosing IoT-connectivity? A guiding methodology based on functional characteristics and economic considerations. Trans. Emerg. Telecommun. Technol. **29**(5) (2018). https://doi.org/10.1002/ett.3308
23. Vogel-Heuser, B., Hess, D.: Guest editorial industry 4.0-prerequisites and visions. IEEE Trans. Autom. Sci. Eng. **13**(2), 411–413 (2016). https://doi.org/10.1109/TASE.2016.2523639
24. Wölfle, M.: Kontextsensitive Arbeitsassistenzsysteme zur Informationsbereitstellung in der Intralogistik. Dissertation, Technical University of Munich, Munich (2014)
25. Zezulka, F., Marcon, P., Vesely, I., Sajdl, O.: Industry 4.0 - an introduction in the phenomenon. IFAC-PapersOnLine **49**(25), 8–12 (2016). https://doi.org/10.1016/j.ifacol.2016.12.002

A Gamified Mobility Experience

Andrea Vesco[1]([⊠]), Salvatore Di Dio[2], Enza Lissandrello[3],
and Domenico Schillaci[2]

[1] LINKS Foundation, Turin, Italy
andrea.vesco@linksfoundation.com
[2] PUSH Design Lab, Palermo, Italy
{s.didio,d.schillaci}@wepush.org
[3] Aalborg University, Aalborg, Denmark
enza@plan.aau.dk

Abstract. We believe in the use of urban games to define new enjoyable experiences, change citizens' unsustainable habits and educate them to new environment-and social-friendly ones. This paper presents MUV, an innovative action that has the power to engage citizens and foster sustainable mobility behaviors. MUV complements engaging HMIs with a participatory method within an iterative innovation process called the virtuous cycle (understand, involve, co-create, implement, experiment). The innovation process has led to a new game dynamic: *Mobility as a Sport*. It results in a rewarding personal mobility experience; the same rewarding sensations the athletes feel when they improve their results.

Keywords: Urban mobility · Sustainability · Urban games · Human-Machine Interaction

1 Introduction

Issues related to the growth of the urban population are among the most important challenges of our time. But the recurring question is why it is so important to address sustainability at city scale and our answer is quite simple: the bulk of non-renewable resource consumption occur in cities, this implies that they are the first place where the innovations which must guide us towards a new model of sustainable development, *i.e. the development that meets the needs of the present without compromising the ability of future generations to meet their own needs* [1], must be experimented. The main issue is therefore planning and managing cities so that all the processes that take place inside them become fully sustainable from a social, economic and environmental point of view, the so-called *Triple Sustainability* [2].

We are convinced that the most successful actions within an urban context today are the ones where citizens are active agents in the innovation process [3]. The evidence of the importance of the social dimension reminds us that sustainable development and growth is not possible without the engagement of citizens [4], their awareness of the importance of sustainable behavior and their willingness to play an active role in the change. Urban Mobility is indeed an organizing factor of city structure but also an

© Springer Nature Switzerland AG 2020
M. Kurosu (Ed.): HCII 2020, LNCS 12183, pp. 658–670, 2020.
https://doi.org/10.1007/978-3-030-49065-2_45

organizing factor of the lifestyle of citizens that through the everyday practice of mobility, shape the values of their surrounding and therefore their cities. Mobility is therefore a factor for transforming areas into more inclusive, safe, resilient and sustainable environments [5].

The authors are designing and experimenting a participatory process to make urban mobility sustainable. The process aims at increasing the level of acceptance of sustainable transport modes; hence it can be seen as a sparkle that create the precondition for the operators to deploy sustainable transport services and make them available to all. To start achieving this ambitious objective the authors asked themselves the following research question: *How to support people from different cultural backgrounds and different contexts, in the transition toward a healthier and environmentally friendly lifestyle?*

The focus of the discussions on mobility were often on how to exploit new infrastructures to improve the urban transport system. The prevailing attempt was to innovate the exploitation of existing infrastructures and services (or add new ones) to accommodate the demand regardless the sustainability-related implications of these choices. The focus of the discussions changed when the awareness about sustainable mobility and sustainable targets to be reached have shifted the public attention from infrastructure and service management within city structure (the hardware) to mobility management as travel behavior (the software). This has implied a paradigm shift from rational to participative and diffuse mobility planning and design disciplines. The changes in urban mobility are no longer understood as issues for expert-driven transport engineers alone but instead new methods needed to generate co-created and more people-centered solutions, *i.e.* methods that enable citizens to travel more sustainably and also raise their awareness about the impact of their travel behavior on issues of urban livability and sustainability.

Under this new way of reasoning and mindset goals as reducing car-mobility in urban centers [6] and visioning a post-car future society [7] are therefore not just referring to an expert utopia. Many initiatives towards mobility low-carbon choices [8–10] and the shaping of new societal mobility values are indeed nowadays already changing the street level in European cities. There is a desire from the society to move towards a long-term radical change for more sustainable and livable cities. Listening and leveraging on this desire is key for mobility planning in view of considering not just technical consequences of the current trends but to enable citizens to shape new visions of a sustainable future. The willingness of listening to society and take into account its desires and needs requires to work at the interplay of hard infrastructural planning and soft practices of social innovation.

On that direction, nowadays, researchers and practitioners are drawing on lessons from the social sciences [11], trying to understand the behaviors that shape the use of transport services and how people can be persuaded to adopt healthier and sustainable mobility behaviors [12]. People rarely recognize that to improve the quality of urban environment, we need to change daily habits, and even when we know it, we hardly start doing it.

Behavioral sciences highlight gamification of urban mobility as an effective approach to eradicate these beliefs and push for change [13]. The resulting urban games have the power to define through well designed *Human-Machine Interaction*

(HMI) new enjoyable experiences, change citizens' unsustainable habits and educate them to new environment-and social-friendly ones [14].

The MUV innovative action [15] believes in a participatory process to create and share sustainable mobility values and in the adoption of game principles in real urban spaces to concretely answer to the research question set above. MUV intends to start-up a *MUVement* that fosters sustainable urban lifestyles by leveraging a gamified mobility experience implemented by means of an App for mobile phones. All the key actors of urban physical transformation are involved: citizens as individuals and/or local active communities, public authorities and local businesses. All actors actively play:

- a role as goals-values carriers performing their habitual mobility activities and transmitting values within the city;
- an experience of social interaction in which challenges, efforts and mobility choices come together to refine mobility urban values and help in reaching sustainability targets.

MUV project is experimenting in 6 different EU cities (Palermo, Italy – Fundao, Portugal – Barcelona, Spain – Amsterdam, Netherland – Ghent, Belgium – Helsinki, Finland) an innovative action that enables citizens to deliberately meet inclusive and sustainable values by engaging them in a game experience while they are moving around the city during their daily life. The MUV game is based on the concept of urban mobility as an experience that has more value than the simply A-to-B route aiming to translate the MUV game dynamics in a way that provides added value to the city. The dynamic of the MUV game is *Mobility as a Sport*. It results in a rewarding personal mobility experience; the same rewarding sensations the Athletes feel when they improve their results. The public authorities are the *Trainer* of the *Athletes* and they propose always new challenges to improve their performances. The local businesses are the *Sponsors* of the *Athletes*. The *Sponsor* rewards the best *Athletes* and make them stand out from the crowd/community. By playing the MUV game, *Athletes* are rewarded with a certain amount of points for every trip on foot, by bicycle, by public transportation or by car-pooling. The points earned by *Athletes* enable the rewards. The people-oriented mobility data produced as side effect of the game is used to increase awareness and make new knowledge used by public authorities to develop evidence-based mobility policy making. MUV complements technical innovation with a participatory method within an iterative innovation process called the *virtuous cycle* (understand, involve, co-create, implement, experiment).

2 Approach to Innovation

The MUV innovation is currently implemented through three iterations of the virtuous cycle depicted in Fig. 1.

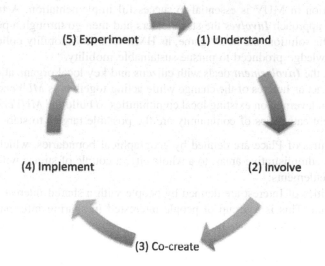

(5) Experiment   (1) Understand

(4) Implement   (2) Involve

(3) Co-create

Fig. 1. The virtuous cycle of innovation.

Within the framework of MUV, the first step of the innovation cycle is *Understand*. It means collect information and data about the mobility process to understand what the challenges are, the barriers and the possible actions to overcome those barriers and the drivers to leverage on to achieve the intended results.

Public participation is widely mentioned and adopted [16] and it has been recently extended in [17] to explore/define three kinds of public participation: (*i*) *Thick* involving groups of citizens (*ii*) *Thin* involving citizens as individuals and (*iii*) *Conventional* often required to adhere to local regulations/laws. *Thick* and *Thin* participation have the purpose of empowering citizens, while the *Conventional*, which covers hearings, has the purpose of providing citizens' accountability for decision making.

The MUV process contributes to frame and facilitate public participation of citizens to help them making informed choices about their mobility option while gaining a sense of ownership on the quality of their cities and contributing to actively feed-back on policy making performed by public authorities. MUV participation includes also public authorities to enable new possibilities of interactions that constitute not just tools but new approaches that tend to flat the relations and open a dialogue between citizens and public institutions. The MUV App is therefore understood as a channel for enabling *Thick* participation involving communities and citizens to use and exchange data with public authorities for the purpose of making mobility policies. Thus, MUV participation has important returns on the progress of knowledge and public legitimation. The progress of knowledge occurs when involving communities, citizens and public authorities into the production of new knowledge whereas public legitimation is the driver of changing urban planning policies [18].

Participation in MUV is essential to successful implementation. A truly effective participatory approach *Involves* the stakeholders and then go through a process of *Co-creation* of the solution: the MUV game, its HMIs and new mobility policies based on the new knowledge produced to pursue sustainable mobility.

In MUV, the *Involvement* deals with citizens and key local organizations that have the power to act as helixes of the change while acting together as *MUVers*. MUV starts from and then leverage on existing local communities to build the *MUVers* community. Three different categories of community are the possible targets to start with:

- Communities of Place are defined by geographical boundaries, which can vary in size from administrative areas, to a whole city, a couple of streets within a town or smaller settlements;
- Communities of Interest are defined by people with a shared interest, behaviors or background. This is a group of people interested in sharing information and discussing a particular topic. Being part of this community is not dependent upon expertise; members only needs to feel the urgency to take action on the topic;
- Communities of Practice are communities that have a practical or professional interest in the topic in common. The purpose of a community of practice is to provide a way for practitioners to share tips and best practices, develop their field of expertise further, ask questions to their colleagues, and provide support for each other. Membership is dependent on expertise.

MUV targets the community of place, where the geographical boundaries are the neighborhoods. The following neighborhoods are involved: the Centro Storico in Palermo, the Historic District of the Portuguese county of Fundao, Sant Andreu in Barcelona, Buitenveldert in Amsterdam, Muide-Meulestede in the harbour of Ghent and the new area of Jätkäsaari in Helsinki. Moreover, MUV involved also mobility experts and decision makers of the existing communities of practice at city level. The community engagement is carried out as an ongoing process enabling relationships and trust over time to build a community of *MUVers* that is sustainable and will last beyond the MUV project grant period. It was extremely important to clearly and transparently communicating the desired level of engagement and the scope of the co-creation activities: (*i*) the MUV game and its HMIs and (*ii*) new mobility policies toward the end of the project when new knowledge is created. At the same time, it is extremely important to provide continuous feedback and fulfill the promises on what the community co-create to maintain high level of involvement [19].

Once established the first community in each neighborhood, the project proceeded to *Co-create* the MUV game. In particular the communities co-created the main features of the game dynamic, the avatars, the training session and the reward schemas trying to capture the sense of feeling and belonging of the people to their neighborhoods/cities.

Implementation in MUV means development of the MUV App the back-end cloud platform underpinning the entire technological ecosystem and awareness creation. The App is developed in accordance to the co-creation inputs from the 6 neighborhoods involved with the final goal to engage *MUVers* into the game dynamic presented in Sect. 3.1. At the same time, Open Days occurs periodically to give evidence of MUV to people. Open Days are hands-on sessions on the streets to show citizens and public authorities how MUV works and its features. The final purpose is to increase awareness and user base. During these events a mentor shows how to use the MUV App. Local web-influencers are also invited to spread the initiative and report through their main digital channels. Digital communication activities are also performed at local and global level to encourage adoption.

Experiment is of paramount importance in MUV. Citizens are leaved free to play the game and the results are evaluated on a weekly basis. Evaluation of the results is the process to develop new knowledge that results in *Understand* something new to start the virtuous cycle again.

The added value of MUV could not be defined only on the basis of the innovativeness of the technological and gaming solution, but also looking at the whole process of deployment of MUV initiative including accompanying activities such as communication dissemination, involvement, co-creation, and the resulting interactions among the local stakeholders. A deep analysis of these factors is expected to lead to new findings about the factors of success, the drivers to leverage on, the barriers and the strategies to overcome them during the project. Moreover it is worth noting that the analysis and valorization of the data collected as a side effect of the MUV game, is the key element to allow the involved communities and cities to understand their challenges and to put them in the pole position to follow the virtuous cycle by themselves at the end of the project. This handover will be an interesting output of MUV initiative for the cities involved, because it pays the way to progress in the knowledge creation and in pursuing sustainability targets.

3   The MUV Game

3.1   The Game Dynamic

The MUV game is proposed as a mobile activity-based game with a sporty narrative:

1. Citizens are involved as *Athletes* and get rewarded for their sustainable mobility choices;
2. Public authorities are the *Trainers* of the *Athletes;*
3. The local businesses are the *Sponsors* of the *Athletes.*

By playing MUV, citizens become *Athletes* of the mobility game. The public authorities act like *Trainers*, providing the Training Session to couch *Athletes* to improve. Local business owners (and all those who want to provide gifts and discounts) are *Sponsors*, aiming to link their brand and their product to the *Athletes* best achievements. This approach aims at defining a space where all the different actors can find meaningful reasons to exchange their values (conscious behaviors, data, rewards, policies, creativity) and, by doing that, they enrich the sense of feeling part of the community and they also improve the livability of their city.

The metaphor of sport has been selected to bound the three values of MUV (1) being active, (2) being sustainable and (3) being happy to common values in sport: fairness, equality, inclusion, respect, perseverance, teambuilding, healthy lifestyle and value of practice and preparation. Thus, to trigger a feeling of self-rewarding and pride for the sole act of moving sustainably around the city and be recognized within the community.

It is worth noting that MUV game does not ask to move around the city performing specific tasks to progress in the sport career. The *Athletes* play as they move around the city for their mobility purpose (*e.g.* going to work, to the gym, carrying child somewhere) during their daily life, not because of the game asking them to move. This choice is very important, and it differentiates MUV from other games; MUV is conceived to help citizens to change their daily mobility habits.

The *Athletes* play with the MUV App, depicted in Fig. 2, by pressing a button when they start moving in a sustainable way and then press it again when they arrive to destination. In case of a multimodal trip, the athletes are requested to change the mode of transport interacting with the same button.

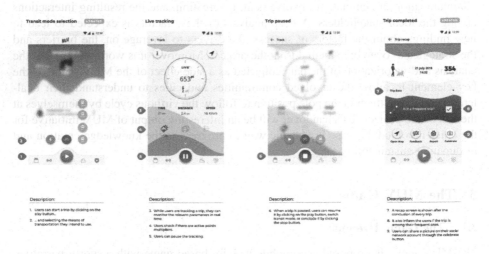

Fig. 2. The MUV App: Start and Stop activities.

As a result, athletes score points by moving sustainably by: *Walking, Biking, using Public Transportation*. Weather and traffic conditions influence points attribution. According to weather data provided by third parties services, in fact, users get extra points if it's Cloudy/Windy (+5%), Rainy/Snowy (+10%), and if it's a traffic peak hour (+15%).

3.2   The User Experience

The experience of playing MUV has 4 different steps related to the player's experience and mastery in the game as depicted in Fig. 3.

Like every successful career in sport, the experience of being an *MUVer* (*i.e.* Athlete) starts with tough trainings and ends with legendary triumphs. At the very beginning, MUVers have to train to be ready to compete with others. They have to complete individual Training Sessions to better learn how to play and measure their potential. Training sessions represent the first game mode: a series of mobility tasks they have to accomplish in a given condition. Training Sessions are divided into programs and each program is made up of single training events; for the sake of example:

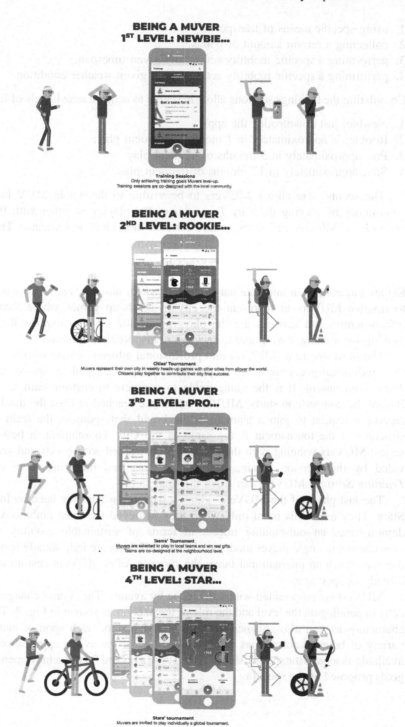

Fig. 3. Level of Experience of the MUV game dynamic.

1. using specific means of transport;
2. collecting a certain amount of points;
3. performing a specific mobility action in a given timespan;
4. performing a specific mobility action with a given weather condition.

Completing the trainings sessions allow MUVers to achieve new Levels of Experience:

1. Newbie: just downloaded the app;
2. Rookie: in approximately in 1 month of frequent play;
3. Pro: approximately in 5 months of frequent play;
4. Star: approximately in 12 months of frequent play.

The second step allows MUVers to be visible to the whole MUV international community by playing the *City Tournament*. By playing together with their cities' community, MUVers can be recognized for their individual performance. This mode is a massive multiplayer game in which two opposing cities face each other in a one vs one match. MUVers in each city contribute to compose the final score of their team. If the city wins, the best MUVers are rewarded with badges and coins. Cities all over the EU are engaged in an international challenge: *who's moving better?* To win they have to involve MUVers to represent the city in heads-up games where local mobility infrastructures and services are the playgrounds for them to express the ability of moving by walking, biking and using mass transportation systems.

The third step turns MUVers into professional athletes. Those who have achieved their individual goals are asked to join new teams, managed by sponsors, to play a *Team Tournament*. It is the game mode to compete in custom team vs team way. Before the competition starts, MUVers who have reached at least the third level may receive a request to join a team from the brand that sponsors the team itself. The structure of the tournament is the same as the City Tournament: a best-of-7-game series. MUVers winning with their teams got rewarded with goods and services provided by the sponsor. Again, only by selecting and finalizing more challenging *Training Sessions* MUVers can reach the final step.

The last phase of the MUVers' journey happens when they become International Stars. They reach this point only when they achieved the most ambitious goals and demonstrated an outstanding impact in terms of sustainable mobility. The *Stars Tournament* is single-player mode one vs one. MUVers are individually sponsored and they can reach an international fame; the sponsors offer MUVers custom sponsorship directly as sport stars.

MUVers are represented within the game by avatars. The Avatar changes automatically depending on the level and the role of the *MUVer* as shown in Fig. 4. The avatar's characteristics can also enhance through a sponsorship. Each sponsor can provide a variety of branded accessories or customizations of the avatar appearance. They are available as soon as the sponsorship is agreed or as a reward for the achievement of specific goals proposed by the sponsor.

Fig. 4. Type and evolution of Avatars of the MUV game.

3.3 The MUV Touchpoints

The MUV game dynamic is implemented in the real world by means of four techno-logical touchpoints. The touchpoints are not meant to be simple tools in accordance to the common instrumental vision of the technology, but they are concrete endpoints to enable sustainable mobility behaviors and empower people [20].

The MUV App represents the service's most important touchpoint because it's meant to foster more active and sustainable mobility lifestyles by enabling the MUVers to play the game. The main feature of the App is the capability for the player to track his/her sustainable trips by pressing the start button when he/she starts moving and the stop button at the end of the travel. Once completed, the trip is validated (*i.e.* means of transport adopted) by the system and all the data are then stored in the MUV back-end cloud platform. In case of success, the player receives his/her points.

The MUV wearable App, depicted in Fig. 5, is designed to enrich the touchpoints of the MUV game as expressed by several people during the co-creation activities. It is developed as a notification system to interact with the MUV app from the wrist.

The MUV Monitoring Stations are easy to build open source devices, installed as urban artistic furniture, to collect environmental data and to enable fancy interactions with MUVers when they are nearby.

Finally, the MUV Analytics, a business intelligence unit that provide local author-ities the capabilities to analyze data collected from the MUVers and produce new knowledge on mobility in their cities.

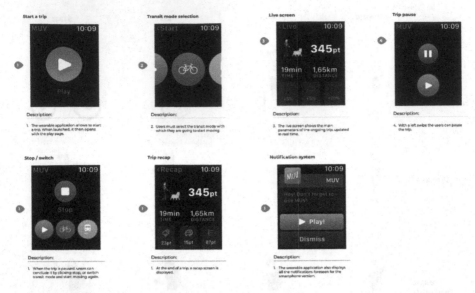

Fig. 5. The MUV wearable App

3.4   The Goals of the Game

MUV can transform daily life urban mobility in a sport that everybody can play. According to the categorization in [21] MUV tries to foster self-motivated, self-rewarding activities in different ways:

1. *Satisfying work*: the exact nature of satisfying work is different from person to person, but for everyone it means being immersed in clearly defined, demanding activities that allow us to see the direct impact of our efforts. MUV's training sessions are meant to empathize with this aspect.
2. *Being successful*: we all want to feel powerful in our own lives and show off to others what we're good at. We want to be optimistic about our own chances for success, to aspire to something, and to feel like we're getting better over time. MUV's LoE is a way to let athletes measure their game mastery.
3. *Social connections*: humans are extremely social creatures, and even the most introverted among us derive a large percentage of our happiness from spending time with the people we care about. We want to share experiences and build bonds, and we most often accomplish that by doing things that matter together. MUV's interactions among friends and during tournaments create a strong sense of community.
4. *Meaning*: we want to feel curiosity, awe, and wonder about things that unfold on epic scales. Most importantly, we want to belong to and contribute to something that has lasting significance beyond our own individual lives. MUV's game dynamic is implicitly about make cities healthier together, this turns more explicit in statistics where CO_2 equivalent emissions avoided are emphasized.

4 Conclusions

MUV is a viable contribution to urban transition based on three fundamental values: *being fit, being green, being happy.* MUV action at large is demonstrating to be an engaging and rewarding experience for citizens especially when they are involved in tournaments. Environmental consciousness, competitive spirits, pleasure of reward, feeling of being fancy and other motivations, are all levers that push citizens to participate in the game. Regardless of what the underlying motivation is, some citizens are now actively contributing to make urban mobility more sustainable in their cities. Behind the scene MUV is also a valuable tool for collecting people-mobility data (not car-mobility data). What is very interesting to us, is that citizens are donating their mobility data for the purpose of better mobility policies. At the time of writing, the consortium is working on the analysis of big amount of data and on the implementation of the analytics to extract the information cities need. This work is performed in strict collaboration with the involved cities to understand with them what are the format of this information and how this information can be used today to make new mobility policy. This is, in the end, the real reward of participating in MUV and the feedback many of us want, as citizens, from our local authorities to continue active participation to public life.

Acknowledgement.   This work has been funded by the European Union's Horizon 2020 research and innovation program, under grant agreement No 723521.

References

1. World Commission on Environment and Development (WCED): Our Common Future. Oxford University Press, Oxford (1987)
2. Vesco, A., Ferrero, F.: Handbook of Research on Social, Economic, and Environmental Sustainability in the Development of Smart Cities. IGI Global, Hershey (2015)
3. Leydesdorff, L., Deakin, M.: The triple helix model of smart cities: a neo-evolutionary perspective. J. Urban Technol. **18**(2), 53–63 (2011)
4. Carayannis, E., Campbell, D.: Mode 3' and 'Quadruple Helix': toward a 21st century fractal innovation ecosystem. Int. J. Technol. Manage. **46**(3), 201–234 (2009)
5. United Nations (UN): Proposal for Sustainable Development Goals. New York, United Nations General Assembly. Open Working Group (A/68/970) (2014)
6. Bertolini, L., Le Clercq, F.: Urban Development without more Mobility by Car? Lessons from Amsterdam, a Multimodal Urban Region. Environ. Plann. A **35**(4), 575–589 (2003)
7. Urry, J., Dennis, K.: After the Car. Wiley (2009)
8. Banister, D.: The sustainable mobility paradigm. Transp. Policy **15**(2), 73–80 (2008)
9. Banister, D.: Cities, mobility and climate change. J. Transp. Geogr. **19**(6), 1538–1546 (2011)
10. Schwanen, T., Banister, D., Anable, J.: Rethinking habits and their role in behaviour change: the case of low-carbon mobility. J. Transp. Geogr. **24**, 522–532 (2012)
11. Zhan, J., Van Acker, V.: Life-oriented travel behavior research: an overview. Transp. Res. Part A **104**, 167–178 (2017)

12. Calastri, C., Hess, S., Daly, A., Carrasco, J.: Does the social context help with understanding and predicting the choice of activity type and duration? An application of the Multiple Discrete-Continuous Nested Extreme Value model to activity diary data. Transp. Res. Part A **104**, 1–20 (2017)
13. Koivisto, J., Hamari, J.: The rise of motivational information systems: a review of gamification research. Int. J. Inf. Manage. **45**, 191–210 (2019)
14. Nakashima, R., Sato, T., Maruyama, T.: Gamification approach to smartphone-app-based mobility management. Transp. Res. Proc. **25**, 2344–2355 (2017)
15. MUV Mobility Urban Value. European Union's Horizon 2020 RIA, GA No. 723521. https://www.muv2020.eu
16. Conrad, E., Cassar, L., Christie, M., Fazey, I.: Hearing but not listening? A participatory assessment of public participation in planning. Environ. Plann. C Gov. Policy **29**(5), 761–782 (2011)
17. Nabatchi, T., Leighninger, M.: Public Participation for 21st Century Democracy. Wiley, Hoboken (2015)
18. Blanchet-Cohen, N.: Igniting citizen participation in creating healthy built environments: the role of community organizations. Community Dev. J. **50**(2), 264–279 (2014)
19. Schmitz, P.: Community Engagement Toolkit (2017). https://collectiveimpactforum.org/sites/default/files/Community%20Engagement%20Toolkit.pdf
20. Heidegger, M.: The Question Concerning Technology. Essay (1977)
21. McGonigal, J.: Reality Is Broken: Why Games Make Us Better and How They Can Change the World. The Penguin Press, New York (2011)

Author Index